A Companion to
Middle English Prose

A Companion to
Middle English Prose

Edited by A. S. G. Edwards

D. S. BREWER

First published 2004
D. S. Brewer, Cambridge
Paperback edition 2010

Transferred to digital printing

ISBN 978-1-84384-018-3 hardback
ISBN 978-1-84384-248-4 paperback

D. S. Brewer is an imprint of Boydell & Brewer Ltd
PO Box 9, Woodbridge, Suffolk IP12 3DF, UK
and of Boydell & Brewer Inc.
668 Mt Hope Avenue, Rochester, NY 14620, USA
website: www.boydellandbrewer.com

A CIP catalogue record for this book is available
from the British Library

This publication is printed on acid-free paper

Contents

Preface   vii

Contributors   ix

Abbreviations   x

1   The *Ancrene Wisse* Group   1
     BELLA MILLETT

2   Rolle and Related Works   19
     R. HANNA

3   Walter Hilton's *Scale of Perfection* and *The Cloud of Unknowing*   33
     AD PUTTER

4   Nicholas Love   53
     KANTIK GHOSH

5   Julian of Norwich   67
     BARRY WINDEATT

6   Margery Kempe   83
     A.C. SPEARING

7   Mandeville   99
     IAIN MACLEOD HIGGINS

8   John Trevisa   117
     A.S.G. EDWARDS

9   Anonymous Devotional Writings   127
     VINCENT GILLESPIE

10   Sermon Literature   151
     H.L. SPENCER

11   Historical Writing   171
     ALFRED HIATT

12   Wycliffite Prose   195
     FIONA SOMERSET

13   Prose Romances   215
     HELEN COOPER

14   Scientific, Medical and Utilitarian Prose   231
     GEORGE KEISER

15 Saints' Lives   249
         O.S. PICKERING

16 Reginald Pecock and John Fortescue   271
         JAMES SIMPSON

17 Private Letters   289
         RICHARD BEADLE

18 Caxton and After   307
         ALEXANDRA GILLESPIE

Index   327

Index of Manuscripts   333

Preface

The study of Middle English prose has greatly increased over the last quarter of a century. In part this is the consequence of the first systematic bibliographical work in this field, reflected in the researches of those involved in the ongoing *Index of Middle English Prose* (published by Boydell & Brewer). There has also been a steady increase in editorial activity that has made far more texts available (some for the first time) in modern editions. The field has also benefitted from the increasing interest in Middle English codicology through which prose texts have been fruitfully located in contexts of manuscript compilation.

The case for a *Companion to Middle English Prose* is therefore clear. It will be to the benefit of all students in this field to have some compendious introductory guide to the various authors and genres that it encompasses. This volume is designed to serve such a purpose. Each chapter deals with either a significant figure or category and offers an authoritative survey of relevant works. In the case of individual authors there is also a brief biographical overview. Inevitably there are variations in emphasis from chapter to chapter but all seek to convey some sense of the distinctive literary qualities of the work(s) being examined. In addition, all chapters contain bibliographical guides. It is my hope that this volume will thereby be of value to both the beginning and the more advanced student in this field.

Some material has not been included here for compelling reasons. There are no chapters on either Thomas Malory's *Morte Darthur* or the *Ancrene Wisse*, since these works have already been the subject of earlier Companions from Boydell & Brewer, by Elizabeth Archibald and A.S.G. Edwards (1996) and Yoko Wada (2003) respectively. In addition, Chaucer's prose works are not examined here since they have been the subjects of extensive study.

I wish to offer my thanks to all the contributors, who have dealt with punctuality and patience with my requests for revision. I am grateful to Jonathan Boffey for valuable computer assistance. For errors and inconsistencies I must assume the sole responsibility.

A. S. G. Edwards

Contributors

RICHARD BEADLE is Reader in the Faculty of English, University of Cambridge, and a Fellow of St John's College

HELEN COOPER is Professor of Medieval and Renaissance English at the University of Cambridge

A.S.G. EDWARDS is Professor of English, University of Victoria; he will shortly take up a chair at the University of Glamorgan

KANTIK GHOSH is a Fellow of Trinity College, Oxford

ALEXANDRA GILLESPIE is Assistant Professor, University of Toronto

VINCENT GILLESPIE is a J.R.R. Tolkien Professor, University of Oxford and a Fellow of Lady Margaret Hall

R. HANNA is Professor of Palaeography at the University of Oxford and a Fellow of Keble College

ALFRED HIATT is a Lecturer in the School of English, University of Leeds

IAIN HIGGINS is Associate Professor of English, University of Victoria

GEORGE KEISER is Professor of English, Kansas State University

BELLA MILLETT is Reader in English, School of Humanities, Southampton University

AD PUTTER is Reader in the Department of English, University of Bristol

OLIVER PICKERING is Deputy Head of Special Collections, Brotherton Library, University of Leeds, and Associate Lecturer in English

JAMES SIMPSON is Professor of English, Harvard University

FIONA SOMERSET is Associate Professor of English, Duke University

A.C. SPEARING is Professor of English, University of Virginia

H.L. SPENCER is a Fellow of Exeter College, Oxford

BARRY WINDEATT is Professor of English, University of Cambridge, and a Fellow of Emmanuel College

Abbreviations

BL	British Library
Bodl.	Bodleian Library, Oxford
CUL	Cambridge University Library
EETS	Early English Text Society
	es extra series
	os ordinary series
fol./fols	folio/folios
IMEP	*The Index of Middle English Prose*, gen. ed. A.S.G. Edwards (Cambridge, 1984–)
IPMEP	*An Index of Printed Middle English Prose*, N.F. Blake, A.S.G. Edwards and R.E. Lewis (New York, 1985)
Jolliffe	P.S. Jolliffe, *A Check-List of Middle English Prose Writings of Spiritual Guidance* (Toronto, 1974)
Manual	*A Manual of the Writings in Middle English*, rev. ed., ed. J.B. Severs and A. Hartung, 10 vols to date (New Haven, Conn., 1968–)
MED	Middle English Dictionary
MMTE	*The Medieval Mystical Tradition in England*, ed. Marion Glasscoe
MS/MSS	Manuscript/Manuscripts
New DNB	New Dictionary of National Biography
New IMEV	New Index of Middle English Verse
ns	new series
OED	*Oxford English Dictionary*
PL	*Patrologia latina*, ed. J.P. Migne
STC	*A Short-Title Catalogue of Books Printed in England, Scotland, & Ireland . . . 1465–1640*, 2nd ed., by W.A. Jackson, F.S. Ferguson and Katharine F. Pantzer, 3 vols (London, 1976–90)
UL	University Library
Wells	See Manual, above

1

The *Ancrene Wisse* Group

BELLA MILLETT

The Early Middle English religious prose works collectively described here as 'the *Ancrene Wisse* Group' occupy an important but still not fully explained position in the history of Middle English prose. At a time when relatively little was being written in English, and still less written well, this substantial body of prose draws on a variety of stylistic traditions with unexpected skill and confidence; but we do not have enough evidence to establish its authorship, audience, date, or place of composition with any certainty, and there is no scholarly consensus even on the institutional context in which it was produced. Although the early manuscripts give some clues to its origin, palaeographical and linguistic criteria cannot be used as precision tools for dating and localization in this period; and the internal evidence of the works themselves is limited and sometimes ambiguous. Even fragmentary evidence, however, may take on new meaning if it can be identified as part of a larger pattern. Over the past few decades, the focus of research on the works of the *Ancrene Wisse* Group has shifted from its debt to Anglo-Saxon literary tradition towards its links with contemporary Continental Europe, providing new evidence for its context and suggesting alternative interpretations of the existing evidence.

The phrase '*Ancrene Wisse* Group' is one of several terms used by modern scholars to classify this group of works.[1] The assumption that they constitute a distinct group is itself modern; but it is given some plausibility by a shared manuscript tradition, by verbal, stylistic, and thematic parallels, and by a few apparent cross-references.

The longest and most influential work of the Group is *Ancrene Wisse*,[2] an unofficial 'rule' or 'guide' for anchoresses – women who had chosen to be enclosed in a cell (usually built on to a church) to lead a solitary religious life. It is made up of a Preface and eight parts (*distinctiones*). Parts 1 and 8 constitute an 'Outer Rule', prescribing the anchoresses' devotional observances and their external routine; they enclose an 'Inner Rule' of more general moral instruction, with sections on the custody of the senses, the solitary life, the seven deadly sins and their remedies, confession, penance, and the love of Christ.

Ancrene Wisse has no single Latin source; it borrows eclectically from a variety of written and oral traditions. The structure and content of the 'Outer

---

[1] See further pp. 3–5 below.
[2] This title is found in Cambridge, Corpus Christi College, MS 402; the alternative title sometimes used by editors, *Ancren(e) Riwle*, has no medieval authority (see further Millett 1996, 5).

Rule' – and, to some extent, of the work as a whole – are influenced by a number of earlier Rules, monastic as well as anchoritic (see Millett in Wada 2003); the 'Inner Rule' draws on Christian Latin writers from the patristic period onwards (particularly Augustine, Gregory, and Bernard of Clairvaux), and also reflects the influence of contemporary developments in preaching and pastoral literature. The anonymous author handles his sources with considerable freedom, weaving them into more extended arguments, amplifying them with additional material, and sometimes adapting them quite radically for their new audience. There is a striking instance of this in the section on penance, where he modifies a sermon by Bernard of Clairvaux to imply that anchoritism and penance (rather than, as in Bernard's sermon, monasticism and mystical experience) constitute the highest form of religious life. Although *Ancrene Wisse* addresses women leading a contemplative life, it is more concerned with general moral and spiritual advice than with the higher levels of contemplation, what in modern terms would be described as 'mysticism'; the anchoritic life is presented as essentially penitential, rewarded by union with God in the next world rather than this. The accessibility of the spirituality of *Ancrene Wisse* is matched by the accessibility of its style. Although its prose shows some influence from a native English tradition of rhythmical and alliterative prose, and considerably more from the techniques of Latin rhetoric, it is less formal and ornate than that of the other works of the Group; eloquent, lively, and colloquial, it exploits contemporary preaching methods and materials with professional skill, aiming 'not to prove but to move' (Shepherd 1959, lx).

The earliest manuscripts of *Ancrene Wisse* date from the second quarter of the thirteenth century; a passage which was certainly part of the original work, although it survives in full in only one manuscript (BL, Cotton Nero A. xiv, fol. 50r), indicates that it was initially composed for three well-born (*gentile*) sisters who had withdrawn from the world as young women to become anchoresses. From the beginning, however, the author seems to have had in mind a wider potential audience, both anchoritic and non-anchoritic. At one point he says, 'Ich write muchel for oþre þet nawiht ne rineð ow, mine leoue sustren' ('I write much for others [i.e., other anchoresses] which does not concern you, my dear sisters', Cambridge, Corpus Christi College 402, fol. 13r); and towards the end of the section on confession, he says, 'Mine leoue sustren, þis fifte dale . . . limpeð to alle men iliche; for-þi ne wundri ȝe ow nawt þet Ich toward ow nomeliche nabbe nawt ispeken i þis dale. Habbeð þah to ower bihoue þis lutle leaste ende . . .' ('My dear sisters, this fifth part . . . is relevant to everybody alike; so do not be surprised that I have not addressed you in particular in this part. But here is a short final section for your use . . .', Corpus 402, fol. 93r). From a very early stage, the work began to be revised, adapted, and even translated (once into Latin, twice into French) for different contexts, and for different audiences. Some major early revisions were probably authorial. The carelessly copied text in BL, Cotton Cleopatra C. vi was corrected and revised by someone who may have been the author himself (Dobson 1972, xciii–cxl); and the much better text in Corpus 402 (now generally used, in the 1962 edition by Tolkien, as the standard version for reference) reflects a fairly extensive updating of the original, incorporating earlier revisions and adding more in a similar style, for a larger and more geographically scattered group of anchoresses, 'twenti nuðe oðer ma' ('twenty now or more', fol. 69r) . The work was also adapted and revised for non-anchoritic audiences. The compilation of extracts in Cambridge, Gonville and Caius College 234/120 seems to have been modified for a male mendicant community: on p. 59 *recluses* is replaced by *men of religiun*, and on p. 68 a comment on the shame of having to beg for one's living and be dependent on others 'as ȝe beoð, leoue sustren' ('as you are, my dear sisters', Corpus 402, fol. 96v) is modified to address 'breþren' ('brothers'). An early adaptation for a male religious house (changing, for instance, the prescription of four haircuts a year to fifteen) underlies a number of the surviving texts, although in BL, Cotton Titus D. xviii the adaptation seems to have been partially reversed (the Titus text sometimes has feminine pronouns where the other manuscripts have masculine ones). The Latin translation, which survives in manuscripts from the early fourteenth century onwards, is modified at some points to apply more generally to male and female religious; and the late thirteenth-century 'Trinity French' translation, incorporated in a larger Franciscan compilation, addresses a mixed readership of religious and laity. The later fourteenth-century text in Cambridge, Magdalene College, Pepys 2498 has been extensively rewritten (probably more than once), with some unorthodox modifications to the doctrine of the original (see Colledge 1939, and Christina von Nolcken in Wada 2003); and the fifteenth-century extracts in BL, Royal 8 C.i have been adapted for a general lay audience. Even texts of *Ancrene Wisse* not revised for non-anchoritic audiences might reach a wider readership. At some point between 1284 and 1289, Cleopatra C. vi was presented to the Augustinian nuns of Canonsleigh in Devon; about 1300, Corpus 402 was acquired by the Victorine canons of Wigmore Abbey in Northern Herefordshire; the earlier French translation in BL, Cotton Vitellius F. vii was presented to Eleanor, Duchess of Gloucester, by the widow of the Earl of Kent between 1433 and 1441; and the modernized but otherwise faithful text in the late fourteenth-century 'Vernon manuscript', Bodl. Eng. poet. a. 1, is part of a physically massive, expensively produced compilation of devotional literature certainly not designed for an anchoritic reader. In all, *Ancrene Wisse* survives in seventeen medieval manuscripts or manuscript fragments (nine of the Middle English version, four of the Latin translation, one of the earlier French translation and three of the later), and borrowings from it also appear in some late-medieval devotional works (see Millett 1996, 31–34, and Nicholas Watson in Wada 2003).

The other works of the *Ancrene Wisse* Group are sometimes subdivided into the Katherine Group and the Wooing Group. The term 'Katherine Group' is ambiguous: it has sometimes been used to cover the *Ancrene Wisse* Group as a whole, sometimes all the works of the Group except *Ancrene Wisse*. It is most often used, however, to describe the five works found together in Bodl. Bodley 34: three lives of virgin martyrs (*Seinte Katerine*, *Seinte Margarete*, and *Seinte Iuliene*), a work usually called by its editors '*Hali Meiðhad*' but in Bodley 34 'Epistel of meidenhad meidene froure' ('Letter on virginity for the encouragement of virgins'), and a work on the custody of the soul, *Sawles Warde*.

The saints' lives are free translations of earlier Latin sources. They show little

stylistic influence, however, from their Latin originals; their prose is mannered
and elaborate, a sequence of mainly two-stress phrases highlighted and/or
linked together by heavy alliteration. It is probably indebted to the rhythmical
and alliterative sermon prose developed by Ælfric and Wulfstan in the late
Anglo-Saxon period; although there are no verbal parallels close enough to
demonstrate direct influence from either writer, there are evident similarities in
stylistic technique, particularly with Wulfstan's prose (see Millett 1988,
Schaefer 1996). The content of the Latin originals has also been modified:
comic, erotic, and sensational elements have been heightened, and the more
intellectually demanding passages simplified and clarified. The 'baroque'
features of the English versions, their ornate style and uninhibited exploitation
of the audience's emotions, have made many critics uneasy (see Millett 1996,
41–42); but they reflect less a provincial coarsening of the originals than a
purposeful and assured reworking for a different kind of audience.

     Sawles Warde is also a free adaptation of a Latin original, the twelfth-century
pseudo-Anselmian dialogue *De custodia interioris hominis*, which takes as its
framework the allegorical image of the body as castle of the soul, recommending the fear of hell and the hope of heaven as a protection against the
attacks of the devil. The descriptions of hell and heaven in the original are
considerably amplified in the English version; the author at times imitates the
rhetorical patterning of his Latin original, but he also draws on the older native
tradition of sermon prose, and his description of hell echoes its phrasing as well
as its stylistic devices (see Millett 1983).

     Epistel of Meidenhad, unlike the other works of the Katherine group, has no
single Latin source; it weaves together material from a variety of different
sources into a *writ* ('treatise') in praise of virginity, addressed to an unspecified
(and probably non-specific) female virgin. Its most striking feature to a modern
reader is its vehement denunciation of marriage as inevitably unhappy, and
sexual activity (even within marriage) as inevitably sinful. This approach, which
sometimes risks overstepping the limits of contemporary theological orthodoxy,
has been criticized as intemperate and unsubtle; but the author's exclusive focus
on the woes of marriage, his implication that even marital intercourse is a form
of prostitution, and his stress on the practical advantages of virginity are rhetorical strategies which have precedents in a tradition of virginity literature going
back to the patristic period (see Millett 1982, xxx–xxxviii).

     The works of the Katherine Group seem to have been composed for more
than a single audience. Two of the three saints' lives, *Seinte Iuliene* and *Seinte
Margarete*, explicitly address a general audience of listeners; *Seinte Iuliene*
invites 'alle leawede men þe understonden ne mahen Latines ledene' ('all
lay-people who cannot understand Latin', Bodley 34, fol. 36v) to listen to
Juliana's life. It is possible that *Seinte Katerine* and *Sawles Warde* (which is
more homiletic in form than its Latin source; see Becker 1984) were also
designed primarily for delivery as sermons. *Epistel of Meidenhad*, however, was
composed to be read individually by the virgins it addresses, and the other works
of the Katherine Group probably also had a secondary function as devotional
reading. All of them are concerned, to a greater or lesser extent, with the theme
of virginity, particularly female virginity; even *Sawles Warde*, where virginity is

not a central theme, replaces a passage in its monastic source on the heavenly reward of monks by a more extended description of the reward of virgins (Bodley 34, fol. 79r), and *Seinte Margarete* defines its audience as 'widewen wið þa iweddede, ant te meidnes nomeliche' ('widows with the married, and especially virgins', Bodley 34, fol. 18v). The women for whom *Ancrene Wisse* was written may have been among the readers of some of these other works; its author refers to 'ower Englische boc of Seinte Margarete' ('your English book of St Margaret', Corpus 402, fol. 66r), perhaps the Katherine Group version. The works of the Katherine Group, unlike *Ancrene Wisse*, do not seem to have been widely disseminated; they survive only in Bodley 34 and two other thirteenth-century manuscripts, BL, Royal 17 A. xxvii (*Seinte Katerine, Seinte Iuliene, Seinte Margarete, Sawles Warde*), which also includes a fragment of the Wooing Group *Oreisun of Seinte Marie*, and BL, Cotton Titus D. xviii (*Seinte Katerine, Epistel of Meidenhad, Sawles Warde*), which also includes *Ancrene Wisse* and a Wooing Group work, *Þe Wohunge of ure Lauerd*.

The term 'Wooing Group' was used in W. Meredith Thompson's 1958 edition to link four prayers and meditations in rhythmical and alliterative prose. *Þe Oreisun of Seinte Marie* is a free translation of a prayer to the Virgin in Latin verse by Marbod of Rennes (c. 1025–1133). The other three works seem to be original compositions, 'but original in the medieval sense of free expression within a tradition and a current phraseology' (Thompson 1958, xiv). The '*Lofsong of ure Louerde*' (the title is editorial) is an extended prayer to Christ and the Virgin; the *Ureisun of God Almihti* and *Þe Wohunge of ure Lauerd* are meditations, emphasizing the desirability of Christ as a lover and his sufferings to gain the love of humanity. There are some textual indications that the first-person speakers of these three works are anchoresses, and it has been suggested more than once that the 'meditative and emotional rather than logical' nature of the Wooing Group implies female authorship (see Thompson 1958, xviii–xxii); it is more likely, however, to reflect a clerical response to the pastoral needs of a specific female audience. The works of the Wooing Group are emotive rather than emotional, designed to evoke rather than simply express the love of God; the author of the *Wohunge* concludes, 'Prei for me, mi leue suster; þis haue I writen þe for-þi þat wordes ofte quemen þe heorte to þenken on ure Lauerd . . .' ('Pray for me, my dear sister; I have written this for you because words often sway the heart to meditate on our Lord . . .', lines 645–9).

There are complete texts of all the Wooing Group works apart from the *Wohunge*, together with *Ancrene Wisse*, in BL, Cotton Nero A. xiv; an incomplete text of *Ureisun of God Almihti* in London, Lambeth Palace Library, 487; and a fragment of *Oreisun of Seinte Marie* in BL, Royal 17A. xxvii. The *Wohunge* survives only in Titus D. xviii. As with the works of the Katherine Group, their dissemination seems to have been relatively limited; but the fourteenth-century rhythmical prose treatise *A Talkyng of the Loue of God* reflects the influence of two Wooing Group works, the *Ureisun of God Almihti* and the *Wohunge*.

It is possible that other surviving works are connected with the *Ancrene Wisse* Group; it has been suggested that the first five sermons in Lambeth 487, which share some stylistic similarities with *Ancrene Wisse*, should also be included (for further discussion of this manuscript, see p. 11 below).

It has been generally agreed since the late 1920s that the *Ancrene Wisse* Group originated in the West Midlands, a location suggested not only by the dialect and provenance of the earliest manuscripts, but by the vocabulary (including the Welsh loan-words *baban* 'baby' and *cader* 'cradle') of the works themselves, their use of alliterative collocations also found in later West Midlands works, and references to Shrewsbury and Chester in an address to the larger group of anchoresses in the Corpus 402 text of *Ancrene Wisse* (fol. 69r). There has been less agreement about their dating; but two revisions incorporated in the Corpus 402 text, recommending visits to the anchoresses by Dominican and Franciscan friars, have been accepted as offering at least an approximate 'anchor-date'. They place the Corpus text after 1224, when both orders had settled in England, and probably no earlier than the 1230s, when both had established houses in the West Midlands (see below, p. 10); but also, since they qualify the pessimistic assumption of the original that no clerical visitor could be trusted ('Worltliche leueð lut, religiuse ʒet leas' ('Trust seculars little, religious still less'), Corpus 402, fol. 16v), indicate that the original was written before regular visits by the friars were a practical possibility. Beyond this area of consensus, how far is it possible to pin down the origins of the Group?

The theory that has been most generally accepted was argued in detail by E.J. Dobson in his 1976 study, *The Origins of Ancrene Wisse*. J.R.R. Tolkien, in an influential article of 1929, had drawn attention to the unusually systematic West Midlands scribal dialect shared by Corpus 402 ('A') and Bodley 34 ('B'), which he called the 'AB' language; D.S. Brewer in 1956 had noted parallels in *Ancrene Wisse* to the regulations of the independent congregations of Augustinian canons, and suggested that the connection of Corpus 402 with the house of Victorine canons at Wigmore (see p. 3 above) might be significant. Dobson's cross-disciplinary study pursued both lines of research further, arguing that Wigmore Abbey must have been the centre at which the 'AB language' had been developed and the works of the *Ancrene Wisse* Group produced: 'To assign *Ancrene Wisse* and its group to any other house would be to ignore either the evidence of their language or that of their Augustinian origin; to assign them to a priest (or a series of priests) unconnected with any religious house would be to ignore both *Ancrene Wisse*'s evidence that its author was a member of an order and the obvious fact that only an organized community could have produced a number of authors and scribes trained in a single distinctive but somewhat old-fashioned orthography. Only Wigmore Abbey fits' (Dobson 1976, 172). But the premises underlying this theory, the Victorine origin of *Ancrene Wisse* and the need to assume the existence of an 'AB centre', can both be questioned, and recent research has suggested alternative possibilities.

Although Dobson's own research in monastic rules and customaries reinforced the evidence for Augustinian influence on *Ancrene Wisse*, it did not point conclusively to Victorine authorship; he identified more numerous and extended parallels with the regulations of two other orders following the Rule of St Augustine, the Premonstratensian canons and the Dominican friars, than with the Victorine constitutions (Dobson 1976, ch. 2). The Fourth Lateran Council of

1215 had prohibited the foundation of new orders, requiring any new religious houses to adopt the rule and customs of an existing order; in 1216, the newly founded Dominicans adopted the Rule of St Augustine and the Premonstratensian statutes, which they modified for their own use. Within the Premonstratensian/Dominican legislative tradition, Dobson found the closest parallels in the Dominican constitutions; he also noted some apparent parallels with the regulations provided by the Dominicans in 1220 for the new women's house of St Sixtus in Rome. He argued that these parallels reflected legislative traditions which must have been shared by the Victorines; but later research has not supported this view, and the evidence now seems to be pointing increasingly towards Dominican rather than Victorine origin (Millett 1992, 2000).

The premise that the 'AB' language must have been developed in a religious house seems to have been universally taken for granted, but it is not a necessary assumption. The twelfth century had seen an increase in the intellectual activity and influence of cathedral schools,[3] the multiplication of other local schools,[4] and an expansion in the number of commercial scribes (usually clerics in minor orders). The library of Hereford Cathedral, which was run by a college of secular canons, includes a number of twelfth-century manuscripts produced locally; R.A.B. Mynors notes, 'There are a number of records of professional scribes, painters (though not necessarily of books) and parchmenters working in Hereford during the twelfth and thirteenth centuries . . . Surely it was to men such as these, commercial scribes operating in the town, that the Cathedral turned when it needed books made.'[5] It could also be argued that there were fewer incentives for the development of vernacular writing in an enclosed religious community than in a milieu where the clergy worked closely with the laity.

More radically, Merja Black, Margaret Laing, and Jeremy Smith have recently questioned Tolkien's claim that the 'AB' language constituted a distinctive West Midlands written standard, 'a cultivated and taught medium' (Black 1999, 157), and suggested an alternative reading of the evidence: 'we are dealing not with a "standard" surrounded by deviant usages, but rather with various local attempts to reorganize the traditional spelling of the area', resulting in 'a variety of similar but distinct usages, derived from the same basic conventions' (Smith 2000, 130, 131). 'AB' as defined by Tolkien is found in only two manuscripts, one (Bodley 34) written by a *literatim* copyist who, when he changes to another exemplar for the first four folios of *Seinte Margarete*, ceases to follow 'AB' conventions consistently (see Benskin and Laing 1981); Black notes further that the Bodley 34 scribe's own orthography, judging by his variant forms and corrections, seems to have differed significantly from 'AB' (Black 1999, 164–5). This raises the possibility that 'AB' may have been a scribal idiolect rather than a dialect, the unusually, but not uniquely, systematic

---

3   See Joseph Goering, *William de Montibus (c. 1140–1213): The Schools and the Literature of Pastoral Care*, Studies and Texts 108 (Toronto, 1992), pp. 42–57, and the further references p. 18, fn. 57.
4   See R.W. Southern, *Robert Grosseteste: The Growth of an English Mind in Medieval Europe* (Oxford, 1986), ch. 3, 'Two Patterns of Education'.
5   See R.A.B. Mynors and R.M. Thompson, *Catalogue of the MSS of Hereford Cathedral Library* (Cambridge, 1993), pp. xvii–xix.

usage of a single scribe (see further Smith 2000, 129–30). Black also questions the assumption that the archaic features of 'AB' orthography indicate a continuous scribal tradition going back beyond the Conquest, either to Late West Saxon or to a hypothetical Mercian written standard; instead, she suggests the continuing influence of Late West Saxon spelling-conventions in an area where pre-Conquest vernacular works were still being studied and modernized in the early thirteenth century.[6]

The recent work summarized above reopens the questions about authorship, audience, date, and place of composition which Dobson had aimed to resolve. But it also suggests other possible ways of interpreting the surviving evidence, which might in turn involve a reassessment of the position of the *Ancrene Wisse* Group in the history of English prose.

For much of the twentieth century, literary historians focused primarily on the continuity of this group of works with the pre-Conquest tradition of English prose writing. There was a critical tendency, particularly in the period between the two World Wars, to see the *Ancrene Wisse* Group as a 'well of English undefiled', protected (not unlike the anchoresses it addressed) from potentially corrupting outside influences by its physical and cultural isolation. R.W. Chambers, in his 1932 essay on 'The Continuity of English Prose', saw *Ancrene Wisse* as a key link in a chain of religious works extending through the Middle Ages, reviving and sustaining the native tradition of vernacular prose writing threatened by the Norman Conquest:

> We begin with the greatest and noblest of all English kings [Alfred] building up (upon what foundations we do not know) a King's English. We see the civilization of which this English prose was the instrument developing for nearly two centuries; then suffering sudden and catastrophic overthrow; then fighting a losing battle steadily but hopelessly, until, two centuries after the Conquest, the glories of romance and the niceties of the law had become the province of the French tongue, history and theology of the Latin. Yet, when we might expect to find the English tongue surviving as a mere peasants' speech, and English prose ceasing altogether, we see it consecrated in a series of noble books, written for or by those who had withdrawn to cloister or hermitage in search of a peace which they could not find in feudal England . . . And so the cadences of the English tongue were preserved. (clxxii–clxxiii, clxxiv)

Similarly, J.R.R. Tolkien characterized the 'AB' language as 'an English . . . that has preserved some of its former cultivation . . . and has contrived in troublous times to maintain the air of a gentleman, if a country gentleman' (Tolkien 1929, 106).

From the 1950s onwards, however, this stress on the 'Englishness', even the provincialism, of the *Ancrene Wisse* Group gradually began to be replaced by a recognition of its stylistic heterogeneity. One aspect of this tendency was a

---

[6] See Christine Franzen, *The Tremulous Hand of Worcester* (Oxford, 1991), R.M. Thomson, *A Descriptive Catalogue of the Medieval Manuscripts in Worcester Cathedral Library* (Cambridge, 2001), p. xxiv, and the discussion of Lambeth 487 below, p. 11.

greater emphasis on the influence of Latin rhetoric on the works of the Group, either as a general stylistic model (e.g. Shepherd 1959, lix–lxxiii, and Clark 1977, on *Ancrene Wisse*) or through direct adaptation of their twelfth-century and earlier Latin sources (e.g. Millett 1983, on *Epistel of Meidenhad* and *Sawles Warde*). Another was an increasing readiness to look outwards as well as back-wards for stylistic influences, particularly to current developments in preaching in Continental Europe. Shepherd 1959, xxviii–xix, noted the close similarities of approach between the author of *Ancrene Wisse* and the Paris master Peter Cantor (d. 1197), who with his followers played a key role in the development of popular preaching in the late twelfth century; G.V. Smithers in 1966 claimed that the main stylistic debt of *Ancrene Wisse* was not to Anglo-Saxon models but to the preaching methods being developed in the emergent universities, and that the 'dogma' of its central position in the continuity of English prose was there-fore 'a major error of literary history' (Bennett and Smithers 1966, 224). Later research has confirmed the influence on *Ancrene Wisse* – and also some other works of the *Ancrene Wisse* Group – of Continental preaching techniques of the late twelfth and early thirteenth centuries. The *Epistel of Meidenhad* bases its structure partly on two model sermons from the *Summa de Arte Praedicatoria* of the Paris master Alan of Lille (d. 1203), a work which probably also influ-enced *Ancrene Wisse* (Millett 1982, 1996b); *Þe Wohunge of ure Lauerd* uses a extended sermon-*topos*, a list of the conditions which make Christ an eligible lover, found in a very similar form in mid-thirteenth-century Paris sermons (Bériou and d'Avray 1994); and the treatment of confession in *Ancrene Wisse* reflects early thirteenth-century Continental developments in preaching and pastoral writing (Millett 1999).

What still needs to be developed is a 'unified theory' of the origins of the *Ancrene Wisse* Group which would account for this combination of stylistic influences. To explain its mixture of old and new, of native English and Conti-nental elements, it may be necessary to go beyond the search for a single point of origin and look at the broader historical context within which the Group was produced.

In 1215, the Fourth Lateran Council initiated a major programme of pastoral reform. Canon 21 of the Council required all Christians, on pain of excommuni-cation, to confess to their own priest at least once a year, complete the penance imposed, and take communion at Easter. Canon 10 instructed bishops, again under the threat of severe penalties, to recruit suitably qualified assistants to support the increased workload of preaching and hearing confessions involved; and within a few years the newly founded mendicant orders, Dominicans and Franciscans, were being actively recommended by the Papacy to fill this func-tion. Marion Gibbs comments on the commitment of bishops trained in the schools to this process of reform:

> Learned bishops made especial efforts to recruit for services in their dioceses learned seculars and friars, men of their academic acquaintance, canonists and theologians from the schools. Again, some *magistri*, on becoming bishops, made earnest attempts to enforce canon law in face of opposition, were fore-most among the episcopate in the instruction of clergy by issuing synodal

constitutions or articles of visitation, and strenuous in visiting, preaching, and reforming throughout their dioceses.[7]

In the period following the Fourth Lateran Council, a number of bishops were active in pastoral reform in the West Midlands area: William of Blois, Bishop of Worcester (1218–36), and his successor Walter Cantilupe (1237–66); Hugh Foliot, Bishop of Hereford (1219–34), and his successor Ralph of Maidstone (1234–9); and Alexander Stavensby, Bishop of Coventry and Lichfield (1224–38). All but one (Hugh Foliot) were *magistri*; all but one (William of Blois, a protégé of Stephen Langton) were linked in one way or another with a more well-known reformer, Robert Grosseteste, Bishop of Lincoln (1235–53), who earlier in his career had worked in the diocese of Hereford under Hugh Foliot.[8] The earliest mendicant houses in the West Midlands were founded in this period, Franciscans in Worcester (1227) and Hereford (1228), and Dominicans in Shrewsbury (before 1232) and Chester (before 1236); Alexander Stavensby, in whose diocese the Dominican priories were founded, had taught St Dominic and his earliest followers at Toulouse in 1214, and remained a committed supporter of the Dominicans.

It is possible that these bishops acted as catalysts for a revival of vernacular preaching and devotional literature in the West Midlands, introducing Paris-trained preachers familiar with new techniques and themes, but also encouraging the repackaging of older native preaching resources for new purposes. There has been a tendency among scholars to assume that the relationship between older and newer preaching traditions, and between monastic and mendicant culture, would necessarily be one of opposition rather than collaboration; but there is some evidence in the surviving manuscripts that this was not always the case.

Christine Franzen has recently noted the close similarity (though not identity) of the language and orthography of the scribe who wrote the text of *Ancrene Wisse* in BL, Cotton Nero A. xiv (which also includes three of the works of the 'Wooing Group'), to that of the 'tremulous hand' which annotated ninth- to twelfth-century manuscripts of Old English works in the cathedral library of Worcester (Franzen 2003). Worcester Cathedral, whose library included an exceptionally large collection of pre-Conquest vernacular works, and whose surviving manuscripts suggest a continuing interest in both Latin and vernacular preaching,[9] was served by a priory of Benedictine monks; Franzen suggested in 1991 that the 'tremulous scribe' might represent the last stirrings of an older tradition of monastic preaching as opposed to the newer preaching methods of the friars,[10] but the similarities between the two hands may suggest that both traditions were current in the same milieu.

---

[7] Marion Gibbs and Jane Lang, *Bishops and Reform 1215–1272: with special reference to the Lateran Council of 1215*, Oxford Historical Series (London, 1934), p. 49.

[8] See Gibbs and Lang, *Bishops and Reform 1215–1272*; and, on Grosseteste's association with the diocese of Hereford between 1195 and 1220, Southern, *Robert Grosseteste*, pp. 65–69.

[9] See Thomson, *A Descriptive Catalogue of the Medieval Manuscripts in Worcester Cathedral Library*, pp. xix–xx, xxi, xxix.

[10] Franzen, *The Tremulous Hand of Worcester*, p. 193.

A more striking illustration of their *rapprochement* can be found in London, Lambeth Palace Library 487, an early thirteenth-century compilation of sermons and other pastoral material of various origins, copied by a West Midlands scribe whose dialect has been localized by Michael Samuels to the same area (Northern Herefordshire or Southern Shropshire) as that of Corpus 402. This compilation includes some modernized pre-Conquest material: a sermon by Wulfstan incorporated in Sermon 2, two sermons (9 and 10) by Ælfric, and another passage borrowed from Ælfric in Sermon 11 (see Sisam 1951). But some of its material reflects the influence of late twelfth- and early thirteenth-century Continental developments in preaching and pastoral care. Four of the five sermons it shares with the late twelfth-century collection of homilies in Cambridge, Trinity College B. 14. 52 (the 'Trinity Homilies') make use of *distinctiones*, a preaching technique developed in the Paris schools in the second half of the twelfth century, in two cases (Sermons 13 and 17) using them as a structuring device in a way which anticipates the fully-developed 'thematic sermon' of the early thirteenth century.[11] It is also possible that Sermon 3 reflects the embedding at parish level of the prescriptions of the Fourth Lateran Council on annual confession and communion (see p. 9 above). Warning against confessing for the wrong reasons, it dramatizes the penitent's dubious motives: 'Ic wulle gan to scrifte for scome, alswa doð oðer men – ʒif Ic forlete, þe preost me walde eskien on Ester Dei hwa me scriue er he me ʒefe husul – and ec for monne weordes ðing' ('I will go to confession to avoid embarrassment, as other people do – if I neglected to do it, the priest would ask me on Easter Day who confessed me before he gave me communion – and also because people would talk', Morris 1868, 25). Celia Sisam suggests, because Lambeth 487 shows little sign of use, that it reflects the 'last flicker' of an older pastoral tradition (Sisam 1951, 110 fn. 2), but its combination of older and newer material, sometimes within the same sermon, implies a more collaborative relationship between the two traditions – as does the addition in a later hand of an incomplete copy of one of the works of the 'Wooing Group', the *Ureisun of God Almihti*.

If the *Ancrene Wisse* Group formed part of a wider West Midlands programme of pastoral education, we may not need to think in terms of a single 'centre', either of manuscript production or of literary production. The early manuscripts of the *Ancrene Wisse* Group vary quite widely in their scribal dialects, the technical skill with which they are written, and the freedom with which their text is treated; we cannot assume that they (or even their lost predecessors; see Laing and McIntosh 1995) were copied in the same place, or by the same kind of scribe. The place of composition of the works of the Group may similarly be more difficult to localize than has sometimes been assumed; the friars in particular were itinerant by profession, and might be transferred from

---

11 The use of *distinctiones* was first noted by S.M. O'Brien, 'An Edition of Seven Homilies from Lambeth Palace Library MS 487' (unpublished doctoral dissertation, Oxford University, 1986); on the historical development of this technique, see R.H. and M.A. Rouse, '*Statim invenire*: Schools, Preachers, and New Attitudes to the Page', in *Renaissance and Renewal in the Twelfth Century*, ed. Robert L. Benson and Giles Constable (Oxford, 1982), pp. 201–25..

one priory to another, or be seconded to a bishop's household, rather than working from a single base.

It is also possible that we should be thinking in terms of more than one author, or even more than one type of author (only *Ancrene Wisse* provides enough internal evidence to suggest a specific institutional origin). Although there are resemblances between the works of the *Ancrene Wisse* Group, there are also differences, especially of style. At one extreme, the saints' lives of the Katherine Group follow a native tradition of rhythmical and alliterative prose, showing almost no influence from the style of their Latin sources; at the other, *Ancrene Wisse* is written in a style whose closest affinities are with contemporary Continental Latin pastoral literature, particularly the works of Odo of Cheriton and James of Vitry. Although there is no conclusive evidence to rule out common authorship, it may not be necessary to assume 'one busy author and universal provider of devotional literature' (d'Ardenne 1936, xliii).

The internal evidence of the works of the Group certainly suggests that we should be thinking in terms of more than a single audience. It is possible that the texts which have survived to us reflect only one aspect of the post-1215 programme of pastoral instruction for 'all lay-people who cannot understand Latin', the recording of Middle English religious works in writing. The contents of Lambeth 487 suggest one possible group of readers, the clerics (whether friars, cathedral clergy, or parish priests) entrusted with the basic religious education of the laity through the vernacular; the anchoresses addressed in *Ancrene Wisse* and *Þe Wohunge of ure Lauerd* represent another, relatively new, type of literate user. The internal evidence of *Ancrene Wisse* indicates that they were 'lay-anchoresses' rather than 'nun-anchoresses': that is, women who had entered the anchor-house directly from the world rather than, as was the recommended practice in the early Middle Ages, entering it only after an extended apprenticeship as a nun in an enclosed community. These 'lay-anchoresses' were supervised directly by the local bishop; their numbers increased sharply in thirteenth-century England, as a decline in the rate of foundation of women's religious houses and the prohibition by Canon 14 of the Fourth Lateran Council of new religious orders limited the opportunities for women to follow a religious vocation in other ways.[12] The literacy of such anchoresses might vary considerably, from complete inability to read to a good reading knowledge of Latin, but the anchoresses addressed in *Ancrene Wisse* seem to have been literate in English (and, at least in some cases, French) rather than Latin (see Millett 1993). In some of the works of the Group, these literate women are the primary audience; but even *Ancrene Wisse* itself was not designed solely for them, and most of the works of the Katherine Group seem to have been intended primarily for

---

[12] On the rise of the lay-anchoress in this period, see Patricia J.F. Rosof, 'The Anchoress in the Twelfth and Thirteenth Centuries', in *Medieval Religious Women*, vol. 2, *Peaceweavers*, ed. John A. Nichols and Lillian Thomas Shank, Cistercian Studies Series 72 (Kalamazoo, Michigan, 1987), pp. 123–44, and Ann K. Warren, *Anchorites and their Patrons in Medieval England* (Berkeley, 1985), pp. 18–29; on the foundation of women's religious houses, Bruce L. Venarde, *Women's Monasticism and Medieval Society: Nunneries in France and England, 890–1215* (Ithaca, 1997), pp. 170–86; on the implications of Canon 14 of the Fourth Lateran Council, Millett 2002.

delivery to a wider audience of lay listeners. Much of the *Ancrene Wisse* Group is multi-purpose, offering approachable forms of spiritual instruction in the vernacular for both readers and listeners.

This theory of the origins of the Group has implications for its position in the history of English prose. The West Midlands bishops who implemented the programme of pastoral reform initiated by the Fourth Lateran Council were in a position to draw on both existing local resources (including the surviving records of an earlier English tradition of vernacular preaching) and the assistance of the friars for the religious education of 'all lay-people who cannot understand Latin'. The works of the Group may represent less the 'continuity of English prose' than the deliberate revival of an earlier tradition in a new situation; and their stylistic variety reflects the convergence of the native English tradition of religious prose with the newer preaching techniques developed in the Paris schools of the late twelfth century. The *Ancrene Wisse* Group may have emerged from a context which was more urban, more institutionally heterogeneous, and more responsive to international developments than has generally been assumed.[13]

BIBLIOGRAPHY

For a bibliographical survey of work on the *Ancrene Wisse* Group up to the end of 1993, with full annotations of individual items, see Millett 1996a; this is supplemented and updated (to 1995) by Dahood 1997.

The list below is therefore not comprehensive: it covers most post-1995 publications on the *Ancrene Wisse* Group, a few earlier items not included in the bibliographies above, and all publications on the Group mentioned in the article itself.

Primary Sources

Bennett, J.A.W., and G.V. Smithers, ed., *Early Middle English Verse and Prose* (Oxford, 1966)

D'Ardenne, S.R.T.O., ed., *An Edition of Þe Liflade ant te Passiun of Seinte Iuliene*, Bibliothèque de la Faculté de Philosophie et Lettres de l'Université de Liège 64 (Paris, 1936); repr. (with corrections) EETS os 248 (London, 1961)

Dobson, E.J., ed., *The English Text of the Ancrene Riwle: Edited from B.M. Cotton MS Cleopatra C. vi*, EETS os 267 (London, 1972)

Hasenfratz, Robert, ed., *Ancrene Wisse*, TEAMS Middle English Texts Series (Kalamazoo, Michigan, 2000)

Millett, Bella, ed., *Hali Meiðhad*, EETS os 284 (London, 1982)

---

13 I am grateful to Dr Brian Golding and Professor Malcolm Parkes for their generous advice and help when I was working on the early stages of this chapter; all remaining errors, and the views expressed, are solely my responsibility.

Morris, Richard, ed. and trans., *Old English Homilies and Homiletic Treatises . . . of the Twelfth and Thirteenth Centuries: Edited from Mss in the British Museum, Lambeth, and Bodleian Libraries . . . First Series*, EETS os 34 (London, 1868)

Shepherd, Geoffrey, ed., *Ancrene Wisse: Parts 6 and 7*, Nelson's Medieval and Renaissance Library (London, 1959)

Thompson, W. Meredith, ed., *Þe Wohunge of ure Lauerd*, EETS os 241 (London, 1958)

Tolkien, J.R.R., ed., *The English Text of the Ancrene Riwle: Ancrene Wisse: Edited from MS Corpus Christi College Cambridge 402*, introd. N.R. Ker, EETS os 249 (London, 1962)

Zettersten, Arne, and Bernhard Diensberg, ed., *The English Text of the Ancrene Riwle: The 'Vernon' Text: edited from Oxford, Bodleian Library MS Eng. poet. a. 1*, EETS os 310 (Oxford, 2000)

Secondary Sources

Amsler, Mark, 'Affective Literacy: Gestures of Reading in the Later Middle Ages', *Essays in Medieval Studies* 18 (2001), 83–110

Ayto, John, and Alexandra Barratt, eds, *Aelred of Rievaulx's De Institutione Inclusarum: Two English Versions*, EETS os 287 (London, 1984), pp. xxxviii–xliii ('The "De Institutione Inclusarum" and Ancrene Wisse')

Bartlett, Anne Clark, *Male Authors, Female Readers: Representation and Subjectivity in Middle English Devotional Literature* (Ithaca, 1995)

Becker, Wolfgang, 'The Literary Treatment of the Pseudo-Anselmian Dialogue *De custodia interioris hominis* in England and France', *Classica et Mediaevalia* 35 (1984), 215–33

Beckwith, Sarah, 'Passionate Regulation: Enclosure, Ascesis, and the Feminist Imaginary', in *Materialist Feminism*, ed. Toril Moi and Janice Radway, *The South Atlantic Quarterly* 93.4 (Fall 1994), 803–24

Benskin, Michael, and Margaret Laing, 'Translations and *Mischsprachen* in Middle English Manuscripts', in *So Meny People Longages and Tonges: Philological Essays in Scots and Mediaeval English presented to Angus McIntosh*, ed. Michael Benskin and M.L. Samuels (Edinburgh, 1981), pp. 55–106

Bériou, Nicole, and D.L. d'Avray, 'The Image of the Ideal Husband in Thirteenth Century France', in *Modern Questions about Medieval Sermons: Essays on Marriage, Death, History, and Sanctity*, ed. Nicole Bériou and D.L. d'Avray, Biblioteca di Medioevo Latino 11 (Spoleto, 1994), pp. 31–69

Bernau, Anke, 'Virginal Effects: Text and Identity in *Ancrene Wisse*', in *Gender and Holiness*, ed. Sarah Salih and Sam Riches (London, 2002), pp. 36–48

Black, Merja, 'AB or Simply A? Reconsidering the Case for a Standard', *Neuphilologische Mitteilungen* 100 (1999), 155–74

Brewer, Derek S., 'Two Notes on the Augustinian and Possibly West Midland Origin of the *Ancren Riwle*', *Notes and Queries* ns 3 (1956), 232–35

Cannon, Christopher, 'The Form of the Self: *Ancrene Wisse* and Romance', *Medium Ævum* 70 (2001), 47–65

Chambers, R.W., 'On the Continuity of English Prose from Alfred to More and his School', in the Introduction to *The Life and Death of Sʳ Thomas Moore . . . by Nicholas Harpsfield*, ed. Elsie Vaughan Hitchcock, EETS os 186 (London, 1932), pp. xlv–clxxiv

Chewning, Susannah, 'Mysticism and the Anchoritic Community: "a time . . . of veiled infinity" ', in *Medieval Women in their Communities*, ed. Diane Watt (Cardiff, 1997), pp. 116–37

———, 'The Paradox of Virginity within the Anchoritic Tradition: The Masculine Gaze and the Feminine Body in the *Wohunge* Group', in *Constructions of Widowhood and Virginity in the Middle Ages*, ed. Cindy Carlson and Angela Weisl (New York, 1999), pp. 113–31

Clark, Cecily, 'As Seint Austin Seith . . .', *Medium Ævum* 46 (1977), 212–18

Colledge, Eric, '*The Recluse*: A Lollard Interpolated Version of the *Ancren Riwle*', *Review of English Studies* 15 (1939), 1–15, 129–45

Dahood, Roger, 'The Current State of *Ancrene Wisse* Group Studies', *Medieval English Studies Newsletter* 36 (June 1997), 6–14

Dance, Richard, 'Two Difficult Words in "AB" ' [*keaft, onont*], *Neophilologus* 85 (2001), 635–46

Diensberg, Bernhard, 'The English Text of the *Ancrene Riwle* Edited from Bodleian MS Eng.Poet.a.1. (Vernon) by A. Zettersten and B. Diensberg', *Medieval English Studies Newsletter* 37 (1997), 6–20 [see also Laing 1998, below]

Dobson, E.J., *The Origins of Ancrene Wisse* (Oxford, 1976)

Dusel, Sister Juliana, 'The Bride of Christ Image in the *Ancrene Riwle*', in *Sovereign Lady: Essays on Women in Middle English Literature*, ed. Muriel Whitaker, Garland Medieval Casebooks 11 (New York, 1994), pp. 115–32

Franzen, Christine, 'The Tremulous Hand of Worcester and the Nero Scribe of the *Ancrene Wisse*', *Medium Ævum* 72 (2003), 13–31

Gunn, Cate, ' "Efter the measse-cos, hwen the preost sacreth": When is the Moment of Ecstasy in *Ancrene Wisse*?' *Notes and Queries* ns 48 (2001), 105–8

———, '*Ancrene Wisse*: A Modern Lay Person's Guide to a Medieval Religious Text', *Magistra* 8 (2002), 3–25

Hassel, Julie B., *Choosing Not to Marry: Women and Autonomy in the Katherine Group* (London, 2002)

Hornero Corisco, Ana Maria, 'French Influence on English Prepositions: A Study of *Ancrene Wisse*', *Studia Anglica Posnaniensia* 32 (1997), 33–45

———, 'An Analysis of the Object Position in *Ancrene Wisse* and The Katherine Group', *SELIM: Journal of the Spanish Society for Medieval English Language and Literature* 4 (1994), 74–93

Hostetler, Margaret M., 'Designing Religious Women: Privacy and Exposure in *The Life of Christina of Markyate* and *Ancrene Wisse*', *Mediaevalia* 22 (1999), 201–31

Hughes-Edwards, Mari, 'Hedgehog Skins and Hairshirts: The Changing Role of Asceticism in the Anchoritic Ideal', *Mystics Quarterly* 28.1 (March 2002), 6–25

Imai, Mitsunori, and Hideki Watanabe, eds, *Reading the* Ancrene Riwle*: Proceedings of the International Symposium held on 25 January, 1997 at Osaka University* (Osaka, 2000)

Innes-Parker, Catherine, 'Fragmentation and Reconstruction: Images of the Female Body in *Ancrene Wisse* and the Katherine Group', *Comitatus* 26 (1995), 27–52

———, ' "Mi bodi henge with thi bodi neiled o rode": The Gendering of the Pauline Concept of Crucifixion with Christ in Medieval Devotional Prose for Women', *Studies in Religion: Canadian Journal/ Sciences religieuses: Revue canadienne* 28:1 (1999), 49–61

Johnson, Lesley, and Jocelyn Wogan-Browne, 'National, World and Women's History: Writers and Readers of English in post-Conquest England', in *Cambridge History of Medieval English Literature*, ed. David Wallace (Cambridge, 1999), pp. 92–121

Kalve, Kari, ' "The Muthes Wit": Reading, Speaking, and Eating in *Ancrene Wisse*', *Essays in Medieval Studies* 14 (1998), 39–49

Kauth, Jean-Marie, 'Book Metaphors in the Textual Community of the *Ancrene Wisse*', in *The Book and the Magic of Reading in the Middle Ages*, ed. Albrecht Classen, Garland Medieval Bibliographies 24 (New York, 1999), pp. 99–121

Kubouchi, Tadao, 'The Decline of the S. Noun O.V. Element Order: The Evidence from Punctuation in Some Transition-Period Manuscripts of Ælfric and Wulfstan', in *Back to the Manuscripts: Papers from the Symposium "The Integrated Approach to Manuscript Studies: A New Horizon" held at the Eighth General Meeting of the Japan Society for Medieval English Studies, Tokyo, December 1992*, ed. Shuji Sato, Centre for Medieval English Studies Tokyo, Occasional Papers 1 (Tokyo, 1997), pp. 51–68

——, *From Wulfstan to Richard Rolle: Papers Exploring the Continuity of English Prose* (Cambridge, 1999)

—— et al., eds, *Electronic Parallel Diplomatic Manuscript Texts of Ancrene Wisse, Preface and Parts 1–4: A Printed Trial Version* (Tokyo, 2000, 2001)

——, 'Relative Pronoun Selection in the *Ancrene Wisse*', in *Studies in English Historical Linguistics and Philology: A Festschrift for Akio Oizumi*, ed. Jacek Fisiak (Bern, 2002), pp. 225–37

Laing, Margaret, 'Linguistic and Textual Relationships between the Corpus, Nero and Vernon Manuscripts of *Ancrene Riwle* – a Response', *Medieval English Studies Newsletter* 38 (1998), 4–16 [see Diensberg 1997, above]

——, ' "Never the twain shall meet": Early Middle English – the East-West Divide', in *Placing Middle English in Context*, ed. Irma Taavitsainen et al., Topics in English Linguistics 35 (Berlin, 2000), pp. 97–124

—— and Angus McIntosh, 'The Language of *Ancrene Riwle*, the Katherine Group Texts and *The Wohunge of Ure Lauerd* in BL Cotton Titus D XVIII', *Neuphilologische Mitteilungen* 96 (1995), 235–63

Millett, Bella, ' "Hali Meiðhad", "Sawles Warde", and the Continuity of English Prose', in *Five Hundred Years of Words and Sounds: A Festschrift for Eric Dobson*, ed. E.G. Stanley and Douglas Gray (Cambridge, 1983)

——, 'The Saints' Lives of the Katherine Group and the Alliterative Tradition', *Journal of English and Germanic Philology* 87 (1988), 16–34

——, 'The Origins of *Ancrene Wisse*: New Answers, New Questions', *Medium Ævum* 61 (1992), 206–28

——, 'Women in No Man's Land: English Recluses and the Development of Vernacular Literature in the Twelfth and Thirteenth Centuries', in *Women and Literature in Britain, 1150–1500*, ed. Carol M. Meale (Cambridge, 1993; 2nd ed. 1996)

—— (with the assistance of Yoko Wada and George Jack), *Ancrene Wisse, The Katherine Group, and the Wooing Group*, Annotated Bibliographies of Old and Middle English Literature 2 (Cambridge, 1996a)

——, '*Peintunge* and *schadewe* in *Ancrene Wisse* Part 4', *Notes and Queries* ns 43 (1996b), 399–403

——, '*Ancrene Wisse* and the Conditions of Confession', *English Studies* 80 (1999), 193–215

——, '*Ancrene Wisse* and the Book of Hours', in *Writing Religious Women*, ed. Denis Renevey and Christiania Whitehead (Cardiff, 2000), pp. 21–40

——, '*Ancrene Wisse* and the Life of Perfection', *Leeds Studies in English* 33 (2002), 53–76

O'Mara, Veronica M., 'Preaching to Nuns in Late Medieval England', in *Medieval Monastic Preaching*, ed. Carolyn Muessig, Brill's Studies in Intellectual History 90 (Leiden, 1998), pp. 93–119

Renevey, Denis, 'Enclosed Desires: A Study of the Wooing Group', in *Mysticism and*

Spirituality in Medieval England, ed. William F. Pollard and Robert Boenig (Wood-bridge, Suffolk, 1997), pp. 39–62

Robertson, Elizabeth, ' "This Living Hand": Thirteenth-Century Female Literacy, Materialist Immanence, and the Reader of the *Ancrene Wisse*', *Speculum* 78 (2003), 1–36

Salih, Sarah, 'Performing Virginity: Sex and Violence in the Katherine Group', in *Constructions of Widowhood and Virginity in the Middle Ages*, ed. Cindy Carlson and Angela Jane Weisl (New York, 1999), pp. 95–112

——, 'Queering *Sponsalia Christi*: Virginity, Gender and Desire in the Early Middle English Anchoritic Texts', *New Medieval Literatures* 5 (2001), 156–75

——, *Versions of Virginity in Late Medieval England* (Cambridge, 2001)

Savage, Anne, 'The Solitary Heroine: Aspects of Meditation and Mysticism in *Ancrene Wisse*, the Katherine Group, and the Wooing Group', in *Mysticism and Spirituality in Medieval England*, ed. William F. Pollard and Robert Boenig (Woodbridge, Suffolk, 1997), 63–83

Scahill, John, 'Lexicographical Notes on Fourteenth-Century Copies of Ancrene Wisse', *Seikei Review of English Studies* 1 (1997), 107–14

Schaefer, Ursula, 'Twin Collocations in the Early Middle English Lives of the Katherine Group', in *Orality and Literacy in Early Middle English*, ed. Herbert Pilch, *ScriptOralia* 83 (1996), 179–98

Shinoda, Yoshihiro, 'Double Verb Phrases in *Saint Juliana* and *Hali Meiðhad*', in *Language and Style in English Literature: Essays in Honour of Michio Masui*, ed. Michio Kawai (Tokyo, 1991), pp. 191–210

Sisam, Celia, 'The Scribal Tradition of the *Lambeth Homilies*', *Review of English Studies* ns 2, 6 (1951), 105–13

Smith, Jeremy, 'Standard Language in Early Middle English?' in *Placing Middle English in Context*, ed. Irma Taavitsainen et al., Topics in English Linguistics 35 (Berlin, 2000), pp. 125–39

Stevenson, Lorna, and Jocelyn Wogan-Browne, eds, *Concordances to the Katherine Group, MS Bodley 34, and the Wooing Group, MSS Nero A XIV and Titus D XVII* (Cambridge, 2000)

Tolkien, J.R.R., '*Ancrene Wisse* and *Hali Meiðhad*', *Essays and Studies* 14 (1929), 104–26

Wada, Yoko, ed., *A Book of Ancrene Wisse* (Osaka, 2002)

——, ed., *A Companion to Ancrene Wisse* (Cambridge, 2003)

Wogan-Browne, Jocelyn, *Saints' Lives and Women's Literary Culture: Virginity and its Authorizations* (Oxford, 2001)

2

Rolle and Related Works

R. HANNA

Richard Rolle, the Yorkshire hermit-visionary-purveyor of spiritual counsel (d. 1349), is the first real 'author' in Middle English. And his author(ial)ity was well recognised in the period, for he was widely known by name and, on the basis of manuscript survivals and references, the most popular English spiritual writer of the later Middle Ages. Indeed, during the period, Rolle was ascribed a wider range of religious texts than even a very prolific literary career had managed to produce. If not the first Middle English writer to produce a literal biblical translation and commentary,[1] he was certainly the most important and a model regularly invoked by later writers (see Hudson 1985).

The only real information about Rolle's biography is provided by the *lecciones* prepared late in the fourteenth century in anticipation of his canonisation. This liturgical office gives at best only approximative information, the actual events now visible only through a hagiographic sheen. In 'St Richard, [hermit] of Hampole', his customary denomination, his chosen vocation has obscured his surname, and the variousness of his residences has been subsumed under the name of the south Yorkshire Cistercian nunnery where he died and was buried in 1349. (Since the projected canonisation did not occur, this office was never publicly celebrated but communicated for private devotion; see 'Officium' and Comper for a translation.)

The Office tells that Rolle was born at Thornton Dale, on the edge of the North Yorkshire moors (perhaps, as Watson compellingly argues, so late as 1310). He was sent to Oxford, under the patronage of Thomas Neville, later an archdeacon of Durham, but a younger son of the prominent Northern family, the Nevilles of Raby (co. Durham). However, at age eighteen, Rolle seems to have thrown over academic life (cf. 'For sum þat semes wysest er maste foles, for al þar wysdom þai spyll in covayties and bisynes abowte þe worlde')[2] and to have returned secretly to the area of his birth (so as not to alert or anger his father, now living further north in Yafforth).

Rolle then consecrated himself as a hermit. He signified this new life of

---

[1] One manuscript of the (lightly glossed) 'Early English Prose Psalter' (IMEP 114, the printed text does not signal the glosses) may have been copied within Rolle's lifetime, and this text, as well as two further extensive works of biblical commentary, the prose Apocalypse (IMEP 584) and unedited prose *Mirror*, partly dependent upon the Apocalypse, most probably predate 1320.

[2] 'Form' 112/142–44; 737–39: my customary form of citation, first page/line to Allen's edition (in Yorkshire language), second Ogilvie-Thomson's lineation (a better text, from which I have derived bracketed corrections).

devotion by reclothing himself in a parti-coloured habit made from his sister's castoff clothing. (Such self-creation is not unusual for those feeling such a calling.)[3] He was, the Office says, for a short time patronised as local holy man by the Dalton family of nearby Pickering, but seems to have spent most of his life as a hermit-solitary in variously mobile hermitages in 'Richmondshire' (northwest Yorkshire), before retiring to a cell near Hampole.

This choice of residence appears to depend upon Rolle's relation as spiritual advisor to Margaret Kirkby, who became a nun at Hampole c. 1343 (on such relationships, see Riddy). The one discernible date in Rolle's life falls in its last year, his composition for Kirkby of the epistle of spiritual counsel 'The Form of Living'. This work is associated with her leaving Hampole to be enclosed as an anchorite in a cell at East Layton (North Riding; cf. 'Form' 122–24, lines that identify the occasion).

Most of Rolle's writings, indeed all the early materials, are in Latin and had, in many cases, a considerably greater circulation (and more extensive printing history) than even his widely dispersed English ones (see Sharpe). These include not simply a full commentary on the Psalter but two contemplative tracts, *Incendium amoris* and *Melos amoris*, frequently written in an ecstaticly mannered Latin prose, and the popular instructional tract, *Emendatio vite*. (*Incendium* and *Emendatio* were both eventually translated into English, the latter eight times.) The vernacular writings appear to come from the last years of Rolle's life. Here, although there is a large group of short texts, pre-eminent are a second, English commentary on the Psalter and three prose epistles of counsel, 'Ego dormio', 'The Commandment', and 'Form of Living'.

'Tradition', in this case represented by the poem prefaced to the copy of the Psalter in Bodl. MS Laud misc. 286, identifies the work as having been addressed to Margaret Kirkby. The poem further alleges that the autograph was preserved at Hampole.[4] However produced, the prose Psalter is an academic text – commentary is a learned clerical genre (one Rolle ceaselessly pursued in Latin), and the work is drawn from a standard Latinate authority, the common gloss of Peter Lombard (itself a compendium of accepted patristic readings, cf. 'In expounynge I folew haly doctours', 7/97–8). Moreover, the work is preceded by a prologue, a specifically learned and academic genre, here one that takes up, albeit in deliberately parodic and disordered fashion, those topics conventional in academic reading strategies: the title of the work, its author, his intention, the material treated, the type of procedure used in argument, the ordering and parts

---

3   Cf. the discussions in *Piers Plowman*, e.g. 'I *shoop* me in shroudes . . ./ In habite as an heremite' (B Pro. 2–3); see Hanna 1997.
4   See Bramley, pp. 1–2, lines 23–32, which begin by stating that Rolle:
        Glosed þe sauter þat sues here in Englysch tong sykerly
        At a worthy recluse prayer, cald dame Merget Kyrkby.
     The poem was composed no earlier than the opening years of the fifteenth century (and perhaps after 1409); this dating depends on the author's objections (lines 45–60) to circulating versions of the Psalter expanded with Lollard interpolations. However, this insistence on orthodoxy and the necessary precision of reproducing Rolle's words might qualify the provided information, for this is an interpolated copy. The manufacturers of the book were either using the poem to shield and authenticate their actual work, or could not recognise the interpolations included in the copy they transmitted.

of the book, its usefulness, the branch of learning to which it pertains (cf. Minnis).

This will indicate an important paradox, especially germane to Rolle's English writings. Although Rolle writes informally, and frequently alludes to his own experience, this presentation largely represents an act of rhetorical positioning. Whatever his sometime dismissiveness about the value of books, he had either absorbed (or carried about with him) a very large number of them (cf. Bennett). As recent treatments (notably Renevey) show, he alludes to books, often silently but pretty constantly, and his various cells are apt to have featured not just spartan pallets but both book-chests and writing equipment. Merely to note one example, at 'The Commandment' 198–213, what appears the rhetorically climactic and earnest entreaty against worldlyness in fact cites or adapts closely a short meditation often ascribed to Bernard of Clairvaux. This Rolle is most apt to have known from the excerpt in the *Summa iusticie* often ascribed to Robert Grosseteste.[5]

Academic commentary is a public mode of writing, and Rolle's Psalter, especially given its great length, had a very large circulation, a good deal of it in Wycliffite adopted versions (see Hudson 1988). In contrast, the epistles seem a more intimate form of writing. Although the important anthology, Longleat House, Marquess of Bath, MS 29, implicitly presents the three texts as if all were addressed to 'Margareta de Kyrkby', their headings in the collection in CUL, MS Dd.5.64 (III) would indicate a more various, but nonetheless originally private, audience. Although Dd identifies 'The Form' as 'scripta . . . ad Margaretam annachoritam, suam dilectam discipulam', it also states that 'The Commandment' was 'scriptus cuidam sorori de Hampole' and 'Ego Dormio', 'cuidam moniali de ӡedyngham', i.e. Yedingham, a small house of Benedictine nuns just east of Pickering and Thornton Dale.

The manuscript record offers similar difficulties in terms of viewing the epistles as a unified group. These have been obscured by a history of editorial presentation focussed upon witnesses in which all three texts appear together (Longleat and Dd; Bodl. MS Rawlinson A.389, from which are derived most other examples of this presentation, Ogilvie-Thomson's GSVW). But in the extensive record of these texts, involving something like seventy separate copies, 'The Form of Living' seems always to have been perceived as central to spiritual life, and the circulation of the others diffused and a bit hit or miss.

This view would confirm what seems evident on any inspection, that the three epistles address different situations and imperatives. 'The Commandment' has certainly been composed for someone in a monastic situation (see 152–60). And while it broaches a number of themes Rolle ceaselessly repeats, it is not involved, as the other epistles are, with issues of the contemplative life. In this emphasis, 'The Commandment' follows the text cited at its opening, 'the greatest commandment of the law' (Matt. 22:37–40, a quotation of Deut. 6:5), a general prohibition against worldlyness in fact applicable to every Christian.

---

5   The same passage appears, independently, elsewhere in prose and verse, as 'The Meditation of St Augustine' (IPMEP 338, ed. Horstman, 2:374–5) and as IMEV 3310.

Rolle urges here the most ubiquitous of all topics in his writing, turning from worldlyness in order to experience the fire of love. But equally, he here regularly presents the fire as that of penitential purgation, not that of heavenly presence, e.g. 'þe fyre of lufe þat sal byrn in þi hert wil bryn til noght al þe rust of syn and purge þi sawle of al fylth, als clene as þe golde þat es proved in þe fournes' (80/240–43; 185–87). Generally, divine presence is imagined in the work as an experience to anticipate only in eternity (lines 50–3, on making one's thoughts companions to angels, may involve the most expansive claim made here), and the frequent (in Rolle's English writing, unusual) gospel emphases of the piece (e.g. 86–101) mark it as admonitory general instruction, perhaps to a novice, on the difference between religion and the *saeculum*.

In contrast, the claims advanced in the other epistles are far from so routine. 'Ego dormio' has a favoured addressee: 'Til þe I write [þis] specialy, for I hope[6] mare godenes in þe þan in another' (62/39–40; 33–44). And this tract provides ecstatic instruction in contemplative experience, signalled by its governing text, 'Ego dormio, et cor meum vigilat' (Song 5:2), as Renevey argues, central to a Latin commentary tradition Rolle had thoroughly absorbed and assimilated. From the beginning, Rolle expects that his addressee will be joined, not just with angels but 'intill þe heest, þat maste lufed God and byrnandest es in hys lufe – Seraphyn, es at say "brynand" ' (62/33–35; 28–29).

'The Form of Living' is the only one of the three letters with a recorded medieval title (derived from 94/42; 265, 119/76–77; 894 and repeated in a few manuscript copies).[7] Its canonical status in the late medieval spiritual community is well deserved, since it is a comprehensive guide to spiritual conduct, beginning with 'ilka synful man or woman þat es bunden in dedly syn' and extending to instruction in contemplation of divinity itself. The text, written on Margaret Kirkby's inclaustration, provides a full model of religious life from its beginnings – in the first half Margaret is in The Life, not worldly, yet potentially susceptible to demonic temptation and not perfect (but in need of advice on 'discretion of spirits' and of visions).

'The Form', with its references to a path or way, outlines succintly 'how þou may come til perfeccion' (119/77; 894–5). The tract, an expression of the wish 'þat þou be ay clymbande tyll Ihesuward and ekand þi luf and þi servys in hym' (96/1–2; 311–2), uses clear instructional paradigms and has a clarity of structure absent from the other writings. The first half demonstrates 'how þou may dispose þi lyfe and rewle it to Goddes will' (102/213–14; 485–66) and is succeeded by the discussion of (contemplative) love, introduced by the citation 'Amore langueo' (Song 2:5, 103/1; 489). This text will be replaced, in the highest stages of love, by the definitive 'Ego dormio' (106/51–52, 61–71; 564, 571–78). Precisely this carefully structured comprehensiveness made the work a vernacular spiritual classic.

But whatever the state of the addressee or the occasion, the English treatises display a certain constancy of theme and discussion. Rolle persistently returns

---

6   The customary Northern sense 'think, believe', not 'expect'.
7   Dd calls the tract 'Forma vivendi', the pair Vernon/Simeon 'þe fourme of parfyt liuyng'.

to a few basic issues (best outlined, within the context of the whole English mystical tradition, in Gillespie's series of articles). Most basic to all the tracts is a simple distinction between the life of the world and that of the spirit. This is predicated on both Jesus's 'great commandment' and upon the claim 'Qui non diligit, non novit Deum, quoniam Deus caritas est' (1 John 4:8, cf. 15). Rolle's favourite word is 'lufe', and it always defines a life of devotion, as opposed to one not knowing God, of worldlyness, vanity and sin. And as love approaches being the totality of the addressee's experience, she will approach a rapturous unity with the divine nature.

Implicit in this formulation and in the insistence upon withdrawal from worldly concerns is a dialectical distinction between two ways of living. This Rolle tends to present in both the positive and negative, through the inclusion of satirical attacks, especially upon the detraction the godly might expect from the worldly (e.g. 'Commandment' 14–23, 'Form' 731–2). In the sometimes more pronounced form of the Latin writings, Watson construes such statements as Rolle's anxiety about his own authority as spiritual teacher.

If, as Rolle sees it, the world and the social relations it enjoins are all 'busyness', the life of love is the strange inaction of solitude, and preferably the solitude of eremetic withdrawal or literal inclaustration. Rolle grudgingly acknowledges the limitations of his addressee in 'The Commandment', 'If þow may not dreghe to syt by þin ane' (75/74–5; 58), and, early in 'The Form', he instructs Kirkby directly, 'þe state þat þou ert in, þat es solitude, es maste abyll of all othyr til revelacion of þe Haly Gaste' (90/23–4; 138–9).[8] Although withdrawal, in Kirkby's case the utter physical isolation of inclaustration, literally dead to the world, seems senseless in conventional terms, the worldly simply do not comprehend:

> Men wenes þat we er in pyne and in penance grete, bot we have mare ioy and mare verray delyte in a day, þan þai have in þe worlde all þar lyve. þai se oure body, bot þai se noght oure hert, whare oure solace es. (89/12–16; 130–33)

> (Indeed, 'pyne and penance grete' are strikingly absent from Rolle's thinking, and he tends to deprecate, rather than encourage, ascetic rigour, in favour of opening oneself to love; cf. 'Form' 48–86.)

'Sit', the powerfully inactive verb Rolle uses to describe the apparent inaction of love, functions as an emblem for the acts of eternity. In that future of full bliss, one gains a seat where full vision and coparticipation with the divine will become all: 'þai er Goddes trone þat dwelles still in a stede, and er noght abowte rennand . . . and I have lufed for to sytt' (116/258–9; 827–9). Similarly, measured physical pauperisation here opens the way to a higher experience, that of an existence self-sufficient apart from the world, sustained in the presence of God.

---

8   Cf. also 'mare delyte to be by þin nane and speke till þi luf' (89/9–10; 128–29); and in 'Ego dormio', '[to] go [þyn] ane to walk [i.e. wake] and pray and thynk þe joy of heven and [to have compassyon] of þe passyon of Ihesu Criste' (62/54–55; 44–45); 'euer þe wil list sit þat þou be euer louynge [a common Rolle pun, 'loving'/'lowing' praising] thy Lord' (245–46; omitted at 70/299).

Yet, such behaviours, essentially the emulation of Rolle's personal eremetic practise, are far from actionless. Typically, Rolle imagines the solitary as proceeding by degrees, passing through various stages of the spiritual life. While perhaps unsurprising as a conceptualisation, this view is presented in a language learned and appropriated, the triad of insuperable, inseparable, and singular love derived from the writings of the twelfth-century Parisian theorist, Richard of St Victor (cf. the explicit listings of 'Commandment' 24–41, 'Form' 525–626). But categories are far from a system, and Rolle fills them in variously, depending on the instructional context. At 'Ego dormio' 66–138, where they comprise the body of the tract, for example, the states are unnamed, but described as general actions. The lowest is keeping the commandments and avoiding sins, essentially the life of common Christians and that enjoined in 'The Commandment'; the second, 'perfite life', one of withdrawn spiritual occupations leading to the third, contemplative life, direct contact with the heavenly itself.

Advance in this process does not simply reflect an effort at purging worldlyness. The solitary life, as Rolle describes it, may not include the worldling's 'busyness', but it certainly relies on work, the traditional monastic devotional order of reading, prayer, and meditation (leccio, oracio, meditacio).[9] Thus, 'Ego dormio' initially describes the second state as given over to spiritual things, including 'thynkyng of his passyon' (65/152; 121). But as one progresses, 'þan wil þe liste stele by þe alane, to thynk on Criste and to be in mykel praying' (65–6/158–9; 125–6). And the subsequent description of prayer, 'when þou ert by þe alane, gyf þe mykel to say þe psalmes of þe Psauter and Pater Noster and Ave Maria' (6/164–5; 129–30), implies the prior absorption of the written text. This injunction explains why Rolle thought the Psalter important enough to translate for Kirkby's use and to comment upon twice. In Rolle's thought, this basic book of biblical devotion enjoins two modes, both the penitential and the faithfully amatory.

But Rolle is far more interested in exceeding these exercises to arrive at contemplacion:

> Contemplatife lyf hase twa partyes, a lower and a heer. þe lower party es meditacion of haly wrytyng, þat es Goddes wordes, and in other gude thoghtes and swete, þat men hase of þe grace of God abowt þe lufe of Jhesu Criste, and also in lovyng of God in psalmes and ympnes, or in prayers. þe hegher party of contemplacion es behaldyng and ȝernyng of þe thynges of heven.
>
> ('Form' 118/35–42; 861–66)

Meditative prayer functions as a springboard to contemplation. Here Rolle is prone to emphasise the love inspired by thought of the Passion and a responsive emulation of the love that Jesus showed in his voluntary suffering. But equally prominent is what one might consider the nonverbal (or the only fragmentarily

---

[9] Perhaps the classic English statement appears in the Carthusian Adam of Dryburgh (d. 1212), 'De quadripartito exercitio cellae', ed. *PL* 153:799–854.

verbal), the name of Jesus. The tacked-on final paragraph of 'The Commandment' (214–24) urges the practise of this devotion, as does 'Ego Dormio':

> Nathyng pays God swa mykel als verray lufe of þis nam Ihesu. If þou luf it
> ryght and lastandely and never let for nathyng þat men may do or say, þou sal
> be r[ayvyst] intil a heghar lyfe þan þou can covete. (66/182–66; 144–47)

And 'Oleum effusum', a translated fragment of Rolle's partial exegesis of the
Song, offers a thoroughly expansive commendation:

> Sothely nathynge slokyns sa fell flawmes, dystroyes ill thoghtes, puttes owte
> venemous affeccyons, dos awaye coryous and vayne ocupacyons fra vs. This
> name Ihesu lelely haldyn in mynde drawes by ye rote vyces, settys vertus,
> inlawes charytee, inȝettis sauo[u]re of heuenly thynges, wastys discorde,
> reformes pese, gyffes inlastande ryste, dose awaye greuesnes of fleschely
> desyris, turnes all erthely thynge to noye, fyllys ye luffande of gastely ioye.
>
> (Lincoln Cath 91, fol. 192v)

The expansiveness of praise, both for the prayer and its referent, expresses itself
in the great rush and tumble of serial presentation. This embodies a(n inconsistent) tendency toward palpable English verbal roots, very physical acts, in
conjunction with the abstract romance vocabulary of spiritual life.[10]

Just as 'the name of Jesus' threatens to escape verbality, so the height of
unific contemplation of/participation in divinity to which it leads can also be
defined only gesturally. Rolle typically 'describes' the height of spiritual experience by a language pointing toward a distinct and complicated variety of sensation, physical terms doing duty as purified spiritual metaphor:

> A mans hert þat verraly es byrnand in þe lufe of God . . . hase myrth and ioy
> and melody in aungels sang ('Ego dormio' 63/65–67; 53–54)

> He gyves hymself till þaime in swetnes and delyte, in byrnyng of luf and in
> ioy and melody' ('Form' 90/29–31; 143–44)[11]

Here the repeated epithets 'joy/burning/song', with their contextual synonyms,
provide the English equivalents for Rolle's favourite Latin triplet, 'dulcor/calor/
canor'. More pregnantly than the English, the Latin alliteration and rhyming
terminations re-enforce the unitive experience, both a complex simplicity in the
worshipper *and* in her juncture with the celestial.

Uniquely, Rolle insists upon the enduring quality of this mystic ecstasy. The
epistles differ strikingly from most medieval discussions, with their attention to
'the dark night of the soul' when God does not return, and their accounts of

---

[10] Cf. the great definition of love, reminiscent of Herbert's 'Prayer': 'Luf es perfeccion of letters, vertu
of prophecy, frute of trowth, hel[e] of sacramentes, stablyng of witt and conyng, rytches of pure men,
lyfe of dyand men' ('Form' 109/30–2; 649–51); for another discussion that might anticipate early
modern devotional language, see the elaboration of the perforations of the Passion in 'Meditation B'.

[11] Cf. further 'Ego dormio' 224–36 (a product of the preceding passion meditation); the opening of the
prologue to the Psalter (Allen 4–5/1–15 or so); or 'Form' 551–64 (associated with moving beyond the
general description of love, 'Amore langueo', to the fully fledged union signalled by the verse 'Ego
dormio').

ascetic exercises that may hasten His reappearance. For Rolle, burning musical joy never partakes of a repeatable exercise; rather, he assumes that, once gained, the state is preserved and becomes the automatic and ceaselessly available end of the solitary's endeavour:

> þan þe fire of lufe verrali ligges in þair hert and byrnes þarin . . . and sithen forward þai er contemplatife men and ravyst in lufe
>
> ('Form' 119/65–68; 885–88)

The accomplished hermit or recluse lives ever in love, in the sweetness of heaven. Her continuous ecstasy poises herself both against *and* longing for death and the full consummation of love. Hence Rolle is fond of the proverb, that love is strong as death and hell (even in 'The Commandment'; see 36–41).

These ideas are couched in a prose of often extravagant and certainly various stylistic virtuousity (ably discussed by Copeland). As someone well trained in the trivium, Rolle has a keen sense of a suitably diverse form of literary statement that will parallel the diverse situations and subjects of his writing.

The prose Psalter, whose prologue includes an important stylistic statement (Allen 7/91–7), shows a deliberately greater roughness than any of the epistles. Rolle promises to 'seke no strange Inglis', by which he means no language that will alienate or estrange the reader from the Latin.[12] In encouraging the vernacular reader to 'come to the Latin', Rolle implies the potential use of the translation as liturgical primer. And the carefully non-English word order of the actual translation, a practise that may have influenced the first Wycliffite biblical translation, is frequently evident:

> **Auditui meo dabis gaudium et leticiam; et exultabunt ossa humiliata** ¶ *Til my heryng þou sall gif ioy and faynes; and glade sall banes mekid*
>
> (Ps. 50:9, Bramley 186)

Such meticulous literalism extends to vocabulary, and Rolle relies especially heavily on calque translation, e.g. prayabill/deprecabilis 89:15, vptaker/susceptor 90:2, huntand/venancium 90:3, inras/incursis 90:6. The style of the commentary portions is equally constrained (if somewhat freer), but in this case by standard techniques of glossing, with sentence grammar adjusted to accommodate the biblical lemmata:

> ¶ *Til my heryng* with men *þou sall gif ioy* of remyssion, sayand, 'þi syn is forgifen þe', *and faynes* of endles life þat I hope. *And glade sall banes*, þat is all þe vertus of my saule *mekid*, for þai er withouten pride.[13]

---

12 Hence, he promises to provide a translation 'mast like vnto þe Latyn' and claims, 'I folow þe letter als mekil als I may'.

13 Some sense of the customary compression and rearrangement can be gained by comparing the source (*PL* 191:489):

  Nota istum humilem esse, quasi dicat, 'Audiam te humilis, non loquar contra te superbus defendendo culpam'. Et huic *auditui meo dabis gaudium* de absolutione peccati, dicendo 'Dimissum est tibi peccatum tuum' [cf. 2 Reg. 12:13]. *Et laetitiam* de aeternis quae promittis mihi. Qui enim humilis audit et discit, intus gaudet de veritate [Rolle's source had, or he read it as, 'virtute'] . . . *Et* quia iam humilis sum *exsultabunt ossa*, id est interiora mea *humiliata*, quia sunt sine fastu, non habent tumorem.

The only other fairly persistent example of 'plain style' occurs in 'The Commandment'. Here Rolle does not present the 'rough style', the constrained literalism of translation, but rather what one understands as the traditional plain style of moral instruction. The tract relies on the repeated imperative mode, often embodied in a clipped and frequently staccato series of directives.

But in general, the epistles display a considerably more elegant sense of diction and phrasing. One typically elevated example of a 'middle style' occurs in a 'name of Jesus' passage in 'The Form':

> And when þou spekes til hym and says 'Ihesu' thurgh custom, it sal be in þi ere ioy, in þi mouth hony, and in þi hert melody. For þe sall thynk ioy to here þat name be nevened, swetnes to speke it, myrth and sang to thynk it. If þou thynk Ihesu contynuly and halde it stabely, it purges þi syn and kyndels þi hert; it clarifies þi sawle, it removes anger and dose away slawnes; it woundes in lufe and fulfilles of charite; it chaces þe devel and puttes oute drede; it opens heven and makes a contemplatif man. Have in mynde Jhesu, for al vices and fantomes it puttes owte fra þe lover. And haylce oft Mary, bath day and nyght. Mikel lufe and ioy sal þou fele, if þou wil do aftyr þis lare. þe thare noght covayte gretely many bokes; halde lufe in hert and in werke, and þou hase al [done] þat we may say or wryte. For fulnes of þe law es charite; in þat hynges all. (108/4–20; 612–25)

As several citations above will have indicated, such serial presentation is endemic in the epistles. Although much of the passage shows that same rush of epithet I have previously described, the whole is plotted and controlled. Although carefully balanced (and one might note the terminals of ioy/hony/melody at the head as an 'Englishing' of the terminal -or's of the underlying Latin triplet), the balance is varied, both in terms of the number of members in each unit, and in alternations between complete and incomplete repetition of detail within those members. And as in my earlier citation of 'Oleum', there is an attractive and deliberated alternation of foreign and native roots. But whatever the degree of carefully expansive balance (Dd emphasises it in this passage, whereas Lt attempts a more serial presentation), the conclusion is drawn plainly and directly. The prose quiets near the end, the members shorten, affective description is replaced by a direct turn to the reader, and the whole is rounded off by plain proverbial biblicism (cf. Alford 1973).

Rolle reserves his truly 'high style', in essence a translation of the mannerism of the Latin writings, for specific effects. It is the property of incantatory meditative texts and reserved for specific model contexts, notably descriptions, designed to lift the reader toward ecstasy, of the Passion and of the power of the name 'Jesu'. Here one might single out the pyrotechnics of 'Meditation on the Passion A' (Allen 24–25), or of another Passion account, 'Ego dormio' 175–211. On such occasions, Rolle writes in rhythmic cadences hanging rather ambiguously between prose and verse (see Smedick), and between the traditional line of alliterative poetry (my preferred way to read it) and septenary verse. In addition to the rhythmic exaltation, the lines are embellished with sporadic decorative alliteration and medial- and/or end-rhyme.

'Richard hermit' had an enormous medieval circulation, both real and suppositious. He was ascribed in manuscript a wide swathe of Middle English literature, including the extensive and widely disseminated Northern instructional poems *The Prick of Conscience* and *Speculum vite*. But in spite of this very great medieval popularity, Rolle seems to have been deselected from the vernacular canon precipitately and at a very early date (c. 1510). Only two English bits, both short excerpts from 'The Form of Living', appeared in early modern prints, that in the Latin *Speculum spiritualium* (Jones, not in IPMEP); and that prefaced to de Worde's edition of an Englished version of William Flete's *Remedies against Temptations* (IPMEP 528).

Rolle was only re-discovered as a Middle English writer in the nineteenth century. G.G. Parry first signalled the importance of the English work by printing (in EETS 20, 1866) the bundle of short texts found in the Yorkshire miscellany, compiled by the gentryman Robert Thornton, Lincoln Cathedral, MS 91, fols 192–196v. And the English writings were first extensively provided in Horstman's anthology, complete with elaborate and extended misascriptions. Whereas medieval readers were fond of crediting the hermit with extensive Northern verse texts, Horstman's Victorian expansiveness concentrated on any spiritual prose that appeared remotely proximate to genuine Rolle in manuscript. Hope E. Allen sorted most of the broad problems associated with this misplaced enthusiasm, although as Jones shows, not altogether fully.

Although his sense of its distribution might be questioned, Horstman did correctly see one important mechanism underlying Rolle's medieval popularity. His work persisted and remained broadly influential throughout a range of Middle English devotional prose. Such writing – including texts such as *The Holy Book Gracia Dei*, the Yorkshire translation of *Vitae patrum* selections (sayings and anecdotes associated with the first hermits, the Desert Fathers), *Contemplations of the Dread and Love of God*, to name prominent examples – does not simply recall Rolle's themes, but is frequently quotational, recycling Rolle's own words for new audiences. Far from all examples of this direct indebtedness have been discovered; for example, the ascription of *Speculum vite* to the hermit may rest on a recognition that about two hundred lines of the text versify quite directly 'The Form of Living' 329–98.

But equally, such widespread quotational appropriation reflects the state of Rolle's text itself. For his writings frequently do not circulate in manuscript as authorially promulgated works, but as the products of selective quotation. The two early printings are in a certain way prescient, for most copies of 'The Form' are excerpted in some way or another, often following convergent quotational patterns. At some point, the most extensive evidence of his influence, its appropriation by others, becomes indistinguishable from relatively faithful (if selective) handlings of his own text.

BIBLIOGRAPHY

Primary Texts in English

Where possible, texts are linked to Ogilvie-Thomson's edition (OT); this volume appeared after IPMEP and provides only those texts in Longleat House, Marquess of Bath, MS 29. Moreover, although OT's texts are better than those printed elsewhere, they do not appear in the North Yorkshire language one supposes authorial; this can be savoured in Allen's (often textually inferior) edition.

The prose psalter (IPMEP 271, Wells 23/2, i.e. Lagorio et al.), ed. Bramley; selections ed. Allen, pp. 1–16

Meditations on the Passion (IPMEP 618, ? 367, Wells 23/3), ed. OT, pp. 64–83, an earlier version of 'Meditation A' ed. Allen, pp. 19–27

The Bee and the 'Stork' [the bird is actually a 'struk' ostrich] (IPMEP 657, Wells 23/4), ed. Allen, pp. 54–56

Desire and Delight (IPMEP 863, Wells 23/5), ed. OT, p. 40

Ghostly Gladness (IPMEP 253, Wells 23/6), ed. OT, p. 41

The Seven Gifts of the Holy Spirit (IPMEP 700, Wells 23/7), ed. Allen, pp. 116–17, in the form intruded as ch. 11 into her base MS of 'The Form of Living'

The Ten Commandments (IPMEP 667, Wells 23/8), ed. Horstman, 1:195–6

Ego dormio (IPMEP 160, Wells 23/9), ed. OT, pp. 26–33

The Commandment (IPMEP 660, Wells 23/10), ed. OT, pp. 34–39

The Form of Living (IPMEP 351, Wells 23/11), ed. OT, pp. 1–25

Richard Misyn's translation of Incendium amoris (IMPEP 92, Wells 23/13), this text and the next ed. Harvey

Richard Misyn's translation of Emendatio vite (IPMEP 652, Wells 23/14)

Other translations of Emendatio vite (cf. IPMEP 651–52, Wells 23/15), only two of these versions have been published; see Hulme and Harford

Oleum effusum (IPMEP 506, Wells 23/16), ed. Horstman, 1:186–91

Prose exempla (cf. Wells 23/17), probably Rollean are IPMEP 821, 564, 58, 59, ed. in that order, Horstman, 1:192–94; perhaps Rollean are IPMEP 126 and 8, ed. in that order, Horstman, 1:157

Lessouns of Dirige (not in Wells and unpub.), certainly a translation from Rolle's popular *Super novem lectiones mortuorum*, perhaps an authentic English text; see Hargreaves

Editions

Allen, Hope E., ed., *The English Writings of Richard Rolle, Hermit of Hampole* (Oxford, 1931, 1963)

Bramley, H.R., ed., *The Psalter or Psalms of David and Certain Canticles* (Oxford, 1884)

Comper, Frances M.M., *The Life of Richard Rolle* (1928; repr. New York and London, 1969), the Office translated, pp. 301–14

Horstman, C., ed., *Yorkshire Writers*, 2 vols (London, 1895–96); repr. ed. Anne C. Bartlett (Cambridge, 1999)

'Officium de S. Ricardo de Hampole', *Breviarium ad usum insignis ecclesie Eboracensis, Vol. II*, Surtees Society 75 (1880), cols 785–820

Ogilvie-Thomson, S.J., ed., *Richard Rolle, Prose and Verse*, EETS 293 (Oxford, 1988)

Windeatt, B.A., ed. *English Mystics of the Middle Ages* (Cambridge, 1994), pp. 15–66

Some Related Texts

Aarts, F.G.A.M., ed., *Þe Pater Noster of Richard Ermyte: A Late Middle English Exposition of the Lord's Prayer* (Nijmegen, 1967)

Arntz, Mary L., ed., *Richard Rolle and Þe Holy Boke Gratia Dei: An Edition with Commentary*, Elizabethan and Renaissance Studies 92 (Salzburg, 1981)

Connolly, Margaret, ed., *Contemplations of the Dread and Love of God*, EETS 303 (Oxford, 1993)

Harford, Dundas, ed., *The Mending of Life, Being an Anonymous Version . . .* (London, 1913) [a modernisation, rather than edition or translation, of the 'Emendatio vite' translation in CUL, MS Ff.v.40 and BL, MS Harley 2406]

Harvey, Ralph, ed., *The Fire of Love, and the Mending of Life . . .* , EETS os 106 (London, 1896)

Hulme, William H., 'Richard Rolle of Hampole's *Mending of Life*, from the Fifteenth Century Worcester Cathedral Manuscript F.172', *Western Reserve University Bulletin* ns 21 (Cleveland, OH, 1918)

Discussions

Alford, John A., 'Biblical *Imitatio* in the Writings of Richard Rolle', *ELH* 40 (1973), 1–23

———, 'Richard Rolle and Related Works', in *Middle English Prose: A Critical Guide to Major Authors and Genres*, ed. A.S.G. Edwards (New Brunswick, NJ, 1984), pp. 35–60

Allen, Hope E., *Writings Ascribed to Richard Rolle, Hermit of Hampole, and Materials for his Biography* (New York, 1927)

Allen, Rosamond S., trans., *The English Writings* (London, 1989), with an extensive basic introduction, pp. 9–63

Bennett, J.A.W., and Douglas Gray, *Middle English Literature*, The Oxford History of English Literature 2, i (Oxford, 1986), pp. 301–10, 324, 383–84

Blake, N.F., '*The Form of Living* in Verse and Prose', *Archiv für das Studium der neueren Sprachen und Literaturen* 211 (1974), 300–08

Brady, M. Teresa, 'Rolle and the Pattern of Tracts in *The Pore Caitif*', *Traditio* 39 (1983), 456–65, with references to several earlier studies of Rolle's influence on this popular prose devotional manual

Copeland, Rita, 'Richard Rolle and the Rhetorical Theory of the Levels of Style', *MMTE* 3 (Cambridge, 1984), pp. 55–80

Gasse, Rosanne, 'Dowel, Dobet, and Dobest in Middle English Literature', *Florilegium* 14 (1995–96), 171–95

Gillespie, Vincent, 'Mystic's Foot: Rolle and Affectivity', *MMTE* 2 (Exeter, 1982), pp. 199–230

———, '*Lukynge in haly bukes: Lectio* in Some Late Medieval Spiritual Miscellanies', in *Spätmittelalterliche geistliche Literatur in der Nationalsprache 2*, ed. James Hogg, Analecta Cartusiana 106 (Salzburg, 1984), pp. 1–27

————, 'Strange Images of Death: The Passion in Later Medieval English Devotional and Mystical Writing', *Zeit, Tod und Ewigkeit in der Renaissance Literatur*, ed. James Hogg, 3 vols, Analecta Carthusiana 117.3 (Salzburg, 1987), pp. 111–59

————, 'Vernacular Books of Religion', *Book Production and Publishing in Britain 1375–1475*, ed. Jeremy Griffiths and Derek Pearsall (Cambridge, 1989), pp. 317–44

————, 'Postcards from the Edge: Interpreting the Ineffable in the Middle English Mystics', in *Interpretation: Medieval and Modern . . .*, ed. Piero Boitani and Anna Torti (Woodbridge, 1993), pp. 137–65

Glasscoe, Marion, *The English Medieval Mystics: Games of Faith* (London, 1993), esp. pp. 58–115

Hanna, Ralph, 'The Middle English *Vitae Patrum* Collection', *Mediaeval Studies* 49 (1987), 411–42

————, 'Will's Work', in *Written Work: Langland, Labor, and Authorship*, ed. Steven Justice and Kathryn Kerby-Fulton (Philadelphia, 1997), pp. 23–66

Hargreaves, Henry, '*Lessouns of Dirige*: A Rolle Text Discovered', *Neuphilologische Mitteilungen* 91 (1990), 511–19

Hudson, Anne, *Lollards and their Books* (London, 1985), esp. pp. 67–84 and 141–63 passim

————, *The Premature Reformation: Wycliffite Texts and Lollard History* (Oxford, 1988), esp. pp. 259–64 on Lollard adaptations of the Prose Psalter

Jones, E.A., 'A Chapter from Richard Rolle in Two Fifteenth-Century Compilations', *Leeds Studies in English* ns 27 (1996), 139–62

Keiser, George R., 'Þe Holy Boke Gratia Dei', *Viator* 12 (1981), 289–317

Lagorio, Valerie M., Michael G. Sargent, and Ritamary Bradley, 'English Mystical Writings', ch. 23 of *A Manual of the Writings in Middle English 1050–1500* [Wells' Manual], ed. Albert E. Hartung, vol. 9 (New Haven, 1993), pp. 3051–68, 3411–25

Minnis, A.J., *Medieval Theory of Authorship* (London, 1984), pp. 17–28 on academic prologues

Renevey, Denis, *Language, Self and Love: Hermeneutics in Richard Rolle and the Commentaries on the Song of Songs* (Cardiff, 2001)

Riddy, Felicity, ' "Women Talking About the Things of God": A Late Medieval Subculture', in *Women and Literature in Britain 1150–1500*, ed. Carol M. Meale (Cambridge, 1993, 1996), pp. 104–27

Riehle, Wolfgang, trans. Bernard Standring, *The Middle English Mystics* (London, 1981)

Sargent, Michael, 'Contemporary Criticism of Richard Rolle', *Kartusermystik und -Mystiker 1*, Analecta Cartusiana 55 (Salzburg, 1981), pp. 160–205

Sharpe, Richard, *A Handlist of Latin Writers of Great Britain and Ireland before 1540*, Publications of the Journal of Medieval Latin 1 (Turnhout, 1997), pp. 501–03

Smedick, Lois, 'Parallelism and Pointing in Rolle's Rhythmical Style', *Mediaeval Studies* 41 (1979), 404–67

Watson, Nicholas, *Richard Rolle and the Invention of Authority* (Cambridge, 1991)

————, 'Conceptions of the Word: The Mother Tongue and the Incarnation of God', *New Medieval Literatures* 1 (1997), 85–124

————, 'The Middle English Mystics', in *The Cambridge History of Medieval English Literature*, ed. David Wallace (Cambridge, 1999, 2002), pp. 539–65

3

Walter Hilton's *Scale of Perfection* and *The Cloud of Unknowing*

AD PUTTER

The *Cloud of Unknowing* and Walter Hilton's *Scale of Perfection* stand in an uncertain relationship to each other.[1] Both Hilton and the *Cloud* author were active in the East Midlands in the latter half of the fourteenth century, and a number of verbal echoes would suggest that one (or each) was familiar with the other's work (Taylor 2002), though the directions of influence are matters of dispute.[2] The similarities of thought and phrasing have even led some scholars to conclude that Walter Hilton and the *Cloud* author are one and the same man (Riehle 1977), but this hypothesis is implausible. The only medieval warrant for it is an annotation by the Carthusian theologian James Greenhalgh in a late manuscript of the *Cloud* (Bodl. Douce 262; c. 1500), ascribing it to Hilton, but the differences in temperament and theology between the *Scale* and the *Cloud* argue against common authorship.[3] For this reason, I shall discuss these works separately, making the occasional comparison to highlight the distinctiveness of their respective achievements.

I begin with the work that is the more welcoming to beginners, Hilton's *Scale of Perfection*.

The biographical facts concerning Hilton are few. According to most of the

---

[1] For the *Cloud* and associated works I have used the edition by Phyllis Hodgson, *'The Cloud of Unknowing' and Related Treatises* (Salzburg, 1982); this edition incorporates a number of corrections to the texts as printed in the two earlier EETS editions on which it is based: *The Cloud of Unknowing*, EETS os 218 (London, 1944) and *Deonise Hid Diuinite*, EETS os 231 (London, 1955). Unless otherwise stated, all references to Hodgson are to the 1982 edition. Hilton's *Scale* is cited from the edition by Thomas H. Bestul, *Walter Hilton: The Scale of Perfection* (Kalamazoo, MI, 2000), based on the text of Lambeth Palace, MS 472. References to Hilton's Latin works are to the edition by J.P.H. Clark and C. Taylor, *Walter Hilton's Latin Writings*, 2 vols (Salzburg, 1987). Arabic numbers indicate page and line numbers in these editions; roman numerals are used for references to the *Cloud* and the *Scale* to indicate books and/or chapters.

[2] Compare 'And in þis oonheed is þe mariage maad bitwix God and þe soule, þe whiche schal neuer be broken. . .' (*Epistle of Prayer*, 106.14–15) with 'And sotheli in this onynge is the mariage maad bitwixe God and the soule, which schal nevere be brokyn' (*Scale*, 38.159–60 [I.viii]); '& ʒif any þouʒt rise . . . & asche þee seiing: "What sekist þou, & what woldest þou haue?" sey . . . "Him I coueite, him I seche, & noʒt bot him."' (*Cloud*, 14.31–35) with 'Therfore yif it come to thy mynde as it were askand what thou hast lost and what sekest thou . . . seie Hym hast thu lost, and Hym wolde thou have, and nothynge but Hym' (*Scale*, 84.1337–41 [I.xlvi]), and 'þees men willen sumtyme wiþ þe coriouste of here ymaginacioun peerce þe planetes, make an hole in þe firmament to loke in þerate' (*Cloud* 58.29–31 [lvii]) with 'Not as summe men wenen, þat þe openynge of heuen is yif a soule miʒt seen by ymaginacioun þurʒ þe skies abouen þe firmament' (*Scale*, 214.2222–24 [II.xxxiii]).

[3] On these differences see Clark 1978 and Minnis 1983.

manuscript colophons, he died on 24 March 1396, in the Augustinian priory of Thurgarton (Nottinghamshire). In his younger years he had trained as a lawyer, probably at the University of Cambridge (Clark 1992), but he abandoned law to become a hermit. Two manuscripts refer to Hilton as a candidate for a Mastership in Canon Law, and one Walter Hilton, Bachelor of Civil Law, is mentioned in two documents dated 1371 and 1375 (Russell-Smith 1954). This documentary evidence fits with what Hilton reveals about himself in his Latin writings. In a Latin epistle (*Epistola ad Quemdam Seculo Renunciare Volentem*) addressed to a lawyer friend, John Thorpe, Hilton emboldens the lawyer to embrace the religious life and renounce his worldly occupation, admitting sympathetically that he, too, had to disappoint friends who thought he had a brilliant legal career ahead of him (262.266–77). In his *De Imagine Peccati*, Hilton speaks of himself as a solitary (97.445–46), while in a later work, *Epistola de Utilitate et Prerogativis Religionis*, he implies that the solitary life does not altogether suit him, and hopes that he may one day join a religious community (146.465–73). The *Epistola de Utilitate* is the only work by Hilton that can be securely dated, to c. 1383;[4] presumably he joined Thurgarton priory not very long afterwards.

The Latin language remained throughout the fourteenth century the obvious medium for theological writings, and was indeed Hilton's choice for most of his works (which include an anti-Lollard defence of the veneration of images). This explains why Hilton's English *Scale of Perfection* was translated into Latin (c. 1400) by the Carmelite friar Thomas Fishlake (Hussey 1973), in whose translation the *Scale* circulated in monastic circles on the continent. Hilton's shift to English was evidently prompted by the demand for guidance from lay and religious folk, particularly women, whose literacy did not extend to Latin. *The Epistle of the Mixed Life* was written for a lord occupied in 'bisynesse of þe world' (9.98),[5] who wishes to follow his inner spiritual calling without abandoning his worldly estate. The *Scale* is addressed to a female recluse, who has only just embarked on the contemplative life; she can read, but does not have the Latin to study the Bible: 'Redynge of Holi Writ mai thu not wel use' (45.334). The demand for English translations of Hilton's works is also attested by an anonymous Middle English exposition of a Latin epistle by Hilton (now lost), addressed to a Gilbertine nun, and an adaptation into English of a large chunk of the *Epistola ad Quemdam Seculo Renunciare Volentem*.[6] This adaptation, *A Pystille Made to a Cristene Frende*, is generally credited to an anonymous translator, and certainly the dialect of the extant version (BL, Add. 33971) is distinctly more northerly than Hilton's, but I think that the possibility that the *Pystille* was actually by Hilton himself should not be discounted. Hilton's *Eight Chapters on Perfection* (on how our love of Christ may be perfected) is a trans-

---

4 The *Epistola* refers to 'heretics' who impugn the vowed religious life, so must have been written after 1382, when Wycliffe's opinions on the religious life were officially condemned at the Blackfriars Synod; the terminus *ante quem* is 1386, when the addressee (Adam Horsley) joined a religious community (the Charterhouse of Beauvale), as the letter urges him to do.

5 *Walter Hilton's Mixed Life Edited from Lambeth Palace MS 472*, ed. S.J. Ogilvie-Thomson (Salzburg, 1986).

6 Both these works have been edited by Clark and Taylor, *Walter Hilton's Latin Writings* (see n. 1).

lation of a (no longer extant) Latin treatise by Lluis de Font, a Spanish Franciscan who taught theology at Cambridge in the 1380s.[7] Like the *Scale*, *Eight Chapters* was primarily intended for contemplatives who could not read Latin. Other works plausibly attributed to Hilton are *Of Angel's Song*[8] and the commentaries on *Qui habitat* (Ps. 90) and *Bonum est* (Ps. 91).[9] The ascriptions to Hilton of *The Prickynge of Love* (a translation of the *Stimulus Amoris* by James of Milan)[10] and of a commentary on the *Benedictus* (Luke 1.68–80) are uncertain.[11] Our problem is that Hilton's reputation as a theologian was such that later medieval English scribes fathered on him any number of anonymous mystical writings (*Remedies against Temptations*, *Chastising of God's Children*, the *Cloud*, and so on).

The *Scale of Perfection* is thought to belong to Hilton's later years at Thurgarton. Because it survives in over forty manuscripts (plus a number of early printed editions), the textual history of the *Scale* is intricate and further complicated by the fact that Book I circulated independently from Book II in the early manuscript tradition.[12] Indeed, there are almost as many manuscripts containing Book I alone (twenty-one) as there are manuscripts of the entire work (twenty-three);[13] only three manuscripts contain Book II alone. The scribes of the manuscripts containing only Book I seem to have been completely unaware that a second book existed (Gardner 1936). This suggests that Book I was originally published by Hilton as a free-standing work, Book II being added later as a supplement. Differences in style and matter between Books I and II also point to an interval between their composition. For example, while Book I has nothing to say about the role of biblical reading in the progress of the contemplative (since this path to perfection is not open to Hilton's addressee), Book II devotes a lengthy chapter to the sustenance to be drawn from Holy Writ, and to the special insight and inspiration that God gives to 'hem that aren speciali enspired for to

---

7 Ed. Fumio Kuriyagawa and Toshiyuki Takamiya, *Two Minor Works of Walter Hilton* (Tokyo, 1980).

8 Ed. Carl Horstman, in *Yorkshire Writers: Richard Rolle of Hampole and his Followers*, 2 vols (London, 1895–96), I, pp. 175–82.

9 Ed. Björn Wallner, *An Exposition of 'Qui habitat' and 'Bonum est' in English* (Lund, 1954). Hilton's authorship of the *Commentary on 'Bonum est'* has been questioned by Clark 1983, who argues that most of the ideas common to both *Bonum est* and Hilton's canonical works are religious commonplaces, but common authorship is, I think, indicated by stylistic similarities. For example, while there may be nothing strikingly original about the idea (common to *Bonum est* and the *Scale*) that God's withdrawal of sensible comforts from the soul may be the prelude to greater spiritual grace, the expression of this idea in *Bonum est* is markedly Hiltonian in style: 'He knoweþ wel þat grace is with-drawen from him in o manere. But hit is ʒiuen to him in a-noþur manere as god wole. Not so sweteli ne so felabli as hit was, but more prieuli and more miʒteli and more godly' (57.1–4). Typical of Hilton are calques on Latin words and constructions (e.g. *sensibiliter > felabli*, according to *MED* only recorded in *Scale*, 174.1060 [II.xxi]) and the striking preference for periphrastic comparative adverbs and adjectives, which reflect his careful emphasis on spiritual transcendence as a gradual process. Cf. *Scale* 240.2979–80 [II.lx]: 'the more clene that the soule is . . . the more myghti is the grace, more inward and moore goostli schewand the presence of our Lord Jhesu'. The periphrastic mode of comparison is still uncommon in fourteenth-century English (Hosic 1906).

10 Ed. Harold Kane, *The Prickynge of Love*, 2 vols (Salzburg, 1983).

11 *A Commentary on the 'Benedictus'*, ed. Björn Wallner (Lund, 1957).

12 For a full list of manuscripts and early printed editions, see Lagorio and Sargent 1993, 3430–31.

13 Amongst the twenty-three manuscripts containing both books, at least two – Bodl. 12143 (Rawlinson 285) and Cambridge, Corpus Christi College, 268 – separate Books I and II as if they were independent works.

seken sothfastnesse in Hooli Writ, with gret devocion in prayinge *and with moche bisynesse in studyinge goynge bifore*' (252.3342–44 [II.xliii]). In other respects, too, Book II is more ambitious, the final chapters transporting the reader to the sublime heights of contemplation. Hilton sets his sights much lower in Book I, for the simple reason that his addressee is a novice. If the addressee in Book II is the same person, she must have made much progress in the meanwhile. Evelyn Underhill thought that Hilton's writing in Book II 'showed signs of greater spiritual maturity' (Underhill 1923, p. xx); I am not qualified to read such signs, but there are many others that indicate a time-lag between books I and II. Thus the chapters in Book I are short and expository, while those of Book II are much longer and more diffuse. And while the argument and organisation of the chapters in Book I are dominated by scholastic divisions, the tenor of Book II is deeply influenced by the expressive possibilities which Hilton discovers in allegories, imagery and verbal paradoxes (Hussey 1980).

Qua literature, Book II is therefore much more interesting. Particularly good is the allegory of the pilgrimage to Jerusalem (representing the progress of the contemplative). This allegory is admirable not merely for the ingenuity with which Hilton adapts this conventional allegorical exemplum to suit the mystical situation, but also, *vice versa*, for his readiness to reshape his ideas in order to take advantage of the accidental associations of the comparison. On occasion, Hilton gives the metaphorical vehicle free rein and enjoys the ride, as in the final vision of Jerusalem (the sight of God), which can be glimpsed in the distance like a city approached in darkness:

> Thou art not yit at it, but by smale sodeyn lightnynges that gliteren oute thorugh smale cranés fro the cité schalt thou mowen see it from feer, or thou come therto. (189.1492–93 [II.xxv])

The 'sodeyn lightnynges' represent the touches of grace that may precede the mystical vision, but the 'small crannies' that emit the light are there to be relished for their own sake. They represent nothing more (or less) than what John Crowe Ransom terms the 'irrelevant texture' that gives the metaphor its power of suggestion. Close attention to Hilton's prose style would, I think, show that he has in Book II become more comfortable writing in English, but nothing definitive can be said about this until we have a proper critical edition that can assure us that we are reading Hilton rather than his scribes.[14]

But although Books I and II must have been separated by a significant interval, it is misleading to suggest that they have no direct connection with each other. In fact, Book II was occasioned by a request from a reader about the image of God discussed by Hilton 'before tymes' (134.4 [II.i]) in Book I. Book II thus arises out of Book I and, given the time lapse, it is surprising how 'connected' Hilton still was with Book I. When, for example, in II.xx, he writes that we can only achieve cleanness of heart and 'felynge of grace' through a constant struggle against all manner of vice, he refers us back to his exposition of the

---

[14] A critical edition for the Early English Text Society has long been in progress.

deadly sins in Book I ('as I have seid heer biforn in the first partie of this writynge', 172.1005). Hilton plainly thought of the *Scale* as one work ('*this writynge*'), and the ideal reader of Book II therefore needs a good recall of Book I. Another casual cross-reference at the end of Book II.xxx – 'For summe [outward feelynges] mowen ben trewe and summe mowen be feyned, as I have seide bifore' (210.2092–93) – is meant to bring to mind his extended treatment of this topic in Book I, x. As we shall see, the relationship between Hilton's two Books is similar to that of other divisions in Hilton: the higher *partie* does not supersede the lower one but both are elevated into a new synthesis. It therefore makes sense to treat Books I and II as one work.

The argument of this work may be summarised as follows:

Book I is an introduction to the contemplative life and the stages by which Hilton's addressee, an anchoress, may progress to the highest degree of contemplation, which lies in 'cognicion and in affecion, that is for to seie, in knowynge and in perfight lovynge of God' (37.146–48 [I.viii]). By 'affection' Hilton does not mean 'bodily sensations', for he is careful to distance himself from contemplatives (probably Richard Rolle and his followers) who dramatise their religious 'feelings' as if these were the index of their proximity to God. In fact, bodily feelings may not be God-sent, and, even supposing they were, they would only be valuable if they spurred us on to 'goostly' [spiritual] experiences of God. The three 'meenes that bryngen a man to contemplacioun' (45.331 [I.xv]) are reading (of the Bible and related material), meditation and prayer, but these should not be attempted without meekness, true faith in God and in Holy Church and 'an hool wille and a desyre oonli to plese God' (55.579 [I.xxii]). After further discussions of prayer and meditation, Hilton develops the point that our sinful souls require reform. Baptism and confession wipe out the devil's 'image' in our souls, and the gift of salvation may be ours if we hold out against deadly sins. None of us are immune to sinful 'stirrings', but as long as we do not give in to them they represent venial sins for which we may be forgiven. In an original image, Hilton likens the seven sins to stinking rivers that run through the human soul; it is right that we should be repelled by them, but, try as we may, we cannot keep the garden of our soul clean unless 'bi the grace of Jhesu in a meke soule, the ground mai be stoppid and distroied, and the springe mai be dried' (116.2184–86 [I.lxxiii]). It follows that we should not strive obsessively with our sins as if it were up to *us* to destroy them; it is better to fasten our hopes on Christ, who may fight and destroy sin on our behalf.

As this summary shows, Book I hardly seems to be a 'mystical' work at all, but then medieval thinkers had no notion that 'mysticism' existed as a specialised brand of theology (Watson 1999). The tradition to which Book I of the *Scale* belongs is broadly that of the religious handbook for the layman (Milosh 1966). About the climax of contemplation it has little to say, and the mystical union with God figures as a distant prospect rather than an immediate objective. Indeed, Hilton expresses himself well satisfied should his addressee only reach the lower stages of contemplation: his purpose in describing the long road to the ultimate experience is 'that thu myght knowe it and sette it as it were a mark before the sight of thi soule, and for to desyre al thy lyvetyme for to come to *ony partie* of it bi the grace of oure Lord Jhesu Crist' (44.311–13 [I.xiv]).

At the beginning of Book II Hilton announces that he will say more about the 'reformynge' of the soul. Two kinds of reform are distinguished: full reform, which awaits us in the life beyond, and reform *in partie*, which is achievable here and now. The latter is in turn divided in two: reform in faith and reform in faith *and* feeling. Reform in faith is the minimum entry requirement for heaven; it is within the reach of all good Christians who lead decent lives and put their faith in Holy Church. The higher reform in faith and feeling, which contemplatives seek, is an inner transformation leading to an awareness of God's immanence in the soul. This idea is dimly foreshadowed in Book I, where Hilton mentions briefly that our soul's original glory 'myght bi grace and bisi travaile sumwhat be recovered agen in partie of felynge' (89.1478–79 [I.lii]). How would our lives change as a consequence? First our flawed sentiments – e.g. feeling attracted by sin, uninspired by the exercise of virtue, or uncomprehending before the articles of faith – will disappear and make way for 'newe gracious feelynges thorugh wirkynge of the Holi Gost' (143.224 [II.v]). Without the benefit of this inner illumination, Christians must take things on trust and put their faith in the efficacy of the sacraments of the Church (baptism, confession, and so on), which Hilton is at pains to defend against heretical attack.

Reform in feeling is a long process. Hilton likens it to a pilgrimage to Jerusalem in which the pilgrim will find many obstacles in his way; these can only be overcome by the pilgrim if he pursues his goal single-mindedly. The process of inner reform may be facilitated by various 'meenes and weies' (170.961 [II.xix]), as long as we remember that they are means to an end. The contemplative who loses sight of the end 'binds himself to custom' like a lazy apprentice who, having learned 'sympil craft' (170.964 [II.xix]), does not attempt to progress any further. As we leave behind the 'false light' of the world, we enter into a darkness, beyond which lies the light of God. This darkness is disorientating, but our eyes adjust to it if we are content to remain in the dark and look for the true light. The final chapters are devoted to the ultimate mystical experience, when the soul, having reached within and above itself, no longer encounters any intermediary between itself and God. Then, with our senses purified, Christ may be seen, heard, and touched in the soul; the hidden secrets of scripture and doctrine will be unlocked; we will comprehend the mysterious ways of God's judgement, his providential plan for the world, the destiny of Holy Church, the blessed state of angels – and realise that any description of these matters is totally inadequate. 'For a soule that is clene, stired bi grace to use of this wyrkynge, mai seen more in a hour of siche goostli matier than myght be writen in a grete book' (261.3594–5 [II.xlvi]). In this humble *explicit*, Hilton anticipates a time when his own 'grete book', too, will seem trivial, its matter entirely superseded by our experience of the real thing.

While Book I seems to have circulated without a title, the name chosen by Hilton for the combined books was *Scala Perfectionis*. We may gain some insight into Hilton's thought by reflecting on the title, which has with equal justice been considered apt (Hodgson 1967) and ridiculously inept (Hussey 1980). *Scala Perfectionis* recalls the title of a very popular treatise by the Carthusian Guigo II, the *Scala Claustralium*, which likens the *via contemplative* to scaling a ladder, composed of four rungs: reading (for beginners), meditation (for the advanced), prayer (for the devout) and contemplation (for the blessed).[15] By comparison with Guigo, Hilton does very little with the image. He uses it only once:

> For reformynge in feith is the lowest staat of alle chosen soulis, for binethe that myght he not wel ben, but reformynge in feelynge is the highest staat in this liyf that the soule mai come to. But fro the loweste to the higheste mai not a soule sodeynli stirte, ne more than a man that wole clymbe upon an high laddre and setteth his foot upon the loweste stele mai atte the nexte fleen up to the higheste; but hym behoveth bi processe gon oon aftir another, til he mai come to the overeste. Right so it is goostli: no man is maad sodeynli sovereyne in grace, but thorugh longe exercise and sligh wirkynge a soule mai come therto, namely whanne He helpeth and techeth a wrecchid soule in whom al grace liggeth. For withoute special help and inli techynge of Hym mai no soule come therto. (167.880–89 [II.xvii])[16]

What prompts the image of the ladder here is Hilton's insistence that the mystical ascent is long and hard work. On the one hand, the image is meant to put off mystical enthusiasts who are starry-eyed but have no stomachs for 'long exercise'; on the other, it encourages serious contemplatives by making the distance separating God from his creatures less daunting. Instead of having to 'stirte' across this vast divide, we can go 'step by step' until 'bi process' we reach the top.

The main reason why here, as in other mystical treatises, the inner conversion to God is externalised – as an ascent up a ladder or a journey in several stages[17] – is that gradual internal transformations are extremely difficult to capture in non-figurative words. The vernacular tradition bequeathed by Richard Rolle cannot have given Hilton much help, since Rolle does not generally talk (and probably did not think) of mystical experiences as the outcomes of gradual processes. In a very different context, Chaucer confronted a comparable problem when he wished to describe Criseyde's conversion to love as a slow process, in the teeth of a dominant tradition of love-at-first-sight. Chaucer proceeded both negatively – by vigorous denials: Criseyde's love was *not* 'sodeyn'; it did *not* happen 'lightly for the firste syght' – and positively, expressing his sense of change (as the outcome of progressive inner adjustments) in painstakingly precise syntactical successions: e.g. not 'she converted' but 'she wex sumwhat able to converte'. Hilton accomplishes something similar in his own field. Negatively, he distances himself from Rolle's rapturous spirituality – 'I sey *not* that thou so lightli on the first day may be turnyd to Hym' (31.17 [I.i]) – but, like Chaucer, he also strives to communicate his sense of spiritual perfection as a continuous process constructively. When, for example, he considers the role of active deeds in the mystical ascent he writes: 'Thise werkes, though thei ben actif, not for thi they helpen mykel and ordaynen a man

---

15 Guigo, *Scala Claustralium*, ed. E. Colledge and J. Walsh (Paris, 1970). A Middle English adaptation, *A Ladder of Foure Ronges*, is edited by Hodgson in an appendix to *Deonise Hid Diuinite* (see n. 1).

16 'He' and 'Hym' must refer to God; the pronouns erroneously appear in lower case in Bestul's edition.

17 This most influential development of this metaphor is Bonaventure's *Journey of the Mind to God* (*Itinerarium mentis in Deum*).

in the bigynnynge to come to contemplatif lif'. (33.40–41 [I.ii]). The inadequacy of a short paraphrase of this – 'active deeds prepare a man for the contemplative life' – highlights the precision of Hilton's formulation, which begins by
commending the benefit of good works ('they helpen *mykel*') and continues,
without suggesting any adversative relation, by emphasising the strictly prepara-
tory and provisional nature of their contribution in the grander scheme of things.
Active deeds do not produce contemplation, but 'ordeynen [dispose] a man',
when he is just starting out ('in the bigynnge'), to get *closer* to ('come to')
contemplative life.

In a similar vein, Hilton cautions that the restoration of the soul's divine
image can only come about slowly, 'not al at oonys but litil and litil, til thou be
sumdel reformed to His liknesse' (130. 2535–6 [I.lxxxviii]; cf. 212.2161
[II.xxxii]). The adverbial phrases, which risk sounding hesitant, fulfil very
precise functions in Hilton's prose. 'Litel and litel' and the variation 'bi litil and
litil' (apparently first recorded in the *Scale*: 189.1485 [II.xxv], 220.2398
[II.xxxiv]), envisage progress as the cumulative effect of minuscule advances,
and *sumdel* ('partially') is precise rather than vague because it reminds us that
complete reform is only possible after death. The ladder that will lead us to
perfection is both long and not nearly long enough, but we can at least move
sumdel in the right direction.

Hilton's self-presentation and pedagogical method show the same attractive
acceptance of insufficiency. He admits freely to the limitations of his own
powers to enlighten ('By this that I have seid myght thu *sumwhat* undirstonde',
40.200 [I.x]; 'Now have y toolde thee *a litil* of countemplacion', 44.311 [I.xiv]),
but this is coupled with an optimistic belief in the possibility of systematic progress. This belief is reflected structurally by the provision both of recapitulatory
sections ('a litil rehersynge of thynges biforseid', 56.612 [I.xxiii]), which allow
us to rest whilst ensuring that we progress on the basis of what has gone before,
and of divisions and subdivisions, which parcel out our task in smaller units and
so make it manageable.

It would be tempting to think of these divisions as rungs on a ladder but,
unlike Guido II, Hilton refuses to sacrifice the practical convenience of his tools
for the sake of metaphorical consistency. For unlike rungs on a ladder, which are
fixed and separate, Hilton's divisions offer a remarkable amount of flexibility
and overlap. For example, at the beginning of Book I, Hilton distinguishes 'two
maner of lyves', one the active life, the other the contemplative life. He then
divides the contemplative life into three *parties*: the first and lowest *partie* is
contemplation through study and reason; the second, through feeling; the third,
through reason and feeling. The second *partie* (contemplation through feeling)
itself consists of two *degrees*. In the lower degree the feeling is weak and inter-
mittent; in the second it is fuller and more spiritual, and will stimulate us to
reach the third *partie* of contemplation. Looked at closely, these 'divisions' are
not in the least divisive. Not only can active deeds lead us toward the contemplative life (as we have seen), 'actif men' can, according to Hilton, participate in the
second *partie* of contemplative life, if only at the lower *degree*. The *parties* of
the contemplative life also do not work hierarchically. Thus the first *partie* (the
life of learning) is no prerequisite for the second, since Hilton's addressee, who

is not qualified for the first, is evidently not debarred from the others. There is further elasticity in the way Hilton overlays one set of divisions with another. A recurrent division in the *Scale*, derived from Thomas Aquinas (*Summa Theologica*, II, q. 24, art. 9), is that of Christ's followers into beginners (who are like little children in need of milk), the proficient and the perfect. In Book II Hilton maps this Thomist division onto his own division between 'reform in faith' and the higher 'reform in feeling': 'The firste reformynge is oonli of bigynnynge and profitynge soulis, and of actif men. The secunde is of perfight soulis and of contemplatif men' (142.220–21 [II.v]). Soon afterwards, however, Hilton appears to contradict himself when he distinguishes simple folk (who must believe blindly what Holy Church tells them) from people who are reformed in feeling and have true belief 'quykened with love and charité' (151.431 [II.x]): the former are beginners, who have 'but a childisch knowynge of God', while the latter, 'the which aren reformed in goosteli feelynge', are '*profitande* in grace, or ellis in love *perfight* of God'. First contemplatives reformed in feeling were designated as 'perfight soules'. Now they are downgraded to being proficient *or* perfect. The terms 'beginner' (or 'child'), 'proficient' and 'perfect' are re-adjusted on more than one occasion, but there is no contradiction if we accept that whenever we graduate to a higher stage of contemplation we become, as it were, beginners all over again.

Hilton's 'ladder' thus turns out to be a flexible instrument: it has different points of entry and, depending on where you stand on it, different rungs can be regarded as the 'beginning'. And unlike any literal ladder, the higher rungs tend in Hilton's thinking to include the lower ones. Thus the highest *partie* of contemplation, based on knowing and feeling, contains within it both the lower *partie* (based on knowing) and the middle one (based on feeling). Similarly, the higher 'reform in faith *and* feeling' subsumes the lower 'reformynge in faith'. There is something similarly accretive about the ultimate mystical experience. We will see and feel many things when God has finally opened our inner eyes, but in Hilton's account these include the things we thought and saw when those eyes were still shut. Thus, even as we behold God, we may still love and think (in spiritual fashion) of 'othere creatures' (239.2944 [II.xl]). God's grace will move us in our prayers, yet the Pater Noster will remain our favourite (246.3167–68 [II.xlii]). Hilton had earlier likened the Pater Noster to the walking stick of the spiritually infirm (60.706 [I.xxvii]); now we will run with it, and we will utter it in our soul, though naturally the 'soule praieth thanne not in manere as it dide bifore' (247.3170 [II.xlii]). When we now read the Bible, we will apprehend it instantly as the expression of Christ's essential being: his wisdom, goodness, mercy, holiness, righteousness and truth – 'al this . . . seeth a soule in Hooli Writ *with alle other accidentis that fallen therto*' (254.3381–82 [II.xliii]). Hilton's ultimate mystical experience seems, in other words, to absorb all the sensations that led up to it – which is very different from the *Cloud* author's conviction that the mystical moment has no connection with anything thought or felt before.

However, what is most misleading about the ladder image is the suggestion that going up it is a measure of our own strength. Hilton was aware of this when he introduced the metaphor, warning that 'withoute special help and inli techynge of Hym mai no soule come therto.' The most penetrating discussion of the interrelationship between human effort and divine grace is the chapter on 'created love' (i.e. human love, including our love of God) and 'unformed love' (i.e. God's love, which 'loveth us er than [before] we loven Him', 220.2384–85 [II.xxxiv]). Emphasizing the priority (in every sense) of 'unformed love', Hilton writes:

> We doon right nought but suffre Him, and assente to Him, for that is the mooste that we doon, that we assente wilfulli to His gracious werkynge in us. And yit is not that wille of us, but of His makynge, so that me thenketh He dooth in us al that is wel doon, and yit we seen hit nought.
>
> (220.2392–95 [II.xxxiv])

From Hilton's ease of manner and expression one would hardly know that he is treading a theological minefield. At one end of it lies the position, which Hilton knew to be associated with the heresy of the Free Spirit (Clark 1978), that God's special grace saves its recipients from a life of effort. Hilton's insistence that the soul must never cease to exert itself (though God may make its exertions light and easy) firmly puts this view beyond the pale. Even within the bounds of orthodoxy, however, theologians disputed whether the mystical grace was co-operant (requiring the active participation of the human will) or operant (with God acting directly on the soul). Hilton was evidently sensitive to the distinction – indeed, the above-cited passage has been admired for offering an accurate definition of these two kinds of grace (Knowles 1961, 112). But perhaps the real subtlety lies in the way Hilton conjures up the distinction only to make it disappear again. The contemplative assents *wilfully* (and so co-operates), only to discover in *that wille* God's prior operation. The scale of perfection, to pursue the metaphor, conceals an escalator that is operated by God but that will not work for us unless in our 'will' and our 'werkynge' we continue to treat it as a gruelling staircase.

In conclusion, the key word that sums up the distinctive accent of Hilton's thought is *process*. The English language managed without the word for a surprisingly long time (until c. 1375), but Hilton's theology can hardly operate without it. As we have seen, he uses it in Book II, xvii, when introducing the image of the ladder that must be ascended 'bi process'; and this whole passage is echoed in *Mixed Life*, which tells us that 'we mai not sodeynli stirte oute of þis mirk niȝt of þis fleschli corrupcion in to þat goostli liȝt . . . And þerfore me mosten abide and worche bi process of tyme' (3–4.23–28). In this respect, the works of the *Cloud* author provide a striking contrast, for the word is conspicuously absent, with the exception of a passage in *Deonise Hid Diuinite*, which argues, significantly, for the irrelevance of the concept, God having nothing to do with 'temporeel flowyng bi proces of tymes' (127.22).[18] Hilton emphasises continuity, the *Cloud* author discontinuity. But before turning to the latter's works, a short introduction to his life and works is required.

---

[18] I disregard the use of the word in the *Book of Privy Counselling*, 83.23, where it refers to a textual passage.

The only plausible external evidence of the *Cloud* author is a colophon by Richard Methley, who in his late fifteenth-century Latin translation of the *Cloud* assumed the author to be a Carthusian monk.[19] This is still our best guess.[20] Phyllis Hodgson has pointed out that many of the early manuscripts of the *Cloud* and its related treatises are of Carthusian provenance;[21] she also notes many connections between the *Cloud* author's work and other works of Carthusian spirituality.[22] For a clearer portrait of the author we must rely, however, on the internal evidence of the writings that have been identified as his: *The Cloud of Unknowing, The Book of Privy Counselling, An Epistle of Prayer, An Epistle of Discretion of Stirrings, Deonise Hid Divinite, A Treatise of the Study of Wisdom called Benjamin* (henceforth *Benjamin*) and *A Treatise of Discretion of Spirits*. We can be reasonably confident about these attributions since (with the exception of the problematic *Benjamin*), the *Cloud* author's works are closely associated in the manuscript tradition and in thematic and stylistic respects. Moreover, the author makes a number of cross-references to his other works. Thus in *Deonise Hid Divinite*, a translation of a Latin version of pseudo-Dionysius' *De mystica theologia*, he says that he has translated not only the 'letter' but also the 'sentence' (the deeper meaning), as expounded by the commentator Thomas Gallus (d. 1246), *because* 'it is mad minde in þe 70 chapter of a book wretin before (þe which is clepid *Þe Cloud of Vnknowing*) how þat Denis sentence wol cleerli afferme al þat is wretyn in þat same book' (119.4–6). In *The Book of Privy Counselling*, apparently written to clarify some of his ideas in the *Cloud*, he refers his reader to 'oþer diuerse places of myne owne wryting'; he mentions by name 'þi lityl pistle of preier' (a short treatise on how to pray to God in the right spirit) and alludes to 'þe cloude of vnknowyng' and 'Denis deuinite' (87.41–88.1). This leaves just three of his works unmentioned. The most appealing of these is *An Epistle of Discretion of Stirrings*, a devastatingly incisive response to a young contemplative struggling with the problem of which observances (fasting, silence, solitariness?) he should adopt. The *Cloud* author suspects that his friend's concern to strike the right pose is a convenient substitute for the proper business of loving God. If he did that, his outward behaviour would fall into place as a matter of course. *A Treatise of Discretion of Spirits*, loosely based on two of St Bernard's *Sermones de Diversis*, is about how we may distinguish, firstly, between spiritual apparitions that are God's work and those that are the work of the devil (we can tell from their appearance and their effect on us), and, secondly, between evil suggestions that come from without, by the suggestion of the flesh, the world or the devil, and those that come from within, by the suggestion of the soul (we can tell by cleansing our souls completely, for this will prove any subsequent wicked prompting to have come from without). Finally, there is *Benjamin*, an adaptation

[19] There is no edition of this translation, which survives in Cambridge, Pembroke College, 221. An earlier Latin translation is also extant (see Hogg 1984).
[20] A range of different opinions is surveyed in Hodgson's EETS edition of the *Cloud*, pp. lxxxii–lxxxiii (see n. 1).
[21] It should be noted, however, that the Charterhouses were the specialist 'publishing houses' of mystical and visionary writings in general (Sargent 1976).
[22] *'The Cloud of Unknowing' and Related Treatises*, pp. xi, xlv–xlix. See also Lees 1983.

of Richard of St Victor's *Benjamin Minor*, a tediously contrived allegory culminating in the birth of Benjamin (personifying contemplation) and the death of
his mother Rachel (personifying reason) in childbirth. Because *Benjamin* is only
associated with other works by the *Cloud* author in four of its thirteen manuscripts, its ascription to the *Cloud* author is more speculative, and has recently
been called into question by Roger Ellis (1992, 1994), mainly on the grounds
that the Bible translations in *Benjamin* are 'considerably more literal than
anything we observe in the original works of the *Cloud* author' (Ellis 1992, 205).
But this argument is not altogether convincing. Firstly, the biblical quotations in
Benjamin are generally second hand: they form part of the Latin text which the
Cloud author was translating. In most of his other works, however, the *Cloud*
author was himself responsible both for finding the appropriate biblical quotations and for accommodating these into his discourse; it would only be natural
for him to translate his own quotations more creatively than Richard of St
Victor's. Secondly, there are some striking verbal similarities between *Benjamin*
and the *Cloud* author's other works, which are unlikely to be coincidental.[23] If
Benjamin were by a different author, he must have been deeply influenced by
the works of the *Cloud* author. Of course, the simpler explanation is that the
latter did indeed write all seven of the texts I have mentioned above.

From these texts, it appears that the *Cloud* author was himself a solitary and
had acted as a spiritual adviser to a number of contemplatives long before he
came to write the *Cloud* (see 49.1–4 [xlvii]), which must be one of the earliest of
his surviving works, judging by the cross-references. In most of his works, the
author addresses a personal acquaintance. In the case of the *Cloud* this is a
twenty-four year old, who, after living the 'common life', chose the 'special life'
(i.e. the religious life), in order 'to be a seruaunt of the special seruauntes of his'
(8.8 [i]). The phrase plays on the title of the pope (*servus servorum*), but would
suit a layman who had joined a community of religious ('special servants') as a
lay-brother ('servant') (Glasscoe 1993, 168–69). Subsequently this young man
felt called to the 'singular ['solitary'] life', and now the *Cloud* author writes to
help him achieve the 'perfect life' (a life centred exclusively on the love of God).
Since the *Cloud* author even takes the trouble of translating the terms '*Lesson,
Meditacion, & Oryson*' into plain English – 'to þin vnderstondyng þei mowe be

---

[23] For example, the unusual word *erles* ('pledge, foretaste') is apparently only once attested in Middle
English before the *Cloud*, which informs us that we may feel the 'swetenes' of God's love as a foretaste (*in erles of*) of heaven (8.32 [ii]). *MED* omits the attestations in *Benjamin*, which also mentions
the 'swetnes' that God may give us 'in erles of þe souereyn ioie and mede of the hiȝe kyngdome of
heuen' (138.9–10). Also missing from *MED* are any attestations before 1400 of *fagen*, 'to cajole', so it
is noteworthy that the word is found in *Benjamin* and *An Epistle of Prayer*, both times in alliterative
collocation with *flatter*: 'bot ȝif it so be (þe whiche God forbede!) þat þou flater and fage þi fals,
fleschly, blinde herte' (*Pistle of Preier*, 101.17) and 'And outrageous loue is flateryng and fagyng'
(*Benjamin*, 141.22–23). Another revealing instance in *Benjamin* is the passage 'For betir is a sley man
þan a strong man, ȝe, and betyr is list þen liþer strengþe. And a sley man spekeþ of victories'
(142.19–21). As noted by Hodgson (p. 199), this faithfully renders Richard of St Victor's 'Quia
melior est vir prudens viro forti. Vir enim prudens loquitur victorias' – except that the *Cloud* author
has added both alliteration (which he liked) and the italicised saying, which happens to be a favourite
of his (cf. *Cloud*, 48.17–18 [lxiv] and *Epistle of Prayer*, 107.5–6).

clepid: Redyng, þinkyng & Preiing' (39.25–26 [xxxv]) – his reader cannot have been a Latinist or a monastic insider.

The *Cloud* author is thus in one sense non-élitist: he expects no specialist knowledge in his readers, and indeed espouses the view that any exercise of the intellect is counterproductive 'in þis werk' (his deliberately untechnical term for the mystical endeavour). But he is nevertheless fiercely élitist in another sense: he writes for a select few who already know that they are called to 'the work', not for those who are curious about it or earnestly aspire to qualify themselves for it. For such aspirants, the *Cloud* author has the bad news that aptitude for 'the work' cannot be cultivated: 'þe abilnes to þis werk is onyd to þe selue werk, withoutyn departyng; so that whose feliþ þis werk is abil þerto, & elles none' (38.32–33 [xxxiv]). In exactly the same way, he says, his own 'werk' will be right only for those who recognise it as such and feel, as they read it or hear it read, 'a verrey accordaunce to þe effecte of þis werk' (72.37–38 [lxxiv]). All others are advised not to meddle with the author's writings – for their own sake as well as his.

Unlike Hilton, whose friendly invitations to the religious life sought (and found) a broad appeal, the *Cloud* author had no wish to make converts. Unlike Hilton, too, he speaks with the authority of someone who has himself achieved the soul's mystical union with God. Thus he tells us that, if some of his advice sounds silly, it is because we are not divinely inspired as he is: 'þis is childly and pleyingly spoken, þee think, parauenture. Bot I trowe whoso had grace to do & fele as I sey, he schuld fele God gamesumli pley wiþ hym, as the fadir doþ wiþ þe childe, kyssyng and clippyng, þat weel were him so' (48.34–37 [xiiv]). The *Cloud* author has God's grace; if it were so with us we would recognise that his 'child-like words' are, as it were, the toy that God uses to play with his children.

The *Cloud* author knows what he is talking about, and his writings, especially the *Cloud of Unknowing*, are distinguished by an unexpected rigour and precision of observation and expression. In the remainder of this chapter I shall discuss the central ideas of the *Cloud* and some of the stylistic consequences that follow from these ideas.

The *Cloud* author's fundamental starting point is that God exists on the other side of our reason and our senses. Uncreated, he belongs to a different order from that of created things, and he is reached, not positively by a process of 'reforming our faith and feeling' (as in Hilton), but negatively by ridding the 'will to God' from any interference of reason, imagination and feeling. The *Cloud* author has a lengthy 'scientific' discussion of the powers of the human soul (lxiii–lxvii), which makes clear why in our fallen condition we are naturally ill-equipped for 'the werk'. The mind contains within it both reason and will, and their respective handmaidens, imagination and sensuality. Sensuality is the domain of the 'bodily wits' (i.e. the senses); and since these are directed outward towards the world they are useless for work that is 'ghostly'. However, the 'ghostly wittes' (i.e. our mental faculties) are also contaminated by 'bodily' influences. For example, images seen by the mind's eye will be based on (or modelled after) things that we have seen with our outer eyes, and so the domain of what we call 'spiritual' or 'immaterial' is actually contaminated by 'bodily' experiences. This problem of the vestigial physicality of the 'spiritual' does not much trouble Hilton, who generally thinks of the material world as a hospitable arena for spiritual progress, and sets store by various 'ghostly werkes' (typically various and plural for Hilton: see 172.1009–10 [II.xx], 196.1701–02 [II.xxvii]) that the *Cloud* author regards as inimical to 'þe werk' (singular and indivisible) because they smuggle the material world in through the backdoor. Accordingly, traditional activities associated with purgation and meditation, like ransacking one's conscience or reflecting on God's humanity, are valued by the *Cloud* author only as stages that must be traversed before 'the werk' can start; after that they should play no further part, for they will stimulate the very powers of sense and reason that must be evaded if 'the werk' is to succeed.

It follows from the *Cloud* author's distrust of intellectual approaches to God that he offers us no systematic 'course' in contemplation and (in striking contrast with Hilton) no logical method in the organisation of chapters (Tixier 1997). What he does offer are some guiding metaphors and some practical hints that will have to prove their value to us in experience. A recurrent metaphor in the *Cloud* is that our will must be 'naked' or 'blind', that is, stripped of all thoughts and images, without 'regard' to anything other than God. Everything known or conceivable must be placed under a 'cloud of forgetting', in order that we may arrive in the 'cloud of unknowing', the final and impassable frontier that separates us from God. To those who manage to remain in this 'cloud of unknowing' God may 'sumtyme parauenture seend oute a beme of goostly liȝt, peersyng þis cloude of vknowing þat is bitwix þee and hym, & schewe þee sum of his priuite' (34.31–32 [xxvi]).

These reflections should not be regarded as metaphysical speculations but as the basis of a 'maner of worching' (72.26 [lxxiv]). To help us get the hang of it, the *Cloud* author gives us a number of strategic tips, or, in his own carefully chosen word, 'sleiȝtes'. The author's frequent recourse to words describing devious cunning[24] ('list', 'listely', 'sley', sleiȝt, etc.) and his liking for the saying that it is better to proceed with cunning rather than strength (see n. 23) must here be considered not merely as stylistic habits but also as his way of dealing with the problem that we cannot put our faith in our *natural* resources (i.e. our bodily and ghostly wits). Perversely, our success will depend on our ability to outwit these wits, or, more precisely, on the possibility that our wits may outwit themselves (for we have no abilities other than the ones we were born with).

This predicament bears on a problem that has much exercised critics of the *Cloud*: the apparent contradiction that in his fight against the imagination the *Cloud* relies constantly on images.[25] In the same way, it might be objected that his case against the use of 'reason' in contemplation relies a good deal on the application of that faculty. But these are ultimately pseudo-problems. For unless the *Cloud* author thought we possessed some occult powers besides our inborn 'myȝtes of the soul' – and he is too hard-nosed for that – it is hard to see what else he could do other than appeal to human minds as they are constituted. His

---

[24] This sense is sometimes obscured by Hodgson's glossing of these words.
[25] The problem is brought into clear focus by Burrow 1977.

challenge, and ours in 'the werk', is therefore to turn the bodily and the ghostly wits against themselves or against each other.

To take the 'ghostly wits' first. In devising ways to sabotage their workings, the *Cloud* author's formative debt is to the negative (or cataphetic) tradition of mysticism, transmitted to the West by the writings of the pseudo-Dionysius, one of which (*Mystica Theologia*) the *Cloud* author translated into English as *Deonise Hid Diuinite*. The *via negativa* to God is often misunderstood as privileging negation over affirmation, on the mistaken assumption that the 'normal faculties of intelligence attain to a more complete truth in the statement of what God is not than of what he is',[26] but the *Cloud* author knows very well that a negative statement about God is as much a proposition about him as a positive one and therefore just as misleading, God being 'vn-understondabely abouen alle affermyng *and deniinge*' (*Deonise Hid Diuinite*, 128.18–19; my italics). The truly effective 'sleiȝt' is therefore not to negate the proposition but rather to 'negate the propositional'.[27] A succinct example is the *Cloud* author's suggestion that we should pray to God 'in þe depnes of spirit, þe whiche is þe heiȝt' (41.24–25 [xxxvi]). Here the first notion (praying 'in depth') is logically cancelled out by the second (praying 'on high'), so that the proposition undoes itself by virtue of the law of non-contradiction. But inasmuch as God appears precisely in the breakdown of understanding – 'for whi that þing þat it failiþ in is noþing elles bot only God' (70.3–4 [lxx]) – auto-destructive utterances like this can after all say something about God, in this case that God is beyond contradictions: 'for in goostlynes alle is one: heiȝt & depnes, lengþe & brede' (41.25–26 [xxxvi]). (Note the deceptive simplicity of 'alle is one', which does not just introduce the contradictions but already *is* one.[28])

The 'philosophical' error exposed by the deliberate short-circuiting of sense is the assumption that the rules of our familiar 'language-games' continue to apply to 'the werk'.[29] And if this is not an error which intelligent people *think* they would make it is because they commit it unthinkingly in their actions. For example, encouraged to 'show' their desire to God, they make emotive displays – as if 'showing' in 'showing to God' could still mean what that verb normally means. To fend off such misunderstandings, the *Cloud* author turns common sense on its head and advises his disciple to *hide* his purpose from God [xlvii]. Since God is all-seeing, this plainly is physically impossible, but this is precisely why the *Cloud* author suggests it. For if we try to put his advice into practice, we at least know we cannot do so 'bodily', and are thus saved from the mistake of treating our purpose as something internal ('hidden') or external ('shown'), when it should be 'naked' of such categories and preconceptions.

---

[26] Hodgson, ed., *Cloud*, EETS, p. lx.

[27] I borrow these words from Turner 1985, p. 35, taking this opportunity to register my general indebtedness to his illuminating study of the *via negativa*.

[28] As noted by Hodgson (*Cloud of Unknowing and Related Treatises*, p. xxxvi), the idea may be due to Richard of St Victor's *Benjamin Major*: 'Sed in humano procul dubio animo idem est summum quod intimum, et intimum quod summum' ('But undoubtedly in the human soul what is highest is deepest and what is deepest is highest', *PL* 196, col. 167) – but *idem* lacks the force of 'alle is one'.

[29] I use the term 'language-games' in Wittgenstein's original sense, to refer not only to forms of expression but also to the forms of life with which the former are bound up (Wittgenstein 1953, §7).

This 'nakedness' extends to the realm of our 'bodily wits'. The *Cloud* author's insistence that God must be sought with 'love' – 'will' or 'affection' are used as roughly equivalent terms – is consistent with a 'manner of working' that seeks to circumvent the powers of the 'ghostly wits'. It is consistent also with the required detachment from our senses and emotions, again provided we do not confuse 'language-games' and mistake the meaning of 'love' in 'loving God' with that in, say, 'loving your spouse'.[30] In the latter case, affection is mediated by the 'bodily wits'; in the former, it must work 'nakedly', without the encouragement of the senses or the imagination. Moreover, when we love God, we do not even know what we love, so our difficulty lies in continuing to 'wilne and desire þou-wost-neuer-what' (38.37–38 [xxxiv]),[31] without falling back on any sensible or cognitive support or focus. The *Cloud* author's characteristic encouragements – '*Do on* þan, I preie þee, fast' (8.34 [ii]), '*Put on* þan . . . Bot . . . how schalt þou *put*?' (9.8–10 [ii]), '*Do forth* euer more & more, so þat þou be euer *doyng*' (38.38–39 [xxxiv]), '*Step vp* þan stifly' (*Book of Privy Counselling*, 77.34) – are ingeniously phrased to confront and overcome that difficulty, for they manage to urge us on to vigorous action without setting any object in our view (hence the author's liking for intransitive usages of normally transitive verbs). The same desired effect of de-specification is achieved by making God the grammatical object of a verb that normally takes a complex clause ('*mene God* . . . and resseiue none oþer þou3t', 15.26–28 [vii]).[32] In vocal prayer, too, sense and imagination must be by-passed. A good ploy is to exclaim 'God!' (the goal) and 'sin!' (the obstacle) in the same way as a man whose house is on fire would shout 'fire, fire!' (41.21 [xxxvii]). The analogy is most illuminating, since 'fire' does not function *in this context* to signify or evoke an object but purely to trigger a response. In exactly the same way, words in prayer will be the more effective the less they 'signify' or 'evoke' (so the shorter the word the better).

At this point, the *Cloud* author is most vulnerable to the criticism that he plainly *does* use evocative words, be it by employing images – '*þis cloude* of vnknowyng (13.25 [v]), a '*cloude* or for3etyng' (13.30–31 [v]), 'a *scharp darte* of longing love' (14.29 [vi] etc.) – or by using kinetic verbs figuratively – e.g. 'sche *heng up* hir loue . . . in þis cloude of unkowing' (25.36 [xvi]), '*schere away* couetyse of knowyng' (39.6 [xxxiv]), '*wrastlyng* wiþ þat blynde nou3t' (68.8 [lxviii]). The evocative pull of these concrete nouns and verbs is not to be denied, but nor are the deliberate contradictions of the metaphors (how do you 'hang' something in a 'cloud'?[33]) and the countervailing drift towards abstract

---

30 Simon Tugwell's excellent point about the *Cloud* author deserves quoting here: 'Our author is plainly sensitive to the impropriety of simply trying to transfer our love to God as if this did not require a radical transformation in the nature as well as the object of our love' (Tugwell 1984, 173).

31 I add the hyphens (not in Hodgson's text) to draw attention to the author's striking use of 'rank shifting', the conversion of words from one grammatical 'rank' to another (Turner 1973, 81). In this instance, a complex negative clause, 'þou wost never what', acts as if it were a simple direct object. This 'rank shifting' is the verbal realisation of the paradox that we positively love God when, negatively, we do not know what we love.

32 Forman 1987 has some interesting remarks on the *Cloud* author's peculiar use of 'intentional verbs'.

33 On the *Cloud* author's use of 'antagonistic metaphors' see Spearing 2001, p. xxxii.

nouns or notions ('vnknowyng', 'forʒetyng', 'love', 'couetyse of knowyng'). There is consequently no question of the reader succumbing to the temptations of visualisation or 'fantasy', for the mixing of metaphors spoils any attempt at imaginative elaboration, and in any case the invitation to imagine physical realities is immediately countermanded by the opposite one to think abstractly. In this dazzling alternation between abstract and concrete nouns, which is the hallmark of his style, the *Cloud* author takes the measure of the two powers of the soul: the bodily wits that demand *sensibilia*, and the ghostly wits that demand abstract ideas. While no writing can be comprehensible without engaging these two powers, writing of this stature reveals the astonishing possibility of doing so while confounding both, for the *Cloud* author manages to frustrate both the intellect (by turning ideas into things) and the senses (by turning things back into ideas). In the *Cloud*, we might say, the concrete remains abstract and the abstract concrete. And that is how it should be, for 'in þis werk alle is one'.

BIBLIOGRAPHY

This bibliography lists all works referred to in the text above. For a full bibliography see Valerie M. Lagorio and Ritamary Bradley, *The Fourteenth-Century Mystics* (New York, 1981), Alastair Minnis, '*The Cloud of Unknowing* and Walter Hilton's *Scale of Perfection*', in *Middle English Prose: A Critical Guide to Major Authors and Genres*, ed. A.S.G. Edwards (New Brunswick, NJ, 1984), 61–81, and Lagorio and Sargent 1993, 3425–38. Updates can be found in *The Fourteenth-Century Mystics Newsletter*.

Primary Texts

Bestul, Thomas H., ed., *Walter Hilton: The Scale of Perfection* (Kalamazoo, MI, 2000)
Clark, J.P.C., and C. Taylor, eds, *Walter Hilton's Latin Writings*, 2 vols (Salzburg, 1987)
Colledge, E., and J. Walsh, eds, *Guigo: Scala Claustralium* (Paris, 1970)
Hodgson, Phyllis, ed., *The Cloud of Unknowing*, EETS os 218 (London, 1944)
———, *Deonise Hid Diuinite*, EETS 231 (London, 1953)
———, '*The Cloud of Unknowing' and Related Treatises* (Salzburg, 1982)
Horstman, Carl, ed., *Yorkshire Writers: Richard Rolle of Hampole and his Followers*, 2 vols (London, 1895–96)
Kane, Harold, ed., *The Prickynge of Love*, 2 vols (Salzburg, 1983)
Kuriyagawa, Fumio, and Toshiyuki Takamiya, *Two Minor Works of Walter Hilton* (Tokyo, 1980)
Ogilvie-Thompson, S.J., *Walter Hilton's Mixed Life Edited from Lambeth Palace MS 472* (Salzburg, 1986)
Wallner, Björn, ed., *An Exposition of 'Qui habitat' and 'Bonum est' in English* (Lund, 1954)

Secondary Texts

Burrow (1977) J.A. Burrow, 'Fantasy and Language in the *Cloud of Unknowing*', *Essays in Criticism* 27, 283–98

Clark (1977) John. P.H. Clark, 'Walter Hilton and "Liberty of Spirit" ', *Downside Review* 95, 61–79

Clark (1978) '*The Cloud of Unknowing*, Walter Hilton and St John of the Cross: A Comparison', *Downside Review* 96, 281–98

Clark (1985) 'Walter Hilton in Defence of the Religious Life and the Veneration of Images', *Downside Review* 103, 1–25

Clark (1992) 'Late Fourteenth-Century Cambridge Theology and the English Contemplative Tradition', in *The Medieval Mystical Tradition in England: V*, ed. Marion Glasscoe (Cambridge), pp. 1–16

Ellis (1992) Roger Ellis, 'Author(s), Compliers, Scribes and Bible Texts: Did the *Cloud* author Translate *The Twelve Patriarchs*?' in *The Medieval Mystical Tradition in England: V*, ed. Marion Glasscoe (Cambridge), pp. 193–221

Ellis (1994) 'Second Thoughts on the Authorship of *Tretyse of þe Stodye of Wysdome*', *Neuphilologische Mitteilungen* 95, 307–17

Forman (1987) Robert K. Forman, 'Mystical Experience in the *Cloud*-Literature', in *The Medieval Mystical Tradition in England: IV*, ed. Marion Glasscoe (Cambridge), pp. 49–61

Gardner (1936) Helen Gardner, 'The Text of *The Scale of Perfection*', *Medium Aevum* 5, 11–30

Glasscoe (1993) Marion Glasscoe, *English Medieval Mystics: Games of Faith* (Harlow)

Hodgson (1967) Phyllis Hodgson, *Three Fourteenth-Century English Mystics* (London)

Hogg (1984) James Hogg, 'The Latin *Cloud*', in *The Medieval Mystical Tradition in England: Exeter Symposium III* (Cambridge), 104–15

Hosic (1906) Alma Hosic, 'On the Comparison of Adverbs in English in the Fourteenth Century', *University Studies* (University of Nebraska) 6, 251–76

Hussey (1973) S.S. Hussey, 'Latin and English in *The Scale of Perfection*', *Mediaeval Studies* 35, 456–76

Hussey (1980) 'Walter Hilton: Traditionalist?' in *The Medieval Mystical Tradition in England: I. 1980*, ed. Marion Glasscoe (Exeter), pp. 1–16

Knowles (1961) David Knowles, *The English Mystical Tradition* (London)

Lagorio and Sargent (1993) Valerie Lagorio and Michael Sargent, 'English Mystical Writings', in *Manual*, vol. IX, pp. 3049–137, 3405–71

Lees (1983) Rosemary A. Lees, *The Negative Language of the Dionysian School of Mystical Theology: An Approach to The Cloud of Unknowing*, 2 vols (Salzburg)

Minnis (1983) Alastair Minnis, 'Affection and Imagination in the *Cloud of Unknowing* and Hilton's *Scale of Perfection*', *Traditio* 39, 323–66

Riehle (1977) Wolfgang Riehle, 'The Problem of Walter Hilton's Possible Authorship of the *Cloud of Unknowing* and its Related Tracts', *Neuphilologische Mitteilungen* 78, 31–45

Russell-Smith (1954) Joy M. Russell-Smith, 'Walter Hilton and a Tract in Defence of the Veneration of Images', *Dominican Studies* 7, 180–214

Sargent (1976) Michael G. Sargent, 'The Transmission by the English Carthusians of Some Late Medieval Spiritual Writings' *Journal of Ecclesiastical History* 27, 225–40

Spearing (2001) A.C. Spearing, 'Introduction', in *'The Cloud of Unknowing' and Other Works*, trans. A.C. Spearing (Harmondsworth), pp. ix–xliv

Taylor (2002) Cheryl Taylor, 'A Contemplative Community? The *Cloud* Texts and *Scale* 2 in Dialogue', *Parergon* ns 19, 81–100

Tixier (1997) René Tixier, 'Contemplation in *The Cloud of Unknowing*', in *Mysticism and Spirituality in Medieval England*, ed. William F. Pollard and Robert Boenig (Cambridge), pp. 122–37

Tugwell (1984) Simon Tugwell, 'The Cloud of Unknowing', in his *Ways of Imperfection* (London), pp. 170–86

Turner (1973) G.W. Turner, *Stylistics* (Harmondsworth)

Turner (1995) Denys Turner, *The Darkness of God: Negativity in Christian Mysticism* (Cambridge)

Underhill (1923) Evelyn Underhill, trans., *The Scale of Perfection* (London)

Watson (1999) Nicholas Watson, 'The Middle English Mystics', in *The Cambridge History of Medieval English Literature* (Cambridge), pp. 85–124

Wittgenstein (1953) Ludwig Wittgenstein, *Philosophical Investigations*, trans. G.E.M. Anscombe (Oxford)

4

Nicholas Love

KANTIK GHOSH

And as it is seide þe deuoute man & worthy clerke *Bonauentre* wrot hem
[deuovte meditacions of cristes lyfe] to A religiouse woman in latyne þe
whiche scripture ande wrytyng for þe fructuouse matere þerof steryng
specialy to þe loue of Jesu ande also for þe pleyn sentence to comun
vndirstondyng semeþ amonges oþere souereynly edifiyng to symple creatures
þe whiche as childryn hauen nede to be fedde with mylke of lyȝte doctryne &
not with sadde mete of grete clargye & of hye contemplacion.[1]

Thus Nicholas Love in his *apologia pro arte sua* attached, in the form of an
original preface, to his free translation of the medieval Latin *Meditaciones vitae
Christi* generally attributed to St Bonaventura in the Middle Ages.[2] The
Meditaciones, a set of pronouncedly affective meditations on the life of Christ,
formed one of the most popular of medieval devotional texts. Regularly and
often multiply translated into almost every major European tongue, it constituted one of the most influential expressions of Franciscan spirituality in the
later Middle Ages, and had a significant impact on both religious art and
drama.[3] However, Nicholas Love's is more than just a simple translation. What
distinguishes his rendition, named by him the *Mirrour of þe blessed life of Jesu
criste* (11/19), is an extraordinary degree of self-consciousness about his undertaking. This self-consciousness arises out of, and is a defensive response to, the
contemporary politicisation of the issue of lay interpretation of Biblical and
other religious writings by the followers of the Oxford philosopher and heretic,
John Wyclif (d. 1384), known as the Lollards. It is therefore not adequate to
consider Love as a mere participant in an affective tradition of venerable pedigree,[4] for such affectivity and its literary formations are explicitly identified by
him, as in the quotation above, as especially appropriate for the intellectually
unsophisticated, the *puerile*.[5] Indeed, the *Mirror* offers fascinating evidence of

---

[1] Ed. Sargent (1992), p. 10/9–17. All further references will be to this edition by page number followed
by line number.
[2] Ed. Peltier (1868); Stallings-Taney (1997). On its possible composition in the early fourteenth
century by John de Caulibus, a Franciscan friar from San Gemingnano, see Sargent 1992, pp. xv–xvi;
Deanesly 1922. On dating, see McNamer 1990. On translations of the *Meditaciones*, see Sargent
1984; Ruh 1956; Vaccari 1952; Salter 1974.
[3] See Beadle 1997; also see Mâle 1986, 28–48.
[4] This aspect of the *Mirror* has been most thoroughly studied by Salter 1974, esp. chs 4 and 5; for the
location of the *Mirror* within the tradition of the Middle English lives of Christ, see Johnson 1990.
[5] See Watson 1997.

the changing valences of inherited religio-literary traditions in an environment in which religious meanings, and the competence of the laity to access and determine such meanings, had become the objects of fierce partisan zeal. The *Mirror* therefore emerges as not only an exercise in traditional devotional writing, but also, by the same token, in contemporary religious polemics.

Nicholas Love was the first Prior of Mount Grace Charterhouse in Yorkshire, founded in 1397 by Thomas de Holand, Duke of Surrey, and nephew of Richard II. As Michael Sargent has pointed out, 'nothing is known of Love's origins and little of his life'. As first Prior of a newly founded Carthusian house, he must have been, as Sargent suggests, 'a man of great prudence and strict personal discipline'. The pronounced anti-Lollard stance of the *Mirror* as well as its foregrounded devotion to ecclesiastical hierarchy and authority indicate that he was 'an ecclesiastical conservative'.[6]

Love's conservative politics informs the *Mirror* and its reception history from the very beginning. In 1407–1409, Thomas Arundel, Archbishop of Canterbury, drafted and promulgated a set of anti-heretical censorship laws known as the *Constitutions*. Among various other restrictions on preaching, on theological research and on academic freedom, the *Constitutions* forbade the translation or reading of the scriptures without prior diocesan permission:

> no one from now on should translate any text of holy scripture on his own authority into the English language or any other, by way of book, pamphlet or tract, nor should anyone read such a book, pamphlet or tract newly composed since the time of John Wyclif, or in the future to be composed, in part or in whole, publicly or privately, under pain of excommunication, until that translation was approved by the local diocesan, or, if need be, by provincial council.[7]

The extent to which this particular law of Arundel's was enforced still remains unclear. Over 250 copies of the Wycliffite Bible survive, and none contains any evidence of official episcopal approval. However, although many Wycliffite Bibles were produced after 1409, none gives a precise date of production, and several betray attempts – through erasures and patently false dates – to appear to be of much earlier provenance, and therefore exempt from the archbishop's mandate.[8] The consciousness of Arundel's promulgation thus seems to have been fairly widespread in the early fifteenth century, and Love, in keeping with his conservative political stance, exploited it. Seventeen manuscript copies of the *Mirror* have a 'Memorandum' attached to them which claims that Archbishop Arundel examined the text before it was 'freely communicated' ('libere

---

6 Sargent 1992, xxii–xxiii. Sargent provides the few tentative details that we do have about Love's life, pp. xxii–xxv.
7 For the full text of the *Constitutions*, see Wilkins 1737, vol. III, pp. 314–19; the translation cited here is by Sargent 1992, xlv; for discussion of Arundel's laws see Spencer 1993, Watson 1995, Copeland 2001.
8 See Christopher de Hamel, *The Book: A History of the Bible* (London and New York, 2001), pp. 177–78. De Hamel cites some instances: Oxford, Bodl. MS Fairfax 2 changes its original date of 1408 to 1308; Manchester, John Rylands Library, MS Eng. 80 dates itself 1343 though the manuscript was made in the mid-fifteenth century.

communicata') and found it to be ideal for 'the edification of the faithful and the confutation of heretics or Lollards' ('ad fidelium edificacionem, & hereticorum siue lollardorum confutacionem') (7/16, 7/21–22).

The *Mirror* thus invites us to consider its significance in the context of contemporary religious politics. One of Lollardy's fundamental aims was to equip lay readers and listeners, both male and female, primarily from non-aristocratic backgrounds, with basic skills in the interpretation of the actual words of the Bible translated into the vernacular, typically conceptualised as the ability to access, through devoted study, 'open reason' and inspiration from the Holy Ghost, the 'literal sense' of scripture. The contemporary Church and academia (as represented by the University of Oxford) were castigated as authorities more interested in distorting the word of God through a concupiscent hermeneutics for their corrupt worldly ends than in fostering the primitive simplicity of the *vita apostolica*.[9] Lay discernment of authority, in particular textual authority, thus became (from the 1390s onwards) a sensitive political issue. Love's religio-textual methodology, while of ancient pedigree, emerges in this context as a self-consciously reactionary gesture. The *Mirror* takes the form of a series of emotive 'imaginations' of Christ's life and the feelings of those who surrounded him and witnessed his Passion. What it conspicuously does not offer are the exact words of scripture. Instead, the biblical words and the author's meditations on them are welded into a near-inseparable unity, the emphasis falling on an imaginative emotional participation in the fundamental events of Christian history rather than on the reader's ability to assess the validity or otherwise of particular interpretations (and methodologies of inter-pretation) of scripture. For instance, in the climactic episode of the crucifixion, actual Gospel passages and the imagined prayers of Mary and Jesus on each other's behalf form a seamless whole drawing from the affective reader an intense emotive response to the tortured humanity of Christ and his mother: 'And so stode þe moder byside þe crosse of hir sone, bytwix his crosse & þe þefes crosse; she turnede neuer hir eyene fro him, she was full of anguysh as he was also' (see 178/6–42).

The laity, as visualised by Love, is characterised by 'ignorance, intellectual simplicity, spiritual childishness and carnality' (Watson 1997, 95), and therefore incapable of participating in mature discourses of religious understanding, the 'sadde mete of grete clargye' (10/16). Instead, affective meditation on the humanity of Jesus is the 'milk' that such children require. The implication – in direct conflict with Lollard visions of lay empowerment – is that such children remain children, in a state of perpetual intellectual disenfranchisement, and therefore entirely dependent on the loving ministrations of Holy Mother Church. It is worth bearing in mind here that the *Mirror*'s original, the pseudo-Bonaventuran *Meditaciones*, was addressed specifically to a woman religious, and generally to those who had chosen the contemplative life. Salter (1974, 42) points out that the 'many references to the contemplative life, and the long digression on the subject inserted into the account of the Ministry of Christ,

---

9   See Hudson 1988, Copeland 2001, Ghosh 2002.

point to a specialised public'. Love's version explicitly recasts the original's stated and implied audience through a series of changes designed to adapt the text to the alleged intellectual and spiritual (in)capacities of a lay audience of 'simple souls'.[10] In the process, he aligns the affective tradition of 'carnal' meditation on Christ's humanity[11] with intellectual and religious infancy much more sharply that does his source. The *Meditaciones* itself considers affective meditation as a spur which initiates a process having as its aim the highest levels of spiritual illumination. Indeed, it points to St Francis himself as the prime example of the achievement of a 'luminous understanding of the Scriptures' ('luculentam intelligenciam scripturarum', Peltier 1868, 519; Stallings-Taney 1997, 9/65) through meditation on the life of Christ.

The *Mirror* rapidly achieved immense popularity. Sargent lists well over sixty manuscript copies, most of them produced 'far away from Mountgrace, and chiefly in the main centres of vernacular book-production' (Doyle 1983, 87), in which the text is preserved either fully, fragmentarily or as an excerpt. It therefore forms, along with the Wycliffite Bible, the Brut Chronicle, Walter Hilton's *Scale of Perfection*, and John Mirk's *Festial*, one of the most widely disseminated works in Middle English prose. The *Mirror*'s popularity had doubtless to do both with its relevance to contemporary religious politics and the fine literary expression it gives to 'the particular form of affective piety most effectively popularised through the writings of the Franciscans' (Meale 1997, 20). Evidence of early ownership is sparse, and has been studied most extensively by Carol Meale. She underlines the *Mirror*'s vogue amongst members of both the religious and the secular elite, ascribing this, in part, to the then fashionable upper-class predilection for Carthusian spirituality.[12] One of the earliest copies, the former Foyle manuscript, belonged to Sibyl de Felton, abbess of Barking, who died in 1419. Another early copy, Tokyo, Takamiya MS 8, was in the possession of Joan, Countess of Kent. Indeed, some copies such as Tokyo, Waseda University Library, MS NE 3691 and Edinburgh, National Library of Scotland, Advocates' MS 18.1.7 (by the same scribe), can be categorised as 'luxury books' (Meale 1997, 23). As a corollary to this upper-class interest in the *Mirror*, it may be noted that 'with some few exceptions, the material standard of production of early copies of the text was consistently high' (Meale 1997, 27), though there are extant copies from the mid-fifteenth century such as San Marino, Huntington Library, MS HM 149, revealing considerable efforts at economy (Furnish 1990). The manuscripts also suggest that much attention was paid to decoration, especially in the early decades of the fifteenth century, as documented by Kathleen Scott (1997). Scott's analysis points to greater interest in the decoration of the text when fears of Lollardy were particularly potent (around the time of the Oldcastle rising of 1414, for instance) than in the later

---

[10] See Sargent 1992, xxx–xliv; Salter 1974, ch. 3.

[11] This tradition of meditation found one of its most influential exponents in Bernard of Clairvaux, who said, in one of his sermons on the Song of Songs, that the 'love of the heart is, in a certain sense, carnal, because our hearts are attracted most toward the humanity of Christ and the things he did or commanded while in the flesh'; quoted by Cousins 1988, 378.

[12] See Tuck 1984; Knowles 1955–59, vol. II, 129–138.

decades of the century, when the *Mirror*'s readership seems to have become 'socially more diverse' (Meale 1997, 27–28). As she points out:

> If official church approval of the text was perhaps an impetus to decoration of *Mirror* manuscripts, then the display of miniatures and the sequences of borders. . .may have been a gentle nudge to the Establishment by patrons: we take your point and take it one step further in making our pride in owning the text visually ostensible. (p. 76)

All this may point to an apparent paradox. A text explicitly identified by its author as catering to the needs of orthodox 'symple creatures' in an embattled heretical environment seems to have found part of its initial readership among the very highest in the land who were sometimes prepared to spend significant amounts on parchment manuscripts of a high quality. Of course, there is always the possibility that a disproportionate number of such manuscripts survives (parchment is much more durable than paper, decorated manuscripts have a greater chance of being treasured). Indeed, Ian Doyle (1997, 164) has pointed out that 'the sixty-odd complete or partial manuscripts which survive show, by their textual variations and groupings that, like many much-multiplied medieval compositions, there must have been formerly several (perhaps many) times copies made and in use, probably hundreds'. But it is equally plausible, to develop Scott's suggestion cited above, that a text such as Love's, explicitly advertising its orthodoxy, would have appealed in particular to an upper-class readership not averse to displaying its religious conformity in times of social upheaval encompassing even the aristocracy.[13]

Love's assertion of the *Mirror*'s orthodoxy was not just a rhetorical gesture. Significant effort seems to have been made to ensure that the text was transmitted without change, and extant copies, though they do show some variation, are on the whole remarkably uniform. Michael Sargent has studied the *Mirror*'s textual affiliations in a series of articles, his seminal suggestion being that the extant manuscripts fall into two main groups which he designates as the β- and α- recensions of the text. The former he considers to be a 'pre-publication' version of Love's text, circulating before it had been examined officially, and betraying, through certain textual disruptions, an on-going process of composition and revision, the latter being a more finished, 'post-publication' version circulated after the approbation of Arundel had been obtained (Sargent 1995a, 1997). The text in both versions shows remarkably little variation, especially when compared to other contemporary texts such as Hilton's *Scale of Perfection*, William Flete's *Remedies Against Temptations*, or the works of Richard Rolle (Sargent 1992, cvi). This interest in uniformity is significant both of the *Mirror*'s Carthusian origins and of its polemical stance. The Carthusians took considerable pains to ensure that their texts were copied correctly, particularly in times of troubled internal politics arising out of the papal schism of 1378 and the subsequent division of the Order into two obediences (Sargent 1995b). The Lollards were avid book-producers devoting scrupulous attention to textual

---

[13] On the relationship of Lollardy and the gentry, see the various articles in Aston and Richmond 1997.

uniformity, and self-consciously aware of the importance of ensuring that their books were transmitted correctly, without any change (Hudson 1985, 1988, 1989). Opponents of Lollardy had to acknowledge and respond to their emphasis on textual authority.

The *Mirror*'s anti-heretical endeavour finds expression in a number of ways. First, Love embellishes the pseudo-Bonaventuran text with a number of polemical additions, preeminently on the Eucharist – in the form of a 'Treatise on the Sacrament' appended to the *Mirror* – as well as on other topics made controversial by the Lollards such as oral confession, the giving of tithes, priestly morality and the spiritual validity of ecclesiastical hierarchy. Many of these original passages are sign-posted in the manuscripts by a marginal reference 'contra lollardos' ('against the Lollards'). Second, as pointed out above, the exact words of the Bible almost disappear into the highly emotive texture of a series of meditations on the life of Christ. The kind of scripturally informed polemical argumentation so beloved of the Lollards – as for instance in the English Wycliffite Sermons[14] – is rigorously eschewed in favour of 'imaginative' meditations. Third, Love is highly self-conscious, and defensive, of his meditative and (by implication) scriptural methodology, and he repeatedly guides his readers to an authoritative tradition of scriptural exegesis embedded in and inseparable from the authority of ecclesiastical history and tradition. Moreover, his attempts to counter a heterodox hermeneutics ultimately betray an uneasy and uncertain accommodation of certain fundamental Lollard emphases, in particular of those which have to do with the discernment of authority. I will consider these various elements in Love's conservative religious polemics in order.

First, Love's treatment of the sacrament of the Eucharist. The most sensational and controversial question at the heart of the Lollard heresy, the nature of the Eucharist – whether the sacrament was merely symbolic and commemorative or involved the real presence of the flesh and blood of Christ, and whether the substance of the bread and wine remained after consecration – rapidly emerged as one of the most unacceptable sites of heretical debate (Hudson 1988, 281–90). In response to rationalist Wycliffite questioning of the alleged annihilation of the material bread and wine, Love stresses the centrality of the 'marvellous' to all Christian doctrine. Christ was 'merueilously' conceived and born; his incarnation and passion were both 'merueylous', his resurrection was 'merueilous', his Ascension 'merueylous & gloriouse', his works and deeds 'merueilous' (225/16–30). The implied emphasis on the supra-rational nature of Christ's mission is central to Love's dismissal of Lollard emphasis on 'open reason' as a valid means of understanding religious truth: 'god almihty wrouht alle þees merueiles & many moo, aboue þe reson of man' (228/43–44). The Eucharist is thus the preeminent sign that God gave to man of the necessity of the subordination of reason to the authority of the Church; 'curious' seeking must be replaced by a 'buxom' submission to what the 'holy doctours tauht, & holi chirch determinede' (229/36–37). Indeed, Wyclif, the 'maister of Lollardes', 'þorh his grete clergy & kunnyng of philosophye' trusted more in the

---

[14] Ed. Anne Hudson and Pamela Gradon, *English Wycliffite Sermons*, 5 vols (Oxford, 1983–96).

'doctrine of Arestotele þat stant onely in naturele reson of man' (238/32–239/14).

However, this apparently decisive assertion of the inadequacy of reason in matters of faith, and the consequent necessity of abiding by the determinations of Holy Church, is accompanied in Love by an uneasy capitulation to Lollard demands that the faith be 'open', evident, credible, and independent of the interpretative authority of the Church. After narrating a eucharistic miracle from the life of St Hugh of Lincoln, Love says:

> Þere was þan to see & ʒit now is, a wonderfull myracle, þat is to sey, wyne turnede opunly to mannus siht in to blode & brede in to flesh, declaring expressely þe forme & þe soþenes of þat blessede sacrament. (234/11–14)

Note how Love uses standard elements of vocabulary particularly favoured by the Lollards: 'openly' and 'expressly', both adverbs eliding the interpretative agency of the Church.[15] The real meaning of the sacrament is made 'open' by the miracle; its form and truth emerge 'expressly', independent of interpretation. Indeed, the 'makyng & ordinance of þat blessede sacrament' can therefore be simultaneously 'aʒeynus mannus reson' (153/41) and yet 'resonable' (152/24).

The tension that I have gestured towards above – a tension between an outright dismissal of Lollard approaches to scripture and religious traditions as misguided and invalid, and an acceptance and accommodation of their critiques of authority – also informs Love's treatment of his inherited affective scriptural methodology. The Bible and its expositions are regarded by Love as a unity. This is in direct opposition to the Lollard idea that the Bible is a unique text which must be consistently and rigorously distinguished from its interpretations. The Wycliffite Bible, the Long English Sermon Cycle, and the *Glossed Gospels* – all major pieces of Lollard scholarship – are scrupulously discriminatory of textual authority. Love, on the contrary, chooses to write within a tradition where the biblical text and its expositions are treated as a pied-à-terre for the affective outpourings of the meditative reader. Scripture, patristic and other interpretation and commentary, anti-Lollard polemic and non-biblical devotional material are welded into one indivisible whole, through a constant violation of what Vincent Gillespie calls 'the decorums of textual boundaries' (Gillespie 1984, 23). Indeed, Love translates in full the pseudo-Bonaventuran assertion that Holy Writ may be interpreted and reinvented in diverse ways, as long as all such reinventions are in accordance with the faith and 'stir devotion':

> Wherfore we mowen to stiryng of deuotion ymagine & þenk diuerse wordes & dedes of him [Christ] & oþer, þat we fynde not writen, so þat it be not aʒeyns þe byleue, as seynt Gregory & oþer doctours seyn, þat holi writte may be expownet & vndurstande in diuerse maneres, & to diuerse purposes, so þat it be not aʒeyns þe byleue or gude maneres. (10/43–11/4)[16]

---

15 For the notion of a 'Lollard sect vocabulary', see Hudson 1985, 165–80; for the use of such words in the Lollard–Church conflict, see Ghosh 2002, passim.

16 Love's source runs: 'Nam circa diuinam Scripturam meditari, exponere et intelligere multifarie, prout expedire credimus possumus: dummodo non sit contra ueritatem uite, iusticie aut doctrine, id est non sit contra fidem uel bonos mores' (Peltier 1868, 511; Stalling-Taney 1997, 10/95–98).

What is of governing importance is edification, 'fruitfulness', and to this purpose it is allowable to read the Bible selectively, and to create one's own edifying (but not necessarily scripturally supported) narratives. One of Love's favourite words is 'fructuose', referring to the spiritual fruit that one can gain through meditation on the events in Christ's life. Another is 'processe', meaning both 'sequence of events/progression' and 'purpose/goal'.[17] The progression of Biblical events has as its inscribed 'fructuose processe' the stimulation of prayer and 'imaginative' meditation and the giving of 'ensaumples' to the devout. The pattern most often followed by Love tends to include the citation of a Biblical passage (the 'ground'); a 'historical', often memorably dramatic reconstruction or invention based on this; a contemplative passage, usually of heightened tone, drawing attention to the affective potential of the invented scene and to its exemplary value, followed by a passage of prayer or homiletics, accompanied, if possible, by some polemics. Of course, the various elements might occur in a slightly different order, but this forms the general pattern. A fairly typical example would be the chapter entitled 'How þe child Jesus laft alone in Jerusalem' (57–60). It begins with the gospel story of Jesus's journey to Jerusalem with his parents when he was twelve and his staying behind there; is followed by an affective emphasis on Mary's sorrow ('Wherfore here we mowen haue resonably gret compassion of þe gret anguyshe'); a pointer to the *ensaumple* offered ('here mowe we lern, what tyme tribulacion & anguysh fallen to vs not to be . . . miche disturblet þerby'); a prayer uttered by Mary in which the reader is expected to participate; a passage of 'historical' invention ('In þis forseid processe of Jesu what hope we þat he dide?'); more *ensaumples* ('we mowe note & lerne þre notable þinges'); and finally a piece of homiletic addressed to the religious. Love also manages to introduce, independently of his original, a piece of polemics suggesting that Christ begged: 'And some doctours seyn þat he begget in þo þre dayes' (60/7–8). The mendicant orders had been one of the prime targets of the Lollards, one of the main arguments being that the friars' claim to *imitacio Christi* was false as Christ had never begged. Indeed, the episode from Christ's childhood that Love suggests may indicate his possible mendicancy had been explicitly dismissed as a sufficient basis for such suggestions by the Lollard William Taylor in his sermon of 1406 delivered at St Paul's Cross in London.[18] Love's casual interpolation of a piece of sensitive polemic is typical of the freedoms afforded by an 'imaginative' meditative discourse. Love however seems to be somewhat uneasy with this suggestion of his, and quickly moves on: 'But þerof litel forse, so þat we folowe him in perfite mekenes & oþer vertues. For beggyng withoutforþe bot þere be a meke herte withinneforþe is litel worþ als to perfeccion' (60/8–11).

The various stages of a meditative 'processe' such as the one we have just examined are often emphasized by marginal notes. In most manuscripts of the *Mirror*, the text is accompanied by a marginal apparatus, pointing out important passages as well as identifying cited texts. In the rhetorical presentation of

---

[17] Senses 1a and 1e in *MED*.
[18] See Anne Hudson, ed., *Two Wycliffite Texts*, EETS os 301 (1993), p. 21/669–689.

Magdalen's conversion, for instance, the marginal notes are detailed. At the beginning, there is a 'nota verba magdalene intima' to indicate Magdalen 'þenkynge as it were in þis manere'; a further 'nota' to signal the affective passage and 'the gostly fruite' to be plucked; 'notabilia' pointing to the 'grete notabilities to oure edificacione'; a reference to St Bernard as the authority for the homiletic passage; and a 'contra lollardos' to indicate how Magdalen's conversion suggests that oral confession is necessary, as opposed to 'þe fals opinyon of lollardes þat shrift of mouþe is not nedeful' (90–92).

However, Love's appropriation of the inherited discourses of affectivity and scriptural reinvention is polemical and self-conscious. As a result, there is an abiding unease in the *Mirror* with the meditative predilection for imaginative reinventions of scripture: after all, a central tenet of Lollardy was that such interference with the precise words of the Bible is part of the 'cautela diaboli' ('devil's tricks')[19] by means of which the establishment attempts to support its corrupt claims to authority and beguile the laity. Significantly expanding the pseudo-Bonaventuran explanation of meditative methodology,[20] Love repeatedly introduces cautious explications and *caveats* original to him to ensure that his meditative techniques cannot be accused of leading the simple astray. The imaginative 'process' of the *Mirror* must both be recognised as 'imaginative', functioning by analogy and 'likeness', and be confined to the limits prescribed by faith: 'þe which processe sal be taken as in liknes & onlich as a manere of parable & deuoute ymaginacion' (18/1–2); 'beware þat þou erre not in imaginacion of god' (22/7); 'we shole here more specialy gedere in oure entent, & make vs by ymaginacion, as þei we were present in bodily conuersacion' (128/6–8); 'Nowe go we vp by deuout contemplacion to oure lorde Jesu beholdyng in ymaginacion of heuenly þinges by likenes of erþely þinges' (216/30–32). Indeed, Love virtually introduces into the *Meditaciones* the concepts of 'reasonable imagination' and 'devout imagination' in relation to the Gospels. 'Vnresonable ymaginacion' (161/9) can blind men spiritually, and must be guarded against. 'Reasonable' and 'devout' imaginations, 'supposings' or 'trowings' are however acceptable as a valid means of biblical reinvention. The exact methodology and limits of such reinvention are left vague, the suggestion being that it is in the devout *intention* of the reader that the orthodoxy of the whole 'process' is anchored.[21] The vulnerability of such a vision of valid reading (described by Richard Beadle as 'essentially a self-validating rhetorical strategy', Beadle 1997, 11) to Wycliffite textual-fundamentalist criticism is evident, and indeed, Love is uneasily aware of this. One consequence of this resisted awareness of the pitfalls in his version of 'orthodox' hermeneutics is a repeated attempt to justify his interpretations in terms of Lollard positives: readings are therefore defended as 'open', 'express' and 'reasonable' (Ghosh 2002, 158–68).

This conflicted and defensive self-consciousness of Love's scriptural methodology finds expression in the lay-out of the manuscripts. Unlike medieval manuscripts of the pseudo-Bonaventuran *Meditaciones*, which vary consider-

---

19 The phrase is Wyclif's; see G. Lechler, ed., *De Officio Pastorali* (Leipzig, 1863), p. 35.
20 See Peltier 1968, 511; Stallings-Taney 1997, 10/90–103.
21 For discussion of 'devout imagination', see Beadle 1997.

ably in appearance and lay-out, manuscripts of the *Mirror* show a remarkable
degree of consistency. As we have noted above, most manuscripts contain a
marginal apparatus. In large part, this apparatus is devoted to the identification
of cited authorities, often in great detail. There is also a significant attempt at
rubricating biblical words to distinguish them from the surrounding text.
Furthermore, twenty-seven manuscripts of the *Mirror* are prefaced by the
following notice:

> Attende lector huius libri prout sequitur in Anglico scripti, quod vbicumque in
> margine ponitur litera N verba sunt translatoris siue compilatoris . . . Et
> quando peruenitur ad processum & verba eiusdem doctoris [Bonaventura]
> inseritur in margine litera B . . . (7/1–9)

> (Note, reader of the following book written in English, that wherever the letter
> 'N' is placed in the margin, the words are added by the translator or compiler
> . . . And when it returns to the narrative and words of that doctor
> [Bonaventura], then the letter 'B' is inserted in the margin. . .[22])

What does such a *mise-en-page*, transmitted with great fidelity in most extant
manuscripts, suggest? Its major aim seems to be one of which the Lollards
would have approved: the discernment of authority. Doctors cited must be identified; scriptural words must be given a separate visual status through under-
lining or other forms of rubrication; the words of the original *auctor* – in this
case, St Bonaventura – must be distinguished from the additions of the translator. These emphases would have been unremarkable in a Lollard text or in an
academic text. What is surprising is their presence in an avowedly 'orthodox'
and 'popular' meditative work, the very form of which – an inextricable
mingling of the scriptural and the non-scriptural, of the authorial and the interpolated – militates against precise textual distinctions. Indeed, the 'N-B'
distinction is not (and given the minutely pervasive nature of the changes introduced by Love, cannot be) particularly rigorous or successful. But the fact that
the attempt should have been made at all is revealing: it suggests how the
methodological emphases of Lollardy have begun to be internalised within what
presents itself as its opposite, and how the orthodox establishment is forced to
recognise that the laity is much more than simple children incapable of intellectual labour and therefore necessarily reliant on unqualified ecclesiastical
assertion.

Much of the contemporary 'meaning' of the *Mirror* thus emerges from its
polemical situation within a particular conflict, a conflict whose reverberations
extended well into the fifteenth century. But of course, the *Mirror* is much more
than a polemical tract. Its stylistic graces, at once colloquial and elevated, have
often been noted, and studied in depth by Salter (1974).[23] Salter pays particular
attention to Love's masterly fusion of native English rhythms with Latin rhetorical structures. She points to his use of 'balanced sentence construction', the use
of parallelisms and repetitions, and the accumulation of clauses and sentences in

22 Trans. by Sargent 1992, xxx.
23 See especially ch. 7; also see Nolan 1984; Blake 1997.

NICHOLAS LOVE   63

the manner of a rhetorical catalogue as some of his favourite devices to heighten emotional tension and to induce emotional crises. However, though Love often relies on Latin rhetorical models, he avoids the complex periodic sentence, preferring instead, even in passages of heightened emotional tone, a relatively simple sentence construction (Salter 1974, 267–73). For instance:

> And after þat tyme oure lorde began to faile in siht in manere of diynge menne, & was alle pale now stekyng þe eyene & now opunyng, & lowde his hede now in to one side & now in to a noþer side, failyng alle þe strenghes, & alle þe vaynes þan voide. (180/17–21)

> Þis is a pitevouse siht & a ioyful siht. A pitevous siht in him, for þat harde passion þat he suffrede for oure sauacion, bot it is a likyng siht to vs, for þe matire & þe effecte þat we haue þerbye of oure redempcion. (181/12–15)

> Aa lady what do ȝe? ȝhe lowene ȝow // to þe feete of hem þat bene moste wikkede, & preyne hem, þat hauene no rewarde to any gude praiere. Suppose ȝhe to bowe by ȝour pite, hem þat bene moste cruele & most wikkede & wiþoute pite? Or to ouercome hem þat bene alþere priddest wiþ mekenes? Nay, for proude men hauen abominacion of mekenes. Wherfore ȝe trauaile in vayne. (182/30–36)

As the above quotations indicate, the rhythmic prose of the *Mirror* would have been especially suited to oral delivery, and indeed, the evidence of the extant manuscripts bears this out. Many of the volumes are very large, 'meant for stability, not portability, for communal lessons rather than private meditations' (Doyle 1953, 148). The careful and varied scribal attention paid to details of punctuation, as recently studied by Malcolm Parkes (1997), also bears witness to contemporary recognition and appreciation of Love's rhetorical intentions.

The *Mirror*'s stylistic achievement, its pronounced dramatic imagination, and its limpid vernacular rendering of one of the consummate achievements of Franciscan spirituality ensured that it had a long afterlife. In particular, it seems to have struck a most resonant chord with late-medieval female readers, as recently documented by Carol Meale (1997). Meale points to Love's simple vocabulary, his emphasis on a meek, tender and 'feminine' Christ as also 'the privileging of female experience in the *Mirror*' as part of the appeal of the text for women from a range of social classes over the fifteenth century, from the upper reaches of the aristocracy to the lower bourgeoisie. The dramatic visualisation of the life of Christ which informs the pseudo-Bonaventuran text and is further developed by Love must also have had a particular appeal for the theologically unsophisticated. Richard Beadle discusses the *Mirror* 'as an especially eloquent expression of the dramatic sensibility in late-medieval culture', and points to the undoubted impact it had on the Middle English N-Town Plays (Beadle 1997). The *Mirror*'s appeal seems not to have waned over the fifteenth century; indeed, extant manuscripts suggest that its readership became wider, more socially inclusive, a process further consolidated by printing. Caxton brought out his editions c. 1484 and c. 1489, followed by further editions from Wynkyn de Worde and Richard Pynson. The visual dramatic element of the text remained in the foreground, for these early printed editions are accompanied by woodcuts illustrating the life and passion of Christ. The publication of the text in England apparently ended in 1530, and Lotte Hellinga (1997, 146) considers it 'very unlikely' that any further editions appeared in post-Reformation England. However, the text retained its appeal for Catholic sensibilities and two further, recusant, editions were brought out from Douai and Saint-Omer in the early seventeenth century. These editions, along with the post-Reformation prove-nance of some of the extant manuscripts, suggest that Love's work 'continued to be kept and known (yet not under his name) by Catholics in England and in exile on the continent of Europe, lay-people, clergy and members of religious orders, a mixed public, as in the Middle Ages' (Doyle 1997, 164–65).

BIBLIOGRAPHY

For a full list of manuscripts and early printed editions, see Sargent 1992, 1995a, 1997.

Primary

MODERN EDITIONS

Powell, Lawrence F., ed. (1908) *The Mirrour of the Blessed Lyf of Jesu Christ* (Oxford) [Reprinted as: Hogg, James, and Lawrence F. Powell, eds, *Nicholas Love's Mirrour of the Blessed Lyf of Jesu Christ*, Analecta Cartusiana 91 (Salzburg, 1989)]
Sargent, Michael G., ed. (1992) *Nicholas Love's Mirror of the Blessed Life of Jesus Christ: A Critical Edition Based on Cambridge University Library Additional MSS 6578 and 6686* (New York and London)

OTHER PRIMARY TEXTS

Pseudo-Bonaventura, *Meditationes Vitae Christi*, in:
Peltier, A.C., ed. (1864–71), *S. Bonaventurae Opera Omnia*, 15 vols (Paris), vol. XII (1868), pp. 509–630
Ragusa, Isa, and B. Rosalie, eds and trans. (1961) *Meditations on the Life of Christ: An Illustrated Manuscript of the Fourteenth Century* (Princeton)
Stallings-Taney, M., ed. (1997) *Ioannis de Cavlibus Meditaciones vite Christi, Corpus Christianorum (Continuatio Mediaevalis)* 153 (Turnhout)
Wilkins, David, ed. (1737) *Concilia Magnae Brittaniae et Hiberniae*, 4 vols

Secondary

Aston, Margaret, and Colin Richmond, eds (1997) *Lollardy and the Gentry in the Later Middle Ages* (New York)
Beadle, Richard (1997) ' "Devoute ymaginacioun" and the Dramatic Sense in Love's *Mirror* and the N-Town Plays', in Oguro, Beadle and Sargent (1997), pp. 1–17

Blake, N.F. (1997) 'Some Comments on the Style of Love's *Mirror of the Blessed Life of Jesus Christ*', in Oguro, Beadle and Sargent (1997), pp. 99–114

Copeland, Rita (2001) *Pedagogy, Intellectuals and Dissent in the Later Middle Ages: Lollardy and Ideas of Learning* (Cambridge)

Cousins, Ewert (1988) 'The Humanity and the Passion of Christ', in Jill Raitt, ed., *Christian Spirituality: High Middle Ages and Reformation* (New York), pp. 375–91

Deanesley, Margaret (1920) *The Lollard Bible and Other Medieval Biblical Versions* (Cambridge)

———— (1922) 'The Gospel Harmony of John de Caulibus, or S. Bonaventura', in C.L. Kingsford, ed., *Collectanea Franciscana II*, British Society of Franciscan Studies 10 (Manchester), pp. 10–19

Doyle, A.I. (1953) 'A Survey of the Origins and Circulation of Theological Writings in English in the Fourteenth, Fifteenth and Sixteenth Centuries', 2 vols, Ph.D. thesis, University of Cambridge

———— (1983) 'Reflections on Some Manuscripts of Nicholas Love's *Myrrour of the Blessed Lyf of Jesu Christ*', *Leeds Studies in English* ns 14, 82–93

———— (1997) 'The Study of Nicholas Love's *Mirror*, Retrospect and Prospect', in Oguro, Beadle and Sargent (1997), pp. 163–74

Furnish, S. (1990) 'The *Ordinatio* of Huntington Library, MS HM 149: An East Anglian Manuscript of Nicholas Love's *Mirrour*', *Manuscripta* 34, 50–65

Ghosh, Kantik (2002) *The Wycliffite Heresy: Authority and the Interpretation of Texts* (Cambridge)

Gillespie, Vincent (1983–84) '*Lukynge in haly bukes*: *Lectio* in Some Late Medieval Spiritual Miscellanies', in Hogg (1983–84), vol. II, pp. 1–27

———— (1989) 'Vernacular Books of Religion', in Griffiths and Pearsall (1989), pp. 317–44

Griffiths, Jeremy, and Derek Pearsall, eds (1989) *Book Production and Publishing in Britain 1375–1475* (Cambridge)

Hellinga, Lotte (1997) 'Nicholas Love in Print', in Oguro, Beadle and Sargent (1997), pp. 143–62

Hogg, James (1980) 'Mount Grace Charterhouse and Late Medieval English Spirituality', in *Collectanea Cartusiensia 3*, Analecta Cartusiana 82/3 (Salzburg), pp. 1–43

————, ed. (1983–84) *Spätmittelalterliche geistliche Literatur in der Nationalsprache*, 2 vols, Analecta Cartusiana 106 (Salzburg)

Hudson, Anne (1985) *Lollards and their Books* (London and Ronceverte)

———— (1988) *The Premature Reformation: Wycliffite Texts and Lollard History* (Oxford)

———— (1989) 'Lollard Book Production', in Griffiths and Pearsall (1989), pp. 125–42

Johnson, I.R. (1990) 'The Late Medieval Theory and Practice of Translation with special reference to some Middle English Lives of Christ', Ph.D. thesis, University of Bristol

———— (1997) 'Vernacular Valorizing: Functions and Fashionings of Literary Theory in Middle English Translation of Authority', in Jeanette Beer, ed., *Translation Theory and Practice in the Middle Ages* (Kalamazoo, MI), pp. 239–54

Knowles, David (1955–59) *The Religious Orders in England*, 3 vols (Cambridge)

Mâle, Émile (1986) *Religious Art in France: The Late Middle Ages*, trans. M. Mathews (Princeton)

McNamer, Sarah (1990) 'Further Evidence for the Date of the Pseudo-Bonaventuran *Meditationes Vitae Christi*', *Franciscan Studies* 50, 235–61

Meale, Carol (1997) ' "oft siþis with grete deuotion I þought what I miȝt do plesynge to god": The Early Ownership and Readership of Love's *Mirror*, with special reference to its Female Audience', in Oguru, Beadle and Sargent (1997), pp. 19–46

Nolan, Barbara (1984), 'Nicholas Love', in A.S.G. Edwards, ed., *Middle English Prose: A Critical Guide to Major Authors and Genres* (New Brunswick, NJ)

Oguro, Shoichi, Richard Beadle and Michael G. Sargent, eds (1997) *Nicholas Love: Waseda, 1995* (Cambridge)

Parkes, M.B. (1997) 'Punctuation in Copies of Nicholas Love's *Mirror of the Blessed Life of Jesus Christ*', in Oguro, Beadle and Sargent (1997), pp. 47–59

Ruh, Kurt (1956) *Bonaventura deutsch: Ein Beitrag zur deutschen Franziskaner-mystik und -scholastik* (Bern)

Salter, Elizabeth (1974) *Nicholas Love's "Myrrour of the Blessed Lyf of Jesu Christ"*, Analecta Cartusiana 10 (Salzburg)

——— (1981) 'The Manuscripts of Nicholas Love's *Myrrour of the Blessed Lyf of Jesu Christ* and Related Texts', in A.S.G. Edwards and Derek Pearsall, eds, *Middle English Prose: Essays on Bibliographical Problems* (New York), pp. 115–27

Sargent, Michael G. (1983–84) 'Bonaventura English: A Survey of the Middle English Prose Translations of Early Franciscan Literature', in Hogg (1983–84), vol. II, pp. 145–76

——— (1995a) 'Versions of the Life of Christ: Nicholas Love's *Mirror* and Related Works', *Poetica* 42 (for 1994), 39–70

——— (1995b) 'The Problem of Uniformity in Carthusian Book-Production from the *Opus Pacis* to the *Tertia Compilatio Statutorum*' in Richard Beadle and A.J. Piper, eds, *New Science Out of Old Books: Studies in Manuscripts and Early Printed Books in Honour of A.I. Doyle* (Aldershot), pp. 122–41

——— (1997) 'The Textual Affiliations of the Waseda Manuscript of Nicholas Love's *Mirror of the Blessed Life of Jesus Christ*', in Oguro, Beadle and Sargent (1997), pp. 175–274

Scott, Kathleen (1997) 'The Illustration and Decoration of Manuscripts of Nicholas Love's *Mirror of the Blessed Life of Jesus Christ*', in Oguro, Beadle and Sargent (1997), pp. 61–86

Spencer, H. Leith (1993) *English Preaching in the Late Middle Ages* (Oxford)

Tuck, J. Anthony (1984) 'Carthusian Monks and Lollard Knights: Religious Attitudes at the Court of Richard II', *Studies in the Age of Chaucer* 1, 149–61

Vaccari, Alberto (1952) 'Le "Meditazione della vita de Cristo" in volgare', in *Scritti di erudizione e di filologia I: Filologia biblica e patristica* (Rome), pp. 341–78

Watson, Nicholas (1995) 'Censorship and Cultural Change in Late Medieval England: Vernacular Theology, the Oxford Translation Debate, and Arundel's *Constitutions* of 1409', *Speculum* 70, 822–64

——— (1997) 'Conceptions of the Word: the Mother Tongue and the Incarnation of God', in Wendy Scase, Rita Copeland and David Lawton, eds, *New Medieval Literatures* 1, 85–124

——— (1999) 'The Politics of Middle English Writing', in Jocelyn Wogan-Browne, Nicholas Watson, Andrew Taylor and Ruth Evans, eds, *The Idea of the Vernacular: An Anthology of Middle English Literary Theory 1280–1520* (Exeter), pp. 331–52

5

Julian of Norwich

BARRY WINDEATT

Dying in Norwich in May 1373, a young woman is gazing at a crucifix held before her eyes. Suddenly, blood trickles down from under the crown of thorns. The painted artefact of the crucifix dissolves, filmlike, into moving image: a montage of vivid and singular revelations or 'shewings', whose defamiliarizing readings of the Passion invite deconstructive reassessment of meditative tradition. Duly recovered, the woman compiles a book out of her experience in meditating on the meaning of these revelations over subsequent years. To her, the shewings bring both joyous serenity and some anguishing bafflement: she can hardly doubt them, yet in their exaltation they seem to promise more than orthodox church teaching.

From this experience derives the work of Julian of Norwich, the earliest woman whose writing in English can be identified. Although Julian discloses few details about herself – preferring her readers to focus on the revelations and not on their first recipient – she does document precisely the dates of her shewings and of her two later breakthroughs in interpreting them. The longer version of her shewings records that they occurred on 8 or 13 May 1373,[1] when she was thirty and a half years old. She was born, therefore, in late 1342 and was thus an almost exact contemporary of Chaucer. Her text also records how it was 'xv yer after and more' (i.e. in 1388 or later) before she gained insight into the key overall significance of her revelations (ch. 86; p. 135), and not until 'xx yeres . . . save iii monethis' after the time of the shewings (i.e. February 1393) that she finally interpreted her vision of the Lord and Servant (ch. 51; p. 74). A name for the author is supplied, and identified with a place, when the rubric to one version of her text opens by declaring: 'There es a vision schewed be the goodenes of God to a devoute woman and hir name es Julyan that is recluse atte Norwyche and yitt ys on lyfe anno domini millesimo CCCCxiii [i.e. 1413] . . .' (p. 182).[2] Four wills variously provide evidence of an anchoress named Julian at Norwich and at St Julian's Church in Conisford, Norwich, between 1393/4 and at least 1416, although Julian was probably an anchoress well before 1394.[3]

---

1   The manuscripts give different dates (S1 has 'viii'; P has 'xiii') probably deriving from scribal error over roman numerals. All reference to the longer version is by chapter and page number to the edition in Glasscoe 1993.
2   All reference to the shorter version is by chapter and page number to the edition in Windeatt 1994.
3   For the wills, see Colledge and Walsh 1978, 33–8, 'Julian: Biographical Data'. On 20 March 1393/4 Roger Reed, rector of St Michael's, Coslany in Norwich, bequeathed two shillings to 'Julian anakorite'. In 1404 Thomas Emund, chantry priest of Aylsham, Norfolk, bequeathed one shilling to

Even her own name is uncertain, for the anchoress would be likely to have taken 'Julian' as her name in religion from the patronal saint of the church to which her anchorhold was attached.[4] Nor does her book give itself a name, and the titles of all editions of Julian's work since the nineteenth century are editorial.

It was probably in 1413, while visiting Norwich, that Margery Kempe felt herself divinely bidden 'to gon to an ankres in the same cyte, whych hyte Dame Jelyan'. According to this contemporary witness, it was on account of Julian's reputation as a spiritual adviser that Margery confided some of her own 'wondirful revelacyons whech sche schewyd to the ankres to wetyn yf ther wer any deceyte in hem, for the ankres was expert in swech thyngys and good cownsel cowd yevyn' (ch. 18).[5] Although Margery gives Julian the title of 'dame', which was customary for nuns, all the wills naming Julian as a benefi-ciary refer to her as an anchoress or recluse rather than as a nun. Indeed, Julian may have been still in secular life at the time of her revelations, for her account mentions her mother and others around her. Whether this would be likely if Julian were already an anchoress remains a matter of dispute: it is unclear whether an anchorhold could accommodate these onlookers, and whether the rules of enclosure would be waived in the event of grave illness. It may be that after the revelations, influenced by them, Julian entered religious life as an anchoress. It has been argued that Julian may have been a widow at the time of her shewings, not least because to be an unmarried laywoman aged thirty and a half would be highly unusual.[6] The possibility of Julian's widowhood has also allowed for speculation that she had been a mother herself, not that this is neces-sary to explain the special place of Christ as our mother in her meditations. If a laywoman, Julian evidently had the circumstances and the leisure to allow for devotion. The manuscripts variously describe her as 'leued', and as a simple creature 'vnlettyrde' or 'that cowde no letter',[7] and although the latter may be a claim to ignorance of Latin rather than to illiteracy, it was no doubt prudent at times for Julian to claim both. It may be that she refers simply to her lack of literacy at the time of her revelations rather than the education she later attained. Her likely revisions of her work make it seem improbable that Julian could not write even in English, as does her reference to the alphabet ('in this mervelous example I have techyng with me, as it were the begynnyng of an ABC, wherby I may have sum vnderstondyng of our lordis menyng', ch. 51; p. 79). Her text is a witness to its author's intellect and her knowledge of spiritual writings, but its learnedness is suffused and implicit, without direct citation of sources. Even biblical reference – with many echoes of John and Paul – does not always follow

---

'Juliane anchorite apud St Juliane in Norwice'. On 24 November 1415 John Plumpton, a citizen of Norwich, bequeathed forty pence to 'le ankeres in ecclesia Sancti Juliani de Conesford in Norwice', and twelve pence each to her serving maid and to Alice, her former maid. In the will of Isabel Ufford, Countess of Suffolk (d. 1416), is 'Item jeo devyse a Julian recluz a Norwich 20s.'

4   St Julian's Church was mostly destroyed in the German bombing of Norwich on 27 June 1942. For a pre-war account of the church, see Flood 1937, and for anchorites in medieval Norwich, see Dunn 1973.

5   See further in Barry Windeatt, ed., *The Book of Margery Kempe* (Harlow, 2000), pp. 119–23.

6   For discussion, see Ward 1988, 1992.

7   'leued' in A (Windeatt 1994, 189); 'vnlettyrde' in P (Colledge and Walsh 1978, 285); 'that cowde no letter' in S1 (Glasscoe 1993, 2).

the letter so much as the spirit of the original, possibly because Julian's awareness of texts often derived from hearing them read and from conversation with
spiritual advisers, and so is reexpressed later in her own words. How Julian
came by her learning remains a matter of speculation, but the Norwich of her
day was no intellectual backwater.[8]

Julian's work survives in a shorter and a longer form. The shorter text is
found only in one mid-fifteenth-century manuscript – BL, MS Add. 37790 (A)
– possibly of Carthusian provenance. This comprises an anthology of spiritual
reading, all but one item in English and including, among other things, much
Richard Rolle, the *Mirror of Simple Souls*, an extract from Suso's *Horologium
Sapientiae*, a note on the visions of St Bridget of Sweden, and the unique copy
of an English translation of Ruysbroeck's *Treatise of Perfection*.[9] Some six
times longer, the longer version is preserved complete in three post-Reformation
manuscripts copied, perhaps directly from medieval manuscripts in their
keeping, by the communities of English nuns exiled on the continent.[10] The
earliest is that in Bibliothèque nationale, Paris, MS fonds anglais 40 (P), of
which the paper has been dated on the basis of watermarks to c. 1580;[11] it may
have been written in Flanders, possibly at Antwerp. The text in BL, MS Sloane
2499 (S1) has been dated, on the basis of its Dutch watermarks, to the later
seventeenth century.[12] This would make S1 somewhat later than BL, MS Sloane
3705 (S2), hitherto discounted as an early eighteenth-century copy, but recently
dated by its Amsterdam watermarks to the second half of the seventeenth
century (not that S2's revised dating alters its perceived textual inferiority to
S1). Both these Sloane manuscripts may be copies of the same vanished archetype and are of much the same period as the first printed edition of 1670 by the
English Benedictine monk Serenus Cressy. Entitled *XVI Revelations of Divine
Love* and described as 'revived from an ancient copy' (probably P), this edition
was almost certainly printed in England.

Although the complete longer text is thus extant only in copies made centuries after its composition, there does survive – in Westminster Cathedral Trea-
sury MS 4 (W) – a unique medieval copy of what are usually taken to be
excerpts from the longer version of Julian edited into a continuous text.[13]
Copied c. 1500 from an exemplar of c. 1450, W is a florilegium of excerpts
from the Psalm commentaries *Qui Habitat* and *Bonum Est*, Walter Hilton's
Scale of Perfection, and the Julian text.[14] None of the four texts is attributed to

---

8   For a survey of church and society in late medieval Norwich, see Tanner 1984. The nearby Benedic-
    tine convent of Carrow Abbey held the advowson of St Julian's church but had no school, library, or
    record of concern with education or spirituality (according to Ward 1988, 19). The introduction and
    apparatus to Colledge and Walsh 1978 constructs a learned, scholarly Julian.
9   For descriptions of BL, MS Add. 37790 and its contents, see Beer 1978, 9–13, and Colledge and
    Walsh 1978, 1–5.
10 On preservation of English medieval spirituality among the recusant communities, see Spearitt 1974,
    Birrell 1976, and the introduction to Colledge and Walsh 1978.
11 By A.I. Doyle, as reported in Reynolds and Holloway 2001, 136 n. 1.
12 By W.H. Kelliher, as reported in Reynolds and Holloway 2001, 495, 508 n. 6.
13 W's text of Julian comprises selections from the first, second, ninth, tenth, fourteenth and fifteenth
    revelations (chs 4–7, 10, 22–24, 41–44, 53–56, 59–61, 63–64 of the longer version).
14 For a modernization of the whole florilegium, see Walsh and Colledge 1961; for an edition of the W
    text of Julian, see Kempster 1997.

its author, and the effect of W's selection is to elide (apart from what is probably one brief oversight) all trace of the female authorship of Julian's work. In its language W offers a valuable check on the fidelity of the post-Reformation copies of Julian to the Middle English language of the original. Although W has been interpreted as a symptom of fifteenth-century readership of Julian, or even claimed as an authentic *ur*-text of the shewings, its origins may lie somewhere between the two and derive scribally from a copy of Julian's text at a stage no longer extant.[15]

The relative merits of the texts in P and S1 as the basis for editing the longer text remain a puzzle for would-be modern editors of Julian. The Paris text is an exercise in calligraphic imitation, striving to emulate a simplified late-medieval script. Its language, however, represents some modernization and sophistication of the medieval original.[16] By contrast, S1 is rather untidily written in a seventeenth-century cursive hand. Yet while in looks S1 makes no pretence to be other than of its age, it does preserve medieval English linguistic forms more faithfully and consistently than the text in P (or S2), and hence has been preferred over P as the basis of modern editions.[17] Both P and S1 occasionally contain material not present in the other, and S1 contains (as P does not) summary chapter contents as the heading to each chapter (which are perceptive readings, but not necessarily an authorial apparatus – they largely refer to Julian in the third person). Many of the differences between P and S1 appear to stem from no more than the familiar and characterizable patterns of scribal error.[18] Comparison with A and W, where these overlap with the longer version, points to some inevitable textual corruption in both P and S1, which is often to be suspected on grounds of sense where comparison with A or W is not available as a control. Future editions of Julian's text might profitably be more eclectic between the surviving witnesses.

On balance, the nature of the shorter version (S) points to its being an authentic earlier version of Julian's work. True, S survives in a manuscript containing some abridgements of other contemplative texts, which raises the possibility that it is an abridgement itself. However, only S includes certain circumstantial details about the shewings as an event: the priest who brings the crucifix has a child with him and addresses Julian as 'daughter' (p. 184); the posture of Julian's head and hands is specified (p. 184); her mother is present at the sickbed (p. 194); she recalls how her wish for three wounds was prompted by hearing in church the story of St Cecilia (p. 183). Such details seem more likely to occur in an earlier text, nearer in time to the original experience, than to be inserted into one abridged later, whether by a scribal editor or by Julian herself. Taken as a whole, the features of S suggest a version earlier in that lengthy process of understanding the shewings which Julian's longer version (L) acknowledges to have occurred. By comparison with L, the shewings in S are

---

[15] Kempster 1998 argues for lay readership; Walsh and Colledge 1961 argue, more convincingly, for an advanced contemplative readership. On W as a Julian *ur*-text, see Reynolds and Holloway 2001, 21.

[16] P is the base text of Colledge and Walsh 1978.

[17] S1 is the base text of Glasscoe 1976, 1986, 1993, and of Crampton 1994.

[18] See the examples discussed in Glasscoe 1989.

quite sparely narrated, closer to speech than L and possibly dictated; they are introduced with little preface or context, and unlocated in time. Some of Julian's more striking visual insights do not figure in S, including some details of her Passion shewings, but her vividly visualizing powers of description apparently reflect the serene and assured outcome of intervening meditation rather than closeness to the immediate experience. S is more tentative than L in presenting its account of the revelations, and more defensive in asserting its conformity to orthodox church teaching. A sense of sin, as too of the devil, seems always near, and S gives a compelling testimony of an unforgettable experience.[19]

The date and purpose of S can only be established from internal evidence, and this has been variously interpreted. Its relatively unelaborated commentary on the shewings, together with its circumstantial details, have suggested that S was written down not long after Julian's revelations as a form of memorandum, perhaps in the mid 1370s, and possibly in connection with her entering religious life. However, a passage near the beginning of S (and absent from L), which refers to 'the payntyngys of crucyfexes that er made be the grace of God aftere the techynge of haly kyrke to the lyknes of Crystes passyon' (ch. 1; p. 182) has been taken to reflect a concern not to be identified with heretical Lollard hostility to images. If so, this concern would belong more to the 1380s than earlier. Given the very substantial revision occurring between S and L, this dating of S might then imply a later composition of L than around 1393, when Julian declares she was vouchsafed her latest understanding of her shewings.[20] On the other hand, granted a cautious and conservative tradition in medieval England concerning claims to visionary experience, especially by women, and given Julian's larger caution in S, the reverent claim of her shewings to have seen so very much more than the crucifix held before her dying gaze is rather different from, and may not necessarily be linked to, contemporary nervousness about Lollard contempt for graven images.

Although Julian indicates dates for her own contemplative progress in understanding (May 1373, 1388, February 1393), this is not the same as dating the texts in which that understanding was written down. The germ of some of what is later developed very characteristically in L is already present in S. Whatever may have been the purpose of compiling S's succinct account, it was still thought worth copying as late as 1413, and the rubric implies it was copied by someone who knew or knew of Julian, by then in her seventies. In view of the absence of medieval witnesses to the completed longer version, it may be that Julian left this uncirculated and hence 'unpublished' in her lifetime. By the early fifteenth century there were ample grounds for a female visionary to hesitate before publishing so profound and audaciously original a work as Julian's longer text.

Unlike some visionaries (including Margery Kempe), Julian does not record in so many words that she was divinely charged to write down her revelations,

---

[19] For studies of the differences between S and L, see Windeatt 1977, 1992, and Watson 1993.

[20] For arguments for so re-dating S and L, see Watson 1993; for objections, see Aers and Staley 1996: 'Julian's often radical vernacular theology is most unlikely to have been possible after Arundel's Constitutions of 1407/9' (79 n. 4; also 111).

but she does understand, clearly and firmly, that God wants them to be made known. This is the context of her declaration confronting and rejecting the notion that, because she is a woman, she should not make public what she has learned by revelation, while distancing herself from any problematic claim to be a woman who teaches:

> Botte God forbede that ye schulde saye or take it so that I am a techere, for I meene nought soo – no, I mente never so! For I am a woman, leued, febille and freylle . . . Botte for I am a woman, schulde I therfore leve that I schulde nought telle yowe the goodenes of God, syne that I sawe in that same tyme that [it] is his wille that it be knawen? (ch. 6; p. 189)

That this passage no longer appears in the much fuller and more ambitious text of L suggests that Julian moved so far beyond such defensiveness about her vocation as thinker and writer that she no longer felt the need to address it. Yet her last chapter declares: 'This booke is begunne be Gods gift and his grace, but it is not yet performid, as to my syte' (ch. 86; p. 134), and it may well be that Julian kept her full text to herself as work-in-progress. It is not necessary to posit a distinct version completed after the understanding she attains in 1388, and then revised after that of 1393, in order to imagine that Julian's text developed through a number of stages and layers. There was only ever one book for Julian to write, because there was only one subject: her revelations of 1373, understood cumulatively over time in response to the various unclarities, problems and challenges that Julian encountered in them. If two authentic states of Julian's text survive, their differences can chronicle the pilgrimage of a mystic's mind. To chart the evolution of Julian's contemplative commentary on her original revelations is to understand them better by comprehending something of Julian's method as a contemplative and a writer.

Some of the differences between S and L represent moves to edit her shewings for a readership, a wider audience than that envisaged in S. Implications in S that the text is aimed at contemplatives are dropped from L.[21] Much of Julian's shorter text is carried forward, its phrasing relatively unchanged, into the longer version, as if Julian works on and from a copy in front of her. L treats S curatorially, as if the words of S embody the core documentary testimony of the revelations, and it is around S's text that L constructs the apparatus of an edition in a process of 'self-textualization'.[22] The numbering of the shewings, division into numbered chapters, chapter summaries (if authorially sanctioned), and a first chapter setting out a table of contents, are in L but not in S. Along with these articulated divisions comes more of a chronological continuum smoothing over some of the terse transitions in S, and a timetable of the first day's shewings is added in retrospect (chs 65–66). Some connections across the

---

[21] Cf. 'of this nedes ilke man and woman to hafe knawynge that desyres to lyeve contemplatyfelye' (S; ch. 4; p. 186; omitted from L); 'and in this was I lerede that ilke saule contemplatyfe to whilke es gyffen to luke and seke God schalle se hire and passe unto God by contemplacion' (S, ch. 13; pp. 197–8); L rewrites into 'wherin I was lernyd that our soule shal never have rest til it comith to hym' (ch. 26; p. 37). These passages imply that at least by the time of S's composition Julian was herself vowed to contemplation.

[22] On 'self-textualization' in Julian, see Riddy 1993, 125. On self-presentation, see Johnson 1991.

text between shewings are starting to be made in S, but by the stage of L the meditations are interlinked by precise cross-references facilitated by citation of shewing or chapter numbers. In effect, the investiture of S's account with the sustainedly more analytical and patterned prose of L in itself represents a reading and editing.

Notwithstanding all such careful editing, the mixture of comfort and bafflement in the original revelations makes provisional any written text that Julian attempts to translate from the medium of moving image and visualization in her shewings. Turning shewing into writing confronted Julian with intractable problems in both form and content that remain part of the challenge in reading her work. The original revelations do not immediately present a connected thematic sequence: they seem fragmentary, even disjointed; a series of segments, without much foreground or background, and in no particular order.[23] Absence of formal sub-division in S perhaps retains Julian's earlier sense of her experience as a stream of revelatory consciousness where boundaries between shewings are merging and emerging to her perception. As an answer to Julian's earlier prayer to have more bodily sight of the Passion, this cinematically vivid, montage-like series of images and impressions, sensations and heard words, is so singular and deconstructive of traditional expectation as to pose real challenges to interpretation. While in some ways the contemplative has gone to work on her material like the film-editor – splicing, pacing, shaping what is seen, and creating continuity in her edited later version – this is art-house cinema and the defamiliarizing uniqueness of the content and its structure remains central.

As visions, Julian's shewings are strikingly dissimilar: they are unequal in length, type or content. Not all are of the Passion, not all are primarily visual, and they prompt different kinds of contemplative revision. The 1st and 8th Shewings present almost cinematic close-ups of the bleeding of Christ's head, and the congealing and drying of his body. This pathological focus is not for its own sake, but offers a cue for contemplation on the spiritual implications of these quasi-photographic details. The 2nd Shewing develops an extended contemplation from just one intently observed visual shot of Christ's face discolouring on the cross. With meditation, the 4th Shewing of Christ's body bleeding, as if at his flagellation, is developed literally in another dimension, so as to understand his blood streaming through the firmament, descending into hell and ascending into heaven for us. Mysterious transformations of normal space and dimension are deployed in other shewings, like the 10th, which opens out from its initial focus on the wound in Christ's side. The 3rd Shewing of God 'in a point', or the 1st Shewing's vision of something as small as a hazelnut yet understood to be 'all that is made', work by challenging normal ideas of space and form. The concluding 16th Shewing of Christ enthroned in majesty in the human soul is the culmination of Julian's pervasive spatial discourse of enclosing and inclusion. Fundamental to her interpretation of her revelations, this vision prompts recurrent cross-references in her contemplations, as does the 12th Shewing of Christ glorified. For Julian, this shewing defeats all attempts to

---

23 For classifications of the revelations, see Molinari 1958 and Pelphrey 1989, 80–91.

picture it but presents God proclaiming himself in a prose poem of
self-description ('I it am that is heyest . . . I it am that is al . . .' ch. 26; p. 37).
Such understandings vouchsafed in words also form the core of a number of
shewings, where further insights may be developed in visual terms. Julian
understands that: the devil is vanquished (5th Shewing); Christ thanks her for
her youthful suffering (6th Shewing); if it were possible for Christ to suffer
more, he would willingly do so (9th Shewing); Christ's question 'Wilt the se
her?' introduces the vision of Mary at the Passion (11th Shewing); she will be
taken suddenly from her suffering and come to heaven (15th Shewing). It is two
non-visual revelations – the 13th (on sin) and the 14th (on prayer) – that prompt
the most extended contemplative commentary, culminating in Julian's analysis
of her layered vision of the Lord and Servant. The 7th Shewing – without a
visual focus and consisting of rapidly alternating feelings of exaltation and
desolation – is exceptional in remaining unsupplemented by subsequent meditation, whether because Julian moved beyond such fluctuating feelings or because
she saw them as worked through in the production of her revised text in L.

With the insights of intervening meditation, Julian's response to the earlier
text recording her shewings is to interpolate material analyzing and expanding
on the original's significance. Many interpolations are responses to challenging
aspects of the shewings (such as that 'synne shal be no shame, but worship to
man', ch. 38; p. 52) which have provoked lengthy meditations to arrive at their
interpretation. Many other interpolations are on a much smaller scale:

> Here I saw a part of the compassyon of our lady Seynt Mary, for Christe and
> she were so onyd in love that the gretnes of his lovyng was cause of the
> mekylhede of hyr payne; *for in this I saw a substance of kynd love, continyyd
> be grace, that creatures have to hym; which kynde love was most fulsomely
> shewyd in his swete moder and overpassyng*, for so mech as she lovid him
> more than al others, hir panys passyd al others; *for ever the heyer, the
> myghtyer, the sweter that the love be, the mor sorow it is to the lover to se that
> body in payne that is lovid*
>
>   (ch. 18; p. 27; the italicized words appear only in L).

Here as elsewhere, Julian weaves new matter into existing sentences so as to
transform them in content and style through her fuller analysis of love's role,
expressed in her characteristically ordered and cadenced prose patterning, often
in triads ('the heyer, the myghtyer, the sweter'), redolent of her pervasive devotion to the Trinity.[24]

Julian's two versions of her compact 10th Shewing in S and L can serve to
encapsulate her characteristic editing and deepening of visuality and interpretative frame. The core of the original tenth revelation in S is that a vision into
Christ's wounded side – seeing there his flowing blood and the sacred heart –
substitutes for an inability to see into the Godhead. In insight and style this has
been transformed as both vision and interpretation in L. Here, in cinematic
fashion, the audience's looking now follows and responds to the presented looks

---

[24] Julian's prose has received little sustained analysis: see Wilson 1956, Stone 1970, and the (somewhat
overdone) attention to rhetoric in the annotations to Colledge and Walsh 1978.

of those on screen ('our Lord loked into his syde and beheld . . . with his swete lokyng he led forth the understondyng of his creture', ch. 24; p. 35). The camera then pans out into a mysterious perspective inside Christ's side, visualized as an interior so vast as to confound any earthly sense of space ('And than he shewid a faire delectabil place, and large enow for al mankynd that shal be save to resten in pece and in love'). What at first Julian had merely supposed Christ might be saying about his heart and blood is now reported with assurance ('he browte to mende . . . he shewid . . .'). Where the 10th Shewing in S had implicitly disclaimed vision of the Godhead ('yyf thow kan nought loke in my godhede', ch. 13; p. 197), in L the same tenth revelation has been rewritten into a claim to precisely such a vision ('And with this swete enioyyng he shewid onto myn vnderstondyng, in party, the blissid Godhede'). In the remainder of this brief shewing the five-word divine locution from S ('Loo, how I lovyd the') is interpreted through Julian's habitual technique, whereby revelation merges with commentary in an expansive meditative paraphrase that allows considerable interpretative license to the contemplative author ('as if he had seid . . . And also for more vnderstondyng this blissid word was seyd').

If L can be construed as an edition of S, it is one that includes such extensive commentary on the earlier narrative of her experience as to shift the balance and focus of her earlier self-account and re-make its genre.[25] The predominance of a narrative line gives way to the more exploratory continuum of commentary that displays all the analytical subtlety of a mind that discerns patterns, categorizes and sub-divides.[26] Indeed, the 13th and 14th shewings each provoke such a major excursus of commentary that the narrative of the first day's fifteen shewings can barely re-establish itself before the commentary on the completed revelations as a whole takes over until the end of the book. What had been at first the story of her visions becomes the history of how she came to understand them, with attempted categorizations of the different aspects of bodily sight, spiritual sight, 'words formed in my understanding', and so on.[27] A brief observation jotted down like a memo in S ('luffe was moste schewed to me, that it is moste nere to us alle', ch. 24; p. 212) will be rewritten in L in terms of what the soul now understands of God's will in the original insight ('the soule toke most vnderstonding in love; ya, and he will in allthing that we have our beholding and our enioyeyng in love', ch. 73; pp. 117–18). Her perplexing but crucial revelation of the Lord and Servant is presented through the problematic process of how she learns to analyze it and then applies the lesson ('I had techyng

---

25 On the structure and procedure of Julian's book, see Windeatt 1980.

26 Of many possible examples, cf.: 'I had iii manner of vnderstondyng in this light, charite: the first is charite onmade; the second is charite made; the iii is charite goven. Charite onmade is God; charite made is our soule in God; charite goven is vertue; and that is a gracious geft of werkyng in which we loven God for himselfe and ourselves in God and that God loveth, for God' (ch. 84; p. 133). Cf. also: 'These arn two werkyng that mown be seene in this vision: that on is sekyng, the other is beholdyng . . . It is God wil that we have thre things in our sekyng: the first is . . .' (ch. 10; p. 17); 'Our lord God shewid to manner of privytees: on is . . .' (ch. 34; p. 46); 'in which shewing I se ii conditions in our Lordis menyng: on is rytfulnes . . .' (ch. 41; p. 56).

27 Cf. also 'ghostly in bodily likeness' (ch. 4; p. 6); 'more gostly without bodyly lyknes' (ch. 51; p. 72); 'And in this an inward gostly shewing of the lords menyng descendid into my soule' (ch. 51; p. 73); 'Than he, without voice and openyng of lippis, formys in my soule these words' (ch. 13; p. 20).

inwardly'), although the endpoint concerns Julian more than intervening stages of enlightenment: her original and subsequent understandings of this shewing and of all the shewings as a whole 'arn so onyd, as to my vnderstondyng, that I cannot, ner may, depart them' (ch. 51; p. 74). Julian's work retains something of the layered, interleaved structure of a private working draft. It has not been reconstructed into a logical linearity for the benefit of readers who have not shared the author's experience, and is interlaced with cross-references in the meditations to revelations that have not yet been narrated.

Driving this exploratory and experimental nature of Julian's text is a concern over authority. Her visions represented a privileged insight uniquely vouchsafed to her, which she, a woman, felt called to communicate, necessarily in the vernacular, to a wider audience than her local circle of clerical contacts. Whether or not her visions had motivated Julian to become an anchoress, they must have been central to her sense of herself, yet aspects of the shewings, especially in hinting at universal salvation, appeared to go beyond orthodox teaching.[28] In unsettled times, and with no settled English tradition of female visionaries or female authorship, this may well have felt like an exposed position, which seems to be reflected in the authorial voice in Julian's text. Studiedly anonymous and self-effacing, yet with the intensely inward focus of a personal testimony in first-person narrative, the text cannot but have an intrinsically autobiographical quality, while striving to present itself more generally as the progress of a soul ('for thus have I felt in myselfe', ch. 41; p. 56; 'Here may you sene what I am of myselfe', ch. 66; p. 108).[29] Julian's selectivity in disclosing information gives the text a distinctive voice, at once individual yet universal. Any context in place, circumstance or status has been occluded, but her gender and her age at the time of the shewings are divulged. The precise dating of the revelations to the very day and hour ('erly on the morne, aboute the howre of fowre . . . ich folowand other, till it was none of the day overpassid', ch. 65; p. 107) lends the historicity of a documentary deposition to an account of what transcends time and defies description. Yet acknowledgement within the text of the fifteen and twenty year gaps needed for its understanding only confirms explicitly what the whole work implies of a protracted and anxious spiritual journey towards understanding ('And yet I stond in desire, and will into my end', ch. 45; p. 64). It is this uncompleted project shared with the reader, that subsumes any more direct claim to didactic intent in her earlier text. Julian offers no scheme or programme for her readers to borrow and develop for themselves. She deploys no overarching metaphors of spiritual progress as a journey, pilgrimage, or ascent, and does not analyze advancement (for herself, or potentially, for her readership) through successive stages of purgative, illuminative or unitive contemplation. In essence, Julian offers her own experience as a witness, and her only claim on her reader lies in her conviction that her testimony's value lies not in any endorsement of herself but in its import for all her fellow-Christians.

When Julian rather exceptionally seeks to learn more by revelation about a

---

[28] On universal salvation, see Watson 1997.
[29] On 'intrinsic autobiographicality' in Julian's work, see Abbott 1999.

particular acquaintance (as Margery Kempe does habitually) she rapidly understands that she hinders herself by such a particular focus (ch. 35). A significant
movement of the longer version as a whole is for Julian to learn from what she is
not shown and to be reconciled to what is not going to be revealed ('I saw and
understode that every shewing is full of privities', ch. 51; p. 74). Since Julian is
not shown sin at any point in her revelations, she is both comforted by its noth-
ingness yet remains fearful of its perils. The style of a passage in S, staccato and
insistent, betrays her anxiety:

> for alle thynge is goode botte synne, and nathynge is wikkyd botte synne.
> Synne es nowthere deed no lykynge, botte when a saule cheses wilfully synne
> that is payne as fore his God, atte the ende he hase ryght nought. That payne
> thynke me the herdeste helle, for he hase nought his God. In alle paynes a
> saule may hafe God botte in synne . . . (ch. 18; p. 203)

which in L has been rewritten into one of Julian's most characteristic insights, as
serenely assured in style as it is optimistic in theme:

> And to me was shewid no herder helle than synne, for a kynde soule hath non
> helle but synne. And we govyn our intent to love and mekenes, be the werkyng
> of mercy and grace we arn mad al fair and clene. (ch. 40; pp. 55–56)

Nor can it be an accident that Julian's revision to her 3rd Shewing adds a
Boethian distinction between God's vision outside time and what humankind
may perceive as chance ('we seyen these ben happis and aventures; but to our
lord God thei be not so', ch. 11; p. 18), because some of the wisdom of her
longer version is to accept that her revelations cannot be completely revelatory
during this life and within time. Part of what Julian comes to see in her 14th
Shewing on prayer explodes any human concept of prayer within time – as prior
petition and subsequent granting – for as the shewing reveals, before we want
something and pray for it, God's will is that we have it and then that we want and
pray for it: 'how shuld it than be that thou shuld not have thyn besekyng?' (ch.
41; p. 56). Despite fallen humanity's sins, Julian famously learns that 'all shall
be well', but she also comes to realize that she cannot yet comprehend the 'great
deed' by which God will indeed make all things well at the end of time. By
implication, this is likely to involve a universal salvation that will transcend
notions of sin and blame and will fulfil the redemptive potential in our fallen
bodiliness revealed to Julian in her shewings ('For in every soule that shal be
savid is a godly wil that never assentid to synne ne never shal', ch. 37; p. 51).

Semi-modernized ('Sin is Behovely, but/ All shall be well, and/ All manner
of thing shall be well'), it is this sublimely hopeful aspect of the thirteenth revelation that is echoed at the close of T.S. Eliot's *Little Gidding* (1942), and also at
the end of Aldous Huxley's *Eyeless in Gaza* (1936). Largely overlooked before
the twentieth century, Julian's work is known to have been read by W.B. Yeats,
May Sinclair and Charles Williams, and is echoed in Iris Murdoch's novel, *Nuns
and Soldiers* (1981).[30] A devotional centre, and something of a shrine, has been

---

[30] For surveys of Julian's reception, see Birrell 1976 and Barratt 1995. In the absence of a scholarly

built in Norwich near the site of her anchorhold, and since 1980 Julian of
Norwich has had her feast day on 8 May in the Church of England's calendar.
Popularizations and selections published by religious presses testify to her
continuing appeal to a devout readership. Along with general recognition has
come acknowledgement of Julian's achievement as a theologian,[31] while
comparison with other medieval English contemplatives has only highlighted
Julian's specialness.[32] Most special of all – to modern perceptions – her spiritually imaginative and wonderfully tender analysis of God as our mother has
propelled Julian to celebrity as a woman writer who re-genders the Christian
God, although this tends to overlook her inconvenient insistence in context that
the maternal is one among other divine aspects, for God is our father, mother,
spouse, brother and lord (chs 52, 57).[33] In the academy, the later twentieth
century has often read in its own humanist image Julian's profound spiritual
optimism and her magnanimous understanding of the incarnation's implications
for humankind in bodily nature ('we arn all in him beclosid and he is beclosid in
us', ch. 57; p. 93). Her theological independence of spirit is read as radical,
polemical and hence political, in a discourse where salvation constitutes incorporation into a new polity and perfected sociality. Indeed, fully politicised,
Julian's text can now be seen to interrogate hegemonies so very subversively
that uninformed modern readers may even have imagined otherwise. That Julian
could be so otherworldly and apolitical as to be a mystic – or that as a visionary
her text might claim any authority beyond her own authorship – have become for
some an embarrassment, and are downplayed or denied. The audacious theological implications of Julian's humanity remain to be integrated with a balanced
view of her writing as a visionary and contemplative for whom 'this place is
prison and this life is penance', and who longs for the fullness of perception and
knowledge that is beyond this world: 'and than shal we sen God face to face,
homly and fulsumly' (ch. 43; p. 62).

Confronted with what is unknown about Julian herself yet known about her
work's development, any devil's advocate would certainly ask whether it isn't
actually more likely that the book of this great 'foremother' was penned – at
least to some degree – by a man? Margery Kempe's acknowledgement of her
inability to write, and her description of dictating her text to an amanuensis,
leads her modern interpreters to credit that man not so much with the transcription as the authorship of 'her' book. Julian describes herself as unlettered but
has produced a profoundly original theological work, derived from her claim to
have seen visions, yet presented so surefootedly as to be proof against
narrowmindedly orthodox criticism. Might Julian not only have dictated her

---

edition, the modernization by Grace Warrack (London, 1901), frequently reprinted for half a century,
had a decisive impact on perceptions of Julian.

[31] For Julian as theologian, see especially: Bauerschmidt 1999; Clark 1981, 1982a, 1982b, 1991; Jantzen
1987; Nuth 1991; Pelphrey 1982, 1989. For further literary implications, see Baker 1994; Gillespie
and Ross 1992; Glasscoe 1993.

[32] For some comparative studies, see Baker 1998; Glasscoe 1993; Park 1992; Pezzini 1989.

[33] On the theme of God as our Mother and its tradition, and on aspects of gender raised by Julian's work,
see Barker 1982; Bradley 1978; Bynum 1982; Cabassut 1949; Heimmel 1982; Robertson 1993;
Watson 1996.

meditations but composed the polished longer text in collaborative interchange with some of the learned spiritual directors to whom she could have had access in contemporary Norwich? Could this explain where her implicit learnedness derives from, especially in her longer version? Might this explain the transformation between the two versions in penetration of theological analysis as well as in rhetorical accomplishment and editorial textualization? It might indeed, and yet those tantalizingly faint but precious echoes in *The Book of Margery Kempe* of Julian's reported conversation with her visitor on those days in 1413 suffice to testify that Dame Julian spoke much as her text is written – luminously, with compassionate wisdom, and inflected with scripture – and that her mind and her book were essentially one.

BIBLIOGRAPHY

Editions

THE LONG TEXT

Colledge, Edmund, and James Walsh, eds, *A Book of Showings to the Anchoress Julian of Norwich*, 2 vols, Pontifical Institute of Mediaeval Studies: Studies and Texts 35 (Toronto, 1978), pp. 281–734

Crampton, Georgia Ronan, ed., *The Shewings of Julian of Norwich*, TEAMS Middle English Texts Series (Kalamazoo, MI, 1994)

Cressy, R.F.S., ed., *XVI Revelations of Divine Love, Shewed to a Devout Servant of our Lord, called Mother Juliana, an Anchorete of Norwich: Who lived in the Dayes of King Edward the Third* (London, 1670), reprinted 1843, 1864, 1902, with prefaces by, respectively, G.H. Parker, I.T. Hecker, and George Tyrell

Glasscoe, Marion, ed., *Julian of Norwich: A Revelation of Love*, Exeter Medieval English Texts and Studies (Exeter, 1976; rev. ed. 1986; rev. ed. 1993)

Reynolds, Sister Anna Maria, and Julia Bolton Holloway, eds, *Julian of Norwich: Extant Texts and Translation* (Florence, 2001), pp. 121–682

THE SHORT TEXT

Beer, Frances, ed., *Julian of Norwich's Revelations of Divine Love: The Shorter Version, ed. from BL Add. MS 37790*, Middle English Texts 8 (Heidelberg, 1978)

Colledge and Walsh (1978), see above under 'The Long Text', pp. 201–78

Reynolds and Holloway (2001), see above under 'The Long Text', pp. 685–783

Windeatt, Barry, ed., *English Mystics of the Middle Ages* (Cambridge, 1994), pp. 181–213

MANUSCRIPT SELECTIONS

Kempster, Hugh, ed., 'Julian of Norwich: The Westminster Text of *A Revelation of Love*', *Mystics Quarterly* 23 (1997), 177–245

Reynolds and Holloway (2001), see above above under 'The Long Text', pp. 5–117

Walsh, James, and Eric Colledge, trans., *Of the Knowledge of Ourselves and of God: A Fifteenth-Century Spiritual Florilegium* (London, 1961)

Secondary Works

Abbott, Christopher, *Julian of Norwich: Autobiography and Theology* (Cambridge, 1999)

Aers, David, and Lynn Staley, *The Powers of the Holy: Religion, Politics and Gender in Late Medieval English Culture* (Philadelphia, 1996), chs 3 and 4

Baker, Denise Nowakowski, *Julian of Norwich's Showings: From Vision to Book* (Princeton, 1994)

———, 'The Image of God: Contrasting Configurations in Julian of Norwich's *Showings* and Walter Hilton's *Scale of Perfection*', in McEntire (1998), 35–60

Barker, Paula S. Datsko, 'The Motherhood of God in Julian of Norwich's Theology', *Downside Review* 100 (1982), 290–304

Barratt, Alexandra, 'How Many Children had Julian of Norwich? Editions, Translations and Versions of her Revelations', in Anne Clark Bartlett, ed., *Vox Mystica: Essays on Medieval Mysticism* (Cambridge, 1995), 27–39

Bauerschmidt, Frederick Christian, *Julian of Norwich and the Mystical Body Politic of Christ* (Notre Dame, 1999)

Beer, Frances, *Women and Mystical Experience in the Middle Ages* (Woodbridge, 1992)

Birrell, T.A. 'English Catholic Mystics in Non-Catholic Circles', *Downside Review* 94 (1976), 60–81, 99–117, 213–31

Bradley, Ritamary, 'Patristic Background of the Motherhood Similitude in Julian of Norwich', *Christian Scholar's Review* 8 (1978), 101–13

Bynum, Caroline Walker, *Jesus as Mother: Studies in the Spirituality of the High Middle Ages* (Berkeley, 1982)

Cabassut, A., 'Une dévotion médiévale peu connu: la dévotion à Jésus notre mère,' *Revue d'ascétique et de mystique* 25 (1949), 234–45

Clark, J.P.H., '*Fiducia* in Julian of Norwich', *Downside Review* 99 (1981), 97–108, 214–29

———, 'Predestination in Christ according to Julian of Norwich', *Downside Review* 100 (1982a), 79–91

———, 'Nature, Grace and the Trinity in Julian of Norwich', *Downside Review* 100 (1982b), 203–20

———, 'Time and Eternity in Julian of Norwich', *Downside Review* 109 (1991), 259–76

Dunn, F.I., 'Hermits, Anchorites and Recluses: A Study with Reference to Medieval Norwich', in *Julian and her Norwich: Commemorative Essays and Handbook to the Exhibition 'Revelations of Divine Love'*. ed. Frank Dale Sayer (Norwich, 1973), 18–26

Flood, Robert H., *A Description of St Julian's Church, Norwich, and an Account of Dame Julian's Connection with It* (Norwich, 1937)

Gillespie, Vincent, and Maggie Ross, 'The Apophatic Image: The Poetics of Self-Effacement in Julian of Norwich', in Glasscoe (1992), 53–77

Glasscoe, Marion, ed., *The Medieval Mystical Tradition in England* (Exeter, 1980)

———, 'Visions and Revisions: A Further Look at the Manuscripts of Julian of Norwich', *Studies in Bibliography* 42 (1989), 103–20

———, ed., *The Medieval Mystical Tradition in England: Exeter Symposium V* (Cambridge, 1992)

———, *English Medieval Mystics: Games of Faith* (Harlow, 1993), ch. 5

Heimmel, Jennifer, *'God is Our Mother': Julian of Norwich and the Medieval Image of Christian Feminine Deity* (Salzburg, 1982)

Jantzen, Grace, *Julian of Norwich: Mystic and Theologian* (London, 1987)

Johnson, Lynn Staley, 'The Trope of the Scribe and the Question of Literary Authority in the Works of Julian of Norwich and Margery Kempe,' *Speculum* 66 (1991), 820–38

Kempster, Hugh, 'A Question of Audience: The Westminster Text and Fifteenth-Century Reception of Julian of Norwich', in McEntire (1998), 257–89

McEntire, Sandra J., ed., *Julian of Norwich: A Book of Essays* (New York, 1998)

Molinari, P. *Julian of Norwich: The Teaching of a 14th Century English Mystic* (London, 1958)

Nuth, Joan M., *Wisdom's Daughter: The Theology of Julian of Norwich* (New York, 1991)

Park, Tarjei, 'Reflecting Christ: The Role of the Flesh in Walter Hilton and Julian of Norwich', in Glasscoe (1992), 17–37

Pelphrey, Brant, *Love Was His Meaning: The Theology and Mysticism of Julian of Norwich* (Salzburg, 1982)

———, *Christ Our Mother: Julian of Norwich* (London, 1989)

Pezzini, Domenico, 'The Theme of the Passion in Richard Rolle and Julian of Norwich', in *Religion in the Poetry and Drama of the Late Middle Ages*, ed. Piero Boitani and Anna Torti (Cambridge, 1989), 29–66

Riddy, Felicity, ' "Women talking about the things of God": A Late Medieval Sub-culture', in *Women and Literature in Britain, 1150–1500*, ed. Carol M. Meale (Cambridge, 1993), 104–27

Robertson, Elizabeth, 'Medieval Medical Views of Women and Female Spirituality in *Ancrene Wisse* and Julian of Norwich's *Showings*', in *Feminist Approaches to the Body in Medieval Literature* ed. Linda Lomperis and Sarah Stanbury (Philadelphia, 1993), 142–67

Spearitt, Placid, 'The Survival of Medieval Spirituality among the Exiled English Black Monks', *American Benedictine Review* 25 (1974), 287–309

Stone, Robert Karl, *Middle English Prose Style: Margery Kempe and Julian of Norwich* (The Hague, 1970)

Tanner, N.P., *The Church in Late Medieval Norwich 1370–1532* (Toronto, 1984)

Ward, Sister Benedicta, 'Julian the Solitary', in *Julian Reconsidered* ed. K. Leech and Sister Benedicta (Oxford, 1988), 11–29

———, 'Lady Julian and her Audience: Mine Even-Christian', in *The English Religious Tradition and the Genius of Anglicanism* ed. G. Rowell (Oxford, 1992), 47–63

Watson, Nicholas, 'The Composition of Julian of Norwich's *Revelation of Love*', *Speculum* 68 (1993), 637–83

———, ' "Yf women be double naturally": Remaking "Woman" in Julian of Norwich's *Revelation of Love*', *Exemplaria* 8 (1996), 1–34

———, 'Visions of Inclusion: Universal Salvation and Vernacular Theology in Pre-Reformation England', *Journal of Medieval and Early Modern Studies* 27 (1997), 145–88

———, 'The Trinitarian Hermeneutic in Julian of Norwich's *Revelation of Love*', in Glasscoe (1992), 79–100; reprinted in McEntire (1998), 61–90

Wilson, R.M., 'The Middle English Mystics', *Essays and Studies* 9 (1956), 87–112

Windeatt, B.A., 'Julian of Norwich and her Audience', *Review of English Studies* ns 17 (1977), 1–17

———, 'The Art of Mystical Loving: Julian of Norwich', in Glasscoe (1980), 55–71

———, ' "Privytes to us": Knowing and Re-vision in Julian of Norwich', in *Chaucer to Shakespeare* ed. T. Takamiya and R. Beadle (Cambridge, 1992), 87–98

6

Margery Kempe

A. C. SPEARING

All we know about Margery Kempe comes from the text of the 1430s called *The Book of Margery Kempe*. The original is lost, but a manuscript copy made about 1450 by one Salthows was discovered in 1934. In the late fifteenth century it had belonged to a Carthusian monastery, Mount Grace Priory, and annotations indicate that it was read there as a valuable account of religious experience. It was first published in 1936 in an adaptation by Colonel William Butler-Bowdon, the then owner of the manuscript (now BL, Add. MS 61823). The first scholarly edition appeared in 1940; Hope Emily Allen's notes remain of great value despite the absence of an intended second volume.[1] The *Book* has since appeared in further editions and more than one translation, and been read increasingly widely; it is now one of the best-known works of ME prose, valued for the pungency of its narrative and dialogue, for the light it throws on late-medieval religious and social life, and especially because its central figure is a woman – one of forceful character and what now seems striking eccentricity. Though often called the first autobiography in English, it differs greatly from autobiography as now understood, focusing solely on Margery's religious experiences and her life as an ambulatory holy woman, and recounting events not 'in ordyr, euery thyng aftyr oþer as it wer don, but lych as þe mater cam to þe creatur in mend whan it schuld be wretyn' (5/12–15). Moreover, it was written not by Margery herself, described in it as illiterate and shown relying on others to write for her (e.g. 111/20–22), but by an unnamed priest with her collaboration. The complicated question of authorial agency will be discussed below.

The *Book*'s heroine travels widely and meets many historical figures, including both archbishops, the bishops of Lincoln and Worcester, and Julian of Norwich, always at credible times and places. There are no discrepancies with the historical record, but for the protagonist there are no other sources, except that a Margery Kempe is mentioned in the 1438 account roll of the Trinity Guild of Lynn, Norfolk. In the manuscript the *Book* has no title. It opens 'Here begynnyth a schort tretys and a comfortabyl for synful wrecchys' (1/1–2) and refers to its protagonist as *the/this creatur*. Once named as 'Mar. Kempe of

---

1   *The Book of Margery Kempe*, ed. Sanford Meech Brown and Hope Emily Allen, EETS os 212 (London, 1940). Quotations are from this edition, with references given by page/line. Italics in quotations from this and other sources are my own. A few sentences of the present chapter are repeated from Spearing 2002.

Lynne' (243/19), she is addressed in the many reported conversations as 'Margery', which is how I refer to her here, accepting this 'offer of intimacy' made by the *Book* itself (Salih 2001, 173). Its modern title derives from a devotional pamphlet printed by Wynkyn de Worde about 1501, 'taken out of the boke of Margerie kempe of lynn'; a 1521 reprint by Henry Pepwell describes her as 'a deuoute ancres' (Meech and Allen 1940, 353, 357 n11). On this basis, Margery Kempe was supposed until 1934 to be a minor devotional writer typical of her period, but the manuscript reveals something very different.

Margery is known to the bishop of Worcester as 'Iohn of Burnamys dowtyr of Lynne' (109/29), and identifies herself to the mayor of Leicester as 'a good mannys dowtyr of . . . Lynne, whech hath ben meyr fyve tymes of þat worshepful burwgh' (111/28–29). John Burnam or Brunham was a leading citizen of (King's) Lynn, a major port in the most prosperous part of late-medieval England, East Anglia. His daughter was born about 1373, and at 'xx ʒer of age or sumdele mor' (6/25) married John Kempe, 'also a burgeys of þe seyd town, Lynne' (111/31), and, as he appears in the *Book*, 'euyr a good man & an esy man to hir' (32/26), less successful than her father, but a kindly husband to a difficult wife. After the birth of the first of fourteen children she suffered a period of madness and diabolic temptation, but one day Jesus appeared to her, sitting at her bedside as a handsome man clad in purple silk, and asked her, 'Dowtyr, why hast þow forsakyn me, and I forsoke neuyr þe?' (8/20–21). Then he rose slowly through the air and vanished. This, the first of her religious experiences, cured her madness, but did not conquer her desire 'to be worshepd of the pepul' (9/27): she wore ostentatious clothes, was dissatisfied with her husband's status, and attempted unsuccessfully to make careers for herself in brewing and milling. Her conversion did not occur until about 1409, when, in bed with her husband, she had the first of many experiences of heavenly music, and leapt out of bed, crying, 'Alas, þat euyr I dede synne, it is ful mery in Hevyn' (11/15–16). She had previously taken great pleasure in their sexual relations, but thenceforward 'þe dette of matrimony was so abhominabyl to hir þat sche had leuar, hir thowt, etyn or drynkyn þe wose, þe mukke in þe chanel' (11/35–12/2). She did not fail to inform her husband of this reversal, and eventually, after a period of sexual temptation and a particular humiliation when she consented to adultery but was rebuffed, she struck a bargain with him: she would settle his financial debts if he would forgo payment of the matrimonial debt. In the same year, 1413, the couple visited the bishop of Lincoln and the archbishop of Canterbury to obtain authorization to live in chastity, and then, fulfilling a divine command, Margery embarked on a pilgrimage to the Holy Land.

This journey is described in some detail. Wintering in Venice, she reached her destination in spring 1414, returned via Rome, and was back in Norfolk the following spring. The trip was full of troubles, described from Margery's point of view, and all the more piquant because of her inability to grasp to what extent she brought them on herself. In Zeeland on the outward journey she was first visited with 'abundawnt teerys of contricyon', which became 'gret wepyngys & boystows sobbyngys þat many men merueyled & wonderyd' (61/1–7). Copious weeping became the keynote of her devotion, and this, and her insistence on talking incessantly about God's love 'as wel at þe tabyl as in oþer place' (61/20), so annoyed her fellow-pilgrims that they abandoned her. She pursued them, and was allowed to rejoin the party on condition that she should 'syttyn stylle & makyn mery, as we don, boþin at mete & at soper' (65/34–36); but then, unable to resist quoting a Gospel text, she was again banished. Her maidservant stopped doing her cooking and washing, preferring to serve the other pilgrims; of twenty pounds in gold given her by the papal legate – a striking sign of respect – a fellow-pilgrim 'wythhelde wrongfully a-bowte xvj pownd' (64/16); and on the ship from Venice a priest 'toke a-wey a schete fro þe forseyd creatur & seyd it was hys' (67/4–5). On Calvary, she saw Christ's Passion 'in hyr sowle' (68/10), and was unable to prevent herself 'krying & roryng . . . And þis was þe fyrst cry þat euyr sche cryed in any contemplacyon. And þis maner of crying [i.e. screaming] enduryd many ȝerys aftyr þis tyme for owt þat any man myt do, & þerfor sufferyd sche mych despyte & mech reprefe' (68/22–27). Uncontrollable screaming, especially in church, and the disgrace into which it brings her form a leitmotif in what follows. Margery had been given to 'empathetic visual meditations on the Manhood of Christ . . . in the Bonaventurean mode promoted by Nicholas Love's *Mirror of the Life of Christ*' (Holbrook 1986, 276), to conversations with Jesus, and to bodily sensations that he explained were tokens of his love: sweet smells, fire in her breast, sights of white things floating 'as thykke in a maner as motys in the sunne' (88/8–9), blowing sounds 'as it had ben a peyr of belwys' (90/35–36), and bird-like singing in her ear. In Rome a more extraordinary religious experience awaited her: though her devotion to Jesus made her a reluctant bride, God the Father took her as his wife, 'for fayrar, for fowelar, for richar, for powerar' (87/19). Subsequently Jesus explained that he too must be intimate with her, '& þu mayst boldly, when þu art in þi bed, take me to þe as for þi weddyd husbond . . . & þerfor þu mayst boldly take me in þe armys of þi sowle & kyssen my mowth, myn hed, & my fete as swetly as thow wylt' (90/19–26).

Back in England, Jesus insisted that Margery must wear white clothes, marking his seriousness with a thunderstorm, and subsequently this garb, conspicuous but of uncertain meaning, caused her 'meche despyte & meche schame in many dyvers cuntreys, cyteys, & townys' (104/24–26). And English people were truly amazed at her sobbing and screaming, because 'þei had neuyr herd hir cryen before-tyme, & it was þe more meruyel on-to hem' (105/8–9). Almost immediately, she decided to undertake a second pilgrimage to Compostela; this took only a few weeks, and is passed over in a few sentences.

In England once more in 1417, Margery found herself seriously endangered by a Lollard scare. The heresies of Wyclif and his followers, the Lollards, had been condemned (1382), an act of Parliament permitted the burning of heretics (1401), and a recent Lollard rebellion led by Sir John Oldcastle had linked heresy with sedition (1415). Now, while the king was in France, leaving England in charge of his brother the duke of Bedford, a second rebellion led by Oldcastle coincided with a Scottish invasion. Margery's beliefs were evidently not heretical, but Lollardy encouraged laymen and women to engage in religious teaching, and, as a fervently and vociferously religious woman who attracted attention by conduct perceived as eccentric, she was automatically suspect. In

Leicester, a Lollard stronghold, the sight of a painted crucifix caused her 'to breken owte wyth a lowde voys & cryen merueylowslyche & wepyn & sobbyn ful hedowslyche, þat many a man and woman wondryd on hir þerfor' (111/12–15). She was summoned before the mayor and then the abbot and dean, put in custody, interrogated as to her Eucharistic belief and her white clothes, which made the mayor suspect she had come 'to han a-wey owr wyuys fro us & ledyn hem wyth þe' (116/13–14), and told that she could not be released without the bishop of Lincoln's consent. This she obtained, and then left for York, probably on pilgrimage to the shrine of St William. There, after violent sobbing and screaming at Mass in the minster, she was detained, brought before the archbishop, a zealous anti-Lollard, and again interrogated about her clothing and her beliefs. She was understandably terrified, but answered so effectively that the archbishop was driven to ask, 'Wher schal I haue a man þat myth ledyn þis woman fro me?' (128/12–13), and to pay a servant five shillings to take her away. But then at Hull she was rearrested by Bedford's men, accused once more of Lollardy, and at real risk of being burned. Detained in the house of one of her captors under his wife's supervision, she preached through the window to other women to such good effect that they smuggled wine to her. Much to the archbishop's irritation, she was brought before him again in the Beverley chapterhouse, accused of being a spy for Oldcastle and of urging John of Gaunt's granddaughter to leave her husband. 'I wote not what I xal don wyth þe' (134/19–20), sighed the archbishop, but at last she was released, and, after further wanderings, probably returned to Lynn in 1418.

There, enduring a period of ill health, she reached a further low point about 1420, on the arrival of a Franciscan friar famous for his preaching, who objected to having his sermons interrupted by Margery's sobbing and screaming. This brought to a head antagonism between 'reactionary and radical forces within Lynn' (Wilson 1997, 175), the latter seeing her conduct as divinely inspired, the former as deliberate attention-seeking. Sympathizers, both clerical and lay, urged the friar to be tolerant, but he continued to denounce Margery publicly, 'not expressyng hir name, but so he expleytyd hys conseytys þat men vndirstod wel þat he ment hir'. Then, 'smytyng hys hand on þe pulpit, . . . "ȝyf I here any mor þes materys rehersyd, I xal so smyten þe nayl on þe hed," he seyd, "þat it schal schamyn alle hyr maytenowrys"' (152/18–29). Her own confessor, who thought her experiences 'but tryfelys & japys' (44/22), doubted her authenticity, though he eventually came round. Jesus abated her screams, but that only caused allegations of hypocrisy, '&, as summe spoke euyl of hyr aforn for sche cryed, so sum spoke now euyl of hir for sche cryid not' (156/4–6).

From then on, though, Margery's position seems to have stabilized, and few events recounted in the *Book* can be dated to the decade 1421–31. Along with her ostentatious devotion, God granted prophetic gifts which demonstrated 'her spiritual value to her society' (Wilson 1997, 168). In 1421 a conflagration burned down the Lynn guildhall and threatened St Margaret's, the parish church, but on her advice the Sacrament was borne to the fire, a sudden snowstorm extinguished it, and the church was saved. She foretold that the prior of Lynn would be replaced, '& so it was in dede' (171/2). Despite rumours that the bishop of Winchester was dead, 'sche had felyng that he leuyd. & so it was in trewth' (172/6–7). And, recounted earlier in the *Book*, though 'it befel long aftyr þe materys whech folwen' (58/28–29) – in fact, not till 1431 or 1432 – there was controversy as to whether two chapels annexed to St Margaret's should be allowed to conduct baptisms and purifications (thus competing with the parish church for fees), and Margery, consulted by her confessor, correctly prophesied that the innovators would be disappointed.

Meanwhile John Kempe, aged over sixty and left alone as his wife devoted herself to God's purposes, fell downstairs, injuring his head. Many said that if he died it would be her fault for abandoning him, even though when they lived together 'þe pepil slawndryd hem' (179/32) with claims that they did not live in chastity. She prayed that 'hir husbond myth leuyn a ʒer & sche to be deliueryd owt slawndyr' (180/17–19), and God ordered her, despite her reluctance to be distracted from serving him, to look after John. She did so until his death about 1431, even though he became incontinent and disgusting and the work 'lettyd hir ful meche fro hir contemplacyon' (181/8–9), consoling herself with the thought that this was appropriate punishment for the inordinate pleasure she had once gained from his body.

It was probably about now, 'xx ʒer & mor fro þat tym þis creatur had fyrst felyngys & reuelacyons' (3/29–30), that God told her to have them written down. Her first writer was an Englishman long resident in Germany, who came to live with her and wrote as much possible at her dictation till he died. His writing was hard to understand, and in 1436 a priest rewrote his version, 'sche sum-tyme helpyng where ony difficulte was' (5/11–12). In 1438 the priest added, as a brief Book II, an account of Margery's subsequent life 'aftyr hyr owyn tunge' (221/11–12). He began with information about her son, who, after a scapegrace youth, reformed, lived and married in Germany, brought his wife to visit Margery, and died in Lynn shortly before his father. (These details suggest that the son was the first scribe.) Escorting his widow to Ipswich, Margery decided to accompany her on her return to Germany; this was against her confessor's wishes, and also – much to Margery's indignation – against the younger woman's. The remainder of Book II is a kind of picaresque narrative of Margery's third pilgrimage, visiting such relics as the Precious Blood at Wilsnak and Our Lady's smock at Aachen, 'wepyng & sobbyng as wel as yf sche had ben at hom' (231/7–8), finding that many of those she meets avoid her company, though 'What þe cawse was sche wist neuyr' (242/8–9). She finally returned via Calais, Dover, and London to Lynn, where she was reconciled with her confessor.

My attempt (much indebted to Bhattacharji 1997) to reduce the *Book*'s contents to the chronology of an individual life, while inevitably omitting much lively detail, may give the impression of mere personal eccentricity in Margery herself. Contemporaries offered medical diagnoses of her behaviour: the *Book* describes her as going 'owt of hir mende' (7/21) after the birth of her first child; when she nearly falls from her ass for joy in Jerusalem, a priest gives her spices 'wenyng sche had ben seke' (67/29); 'sum seyd [her screaming] was a sekenes' (69/24), some that she had 'þe fallyng euyl' (105/18); and the friar who objects to having his sermons disrupted urges her to acknowledge that her compulsive

screaming derives from 'a cardiakyl er sum oþer sekenesse' (151/8–9). Modern
readers too have favoured explanations in terms of bodily or psychic disorder:
hysteria has been a favourite diagnosis (Partner 1991, Long 1994), and recent
suggestions have included histrionic personality disorder and temporal lobe
epilepsy (Farley 1999, Lawes 1999). There are indications, too, of sexual obses-
sion, a 'dark plot of repressed desire' (Partner 1989, 255). Even in her sixties,
Margery fears for her chastity: lodging en route to Aachen, she asks her hostess
to provide some young women to lie with her for protection – just the opposite
of the normal arrangement (Stargardt 1985, 299) – but still dares not sleep 'for
dred of defilyng' (236/37–237/1). In words conveying both her sense of herself
as a sexually attractive object of shameful looking and the association of sexual
desire with filth indicated in her rejection of John, she tells God, 'I wolde, Lord,
for þi lofe be leyd nakyd on an hyrdil, alle men to wonderyn on me for þi loue,
so it wer no perel to her sowlys, & thei to castyn slory & slugge on me, & be
drawyn fro town to town euery day my lyfe-tyme, ȝyf þu wer plesyd þerby'
(184/19–24). God punishes her unwillingness to believe in damnation with
'fowle thowtys & fowle mendys of letchery & alle vnclennes as thow sche xulde
a be comown to al maner of pepyl', and she imagines she sees men showing
their 'bar membrys'. The devil says she must prostitute herself to one of them,
'& hir thowt þat þes horrybyl syghtys & cursyd mendys wer delectabyl to hir
a-geyn hir wille' (144/34–145/22) – a striking sign of awareness of inner
conflict. Her relation to God is strongly eroticized throughout, and her mystic
marriage to the Father is sealed with his promise to 'schewyn þe my preuyteys'
(86/17), with a pun, as in Chaucer's *Miller's Tale*, though doubtless unconscious,
on mysteries and private parts.

Such eroticization, however, is a normal element in later medieval religious
devotion, and scholarship shows that even behaviour now appearing pathological was not unparalleled. Margery's association of sex with 'wose', 'mukke',
'slory & slugge', recalls actual forms of self-mortification practised by continental holy women (Bynum 1987). More important, in her uncontrollable
weeping and screaming Margery was drawing on a well-established tradition of
the signs of holiness. Medieval Christianity attributed 'holy tears' to the Blessed
Virgin and to Mary Magdalene, and tearful praying had a place in the Benedictine rule and in the liturgy (Atkinson 1983). Holy women, especially in parts of
northern Europe with which East Anglia had trade relations, became famous as
passionate weepers through the writings of their clerical patrons. A notable
example is Mary of Oignies, living around 1200 in what is now Belgium, whose
life was written by her confessor, Jacques de Vitry, later a cardinal. His Latin
vita was translated into English, and the English version tells how 'booþ daye
and nyghte contynuelly water wente aweye by hir eyen', and she had to use a
succession of linen cloths to soak it up, 'þat, as on wette, anoþere myghte drye'
(Horstmann 1885, 138). Mary's weeping was not a spontaneous eccentricity but
a devotional practice for which systematic provision had to be made. English
devotion had been more restrained than that of the weeping and visionary
Beguines and Dominican nuns on the continent, and Margery Kempe is the first
such case in England, but by her time the *vitae* of women such as Mary were
circulating in English as well as Latin. The same is true of more recent works by

female visionaries such as the *Revelations* of St Bridget of Sweden, recording her tears and the visions she was granted to supplement Scriptural accounts of the life of the Holy Family.

Margery may have been illiterate, but she received early encouragement from doctors of divinity such as the Carmelite Alan of Lynn and an unnamed Dominican anchorite who was one of her confessors, and she is depicted as habitually 'comownyng . . . wyth clerkys' (29/30–32), revealing her religious experiences 'to many a worthy clerke, to worshepful doctorys of divinyte, boþe religiows men & oþer of seculer abyte' (43/21–23). Through them her life was shaped by books, or rather the book of her life was shaped by the books of others' lives. For example, once when she was hearing Mass the elevated Sacrament 'schok & flekeryd to & fro as a dowe flekeryth wyth hir wengys', and God told her, 'My dowtyr, Bryde, say me neuyr in þis wyse'. He added, 'rygth as I spak to Seynt Bryde ryte so I speke to þe, dowtyr, & I telle þe trewly it is trewe euery word þat is wretyn in Brides boke, & be þe it xal be knowyn for very trewth' (47/17–35). But how did an illiterate woman know what was in 'Brides boke'? About 1413 a new priest came to Lynn, heard of Margery's holiness, and 'red to hir many a good boke of hy contemplacyon, & oþer bokys, as þe Bybyl wyth doctowrys þer-up- on, Seynt Brydys boke [Bridget's *Revelations*], Hyltons boke [probably *The Scale of Perfection*], Bone-ventur, Stimulus Amoris, [Rolle's] Incendium Amoris, & swech oþer' for 'vij ȝer er viij ȝer' (143/25–35), to his own benefit as well as hers. This was how she became acquainted with Latin and vernacular devotional works. The *Book* also recounts how its writer had doubts about her weeping until he read of Mary of Oignies and 'þe plentyuows teerys þat sche wept, þe whech made hir so febyl & so weyke þat sche myth not endur to beheldyn þe Crosse, ne heryn owr Lordys Passyon rehersyd' (153/4–7). Details are given of the chapters in de Vitry's *vita* that mention weeping, and later of references in the *Stimulus Amoris* and the *Revelations* attributed to Elizabeth of Hungary. These clerkly citations must come from the priest himself. There is an intricate collaboration between Margery's devout emotionalism and the writings that both stimulate and justify it, and are in turn authenticated by her experiences. She is protected and encouraged by clerics, and the clerics gain prestige from their privileged access to her 'felyngys & reuelacyons'. An article tellingly entitled 'Holy Women and their Confessors or Confessors and their Holy Women?' (Dillon 1996a) illustrates the mutual dependence of late-medieval clerics, who gained authority from their contact with female recipients of divine revelation, and the women, whose experiences were in turn authenticated by clerical *discretio spirituum*. Through clerical mediation the story of Margery Kempe's life was shaped by books that she could not read. She saw herself as an English St Bridget, a wife restored to the status of virgin in a culture that downgraded marriage in favour of celibacy. In Rome she eagerly pursued associations with Bridget, meeting her maid though 'sche cowd not vndirstondyn what sche seyd', learning that her host knew the saint, and, on her feast-day, hearing a sermon preached in her death-room 'of hir reuelacyons & of hir maner of leuyng' (95/12–25). Margery believed herself to have been promised sainthood: God assures her that her death will be painless, her only purgatory will be earthly slander, and 'what creatur in erth vn-to þe Day of Dom aske þe any bone

& beleuyth þat God louyth þe he xal haue hys bone er ellys a bettyr thyng'
(52/12–14); he foretells that 'Many a man & woman xal seyn it is wel sene þat
God louyd hir wel' (156/27–28); the Blessed Virgin guarantees plenary remission of sins to all present and future believers that God loves her (175/32–34);
and when she aids a woman suffering (like herself) from post-partum madness,
the writer endorses the view that this was 'a ryth gret myrakyl' (178/37) –
crucial evidence of sanctity. Correspondingly, the writer, recording God's
promise that by his book 'many a man xal be turnyd to me' (216/19–20),
perhaps hoped to become an English Jacques de Vitry. None of these aspirations
was realized: Margery did not achieve canonization, the book did not circulate
widely, and the priest did not rise high in the Church or we would know his
name.

In the later Middle Ages forms of affective spirituality originating in monasteries became attractive to laypeople whose earthly responsibilities forbade a
total dedication to contemplative life. The validity of claims to mystical experience must have become increasingly difficult to judge, and clearly in Margery's
case contemporary opinions differed as to the authenticity of her relationship
with the divine. To attempt an assessment now, six centuries later and in a transformed climate of belief, is impossible. But two characteristics of her devotion,
beyond the spectacular practices of sobbing and screaming, are noteworthy. One
is the element of compensatory fantasy. The life of a medieval wife, even at
Margery's privileged social level, and with a husband who pleased her
physically and was 'euyr a good man & an esy man to hir', could be harsh and
frustrating, and Margery's relation to Jesus often appears not as one of
eroticized transcendence but as an escape into fantasies of the kind now stimu-
lated by Harlequin novels. He tells her, 'Dowtyr, 3yf þu knew how many wifys
þer arn in þis worlde that wolde louyn me & seruyn me ryth wel & dewly, 3yf
þei myght be as frely fro her husbondys as þu art fro thyn, þu woldist seyn þat þu
wer ryght mech beheldyn on-to me. & 3et ar þei putt fro her wyl & suffyr ful
gret peyne, & þerfor xal þei haue ryght gret reward in Heuyn, for I receyue
euery good wyl as for dede' (212/15–22). Jesus serves as Margery's fantasy
husband, and with him, unlike John, she can 'gon to bedde . . . wyth-owtyn any
schame er dred of þe pepil' (213/24–25), and without risk of adding to the
number of her children. Moreover, her conviction that God receives every good
will as for deed encourages other substitutions of fantasy for reality. A single
example: in Rome she is invited into a poor woman's house and given wine 'be
hir lytyl fyer'; the woman is suckling a child, and when he runs to Margery, 'þe
modyr syttyng ful of sorwe & sadnes', Margery 'brast al in-to wepyng, as þei
sche had seyn owr Lady & hir sone in tyme of hys Passyon, & had so many of
holy thowtys þat sche myth neuyr tellyn þe haluendel, but euyr sat & wept
plentyvowsly a long tyme þat þe powr woman, hauyng compassyon of hir
wepyng, preyd hir to sesyn, not knowyng why sche wept' (94/10–20). Far from
helping the woman in her 'sorwe & sadnes', she indulges in fantasies that make
her the centre of attention. Every detail of this scene might be designed to reveal
Margery's self-absorption.

Another characteristic of her devotion, strongly emphasized throughout, is her concern with the earthly reputation brought by her practices. Here as elsewhere it is hard to separate what is peculiar to her as an individual from what belongs to her historical milieu. Honour or reputation, a man's standing in the eyes of others, is familiar as a masculine and knightly concern, one that preoccupies Malory's knights, for example, to such an extent that *worship* can be more important than truth (Brewer 1968, 25–30). Margery, daughter of Lynn's mercantile patriciate, is as obsessed as Malory's Lancelot with *worship*, a term the *Book* incessantly repeats. In her pre-conversion life she wore ostentatious clothes so as to be 'þe mor . . . *worshepd*', 'sche wold sauyn þe *worschyp* of hir kynred what-so-euyr ony man sayd', and 'Sche had ful greet envye at hir neybowrs þat þei schuld ben arayd so wel as sche. Alle hir desyr was for to be *worshepd* of þe pepul' (9/17–27). What is confessed here recalls the social pride among prosperous craftsmen and tradespeople satirized in the *Canterbury Tales*, in the *General Prologue* portraits of the Wife of Bath and the Guildsmen and their wives, or in Symkyn and his wife in the *Reeve's Tale*. (Chaucer sees it as especially characteristic of wives, competing to display the status gained from their husbands' success.)

After Margery's conversion, this concern for reputation is transferred to the religious sphere. Its thematic status, as significant to the writer as to Margery, is established in the *Book*'s preface: 'sum men seyden sche mygth wepen whan sche wold & slawndered þe werk of God . . . For euyr þe mor slawnder & repref þat sche sufferyd, þe mor sche incresyd in grace' (2/22–30). When she starts weeping in the Holy Land, her fellow-pilgrims persecute her, cutting her gown short and making her wear a white sacking apron 'for sche xuld ben holdyn a fool & þe pepyl xuld not makyn of hir ne han hyr in reputacyon. Þei madyn hir to syttyn at þe tabelys ende be-nethyn alle oþer'; yet, 'not-wythstondyng al her malyce, sche was had in mor *worshep* þan þei wher-þat-euyr þei comyn' (62/17–22). The crucial issue is *worship*, outwardly marked in clothing and table placement, and Margery is convinced that others' treatment of her is as much determined by thought for her reputation as her own conduct is. The parallel between religious and secular concern with *worship* is tellingly drawn by Jesus himself when he assures her, 'þe mor schame, despite, & reprefe þat þu sufferyst for my lofe, þe bettyr I lofe þe, for I far liche a man þat louyth wel hys wyfe, þe mor enuye þat men han to hir þe bettyr he wyl arayn hir in despite of hir enmys' (81/28–32). *Shame* and *worship* belong as opposites to the same structure of values. In Margery's unfalsifiable system, the normal criteria of status can be inverted, and scorn and slander confirm her holiness as effectively as admiration and praise. Thus when God makes her scream more quietly after the Franciscan preacher objects, 'as summe spoke euyl of hir aforn for sche cryed, so sum spoke now euyl of hir for sche cryid not' (156/4–6) – but at least they spoke of her. Similarly, when God orders her to resume eating meat after long abstinence, her first thought is of what others will think: 'þe pepil, þat hath knowyn of myn abstinens so many ʒerys & seeth me now retornyn & etyn flesch mete, þei wil haue gret merueyl and, as I suppose, despisyn me & scornyn me þerfor' (161/35–162/3).

*

Since its rediscovery, *The Book of Margery Kempe* has generally been read as a record of actual events, spoken in Margery's own words. Given that it is a written text internally attributed to a cleric and that no external means exist of knowing whether any of its events occurred as reported or even at all, this seems strange. When a critic remarks that, 'Uneducated as she is, she *speaks* with wit and wisdom' (McEntire 1992b, 67), one reason is doubtless the phonocentric prejudice diagnosed by Derrida as characteristic of Western culture. More specifically, the rarity of accounts by medieval women of their own experiences means that in this instance female agency has been fiercely defended, with the *Book* seen even as 'an attempt to establish a maternal metalanguage' (Margherita 1994, 36), and any move to investigate authorial agency attributed to a desire to 'banish the woman from her text and to silence the emergent possi-bilities of the female voice' (Bremner 1992, 124). Yet it is a mere fact that the 'female voice' is mediated here through a male text. Though we cannot know for certain who was the priest referred to as Margery's 'writer' (e.g. 216/5), it has been convincingly argued that the several 'sharp' confessors mentioned were all (except possibly the first) the 'Maistyr Robert Spryngolde' (139/8–9) whom she prays to have in heaven with her (20/19–25) and to have rewarded for her weeping 'as thow he had wept hymselfe' (216/30–31), and that this confessor was the writer of the *Book* (Gallyon 1995, Dillon 1996b; questioned by Goodman 2002). For much of the narrative he depended on Margery's oral account of events; but, despite the claim that she 'dede no þing wryten but þat sche knew rygth wel for very trewth' (5/17–18), incidents are included at which she was not present but Spryngolde was. In chapter 57 a monk newly arrived at Lynn priory refuses to enter the chapel if Margery is there; the prior apologizes to 'Maistyr Robert Spryngolde, whech was hir confessowr þat tyme' (139/8–9), and Spryngolde points out that she has the archbishop of Canterbury's permis-sion to confess and receive communion as often as she asks. Chapter 61 recounts a tactful though unsuccessful approach to the hostile Franciscan by a distinguished elderly friar, accompanied by a bachelor of canon law who is 'confessowr to þe sayd creatur' (150/29) and who must be Spryngolde; this is followed by the account of how the priest 'þat aftirward wrot þis boke' (152/33) was convinced of Margery's authenticity by reading about Mary of Oignies and other holy weepers. And chapter 69 tells how she is vigorously defended by a Carmelite, who is commanded by his provincial to have no more dealings with her, and by 'a bacheler of lawe canon'; the former must be Alan of Lynn and the latter 'hir confessowr' (168/3, 14–15), and thus the writer himself, who then feels obliged to forbid her to approach the Carmelite.

Beyond such cases, it is uncertain how far the *Book*'s language is Spryngolde's. At one point the text accidentally preserves the first-person form of Margery's oral narrative: '& þe Bysshop [of Lincoln] dede no mor to *us* at þat day, saue he mad *us* rygth good cher and seyd *we* wer rygth wolcome' (34/24–26). If this scrap is typical – admittedly a big if – her narrative style was simple, monosyllabic and repetitive,[2] and its transformation into writing

---

2   We may get a similar glimpse of the repetitiveness of Margery's oral style in passages such as 104/24–26, where the writer preserves her own perfect tense instead of converting it into the pluper-

involved not just a systematic conversion of her spoken words into third-person forms, but a more fundamental textualization and clericalization. It has been insufficiently recognized that the *Book* contains many constructions that could belong only to prose, not speech. They include colloquialisms reshaped into *oratio obliqua*, such as 'cheys hir as sche cowde' (27/24), participial absolutes such as 'mech pepyl wonderyng on hir' (28/32–33) or 'hir vnwetyng' (200/5), and other examples of compression such as 'Sche thowt þat sche louyd God mor þan he hir' (13/36–14/1). Much of the language appears clerkly, whether technical – 'ȝyf þu wylt be partabyl in owyr joye, þu must be partabil in owyr sorwe' (73/18–20) – or bureaucratic: 'Whan þe seyde Meyr receyued þe forseyd lettyr . . .' (119/12–13). There are patches of heavy alliteration, especially in chapters 41–42, that clearly belong to a tradition of Latinate rhythmic prose: 'Crist Ihesu, whos melydiows voys swettest of alle sauowrys softly sowndyng in hir sowle, seyd . . .' (98/24–26). The many *now*s in the narrative text invariably refer to the temporal location of the writer, whether he is stating that Margery's story shows how Christ reveals his grace to humanity 'now in ower days' (1/6, 41/16) or adding an informative scholarly note about St Jerome's body, 'whech was myraculosly translatyd fro Bedlem in-to þat place & þer now is had in gret worshep be-syden þe place where Seynt Lauerawnce lyth berijd' (99/15–18). He frequently offers his own authoritative commentary: on Margery's behaviour – 'It is nowt to be meruyeled ȝyf þis creatur cryed & made wondirful cher & cuntenawns, whan we may se eche day at eye boþe men and women . . . cryen & roryn and wryngyn her handys [for earthly reasons] . . . &, ȝyf a man cownsel hem to leevyn er seesyn . . ., þei wyl seyn þat þei may not . . .' (70/22–33) – or on that of opponents, as when the mayor of Leicester addresses her in terms 'þe whiche is mor expedient to be concelyd þan expressyd' (115/25–26), or on general problems such as *discretio spirituum*, 'for reuelacyons be hard sumtyme to vndirstondyn, & sumtyme þo þat men wenen wer reuelacyonis it arn deceytys & illusyons' (219/33–35). Even the repeated references to the text's divergence from the chronological order of events, as in the direction 'Rede fyrst þe xxi chapetre & þan þis chapetre aftyr þat' (38/4–5) or the explanation that the story about the controversy over the two chapels 'is wretyn her for conuenyens in-as-mech as it is in felyng leche to þe materys þat ben wretyn be-forn' (58/26–28), remind us that this is a book and imply a clerical preference for rational chronology. It was stated in 1984 that 'The style needs further examination, perhaps in the light of authorial considerations' (Hirsh 1984, 112), and that is still true. So far there has been little more than sub-Bakhtinian babble about 'voices', and detailed stylistic analysis of the *Book* remains a major desideratum. Whatever the outcome, our understanding would surely be improved by an experimental envisaging of *The Book of Margery Kempe* as *The Book of Robert Spryngolde about Margery Kempe*.

Authorial considerations aside, a crucial consequence of the *Book*'s textuality is that it produces radical uncertainties of tone and intention (Wright 1995). Two instances out of many must suffice. The archbishop of York's clerks reportedly

fect that would be appropriate to *oratio obliqua*: '& sithen hath sche sufferyd meche despyte & meche schame in many dyvers cuntreys, cyteys. & townys, thankyd be God of alle'.

say of Margery, 'her wot we wel þat sche hath a deuyl wyth-inne hir, for sche spekyth of þe Gospel' (126/14–15). First, we cannot tell whether they really said this, or whether the remark is a satirical invention by Margery, or alternatively by Robert, revealing the corruption of a Church supposedly based on the Gospel. But second, if they did say it, we still cannot tell with what intention. Was it a naïve revelation of the poverty of their religious understanding? Was it intended ironically, pointing to the absurdity of the situation in which they found themselves? There is simply no way of deciding. The other instance is this: the preaching friar who denounces Margery is repeatedly referred to as 'þe good frer'. It has been suggested that the *Book* uses 'good' to designate 'spiritual status . . . in ways similar to such Lollard codes as "trew man" or "known man" ' (Staley 1994, 10). That seems unlikely here, given the friar's unyielding intolerance of Margery's fervour, yet if irony is involved it is hard to see the point of the repetition. Again, there is no way to decide how to take it; and that is true of more of the *Book* than is generally acknowledged.

Finally, we need to attend to the *Book*'s repeated stress on its own writtenness. References to writing and 'bookness' (Burrow 1988, 230) abound – 'Many mo swech reuelacyyons þis creatur had in felyng; hem alle for to wryten it xuld be lettyng perauentur of mor profyte' (54/27–29) – and the story told is not just that of Margery Kempe but that of the complicated process by which Robert Spryngolde came to write her *vita*, transforming her speech into 'þis boke' (38/20, etc.). The tone is set by the preface, with its repeated uses of *write, book*, and *read*, along with many other terms associated with clerical technology – leaf, quire, letter, pen, spectacles, candlelight – and scarcely a chapter passes without some further reminder of textuality, even if it is no more than a cross-reference to what 'xal be wretyn aftyrwarde' (60/31–32) or 'is wretyn be-forn' (106/28). One scholar claims that the book 'denies us the comfort inherent in circular form' (Staley 1994, 4), and certainly its form is not that of a simple circle; but the closing chapters of Book I return emphatically, and it would seem deliberately, to the theme of writing established in the preface. A rare authorial first person – 'Wyth swech maner of thowtys & many mo þan *I* cowde euyr writyn sche worschepd & magnifyed owr Lord' (214/23–25; Uhlman 1994, 62) – leads into praise for 'Maistyr Robert' (217/33) oddly reminiscent of that for Master Nicholas at the end of *The Owl and the Nightingale*, and a closing reference to 'þis lityl boke' (220/24) that, doubtless accidentally, echoes the end of Chaucer's *Troilus*. And Book II begins with a flurry of references to writing and ends with the reconciliation of Margery with her writer-confessor that made possible the addition of this supplement. It is time to read *The Book of Margery Kempe* not as the speech from which it originated but as the written text into which that speech has been shaped.

BIBLIOGRAPHY

Primary

Butler-Bowdon, W., trans. (1936) *The Book of Margery Kempe 1436: A Modern Version* (London)

Horstmann, C., ed. (1885) 'Prosalegenden: Die Legenden des MS Douce 114', *Anglia* 8, 102–96

Meech, S.B., and H.E. Allen, eds (1940) *The Book of Margery Kempe*, EETS os 212 (London)

Staley, L., ed. (1996) *The Book of Margery Kempe* (Kalamazoo)

———, trans. (2001) *The Book of Margery Kempe* (New York)

Windeatt, B., trans. (1985) *The Book of Margery Kempe* (Harmondsworth)

Windeatt, B., ed. (2000) *The Book of Margery Kempe* (London)

Secondary

Aers, D., ed. (1986) *Medieval Literature: Criticism, Ideology and History* (New York)

Atkinson, C. (1983) *Mystic and Pilgrim: The 'Book' and World of Margery Kempe* (Ithaca)

Baker, D., ed. (1978) *Medieval Women: Dedicated and Presented to Professor Rosalind T. Hill*, Studies in Church History subsidia 1 (Oxford)

Beckwith, S. (1986) 'A Very Material Mysticism', in Aers 1986, 34–57

——— (1992) 'Problems of Authority in Late Medieval Mysticism: Language, Agency and Authority in *The Book of Margery Kempe*', *Exemplaria* 4, 171–99

Bhattacharji, S. (1997) *God is an Earthquake: The Spirituality of Margery Kempe* (London)

Boitani, P., and A. Torti, eds (1988) *Genres, Themes, and Images in English Literature* (Tübingen)

Brewer, D.S., ed. (1968) *Malory: The Morte Darthur* (London)

Burrow, J.A. (1988) 'The Poet and the Book', in Boitani and Torti 1988, 230–45

Bynum, C.W. (1987) *Holy Feast and Holy Fast: The Religious Significance of Food to Medieval Women* (Berkeley)

Carruthers, M.J., and E.D. Kirk, eds (1982) *Acts of Interpretation: The Text in its Contexts 700–1600* (Norman)

Chance, J., ed. (1996) *Gender and Text in the Later Middle Ages* (Gainesville)

Dean, J.M., and C.K. Zacher, eds (1992) *The Idea of Medieval Literature: New Essays on Chaucer and Medieval Culture in Honor of Donald R. Howard* (Newark)

Dickman, S. (1980) 'Margery Kempe and the English Devotional Tradition', in Glasscoe 1980, 156–72

——— (1984) 'Margery Kempe and the Continental Tradition of the Pious Woman', in Glasscoe 1984, 150–68

——— (1997) 'A Showing of God's Grace: *The Book of Margery Kempe*', in Pollard and Boenig 1997, 159–76

Dillon, J. (1995) 'The Making of Desire in *The Book of Margery Kempe*', *Leeds Studies in English* ns 26, 114–44

———1996a. 'Holy Women and their Confessors or Confessors and their Holy Women?'. In Voaden 1996. 115–40

————1996b. 'Margery Kempe's Sharp Confessor/s'. *Leeds Studies in English* ns 27, 131–38

Edwards, A.S.G., ed. (1984) *Middle English Prose: A Critical Guide to Major Authors and Genres* (New Brunswick)

Evans, R., and L. Johnson, eds (1994) *Feminist Readings in Middle English Literature: The Wife of Bath and All her Sect* (London)

Farley, M.H. (1999) 'Her Own Creature: Religion, Feminist Criticism, and the Functional Eccentricity of Margery Kempe', *Exemplaria* 11, 1–21

Gallyon, M. (1995) *Margery Kempe of Lynn and Medieval England* (Norwich)

Gibson, G.McM. (1989) *The Theater of Devotion: East Anglian Drama and Society in the Late Middle Ages* (Chicago)

Glasscoe, M., ed. (1980) *The Medieval Mystical Tradition in England: Papers Read at the Exeter Symposium, July 1980* (Exeter)

————, ed. (1984) *The Medieval Mystical Tradition in England: Papers Read at Dartington Hall, July 1984* (Cambridge)

————, ed. (1999) *The Medieval Mystical Tradition, England, Ireland and Wales*, Exeter Symposium 6 (Cambridge)

Goodman, A. (1978) 'The Piety of John Brunham's Daughter, of Lynn', in Baker 1978, 347–58

———— (2002) *Margery Kempe and her World* (London)

Greenspan, K. (1996) 'Autohagiography and Medieval Women's Spiritual Autobiography', in Chance 1996, 216–36

Heffernan, T.J., ed. (1985) *The Popular Literature of Medieval England* (Knoxville)

Hirsh, J.C. (1975) 'Author and Scribe in *The Book of Margery Kempe*', *Medium Ævum* 44, 145–50

———— (1984) 'Margery Kempe', in Edwards 1984, 109–19

———— (1989) *The Revelations of Margery Kempe: Paramystical Practices in Late Medieval England*, Medieval and Renaissance Authors 10 (Leiden)

———— (1996) *The Boundaries of Faith: The Development and Transmission of Medieval Spirituality*, Studies in the History of Christian Thought 67 (Leiden)

Holbrook, S.E. (1992) ' "About Her": Margery Kempe's Book of Feeling and Working', in Dean and Zacher 1992, 265–84

Johnson, L.S. (1991) 'The Trope of the Scribe and the Question of Literary Authority in the Works of Julian of Norwich and Margery Kempe', *Speculum* 66, 820–38

Lawes, R. (1999) 'The Madness of Margery Kempe', in Glasscoe 1999, 147–67

Lochrie, K. (1986) '*The Book of Margery Kempe*: The Marginal Woman's Quest for Literary Authority', *JMRS* 16, 33–55

———— (1994) *Margery Kempe and Translations of the Flesh* (Philadelphia)

Long, J. (1994) 'Mysticism and Hysteria: The Histories of Margery Kempe and Anna O.', in Evans and Johnson 1994, 88–111

Margherita, G. (1994) *The Romance of Origins* (Philadelphia)

McEntire, S.J., ed. (1992) *Margery Kempe: A Book of Essays* (New York)

Medcalf, S. (1981a) 'Inner and Outer', in Medcalf 1981b, 108–71

————, ed. (1981b) *The Later Middle Ages* (London)

Partner, N.F. (1989) ' "And Most of All for Inordinate Love": Desire and Denial in *The Book of Margery Kempe*', *Thought* 64, 254–67

———— (1991) 'Reading *The Book of Margery Kempe*', *Exemplaria* 3, 29–66

Pollard, W.F. and R. Boenig, eds (1997) *Mysticism and Spirituality in England* (Woodbridge)

Salih, S. (2001) *Versions of Virginity in Late Medieval England* (Woodbridge)

Spearing, A.C. (2002) '*The Book of Margery Kempe*; or, The Diary of a Nobody', *Southern Review* 38, 625–35

Staley, L. (1994) *Margery Kempe's Dissenting Fictions* (University Park)

Stargardt, U. (1985) 'The Beguines of Belgium, the Dominican Nuns of Germany, and Margery Kempe', in Heffernan 1985, 277–313

Uhlman, D.R. (1994) 'The Comfort of Voice, the Solace of Script: Orality and Literacy in *The Book of Margery Kempe*', *SP* 91, 50–69

Voaden, R., ed. (1996) *Prophets Abroad: The Reception of Continental Holy Women in Late-Medieval England* (Cambridge)

——— (1999) *God's Words, Women's Voices: The Discernment of Spirits in the Writing of Late-Medieval Women Visionaries* (York)

Watt, D., ed. (1997) *Medieval Women in their Communities* (Cardiff)

Weissman, H.P. (1982) 'Margery Kempe in Jerusalem: *Hysterica Compassio* in the Late Middle Ages', in Carruthers and Kirk, 201–17

Wilson, J. (1997) 'Communities of Dissent: The Secular and Ecclesiastical Communities of Margery Kempe's *Book*', in Watt 1997, 155–85

Wright, M.J. (1995) 'What They Said to Margery Kempe: Narrative Reliability in her *Book*', *Neophilologus* 79, 497–508

7

Mandeville

IAIN MACLEOD HIGGINS

Exactly when, where, and by whom *The Book of John Mandeville* was made remain uncertain.[1] Like the narrator's 'Frend' in Chaucer's *House of Fame*, it just suddenly appears: in Paris, on 18 September 1371, at the court of Charles V, in a manuscript copied by Raoulet d'Orléans for Master Gervais Chrétien, the king's physician. We know this because both Raoulet and Charles left autograph records on the manuscript, the earliest extant dated copy (Paris, Bibliothèque Nationale, nouv. acq. fr. 4515; for the records, see Delisle II, 275; Letts, ed., *Mandeville's Travels*, II, 412). It is one of the many ironies in *Mandeville* studies that we know more about Raoulet and his commission than about the copied book's own author or origins, matters once considered 'the nuclei of the Mandeville-question' (Vogels 19 n. 1). By its own account, the book was set down in French from memory in 1356, by a John Mandeville, knight, of St Albans, who having left England on Michaelmas 1322 spent some thirty-four years overseas in the Near East and the Far East before coming to a gouty rest (Deluz, *Le livre des merveilles*, 92–93, 479; Letts, ed., *Mandeville's Travels*, II, 231, 411). Scholars long ago confirmed that French was the book's original language, although, in another mandevillean irony, the influence of the English Cotton translation as edited in 1725 so confused some readers that in the nineteenth century Sir John Mandeville became the 'Father of English prose', and this confusion persisted well into the twentieth century. Having explained why he wrote in French, the author neglects to say where he made his book. Arguing from textual evidence, scholars have proposed three possible places: England, the northern French-speaking regions of Continental Europe, and Liège (source of a singularly odd and later textual tradition – the Interpolated Continental (or Liège or Ogier) Version and its offshoots). Textual history and source studies together suggest that the Continent is the more likely place of origin, but no decisive case has yet been made.

Even more uncertain is how the author occupied himself during those three and half decades abroad, since his *sui generis* book is not a travel memoir in the modern sense. Rather, it is organized geographically as an *impersonal* itinerary tracing the common ways from England through Constantinople, Egypt, and the

---

1 Medieval designations of the work include *The Book of John Mandeville*, *Le livre des merveilles du monde*, and *Itinerarius* (Bennett, *Rediscovery*, Appendix 1). *Mandeville's Travels* has been common English currency since 1568, but sets up misleading expectations. *The Book of John Mandeville* (henceforth *TBJM*) does not prejudge the question of genre.

Holy Land to the far-eastern territories of India, Cathay, and Prester John's Land. Set down in plain but fluent and generally agreeable prose, *TBJM* is a capacious survey – variously engaging, boring, delightful, and thought-provoking – of routes, places, peoples, customs, and marvels, or what the author calls 'choses estranges' (things both foreign and unusual), a survey enlivened by striking anecdotes and the English Knight's occasional, usually memorable personal appearances. Capable of presenting copious information in readable form, the *Mandeville* author can also tell a fine story with both verve and economy, working wonders with a few bold claims and telling details. He claims, for instance, to have received as a special gift one of the thorns from Christ's crown, to have measured the height of both pole stars with his astrolabe, and even to have served as a freelance soldier in the Great Khan's wars against the King of Mancy.

Scholars have failed to find any such Mandeville in the archives, however – not surprisingly perhaps, given that there is no south polar star and that the Khan's wars took place in the thirteenth century. In addition, scholars early on found that this guide-book-cum-'memoir' was put together entirely out of others' works, several dozen in all: in particular Friar William of Boldensele's 1336 memoir of his Palestine pilgrimage, *Liber de quibusdam ultramarinis partibus* (book of certain overseas regions), and Friar Odoric of Pordenone's 1330 *Relatio*, a starry-eyed account of wonders encountered on missionary wanderings in India and China. Spliced together to give the book its basic shape (Odoric after William), these two principal sources were used mainly in Jean le Long of Ypres' 1351 French translation[2] – a fact which, taken together with Raoulet's 1371 complaint about his faulty 'exemplaire' makes the composition date of 1356 the most plausible of the book's 'authenticating' circumstantial data (William's and Odoric's first-person narratives are usually rendered in the third person, except on the rare occasion when they are refashioned as the *Mandeville* author's 'own' experiences).

Although his creative transformation of his sources shows the author to be an avid, intelligent, and frequently discerning reader with a distinct if limited literary gift, such discoveries cannot help but raise suspicions regarding virtually all of his claims. So great have these suspicions been that since the nineteenth century some have tried to make Sir John Mandeville into someone else, reducing an 'absolute Johannes-factotum' to 'an upstart crow beautified with stolen feathers' (to adapt Robert Greene's famous gibe at Shakespeare). The two earliest candidates were Jean de Bourgogne, alias Jean à la Barbe, a Liège physician and author of a plague treatise, and Jean d'Outremeuse, a prolix Liège chronicler and romance-writer. Soon accepted by most late nineteenth- and early twentieth-century scholars, these claims that the 'Father of English prose' had been slain and resurrected as a plagiarist from Liège did not go unchallenged. The result was a fierce 'art versus life' debate, where art meant fraud (the book was a 'mendacious romance' [Hodgen 103]) and life, traveller's truth.

---

2   On the sources, see Deluz, *Le livre de Jehan de Mandeville*, 39–73, 428–91.

The most important document of this debate is Josephine Waters Bennett's *The Rediscovery of Sir John Mandeville* (1954). Hoping to transform the foreign con-artist into an admirable English artificer and his 'mendacious romance' into a 'romance of travel' (*Rediscovery*, 39–53), Bennett produced an archival summa that is still a landmark. In contrast, Malcolm Letts's *Sir John Mandeville: The Man and His Book* (1949) must be used with great caution, since Letts is sometimes confused enough to attribute to the author material clearly added in translation; Giles Milton's recent 'in search of' book (1996) can be safely ignored. Despite her diligence, however, Bennett's case remains no less conjectural than Letts's or Milton's, as does that of the most recent addition to the list of alter egos: Jean le Long of Ypres (Seymour, *Sir John Mandeville*, 23). In fact, important as it was for gathering evidence of the work's early reception, the protracted debate over *TBJM*'s authorship has been largely beside the point. The *Mandeville* author's book is first and last a compilation. Accordingly, then, one should distinguish the *Mandeville* author (the unlocated historical figure responsible for *TBJM*) from the fictional Sir John (the 'I' whose borrowed and invented experiences and adventures the book sometimes details).

Whoever the *Mandeville* author may have been, it is possible to make inferences about him which may have some interpretative value. These can only be made from the French original,[3] of course, which exists in two main versions (discussed briefly later; the Liège Version is clearly unauthorial). Given his somewhat shaky Latin, one scholar thinks him a young nobleman educated in the arts (Deluz, *Le livre de Jehan de Mandeville*, 71), while another, considering the book's sources and the author's biblical knowledge, supposes him to be a French or Flemish Benedictine (Seymour, *Sir John Mandeville*, 23; *Defective*, xi, 173). Both are plausible views, the latter being perhaps slightly more persuasive given the author's habit of citing Scripture, especially the Psalter, in untranslated Latin and his recurrent concern for pious living. The difficulty here is that *TBJM* reveals other habits and concerns that may allow still other inferences which bring scholars no closer to identifying the author: his strenuous anti-Jewishness, for example, and his contrary openness to religious diversity so long as the practice is pious; or his interest in natural phenomena, especially monstrosities, and his 'common-sense' attitude towards speculative scientific questions – whether the antipodes are inhabited, for instance, or whether the earth can be circumnavigated.

What is certain, however, is that this dissembling 'travel memoir' did not suddenly disappear like Chaucer's 'Frend', but became a long-lived figure in the pageant of fame-seekers. Within about a decade of its making, as Raoulet's 1371 complaint suggests, *TBJM* had already been much copied and was fast becoming a 'best-seller'. From its original French the book was soon translated, sometimes more than once and indirectly as well as directly, into Catalan (Riquer), Czech, Danish, Dutch, English, German, Irish, Italian, Latin, and

---

3   Such speculation is paradoxically better founded in the case of a translator like Michel Velser, who can be precisely located in place and time and whose interventions in his German translation are exceptionally interesting (Morrall).

Spanish; there is even a textless pictorial version (Krása).[4] Some three hundred manuscript copies (including fragments, extracts, and epitomes) are still extant (Seymour, *Sir John Mandeville*, 38–49; Higgins 20–25), and there are exemplars and records of printed versions from the 1470s to the present (Seymour, *Sir John Mandeville*, 50–56). Indeed, *TBJM* was printed in eight of its twelve languages before 1515, and had achieved some sixty printings by 1600, after which it continued to appear, mainly in Czech, Dutch, English, and German. Extraordinarily popular and widely circulated in its own day, *TBJM* has found readers almost uninterruptedly throughout its centuries-long afterlife (Bennett, *Rediscovery*, 219–60; Deluz, *Le livre de Jehan de Mandeville*, 267– 361; Moseley, 'Metamorphoses', 1975; Tzanaki), surviving the dismantling not only of its geographical and conceptual worlds in the sixteenth century, but of its authorial and textual integrity in the nineteenth. In England in particular, where its author's claim to Englishness was taken seriously, it has been regularly in print since the fifteenth century. Indeed, as Bennett noted, both book and author have historically occupied 'a special place in English literature' and have long been the objects of 'a proprietary pride' (*Rediscovery*, 9) – in recent centuries largely because of the influence of a single early eighteenth-century printing.

That printing, the most consequential of all for the work's modern reception, took the form of a scholarly edition issued in London in 1725: *The Voiage and Travaile of Sir John Maundevile, Kt. . . . Now publish'd entire from an Original MS. in the Cotton Library* complete with an anonymous 'Editor's Preface', 'An Index of Obsolete Words', and an occasional footnote drawing attention to textual variants. This edition was briefly successful, since it was reprinted in 1727, but its lasting influence dates from 1839, when it was again reprinted. In this context, the crucial facts are that the unique Cotton text (BL, Cotton MS, Titus C. xvi) contains a striking mistranslation, possibly deliberate, of the *Mandeville* author's account of his chosen language, and that this mistranslation, along with the anonymous editor's comment, has long influenced readers (the relevant French wording is given first):

> *Insular.* And know that I *should have* set this writing down [Et sachez qe jeo *eusse* cest escrit *mis*] in Latin to be more concise, but because more understand French [romancz] better than Latin I have put it down in French so that everyone might understand it . . . (Deluz, *Le livre des merveilles*, 93, emphasis added; my translation; cf. Letts, ed., *Mandeville's Travels*, II, 231)

> *Cotton.* And yee schulle vndirstonde that I *haue put* this boke out of Latyn into Frensch and translated it ayen out of Frensch into Englyssch, that euery man of my nacoun may vnderstonde it. (Seymour, ed., *Mandeville's Travels*, 3–4, emphasis added)

> *Editor's Preface.* This Edition agrees with the *Latin* and *French MSS.*; and appears to be the genuine Work of the Author; who says, that he translated it out of *Latin* into *French*, and out of *French* into *English*; whereas all other

---

4   Tzanaki (16) has drawn attention to an unnoticed early sixteenth-century Welsh rendering (BL, MS Additional 14921) made from an English edition of Defective.

printed Editions are so curtail'd and transpos'd, as to be made thereby other Books. (*Voiage* 1725, iv)

When in 1839 the 1725 text was reprinted unrevised for a second time, 'with an Introduction, Additional Notes, and Glossary by J.O. Halliwell', its new introduction implicitly confirmed the earlier editor's view of Cotton's trilingual genealogy: 'This passage . . . I find only in the Cotton manuscript. In the Latin copies nothing is said on this point; but in MS. Sloan. 1464, and in many of the French versions, I find the following: – "Et sachetz que jeo usse mis ceste liverette en Latyn . . ." ' (*Voiage* 1839, vii). By phrasing his remark so tentatively and not translating the difficult 'usse mis', Halliwell allowed what had since 1725 become received opinion to stand unchallenged,[5] as did his scholarly contemporaries (cf. Schönborn 11 and Wright xxvii; Ashton, *Voiage*, xvii, was the first edition to correct them). Scholars had known since at least the late eighteenth century that the original was set down in French, but only in 1869 did Edward Mätzner show that by virtue of its translator's errors Cotton could not be authorial.

Independently confirming Mätzner was Edward B. Nicholson, who in 1876 called Cotton 'a forgery' ('Mandeville's Travels', 477) and soon after announced an 'anti-Mandevillian criticism' ('John', 261) whose central aim was to demolish the received views of *TBJM*, particularly in England, where Cotton's genealogical claim was repeated uncritically. In 1886, for example, the *Mandeville* author was still being honoured as 'the Father of English Prose' (Minto 183, who first used the phrase in 1872), an honour going back, implicitly, at least to 1790 (Bennett, *Rediscovery*, 3 n. 1). So tenacious has this claim been that it was taken seriously as recently as the 1970s and 80s in the excellent literary criticism of Howard ('World', 4 n. 1; but corrected in *Writers*, 62) and Campbell (137 and n. 14). There are presumably many reasons why demonstrable falsehoods become canonical, but one must be the tendency of literary studies to ignore textual scholarship. Indeed, accounts of *TBJM* are speckled with small confirming examples, one of which will suffice as evidence: the papal interpolation (see Higgins 254–60). Revealed in 1840 as an interpolation (Schönborn 22–23), the passage has recently been read as authorial by both critics (Zacher, *Curiosity*, 135) and historians (Phillips, *Medieval*, 206).

Given such confusions, one must first outline what is known about *TBJM*'s complex textual situation, proceeding from the relevant French traditions to the English. Having generally agreed since the 1870s that French alone was the original language, scholars have still not finished the task of sorting the some sixty extant French manuscripts. As Bennett noted in 1954, studies and editions

---

5 Richard Hakluyt did a similar thing when in 1589 he printed John Bale's 'biography' of Sir John Mandeville with the Vulgate Latin Version. The author, Bale asserts, 'committed his whole travell . . . to writing in three divers tongues, English, French, and Latine' (Bale fol. 149b; in Hakluyt 24); but Hakluyt's text states in its *explicit* that the book was 'editum primo in lingua Gallicana', 'first set down in French' (77). Bale must therefore have had access to Cotton, but his claim never had the influence of the 1725 edition, largely because Hakluyt omitted *TBJM* from the second edition of his collection (Tadie). A supposed late fourteenth-century reference to trilingual composition in Radulphus de Rivo's *Chronicle* has been convincingly called into question on textual grounds (Lejeune 414–16).

of various translations had by then appeared, but 'no study of the original text
ha[d] ever been published' before hers (111), nor were scholars yet aware that
the French manuscripts comprised three separate versions, a conclusion also
reached in 1955 by Guy de Poerck: Insular (25 mss: 14 in Anglo-Norman, 11 in
Continental French, in English and Continental hands, respectively), Continental (30 mss), and Interpolated Continental (or Liège or Ogier; 7 mss).[6]
French critical editions had been projected since at least 1877, but despite
further projections subsequent to Bennett's study, none appeared until
Christiane Deluz's 2000 edition of Insular. It is this version from which directly
or indirectly all the English and other Insular translations (four Latin, one Irish,
one Welsh) derive. Prior to Deluz's edition, the only available text of Insular was
that of Warner's monumental but highly restricted 1889 edition (based on four
manuscripts).

Between Bennett's and de Poerck's pioneering work and Deluz's edition, only
one other scholar worked extensively on the French manuscripts: M.C. Seymour
('Scribal Tradition: Insular'; see also Schepens). Bennett had argued, on (shaky)
stylistic grounds, for the priority of Insular (*Rediscovery*, 135–46), while de
Poerck, considering the state of the 1371 manuscript, argued for the priority of
Continental ('La tradition', 155). Seymour has sided with de Poerck ('Scribal
Tradition: Insular', 48; *Defective*, xi, 173), but Deluz has recently reasserted
Bennett's position, that the Anglo-Norman text is prior. Even if living in Liège,
she notes, the *Mandeville* author could have produced his work in his 'langue
maternelle' (*Le livre des merveilles*, 33). Dialect and idiom are Deluz's strongest
evidence: scribal translations, for example, of Anglo-Norman forms into Continental French (*Le livre des merveilles*, 33–35). She concludes, however, that
only a critical edition of Continental can help settle this long-standing uncertainty (*Le livre des merveilles*, 35). Even in the original language, then, it
remains uncertain what the authorial text looked like, particularly since Continental and Insular differ in one major respect – Sir John's account of his journey
through the Val Perilleux (see Higgins 206–16) – and several minor ones
(Bennett, *Rediscovery*, 135–38; de Poerck, 'La tradition', 135–38).[7]

Including fragments and excerpts, the English versions survive in some
forty-four manuscripts (Seymour, *Sir John Mandeville*, 43–45). Thirty-five of
these were first listed, briefly described, and classified in 1891 by Johann
Vogels (esp. 8–18). The most recent sorting was in 1966 by Seymour ('English
Manuscripts'), who knew of some forty-one manuscripts, and described forty. A
fragment (Robbins 17), an extract (Horner), and one full manuscript have since

---

6   The names used here are de Poerck's (Bennett's are less helpful). The numbers come from Deluz, *Le
    livre des merveilles*, 29–30, whose census – the most recent to date – updates and corrects those of
    her predecessors (see 36–58 for her useful description of the Insular manuscripts).
7   Further textual history is unnecessary here, except to note that Seymour ('Scribal Tradition: Insular')
    has sorted the Insular manuscripts into three subgroups (A, B, C); Deluz accepts Seymour's stemma
    with a few minor modifications (*Le livre des merveilles*, 36, 60–81). Cotton, Defective, and Egerton
    all derive, directly or indirectly, from subgroup B. Warner's and Deluz's editions are based on group
    A manuscripts; Deluz's base manuscript (BL, Harley 212) contains numerous English and French
    marginalia (usefully edited with the text), often in the hand of the Elizabethan scientist John Dee (see
    also Tzanaki 25, 274–75).

been added to Seymour's account (Hanna 129), bringing the total to forty-four. Six separate recensions are represented in the extant manuscripts: four in prose (Bodley [2 mss], Cotton [1 ms], Defective [approx. 38 mss],[8] Egerton [1 ms]), two in verse (Metrical [1 ms], Stanzaic Fragment [1 ms]). Although the southeast midlands dialect of the best-known recension (Cotton) might suggest that *TBJM* began its English career in the London area, there is evidence to suggest that all of the English versions, including the verse redactions, may ultimately be of northern origin (Seymour, 'English Manuscripts', 173–74). Of the prose recensions, two (Cotton, Defective) contain translations of Insular, one (Bodley) contains an abridgement of an English recension of a Latin translation of Insular, while the fourth (Egerton) contains a translation of Insular supplemented by the lost English source of Bodley. Without exception, scholars have accepted this grouping of the extant manuscripts into six separate recensions[9] and agreed that the three prose recensions with an Insular French source (Cotton, Defective, Egerton) represent in effect a single translation twice revised. Disagreement remains, however, on the precise filiation of these latter three renderings (see below).

The Defective Version

Defective survives in some thirty-eight manuscripts, of which thirty-three are complete.[10] Vogels and Seymour agree on its being a direct translation from Insular, but Seymour considers it the first English translation, whereas Vogels thinks it a *revision* of an earlier English translation made c. 1400 (Seymour, 'Scribal Tradition: England', 194; 'English Manuscripts', 169; Vogels 35–37, 52). On the available evidence, the matter is uncertain, as is the question of its date.

What distinguishes Defective from the other English prose recensions are numerous small lacunae, especially in the latter two-thirds of the text (Vogels 41–42), and the so-called Egypt gap: the omission in the account of Egypt of roughly ten percent of the text, or enough material fill a single manuscript quire. No convincing explanation of the Egypt gap's origin has yet been offered. Despite its flaws and whether it represents an original translation or a revision, Defective offers a fairly accurate and smooth Englishing of Insular's own quite fluent, mainly expository prose and its easy address to the reader. The following brief excerpt from the closing remarks about the nature of religious belief

---

8   Seymour adds Oxford, Trinity College, MS 29 to the list, describing it as 'scattered extracts within a larger text' (*Defective*, xxvi); this would bring the Defective total to thirty-nine manuscripts and the overall English count to forty-five. Whether 'scattered extracts' constitute a *Mandeville* manuscript is an open question. To get a complete picture of the English manuscripts one has to collate three separate lists by Seymour – in 'English Manuscripts'; *Sir John Mandeville*; and *Defective* – in which information is inconsistently presented and small changes are typically unannounced.

9   Noting that it does not claim to be *TBJM*, Ruddy argues for seeing Metrical not as a version of *TBJM*, but as a separate work (34); Kohanski makes the same case for the Stanzaic Fragment (xiv n. 11). For obvious reasons, neither rendering is discussed here.

10 This count includes the lost Sneyd Manuscript noted in Seymour, *Sir John Mandeville*, 44 (MS no. 60) and counted but not noted in Seymour, *Defective*. See also note 9 above.

beyond Christendom gives a good indication of the book's attitudes as well as its
stylistic strengths (directness, fluency) and weaknesses (lists, redundancies).
Insular is given first for comparison, which reveals Defective not only simpli-
fying the prose but qualifying the *Mandeville* author's original bold claim about
universal faith, supported as so often by the Psalter (translators and scribes
often silently toned down such speculative boldness, in some cases – notably
that of the Vulgate Latin – even opposing it altogether):

> Et sachez qe de touz ces pays dont j'ay parlé at de toutes celles isles, et de touz
> ces diverses gentz qe jeo vous ay deviseez et de diverses lois et des diverses
> creaunces qu'ils count, il n'y ad nul gent, pur quoy ils aient en eux resoun et
> entendement, qe n'aient ascuns articles de nostre foy et ascuns bons pointz de
> nostre creaunce, et q'ils ne croient en Dieu qy fist le mounde q'ils appelent
> dieu de nature, solonc le prophete qe a dit: '*Et metuent [eum] omnes fines
> terre*' [Ps. 67.7]. Et aillors: '*Omnes gentes servient ei*' [Ps.72.11].
>
> (Deluz, *Le livre des merveilles*, 477)

> And ȝe schal vndirstonde þat alle þese men and folk of whom Y haue spoke
> þat beþ resonable haueþ somme articlis of oure treuþe. If al þei be of dyuerse
> lawis and dyuerse trowynges, þei haueþ somme gode poyntes of oure treuþe.
> And þei trowiþ in God of kynde whiche made al the world, and hym clepe þei
> God of kynde as here prophecys seiþ,[11] *Et metuent eum omnes fines terre*, þat
> is to say, And alle endis of erþe schal drede hym; and in anoþer place þus,
> *Omnes gentes seruient ei*, þat is to say, Alle folk schal serue to him.
>
> (Seymour, *Defective*, 134)

It was doubtless material like this, presented in such plain yet generally
pleasant prose, that led to *TBJM*'s widespread international success. Defective's
own success, it is important to note, was not limited to the fifteenth century and
manuscript circulation. An edition by Richard Pynson appeared probably in
1496 (STC 17246; see now Kohanski's edition), giving, Seymour claims, 'a
better text . . . than any manuscript of the Defective Version still extant' ('Early
English Editions', 204). In 1499 Wynkyn de Worde used Pynson as the copy-
text for another edition (STC 17247) with a corrected and slightly modernised
text enhanced by woodcuts borrowed (and simplified) from Anton Sorg's 1481
edition of Michel Velser's German translation. De Worde's improved edition
was printed again, with a few small changes, in 1503 (STC 17249) and yet again
in perhaps 1510 (STC 17248). Four printings in some fifteen years may have
saturated the market, because the next known edition (by Thomas East) did not
appear until 1568 (STC 17250), its text probably from de Worde (Seymour,
'Early', 205–07). East certainly borrowed de Worde's woodcuts, printing most
of them in reverse from well-used blocks (Bennett, 'Woodcut', 66). These woodcuts, far cruder than many manuscript illustrations and often reprinted down to
the present, have likely been a significant influence on *TBJM*'s negative reputation as the work of a marvel-monger. East's edition itself was also well used.
Martin Frobisher had it aboard ship in 1576, during his first attempt to find the

---

[11] The book's intermediaries often altered such remarks, but not here. Several manuscripts read 'solonc
leur prophetes (ou prophecies) qui dient' (Deluz, *Le livre des merveilles*, 477 textual note e).

Northwest Passage. Some fifteen years later, East printed another 'substantially identical' edition (Seymour, 'Early', 207; STC 17251) which Sir Walter Ralegh may have read, since in his *Discoverie of . . . Guiana* (1595/96) he noted that a nation of people, whose 'heades appeare not aboue their shoulders', were also 'written of by *Maundeuile*' (85–86), the very nation who turn up in Othello's 'travel's history' (*Othello* [1603–04] I.iii.143–44). Within a century, then, Defective had appeared in print at least five times, the last two of which editions made it available to those famous Elizabethan figures involved in expanding English literature as well as their nascent empire.

Throughout the next century or so, Defective was in even greater demand, appearing in print at least fifteen times between 1612 and 1722, all the editions deriving ultimately from East's (Seymour, 'Early', 207). Despite the publication in 1725 of Cotton, which eventually became the received English version, Defective did not disappear. The 1722 edition was reprinted in 1730 and 1745, and may have been the basis of a marvel-mongering chapbook that appeared in 1750 and was four times reprinted (Ashton, *Foreign*). After this, Defective disappeared for more than a century, as Cotton took over. In 1887, however, East's 1568 edition was reprinted as 'a thoroughly representative *English* Edition, which gives Sir John's adventures, with their concomitant "Travellers' Tales," without the apocryphal stories which were introduced into some of the MSS. and foreign editions' (Ashton, *Voiage*, vii; his emphasis). In 1928 East's text appeared yet again, in Ashton's edition for Everyman's Library, its Egypt gap filled and other errors corrected from Cotton (*Voiage* 1928). Some four and a half centuries after its first printing, then, Defective was still readily available. There was no critical edition, however, before Seymour's attempt, based on Queen's College, Oxford, MS 383, at a 'substantial (but not linguistic) reconstruction of the archetype of the extant [Defective] manuscripts' (*Defective*, xxx).

The Cotton Version

A single parchment codex (BL, Cotton Titus C xvi.) in an early fifteenth-century hand is all that survives of Cotton. Exactly when and how the version itself was made is uncertain. Vogels and Seymour agree on a date of 'about 1400', but differ on its making. According to Seymour, who refined Nicholson and Warner's argument, the Cotton maker

> based his version on a [lost] manuscript of the Defective Version (of Sub-Group A), which was translated from a manuscript of the Insular Version (of Sub-Group B), and where his copy-text was abridged, by accident or design, he translated from another manuscript of the Insular Version (of Sub-Group A). (*Mandeville's Travels*, 270; see also xx, 275)

According to Vogels, however, Cotton is no such composite; rather, its text best preserves the first English translation from Insular, a translation also represented, but in revised form, in Defective and Egerton (52). Vogels noticed that Cotton is throughout closer to Insular and contains numerous mistranslations avoided in Defective and Egerton (24); since the three renderings are in a sense one version, Vogels thought it unlikely that a more literal if sometimes inaccurate translation would be a revision of a more accurate if textually defective one. The point is well taken, and unanswered by Seymour, yet itself not decisive.[12]

Whatever the uncertainties here, we do have a clear picture of Cotton as a translation, and that picture does not always flatter the translator. His command of French, as Mätzner first noticed (154–55), was shaky enough that he could translate 'montaignes' as 'the hille of Aygnes', but a comparison of Cotton and Defective with each other and against the French shows how Cotton is as fluent and workmanlike a translation as Defective and a better witness to the fuller French text. In this excerpt of the passage quoted above, however, even the highly faithful Cotton translator baulks somewhat at the *Mandeville* author's boldness, adding the qualifying phrase 'but yif it be the fewere':

> And yee schulle vndirstonde that of alle theise contrees and of alle theise yles and of alle the dyuerse folk that I haue spoken of before and of dyuerse lawes and of dyuerse beleeves that thei han, yit is there non of hem alle but that thei han sum resoun within hem and vderstondynge – but yif it be the fewere – and that han certeyn articles of oure feith and summe gode poyntes of oure beleeve; and that thei beleeven in God that formede alle thing and made the world and clepen Him God of Nature, after that the prophete seyth, *Et metuent* . . . (Seymour, ed., *Mandeville's Travels*, 227)

The Egerton Version

Like Cotton, Egerton survives in only a single parchment manuscript written in an early fifteenth-century hand: BL, Egerton 1982. It remained unprinted until 1889,[13] when Warner brought out an edition whose copious annotations are still unrivalled. As Vogels showed, the Egerton maker filled Defective's lacunae, presumably with occasional use of a French text, up to the Egypt gap, repairing the gap from the lost English source of Bodley, a text also used extensively in restoring the remainder (49–50, 52; see also Seymour, 'Origin of Egerton'). The redactor likewise thoroughly revised Defective, making its prose not only more readable, but by far the most supple and engaging of all the English renderings. The following excerpt shows the redactor tidying the prose ('lands, realms and nations') and qualifying the original in smaller and larger ways, especially in two places ('out-taken [etc.]' and 'thus is the prophecy verified'):

> And ȝe schall vnderstand þat in all þir landes, rewmes and naciouns, outtaken þose þat er inhabited with vnresonable men, es na folk þat ne þai hald sum articlez of oure beleue. If all þai be of diueres lawes and diueres trowyngs, þai hafe sum gude poyntes of oure trowth. And generally þai trowe in Godd þat

12 As Kenneth Sisam long ago noted, while attempting to show why 'the central problem . . . is the relation of C[otton] and D[efective]', no simple formula will explain 'the whole web of relationships', and, furthermore, 'an investigator who wished to clear the ground would have to face the labour of preparing a six-text *Mandeville*, in the order, French, C, D, E[gerton], L [=Bodley], Latin' (241, 242). Seymour's recent edition of Defective (2002) has not solved this long-standing problem.

made the werld, and him call þai Godd of kynde; and þus es þe prophecy verified þat saise, *Et metuent . . .*

(Warner 154; cf. Letts, ed., *Mandeville's Travels*, I, 220–21)

If his handling of *TBJM*'s matter is any indication, the Egerton maker was learned as well as religious, proud of English scholarly and missionary achievements. Regarding the diamond, for instance, where Cotton follows Insular in making passing reference to 'the lapidarye' (Seymour, ed., *Mandeville's Travels*, 116), Egerton displays the 'English' author's acquaintance with the proper *auctoritates*: Isidore of Seville's *Etymologies* and Bartholomaeus Anglicus' *On the Properties of Things* (Warner 79; Letts, ed., *Mandeville's Travels*, I, 114–15).

More interesting than this brief addition, and more telling, is a long interpolation right before the account of Paradise: a curious story set at the other end of the earth, in Ultima Thule, whose Christian kingdom is saved from a plague of beasts by 'a miracle of Saint Thomas of Canterbury' (Letts, ed., *Mandeville's Travels*, I, 212–14). To a modern editor collating manuscripts and versions, this story presents itself as an interpolation, which, by virtue of its length and apparent audacity, requires special treatment. One editor thus relegated it to his notes (Warner 220), while another omitted it altogether, commenting: 'Its only slight interest lies in the further evidence it shows of the way redactors sometimes added what they thought to be germane material' (Moseley, *Travels*, 183 n.). Unique to Egerton, the story of St Thomas in Ultima Thule would not necessarily betray itself as an interpolation to anyone acquainted only with this redaction, and its interest is more than slight, since its matter is in fact germane, revealing the Egerton reviser to be a penetrating reader. For even if the allusion to 'the poete' (Virgil) and the remark that 'I hafe herd and sene [þis myracle] writen in diuerse bukes' ultimately betray the interpolator here – the *Mandeville* author himself cites almost no texts except the Bible, and prefers to claim either personal or secondhand knowledge (in the form 'they say') – the 'miracle' as a whole has been effectively dovetailed into the text. Few readers would likely have thought themselves swerving into obviously foreign matter as they passed from a far country inhabited by giant ants to one inhabited by marvellous and cruel beasts.

Nor would they necessarily have found the curious story itself out of character. Indeed, its English element neatly connects it with several references to English figures or 'facts': the ostensible author's birth at St Alban's, St Helen as the daughter of King Cole of England (ch. 2), Richard I of England (ch. 6), the letters thorn and yogh (ch. 15), and the way in which people of 'our country' travel so much because of the moon (ch. 18).[14] As a story, moreover, the 'miracle' is distinguished from other such longish digressions – e.g., on Hippocrates' daughter who was transformed from a woman into a dragon (ch. 4) – only by

[13] An unsubstantiated note on folio 1 claims that the manuscript passed through the hands of the printers William Caxton and Richard Tottyl (Warner xii; Seymour, 'English Manuscripts', 199).

[14] Chapter numbers are from Cotton – Egerton has no chapter divisions – but for ease of cross-reference are often added to the text in editions of other English versions. Except for Ganser (on the Dutch Version), no one has yet examined the various ways in which chapter divisions and headings are used – information that might have much to say about *TBJM*'s reception.

belonging more to hagiography than romance. Yet *TBJM* does devote at least one similar account to a miracle of God that affects the natural order of the world near Persia (ch. 28), and is occasionally concerned with the doings of saints. Perhaps the most significant fact about the interpolation, however, is that it tells the story of a Christian king in a far country, and, in so doing, not only offers in effect a corroborating witness to the reality of Prester John, who dominates the later sections, but fits neatly in with *TBJM*'s finding Christian or proto-Christian belief even at the ends of the earth. In all these respects, then, the interpolation is highly germane.

The Bodley Version

Extant in two manuscripts (Bodl. e Musaeo 116 and Rawlinson D.99), both written in the first half of the fifteenth century, Bodley differs from the other English prose recensions in descending only indirectly from Insular. Strong evidence for this is its lack of the papal interpolation (Vogels 27). Exactly when Bodley was made is uncertain. Originally considered a 'very badly abbreviated' copy of a revision of Defective (Nicholson and Yule 475), it was shown to be the 'significantly and wilfully shortened . . . form' of a full English translation of a Latin translation, with each manuscript deriving independently from its source (Vogels 47–49) and characterised by a differing order of several common parts and variant wording. The passage on belief beyond Christendom reveals Bodley's deliberate conciseness as well as its closeness to Egerton and the variations between its two witnesses:

> *Musaeo*. Wete ye wel for certeyn that of alle reumys and londis and naciounnys that I haue spokyn of byforn, outakyn [hem] that han non resoun with hem, there arn none maner of men that thei ne holdyn manye artikellis of the feyth, for generally thei trowin alle in God that made the world, whom they honoure and clepyn to for helpe. And ther thour is the prophesie verified where it is said, *Et metuant* [sic] . . . (Seymour, ed., *Bodley*, 143)

> *Rawlinson*. And wete ȝe wel for certeyn, of alle thes cuntrees that I haue spoken off bifore, out take hem that haue noo resoun, with hem ther nys non of hem but that they holden some articulis of our feith. ffor [sic] they trowe in God that made al the worlde, whom they honoure and calle vpon. And ther is the prophecie verified where he seith thus, *Et metuant* [sic] . . .
> (Letts, ed., *Mandeville's Travels*, II, 480)

Both manuscripts were parts of miscellanies, Musaeo accompanying Chaucer's *Treatise on the Astrolabe*, Rawlinson a fifteenth-century collection of mainly practical, moral, and historical works, including a prose *Siege of Thebes* (Smith). Despite its mixed contexts, Bodley is not so heterogeneous as the longer versions, and unlike the epitomes of Defective, it represents more than a haphazard selection. Omitting much detail, the redactor smoothed, shaped, even rearranged what remains. He has, in addition, often re-asserted the truth value of the text's claims, expanding 'I' (did, said, heard) to 'I John Mandeville'; such expansions may have been in the source, but only Egerton makes the same sort of authenticating gestures. Where the longer versions merely state, for example, that 'I' saw the crown of thorns and received the gift of a thorn (Seymour, ed., *Mandeville's Travels*, 9; cf. Letts, ed., *Mandeville's Travels*, II, 235), Bodley insists that 'I myself, Iohn Maundevile, saw3 hit' and 'I hadde oon of the thornes' (Letts, ed. *Mandeville's Travels*, II, 421; Seymour, ed., *Bodley*, 7; cf. Deluz, *Le livre des merveilles*, 103). Such reassurances occur somewhat more frequently in Rawlinson, whose redactor or copyist seems even more concerned with the truth value of his text, asserting the superiority of prose to 'romaunce and ryme' at the end of the Prologue (Letts, ed., *Mandeville's Travels*, II, 419).

The most striking change comes in the Far East, where the redactor has resisted *TBJM*'s roughly west-to-east arrangement that brings the text to a close near Paradise and Prester John's Land. Omitting the account of Paradise, the redactor reverses the accounts of Prester John and the Great Khan such that the latter occupies almost the final pages of this version (a few particularly marvellous marvels occupy the very last pages, as if in a final flourish). Such a change may have already been present in the redactor's source, but Seymour has suggested one plausible reason for the redactor himself to make it: to have his modified text reach its climax in 'an account of the most fabulous emperor in the world' ('Medieval Redactor', 171). The section devoted to the Khan begins with the words that normally end it in the longer versions: that the Khan's greatness is unequalled 'vnder the ffirmament' (Deluz, *Le livre des merveilles*, 402; see also Seymour, ed., *Bodley*, 123; cf. Letts, ed., *Mandeville's Travels*, II, 368; Seymour, ed., *Mandeville's Travels*, 177).

Much has been learned about *TBJM* over the last several decades, as scholars have shifted their attention away from possibly irresolvable circumstantial problems like the authorship enigma to richer questions of interpretation as well as intellectual, literary, textual, and reception history. The studies of Campbell, Deluz, Grady, Higgins, Howard, Ridder, Ruddy, Tzanaki, and Zacher have helped reframe the ways in which this culturally significant (if literarily minor) work might be examined. In addition, the recent appearance of editions of Insular and Defective, whatever their limitations, has begun to provide researchers with the material needed for both basic and further study, including the still open question of the relation between Defective and Cotton. More than a century after the work's Victorian fall from grace, *TBJM* has been picked up, dusted off, and asked to answer a different era's concerns and questions.

BIBLIOGRAPHY

The Book of John Mandeville: A. English Versions

DEFECTIVE

Ashton, John, ed., *The Foreign Travels of Sir John Mandeville*, in his *Chap-Books of the Eighteenth Century* (London, 1882; repr. New York, 1970), pp. 405–16
————, *The Voiage and Travayle of Sir John Maundeville, Knight, Which Treateth of the Way toward Hierusalem, and of Marvayles of Inde with Other Ilands and Countryes* (London, 1887) [reprint of East's 1568 edition with editorial additions]
Cawley, A.C.[, ed.], 'A Ripon Fragment of "Mandeville's Travels" ', *English Studies* 38 (1957), 262–65
Horner, Patrick J.[, ed.], *'Mandeville's Travels*: A New Manuscript Extract', *Manuscripta* 24 (1980), 171–75
Kohanski, Tamarah, ed., *The Book of John Mandeville: An Edition of the Pynson Text with Commentary on the Defective Version*, Medieval and Renaissance Texts and Studies 231 (Tempe, AZ, 2001)
Seymour, M.C., ed., *The Defective Version of Mandeville's Travels*, EETS os 319 (Oxford, 2002)
————, 'The English Epitome of *Mandeville's Travels*', *Anglia* 84 (1966), 27–58
————, 'Secundum Iohannem Maundvyle', *English Studies in Africa* 4 (1961), 148–68
The Travels of Sir John Mandeville: Facsimile of Pynson's Edition of 1496, intro. by Michael Seymour, Exeter Medieval English Texts and Studies (Exeter, 1980)
The Voiage and Travayle of Syr John Maundeville Knight with the Journall of Friar Odoricus, intro. by Jules Bramont, Everyman's Library 812 (London, 1928) [based on East 1568 supplemented by Cotton from 1725 edition]

COTTON

Hamelius, P., ed., *Mandeville's Travels, translated from the French of Jean d'Outremeuse: Edited from MS. Cotton Titus C. XVI, in the British Museum*, EETS os 153–54, 2 vols (London, 1919–23, issued for 1916; repr. London, 1960–61)
Mätzner, Edward, ed., *The Voiage and Travaile of Sir John Maundeville*, in his *Altenglischen Sprachproben nebst einem Wörterbuch*, 2 vols (Berlin, 1869), II, 152–221
Pollard, A.W., ed., *The Travels of Sir John Mandeville* (London, 1900; repr. New York, 1964) ['in modern spelling'; reprint illustrated with Anton Sorg's 1481 woodcuts]
Seymour, M.C., ed., *Mandeville's Travels* (Oxford, 1967)
The Voiage and Travaile of Sir John Maundevile, Kt. Which Treateth of the Way to Hierusalem; and of Marvayles of Inde, with Other Ilands and Countryes (London, 1725)
The Voiage and Travaile of Sir John Maundevile, Kt. Which Treateth of the Way to Hierusalem; and of Marvayles of Inde, with Other Ilands and Countryes (London, 1839)
Wright, Thomas, ed., *The Book of Sir John Maundeville, A.D. 1322–1356*, in his *Early Travels in Palestine* (London, 1848; repr. New York, 1969), pp. 127–282

EGERTON

Letts, Malcolm, ed. and trans., *Mandeville's Travels: Texts and Translations*, Hakluyt
Society 2nd ser. 101–02, 2 vols (issued for 1950; London, 1953), I, 1–223 [modern-
ized text]
Moseley, C.W.R.D., trans., *The Travels of Sir John Mandeville* (Harmondsworth, 1983)
Warner, George F., ed., *The Buke of John Maundeuill being the Travels of Sir John
Mandeville, Knight 1322–56: A Hitherto Unpublished English Version from the
Unique Copy (Egerton MS. 1982) in the British Museum edited together with the
French Text, Notes, and an Introduction* (Westminster, 1889)

BODLEY

Letts, Malcolm, ed. and trans., *Mandeville's Travels: Texts and Translations*, Hakluyt
Society 2nd ser. 101–02, 2 vols (issued for 1950; London, 1953), II, 416–81
[Bodleian MS Rawlinson D 99; modernized text]
Seymour, M.C., ed., *The Bodley Version of Mandeville's Travels from Bodleian MS. e
Musaeo 116 with Parallel Extracts from the Latin Text of British Museum MS. Royal
13 E. ix*, EETS os 253 (London, 1963)

OTHER

Seymour, M.C., ed., 'Mandeville and Marco Polo: A Stanzaic Fragment', *AUMLA*:
Journal of the Australasian Universities Modern Language Association 21 (1964),
39–52
———, *The Metrical Version of Mandeville's Travels from the Unique Manuscript in the
Coventry Corporation Record Office*, EETS os 269 (London, 1973)

The Book of John Mandeville: B. French Versions

Deluz, Christiane, ed., *Le livre des merveilles du monde*, Sources d'histoire médiévale 31
(Paris, 2000) [Insular Version]
———, trans., 'Le Livre de messire Jean de Mandeville', in *Croisades et pèlerinages*,
ed. D. Régnier-Bohler (Paris, 1997), pp. 1393–1435 [Liège Version, excerpts]
———, trans., *Voyage autour de la terre* (Paris, 1993) [Insular Version]
See also Letts (Continental; II, 225–413) and Warner (Insular), both under Egerton
above.

Other Works Cited

Bale, John, *Illustrium Majoris Britanniae Scriptorum . . . Summarium* (Ipswich, 1548)
Bennett, Josephine Waters, *The Rediscovery of Sir John Mandeville*, Modern Language
Association of America Monograph Series 19 (New York, 1954)
———, 'The Woodcut Illustrations in the English Editions of *Mandeville's Travels*',
Papers of the Bibliographical Society of America 47 (1953), 59–69
Bovenschen, Albert, 'Untersuchungen über Johann von Mandeville und die Quellen
seiner Reisebeschreibung', *Zeitschrift der Gesellschaft für Erdkunde zu Berlin* 23
(1888), 177–306

Campbell, Mary B., *The Witness and the Other World: Exotic European Travel Writing, 400–1600* (Ithaca, NY, 1988)

de Poerck, Guy, 'Le corpus mandevillien du ms Chantilly 699', in *Fin du Moyen Âge et Renaissance: mélanges de philologie française offerts à Robert Guiette*, ed. Guy de Poerck et al. (Antwerp, 1961), pp. 31–48

——, 'La tradition manuscrite des "Voyages" de Jean de Mandeville: à propos d'un livre récent', *Romanica Gandensia* 4 (1955), 125–58

Delisle, Léopold, *Recherches sur la librairie du Charles V, Roi de France, 1337–1380*, 2 vols (Paris, 1907; repr. Amsterdam, 1967)

Deluz, Christiane, *Le livre de Jehan de Mandeville: Une 'géographie' au XIVe siècle*, Textes, Etudes, Congrès 8 (Louvain-la-Neuve, 1988)

Ganser, W. Günther, *Die niederländische Version der Reisebeschreibung Johanns von Mandeville: Untersuchungen zur handschriftlichen Überlieferung*, Amsterdamer Publikationen zur Sprache und Literatur 63 (Amsterdam, 1985)

Gradon, Pamela, Review of *The Bodley Version of Mandeville's Travels*, ed. M.C. Seymour, *Review of English Studies* ns 16 (1965), 411–12

Grady, Frank, ' "Machomete" and *Mandeville's Travels*', in *Medieval Christian Perceptions of Islam: A Book of Essays*, ed. John Victor Tolan (New York, 1996), pp. 271–88

Hakluyt, Richard, ed., *Liber Ioannis Mandevil*, in his *The Principall Navigations, Voiages and Discoveries of the English Nation (London, 1589): A Photo-Lithographic Facsimile*, Hakluyt Society extra ser. 39, 2 vols (Cambridge, 1965), I, 23–79

Hanna, Ralph III, 'Mandeville', in *Middle English Prose: A Critical Guide to Major Authors and Genres*, ed. A.S.G. Edwards (New Brunswick, NJ, 1984), pp. 121–32

Higgins, Iain Macleod, *Writing East: The 'Travels' of Sir John Mandeville* (Philadelphia, 1997)

Hodgen, Margaret T., *Early Anthropology in the Sixteenth and Seventeenth Centuries* (1964; repr. Philadelphia, 1971)

Howard, Donald R., 'The World of Mandeville's Travels', *Yearbook of English Studies* 1 (1971), 1–17

——, *Writers and Pilgrims: Medieval Pilgrimage Narratives and their Posterity* (Berkeley, 1980)

Krása, Josef[, ed.], *The Travels of Sir John Mandeville: A Manuscript in the British Library*, trans. Peter Kussi (New York, 1983)

Lejeune, Rita, 'Jean de Mandeville et les Liégeois', in *Mélanges de linguistique romane et de philologie médiévale offerts à Maurice Delbouille*, 2 vols (Gembloux, 1964), II, 409–37

Letts, Malcolm, *Sir John Mandeville: The Man and his Book* (London, 1949)

May, David, '*Mandeville's Travels*, Chaucer, and *The House of Fame*', *Notes and Queries* 232 (1987), 178–82

Metlitzki, Dorothee, 'The Voyages and Travels of Sir John Mandeville', in her *The Matter of Araby in Medieval England* (New Haven, 1977), pp. 220–39

Miller, B.D.H., Review of *The Bodley Version of Mandeville's Travels*, ed. M.C. Seymour, *Medium Ævum* 35 (1966), 71–78

Milton, Giles, *The Riddle and the Knight: In Search of Sir John Mandeville* (London, 1996)

Minto, William, *A Manual of English Prose Literature Biographical and Critical Designed Mainly to Show Characteristics of Style*, 3rd ed. (Edinburgh and London, 1886)

Montégut, Émile, 'Sir John Maundeville', in his *Heures de lecture d'un critique* (Paris, 1891) pp. 235–337

Morrall, Eric John, ed., *Sir John Mandevilles Reisebeschreibung in deutscher*

Übersetzung von Michel Velser nach der Stuttgarter Papierhandschrift Cod. HB V 86 (Berlin, 1974)

Moseley, C.W.R.D., 'The Availability of *Mandeville's Travels* in England, 1356–1750', *Library* 5th ser. 30 (1975), 125–33

———, 'The Metamorphoses of Sir John Mandeville', *Yearbook of English Studies* 4 (1974), 5–25

Nicholson, Edward B., 'John of Burgundy, alias "Sir John Mandeville"', *Academy* 25 (12 Apr. 1884), 261–62

———, 'Mandeville's Travels', *Academy* 10 (11 Nov. 1876), 477

Nicholson, Edward B., and Henry Yule, 'Mandeville, Jehan de', in *Encyclopaedia Britannica*, 9th ed. (London, 1883), XV, 473–75

Phillips, J.R.S., *The Medieval Expansion of Europe* (Oxford, 1988)

———, 'The Quest for Sir John Mandeville', in *The Culture of Christendom: Essays in Medieval History in Commemoration of Denis L.T. Bethell*, ed. Marc Anthony Meyer (London, 1993), pp. 243–55

Ralegh, Sir Walter, *The Discovery of the Large, Rich and Beautiful Empire of Guiana*, ed. Robert H. Schomburgk, Hakluyt Society 3 (London, 1848)

Robbins, Rossell Hope, 'Mirth in Manuscripts', *Essays and Studies* ns 21 (1968), 1–28

Ridder, Klaus, *Jean de Mandevilles 'Reisen': Studien zur Überlieferungsgeschichte der deutschen Übersetzung des Otto von Diemeringen*, Münchener Texte und Untersuchungen zur deutschen Literatur des Mittelalters 99 (Munich, 1991)

Riquer, Martí de, 'El "Voyage" de sir John Mandeville en català', in *Miscel.lània d'homenatge a Enric Moreu-Rey*, ed. Albert Manent i Segimon and Joan Veny i Clar, 3 vols (Montserrat, 1988), III, 151–62

Ruddy, David Wilmot, *Scribes, Printers, and Vernacular Authority: A Study in the Late-Medieval and Early-Modern Reception of Mandeville's Travels* (unpublished doctoral dissertation, University of Michigan, 1995)

Schepens, Luc, 'Quelques observations sur la tradition manuscrite du *Voyage* de Mandeville', *Scriptorium* 18 (1964), 49–54

Schönborn, Carl, *Bibliographische Untersuchungen über die Reise-Beschreibung des Sir John Maundevile* (Breslau, 1840)

Seymour, M.C., 'The Early English Editions of *Mandeville's Travels*', *Library* 5th ser. 19 (1964), 202–07

———, 'The English Manuscripts of *Mandeville's Travels*', *Transactions of the Edinburgh Bibliographical Society* 4 (1966), 169–210

———, 'A Medieval Redactor at Work', *Notes and Queries* 206 (1961), 169–71

———, 'The Origin of the Egerton Version of *Mandeville's Travels*', *Medium Aevum* 30 (1961), 159–61

———, 'The Scribal Tradition of *Mandeville's Travels* in England', in Seymour, ed., *Metrical Version*, 193–97

———, 'The Scribal Tradition of Mandeville's *Travels*: The Insular Version', *Scriptorium* 18 (1964), 34–48

———, *Sir John Mandeville*, Authors of the Middle Ages 1 (Aldershot, 1993)

Sisam, Kenneth, ed., *Fourteenth Century Verse and Prose* (1921; repr. Oxford, 1970)

Smith, Kathleen L. 'A Fifteenth-Century Manuscript Reconstructed', *Bodleian Library Record* 7 (1966), 234–41

Tadie, Andrew A., 'Hakluyt's and Purchas's Use of the Latin Version of Mandeville's "Travels"', in *Acta Conventus Neo-Latini Turonensis: Troisième Congrès International d'Etudes Néo-Latins, Tours, Sept. 1976*, ed. Jean-Claude Margolin (Paris, 1980), pp. 537–45

Tzanaki, Rosemary, *Mandeville's Medieval Audiences: A Study on the Reception of the Book of Sir John Mandeville (1371–1550)* (Aldershot, 2003)

Vogels, Johann, 'Handscriftliche Untersuchungen über die englische Version Mandeville's', *Jahresbericht über das Realgymnasium zu Crefeld*, Schuljahr 1890–91 (Crefeld, 1891), 3–52

Zacher, Christian K., *Curiosity and Pilgrimage: The Literature of Discovery in Fourteenth-Century England* (Baltimore, 1976)

————, 'Travel and Geographical Writings', in *A Manual of the Writings in Middle English 1050–1500*, ed. Albert E. Hartung (New Haven, CT, 1986), VII, 2235–54, 2449–66

8

John Trevisa

A. S. G. EDWARDS

The place of John Trevisa in the history of Middle English prose is hard to convey in summary terms. The amount of original writing in his corpus is extremely small in relation to its overall size. Yet he is arguably among the most important prose writers of the later fourteenth century in England.

Trevisa's major claim to significance lies in the extent of his activities as a translator. The most important of his translations are those of two Latin prose works, Ranulf Higden's *Polychronicon* ('History of the world') and Bartholomaeus Anglicus's *De proprietatibus rerum* ('On the properties of things'). The former was a universal history prepared by a monk at the Benedictine abbey of St Werburgh at Chester between (roughly) 1330 and 1360. The latter, originally compiled by a Franciscan about 1225 in France, is among the most influential of medieval encyclopedias. In addition, Trevisa produced a translation of another important thirteenth-century work, in this case one of political instruction, Aegidius Romanus's *De regimine principum* ('Concerning the rule of princes'), as well a number of shorter translations: of the apocryphal *Gospel of Nicodemus* (still unpublished), and of fourteenth-century controversial works by William Ockham, his *Dialogus inter militem et clericum* and Richard Fitzralph's *Defensio curatorum*. (His possible involvement in another major translation project of his time is discussed below.) His only original works were a brief, introduction and dedicatory epistle to the *Polychronicon*. Translation was evidently the activity that occupied most of his literary energy throughout his life.

The pattern of Trevisa's life is one that seemed to have afforded maximum opportunity and maximum encouragement to such an activity. Little is known about his early life. He was almost certainly born in Cornwall, possibly in Trevessa, the place from which his name may be derived. His first appearance in surviving records comes in 1362, when he was admitted to Exeter College, Oxford, in the Lent term of that year, a date which, supposing he was admitted as an undergraduate (as seems most likely), suggests he was born some fifteen to twenty years before, that is, c. 1340, more or less contemporary with Chaucer. In 1369 he removed from Exeter to Queen's College, seemingly to engage in study for a doctorate in divinity. Trevisa remained associated with Queen's until 1379, when he was expelled from the college for a time. He seems to have subsequently regained his association with Queen's and rented rooms there in the 1380s and 1390s. He had become a priest in 1370.

Possibly at some time in the mid-1370s, perhaps in 1374, Trevisa became vicar of Berkeley, in Gloucestershire. He does not seem to have been always resident there, but he does seem to have held the position until his death. Around 1387, he also became canon of Westbury on Trym near Bristol. He was dead before May 1402.

This summary serves to make clear the scholarly and clerical shape of Trevisa's life. One institution, Oxford, and one man, Thomas, Lord Berkeley, were crucial in establishing that shape. Oxford would have refined his skills as a Latinist, and (as we shall see) provided him with an environment in which the issue of translation into the vernacular was of immediate relevance. It also gave him access to scholarly libraries, particularly that of Queen's College, that contained copies of the Latin *Polychronicon* and *De proprietatibus rerum*, as well as other books he may have drawn on for supplementary information.

But the role of Thomas, Lord Berkeley, as his clerical and literary patron seems to have been of even more crucial importance in the shaping of his career. It was seemingly through Berkeley's influence that Trevisa obtained all his clerical appointments. Berkeley is explicitly identified as the patron of Trevisa's major translations, and is associated by implication with all the others.

We do not know the circumstances that led Berkeley to support Trevisa's clerical and literary careers so extensively. Doubtless in the later fourteenth century there were always prospects of advancement for a well-educated cleric, especially one capable of writing in more than one language. What is clear is that Trevisa was extremely fortunate in gaining the favour of such a patron. Thomas Berkeley was one of the wealthiest and most powerful members of the nobility in the late fourteenth and early fifteenth centuries (for extensive discussion of Berkeley's career and his role as patron see Hanna). But what makes Berkeley's patronage particularly unusual is the extent to which it extended beyond obtaining for Trevisa various clerical appointments to shaping the form of his literary career by commissioning his major translations.

For Trevisa insists on the importance of Berkeley's role in the creation of his translations. In the Preface to what was probably the earliest of them, the *Polychronicon*, which was done between 1385 and 1387, he addresses Berkeley to claim that 'ȝe made me do þys medful dede' (Waldron, 295), and at the end of the *De proprietatibus rerum*, completed in 1398, he makes the same claim: 'Sir Thomas, lord of Berkeley, made me make this translacioun' (p. 1396/12–13). Berkeley's patronal role is also acknowledged in his translation of the apocryphal *Gospel of Nicodemus* which he asserts was undertaken 'at the instaunce of Thomas . . . lord of Berkeley'. The only one of Trevisa's major translations that does not mention Thomas Berkeley as patron is the one that was probably his last, his translation of Aegidius Romanus's *De regimine principum*, which he had possibly not completed at the time of his death; however, the sole manuscript of this, Bodley Digby 233, is associated with the Berkeley family (see Briggs 1998, 1999). Berkeley is not associated explicitly with Trevisa's shorter translations, of William Ockham's *Dialogus inter militem et clericum* and Richard Fitzralph's *Defensio curatorum*, neither of which can be precisely dated. But their appearance only in a number of manuscripts of Trevisa's *Polychronicon* translation suggests that they are likely to have been contemporaneous with it and therefore also associated with Berkeley.

The motives for Berkeley's interest in sponsoring Trevisa's translations resist certain resolution. (For some discussion of the possible factors that may have underlain Berkeley's commissioning of these translations, and particularly their political implications, see Somerset.) What seems likely is that Berkeley's interest seems to have extended beyond patronage to ensure the wider promulgation of Trevisa's works within his own circle. While no copies of Trevisa's works apart from the *De regimine principum* survive that can be directly linked to Thomas Berkeley himself, there are some that can be connected with his family: both a manuscript of the *Polychronicon* (BL, MS Add. 24194), and one containing his *Gospel of Nicodemus* (in BL, MS Add. 16165) have links to Berkeley's son-in-law, Richard Beauchamp.

It seems most likely that all of Trevisa's established corpus of translation was undertaken after he removed to Gloucestershire to become vicar at Berkeley. Such translations very probably began in the mid-1380s with the *Polychronicon*, although a number of his shorter translations lack any indication of date and could possibly have preceded it. But it must seem curious that a scholar in his middle years should suddenly undertake such a massive translation into the vernacular, amounting to over a million words, and should complete it so expeditiously within two years. Such a swift and accomplished achievement suggests a degree of proficiency as translator that cannot be readily accounted for in someone without earlier, considerable experience in rendering Latin into English.

There have been those who have sought to find some explanation for Trevisa's seemingly suddenly revealed fluency as translator in his earlier career at Oxford. His contemporaries at Oxford included John Wyclif (c. 1330–1384), who had rooms at Queen's College between 1363 and 1365, and who became the focus for the protests at Oxford in the 1370s and early 1380s that mark the first beginnings of English religious non-conformity. Another colleague at Queen's was Nicholas Hereford, one of the translators of the Early Version of the Bible into English in the late fourteenth century, which project is associated with Wyclif's name. And in 1482, when William Caxton produced the first printed edition of the *Polychronicon*, he credited Trevisa in his Preface with a translation of 'the Byble', presumably the Wycliffite Bible. It is hard to assess Caxton's casual and unsubstantiated attribution (for an examination of the evidence see Fowler 1961). But it is not unreasonable to suppose that Trevisa was certainly aware of issues connected with vernacular translation that were current during his time at Queen's. It may also to be relevant to note that among the manuscripts in the College library were a number of works relevant to Bible translation (for details see Fowler 1993, 17).

At the very least Trevisa would have found himself at Oxford in an environment where vernacular prose translation was an issue of immediate concern. And, given his later evident developed proficiency in this mode, it is likely that Trevisa's interest in the form significantly antedated his earliest datable effort, the *Polychronicon* translation. Bible translation would have been a natural focus for such an interest during his time at Oxford. But the evidence for his direct involvement in translation of the Wycliffe Bible is wholly circumstantial.

What is clear is that by the time he began his identifiable career as a trans-

lator Trevisa had developed a coherent set of principles for the practice of translation and the techniques to be employed in it. These principles are set out in
what is probably his earliest writing, his most substantial pieces of original
prose, his *Dialogus inter dominum et clericum* and *Epistola*. These works appear
as the prefatory materials to the *Polychronicon*.

At one level, the *Dialogus* is clearly intended to represent some version of
Trevisa's relationship with his patron. It consists largely of the Lord's dismissive
answers ('a blere-yʒed man, bot he were al blynd of wyt, myʒte ysee þe solucion
of þis reson', Waldron, 292) to the questions ('feble argementys', Waldron, 291)
of the Clerk, a figure clearly for Trevisa himself. It begins with a general assertion of the desirability of translation into English, even for those who read Latin,
against the professed resistance of the Clerk to this proposition. It also includes,
interestingly, a specific justification for biblical translation into the vernacular, a
tenet of Wycliffite doctrine. Trevisa sees such translation as part of a natural
historical process, continuing a movement that had already seen the Bible pass
from Hebrew to Greek to Latin to French:

> . . . holy wryt was translated out of Hebrew ynto Gru and out of Gru into
> Latyn and þanne out of Latyn ynto Frensch. Þanne what haþ Englysch
> trespased þat hyt myʒt noʒt be translated into Englysch? (Waldron, 292)

The *Dialogus* goes on to affirm the benefits of prose over verse as a mode for
translation: 'for comynlych prose ys more clear þan ryme, mor esy and more
pleyn to knowe and vnderstonde' (Waldron, 293).

The *Dialogus* is followed by the *Epistola* in which Trevisa sets out his actual
principles of translation:

> For to make þis translacion cleer and pleyn to be knowe and vnderstonde, in
> som place Y schal sette word vor word and actyue vor actyue and passiue for
> passyue arewe ryʒt as a stondeþ withoute changing of þe ordre of wordes. But
> yn som place Y mot change þe rewe and þe ordre of wordes and sette þe
> actyue vor þe passiue and aʒenward. And yn som place y mot sette a reson vor
> a word to telle what hyt meneþ. (Waldron, 294)

These views affirm a basic tenet of translation: fidelity to the source being
translated. They also articulate the parameters of acceptable variation from such
fidelity: changes between the active and passive voices, the necessity for differences in word order, and the need for some elaboration to clarify sense ('y mot
sette a reson vor a word to telle what hyt meneþ').

It is not always easy to assess how closely such claims were enacted in practice since all of Trevisa's major translations were of widely popular Latin works
each of which survives in more than a hundred manuscript copies. Modern
scholarship has not been able to identify the precise manuscript, or manuscripts,
from which he worked for any of his translations. But in general terms there
seem no grounds to doubt either Trevisa's capacity for faithful translation or his
inclination to undertake it. Certainly this has been the view of those who have
offered the most sustained analysis of this matter (see Lawler 1983). But
without identification of the actual manuscripts from which he worked, the

degree of accuracy his translations embodied and a full understanding of his translational techniques cannot be properly assessed.

There is a further problem that needs to be raised but which also cannot be resolved. This has to do with Trevisa's general practice in preparing his translations. Beyond a certain point it is difficult to generalize about his translational techniques. One fundamental problem is that neither of his major translations, *Polychronicon* and *De proprietatibus rerum*, has been edited in ways that seem to take full account of their textual traditions as reflected in the surviving manuscript evidence. The evidence of the manuscripts of his translations seems, at times, to suggest that he may have undertaken them in more than one stage. Some manuscripts of several of them offer evidence that there may have been more than one version of the same translation, or, possibly, of part of the same translation. The general tendency of these different versions is not easy to characterize briefly, but it does suggest a tendency to produce an initial literal translation followed by one that is revised in various ways. Perry saw evidence of such revision in the *Dialogus inter militem et clericum* (Perry, li–liii; though he was unclear whether some, all or any of the revision might derive from Trevisa himself); Fristedt has suggested such revision in part of the *Polychronicon* and argued that 'Trevisa's revisions were made by stages' (Fristedt, 39). And revision has also been suggested as an explanation for the consistent variation between groups of manuscripts of the *De proprietatibus rerum* (see Edwards 2003).

It is not possible to reach any very clear conclusions about the question of revision, given the relatively primitive state of Trevisa textual studies. The *Polychronicon* has not been edited for over a hundred years and the edition was based on imperfect knowledge of the manuscripts (see however now Waldron 2004). The recent *De Proprietatibus Rerum* edition is controlled by unexamined assumptions about Trevisa's practice as translator and his source manuscript. But it would clearly affect our understanding of Trevisa's sense of his role as translator if it could be established that he was concerned to revise what may have been initially quite literal versions of his translations to produce more polished renderings.

What can be examined are the general nature of Trevisa's techniques of translation and the extent to which these created a distinctive style.

It seems certain that Trevisa saw himself, as his *Epistola* suggests, as primarily concerned with faithfully rendering his source text. One indication of this concern with fidelity in translation is his treatment of a number of his own additions to his source. He carefully differentiates these from the source itself by the insertion of his own name immediately before the relevant passage, as in this note on the term 'Olympias' in his *Polychronicon* translation:

Treuisa: The Grees usede somtyme tornementes and dedes of myȝt and of strengþe at þe foot of þe hil mons Olympus, ones in fyve ȝere, and clepede suche dedes and pleyes Olympias; and also þe firste fyve ȝere of suche pleies þey cleped þe firste Olimpias and þe secounde fyue ȝere of suche dedes and pleyes þe secounde Olympias and þe þridde five ȝere þe þridde Olympias, and so forþ of alle þe oþere (IV, 253)

The note typifies both his general way of marking his own contributions to his translations and the usual nature of his additions: to offer supplementary and/or clarifying information absent from his source. This note also offers testimony to Trevisa's economical use of such new material. This passage occurs with minor variations in two of his other translations, the *De proprietatibus rerum* (522/32–523/6), and the unpublished *Gospel of Nicodemus* in BL Add. 16165, fol. 94v. Such passages are not frequent in Trevisa's translations. But they demonstrate at least a degree of willingness to move beyond strict translation to amplify the implications of his source materials as his knowledge permitted.

A few other aspects of Trevisa's style of translation are sufficiently pervasive to be readily identified. One is his tendency to use doublets, to translate one Latin word by two English equivalents. A passage from the *Polychronicon* typifies this practice:

> . . . it is harde for to telle how grete worschippe he dede to Stigandus, for he wold arise aȝenst hym and come aȝenst hym wiþ processioun, and þat wiþ greet boost and array, bote al þat was iclosed and ihid in þat doynge come out afterward clere inow (VII, 251)

Here the doublets 'boost and array' and 'iclosed and ihid' translate the Latin noun and verb 'pompae' and 'tegebatur' respectively. The refusal to be satisfied with a single English equivalent for the Latin permits Trevisa to give a fuller and more nuanced sense of the single Latin word by enumerating distinct aspects of its original sense.

Trevisa also shows himself in the *Polychronicon* to be capable of a narrative style that is simultaneously accurate, but tauter and more fluent than might be expected in what is often an annalistic chronicle. Here, for example, is his description of Henry I:

> He wolde fiȝte more gladly wiþ counsaille þan wiþ swerde; he wolde ete to staunche his honger, and nouȝt for gloteneye; he wolde nevere drinke but ȝif he wer aþurst. In hym self and al his meyne alway he hatede outrage of mete and of drynke. (VII, 419)

Trevisa's version of Higden's Latin was probably quite like this (I quote from the version printed in the Rolls Series edition):

> Libentius bellabat consilio quam gladio. In cibando magis temperans esuriem quam urgens ingluviem, potationi praeter sitim nunquam indulgens, crapulam in se et in suis semper exsecrans.

The translation is clearly close to the Latin, but the changes suggest a careful sense of balance in the parallelism of all three clauses that are introduced by the same construction 'he wolde'. Against this parallelism he varies the translation of 'quam', rendering it first as 'þan' but when it recurs as 'and nouȝt for' so that the underlying syntactic structure remains clear but does not become mechanical. And the syntax is also modified so that the final clause of the Latin, 'crapulam in se et in suis semper exsecrans', becomes a separate sentence. The rhythms of the passage are varied in small but evidently deliberate ways to create clear, distinct syntactic patterns.

Such characteristics can be seen as consistent with Trevisa's broad translational aims as part of his general desire for clarity and accuracy, even if this requires some adjustment or expansion to his sources. At their most positive these attributes create a fluent, flexible style that can function effectively in different modes, both narrative and expository. Here, for example, is an expository passage from the *De proprietatibus rerum*, part of a larger classification of the organs of the body in Book V:

> Also among þe membres is gret diuersite in dignite and order; for somme ȝeueþ of hymself and *takeþ* nouȝt of oþir: as þe herte *takeþ* nouȝt of oþir, as Aristotel seiþ. Neuerþeles þe herte ȝeueþ to oþir lif and meuynge. And somme ȝeueþ and *takeþ*, as þe lyuour and brayne *takeþ* strengþe of þe herte, and be principalles of vertues; for þey ȝeueþ vertues to oþir membres. And somme membres neyþir ȝeueþ ne *takeþ*, and stondiþ in her oune vertue . . .
>
> (167/28–34)

Here there are few doublets; the main concern of the passage is to establish the distinction between the function of various organs, which is expressed in terms of giving and taking. As the italicization makes clear, the words are re-iterated, but not in any mechanical way. The passage is marked by small but deft variations of syntax, sometimes expressed in adjustments of the parallel terms: 'ȝeueþ of hymself and takeþ nouȝt of oþir', 'ȝeueþ and takeþ', 'ȝeueþ ne takeþ', sometimes by suppression of one of these terms: 'þe herte ȝeueþ to oþir lif and meuynge', 'for þey ȝeueþ vertues to oþir membres'. Distinctions are made using a limited lexical range, but they are made in ways that are clear and effective mainly through these changes of syntactic pattern.

But Trevisa's techniques were not always successful. His use of doublets, for example, could prove an impediment to clear translation. At times it both clogs the movement of his prose, and obscures more than it clarifies, as in this passage from his discussion of medicine in the *De proprietatibus rerum*:

> To ȝeue couenable and trewe medicine aȝeynes diuers sikenes and periles, a good physician nediþ to loke wel aboute and be ful ware and ful wel avised, for noþing lettiþ more helþ of seke men þan vnkonnynge and necligense of physiciens. (435/12–15)

Here the doublets occur as adjectives 'couenable and trewe', nouns 'sikenes and periles', 'vnkonnynge and necligense' and verbs 'ful ware and ful wel avised'. None of these offers very exact forms of parallelism: 'couenable' means 'appropriate' not 'true'; 'vnkonnynge' means 'lack of knowledge' hence is not strictly equatable with 'necligence'; 'sikenes' is much more specific than 'periles'. Only the verbal doublets offer close synonyms. It may be that Trevisa's use of doublets increases as he has to deal with more technical matter, as he does in parts of the *De proprietatibus rerum*, and that he found it correspondingly harder to find precise equivalents for terms and concepts that lay outside his general range of knowledge. Sometimes such difficulties seem to have led him to employ triplets rather than doublets, as in this passage from his Bartholomaeus Anglicus translation in the chapter 'On thunder':

And þis ly3tnynge smytiþ, þurliþ, and brenneþ þingis þat he touchiþ, and meltiþ and cleueþ and brekeþ, and no bodiliche þinge wiþstondiþ hit.

(593/1–3)

The effort at precision in such instances clearly required greater prolixity.

At its most effective Trevisa's prose is lucid and unpretentious, conveying information in ways that are deftly cadenced, without seeking to impose any stylistic presence that gets in the way of its essentially factual and expository purposes. Take the following passage from the *De proprietatibus rerum*, which discusses geography:

> Þe men ben bolde and hardy. Þe londe is moyste with waters and ryuers and fayre with plenteuous feldes, wodes, and medes and ful of noble bestes wiþ few beestes wonderlyche shape, with fewe venymous bestes outake frogges and adders. And generalyche and comunelyche þis londe is peysible and quiete. And þis londe Belgica hath many diuers peple and cuntrees with somedele dyuerses langages. (740/14–20)

One notes, of course, the doublets: 'bolde and hardy', 'generalyche and comunelyche', 'peysible and quiete'; but also the appearance of seemingly parallel forms that are not quite doublets – 'waters and ryuers', 'peple and cuntrees' – that expand the scope of these references. Repetition of certain key words becomes here a way of preserving control over the distinctions in subject matter, as in: 'ful of noble bestes wiþ few beestes wonderlyche shape, with fewe venymous bestes', and also of establishing both distinction and parallelism within the sentence: 'diuers peple . . . dyuerses langages'. The overall effect of the passage is one of clarity, whereby various categories of information are clearly discriminated through firm syntactical and lexical control.

The use of repetition in this passage can become elsewhere a controlling technique, a kind of lexical adhesive that keeps the focus of exposition clear:

> Þanne it is nou3t *semeliche* þat housebondes be to gelous of here wyues. Noþer it is *semeliche* þat wyues haue ward and kepyng ordeyned by þe housebondes. Noþer is hit semelich þat housebondes ben gelous, but þei schulde take heede of condiciouns of persones and of vsage and manere of þe contray, and eche housebonde schal be þeweliche besy and redyliche rewle his owne wif. And so it is *semeliche* þat eche housebonde loue ordinatliche his own wif . . . (*Governaunce*, 206/24–30)

Here, of course, the stress of the argument falls on establishing the 'semeliche' parameters of the relationship between husband and wife, the terms of what is proper and appropriate. To this end the word is simply reiterated (as italicized), in each sentence, with no recourse to variation through synonyms or doublets. The focus of Trevisa's concerns here is to give appropriate emphasis to a concept that is amplified through illustration of its various aspects, not through attempts at lexical equivalence.

It is possible to recognize some aspects of Trevisa's overall achievement as a translator. At his best, as I have tried to suggest, he could be an unobtrusive stylist, conveying the import of his source material through what were generally deftly efficient translational techniques and a supple grasp of syntax. His sense of his role as translator required adherence to principles of fidelity and the only occasional intrusion of his identity through his signed additions.

It follows from the nature of the material that he translated that Trevisa's primary achievement was as a transmitter of information, both historical and scientific, particularly in his two major translations. It is not a role that affords much scope for the development of a wide range of stylistic effects. But it is an important one. Trevisa's historical significance lies primarily in his usefulness, in the materials he made accessible to readers in the vernacular in an accessible, generally accurate form.

His importance is reflected in the influence of these major translations. Initially it was probably not very wide. Neither one survives in large numbers of copies. There are fourteen complete manuscripts of the *Polychronicon* and eight of the *De proprietatibus rerum*. I noted earlier the circulation of some copies within Berkeley's own family circle. Such evidence as the earliest histories of the other surviving manuscripts affords suggests that Trevisa's major translations circulated chiefly among an elite audience of the wealthy, among the nobility and gentry, those most obviously able to purchase copies of such large and generally expensively produced works. These owners of manuscripts of the *De proprietatibus rerum* translation included such affluent fifteenth-century bibliophiles as Sir Thomas Chaworth (who owned what is now New York, Columbia University MS 263, together with other vernacular books in verse and prose), and Richard Beauchamp, bishop of Salisbury (who owned New York, Pierpont Morgan MS M 875). The audience for the *Polychronicon* seems to have much the same (see Waldron, especially 282–83).

But these works quickly seem to have assumed a wider, more influential role in the cultural history of later medieval England. The influence of the major translations can be seen in a wide range of medieval English works (see Edwards 1984 and the further examples and references cited there). Both the *Polychronicon* and the *De proprietatibus rerum* were printed in the fifteenth century, by William Caxton in 1482, by Wynkyn de Worde in 1495 respectively. Both had a extensive post-medieval afterlife; they were both reprinted in the sixteenth century, and the *De proprietatibus rerum* achieved an enhanced identity through the expansion of the work by Stephen Batman, published by Thomas East as *Batman vppon Bartholome* (1582). In this guise it became a repository of traditional lore for Renaissance readers. Trevisa's role as a conveyor of various kinds of information into English was thus continued and proved capable of redeployment for later generations and very different ages.

BIBLIOGRAPHY

The most up-to-date and comprehensive account of Trevisa's life and works and of studies of him is by David C. Fowler, *John Trevisa*, Authors of the Middle Ages 2 (Aldershot, 1993). The following listing is therefore highly selective; it is limited to primary works and to those studies cited in the text, which include a number that have appeared since Fowler's work.

Primary Works

Dialogus inter Militem et Clericum, Richard Fitzralph's Sermon: 'Defensio Curatorum' and Methodius: Þe Bygynnyng of þe World and þe Ende of Worldes, ed. A.J. Perry, EETS os 167 (London, 1925)
John Trevisa's Translation of the Polychronicon of Ranulph Higden, Book VI, ed. R.A. Waldron (Heidelberg, 2004)
The Governance of Kings and Princes: John Trevisa's Middle English Translation of the De Regimine Principum, ed. David C. Fowler, Charles F. Briggs and Paul G. Remley, Garland Medieval Texts 19 (New York, 1997)
On The Properties of Things: John Trevisa's Translation of Bartholomaeus Anglicus, De Proprietatibus Rerum, gen. ed. M.C. Seymour, 3 vols (Oxford, 1975, 1988)
Polychronicon, ed. C. Babington and J.R. Lumby, 9 vols (London, 1865–86)
Waldron, R.A. 'Trevisa's Original Prefaces on Translation: A Critical Edition', in *Medieval English Studies Presented to George Kane*, ed. E.D. Kennedy, R. Waldron and J. Wittig (Cambridge, 1988), pp. 285–99

Secondary Works

Briggs, Charles F., 'MS Digby 233 and the Patronage of John Trevisa's *De Regimine Principum*', *English Manuscript Studies 1100–1700* 7 (1998), 249–63
———, *Giles of Rome's De Regimine Principum* (Cambridge, 1999)
Edwards, A.S.G., 'John Trevisa', in *Middle English Prose: A Critical Guide to Major Authors and Genres*, ed. A.S.G. Edwards (New Brunswick, NJ, 1984), pp. 133–46
———, 'The Text of John Trevisa's Translation of Bartholomeus Anglicus' *De Proprietatibus Rerum*', *Text*, forthcoming
Fowler, David C., 'John Trevisa and the English Bible', *Modern Philology* 58 (1961), 81–98
Fristedt, Sven L., *The Wycliffe Bible, Part III: Relationships of Trevisa and the Spanish Medieval Bibles*, Stockholm Studies in English 28 (Stockholm, 1973)
Hanna, Ralph, 'Sir Thomas Berkeley and his Patronage', *Speculum* 64 (1989), 878–916
Lawlor, Traugott, 'On the Properties of John Trevisa's Major Translations', *Viator* 14 (1983), 267–88
Somerset, Fiona, *Clerical Discourse and Lay Audience in Late Medieval England* (Cambridge, 1998)
Waldron, Ronald A., 'The Manuscripts of Trevisa's *Polychronicon*', *Modern Language Quarterly* 51 (1990), 281–318

9

Anonymous Devotional Writings

VINCENT GILLESPIE

> Aske not who seide þus, but take heede what is seide.
> We oweþ in scriptures raþer to seke profitablenes þen highenes of langage.
> We owe as gladly to rede symple and devoute bokes as highe bokes and profounde sentences.
> (*Imitatio Christi*, first translation (c. 1450); ed. Biggs, p. 9)

Anonymity is the norm and the condition of late medieval English devotional writing. It is a state of mind shared between author and audience, a reflex of the humility and meekness that such writing sought to encourage and develop in the minds of its readers. Authors and their texts seek to articulate a truth that is above time, place and individual circumstances, and readers and hearers seek to escape from the here and now by longing to gaze on their God *sub specie aeternitatis*. The chances are that most of those anonymous authors were priests or male religious, exercising remotely and indirectly the *magisterium* of their teaching office. The conventional invocation of the writer's own spiritual incapacity and literary failings in describing matters of high theology, the efface-ment of the writer as only marginally more adept than those for whom he is writing ('helpeþ me wiþ preiers, for me lackiþ kunnynge, aȝens my grete febelenes' *The Orchard of Syon*; ed. Hodgson and Liegey, p. 16), are essential gestures in the spiritual roleplaying that leads to the strategic but controlled empowerment of the text's reader or recipient.

But such gestures of effacement may originally have been nothing more than a pious fiction. The apparent anonymity of writings produced and initially circu-lated in relatively circumscribed textual communities, whether an enclosed reli-gious order or a parochial community, may in fact have been readily identified with their producer, who may often also have been their original performer or reader. When the author of *The Orchard of Syon* plays with the governing meta-phor of his re-organisation of Catherine of Sienna's *Dialogo* for the Birgittine nuns of Syon, his claim that 'Grete laborer was I neuer, bodili ne gostli. I had neuer grete strengþe myȝtli to laboure wiþ spade ne wiþ schouel' (ed. Hodgson and Liegey, p. 16) finesses the tradition of incapacity in a way that suggests that he might have been identifiable to his original audience as one of the Brethren of Syon.

Of course, once such texts find a wider readership, either by transmission of the whole work or through copying of extracts, the anonymity changes from a gestural modesty to a more substantial authorial absence. In this world, especially in the suspicious and sometimes sinister intellectual climate of anti-Lollard polemic and the premature Counter Reformation inaugurated by the Councils of Pisa (1409), Constance (1414–18), and Basle (1431–49), anonymity was both a political weapon (as the studied and sustained absence of named Lollard authors suggests), a potential escape from culpability, and a defence against the misuse of one's writings that might result from Lollard interpolation (considered by the hierarchy and their agents to be one of the defining strategies of the heresy), or from inappropriate selection and juxtaposition. The *auctoritas* of such anonymous writings had to be self-validating. Denied an external authorial guarantee, they derived their authority from the contexts in which they were circulated or from the status and theological integrity of the textual milieux (often monasteries, cathedrals or other centres of clerical activity) from which they were derived (Doyle 1989, 1990; Cannon 1999). Because of this, such materials rarely enjoy a purely lay circulation. Clerical involvement in the production, transmission, circulation and ultimately reception (quite often through bequest of a book that had enjoyed lay circulation back into clerical or religious ownership) of these writings means that it is impossible to identify a distinctively lay devotional ideology. Lay taste in devotional books was usually fostered, supplied and often (perhaps increasingly) controlled by the availability and supply of such texts from and through clerical intermediaries (Doyle 1953).

After 1380 the range of such books would have tentatively but steadily expanded to include, as a first stage, versions of the devotional, paramystical and aspirantly contemplative materials that had earlier been the distinctive preserve of nuns, anchoresses and other women religious (a stage apotheosised by the canon of English prose texts gathered in the Vernon manuscript in the 1390s (Pearsall 1990; Hanna 1997)). Subsequently we find more ambitious adaptations and translations of materials originally targeted at male contemplatives and now repackaged for nuns and occasional well-born (and often female) lay readers whose textual interests and competencies are increasingly difficult to distinguish from those of their sisters under the veil (e.g. Jolliffe 1974 and 1975; Hutchison 1989; Riddy 1996). By the early fifteenth century, such texts are increasingly coming to recognise and make allowances for the fact that their readership may, by accident or design, spill over beyond the confines of the nunnery or parochial library (Gillespie 1989). The role of the Carthusians and Birgittines in this process remains a central focus of study, though the emphasis is now moving away from the Carthusians towards a more sustained exploration of the textual agency of the Birgittines of Syon (Sargent 1976; Doyle 1981; Gillespie 1999; Gillespie 2004).

'Deuoute redyng of holy Bokes ys called one of the partes of contemplacyon for yt causyth moche grace and comforte to the soulle yf it be well and dyscretely vsed' (ed. Blunt, pp. 65–6). This advice in *The Mirror of Our Lady* (probably written c. 1430) is designed to be applied to any kind of religious book encountered by the nuns of Syon Abbey, many of whom would not have understood much Latin. Their literary tastes and abilities probably differed little from those of their family members who remained in the world (many of whom gave them books and may in their turn have acquired books or individual texts from the abbey). So the advice offered to them in the *Mirror* provides an informed view of the kinds of vernacular books likely to come into their hands. Some books are purely affective, 'made to quyken & to sturre vp the affeccyons of the soule' and dealing with the love of God and the fear of damnation. Such texts may be considered a basic component of the vernacular writing for lay audiences that seeks to manipulate the audience into spiritual compliance. Other books:

> ar made to enforme the vnderstondynge. & to tel how spiritual persones oughte to be gouerned in all theyr lyuynge that they may knowe what they shall leue. & what they shall do. how they shulde laboure in clensyng of theyr conscyence. & in gettyng of vertewes how they shulde withstonde temptacyons & suffer trybulacyons. & how they shall pray. & occupy them in gostly excercyse. with many suche other full holy doctrynes. (ed. Blunt, p. 68)

Such diagnostic texts represent a change in the dynamic of devotional writing in English. They rely for their success on an informed and developed sense of self-awareness on the part of their readers, and an embracing by them of spiritual autonomy and responsibility. These new emphases on personal responsibility and encouragement for individual spiritual growth are perhaps the hallmarks of vernacular devotional texts produced after 1380.

Devotional and didactic books had, of course, been being produced in English for a full century and a half before Wyclif and his followers gave a heterodox accent to the voices crying in what must sometimes have felt like the late fourteenth-century wilderness of accelerating institutional decay and increasing social chaos. Ralph Hanna has drawn attention to substantial book-making activity in mid to late fourteenth-century Yorkshire and in the South West Midlands (Hanna 1999; 2003). But before 1380, the kinds of religious books to which a literate laymen might have had access would generally have been more didactic and confessional than devotional and contemplative in nature (*The Book of Vices and Virtues* and other offshoots and offcuts from the French tradition of the *Somme le roi*), more ascetic than affective (with the exception, perhaps, of the English epistles of Rolle); and would more probably have been in verse rather than prose (*The Prick of Conscience, Handling Sin, Speculum vitae*). These are the 'bokes ynowe/ To telle men what Dowel is, Dobet and Dobest bothe' that Ymaginatif mentions to Will in *Piers Plowman* (Passus XII. 17–18, ed. Schmidt). But many of the thirteenth- and early four-teenth- century religious books alluded to by Ymaginatif operated in an austere world of the schematised moral taxonomies of the Deadly Sins, and Will's dissatisfaction with such texts and his search for 'kynde knowyng' signals the beginning of a shift of emphasis from catechesis towards contemplation.

It is, of course, a long way from catechesis to contemplation. The teaching syllabus evolved by the English bishops in the thirteenth century, partly in response to the Fourth Lateran Council of 1215 and parallel developments in pastoral theology, required the laity to know and be examined on the Creeds, the *Pater Noster*, the Commandments and the Deadly Sins, sometimes supplemented by the Sacraments and later joined by the *Ave Maria*. Clerical instruction on these matters from the pulpit and in the confessional was to be undertaken in the vernacular. This catechetic legislation provided an early impetus to the appearance of didactic texts in English in clerical miscellanies and their eventual transfer into lay hands (Russell 1962–63; Boyle 1985; Shaw 1985). In time, devotional texts often joined these didactic materials, frequently employing an emotional (or 'affective') appeal as a catalyst to engage the audience's sympathies with the suffering Christ or his tormented Mother during the events of the Passion. The agenda of such devotional texts is nicely described in one of William Caxton's printed books, *Quattuor Sermones*:

> Deuocion as clerkis sayn is a tendernes of herte wherby thou brekyst lyghtly into tearis, also a wylle of loue lyfte vp to God . . . meuyng the inward and outward to the seruyce of God. Suche deuocion purgyth bothe body and sowle. (ed. Blake 1975, p. 78)

Before 1380, these vernacular affective appeals rarely aspired to the more rarified world of contemplation which seeks to transcend imagery and emotions, and to gaze on God in a timeless and affectless union. Such ambitions were considered to be largely the preserve of enclosed contemplative monks and nuns, and were treated as a 'hid diuinite' (the Middle English translation of *mystica theologia*).

The late fourteenth-century efflorescence of writing by named or identifiable vernacular theologians rebalanced the weight given to contemplative as opposed to catechetic writing and recalibrated the primacy of the devotional over the didactic in vernacular writing. But catechetic and didactic texts remained the foundation for a burgeoning and increasingly colourful spectrum of religious writing and it is by no means unusual to find catechetic and contemplative materials in the same text (as in the various English versions and extracts from Edmund of Abingdon's *Speculum ecclesiae* [*Mirror of the Holy Church*], described in the Vernon copy as 'þe bok sikerly þat techeþ to liuen parfytliche' (ed. Horstman 1895, 1. 240)), or in the same manuscript miscellany (Hanna 1988, 1996). Such instructional materials were among the first religious texts to achieve wider vernacular dissemination, and many of these earlier texts remained in circulation or were adapted and recopied in later manuscripts. Catechetic and penitential texts remained necessary but in the fifteenth century were increasingly unlikely to be regarded as sufficient for the users of vernacular books of religion.

The Book for a Simple and Devout Woman, surviving in two fifteenth-century West Midland copies, extends the catechetic range of the *Somme le Roi* and the Latin penitentials of William Peraldus by the annexation of extracts and sections from a range of other spiritual writings which serve to broaden the utility and the moral scope of the text. Addressed to a specific woman (either lay or religious) apparently well-known to the author, the *Book* tries to move away from the generalised penitential train-spotting of many earlier works to a more rounded view of the dynamics, pathology and anxieties of a particular spiritual life:

> My dere suster, my consaile is þat þu fiȝte aȝeyn vayneglorie, for þerof þu art moste fondud. Dremes and siȝtes þat þu seest in þi slepe, ȝeue to hem no feiþe. Lyft þyn herte holiche from hem and haue hem alle suspecte, ne tel no worde bi hem to non to wite what þey wolde mene. Soþfaste siȝte is, and of parfite mede, knowynge of þyself, þorw þe whiche quykeneþ knowyng of God and vnyte wiþ hym. (ed. Diekstra, p. 300)

This authorial addition to the sources dramatises the difficulty of writing such works for an audience aware of its own spiritual potential, eager to realise it, newly hungry for signs of divine grace and for communion with the deity through dreams and visions, but vulnerable to self-delusion and in danger of error and spiritual pride. Such audiences needed more than catechetics.[1]

Books telling them how to avoid temptation or to deal with tribulation were part of the answer to their needs. The Latin *De remediis contra temptationes* was written by William Flete probably between 1352 and 1358. The text had considerable circulation in Latin and English, undergoing at least three recensions and elaborations of the vernacular text along the way (Hackett 1961; Hackett, Colledge and Chadwick 1964). The ascetic tenor and contents of the work ('suffren mekely and abyden pacyently' (ed. Colledge and Chadwick, p. 221)), the fact the Walter Hilton seems to have used Flete's text in his own writings, and that Hilton's works may have been drawn on for the expansions in the later English recensions, made an eventual ascription to Hilton unsurprising. Augmented and expanded over a century of use, the *De remediis* provides a useful barometer of devotional taste and pastoral need. It is found in manuscripts from the complete spectrum of religious use: from professed religious seeking probation and discretion of their own feelings, through parochial clergy using it in their spiritual guidance of others, to devout and literate laymen self-diagnosing the symptoms of their own spiritual wellbeing. The third and fullest recension is preserved in manuscripts from around the middle of the fifteenth century, including Bodl. MS Douce 322 and the closely related BL, MS Harley 1706 with their close connections to London nunneries and well-born London families (Doyle 1958). The copy in Bodl. MS Holkham Misc 41 survives in a manuscript that seems likely to have been produced for the Birgittine nuns of Syon. Usually addressed to a 'sustir', it also aspires to be gender inclusive ('Sister, alwey quan I speke of man in þis wrytinge, take it bothe for man and woman, for so it is ment in alle suche writinges, for al is mankende' (ed. Colledge and Chadwick, pp. 223–24)). The care and concern shown by the text for the doubts and fears experienced by a spiritually ambitious and advanced person, and the reassurance and support it offers such souls may originally have been targeted at those in religion. But the changed devotional circumstances of the fifteenth century when manuscripts containing such works were commissioned, acquired or even simply read by the laity means that the guidance is applicable to them as much as (if not more than) professed religious:

> And if 3e fele 3et ony dredis be ymagynacion or temptacion or for wordes þat
> 3e haue herde or haue rede in bokes, be þe whiche 3e dowte of sauacion,
> þanne þenketh on tho wordes þat crist hym self taughte to a man þat doutyd
> . . . And þerfore þenk weel þat his myght may do alle þinge, and his wisdam
> kan, and his goodnesse wole, and trusteth fully þer-to he wole saue 3ou.
> (ed. Colledge and Chadwick, p. 227)

---

[1] Likewise *A Myrour to Lewde Men and Wymmen* (ed. Nelson 1981), a fifteenth-century prose version of the popular and influential fourteenth-century Northern verse *summa* the *Speculum vitae*, shares with its parent text a deliberate extension of the catechetic and penitential emphasis of the *Somme le Roi* tradition into a broader and more subtly inflected model of devotional psychology.

The final sentence, with its play on verbal tenses and moods is reminiscent of the cadence of similar phrases in Julian of Norwich's *Shewings*, a reminiscence repeated elsewhere in this version of Flete. Many of the distractions and temptations that are described and prescribed against relate to quite advanced stages of spiritual development where the devil will conspire against those who seek to occupy themselves 'highly in contemplacion or in goode meditacions' and against those who 'haue be custom good sterynges and deuoute þou3tes and felyngis of meditacions and of contemplacions', singling out 'suyche parauenture as ben solatarye' who will be tempted to abandon the discipline of their Divine Office (ed. Colledge and Chadwick, p. 232). But most of the text avoids such specific targeting, addressing 'goddis seruauntes, and also worldly men and women' both of whom may be tempted with fears of their own sinfulness:

> the goostly lyueris he tempteth to dispeir be inputtynge of false dreedys and streyt conscience and be deep ymagynacion of predestinacion and in moo sondry wyses þan I kan telle. (ed. Colledge and Chadwick, p. 235)

The *De remediis* is an important and distinctive part of the textual hinterland of the late medieval manuscript transmission of writers such as Rolle and Hilton, and an interesting para-mystical and stylistic analogue to the spiritual struggles and temptations of Julian of Norwich, whose own text reveals a deep familiarity with the varied registers of contemporary devotional writing.

The Chastising of God's Children (probably written in the 1390s) is one of the most successful of the original Middle English devotional compilations (Sargent 1982; Sutherland 2004). It draws together material from Suso, the *Ancrene Wisse* (through the Latin extracts known as *Quandoque tribularis* (Allen 1923; Sargent 1984), themselves retranslated and widely disseminated in devotional miscellanies, including *Pore Caitif* and the third recension of William Flete's *De remediis contra temptaciones*), the *Stimulus Amoris* of James of Milan (probably translated into English by Walter Hilton in the 1390s as *The Pricking of Love* (ed. Kane 1983)), the important epistle on the discernment of visions by Alphonse of Pecia (produced as part of the process of promoting and conforming the authenticity of the revelations of St Birgitta of Sweden, whose canonisation in 1391 is alluded to in the *Chastising*), and translated extracts from book 2 of a Latin version of Jan Ruysbroeke's *Spiritual Espousals*. *The Chastising*'s success may be gauged not only by the care and coherence of its manuscript transmission but also by its influence on other compilations (especially *Disce mori* which borrows heavily from it (Jones 2000)), and the almost inevitable accolade for any orthodox compilation of a contemporary ascription to Hilton. As with other English adaptations from continental sources (especially Suso's *Orologium sapientiae*), the *Chastising* moves the emphasis from speculation to pragmatism and from abstract contemplation to ambitious devotionalism (Lovatt 1968; 1982). Its watchword, repeated at the end of each chapter, is 'Watch and pray that you may not enter into temptation', a sentiment that is typical of the cautiously permissive mood of the new English devotionalism. Perhaps one of the best examples of non-mystical 'vernacular theology' in England, it uses its sources to make a sober and considered contri-

bution to contemporary debates about heresy, clerical authority and Bible translation. On translating Scripture, for example, the compiler puts devotional utility
ahead of the more scholastic and academic concerns expressed in the contemporary debates on the subject:

> Many men repreuen it to haue þe matyns or þe sautir or þe gospels or þe bible
> in englisshe, bicause þei mowe not be translated into vulgare, worde bi worde
> as it stondiþ, wiþoute grete circumlocucion . . . Naþeles I wil nat repreue
> suche translacion, ne I repreue nat to haue hem on englisshe, ne to rede on
> hem where þei mowen stire ȝou more to deuocion and to þe loue of god; but
> uttitrli to usen hem in englisshe and leue þe latin I holde it nat commendable.
>
> (ed. Bazire and Colledge, p. 221)[2]

He also has sane and rational advice on matters of clerical authority and heresy.
This is typical of the sober, moderate and careful teaching of *The Chastising*,
balancing between encouraging spiritual self-help (providing an outline of the
criteria for identifying and testing a true vision 'aftir þe writeng and opynyons
of doctours', for example) and (unsurprisingly) stressing the continuing intermediary and magisterial role of the Church on the other. With its idiomatic ease
and lucidity of exposition, *The Chastising* achieved the status of a classic, and
retained it throughout the fifteenth century and into print. Its sensible guidance
on sensitive spiritual matters such as temptations and 'ymaginacions' without
alarming a potentially vulnerable recipient were often imitated but rarely
bettered. Flete's *Remedies* and *The Chastising of God's Children* were a significant devotional legacy from the late fourteenth century to the ever-expanding
devotional marketplace of the fifteenth century.

The spiritual emancipation and empowerment of an increasingly literate laity
wrought lasting changes in the ways that such texts were composed, compiled,
targeted, transmitted and policed. At its most local and intensive, it gave rise to
the London networks that paid for, produced and circulated the so-called 'common-profit books' (Scase 1992). Some genetically related groups of manuscripts also suggest that it was possible for lay readers to order bespoke volumes
drawing on a common stock of exemplars inflected to suit their particular needs
or tastes (Gillespie 1984; Gillespie 1989; Connolly 2003). But this lay empowerment was usually metropolitan, largely accidental, and socially circumscribed
as the particular privilege of the gentry and mercantile classes (Hanna 1996;
Dutton 2000). It was also sometimes contested and often problematic in the
eyes of a contemporary church hierarchy responding to the challenges of a
domestic heresy (Lollardy) that was itself marked by a commitment to
vernacularity and lay access to religious texts. Ecbert of Schonau's thirteenth-
century *Soliloquies*, usually pseudonymously ascribed to Augustine and trans-

---

2 The same pragmatic attitude is found in *The Mirror of Our Lady*, composed for and perhaps by the
Birgittines some twenty years after Arundel's decrees of 1409. But there the compiler feels compelled
to report that he has received licence from the bishop to make his scriptural translations (ed. Blunt,
p. 71). He also comments that the nuns are able to access the Psalms in the vernacular in Rolle's
English psalter 'and out of Englysshe bibles if ye haue lysence therto' (ed. Blunt, p. 3). But Syon was
an ultra-orthodox and cautious house and its apparent obedience to the Arundel decrees cannot safely
be taken as a measure of universal practice.

lated from a French version by someone in the South West Midland region sometime between 1365 and 1425, vividly dramatises the anxieties and uncertainties that these emancipatory developments could give rise to.

Both surviving copies date from the first quarter of the fifteenth century. One version appears to be addressed to nuns, whereas the other seems to have been adapted and broadened in its appeal with the addition of affective material drawn from Rolle. In both versions, the prologue recommends the 'meditacyons or prayers' for their ability to 'exite and stere the mynde of the reder to the drede of God and to the love of God, and to veray knowyng of hymsilfe'. They are not to be read in great haste nor 'grete tumultuosite' but in quietness; not quickly but 'moderatly and easely' (ed. Wogan-Browne, Watson et al., p. 225). The prologue also encourages selective reading and sampling of the text, in line with the many other devotional texts produced in this period that recognised the utility of such works as occasional and casual devotional catalysts. But the body of the text in the original translation for religious is more uneasy about the free application of readerly choice and selectivity, especially if that choice is exercised by laymen without clerical supervision or interpretation to hand:

> [I]t is gode for comune pepeylle wheche been none clerkys, that they be wel ware in redynge or heringe of so hyhe materis that they emagyn nat ne enserche nat to ferre in hem. For the enemye, the fende, ys fulle redi to tempte theyme that yuyth hem alle to spiritualte & to the loue of God.
>
> (ed. Bartlett and Bestul, p. 168)

In a passage in the commentary on the *Soliloquies* supplied by the English translator in defence of the honour given to images 'as for a loue tokyn' to God, the text argues that the Old Testament's prohibition of graven images need no longer apply as now 'the pepyl haue more discressioun than they had that tyme', and claims (in a probable reference to contemporary Lollard-inspired debates on the status of images which began in earnest in the 1380s) that men 'mys take' the words of Augustine against image worship and have fallen into error, partly because they lacked the guidance of clerical interpretation. A whole pathology of contemporary neuroses and anxieties shimmers through this passage:

> They take his menyng vpsodowne & turnyth it alle in another kynde than he thouhte. And so they falle in to erroure & euel opynyons & schende hem selfe in folwyng the feendys counsayle, by mys takyng of scripturis. Therfor, whan any creature hath suche conseytes or dowtys in redynge of scriptures, or by ymagynaciouns or temptacioun, they schuld anone take counsayle of clerkys & do by here doctrinis . . . Certis, it makyth many to erre, lacke of gode clergy. Clergy is moche worth, for it is trewe leder to the riht wey of trowth, ther grace is ther amonge. (ed. Bartlett and Bestul, p. 177)

'Clergy' is used here both in the sense of learning or education and, perhaps more emphatically in this context, in the sense of the clerical cadre, at least some of whom felt threatened by the increasing questioning they faced from the laity and who seem to have felt increasingly unsure of their status and authority as 'trewe leder'.

This academic, popular, and sometimes heterodox interest in vernacularity and the processes of vernacularisation, enfleshed in the increasing numbers of manuscripts manifesting a serious interest in vernacular theology, and inflected by the responses of writers and readers to repressive legislative provisions such as Thomas Arundel's Oxford Constitutions of 1407x1409, might give a misleading impression that the ideological ferment of the years 1380 to 1415 saw a previously unprecedented and subsequently unparalleled upsurge in the production and circulation of vernacular books of religion. However, while the readership of such texts expanded dramatically in this period, that expansion continued exponentially in the years after Arundel's decrees. And while the intended effect of Arundel's decrees may have been the effacement of a burgeoning speculative theology in the vernacular and the establishment of a conservative and cautious canon of theologically conventional texts, an unintended consequence of those decrees may have been the accelerated production and circulation of miscellanies and anthologies of religious materials (Watson 1995; Watson 1999).

The contents of such books were increasingly likely to be in prose, to be anonymous or pseudonymously attributed to an author with theological *auctoritas* (like Bernard or Bonaventure) or chronological convenience (like Rolle, who died in 1349: Arundel had prohibited vernacular writing from or since the time of Wyclif), and were frequently short texts often extracted from their original context in a longer work. The ubiquity of Rolle as a privileged *auctor* from before the time of Wyclif suggests that he could be seen as a convenient guarantor of safe passage for texts that lacked obvious pedigree but possessed obvious worth. In a Foucaultian sense, 'the author function [in such books] is therefore characteristic of the mode of existence, circulation and functioning of certain discourses within a society'.[3] BL, MS Arundel 286, for example, ascribes two epistles to Rolle's authorship (they are actually anonymous translations from Bonaventure and Anselm), but the colophons clearly flag the compiler's view that in this context the *intentio auctoris* is less important than the *intentio lectoris*:

> Her bygynneþ a pistle maad of Richard Hampul as somme men supposen but who euer made it myche deuout þinge is þerinne. (fol. 82r)

> Here endiþ þe ij pistle maad of Ric. Hampul eþer somme oþer deuout man in whiche pistle ben many deuout þingis & excelent & profitable. (fol. 99v)

Typically there is in these colophons both a gesture of obedience to the status of Rolle as a spiritual teacher and a gesture of independence that draws attention away from the historicity of the authorising name towards the worth of the text in its new context. Indeed the problematic and contested act of translation from Latin paradoxically here becomes a marker of the translator's confidence and independence:

---

3   Michel Foucault, 'What is an Author?', repr. in *The Foucault Reader*, ed. Paul Rabinow (Harmondsworth, 1984), pp. 101–20, p. 108.

þe latyn book by which y translatide was ful fals in þe lettre and poyntinge
also and þerfore I had þe mor trauel to come to þe open and trewe sentence.

(fol. 99v)

The (linguistically usually authoritative) Latin text was 'ful fals' but has now
been converted by the modern interpreter into a vernacular text that is 'open and
trewe'.

Some late fourteenth-century texts are already making ambitious experi-
ments in such devotional *assemblage*, seeking to blend a range of sources into a
smooth and consistent spiritual narrative. *Pore Caitif*, for example, one of the
most important vernacular religious prose texts still to be without a published
edition, consists of a prologue and fourteen sections of varying length which
show a remarkable stability in their transmission (and which are often accompanied in manuscripts by *The Mirror of St Edmund* and the eschatological *Treatise
of the Three Arrows*). *Pore Caitif* explicitly addresses itself to laymen, seeking to
'teche simple men and wymmen of gode wille the right way to hevene' and to do
so 'wiþouten multiplicacion of many bokes' (ed. Wogan-Browne, Watson et al.,
p. 240). It begins with expositions of the Creed, decalogue and *Pater Noster*,
following the standard catechetic syllabus. But, in a manner typical of these
more ambitious spiritual collections, the prologue explains the devotional
dynamic that underpins this ordering. Without faith it is impossible to please
God. Therefore,

> as a child willing to ben a clerk bygynneth first atte grounde, þat is his a.b.c.,
> so he this desirynge to spede the betir, bigynneth atte ground of heelthe, that is
> Cristen mennes bileve. (ed. Wogan-Browne, Watson et al., p. 240)

But faith 'is not sufficiant bi it self to mannes salvacion withoute gode workes
of charite', which are enshrined in the Commandments. And because it is hard
to purchase sight of God through prayer until a man truly believes and lives
according to the Commandments, therefore the *Pater Noster* helps us to learn to
pray. After this (quite lengthy) catechetic introduction, the remaining tracts
(many of them versions, paraphrases or translations of Rolle, including an
important section in praise of devotion to the Name of Jesus) are simply
described as 'somme short sentences exciting men to heuenly desir':[4]

> For thus it bihovith to stye up, as by a laddir of dyverse runges, fro the grounde
> of bileve into the kepinge of Goddis commaundementes, and so up fro vertu
> into vertu, til he se God of Syon regnyng in everlasting blis.
>
> (ed. Wogan-Browne, Watson et al., p. 240)

There is nothing in itself very innovative about such a progression from moral
conformity to the will of God to more advanced spiritual yearning and desire for
union with God. It is the basic groundplan of much ascetic and anchoritic
writing. But *Pore Caitif* uses that groundplan to create a simple, successful
(there are over thirty complete copies surviving, with almost as many extracts

---

4   Many copies read 'men and wymmen' at this point.

and fragments), and versatile compendium of exhortation and instruction aimed firmly at a lay readership striving to realise and fulfil its spiritual potential (Brady 1954, 1957, 1980, 1981, 1983; Sargent 1979). A similar pattern can be observed in many ad hoc spiritual manuals, where catechetic materials are the point of departure for a collection of texts with affective, devotional, para-mystical or contemplative ambitions (Gillespie 1989).

More ambitious *assemblage* is found in the late fourteenth-century *Þe Holy Boke Gracia Dei*, which now exists in a variety of different states in its four surviving witnesses (Keiser 1981). Its varied and piecemeal transmission saw it adapted for a range of readers from the monastic to the lay gentleman. But the turbulence of its transmission, and its rapid breaking up into anthologised extracts, illustrate the difficulty in assembling a work that could comfortably and adequately address the width of the new audience with the depth required by the topics it sought to address. Drawing on many of the already available vernacular sources (including *Ancrene Wisse*, the *Abbey of the Holy Ghost*, *A Ladder of Four Rungs*, *The Mirror of St Edmund* and parts of the *Pore Caitif*) the compiler added patristic and other Latin materials (especially from Bernard, Gregory and Bonaventure) including extracts from the *Vitae Patrum* to produce a kind of Rule of spiritual life, including instructions for interpolating the day's work with para-liturgical prayer and observance:

> Þi euensonge – when it is tyme, with deuocione þat God to þe sendes, in kyrk or in oratory or whore þou so best may – say out of noise or tariyng of þe werlde; or, if þou lewede be, þe prayers þat þou was wont to say in þat tyde.
>
> (ed. Arntz, p. 106)

The work encourages a form of affective but carefully directed meditation on the passion of Christ (widely found in devotional writing of the period) along-side quite sophisticated instruction on the mechanics of avoiding distraction in meditation and prayer:

> [K]ast þin eghen of-ferre on some-what þou may se, and hald þin eghene on þat thinge whils þou þi prayers makes, for þis helpis mekill to stablynge of þi hert. And paynt þer þi Lorde God als he was done on þe croce. Thinke on þose fete and handes þat nayled were to þe tre, and on þose wide wondes.
>
> (ed. Arntz, p. 72)[5]

The implied user of *Gracia Dei* is considered to be in need of (and capable of responding to) a more reflective and discursive account of the fluctuating dynamics of the spiritual life. The compiler borrows from the (originally Latin and Carthusian) contemplative textbook *A Ladder of Four Rungs* to discuss feel-

---

5   Such directed meditation is often thought of as a distinctive feature of the Pseudo-Bonaventuran tradition, exemplified in English most notably by Nicholas Love's *Mirror of the Blessed Life of Jesus Christ*. But it is important to stress how widespread these manipulative and directed meditations were in devotional writing on the life of Christ and Mary, also occurring, for example, in *Book to a Mother*; the *ABC of Aristotle*; *Speculum Devotorum*; the *Passion of Our Lord Jesus Christ*, and many others. Directed meditation is perhaps a function both of affective manipulation and emancipation and of clerical control.

ings of spiritual dryness and abandonment, appropriately adjusted for a potentially illiterate (and therefore probably lay) audience:

> When þou feles þat þis likynge God fro þe draghes, gyfe þe þene too prayere,
> or meditacione, or redynge of holy wryte, if þou letterd be, or to honeste
> werke as to þe tyme falles. And euer mourne after þi lefe als a ʒonge childe
> þat þe modire mysses. (ed. Arntz, p. 79)

This rejigging of the monastic triad of *lectio, meditatio* and *oratio* into the more
permissive formulation found here illustrates the way that in such books reading
becomes merely one of a range of devotional catalysts rather than the corner-
stone of the scripturally based exegetical rumination found in the monastic
tradition (Gillespie 1984).

Fervor Amoris (edited as *Contemplations of the Dread and Love of God*) was
probably compiled before 1425 in the South West Midlands. It seems to have
been intended for a lay audience though, in the codicologically untidy way of
such things, it also enjoyed quite wide circulation in manuscripts of clerical
provenance or ownership. It is a work of some subtlety and style, comparable to
The Chastising of God's Children in its readability, its clear sense of purpose and
its determination to explore in the vernacular aspects of para-mystical and
contemplative experience while seeking to ground that experience firmly in the
discipline and obedience of the Church's *magisterium*. Prefaced by an analytical
table of contents that allows casual (and non-sequential) consultation, the text
skilfully deploys a series of artful (and unacknowledged) borrowings from other
vernacular contemplative, devotional and para-mystical sources (including
Rolle and Hilton and perhaps Birgitta of Sweden). The opening chapter, apparently authorial, speaks of man's 'kindeliche' desire to come to the love of God,
and delineates an inscribed audience of such eager but unskilled lovers:

> Of þis desir many þer be, boþe men and women, wiche haue ful gret liking to
> speke of þe loue of God, and al day askin how þei schul loue God, and in what
> maner þei schul liue to his pleasaunce for his endles goodnes.
>
> (ed. Connolly, p. 5)

It might be assumed that this target audience is lay. Describing his intention to
narrate the lives of 'holi men bifore þis tyme', he comments that 'it mai be so
þat it ys ful hard for þe more partie of men and women to come to so hye degre
of loue' (ed. Connolly, p. 5). But there is carefully nothing said or done in the
compilation to circumscribe its appeal or to limit its address, while beginning so
emphatically with the example of those who lived 'in old time' might be
regarded as a prudent manouevre to step aside from any contemporary debates
about lay para-mystical ambitions or indeed to avoid any contemporary anxieties (and, indeed, legislation) about the explicit citation of more recent authors.
This contrast with the desire for perfection found in former times is pressed
home by the author in a striking passage (not drawn from his main sources)
which extends conventional laments for the decay in human behaviour into what
feels like a more current and immediate complaint. Perfection in the love of God
requires a 'sad contemplatif man or woman':

And bicause mankinde is now and euer þe lengur more fieble, or percas more unstable, þerfore unneþis schul we finde now a sad contemplatif man or woman. Men of religioun haue take diuerse habitis of contemplatif life. Men also and women wiche ben enclosid, as it semethe liue a contemplatif lif, and so withe Godis grace þei do for þe more partie. But for to speke of hie contemplatif lif, as holi man liuede bifore þis time, it semeþ þer be ful fewe.

(ed. Connolly, p. 6)

This sentiment is hardly a ringing endorsement of the health and diversity of the contemporary contemplative scene, and it is balanced by a recognition that people living the active life may have a legitimate aspiration to share some aspects of the lower levels of the life of contemplation, even if they cannot achieve 'suche hie contemplatif lif':

Many oþer men and women þer be wiche plese God ful wel stonding treweliche in here degre as men and women of þe world, lordis and ladies, oþer housbond-men and wyues. (ed. Connolly, p. 7)

This interestingly balances social stability ('stonding treweliche in here degre') with spiritual mobility and an element of contemplative emancipation: every Christian man 'religious and seculer' should 'holde and kepe, and may performe for þe more partie' four degrees of love 'yif his wil be feruentliche yset to the loue of God' (ed. Connolly, p. 8).

Such emancipation is, however, not without its dangers, and the text stresses the likelihood of tribulation and temptation, especially for those who suffer from 'defauut of knowing' and 'unstabilnes' (stability of heart is a recurrent concern of the book). The remedy for those afflicted in this way is to fall back on the resources of the institutional Church:

chaunge not þerfore þi wil, but stond sadli, and schewe þi diseise to þi gostliche fadur, asking him to yeue þe suche counseil þat mai be most helping to þi soule. (ed. Connolly, p. 22)

Referring back to this advice later in the work, the compiler extends this to include 'or ellis . . . some oþer good man of gostliche leuing' (p. 35), and warns against visions, dreams and other 'ymaginaciouns':

And for to schewe more opinliche, what man ymagineþ uppon hie maters þat ben gostliche, which passe alle erþeliche mannis wit, as uppon þe feiþ of holi chirche or suche oþer þat nedeþ not to specifie at þis time, þat man haþ greuous þouȝtis and perlous. (ed. Connolly, p. 34)

This is an interesting and somewhat anxious rewriting of the normal concept of ineffability: the high ghostly matters that should not be speculated upon are not those issues of divine nature and being which contemplative theory would normally address, but rather matters that relate to the faith of the Church, and other (literally unspeakable) areas of doctrinal speculation. Just as Julian of Norwich finds herself in an uneasy dialogue between her perception of the thrust of her *Shewings*, and the faith of Holy Church, so the author of *Fervor Amoris* envisages (as many of his contemporary churchmen also did) a potentially dangerous overflow from devotional aspiration into doctrinal speculation.

Certainly the crucial dynamic between clergy and laity was tirelessly emphasised in fifteenth-century works of devotional guidance. *The Treatise of Ghostly Battle*, for example, is one of a group of mid-fifteenth-century devotional and para-mystical texts imbricated in an unusually richly documented metropolitan and mercantile circulation (Murray 1970; Morgan1973; Jones 2004). It stresses (under the rubric *Beati pauperes spiritu*) the responsibility of all Christians to further and sustain the Gospel imperatives in word, will and deed. But it goes on to highlight the distinctive functions of clerics and laymen:

> Yef thow be a preste, than preche hit and teche hit dewly and trewly, reuerently and charitabely, with meke herte and parfyte lyuyng, wherethorowgh sympelle men that ben not letterede and haue noo power of prechyng and techyng as thow hast, may be stabeled in trewe feythe of goddis lawe, to encres in vertewe and to hate synne. And yef thow be a layman, the behoueth to helpe and sustayn hem that haue power and trewly techyn hit. Also the behoueth to here and to beleue trewly on hit and in all the sacramentys of Holy Churche, and nat dispute and ymagyn howe they myght be so, but fully beleue in hem, and so to conforme the in the lawes of God and the ordynaunce of Holy Churche. (ed. Horstman 1896, 2. 424–25, corrected against the BL, MS Harley 1706)

The importance of clerical intercession and sacramental ministry is also centrally encoded in fascinating accounts of visits to Purgatory (like the *Vision of William Stranton* (ed. Easting 1991) or that of Edmund Leversedge (ed. Nijenhuis 1991) or the Monk of Eynsham (ed. Easting 2002)) or of visitations from beyond the grave (like the *Spiritus Guidonis* or *Gast of Gy*; ed. Bartlett and Bestul 1999), where the effective agency and guidance of good priests are balanced by lurid portrayals of the torments awaiting priests who do not properly exercise their duties.

BL, Add. MS 34193, for example, a hotchpotch of fifteenth-century manuscripts containing Latin and English devotional texts and a mixture of English verse and prose, preserves several works reporting glimpses of purgatorial suffering intended to encourage moral reformation in this life. Perhaps deriving from the environs of York minster, the book is headed by the vernacular version of Deguilleville's *Pilgrimage of the Human Soul* and also includes English versions of the *Disticha Catonis*, Stephen Scrope's translation of the *Liber de moralibus philosophorum* and the Rule of Celestine for hermits. But its core contents are a series of revelations to men: the vision of Edmund Leversedge (received in 1456); the *Spiritus Guidonis* (recording events in 1323), and the *Vision of William Stranton* (here alleged to have happened in either 1406 or 1409 but in fact a redaction and substantial expansion of the popular twelfth-century tale of *St Patrick's Purgatory*). Such texts, and others like them such as *The Revelation of Purgatory*, apparently received by a woman in 1422, serve to reinforce the doctrine of purgatorial cleansing and stress the need for lifetime repentance to avoid the extreme torments described by the returning spirits or the privileged tourists through Purgatory who live to tell their tales. The interpretation of such visions and dreams remained a worry throughout the period (Voaden 1999). The vernacular lives of the Rhineland women visionaries preserved in Bodl. MS Douce 114 (ed. Horstmann 1885), for example, seem to have been kept on a tight leash by the Carthusians. For *Fervor Amoris*, the preferred solution had been to rely on the interpretative expertise and traditional teachings of the Church (the passage derives largely from Gregory's *Moralia in Job*):

> Also þou schalt not drede suche dremis whateuer þei be; for as y rede, yif þou be stable in þe feiþ of holi chirche, yif þou loue God wiþ al þin herte, yif þou be obedient to God and to þy souereynes, whateuir þou be, as wiel in aduersite as in prosperite, and yif þou putte al þi wil at Godis disposicion, þan schalt þou dred no maner of dremis. (ed. Connolly, p. 35)

Fervor Amoris is a slick, effective and stylishly argued text with a skilful blending of sources and materials to produce a work that is both initially spiritually permissive and ultimately doctrinally controlling. It was a hard act to follow, and proved popular and influential: some sections were themselves abstracted into other devotional compilations (Connolly 2002). The final chapter on prayer and meditation is, in different recensions and forms, one of the most widely occurring vernacular teachings on that subject, and is both sensible, empowering, and spiritually ambitious. Strikingly patristic in its orientation, and rather sparse in its explicit citations of Scripture, *Fervor Amoris* displays aspects of contemporary vernacular contemplative theory (particularly that of Rolle and Hilton) in a setting that is cautious, pragmatic, supportive, theologically traditional, but also realistic in its recognition of a new lay appetite for such spirituality:

> Y sey not þou schalt fle bodili from þe world or from þi wordeli goodis . . . but I counsele þe in herte and in wil þat þou fle al suche vanites, for þay þou be a lord or a laidi, housbond-man or wif, þou maist haue as stable an herte and wil as some religious þat sitteþ in þe cloistre. (ed. Connolly, p. 40)

Lay interest in such para-monastic forms of spirituality is a defining characteristic of vernacular devotional writing in this period. One of the earliest expressions of that interest in is found in *The Abbey of the Holy Ghost*, a popular fourteenth-century English version of a French text that allegorises the psychology of devotion in terms of monastic architecture:

> My dere brother and sister, I se weel that many wolde ben in religioun but they mowe nowt for poverte or for awe or for drede of her kyn or for bond of maryage. Therfore I make here a book of relygyoun of the herte . . . that all tho that mow nout been in bodylyche relygyon mow been in gostly.
> (ed. Blake 1972, p. 89)

Allegorical edifices have a long history as menemonic devices in religious writing and have often been used to provide a schematic framework for discussing catechetics and for presenting the complex psychological interactions that devotional writing strives to generate, shape and control (Whitehead 2003). *The Eight Ghostly Dwelling Places* illustrate how compactly the idea can be deployed:

Blessid is þat religioun of whiche þe temple is holynes, þe scole sooþnes, and þe cloister stilnes, þe chapilte of equite, þe dortoir of chastite, and þe fermary pitee, þe fraitir sobirnes and þe hostrie largenes and charite. þerfore who þat haþ þese viij placis goostly in his soule and outward in hise werkis, his religioun is perfiȝt. (ed. Conlee 1975, p. 142)

An angry version of the allegory is found in the reformist-minded *Book to a Mother*, one of the more radical products of that late fourteenth-century peak in the composition of vernacular religious prose in the South West Midlands (Watson 2000). Perhaps composed just before the first major wave of Lollard activity, and initially addressed as a letter of spiritual direction from a priest to his own mother, but by extension aimed at 'euerych man and woman and child', the text moves rapidly from a rehearsal of the catechetic syllabus to more radical and evangelical concerns, basing itself heavily (and rather unusually) on a deeply ruminative appeal to the authority of Scripture (frequently cited in translation). As part of an anti-feminist rant against female pride and vainglory, the priestly author says that women shall see a time when it would be better that they had observed the Rule of St Benedict 'faste iclosed in a cloister of foure stronge wallis, þat ben riȝtfulnes, strengþe, sleiþe and temperaunce' (ed. McCarthy, pp. 120–21).[6] Warming to his theme in a manner that prefigures or reflects Wycliffite criticism of 'private religions' (that is, enclosed orders), he continues:

Modur, ȝif þou kepe wel þis cloister and holde þe þerinne to þi liues ende, Crist, þat is Abbot and Priour of þis cloister wol euer be þerinne wiþ þe where-euere þou be and teche þe his religioun, þat is mekenes and humilite . . . his religioun is most parfit bi hereself, and euere schal laste in heuene, and non oþer mai be good wiþoute þis. For what abite þer ben of ony religioun; customes, signes, or ony oþer serimonies; but þei acorde wiþ Cristes religioun and helpe þerto, þei ben noiouse, and better hit were to leue such ordynaunces of men. (ed. McCarthy, p. 122)

He goes on to argue that this rule of religion is 'most general' (for all men are bound to hold it on pain of damnation) and most 'fre':

for Crist wiþ his couent axeþ not twenti marc as þou woldest sometime haue ȝeue for me to haue ben a chanoun, and þei wolde not receiue me lasse þan twenti pound. (ed. McCarthy, p. 122)

This personal bitterness at his own rejection powers a passionate denunciation of monastic abuses:

for [Crist] loued none symonie ne axeþ of non þat wolde come to his religioun peces, macers, ne seluerne sponis, ne wheþer he be bonde oþer fre, or comen of grete lordus, forte maintene here possessiouns; but þe lowere, þe porere, þe lasse a man haþ, þe bettur welcome. (ed. McCarthy, pp. 122–23)

---

6   This is strikingly similar to the Monk of Canterbury's later wish that Margery Kempe might be enclosed in a house of stone. Clearly some clerics found women easier to deal with if they were safely enclosed and subject to vows of obedience.

The poverty of spirit and meekness of heart that are usually seen as the essentials of spiritual reformation are here interestingly correlated with low social standing and financial poverty, and the mother is encouraged to read, mark, learn, and inwardly digest only one book: that is, the life of Christ that will serve as an exemplar from which she can copy into the book of her own conscience all that she needs to know (Gillespie 1984, 1987). With this new interior literacy, there is no need for what *Pore Caitif* calls 'multiplicacion of manye bokes':

> [I]t is bettur in þis bok þan in ony oþire, and mony þinges a man mai lerne in þis þat he schal not fynde in non oþir . . . Þerfor muche ben þei folis þat leuiþ þis trewe bok and stidien more in false bokis of false mennys makinge . . . And þus þou maist lerne aftir þi samplerie to write a feir trewe bok and better konne Holi Writ þan ony maister of diuinite þat loueþ not God so wel as þou; for who loueþ best God can best Holi Writ. (ed. McCarthy, pp. 38–39)

This emphatic kind of evangelicalism (parallelled in *The Life of Soul* (ed. Moon 1978), another strikingly austere and self-reliant Gospel paraphrase from the same date and region) pays scant regard to sacramentalism and ecclesiology.

With views like this in circulation, it is unsurprising that the institutional Church, faced first with academic Wycliffism and then with the fast-seeding cockle-weed of Lollardy, became edgy and fearful about unmediated lay access to such materials. But the impact of Arundel's 1409 legislation does not, in fact, seem to have substantially slackened the availability and circulation of sophisticated and ambitious guides to godliness. The translator and adapter of Heinrich Suso's *Horologium sapientiae* (originally written in Latin in the 1330s, and translated into English 'finaliter' by 1419 as *The Seven Points of True Wisdom*) imposed radical re-ordering and substantial omissions on the Latin text. But he seems to have felt no discomfort in retaining and translating the Disciple's appeal to Everlasting Wisdom for direct instruction in 'heuenlye diuinite' because:

> Þere beþ so manye bokes & tretees of vyces and vertues & of dyuerse doctrynes þat þis schort lyfe schalle raþer haue an ende of anye manne þanne he may owþere studie hem or rede hem. (ed. Horstmann 1887, p. 328)

Indeed in his own added prologue the English translator reinforces the sense of a profusion of contemporary books when he says that he hesitated over making the translation 'consideryng þe multitude of bokes & tretees drawne in englische, þat now bene generale cominede' fearing that his work would be wasted (ed. Horstmann 1887, p. 326).

In the Latin text, Suso's ambitious Disciple was safely contextualised as male, Latinate and probably monastic or fraternal in affiliation (Suso was himself a Dominican), and his immortal longings are circumscribed by the framework of liturgical and paraliturgical observance. But the English version, finally completed a full decade after Arundel's decrees, nevertheless feels no anxiety about a radical reconfiguration of the text and wholesale extension of its potential readership. The translator's prologue directs the work to a mixed audience of lay noble women and/or female religious readers ('my moste worschipful lady aftir ȝowre hyȝ worþynesse, & derrest loued goostly douȝhter after ȝour vertuous meekenes') and configures his own relationship to them ('ȝowre trewe chapelleyne'; ed. Horstmann 1887, p. 325) in ways that are paradigmatic of the broadening but still hierarchically configured (and usually clerically supervised) textual communities producing and reading such works in the fifteenth century. As Suso's famous aphorism puts it, 'of makynge bokes is none ende' (ed. Horstmann 1887, p. 328).

BIBLIOGRAPHY

This field is so large that only selective references can be provided here. Readers are advised to consult Jolliffe's *Checklist*, Sargent 1984, and the *Manual* volumes for more detailed bibliographical guidance. Most of the modern editions contain dedicated bibliographies. Under 'Selected Secondary Sources and Critical Studies' I have tended to privilege recent studies that have appeared since the standard bibliographies.

Major Bibliographical Reference Works

Barrett, Alexandra, 'Works of Religious Instruction', in Edwards 1984, pp. 413–432
  * Usefully covers catechetic material and books for parish priests.
D'Evelyn , Charlotte, and Frances A. Foster, 'Saints' Legends', in *Manual* 2 (1970), pp. 410–57, with bibliography pp. 553–649
———, 'Instructions for Religious', in *Manual* 2 (1970), pp. 458–81, with bibliography pp. 650–59
Edwards, A.S.G., ed., *Middle English Prose: A Critical Survey of Major Authors and Genres* (New Brunswick, NJ, 1984)
Jolliffe, Peter S., *A Check List of Middle English Prose Writings of Spiritual Guidance*, Subsidia Mediaevalia 11 (Toronto, 1974)
  * Though many of the lists of manuscripts have been augmented by subsequent research (not least *IPMEP* and the fascicles of *IMEP*), and some works have since been edited, this remains a research tool of primary importance.
Lagorio, Valerie M., and Michael G. Sargent, 'English Mystical Writings', in *Manual* 9 (1993), pp. 3049–137, with bibliography pp. 3405–71
  * Contains much helpful discussion and analysis of mystical, para-mystical and devotional texts.
Raymo, Robert R., 'Works of Religious and Philosophical Instruction', in *Manual* 7 (1986), pp. 2255–378, with bibliography pp. 2467–582
  * Useful lists of manuscripts and bibliography and helpful paraphrases. Not as strong on context.
Revell, Peter, *Fifteenth Century English Prayers and Meditations: A Descriptive List of Manuscripts in the British Library* (New York, 1975)
  * Flawed and incomplete but occasionally useful in its cross-references.
Sargent, Michael G., 'Minor Devotional Writings', in Edwards 1984, pp. 147–75
  * Still an excellent point of departure, with good text-specific bibliography.

Key General and Contextual Discussions

Doyle, A.I., 'A Survey of the Origins and Circulation of Theological Writings in English in the 14th, 15th and early 16th Centuries with Special Consideration of the Part of the Clergy therein' (unpublished doctoral thesis, University of Cambridge, 1953)
  * A classic study, still invaluable: full of insight and perceptive observations about connections between books.
Edwards, A.S.G., Vincent Gillespie, and Ralph Hanna, eds, *The English Medieval Book: Studies in Memory of Jeremy Griffiths*, The British Library Studies in the History of the Book (London, 2000)
  * See especially the essays by Hanna, Doyle, Scott, Gillespie and Watson.
Erler, Mary C., *Women, Reading, and Piety in Late Medieval England*, Cambridge Studies in Medieval Literature (Cambridge, 2002)
  * Includes important new attributions and identifications of devotional book ownership by women.
Griffiths, Jeremy, and Derek Pearsall, eds, *Book Production and Publishing in Britain 1375–1475*, Cambridge Studies in Publishing and Printing History (Cambridge, 1989)
  * Still unsurpassed as an introduction to book production in the period. See especially the essays by Doyle, Hudson, and Gillespie.
Pearsall, Derek, ed., *Studies in the Vernon Manuscript* (Cambridge, 1990)
  * See especially the essays by Doyle, Blake, Hussey, and Henry.
Renevey, Denis, and Christiania Whitehead, eds, *Writing Religious Women: Female Spiritual and Textual Practices in Late Medieval England* (Cardiff, 2000)
  * See especially the essays by Cré, Selman and McGovern-Mouron.
Trapp, J.B., and Lotte Hellinga, eds, *The Cambridge History of the Book in Britain* 3: *1440–1557* (Cambridge, 1999)
  * See especially the essays by Bell, Erler and Orme.
Wallace, David, *The Cambridge History of Medieval English Literature* (Cambridge, 1999)
  * See especially the essays by Cannon, Woods and Copeland, Watson, Boffey, and Cummings.
Wogan-Browne, Jocelyn, Nicholas Watson, Andrew Taylor and Ruth Evans, eds, *The Idea of the Vernacular: An Anthology of Middle English Literary Theory 1280–1520* (Exeter, 1999)
  * An essential collection of well edited and usefully annotated extracts supported by lively and well informed analytical essays.
————, Rosalynn Voaden et al., eds, *Medieval Women: Texts and Contexts in Late Medieval Britain: Essays for Felicity Riddy*, Medieval Women: Texts and Contexts 3 (Turnhout, 2000)
  * See especially the essays by Boffey, Lewis, Watson, and Cullum and Goldberg.

Editions and Primary Sources

Bartlett, Anne Clark, and Thomas H. Bestul, eds, *Cultures of Piety: Medieval Devotional Literature in Translation* (Ithaca, 1999)
  * Includes Middle English extracts from all the translated works.
Blake, N.F., ed. *Middle English Religious Prose*, York Medieval Texts (London, 1972)
Book for a Simple and Devout Woman: A Late Medieval Adaptation of Peraldus's Summa

de Vitiis et Virtutibus *and Friar Laurent's* Somme le Roi, ed. F.N.M. Diekstra (Groningen, 1998)

Book to a Mother: An Edition with Commentary, ed. Adrian James McCarthy, Salzburg Studies in English Literature: Elizabethan and Renaissance Studies 92 (Salzburg, 1981)

The Chastising of God's Children and the Treatise of Perfection of the Sons of God, ed. Joyce Bazire and Eric Colledge (Oxford, 1957)

Conlee, John W., 'The *Abbey of the Holy Ghost* and The *Eight Ghostly Dwelling Places* of Huntington Library HM 744', *Medium Aevum*, 44 (1975), 137–44

Contemplations of the Dread and Love of God (Fervor Amoris), ed. Margaret Connolly, EETS os 303 (1993)

Horstmann, Carl, 'Prosalegenden: Die Legenden des MS Douce 114', *Archiv* 8 (1885), 102–96

Horstmann, Karl, '*Orologium Sapientiae* or The Seven Poyntes of Trewe Wisdom aus MS Douce 114', *Anglia* 10 (1887), 323–89

Horstman, C., ed., *Yorkshire Writers: Richard Rolle of Hampole and his Followers* (London, 1895–6)

The Imitation of Christ: The First English Translation of the 'Imitatio Christi', ed. Brendan Biggs, EETS os 309 (1997)

Jolliffe, Peter S., 'Middle English Translations of the *De Exterioris et Interioris Hominis Compositione*', *Mediaeval Studies* 36 (1974), 259–77

———, 'Two Middle English Tracts on the Contemplative Life', *Mediaeval Studies* 37 (1975), 83–121

Þe *Lyfe of Soule: An Edition with Commentary*, ed. Helen M. Moon, Salzburg Studies in English Literature: Elizabethan and Renaissance Studies 75 (Salzburg, 1978)

Marx, C. William, and Jeanne F. Drennan, eds, *The Middle English Prose Complaint of Our Lady and Gospel of Nicodemus*, Middle English Texts 19 (Heidelberg, 1987)

Morgan, G.R., 'A Critical Edition of Caxton's *The Art and Craft Know Well to Die* and *Ars Moriendi* together with the antecedent manuscript material' (unpublished doctoral thesis, University of Oxford, 1973)

Murray, V., 'An Edition of *A Tretyse of Gostly Batayle* and *Milicia Christi*' (unpublished doctoral thesis, University of Oxford, 1970)

A Myrour to Lewde Men and Wymmen, ed. Venetia Nelson, Middle English Texts 14 (Heidelberg, 1981)

The Myroure of Oure Ladye, ed. John Henry Blunt, EETS es 19 (1873)

The Orcherd of Syon, ed. Phyllis Hodgson and Gabriel M. Liegey, EETS os 258 (1966)

The Prickynge of Love, ed. Harold Kane, Salzburg Studies in English Literature: Elizabethan and Renaissance Studies 92:10 (Salzburg, 1983)

Quattuor Sermones printed by William Caxton, ed. Norman Blake, Middle English Texts 2 (Heidelberg, 1975)

'*Remedies against Temptations*': *The Third English Version of William Flete*, ed. E. Colledge and N. Chadwick, Archivio Italiano per la Storia della Pieta V (Rome, 1967), 203–40

The Revelation of the Monk of Eynsham, ed. Robert Easting, EETS os 2002 (2002)

Richard Rolle and Þe *Holy Boke Gratia Dei: An Edition with Commentary*, ed. Mary Luke Arntz, Salzburg Studies in English Literature: Elizabethan and Renaissance Studies 92:2 (Salzburg, 1981)

St. Patrick's Purgatory: Two versions of OWAYNE MILES and THE VISION OF WILLIAM STRANTON together with the long text of the TRACTATUS DE PURGATORIO SANCTI PATRICII, ed. Robert Easting, EETS os 298 (1991)

The Tretyse of Loue, ed. John H. Fisher, EETS os 223 (1951, repr. 1970)

McNamer, Sarah, ed., *Two Middle English Translations of the Revelations of St. Elizabeth of Hungary*, Middle English Texts 28 (Heidelberg, 1996)

The Vision of Edmund Leversedge, ed. W.F. Nijenhuis, Middeleeuwse Studies 8 (Nijmegen, 1991)

The Vision of Piers Plowman: A Complete Edition of the B-Text, ed. A.V.C. Schmidt (London, 1978)

Selected Secondary Sources and Critical Studies

Allen, Hope Emily, 'Some Fourteenth Century Borrowings from the "Ancren Riwle" ', *MLR* 18 (1923), 1–8

Boyle, Leonard E., 'The Fourth Lateran Council and Manuals of Popular Theology', in Heffernan 1985, pp. 30–43

Brady, M.T., '*The Pore Caitif*: An Introductory Study', *Traditio* 10 (1954), 529–48

———, 'The Apostles and the Creed in Manuscripts of *The Pore Caitif*', *Speculum* 32 (1957), 323–25

———, 'Rolle's "Form of Living" and "The Pore Caitif" ', *Traditio* 36 (1980), 426–35

———, 'The Seynt and his Boke: Rolle's *Emendatio Vitae* and *The Pore Caitif*', *Fourteenth-century English Mystics Newsletter* 7 (1981), 20–31

———, 'Rolle and the Pattern of Tracts in "The Pore Caitif" ', *Traditio* 39 (1983), 456–65

Cannon, Christopher, 'Monastic Productions', in Wallace 1999, pp. 316–48

Connolly, Margaret, 'The "Eight Points of Charity" in John Rylands University Library MS English 85', in *And Gladly Wol He Lerne and Gladly Teche: Essays on Medieval English presented to Professor Matsuji Tajima on his Sixtieth Birthday*, ed. Yoko Iyeiri and Margaret Connolly (Tokyo, 2002), pp. 195–215

———, 'Books for the "helpe of euery persoone þat þenkiþ to be saued": Six Devotional Anthologies from Fifteenth-Century London', *The Yearbook of English Studies* 33 (2003), 170–81

Doyle, A.I., 'Books Connected with the Vere Family and Barking Abbey', *Essex Archaeological Society's Transactions* ns 25 (1958), 222–43

———, 'Carthusian Participation in the Movement of Works of Richard Rolle between England and Other Parts of Europe in the Fourteenth and Fifteenth Centuries', *Analecta Cartusiana* 55 (1981), 109–20

———, 'Publication by Members of the Religious Orders', in Griffiths and Pearsall 1989, pp. 109–23

———, 'Book Production by the Monastic Orders in England (c. 1375–1530): Assessing the Evidence', in *Medieval Book Production: Assessing the Evidence*, ed. Linda L. Brownrigg (London, 1990), pp. 1–21

Dutton, Anne M., 'Piety, Politics and Persona: MS Harley 4012 and Anne Harling', in *Prestige, Authority and Power in Late Medieval Manuscripts and Texts*, ed. Felicity Riddy (York, 2000), pp. 133–46

Gillespie, Vincent, '*Lukynge in haly bukes*: *Lectio* in Some Late Medieval Spiritual Miscellanies', *Analecta Cartusiana* 106 (1984), 1–27

———, 'Strange Images of Death: The Passion in Later Medieval English Devotional and Mystical Writing', *Analecta Cartusiana* 117 (1987), 110–59

———, 'Vernacular Books of Religion', in Griffiths and Pearsall 1989, pp. 317–44

———, 'Dial M for Mystic: Mystical Texts in the Library of Syon Abbey and the Spirituality of the Syon Brethren', in *The Medieval Mystical Tradition in England* VI, ed. Marion Glasscoe (Cambridge, 1999), pp. 241–68

————, 'The Haunted Text: Reflections in *The Mirrour to Deuote Peple*', in *Medieval Manuscripts at Notre Dame*, ed. Jill Mann and Maura Nolan (Notre Dame, 2004)

Hackett, M.B., 'William Flete and the *De Remediis contra Temptaciones*', in *Medieval Studies presented to Aubrey Gwynn S.J.*, ed. J.A. Watt, J.B. Morrall and F.X. Martin (Dublin, 1961), pp. 330–48

Hackett, Benedict, Edmund Colledge, and N. Chadwick, 'William Flete's "De Remediis contra Temptaciones" in its Latin and English Recensions: The Growth of a Text', *Mediaeval Studies* 26 (1964), 210–30

Hanna, Ralph, 'The Origins and Production of Westminster School MS 3', *Studies in Bibliography* 41 (1988), 197–218

————, 'Miscellaneity and Vernacularity: Conditions of Literary Production in Late Medieval England', in *The Whole Book: Cultural Perspectives of the Medieval Miscellany*, ed. S.G. Nichols and Siegfried Wenzel (Ann Aarbor, 1996), pp. 37–51

————, 'Introduction', *IMEP* XII (1997), pp. xi–xxiv

————, 'Notes towards a Future History of Middle English Literature: Two Copies of Richard Rolle's *Form of Living*', in *Chaucer in Perspective: Middle English Essays in Honour of Norman Blake*, ed. G.A. Lester (Sheffield, 1999), pp. 279–300

————, 'Yorkshire Writers', *Proceedings of the British Academy* 121 (2003), 91–109

Heffernan, Thomas J., ed., *The Popular Literature of Medieval England*, Tennessee Studies in Literature 28 (Knoxville, 1985)

Hutchison, Ann M., 'Devotional Reading in the Monastery and in the Late Medieval Household', in *De Cella in Seculum: Religious and Secular Life and Devotion in Late Medieval England*, ed. Michael G. Sargent (Cambridge, 1989), pp. 215–27

Jones, Eddie, 'The Heresiarch, The Virgin, The Recluse, The Vowess, The Priest: Some Medieval Audiences for Pelagius's *Epistle to Demetrias*', *Leeds Studies in English* ns 30 (2000), 205–27

————, 'The Compilation of Two Late-Medieval Devotional Manuscripts', in *Text and Controversy from Wyclif to Bale: Essays in Honour of Anne Hudson*, ed. Helen Barr and Ann M. Hutchison, Medieval Church Studies 4 (Turnhout, forthcoming 2004)

Keiser, George, 'Þe Holy Boke Gratia Dei', *Viator* 12 (1981), 289–317

Lovatt, Roger, '*The Imitation of Christ* in Late Medieval England', *Transactions of the Royal Historical Society* 5th ser. 18 (1968), 117–21

————, 'Henry Suso and the Medieval Mystical Tradition', in *The Medieval Mystical Tradition in England*, Exeter Symposium II, ed. Marion Glasscoe (Exeter, 1982), pp. 47–62

Riddy, Felicity, ' "Women talking about the things of God": A Late-Medieval Sub-Culture', in *Women and Literature in Britain 1150–1500*, ed. Carol M. Meale, 2nd ed. (Cambridge, 1996), pp. 104–27

Russell, George H., 'Vernacular Instruction of the Laity in the Later Middle Ages in England: Some Texts and Notes', *Journal of Religious History* 2 (1962–63), 98–119

Sargent, Michael, 'The Transmission by the English Carthusians of Some Late Medieval Spiritual Writings', *Journal of Ecclesiastical History* 27 (1976), 225–40

————, 'A Source of the *Pore Caitif* Tract, "Of Man's Will" ', *Mediaeval Studies* 41 (1979), 535–39

————, 'Ruusbroec in England: The Chastising of God's Children and Related Works', in *Historia et Spiritualis Cartusiensis: Colloquii Quarti Internationalis Acta* (Destelbergen, 1982), pp. 303–12

Scase, Wendy, 'Reginald Pecock, John Carpenter and John Colop's "Common-Profit" Books: Aspects of Book Ownership in Fifteenth-Century London', *Medium Aevum* 61 (1992), 261–74

Shaw, J., 'The Influence of Canonical and Episcopal Reform on Popular Books of Instruction', in Heffernan 1985, pp. 44–60

Sutherland, Annie, 'Ruusbroec in England: The Chastising of God's Children', in *Text and Controversy from Wyclif to Bale: Essays in Honour of Anne Hudson*, ed. Helen Barr and Ann M. Hutchison, Medieval Church Studies 4 (Turnhout, forthcoming 2004)

Voaden, Rosalynn, *God's Words, Women's Voices: The Discernment of Spirits in the Writing of Late-Medieval Women* (York, 1999)

Watson, Nicholas, 'Censorship and Cultural Change in Late-Medieval England: Vernacular Theology, the Oxford Translation Debate, and Arundel's Constitutions of 1409', *Speculum* 70 (1995), 822–64

——, 'The Politics of Middle English Writing', in *The Idea of the Vernacular* (1999), pp. 331–52

——, 'Fashioning the Puritan Gentry-Woman: Devotion and Dissent in *Book to A Mother*', in Wogan-Browne, Voaden et al. 2000, pp. 169–84

Whitehead, Christiania, *Castles of the Mind: A Study of Medieval Architectural Allegory*, Religion and Culture in the Middle Ages (Cardiff, 2003)

10

Sermon Literature

H. L. SPENCER

What is a sermon?

Although their content is designed to inculcate spiritual and doctrinal order in their listeners, sermons are a notably disorderly group of texts about which to generalise.[1] At the time of writing, medieval English sermons have so far resisted attempts to corrall in any orderly kind of way in a catalogue, as has been achieved with the Latin preaching of the period.[2] They are not always easy to identify. A treatise might be read as a sermon, and a sermon might be read as a treatise. The distinction cannot always be rigidly maintained. It can be said that preachers had a tendency to use certain formulaic expressions, which, up to a point, characterise 'sermons'. It is and was not difficult to parody sermons – usually some variant of the typical vocatives used to address an audience at the beginning is enough to establish the tone. In Middle English, they might run 'Friends,' 'Sirs', 'Good men and women', with occasionally more elaborate variations such as 'Frendes in God, bothe men and wymmen' (Ross 1940, p. 26/5). Sermon imitation with parodic intention has attracted much attention, especially when suspected in writers such as Chaucer (see, among others, Shain 1955, Gallick 1975, Wenzel 1976, Fletcher 1989).

Following such a vocative, a 'theme' is customarily announced, commonly taken from one of the epistle or gospel readings appointed for the day. For example:

> *Amice, quomodo huc intrasti* [Matt.22:12] . . . Good men and wymmen, þe wordes of my teme bethe writte in þe gospell of þis daye, and þus muche on Englissh: 'Frende, how commest þou here, or hydere?'[3]

However, in practice a discourse became a sermon by force of circumstances: if it were delivered by a recognised preacher from a pulpit at a familiar preaching venue. Hence the uncertainty among modern scholars about the extent of verse sermons, which undoubtedly existed, but might also be read for private edification.[4]

---

1 General surveys are offered by Owst 1926; Blench 1964; Spencer 1993. For French sermons of the period, see Martin 1988, Taylor 1992. Preaching in Ireland is surveyed by Fletcher and Gillespie 2001.
2 Schneyer 1973–1980. Handlists are in preparation by P.J. Horner and V.M. O'Mara.
3 Ross 1940, 16/1–17/9.
4 Examples listed in Spencer 2000, 617–20.

Prose sermons, too, might have an afterlife as private reading, especially those which were circulated in multiple copies in formal, well presented manuscripts: the tradition goes back at least to the Carolingian preachers that sermon collections might be used for both preaching and reading as the user saw fit.[5] Many preachers had adopted versions of a mode of discourse specially devised for preaching, and described in the Latin treatises on how to preach: the *artes praedicandi*. A short introduction, the 'protheme' or 'antetheme', might follow the announcement of the theme: 'How þat þou shalte brynge þis a-bowte I shall tell þe somwhat in myn ante-teme'.[6] The antetheme concluded with a prayer and the reannouncement of the theme. Within the main body of the sermon – its 'process' – arguments were arranged by dividing and maybe subdividing them into heads, often called 'principals'. In an elaborate sermon, the antetheme might also be divided. This procedure was thoroughly familiar to a preacher's audiences, who, by the late fourteenth century and fifteenth, had often come to expect it. A simple example, taken from St Paul's words in the epistle for the First Sunday in Advent (Rom.13:11), slightly modified to suit the preacher's purpose, runs thus:

'Now is tyme þat we ryse of slepe,' seynge þus, 'Surgite de sompno viciorum, et induite armatura Dei' – arise,' he seis, 'owt of slepe of synne and clothe you in Goddes armore.' In þe wiche wordes I note too þinges of wisdom – oon ys where he seis, 'A-ryse;' anoþur is when he seys 'Clothe you.'[7]

Such ways of presenting a discourse are especially suitable for oral presentation, but may also be used on occasion for the sake of clarity by those who write for readers. There is no generally accepted name for this way of composing sermons: modern commentators refer to it variously as the 'modern', 'new', 'school', 'university' or 'thematic' method. Among professional preachers and those with academic training, it came at times to be almost synonymous with the act of preaching, yet more informal ways of composition never entirely ceased to be employed. Indeed, a simple form, without divisions, is used in many of the surviving sermons written in English, including the most influential collections.[8] By this method, a preacher might offer a translation into English of the entire gospel reading appointed for that Sunday, and follow it, or intersperse it, with a commentary. The translation of the gospel would constitute an explanation of its literal sense; the commentary was 'spiritual', or 'ghostly', applying the gospel's words to the audience's situation metaphorically. The elucidation of the spiritual sense of the gospel was commonly introduced by a formula such as 'Goostely to oure purpose.'[9] Modern commentators have sometimes attempted to designate sermons of this type 'homilies', though the distinction between 'sermons' and 'homilies' is not observed in the usage of the Middle English

5   Gatch 1977, 27–39.
6   Ross 1940, 31/28–9.
7   Ross 1940, 110/14–20.
8   Surveyed in Spencer 1993, 228–68.
9   Ross 1940, 92/11. See further Fletcher 1984.

preachers, and is not followed here. Some summaries of unpublished sermons, English and Latin, which demonstrate both varieties, may be found in Spencer 1993, 235–38, 247–51, 335–58.

When were Sermons Preached?

Sermons were needed for a variety of occasions: the categories were well established among those who recorded sermons in Latin, and vernacular writers followed these models. However, some kinds of sermons, such as *sermones ad status*, that is sermons directed towards particular groups (for instance clerics, women or merchants) are rarely represented in English vernacular manuscripts. English sermons on the duties of the three estates are the nearest equivalent, and the best known example is the sermon preached at Paul's Cross in London by Thomas Wimbledon in around 1387 on the theme 'Redde rationem villicacionis tue' (Luke 16:2, from the gospel for Septuagesima Sunday).[10] It survives in thirteen manuscripts in English and two in Latin. Its outspoken social commentary and its urgent prophecies from 'Joachim of Fiore' and Hildegard of Bingen also commended it in the early modern period, when it was reissued many times in print in the sixteenth and seventeenth centuries. It is never easy for individuals to question traditional models of analysis, and preachers tended by profession to be conservative, nevertheless some showed an uneasy awareness that this tripartite division was too simple to describe the growing complexities of late medieval society.[11]

There were few opportunities for vernacular preachers to address audiences of clerics or fellow religious alone, but there is some limited evidence of preaching to nuns. A case has been made for identifying sermons intended for the Brigittine nuns at Syon (Powell 2000). Brigittine monks, like other members of religious orders might, and did, preach to mixed and lay audiences, but that is a different matter.[12]

English sermons, like Latin ones, may be organised around the Church's calendar of saints' days (the *proprium sanctorum*), commonly beginning with St Andrew, the saint whose day (30 November) coincides most nearly with the opening of the Church's year on Advent Sunday, although other patterns were available, such as Christmas. Occasionally preachers provided sermons for general categories of saint (the *commune sanctorum*): virgin, martyr, confessor, which could be applied to local or minor saints not provided for by name in the *proprium sanctorum*. The defining collections in English from the period are the *South English Legendary*, John Mirk's *Festial* (c. 1390), the *Speculum sacerdotale*, and the collections whose titles betray their direct debt to the seminal *Legenda aurea* of Jacobus de Voragine (Jacopo da Varazze, c. 1229–98), that is, Caxton's *Golden Legend* and the *Gilte Legende*. From their etymology one might expect legendaries to contain things to be read ('legenda')

---

10 Ed. Knight 1967. For another sermon on the three estates see Doyle 1950.
11 Fletcher 1998, 145–69.
12 O'Mara 1998; Powell 2000; Horner 1989 and 1998.

rather than preached. This may be true of Caxton and the *Gilte Legende*, may, or may not be true of *Speculum sacerdotale*, while Mirk explicitly addressed the needs of preachers. My point is that a distinction between preaching and reading cannot be clearly drawn in this period. Saints' lives constituted *materia praedicabilis*, that is, material which *could* be preached. An author's intention with respect to his text was not always observed. Preachers were on the look-out for suitable material, and sermons and sermon-like writings were public property. Mirk acknowledged his debt to the *Legenda aurea* in his preface; *Speculum sacerdotale*, however, was translated from an intervening Latin sermon collection.[13] The ways in which these compilers provided for specifically British, as well as universal saints, is currently attracting attention.[14] Saints' lives might be preached on the Sunday preceding a given saint's day. Hence the common opening formula used in the *Festial*: 'Good men and weymen, such a day ʒe schull haue Seynt Andrawys daye, and fast þe euen. Þe whech dey ʒe schull come to þe chyrch.'[15] In other words, this sermon gives notice of St Andrew's day, and warns the audience in advance of their duties.

Other sermon collections were commonly organised around the set of readings appointed from the gospels and epistles (including for this purpose some passages from the Old Testament prophets and Revelations) for reading at High Mass on Sundays. Most of the surviving English collections of this kind are organised around the cycle of readings appointed for use in the cathedral of Salisbury – Sarum Use – which, by the late medieval period was in almost general use throughout most of southern England. There are a few signs, especially in older collections, of some local variation. Perhaps surprisingly, given the reputation of the friars as preachers, the collections do not show the influence of the Franciscan calendar, which followed Roman Use and differed from Sarum at a prominent time of the Church's year: Advent. The friars, especially after the anti-heresy legislation of the early fifteenth century, were perhaps more apt to record their sermons in Latin (even if they might have been preached in English), and, if they were preaching in parish churches, rather than their own, are likely to have adapted them to the prevailing local use.[16]

Most influential by far of the Sunday gospel collections was the set which comprised a part of a much larger whole: the Wycliffite collection (ed. Hudson and Gradon 1983–1996), described elsewhere in this volume. Because of their comprehensiveness, the Wycliffite sermons are the only series in English to provide for the entire *quadragesimale* (sermons for each day in Lent). Yet there is plenty of evidence, in the form of small groups of Lent sermons surviving on their own in manuscript, and maybe never part of a larger sermon collection, that preachers were especially busy during Lent. Lent was the traditional period for instructing the people in the rudiments of Christian doctrine in preparation for

---

[13] Editions listed in Bibliography. See also Görlach 1972, 1974 and 1998. Details of the source of *Speculum sacerdotale* are given in Spencer 1993, 123, 129.

[14] Wogan-Browne 2001; Bartlett 1995.

[15] *Festial*, ed. Erbe 1905, 6/3–5. A new edition of the *Festial* is being prepared for the Early English Text Society by Susan Powell.

[16] Heffernan 1985, d'Avray 1985. For a case of a friar (perhaps a Franciscan) whose sermons follow Sarum Use, see Hudson and Spencer 1984.

their 'Easter duties' of confession and communion. The only other collection to approach the fullness of the Wycliffite collection's provision for Lent is *Jacob's Well* which, if we are to believe the writer's prefatory remarks, contained sermons preached over a period of ninety-five days, perhaps the 'Easter cycle' from Ash Wednesday until the vigil of Pentecost.[17] *Jacob's Well* contains a particularly comprehensive exposition of these catechetical rudiments including the articles of excommunication, payment of tithes, penance, deadly sins, virtues, works of mercy, the articles of the creed, commandments, Lord's Prayer and Ave. These diverse materials are brought together in the controlling allegory of the digging of the well which gives the collection its title. Other preachers also used sustained allegory as a means of organising pastoral instruction which was carried on serially from week to week, such as the ten branches of the True Vine (Christ: see John 15:1), which represent the Ten Commandments in an unpublished collection extant in Oxford, Bodleian Library MS Bodley 806. Other instances are discussed by Owst (1966).

There remain sermons for many other occasions. The formal collections, complete for the year, appear to imply that weekly preaching was becoming more common in the fifteenth century; certainly contemporaries' comments, and records of church furnishings suggest that preaching in parish churches was becoming more usual by the late fifteenth century. Some benefactors provided for preaching in towns as a work of piety.[18] Yet there are many manuscripts containing small sets of sermons, or oddments. Some, especially Easter sermons, may have been recorded singly in anthologies for private devotion, rather than for preaching; nevertheless the impression that such small sets give is that preachers found it useful to have sermons noted down for important Sundays and certain seasons of the year (especially Lent).[19] Travelling preachers, including prominent ecclesiastics, have left anthologies of their sermons for particular occasions. However, they were not usually recorded as a whole in English, though they commonly incorporate English verses. Such English scraps suggest that the whole was translated into the vernacular in delivery; some preachers have left records explicitly saying that their sermons were preached in the vernacular: *in vulgari*.[20] Internal self-repetitions are common within sermon collections compiled by named individuals, such as Thomas Brinton, Bishop of Rochester (1373–89), as well as in the anonymous compilations of model sermons made for the use of other preachers. This repetition may leave us to doubt that the formal records of their sermons in manuscripts are actual records of oral performances. Rather, such collections have been worked up for 'publication'. At the same time, it seems likely enough that preachers were no more reluctant than any other public speaker to repeat their effects if a *bon mot* had gone down well on a previous occasion.

---

[17] Carruthers 1984; Longère 1983, 61.
[18] The case of the guild of Kalendars, Bristol, is discussed by Orme 1978. Other examples noted in Spencer 1993, 431 n. 152.
[19] O' Mara 1987 and 1988.
[20] For discussions of the language of preaching see Horner 1978; Fletcher 1994; Fletcher 1998, 41–57; Wenzel 1994.

As well as Sunday preaching, there are funeral and memorial sermons, sermons to particular groups including guilds and fraternities, sermons designed for particular preaching venues, especially the famous cross in St Paul's church-yard in London (sermons which commonly addressed tendentious theological and political issues of the day).[21] The preachers themselves, and chroniclers, may tell us something of the external circumstances associated with such preaching. Hence, for example, the colourful example provided by the contro-versy between the Lollard, William Taylor and his opponent, Richard Alkerton in 1406. On 21 November, Taylor had preached at Paul's Cross against clerical possessions; the following day his arguments were controverted by Alkerton in another Paul's Cross sermon. Unsurprisingly, Alkerton's views were not greeted with general enthusiasm. The notion that the Church might be deprived, by force if needs be, of its wealth could attract popular support, especially at times when it appeared reluctant to pay for royal fiscal need. Such indigence in the early years of the Lancastrian regime, was considerable. A layman, Robert Waterton, one of Henry IV's supporters, sent his servant to Alkerton with a curry comb, a symbol of what Waterton saw as his flattery of prelates by 'currying favour'.[22] The sentence of public penance, which the Archbishop of Canterbury, Thomas Arundel, imposed on Waterton, was commuted to private penance, after the king's intercession, during which his servant was to carry a curry comb in one hand and a candle in the other; Taylor, whom Arundel attempted to bring to trial and excommunicated for non-attendance, managed to evade punishment.

What is an English *Sermon?*

It is impossible to draw a clear line between preaching in Latin and preaching in English at this period. This cannot be overemphasised. Sermons recorded in their entirety in English were no doubt preached in English, if they were preached at all. From what has already been said, it will be apparent on the other hand that sermons recorded in Latin were not therefore necessarily preached in Latin. They were commonly preached in English, and to that extent they are English sermons. Even sermons recorded in English usually retain some Latin: typically the justifying scriptural, patristic and other authorities cited, which were clearly read out in Latin, and might then be translated for the benefit of the unlearned: 'Þis name "Clement" aftur þe exsposicion of þe Catholicon est idem quam nobilis, misericors, pius, et sanctus. It is as muche to youre vndyrstondynge as noble, mercyfull, pitovous, and holy.'[23] Sometimes we know Latin sermon writers preached sermons in English because they told us so; often we infer that the sermons were preached in English, because they contain

---

[21] Examples are edited and discussed in Powell and Fletcher 1981, reprinted and revised in Fletcher 1998, 170–97. O'Mara 1994; *Sermon of William Thorpe*, ed. Hudson 1993; see also Knight 1967. On the Paul's Cross sermons, see *John Fisher*, ed. Hatt 2002, 42–47; MacLure (1958).

[22] *Two Wycliffite Texts*, xiv. See further OED 'curry' v. sense 4 and 5 'curry favel', lit. 'to curry the chestnut horse' (later 'curry favour'). On the historical circumstances, see Aston (1984) 1–47.

[23] Ross 1940, 5/15–17. The *Catholicon* referred to was an alphabetical word list by Johannes Balbus, or de Janua, completed in 1286. It was a popular elementary textbook used in the teaching of Latin.

English words and phrases, short poems and rhyming announcements of the sermons' constituent heads of the argument. However care must be exercised in passing this judgement: a preacher might deliver his sermon in Latin to a learned audience, but retain poems and proverbs in the vernacular to salt his discourse, and it does not seem impossible that bilingual and macaronic sermons might have been preached on occasion. Preachers switched between the two languages very readily, as some of the surviving records of sermons and sermon notes show.[24]

Two Dominant Collections

Material in the Wycliffite Sunday gospel sermons was plundered by other sermon compilers. This set provided copy of varying extents for many of the Sunday gospel collections being put together in the period c. 1390–1409. After the Archbishop of Arundel, Thomas Arundel, had issued legislation in 1407–1409 designed to curb the spread of heresy by radical preachers, its influence appears to decline. Yet, because some of the derivative collections continued in use in the later fifteenth century, subsequent sermon compilers continued to take material from the Wycliffite collection at second hand, from the work of the first generation of borrowers, probably without realising whence it had originally come. The collection edited by W.O. Ross (1940) is a case in point. It is an anthology of small sets of sermons taken from diverse other English sources. Some of them, probably unbeknown to the Ross compiler, were originally of a decidedly radical persuasion. The result is a collection which is of considerable interest to the modern student of the subject, since it represents much of the variety of material which was available to preachers in English in the second half of the fifteenth century.

The Wycliffite Sunday gospel series was rivalled and surpassed in influence only by Mirk's *Festial*. Both strongly influenced subsequent compilers, who were hungry for good preaching material and reluctant to resort to original composition. The suspicion surrounding English preaching, especially after Arundel's 1409 Constitutions, renders this reluctance largely understandable; other contributory reasons are discussed below. Besides piecemeal borrowing, great numbers of copies were made of both dominant collections. The *Festial*, which, unlike the Wycliffite collection, had a long history of revision throughout the fifteenth century, and was printed, perhaps under Brigittine influence, in the early sixteenth century, has some claim to be the primary sermon collection of the period. Because of its greater accessibility and later success, the *Festial* has certainly coloured the views of commentators on late medieval spirituality in the sixteenth century and later. The sensational nature of some of its characteristic *narraciones* (Mirk's stories of miracles) confirmed Protestant commentators in their prejudices about pre-Reformation doctrine. At

---

[24] Wenzel 1978 and 1986, and especially 1994; for a different view, see Fletcher 1994. See also Horner 1989, Haines 1972a and1975; Bataillon 1980.

least some of the *Festial*'s success derives from circumstances as much as its intrinsic merits. Its original compiler, the Augustinian canon, John Mirk, probably intended to provide an orthodox counter to heretical preaching, such as the Wycliffite collection. Arundel's Constitutions can only have assisted it to flourish, and the *Festial*'s success is witnessed by the number of copies surviving from the second half of the fifteenth century. In the course of revision in this later period the *temporale* (the portion of the Church's calendar which provides principally for the Sundays of the year) was much augmented, and its more sensational and uncircumspect *narraciones* were edited.[25]

The English Question

Sermons raise perennial questions about lay education, and, in the late fourteenth century and fifteenth especially, about what we may call 'the English question'. What could people without a clerical training safely be told about theology and doctrine in their native language? How suitable was that language to express such complex ideas, when it was perceived to lack the subtlety and specialised vocabulary of Latin, to which such matters had hitherto been confined? There seems good evidence that the textual transmission of English sermons in the fifteenth century was vitally affected by the effects of these discussions: sermons need to be understood in the light of prevailing historical conditions. Because of the importance of sermons as a vehicle for imparting sensitive doctrinal information, and the emphasis placed on the preachers' power to work on their audiences by emotive and persuasive language, the Church authorities sought throughout the period to exercise control of preaching. Preaching in English, a language which was accessible to the entire population, was an especially delicate matter.

In England, at least in the southern Province of Canterbury, censorship reached its height after the 1409 Provincial Constitutions, promulgated by Archbishop Arundel in an attempt to counter the spread of Wycliffism.[26] The canons affecting preaching were not substantially new, but attempted to enforce a restrictive interpretation of pre-existing principles where there had been ambiguity in practice in the past; nevertheless the legislation was fiercely criticised throughout the fifteenth century by both radicals and those of a more moderate persuasion. It seems probable that the Constitutions inhibited the production of new vernacular sermon collections until late in the fifteenth century. Before their publication there are signs that there had been a conscious effort around 1390–1410, to circulate collections of sermons written in English. Not all were as radical as the Wycliffite Sermons.

The delicacy surrounding the use of English to record sermons may be detected also in some features of their style. Writers who are unconfident in their own powers of expression (and the climate of opinion in many quarters

25 Fletcher and Powell 1978. Full discussion of the *Festial*'s textual history will be presented in Susan Powell's forthcoming edition.
26 Hudson 1988; Watson 1995; Spencer 1993, 163–82; Thomson 1965.

discouraged confidence in the expressive powers of English) are particularly apt to quote a source which they find sympathetic, rather than 'find' words of their own for opinions which might otherwise be less clearly formulated. Some sermons were put together almost entirely from scraps of other men's prose. At times it may seem as though the writers may, indeed, have experienced real difficulty in expressing fully formed views in written prose other than by quotation. This is a time when a reader or listener's understanding of a concept was to be measured by whether they had learned a secure and stable 'form of words', as Pecock put it, rather than by the ability to paraphrase.[27] And, in taking notes, it may be easier to record telling or thought-provoking quotations rather than to attempt a personal paraphrase.The inquisitions into Lollardy also encouraged writers to find ways of hinting at their meaning in veiled or coded ways which usually allowed their utterances to be read as decently conformist (albeit at times appearing to us to sail close to the wind). Use of formalised expressions, having the potential for covert meaning within the movement, again removes us from perceiving the nuances of an individual writer's opinions. And deliberate obfuscation does not make a modern reader's job easier. Then, as now, the decent obscurity afforded by allusion to the third person plural pronoun 'they', 'them', without naming the offender, was a refuge to the disaffected. It was a way of letting off steam without incurring any penalty, or being required to substantiate such vague charges. So a secular priest quoted in the collection from the second half of the fifteenth century edited by Ross (1940), discussing hypocrisy, was able to express resentment at those who 'feigned holiness' in order to secure benefices:

> These confermen theym in all that they may in worde and in berynge as holy men doon, that it is full harde for eny man for to knaw on of theym from theym that been holy in-dede, wyth theyre feyned holynes to gete hem summe benefice. (p. 295/16–20)

Questions of Interpretation

Even before 1409, or the burning of the first heretic in 1401, radical writers who felt themselves to be alienated from the visible manifestation of the Church Militant here on earth, represented themselves as subject to persecution: the myth, deriving from scriptural precepts, that they were a persecuted minority, sent out by Christ on the model of his disciples, 'as sheep in the midst of wolves' was a potent one: persecution was a warrant of their veracity. Scriptural allusions in sermons, as we are increasingly coming to recognise, may well contain veiled contemporary allusions: the habit of reading the bible allegorically and tropologically, and the pertinacity of certain favourite scriptural quotations in polemical discussion ensured that connections were made more or less tacitly.

It has been suggested, furthermore, in connection with sermons from an earlier period, that audiences whose modes of discourse are primarily oral do

---

[27] *Book of Faith*, 249/16–21.

not generally distinguish between the distinctiveness of times past and their own present. No doubt such large assertions need testing, especially when considering the much more complicated states of literacy in the late Middle Ages, but it is at least possible that such habits of mind might have persisted as an 'oral residue' in later preaching to lay audiences.[28] There was certainly no difficulty in applying biblical themes to contemporary occasions, but the Middle English sermons were rarely openly topical, and modern students have to read between the lines. At this distance of time, we cannot be sure that our topical interpretations are correct. For example, a sermon in the collection edited by Ross discusses the story of Moses and the burning bush [Exod.3]. When Moses hid his face, this is interpreted to signify that the nobility should occupy themselves with their proper affairs, and not meddle with theology:

> And so it were ryght sittyng ['appropriate'] þat euery man held hym content to common in ['converse about'] maters of ys faculte, polocy, and gouernaunce, so þat kny3thes and oþur gentils with hem shuld sett her besines abowte þe good gouernaunce in þe temperalltee in þe tyme of pees and also abowte diuers poyntes of armes in þe tyme of werre, as þe lawe and þe cronicle techeþ hem.[29]

Ross is likely to be right to view this as a covert comment on Sir John Oldcastle's rebellion of 1413–1414, not least because the passage somewhat resembles Hoccleve's advice explicitly addressed to Oldcastle, and it occurs in a sermon originally by a dignitary who was addressing the court. He alludes to 'owre soueraygne here presente' (Ross, 224/29–30). But, because this is a sermon, the comment is made as a generalised piece of good advice. If it had been too circumscribed by topical events, it would not have been serviceable to the man who compiled the Ross collection. This kind of resolute anonymity, with hints of topicality for those 'in the know', is typical, not just of Middle English sermons, but of much preaching from any time. It is a matter of pulpit propriety, and it is not necessary to invoke orality as the explanation. Such allusions are the *modus operandi* of political sermons: Chrimes has described the opening addresses, declaring the cause of summons to Parliament by successive Chancellors (who were themselves bishops), and noted the conservative influence of Old Testament ideas of kingship which they describe.[30] These parliamentary sermons, like others demonstrate the pull between conventional utterance and specific contemporary allusion, not least in their discussion of such topics as the three estates of society.[31] Sermons are designed to work at different levels, depending on the individual listeners' capacities to understand and mental furniture.[32] So the presence of contemporary allusion may be impossible to prove – some readings will inevitably seem more inherently persuasive than others.

[28] Amos 1993; Ong 1971, 23–47; Stock 1983, 42–87; Holdsworth 1998.
[29] Ross 1940, 224/3–9. Compare 'Address to Sir John Oldcastle, A.D.1415', in *Hoccleve's Works*, ed. Furnivall 1892, i. 14.
[30] Chrimes 1936, 16; see also 142–45. For a recent survey of the parliamentary sermons, especially those of Bishop John Russell, see Watts 2002.
[31] Fletcher 1998, 145–69.
[32] See discussion in Fletcher 1998, 233–48; also 281–303.

We know about the controversy between Taylor and Alkerton because it attracted the attention of the St Alban's chronicler (who, as a Benedictine, knew which side he supported), and from records in the registers of Bishops Chichele and Morgan, who summoned Taylor on subsequent occasions. The lives of the anonymous vernacular compilers cannot be reconstructed, and one can gauge their chronology only approximately from the palaeographical date of the manuscripts and internal references (subject to the caveat mentioned above).

As has already been suggested, there are difficulties in discussing the concept of 'authorship' of sermons. In theory a sermon was 'God's word', not the preacher's own, though some Latin preachers of repute were certainly familiar with the concepts of copyright and plagiarism. Many sermons, however, were compiled or translated from the words of others. Any quest for a personal 'style' would be anachronistic.This is the case, for example, of the anonymous attack, cited above, on hypocrites who pretend holiness in order to get bene- fices: the compiler of the Ross collection was here quoting an earlier sermon.The use of model sermons, compiled for the use of other preachers, was commonplace, and writers of model sermons might often offer alternatives within a sermon to allow an individual some discretion, as in the following, particularly explicit example:

> For as myche as þis gospel spekeþ principalli of þre synnes (þat is: glotenye, veynglorie, and couetise) þerfore, whoso wole, after þe tyme þat he seeþ þat he haþ disposicion of his auditorie, he mai dilate his matere.
>
> (Cigman 1989, p. 131/1–4)

The preacher goes on to offer optional extra material for others to use on these three vices. His remarks are a useful reminder of the exigencies governing actual delivery of a sermon, as distinct from its appearance on the page. The man using his material must see if his audience is becoming restive. As many preachers acknowledged, audiences liked *short* sermons. Not much has changed.

Even a more informal preacher's handbook which has the appearance of being put together by an individual for his own use might incorporate another man's sermons, just as the Franciscan friar, Nicholas Philip did. While noting the occasions on which he preached some of the sermons in his anthology, he included the name 'Melton' after some, suggesting that the 'Melton' group was the work of another man, perhaps a William Melton, who was a noted Fran- ciscan preacher in the first half of the fifteenth century. This Melton has been tentatively identified with the anonymous Greyfriar who confronted Margery Kempe, when she was creating a pious uproar during his sermons preached in Lynn (one of the destinations noted in Philip's collection).[33]

Because sermons were commonly patched together from diverse sources, and because compilers of sermons written in English were often reluctant to write original prose, discerning their real opinions can often be difficult, especially when they may censor controversial matter from one sermon, but allow its substance to be expressed elsewhere. Their views do not seem to be consistent, and are often to be inferred from what they choose to leave out from their

---

[33] Fletcher 1998, 41–57 (50–51).

sources as much as from what they include.[34] When their debts can be traced, some sermons (English and Latin) can be shown to have been pieced together from surprisingly short passages of other men's prose.The results in the surviving manuscripts often show little apparent concern about the resulting risk of incoherence. Once again, in assessing the style of sermons, a modern reader has to remember that they are pragmatic texts, whose life became apparent in performance, rather than on the page. The impression left by many recent accounts of so-called 'modern' ways of constructing sermons is that preachers attached aesthetic importance to the overall structure of their discourse.This impression is understandable when one is reading sermons that are governed by 'principal' heads and sub-divisions. Yet, even in such cases, preachers would freely abandon their announced structure in order to placate audiences:

> For als mekyll als þe tyme passys fast away and lang sermownys nowondayis are haldyn tedius and yrkesom, leuyng to anoþer tyme þe secunde principall of owre sermown, a schorth worde of þe thyrde, and sone make an ende.[35]

Many sermons can be shown to have been compiled from disparate sources. The prompt which caused a compiler to turn to a short passage from a different source from the one with which he had begun might be simply the need to develop a specific subject further, for example, a wish to find further material relating to one of the Commandments, if a preacher had embarked upon an exposition of them. There were plenty of commentaries available on the Commandments, and, indeed, treatises relating to other areas of pastoral instruction, which might jolt the compiler's memory: 'there's good stuff on theft/honouring one's parents/licentiousness in such and such a treatise'. So, for instance, material from the pastoral treatise known as *Pore Caitiff* is used in some sermon collections.[36] Sometimes titbits from influential treatises were, quite simply, memorable: excerpts from *Ancrene Wisse*, for example, have been found, unacknowledged, in many sermons and devotional writings. They often correspond to passages which a modern reader, too, finds memorable, and which find their way into anthologies.[37] They tend to be striking moralised stories (*exempla*) or metaphorical illustrations (*similitudines*) with evident visual properties: the 'dog of hell', a horse shying at a shadow on a bridge. The 'dog of hell' finds his way into a sermon preached in 1406 by Richard Alkerton (he who 'curried favour') at St Mary Spital, London (ed. O'Mara 1987; compare *Ancrene Wisse*, ed. Tolkien 1962, fol. 79a). Often, however, the cue to change source is that, rather than being intrinsically memorable, it happens that, by coincidence, the compiler was able to turn to a different sermon which contained useful and relevant material, because it was associated with a biblical quotation which the compiler himself was using to support his argument. He

---

[34] Spencer 1986 and 1993, 269–320; Fletcher 1998, 119–33.
[35] Ed. O'Mara 2002, 114/291–4. See further O'Mara 1996; Powell 2000, 238–9.
[36] Spencer 1993, 299, 303, 311.
[37] Examples discussed in Spencer 1993, 86–7, 309 and notes. See also Zettersten and Diensberg 2000, xxii n. 33.

matched up the biblical quotations, which (in Latin, it goes almost without saying) acted as the prompt. Almost invariably such quotations (*auctoritates*) are underlined, or boxed, often in red, by scribal convention, and the eye easily picks them out.

Sermon prose should often be seen as having as its basic unit the *auctoritas* with its accompanying comment. Such strings of short passages can be endlessly rearranged to make new sermons. The practice is dependent on writing, yet it is again arguably a reflex of what Ong (1971) would consider an originally oral habit of mind. Composition is the dismemberment of pre-existing 'bite-size pieces for reassemblage into new configurations'. Such a method of composition in sermons, based upon the *auctoritas*, lends some support to John Alford's suggestions about Langland, although the *auctoritates* in *Piers Plowman* perform several functions, and one may not wish to extend the argument to the entire poem.[38] But the habit of composing around quotations with portions of accompanying commentary can certainly be demonstrated in some sermons and is to be suspected in others. It was fostered in academic circles by the use of formal collections of such material, called *distinctiones*, which supply such strings of quotations relevant to subjects alphabetically listed. The use of *distinctiones* is to be suspected in some of the English sermons, and has been demonstrated in some, although debts to particular sets of *distinctiones* are not always easy to prove.[39] Accordingly, the *auctoritates* are primary; they often do not support a preacher's arguments, but rather the other way about: the preacher's words amplify the *auctoritas*. Thus even a preacher who based his sermon upon only a single Biblical sentence – the 'theme' – and proceeded to develop it by divisions and subdivisions, each given countenance by further *auctoritates*, could quite legitimately be said to preach 'God's word', rather than a human fabrication. One reads this prose (and it must be said, other religious literature, too) often in anticipation of a familiar *auctoritas* even before it is adduced, but which one knows full well to be the foundation for what is being said. The value of *auctoritates* to the construction of *distinctiones* is self-evident; although *distinctiones* structure the quotations by placing them in a skeletal organisation, they can and were themselves used for local, rather than overall, composition in a sermon. The characteristics of this aspect of sermon style and method of construction may be illustrated from part of Sermon 48 in the Ross collection. One paragraph in the modern edition does not seem to follow on very easily from what has gone before, or fit with what follows. It is constructed of a string of quotations from St Bernard, with short intervening comment. It is almost certainly from a different source from other parts of the sermon, and it is witnessed independently by another, as yet unpublished, English collection. It is a sermon for Advent, and the subject of the passage is Christ's coming on the Day of Judgement:

---

[38] Alford 1988, 29–65. See further Ong 1971, 34–5 (on 'rhapsody' (lit. 'a stitching together') in the practice of Humanist writers).

[39] von Nolcken 1981; Fletcher and Powell 1978.

I seid also þat þe þrid maner of commyng shall be at þe Day of Dome, qwen he shall deme man . . . Þer-for spekeþ Seynt Barnard of þis commyng in synnefull mens persons and seyþ, et est in sermone De Adventu Iudicis, ubi sic ['and it is in the sermon "Concerning the Coming of the Judge", where it says thus']: 'Semper,' inquid, 'diem illum exstremum considerans, toto corpore contremesco,' et cetera – 'alwey when I thenke on þe last day, for drede my bodie quakeþ' for I can not fynde oon frend to stond at þat day for me, but my synne and my wickednes aȝeyns me. And þer shall no man pray for oþur, but Goddes oune choson children shall be raueshed vp in þe eyre. And þei þat shall be dampned, þe erthe shall swalow hem. 'Certeyn,' seys Seynt Barnard, 'like as þe clowde letteþ þe liȝthe of þe sonne þat it may not shyne vppon þe vrthe, ryght so þer shall be a clowde of synnefull mans dedis be-tweyn God and hem, þat þei shall not see þe blessed face of God.'

(Ross, p. 317/16–34)

The passage illustrates a number of the features of sermon style already mentioned. Thus the easy commerce between English and Latin is seen in the inclusion of comments directed in the first instance to the preacher about the whereabouts of the quotation from St Bernard; the person recording the sermon simply switches languages mid-sentence. The passage is constructed entirely around quotations from St Bernard, rather than the English preacher's own thoughts. It concludes with instructions to the user of the sermon (advice not to be preached) as to how the subject might be continued by telling the audience about the Fifteen Signs which would appear before the Day of Judgement: 'And þat þis is dredefull, narrate de xv signis' (p. 317/35). The Fifteen Signs were a familiar topos of Advent preaching, which a preacher could supply from his own information or from yet another written source (on the subject see Heist 1952). The prime importance attached to Scriptural quotations as the skeleton around which a sermon was formed can also be seen in sermon notes.[40] In other words, it was not only the preachers, but also the listeners who were conditioned to listen out for them. In the early modern period there are records of listeners taking notes of a sermon which they had heard by finding ways of recording simply the biblical *auctoritates* employed. They could then reconstruct the substance of the rest. The practice was taken to an extreme by an illiterate sermon enthusiast, Robert Pasfield, servant to the puritan Cheshire gentleman, John Bruen (1560–1625), himself a voracious sermon-seeker and voluminous taker of notes. Pasfield devised an elaborate mnemonic belt out of leather, referred to in jest by his master as his 'Girdle of Verity', on which were marked the books, chapters and verses of the Bible, by which he was able to recall biblical quotations used by a preacher, and thus to reconstruct the sermon's substance, 'a matter of such wonder unto all that ever saw it, and heard him repeat a sermon by it'.[41] Pasfield and his Girdle were evidently viewed by contemporaries as quaint rustic originals, yet, although no such custom has been described as such in the medieval period, the principle behind his practice is in

---

[40] As in Cambridge, Trinity College MS B.14.50 (Wycliffite sermon notes).
[41] On early modern sermons and memory see Guite 1993. For Pasfield and Bruen see Hinde 1641; Clarke 1675, ii. 85.

substance a more formalised and elaborated extension of medieval ways of thinking about sermons. It was not a wholly new idea. *Auctoritates*, therefore, acted as a memory prompt to both preachers and listeners, as well as to those compiling new sermons out of pre-existing written materials in a study: the practice is not unknown among those revising for examinations in English literature at the present: candidates memorise quotations from texts studied so that they will act as memory prompts for their arguments about those texts when in examination conditions: they do not act solely as guarantees for the rightness of the arguments.

Preaching and Reading: A Visual Style

The inescapable fact about sermons, as distinct from much other Middle English prose, is that they were amphibious. They were oral as well as literate. Some consequences of this basic defining characteristic have already been considered here. The ground which is common to both listeners and readers is memory – sermons must be memorable, whether heard or read, if they are to have any effect. And the sense which was commonly evoked in order to provide memorable features was vision. One of the most evident features of style in religious prose of this period, including sermons, is the use of moralised images: *similitudines*.

A preacher, like any other public speaker, then or now, was most esteemed, if he appeared to speak without notes or other visible prompts. Memory aids assisted him as well as his audience. Exempla, similitudes, a variant of the similitude called a 'picture', rhymes and *auctoritates* all served towards this end, despite the attendant risks that these things will be remembered for their own sake in isolation from the morals which they were intended to elucidate. Such illustrations were generally collected from other people's books, not a preacher's own collection of edifying anecdotes, although from time to time they are given local colour and authenticity by ascribing them to a named location (the stories may nonetheless be of a common type).[42]

Preachers' use of speaking 'pictures' in their sermons has attracted some attention. Objurations to 'see' some affecting circumstance, especially Christ on the cross, were taken more literally than in our own culture: at least such conscious acts of 'image-ination' appear to have been vividly present to their audiences. Jeremiah's plea to 'Behold and see if any sorrow be like unto my sorrow' (Lam. 1:12) prophesied Christ addressing humankind during his great ordeal, and provided the cue for such appeals. Thus:

A-wake from synne and rise owte of þi fowle lustis and loke abowte and be-hold þi mirrour in þe Cros, and þou may see hym – is bake scourged, þe hede sett with white þornes crowned, þe side perched with a speyre, hondes

---

42 E.g. Oxford, Trinity College MS 86, containing an *exemplum* on the penalties for failure to pay tithes, located at Compton, 'Oxenfordshire'. The story is mocked in a later reader's note, 'Comton I knowe, but Comton never knew this to be true' (fol. 47v).

and feet persched, and non hool parti in all is bodie but is tounge, with þe
wiche he preyed for synnefull men. (Ross, p. 111/13–19)

Margery Kempe, whose hearing of affective sermons on the Crucifixion,
conjured up in her mind 'very beholdyng of hys bittyr Passyon' (*Book*, 151/36)
was merely an extreme example of this tendency to 'see'. Funeral sermons have
also attracted attention for their employment of such techniques, though, in the
following remarkable similitude, the preacher attached more importance to
feeling than sight. Yet seeing is more affecting than hearing: if it is bad enough
to hear a dying man's agony through a wall, it is worse to see him:

> Myche more peynful it is to him if he go into þe house þere þe seek ['the sick
> man'] liþe, and seeþ þe wannes and palenes of his visage, þe staring of his yen,
> þe mouȝing ['grimacing'] of his chere, and froþþing of his mouþe, þe bolnyng
> of his breste, and betyng of his armys, and many oþer signes þat he makiþ
> tofore his deeþ. But ȝit it is most peynful to hym þat it feliþ, and þat may wel
> be schewid by reson, me þinkiþ: If it myȝt be so þat a tre whiche haþe many
> rotis were plauntid inne at þi mouþe into þi body, and þe prinsepal rote set in
> þi herte, and in euery lyme of þi body sette oon of þe rotis, if it so were þen
> þat þis tre by gret violence shulde be pullid oute at þi mouþe at onys, reson
> techiþ þat þis shulde be a passyng peyne. Riȝt so fariþ it at mannys deeþ.
>   (Cigman, p. 215/280–91)

Besides *similitudines*, the vernacular writers also made extensive use of the
verbal 'pictures' popularised by the classicising friars of the earlier fourteenth
century, notably Robert Holcot. Such 'pictures' appealed both for their visual
and fashionably pseudo-antique characteristics as well as for their mnemonic
utility (such devices had their origins in the arts of cultivating the artificial
memory).[43] So, several English sermon compilers made use of an illustration, a
verbal 'picture', from Holcot's *Moralitates*: three shields, one bearing three
roses designated 'Litil,' 'Yuel' and 'Fykyll', the second shield having three
swords, labelled 'Dolyng', 'Endyng', 'Deyng', the third having three trumpets:
'Dome', 'Oppynly', 'Myghtfully'. Together they make up a kind of acrostic:
LYF, DED (i.e. 'death'), DOM.[44] The boundary between 'pictures' and 'words'
is infinitely permeable in medieval writing, and the kinds of interdependence
between words and text greatly varied: use of 'ecphrasis', a 'speaking picture',
has attracted much attention in the writings of such as Chaucer, but is
all-pervasive in, indeed, essential to, devotional or meditational texts, and this
includes affective preaching. As Camille has said of the twelfth century, 'much
of the visual art . . . was not so much an expression of the visible world, as of the
spoken word in a still predominantly oral society'.[45] 'Devotional literacy'

---

[43] Powell and Fletcher 1981, rev. Fletcher 1998, 170–97; Smalley 1960; Yates 1966; Carruthers 1990.

[44] One of the English versions (in an unpublished collection represented by Oxford, Bodl. MS e.
Musaeo 180, with other copies) has been edited by Fletcher 1978, sermon for First Sunday in Advent;
A.J. Fletcher is preparing a further study of the use of Holcot's *Castrum sapiencie* by English sermon
writers. An edition of the e Musaeo sermons is in preparation for the Early English Text Society by
S. Morrison. For a more general account of the relation between verses and visual art see Edwards in
Scattergood and Boffey 1997, 26–43.

[45] Camille 1985, 27.

expresses not merely the advance in religious education by learning one's letters, enabling one to study religious texts, but a means of 'reading' images. According to a notorious clerical adage, stemming from Pope Gregory's letter of 600 to Serenus, Bishop of Marseilles, images constituted the laity's books.The understanding of visual images and of the written word may both be referred back to the spoken word, with which the surviving written-out sermons themselves enjoy a problematic relationship. As Baxendall has said, 'The preacher and painter were *répetiteur* to each other',[46] and this relationship extends not only to sacred persons and events, but even the more nugatory exempla, which, as isolable, small illustrative incidents within a sermon, were offered for light relief and the enjoyment of the less well-educated parts of the audience.

Although the old idea that preachers might have used paintings on the walls in churches to illustrate their sermons is incapable of proof, *exempla, similitudines, picturae* have some counterpart with the motifs of the semi-secular, moralizing visual art found in manuscript illustration and church decoration. Both could and did use material from the bestiaries, for example. A somewhat unfamiliar piece of beast-lore (the notion that a lion may be tamed by the force of example if it sees its trainer beat a puppy), found in Egbert of Liège, and subsequently the *Liber de naturis rerum* of Thomas of Cantimpré, is employed in a sermon for the Second Sunday of Advent by the thirteenth-century Paris master, Odo of Cheriton, who was an influence on the late medieval English preachers. It also occurs in the sketchbook of Villard de Honnecourt, whose drawing of a lion owes much to the established conventions of how to draw lions, even while, perhaps as a sales pitch, he claims that it was drawn from life: 'al vif'.[47] Nevertheless, this claim notwithstanding, both artist and preacher had been reading books. Even the schematised language of gesture employed in visual art has a counterpart in advice occasionally given to preachers to use the same familiar gestures: raising the hands aloft to express joy, pointing with the forefinger to draw attention to solemn matters, to point and gaze heavenwards when speaking of divine or heavenly subjects, to place hands on the breast to express humility, or holding them up more moderately to emphasise words pertaining to devotion.[48] Such particular and schematised advice tends to belong late in the period, into the sixteenth century, but some earlier accounts of preachers' oratorical excesses suggest that the general idea was far from new.[49]

Future Directions

The historical record is incomplete, although more can no doubt be achieved by a more systematic study of the episcopal registers and other documentary

---

[46] Baxandall 1972, 49.
[47] Camille 1985, 42–43; Bucher 1979, i. 138–39; on Odo of Cheriton, see Spencer 1982, 461.
[48] Baxandall 1972, 64–65, citing *Mirror of the World* (c. 1527).
[49] Waleys, ed. Charland, 332–33.

sources.[50] Apart from Lollards, who are to be defined by their championship of the vernacular as much as any single doctrinal belief, many of the named preachers, who were typically members of the Mendicant Orders or ecclesiastical notables, rather than parish priests, recorded their sermons in Latin (or at least mostly in Latin).[51] There are fine studies of some of these individuals, but much remains to be done.[52] It must be said that the most fruitful line of further enquiry lies with the Latin material.

Exclusive concentration on sermons recorded in English will take us so far, but cannot ultimately be defended. Although the choice to write in English must often have been a deliberate one in the circumstances of the late fourteenth century and fifteenth, the question was perhaps, rather, 'why *not* write in Latin?' The English writers were prompted to a modicum of self-reflection by their need to defend their choice of recording language and its capacities to express complex theological ideas for which it did not have a ready-made vocabulary. Nevertheless their writing was closely modelled on the example of the much larger group of Latin sermons – some of the English sermon collections have been shown to be direct translations from Latin, or to contain translations in part, and more such debts are strongly to be suspected.[53] There is much to be done on the sources of the English texts.

Study of sermons is perhaps most profitably conducted in an interdisciplinary way by shifting the emphasis from textual study to historical study of the documentary evidence. Regional study might be a beneficial first step towards any attempt to reconstruct a larger picture of the history of preaching in this period.[54] The oral characteristics of sermons cannot be forgotten, although these features are only available for study by inference from the surviving records, and at second hand from the comments of observers. Sermons derive their meaning from performance in particular times and places: they are not 'literary' texts in the sense of words on the page, even though words on the page constitute the bulk of the surviving evidence. The emphasis on mnemonic and visual devices, together with the use of *exempla* in the sermons (knowledge that lay people appreciated stories and *similitudines* was a cliché in the preachers' handbooks) offer the clearest ways of appreciating their 'orality'. But readers also benefit from mnemonic devices, as well as other features of style suitable for oral performance. Preachers had a penchant for rhetorical questions: ' "But, sir," þou seiste parauntur, "how is þis kyngedom of heven like þis kynge?" Sir, I shall tell þe' (Ross, p. 17/36–37). They are a good way of keeping a cantankerous audience quiet by seeming to anticipate objections. But readers can also be awkward, and writers of treatises will also placate them in this way. Especially in collections put together c. 1400, there is some fondness for local alliteration for heightened effect, for social satire or emotive appeals: 'Alle suche ben maad

[50] Greatrex in Muessig 1998, 257–78; Spencer 1993, 257–78 (258–59); Haines 1968 and1972b.
[51] Hudson 1985,141–63; Somerset 1998.
[52] E.g. Fletcher 1998, 41–57 (Nicholas Philip), 58–118 (John Felton); Friend 1936; Mifsud 1953; Forde 1985; Horner 1978, 1989 and 1990.
[53] For a summary and discussion of translation method in sermons see Spencer 1993, 82–86, 118–33.
[54] Hughes 1988; Dobson 1976; Fletcher 1998, 21–142.

blynde or blyndefeld for a tyme, as men pleyen abobbid, for þei beþ bobbid in hire bileue and in hire catel boþe bi suche lepers ouer londe þat libbeþ bi hire lesyngis' (Cigman, pp. 113/302–114/305). Here the emotive quality of the prose is more important than clarity of sense. A generalised comment about unrepentant sinners who are like men playing blindman's buff turns into a coded assault on vagrants ('leapers over land'), in which category this preacher probably included friars, although he does not openly say so. However, even those not initiated into his code will recognise the strength of his feelings and guess that there may be more going on than is apparent on the surface.

Alliterative prose had, of course, a long and honourable tradition in English religious writing. Yet sermons translated from Latin tolerate (at least in their written form) close, not to say slavish, imitation of characteristic features of Latin syntax, coupled with a penchant for vocabulary which approximates to the form of a Latin word to render unfamiliar concepts. They would not have been easy for an audience unfamiliar with Latin to follow. *Speculum sacerdotale* may furnish one instance out of many. In a discussion of the number of days to be devoted to mourning the dead, the preacher moralises the number seven, with the numbers three and four of which it is the sum, and thence multiples of three:

> The sowle hath thre strengþes: scilicet racionabilite, concupiscibilite, and irascibilite. And the body is i-made of iiii. elamentis, and þerfore for that the synnes may be i-waschid a-way by vii, we celebrate the septenarie ['interval of seven days'] . . . And som takeþ space of ix. dayes þrou3 custom and consideracion that the sowles mowe be delyuered fro peynes and ioyned to the ix. ordres of aungelis. But this custom is no3t a-proued, but it is forbode, for in the ix. day askes ['ashes'] i-brende were. And þerfore is a nonendyual ['interval of nine days'] forbode ['forbidden'] that we ne folowe no3t the Gentiles in that as we folowe the Iewys by celebracion of Paske.
>
> (Weatherly, pp. 231/34–232/14)

Fuller discussion of the toleration of 'hard words' and Latin-derived syntax in Middle English sermon style may be found in Spencer 1993, 118–33.

Despite what one would imagine to be the demands of performance, such sermons are 'bookish'. But, in this period, 'bookishness' cannot be dissociated from the persistence of what have often been diagnosed as 'oral features' of style: parataxis, fondness for aphoristic utterance, various kinds of repetition, formulary construction. The interrelation of bookishness with what Ong has called 'residual orality' in sermons is intimate. Claims have been made for signs of concessions being made to accommodate illiterate habits of thought by literate clerics in Carolingian sermons.[55] Late medieval English preachers were aware of the need to make such allowances in theory. Whether and to what extent they did might repay investigation. Any preacher, from any time, was aware of the need (expressed openly in some of the *artes praedicandi*) to modify one's style of discourse when addressing unsophisticated audiences. However, degrees of competence in letters, including 'pragmatic' literacy, in the late Middle Ages are considerably more complex, and audiences were clearly impa-

---

[55] Amos 1993. See also McKitterick 1989.

tient of being preached at in ways that had traditionally been thought suitable for simple unlettered people.[56] This impatience extended to methods of constructing sermons. Old fashioned simple so-called 'homilies' might no longer be tolerated when people expected a sermon (at least a public sermon in an urban setting) to be composed according to accepted professional principles and to appear before them in proper academic dress.[57] People like to think they are sophisticated, even though there were a few clerics who, on ideological grounds, thought that old ways (the ways practised by Christ and the early doctors of the Church) should be revived. And even urban sophisticates need to be reminded of elementary Christian teaching – the obligation to show common charity, for instance. As is the case with the better-known religious literature, study of late medieval preaching cannot be separated from the stormy questions of the literacy and education of the laity in the period.

BIBLIOGRAPHY

Primary Sources

Ancrene Riwle, *The English Text of the* Ancrene Riwle*: The 'Vernon' Text*, ed. A. Zettersten and B. Diensberg, EETS 310 (2000)
Ancrene Wisse, Edited from MS. Corpus Christi College Cambridge 402 by J.R.R. Tolkien, EETS 249 (1962)
Clarke, Samuel, *The Marrow of Ecclesiastical History . . .*, 3rd ed. (London, 1675)
Brinton, Thomas, *The Sermons of Thomas Brinton, Bishop of Rochester, 1373–1389*, ed. M.A. Devlin, Camden Society 3rd ser. 85, 86 (London, 1954)
Fisher, John, *English Works of John Fisher, Bishop of Rochester: Sermons and Other Writings 1520–1535*, ed. Cecilia A. Hatt (Oxford, 2002)
Hinde, William, *A Faithfull Remonstrance of the Holy Life and Happy Death of John Bruen of Bruen-Stapleford, in the County of Cheshire, Esquire* (London, 1641)
Hoccleve's Works, i: The Minor Poems, ed. F. J. Furnivall, EETS es 61 (1892)
Kempe, Margery, *The Book of Margery Kempe*, ed. S.B. Meech and H.E. Allen, EETS os 212 (1940)
Mirk, John, *Mirk's Festial*, ed. T. Erbe, EETS es 96 (1905)
The Northern Homily Cycle: The Expanded Version in MSS. Harley 4196 and Cotton Tiberius E. vii, ed. S. Nevanlinna, Mémoires de la Société Néophilogique de Helsinki 38, 41 and 43 (Helsinki, 1972–74)
[O'Mara] *Four Middle English Sermons: Edited from British Library MS Harley 2268*, Middle English Texts 33 (Heidelberg, 2002)
Pecock, Reginald, *The Book of Faith*, ed. J.L. Morison (Glasgow, 1909)
[Ross] *Middle English Sermons: Edited from British Museum MS. Royal 18 B.xxiii*, ed. W.O. Ross, *EETS 209* (1940)
The Early South English Legendary, ed. C. Horstmann, EETS os 87 (1887)
The South English Legendary, ed. C. D'Evelyn and A.J. Mill, EETS 235, 236, 244 (1956–59)
Speculum sacerdotale, ed. E.H. Weatherley, EETS 200 (1936)

---

[56] Stock 1983; Parkes 1991, 275–97; Aston 1984, 101–33, 135–92, 193–217; Clanchy 1993.
[57] Spencer 1993, 228–68 and references there given.

Supplementary Lives in Some Manuscripts of the Gilte Legende, ed. R. Hamer and V. Russell, EETS 315 (2000)

Waleys, Thomas, *De modo componendi sermones*, in Th.M. Charland, *Artes praedicandi: contribution à l'histoire de la rhétorique au moyen âge*, Publications de l'Institut d'études médiévales d'Ottawa 7 (Paris and Ottawa, 1936)

Wimbledon, Thomas, *Wimbledon's Sermon: Redde rationem villicationis tue. A Middle English Sermon of the Fourteenth Century*, ed. Ione Kemp Knight, Duquesne Studies, Philological Series 9 (Pittsburgh, Pa., 1967)

English Wycliffite Sermons, ed. Anne Hudson and Pamela Gradon, 5 vols (Oxford, 1983–96)

Two Wycliffite Texts: The Sermon of William Taylor 1406, The Testimony of William Thorpe 1407, ed. Anne Hudson, EETS 301 (1993)

Secondary Sources

Alford, John A., ed., *A Companion to* Piers Plowman (Berkeley and Los Angeles, 1988)

Amos, Thomas L., 'Early Medieval Sermons and their Audience', in Hamesse and Hermand 1993, 1–14

Bartlett, Robert, 'The Hagiography of Angevin England', in Coss and Lloyd 1995, 37–52

Bataillon, L.J., 'Approaches to the Study of Medieval Sermons', *Leeds Studies in English*, ns 11 (1980), 19–35

Baxandall, Michael, *Painting and Experience in Fifteenth Century Italy: A Primer in the Social History of Pictorial Style* (Oxford, 1972)

Bernard, G.W., and S.J. Gunn, eds, *Authority and Consent in Tudor England: Essays Presented to C.S.L. Davies* (Aldershot, 2002)

Blench, J.W., *Preaching in England in the Late Fifteenth and Sixteenth Centuries: A Study of English Sermons 1450–c.1600* (Oxford, 1964)

Bucher, François, *Architector: The Lodge Books and Sketchbooks of Medieval Architects* (New York, 1979)

Camille, Michael, 'Seeing and Reading: Some Visual Implications of Medieval Literacy and Illiteracy', *Art History* 8 (1985), 26–49

Carruthers, L.M., 'The Liturgical Setting of *Jacob's Well*', *English Language Notes* 24 (1987), 11–24

Carruthers, Mary J., *The Book of Memory: A Study of Memory in Medieval Culture* (Cambridge, 1990)

Chrimes, S.B., *English Constitutional Ideas in the Fifteenth Century* (Cambridge, 1936)

Clanchy, M.T., *From Memory to Written Record: England 1066–1307*, 2nd rev. ed. (Oxford, 1993)

Coss, P.R., and S.D. Lloyd, eds, *Thirteenth-Century England V* (Woodbridge, 1995)

d'Avray, D.L., *The Preaching of the Friars: Sermons Diffused from Paris before 1300* (Oxford, 1985)

Dobson, E.J., *The Origins of 'Ancrene Wisse'* (Oxford, 1976)

Doyle, A.I., 'A Treatise of the Three Estates', *Dominican Studies* 3 (1950), 351–58

Edwards, A.S.G., 'Middle English Inscriptional Verse-Texts', in Scattergood and Boffey 1997, 26–43

Fletcher, A.J., 'A Critical Edition of Selected Sermons from an Unpublished Fifteenth-Century *de Tempore* Sermon Cycle' (unpublished B. Litt. thesis, University of Oxford, 1978)

————, 'The Meaning of "Gostly to owr purpos" in *Mankind*', *Notes and Queries* ns 31 (1984), 301–02

————, 'John Mirk and the Lollards', *Medium Ævum* 56 (1987), 217–24

————, 'The Preaching of the Pardoner', *Studies in the Age of Chaucer* 11 (1989), 15–35

————, ' "Benedictus qui venit in nomine Domini": A Thirteenth-Century Sermon for Advent and the Macaronic Style in England', *Mediaeval Studies* 56 (1994), 217–45

————, *Preaching, Politics and Poetry in Late-Medieval England* (Dublin, 1998)

Fletcher, Alan. J., and Raymond Gillespie, eds, *Irish Preaching 700–1700* (Dublin, 2001)

Fletcher, Alan. J., and S. Powell, 'The Origins of a Fifteenth-Century Sermon Collection: MSS Harley 2247 and Royal 18 B. xxv', *Leeds Studies in English* ns 10 (1978), 74–96

Forde, S.N., 'Writings of a Reformer: A Look at Sermon Studies and Bible Studies through Repyngdon's *Sermones super Evangelia Dominicalia*' (unpublished Ph.D. thesis, University of Birmingham, 1985)

Friend, A.C., 'The Life and Unprinted Works of Master Odo of Cheriton' (unpublished D. Phil. thesis, University of Oxford, 1936)

Gallick, Susan, 'A Look at Chaucer and his Preachers', *Speculum* 50 (1975), 456–76

Gatch, Milton McC., *Preaching and Theology in Anglo-Saxon England: Ælfric and Wulfstan* (Toronto and Buffalo, 1977)

Görlach, M., *The South English Legendary, Gilte Legende and Golden Legend*, Braunschweiger anglistische Arbeiten 3 (Brunswick, 1972)

————, *The Textual Tradition of the South English Legendary*, Leeds Texts and Monographs ns 6 (Leeds, 1974)

————, *Studies in Middle English Saints' Legends*, Anglistische Forschungen 257 (Heidelberg, 1998)

Greatrex, Joan, 'Benedictine Sermons: Preparation and Practice in the English Monastic Cathedral Cloisters' in Muessig 1998, 257–78

Guite, A.M., 'The Art of Memory and the Art of Salvation: A Study with Reference to the Works of Lancelot Andrewes, John Donne and T.S. Eliot' (unpublished Ph.D. thesis, University of Durham, 1993)

Haines, Roy M., 'Aspects of the Episcopate of John Carpenter, Bishop of Worcester 1440–1476', *Journal of Ecclesiastical History* 19 (1968), 11–40

————, 'The Practice and Problems of a Fifteenth-Century English Bishop: The Episcopate of William Gray', *Mediaeval Studies* 34 (1972a), 435–61

————, ' "Wilde Wittes and Wilfulnes": John Swetstock's Attack on those "Poyswunmongeres", the Lollards', *Studies in Church History* 8 (1972b), 143–53

————, 'Church, Society and Politics in the Early Fifteenth Century as Viewed from an English Pulpit', *Studies in Church History* 12 (1975), 143–57

Hamesse, Jacqueline, and Xavier Hermand, eds, *De L'Homélie au sermon: Histoire de la prédication médiévale*, Publications de l'Institut d'Etudes Médiévales, Textes, Etudes, Congrès 14 (Louvain-la-Neuve,1993)

Heffernan, T.J., 'The Authorship of the "Northern Homily Cycle": The Liturgical Affiliations of the Sunday Gospel Pericopes as a Test', *Traditio* 41 (1985), 289–309

Heist, W.W., *The Fifteen Signs before Doomsday*, Michigan State College of Agriculture and Applied Science, Studies in Language and Literature (East Lansing, 1952)

Holdsworth, Christopher, 'Were the Sermons of St Bernard on the Song of Songs Ever Preached?' in Muessig 1998, 295–318

Horner, P.J., 'A Sermon on the Anniversary of the Death of Thomas Beauchamp, Earl of Warwick', *Traditio* 34 (1978), 381–401

———, 'Benedictines and Preaching in Fifteenth-Century England: The Evidence of Two Bodleian Library MSS', *Revue bénédictine* 99 (1989), 313–32

———, 'Benedictines and Preaching the *Pastoralia* in Late Medieval England: A Preliminary Inquiry', in Muessig 1998, 279–92

Hudson, Anne, and H.L. Spencer, 'Old Author, New Work: The Sermons of MS Longleat 4', *Medium Ævum* 53 (1984), 220–38

———, *Lollards and their Books* (London, 1985)

———, *The Premature Reformation: Wycliffite Texts and Lollard History* (Oxford, 1988)

Hughes, Jonathan, *Pastors and Visionaries: Religion and Secular Life in Late Medieval Yorkshire* (Woodbridge, 1988)

Kienzle, Beverly Maine, ed., *Models of Holiness in Medieval Sermons: Proceedings of the International Symposium (Kalamazoo, 4–7 May 1995)*, Textes et Etudes du Moyen Age 5 (Louvain-la-Neuve, 1996)

———, ed., *The Sermon*, Typologie des Sources du Moyen Age Occidental 81–3 (Turnhout, 2000)

Longère, J., *La Prédication médiévale* (Paris, 1983)

McKitterick, Rosamond, *The Carolingians and the Written Word* (Cambridge, 1989)

MacLure, Millar, *The Paul's Cross Sermons, 1534–1642*, University of Toronto, Department of English Studies and Texts 6 (Toronto, 1958)

———, *Register of Sermons Preached at Paul's Cross, 1534–1642*, rev. Jackson Campbell Boswell and Peter Pauls, Victoria University of Toronto Centre for Reformation and Renaissance Studies 6 (Ottawa, 1989)

Martin, H., *Le Métier de prédicateur à la fin du Moyen Age, 1350–1520* (Paris, 1988)

Mifsud, G., 'John Sheppey, Bishop of Rochester, as Preacher and Collector of Sermons' (unpublished B. Litt. thesis, University of Oxford, 1953)

Muessig, C., ed., *Medieval Monastic Preaching*, Brill's Studies in Intellectual History 90 (Leiden, Boston and Cologne, 1998)

O'Mara, V.M., 'A Study of Unedited Late Middle English Sermons that Occur Singly or in Small Groups' (unpublished Ph.D. thesis, University of Leeds, 1987)

———, 'A Checklist of Unedited Late Middle English Sermons that Occur Singly or in Small Groups', *Leeds Studies in English* ns 19 (1988), 141–66

———, *A Study and Edition of Selected Middle English Sermons. Richard Alkerton's Easter Week Sermon Preached at St Mary Spital in 1406: A Sermon on Sunday Observance, and a Nunnery Sermon for the Feast of the Assumption*, Leeds Texts and Monographs ns 13 (Leeds, 1994), pp. 141–221

———, 'The "Hallowyng of þe Tabernakyll of owre Sawle" according to the Preacher of the Middle English Sermons in BL MS Harley 2268', in Kienzle 1996, 229–42

———, 'Preaching to Nuns in Late Medieval England', in Muessig 1998, 93–119

Ong, Walter J., 'Oral Residue in Tudor Prose Style', in *Rhetoric, Romance and Technology: Studies in the Interaction of Expression and Culture* (Ithaca and London, 1971)

Orme, Nicholas, 'The Guild of Kalendars, Bristol', *Transactions of the Bristol and Gloucestershire Archaeological Society* 96 (1978), 32–52

Owst, G.R., *Preaching in Medieval England: An Introduction to Sermon Manuscripts of the Period c. 1350–1450* (Cambridge, 1926)

———, *Literature and Pulpit in Medieval England* 2nd rev. ed. (Oxford, 1961)

Parkes, M.B., *Scribes, Scripts and Readers: Studies in the Communication, Presentation and Dissemination of Medieval Texts* (London and Rio Grande, 1991)

Powell, Susan, 'A New Dating of John Mirk's *Festial*', *Notes and Queries* ns 29 (1982), 487–89

————, 'Preaching at Syon Abbey', *Leeds Studies in English* ns 31 (2000), 229–67

Powell, Susan, and Alan J. Fletcher, ' "In Die Sepulture seu Trigintale": The Late-Medieval Funeral and Memorial Sermon', *Leeds Studies in English* ns 12 (1981), 195–228, rev. in Fletcher 1998, 170–97

Scattergood, John, and Julia Boffey, eds, *Texts and their Contexts: Papers from the Early Book Society* (Dublin, 1997)

Schneyer, J.B., *Repertorium der lateinischen Sermones des Mittelalters*, 9 vols (Münster, 1973–80)

Shain, C., 'Pulpit Rhetoric in Three Canterbury Tales', *Modern Language Notes* 70 (1955), 235–45

Somerset, Fiona, *Clerical Discourse and Lay Audience in Late Medieval England*, Cambridge Studies in Medieval Literature 37 (Cambridge, 1998)

Spencer, H.L., 'English Vernacular Sunday Preaching in the Late Fourteenth Century and Fifteenth Century, with Illustrative Texts' (unpublished D. Phil. thesis, University of Oxford, 1982)

————, 'The Fortunes of a Lollard Sermon-Cycle in the Later Fifteenth Century', *Mediaeval Studies* 48 (1986), 352–96

————, *English Preaching in the Late Middle Ages* (Oxford, 1993)

————, 'Middle English Sermons', in Kienzle 2000, 597–660

Stock, Brian, *The Implications of Literacy: Written Language and Models of Interpretation in the Eleventh and Twelfth Centuries* (Princeton, NJ, 1983)

Taylor, Larissa, *Soldiers of Christ: Preaching in Late Medieval and Reformation France* (New York and Oxford, 1992)

Thomson, John A.F., *The Later Lollards 1414–1520* (Oxford, 1965)

von Nolcken, Christina, 'Some Alphabetical Compendia and how Preachers used them in Fourteenth-Century England', *Viator* 12 (1981), 271–88

Watson, Nicholas, 'Censorship and Cultural Change in Late-Medieval England: Vernacular Theology, the Oxford Translation Debate, and Arundel's Constitutions of 1409', *Speculum* 70 (1995), 822–64

Watts, John, 'The Policie in Christen Remes: Bishop Russell's Parliamentary Sermons of 1483–4', in Bernard and Gunn 2002, 33–59

Wenzel, Siegfried, 'Chaucer and the Language of Contemporary Preaching', *Studies in Philology* 73 (1976), 138–61

————, *Verses in Sermons, 'Fasciculus Morum' and its Middle English Poems*, Mediaeval Academy of America Publication 87 (Cambridge, Mass., 1978)

————, *Preachers, Poets and the Early English Lyric* (Princeton NJ, 1986)

————, *Macaronic Sermons. Bilingualism and Preaching in Late-Medieval England*, Recentiores Later Latin Texts and Contexts (Ann Arbor, 1994)

Wogan-Browne, Jocelyn, *Saints' Lives and Women's Literary Culture c. 1150–1300: Virginity and its Authorizations* (Oxford, 2001)

Yates, Frances A., *The Art of Memory* (London, 1966)

11

Historical Writing[1]

ALFRED HIATT

During the period from the Norman Conquest to the late fourteenth century, the principal languages of historical writing in England were Latin and Anglo-Norman. From 1400, however, a trickle of works in English that had begun in the fourteenth century became a veritable deluge. This revival raises some important questions. What kinds of history were written in Middle English? By whom and for whom were they written? And what political and social purposes were served by historical writing in Middle English? In suggesting some answers to these questions with regard to prose texts, I will emphasise the importance of *translation*, as a means of generating a historical literature in English, and of the notion of *continuation*, as a means of interacting with a pre-existing corpus of historical writing. Translation and continuation were the practices that enabled a considerable body of historical matter written in English to emerge by the end of the fifteenth century. At the same time, it is important to emphasise the variety of historical writing in Middle English – the range, that is, not only of genres in which history was written, but also of the physical forms, including rolls and documents, as well as books, by which historical writing was transmitted.

Before going any further it is necessary to discuss what is meant by the term historical writing. This term certainly encompasses types of text that have long been considered the standard vehicles of medieval historiography: chronicles, annals, and genealogies, as well as short accounts of particular historical events. Recent surveys have broadened the definition of historical writing somewhat to include propagandistic and political tracts and narratives, prophetic material, descriptions of ceremonies, and newsletters (Kennedy; Matheson 1984; Gransden). It may also be time to rethink the traditional distinction between 'historical literature' and official documents, texts written for the express purpose of forming a historical record, and which were frequently incorporated into historical narratives (Taylor, 39–40; Spiegel, 14). It can be argued, more-over, that texts such as forgeries, apocrypha and pseudepigrapha, as well as literary adaptations of document form such as the late Middle English charters of Christ are historiographical in their intent and function, since they pose as historical texts (whether with the intent of deception or not) in order to situate a

---

[1] In preparing this essay I have been greatly assisted by the suggestions and comments of Tamar Drukker, A.S.G. Edwards, and Scott-Morgan Straker.

contemporary audience in relation to the past. In the fourteenth and fifteenth centuries themselves there seems on the surface to have been an absence of rigid notions of the subject matter fit for historical writing. John Capgrave's dedication to his *Abbreuiacion of Chronicles* (completed in 1462–63) identifies his material simply and broadly as 'elde stories', and 'þe most famous þingis þat haue be do in þe world' from Creation until 1417 (Capgrave, 7). Under such a criterion, romance narratives and hagiography could equally be considered historical writing, since they tell of both old and famous events – and indeed such genres inform a great deal of medieval historiography, Capgrave's work included.

It is tempting, then, to define historical writing in the Middle Ages simply as writing that displays an interest in the past. However, such a definition could be applied to an almost limitless range of medieval texts. Neither can medieval historical writing be defined by the presence of an overriding concern with fact (though most histories claim that their accounts are true versions of events), since medieval histories routinely include elements that most modern historians would consider fictional, or at least legendary or mythical. Nor can a definition satisfactorily be restricted to texts that show an intention to educate rather than entertain the reader: the content and popularity of much medieval historiography indicates that it was designed to be read for pleasure as well as edification. How, then, can medieval historical writing be distinguished from other categories of medieval literature? One important point to make is that late medieval historical writing in English does not in general rely on literary models of authority. That is, it is not ultimately driven by authorial identity: not only are many histories anonymous or composed by multiple authors, writers of histories tend not to construct themselves as authors (*auctores*) at all. Moreover, they do not seek to construct an authorised, finished, text; indeed, they frequently invite their readers to add or revise information. Crucially, they do not consistently seek to authorise their texts by reference to previous authorities (sources, in fact, frequently go unacknowledged). Historical narrative is ongoing, open to continuation, and it invites interaction, correction, and continuation from numerous sources; authority comes from the narrative itself, and the form in which it is presented, rather than from the name of the author. It may be, then, that a definition of English historical writing in the fourteenth and fifteenth centuries should be based on questions of narration rather than motivation or content. The essential feature of late medieval historical writing in English seems to be the sense of a contribution to an ongoing narrative – a narrative that begins with Creation, continues to the writer's present, and will continue until Judgement. If writing attempts to situate itself within that narrative, whether telling or retelling all or only a small part of it, and if that contribution seems designed to be read *as history*, then we should think of it as historical.

Continuation

For historical writing in Middle English the single most important act (or set of acts) was the translation of the prose *Brut* into English. The *Brut*, composed in

Anglo-Norman in the first half of the fourteenth century (an earlier version had been produced in 1272), offered its audience, for the first time, a consolidated history of Britain from first inhabitation to the recent past, in the form of a linear account of the kings of Britain. In so doing it drew heavily upon Geoffrey of Monmouth's *Historia regum britannie* (History of the Kings of Britain) and Wace's *Roman de Brut*. But where Geoffrey, Wace, and Wace's follower Layamon, took their narrative from the colonisation of the island of Albion by the Trojan exile Brutus and his followers as far as the reign of King Cadwallader (seventh century AD), the *Brut* continued this account to incorporate Saxon, Norman, Anglo-Norman, and finally English kings, including fourteenth- and eventually fifteenth-century monarchs. It also (initially in a Latin version) added a prologue which recounts the pre-Brutus occupation of the island of Albion by the exiled Greek or Syrian princess Albina and her sisters (see further Carley and Crick). The *Brut*, then, provided both a history of the origins of the kingdom of Britain, and a means of connecting those origins with the monarchy of the present day through successive royal genealogies. Divided into chapters, rather than years or reigns, it becomes (unsurprisingly) increasingly detailed from the reign of Edward I (1272–1307); however, prior to the Norman Conquest, considerable attention is lavished on the British kings Brutus, Vortigern, Uther Pendragon and above all Arthur. The *Brut*'s translation into English seems to have taken place in the late fourteenth century: the earliest manuscripts of the Middle English *Brut* date from around 1400, and they do not diverge greatly from manuscripts of their source, the Anglo-Norman Long Version (the narrative of which ends in 1333), which continued to enjoy popularity in England in the late fourteenth and early fifteenth centuries (Matheson 1998, 47). In turn, an English *Brut* itself formed the basis of the 'Second Version' of the Latin *Brut*, which was compiled in the fifteenth century (Matheson 1998, 42–46).

The more than 180 surviving manuscripts of the Middle English *Brut* have been divided into four basic categories: (i) the 'Common Version', which consists of a narrative from Albina until 1333, to which numerous additions were made by different continuators, extending the narrative variously to 1377, 1419, 1430, 1434, 1445, and 1461; (ii) the 'Extended Version', which supplements the early part of the narrative with details from an anonymous metrical chronicle, and which adds to the Common Version a short exordium, giving an account of the composition of the *Brut* (Matheson 1998, 173); (iii) the 'Abbreviated Version', most groups of which contain the exordium of the Extended Version, but which is characterised by significant abbreviations and omissions of material found in both the Common and Extended Versions (Matheson 1998, 204); and (iv) the 'Peculiar Texts and Versions', texts that in some cases include unique interpolations from other historical works, and in others evince a close connection with the Latin *Brut* (Matheson 1998, 256). This category includes a second translation of the Anglo-Norman *Brut* into English, attributed to a John Mandeville (not the 'author' of *Mandeville's Travels*). In 1480 William Caxton printed a text of the Common Version, continued to 1461, as *The Chronicles of England*, which formed the basis for twelve subsequent editions between 1482 and 1528 (Matheson 1998, 339–48). The *Brut*'s appearance in print did not prevent further manuscript continuations. The best illustration of this point is the chronicle traditionally ascribed to John Warkworth, master of Peterhouse, Cambridge, from 1473 to 1500, but now tentatively attributed to another fellow of Peterhouse, the Yorkshireman Roger Lancaster (*'Warkworth's Chronicle'*, 87). 'Warkworth's' *Chronicle* picks up where Caxton leaves off, compiling an account of English history from Edward IV's coronation in 1461 until 1474, and it is clear from manuscript evidence that this chronicle was conceived of explicitly as a continuation of the printed version of the *Brut* narrative. Nevertheless, the printing of the *Brut* does seem to have played an important role in fixing the text, since manuscript continuations dry up fairly quickly thereafter, leaving a relatively stable text (Drukker, 20).

This summary of the versions of the Middle English prose *Brut* inevitably glosses over the complexity of the manuscript traditions of the *Brut*, but it should make one point clear: there is not one *Brut*, or even one Middle English *Brut*, but many (Kelly and O'Rourke, 41). This is, in other words, a fluid text, without an original or a single author, subject to interpolation, omission and addition. On the other hand, it is important to note that a core narrative (from Brutus to at least the Norman Conquest, and in most cases beyond to the thirteenth, fourteenth, and fifteenth centuries) is shared by almost all versions, whether Latin, Anglo-Norman, or English. This last point draws attention to another important aspect of historical writing in late medieval England: its multi-lingual nature. This is an area that requires further investigation, but it is clear that the *Brut* continued in the fifteenth century to be read in its Latin, Anglo-Norman, and English versions. Moreover, while the translation of the *Brut* into English seems to have made English, rather than French, the language of vernacular continuation, there is considerable evidence to suggest the continuing vitality of the Latin *Brut* tradition in the fifteenth century (Matheson 1998, 42–46). It seems likely that the *Brut*'s multiple nature – its existence, that is, in numerous states and versions – coupled with its retention of a solid core of historical information, contributed to its great popularity in the fifteenth century. This was, that is to say, a text that invited interaction from suitably qualified compilers who were able to repackage and above all translate and update its contents without substantially recasting its narrative, and that combination of flexibility and continuity helped contribute to its authoritative status and to its wide-spread dissemination.

This process of flexible continuation is made evident in a scribal comment found in the copy of the *Brut* preserved in BL, Egerton MS 650. The manuscript ends with the description of the siege of Rouen (1419), after which the scribe has written in red ink:

> Here is no more of the sege of Rone and þat is be cause we wanted þe trewe copy þerof bot who so euer owys þis boke may wryte it oute in þe henderend of þis boke or in the forþer end of it whene he gettes þe trew copy. When it is wryttyn wryte in þeis iij voyde lyns where it may be foundyn.
>
> (BL, Egerton MS 650, fol. 111r)

Three ruled lines were indeed left blank beneath this remark; they remained unfilled until the sixteenth century, when a reader inserted a reference to the 1548 edition of Hall's *Chronicle*. However, on fol. 111v the history was continued, in the hand of the very same scribe who had lacked the complete text of the *Brut*, in the form of entries taken from a London chronicle (McLaren 2002, 46). This scribal comment, then, goes some way to explaining how the *Brut* managed to remain a coherent text while never being definitively finished. The scribe, perhaps operating within a workshop, is concerned to pass on to the owner of the book the 'trewe copy'; at the same time, transcription of the text is conceived of as an ongoing process.

That notion of the *Brut* as a living text is also conveyed forcefully in the exordium that is a feature of both the Extended and Abbreviated Versions:

> And þis boke made & compiled men of religioun & oþer good clerkes þat wreten þat bifell in her tymes and made þerof grete bokes and remembraunce to men þat comen aftir hem to heere and to see what bifell in þe londe afore tyme and callid hem Cronycles. And in þis londe haue been from Brute to kynge Edward þe thridde aftir þe conquest C xxxij kynges whos lyues and actes ben compiled shortly in þis boke þe whiche conteyneth CC xxxviij chapitres wiþoute þe prothogoll or prolog   [printed Matheson 1998, 64–65]

The *Brut* is, according to this description, multi-authored, and it is written for the express purpose of informing future generations. The exordium invites, in turn, acts that continue the original goal of making 'great books and remembrance'; it establishes a quasi-genealogical connection between those men of religion and good clerks and their successors. That sense of genealogy is made explicit in the enumeration of the kings from Brutus to Edward, but it is also linked to the production of the book: the chronological division of the history of Britain into 132 reigns is compared with the structural division of the book into 238 chapters, the time of the realm aligned with the space of the book. Both, it is implied, will be subject to continuation.

No less than its value as a historical source, the *Brut*'s literary merit has frequently been derided. Its early twentieth-century editor, Brie, was of the opinion that '[a]s literature, the Chronicle is as worthless – except a few inserted poems – as a mediaeval Chronicle possibly can be' (ix–x). There is no denying the plain and generally unadorned style of the *Brut*, but more recent critics have seen the plainness of the style as contributing to its function as national history. In the first place, its plain style ensured that the *Brut* could be read by a wide range of readers, lay and clerical, male and female. Apart from accessibility, the *Brut*'s use of parataxis, and its combination of brief genealogies with much more detailed chapters, suggest the Old Testament as an important literary model. According to this view, the *Brut*'s chronological format emulates biblical historical writing, 'creating a vertical line connecting mundane history to the Divine Will' (Drukker, 8). In addition, the repetitious nature of much of the *Brut* allows for emphases to be placed on certain key themes. In the following passage, the repetition of the words 'þis land' both echoes Old Testament formulations and establishes very clearly the theme of emergent national identity:

> And while þis kyng Cassibalam regnede, come Iulius Cesar, þat was Emperoure of rome into þis lande, with a power of Romayns, and wolde haue hade þis lande þrough strengþ; but Cassibalam him ouercome in bataile,

þrough helpe of þe Britons, and drof him oute of þis Lande; and went ageyne
to Rome, and assemblede grete power anoþer tyme, and come ageyne into þis
lande forto geue bataile to Cassibalam (*Brut*, 32)

After Caesar's second defeat Cassibalam holds a great feast for his allies, who
thereafter go 'into here owen contree'. The invasion of Caesar thus unifies the
Britons from various 'contreen' (regions) in defence of the land. The use of the
demonstrative 'þis' signals the continuing relevance of the *Brut*'s narrative for
its English readers (this land is still the same), and grounds the text itself in the
British soil.

The continuations to the *Brut* demonstrate its interaction with other historical
narratives. In particular, many of the continuations draw upon the London city
chronicles, evidence of the *Brut*'s strong associations with London and nearby
towns (cf. Matheson 1998, 48; Gransden, 225–27). Such interaction is
intriguing because the *Brut* and the London chronicles serve ostensibly different
purposes: while the former narrates a history of the whole 'island of Britain', the
latter concentrate on its major city, are organised in a year-by-year format rather
than by chapters, strike a different tone, and seem intended to appeal to a
different audience – urban and mercantile, rather than noble (Kennedy, 2648;
Gransden, 222). Of course, a history of London is inseparable from a history of
the realm, and the emblematic nature of the city – expressed most clearly in its
designation as 'New Troy' – is never far from the surface of the London chronicles. Like the *Brut* chronicles, the Middle English civic chronicles of London
are continuations of earlier records, written, from the thirteenth century, in Latin
or Anglo-Norman. The earliest of the surviving manuscripts of the London
chronicles seem to date only from the 1430s (although antecedent lists and
chronicles exist in earlier manuscripts: McLaren 2002, 100), but it seems likely
that they began to be written in English from the reign of Henry IV (Matheson
1984, 220). They may reflect the emergence, in the first quarter of the fifteenth
century, of English as a language of official written record. The complete texts
of the Middle English chronicles of London all begin in the year 1189, a fact
that has been interpreted to reflect their descent from a common ancestor
(Matheson 1984, 220; Kennedy, 2649), or the beginning of the mayoralty in that
year. A recent argument has challenged these assumptions, positing instead that
the origin of the London chronicles lies in the commencement of *quo warranto*
proceedings from 1274, and the need to respond to them through recourse to
historical records (McLaren 2002, 17–18). The significance of 1189, according
to this argument, is that it was 'not only the date at which artificial memory was
defined [by Edward I in 1290] as beginning by law, but also . . . it was the date at
which authority was officially invested in writing' (McLaren 2002, 17). As all
scholars acknowledge, however, the purpose of the chronicles changed between
the thirteenth and fifteenth centuries, so that by the fifteenth, they were no
longer compilations used for legal purposes.

The early part of these chronicles consists of fairly sparse entries under each
year, essentially a record of the names of civic office holders, particularly
mayors and sheriffs. Although there is a continuous record through the thirteenth and fourteenth centuries, it is in their accounts of fifteenth-century events

that the chronicles become most expansive, and of most historical interest. The primary concerns of the London chronicles are diplomacy and politics of a civic, national, and (to a lesser degree) European nature. However, considerable space is also devoted to a range of other subjects: hagiographical narratives; comments on the state of trade and commerce; periodic records of the prices of basic commodities; ecclesiastical records and history; criminal trials and civil law, murders and mishaps; the often fraught ethnic relations between Londoners and the large number of 'alien' communities resident in the city; notes of remarkable or significant meteorological and astronomical happenings; the supernatural; tournaments, ceremonies, and dramatic performances. A running theme concerns relations between the city, as represented by its officers, and the King and his court. There is also a sustained interest in the physical appearance of London, reflected in mentions of the destruction or erection of buildings in the city. In this way prominent officials and citizens could have their contributions to the fabric of the city memorialised. In the section of the 'Great Chronicle of London' for 1438 (during the mayoralty of Stephen Broun) it is stated that:

> In this mayers time was the Conduyt In Fleetstreet begunne, by sir Wylliam Estffeyld mercer which said sir Wylliam was this yere with lowys John of Essex and othir made knygth of the Bath. (*Great Chronicle*, 174)

As this entry shows, the London chronicles have a tendency to operate by association, in this case from urban history to chivalric biography. On the other hand, the annalistic form encouraged the juxtaposition of diverse and apparently disconnected information. Thus an addition to the entry of the 'Great Chronicle' for 1437 records two pieces of information:

> this yere dyed John Franke clarke of ye roles who was holde the rychist man that dyed in many yers

> On estar daye one John gardenar was taken at saynt mary at ax in london, for when he shuld have been hoselyd he wypyd his mouthe with a fowle clout and toke ye blyssyd ost ther in, and so was taken by the parson of ye churche, and ye xiiij day of may he was brent in smythfeld. (*Great Chronicle*, 173)

Blasphemer rubs shoulders with super-rich civic official, the two only juxtaposed, it would seem, because of their deaths in the same year.

Like the *Brut* narratives, the London civic chronicles invited updatings and continuations, and as a consequence they too survive in a number of different versions. The editors of the 'Great Chronicle of London', Thomas and Thornley, decided that the surviving London civic chronicles were mutually dependent: no two chronicles were exactly alike, but none was a wholly original composition, since each version was based upon another London chronicle, as well as other sources (Kennedy, 2650). More recent research on the forty-four extant fifteenth- and sixteenth-century manuscripts of the London chronicles has discerned nine 'clusters' of manuscripts, with a large number of variants and additions; of these texts, thirteen bear no or only slight relationships to another extant text (McLaren 2002, 98–139). Although all the manuscript versions are anonymous, some have been attributed to particular authors, the best known of whom is the draper, alderman and sheriff Robert Fabyan (d. 1513), compiler of part of the 'Great Chronicle of London', as well as the *New Chronicles of England and France* (Thomas and Thornley, lxv–lxix; cf. Bean, 167–85; both attributions are questioned by McLaren 2002, 26–29, 264–65). Other likely continuators of the London chronicles include the scrivener Robert Bale, the goldsmith Miles Adys, and a mayor of London, possibly William Gregory (mayor in 1451) or Stephen Forster (1455), who either annotated or composed sections of a copy of one version of the chronicle (Kingsford, 70–112; Gransden, 230–31; McLaren 1992, 56–60; McLaren 2002, 29–34, 38). If these attributions are correct (and there is ample evidence that these men owned manuscripts of the chronicles, even if they did not compose parts of them), a picture emerges of men of high civic standing – prominent aldermen or guildsmen, but not aristocrats – constructing a record that incorporates some of their own personal experiences of city life, including such notable events as royal entries to London, the trial of Eleanor Cobham, and the Kentish rising led by Jack Cade in 1450 (Gransden, 228–29; McLaren 2002, 51–79). On the other hand, the large degree of variety amongst the extant manuscripts of the chronicles suggests their appeal to a broad-based audience of diverse social status and interests (McLaren 1992, 38). The manuscript evidence suggests, moreover, that there was often no clear distinction between readers and writers of the chronicles: owners of manuscripts clearly felt free to continue and amend a history that existed in multiple versions and that had no named authors, and they were on occasion encouraged to do so by the manuscript format (McLaren 2002, 138–39).

While they themselves do not constitute an official record, the chronicles do make use of official documents and parliamentary records, often citing them at some length (McLaren 1994, 161; cf. Gransden, 237–41). The chronicles also appear to have used as sources the London Letter Books, craft and guild records, eyewitness reports, newsletters and political pamphlets (McLaren 2002, 39–46); they incorporate literary texts, in particular verse, in significant number (see McLaren 2002, 237–38). Above all, compilers of the London chronicles made use of other chronicles (McLaren 2002, 45–46): these were texts, like the *Brut* chronicles, that fed upon themselves. Their success seems due, at least in part, to their construction of an identity for the city in some ways distinct from – but always embroiled in, and at the heart of – national politics and identity. The city emerges from the chronicles as an independent actor in the turmoil of fifteenth-century English politics, yet an actor whose decisions are vital for the outcome of nation-wide disputes and disturbances. Possibly the best example of this capacity to sum up and to change the mood of the broader polity is the story of the parading of Henry VI within the walls of the city in 1470, as a means of ensuring the support of Londoners against the return of Edward IV. Henry's inability to muster any semblance of support from within the city on this occasion both fatally weakens him, and is indicative of his already weak state: 'the progresse . . . was more lyker a play then the shewyng of a prynce to wynne mennys hertys, ffor by this mean he lost many and wan noon or Rygth ffewe, and evyr he was shewid In a long blew goune of velvet as thowth he hadd noo moo to chaunge with' (*Great Chronicle*, 215; discussed McLaren 2002, 59–63).

The chronicle's scathing 'more liker a play' deftly indicates the city's lukewarm response, while subtly invoking traditions of civic drama and pageantry.

The popularity of the civic chronicle was by no means confined to London. Indeed, notable offshoots of the London chronicles appeared in the sixteenth century in Lynn and Dublin (Kingsford, 111–12). The *Bristowe Chronicle*, begun by the town clerk Robert Ricart in 1479, was also inspired by the London chronicle tradition. Ricart enumerates six 'principall matiers' at the beginning of the chronicle to establish its purpose: it is to show the foundation of the town of Bristol; to record the kings of England since the Conquest and their enfranchisement of the town; to list the names of the mayors of the town; to record the manner of election of the mayor; to provide a calendar listing the whereabouts of civic records; and to record the 'ancient usages' of the city of London, since these formed the basis of many of Bristol's franchises and liberties (Ricart, 3–6). Using the model of London, then, and drawing heavily on Geoffrey of Monmouth, Ricart's chronicle seeks to integrate Bristol's history, status, and mode of government into a national history. The city is aligned with, but thanks to its geographical distance kept separate from, London, and this confident assertion of civic identity is given impressive visual form by the plan of Bristol that illustrates the chronicle. The plan appears at the moment that the legendary account of the founding of Bristol by the British king Brennius is first mentioned. It shows four gates of the city (St John's, Newgate, St Leonard's, St Nicholas'), four streets intersecting at the central 'High Cross', and a large number of houses, towers, and churches (Delano Smith and Kain, 183–84; Ralph, 311–16). Primarily of symbolic significance, the plan conveys the integrity of the city, its compact and distinct character.

Translation

Part of the process of consolidating English as a language of literary composition was the translation of a body of historical writing hitherto available only in Latin and French. That corpus of historical writing included not just *Brut*ish history but also 'universal' histories, narratives, that is, that give an account of world history from Creation to the present or near-present (but which, as they go on, become increasingly focussed on western Europe). Higden's *Polychronicon* is the prime example of the importance of the universal chronicle in late medieval England. Translated into English for the first time in the late fourteenth century by Trevisa, it was subsequently subject to another, anonymous, translation (contained in BL, MS Harley 2261); in addition, at least another four translations of parts of the *Polychronicon* survive (Edwards, 99). Of only slightly less importance, however, was the thirteenth-century *Chronicon Pontificum et Imperatorum* (Chronicle of the Popes and Emperors) compiled by Martinus Polonus (Martin of Troppau), an abbreviated version of which was translated into Middle English possibly as early as the 1330s, and certainly by the late fourteenth century (*Popes and Emperors*, 13). Polonus' history was (along with Higden) a major source of the 'Lollard Chronicle' (c. 1380), and the section of John Capgrave's *Abbreuiacion* from Creation until the papacy of John XXI

(1276–77) (Matthews, 277–82). It was also, at one remove, the source of the late fifteenth-century English *Fructus temporum* ('fruit of times') (Kennedy, 2672–73). Originally intended as a handbook for canonists and theologians, the *Chronicon* provided a summary of biblical history up to Augustus, and around 300 biographies of popes and Roman emperors. Its account of the often complex relations between the papal see and the Holy Roman Empire was obviously regarded as immensely useful by subsequent chroniclers, as was its record of important innovations in canon law and ecclesiastical practices. Like Higden's *Polychronicon* it had the advantage over *Brut* narratives of putting British history into a broader, international context. However, it is interesting to note that, in condensing the text, the English translator of the *Chronicon* showed remarkably little bias towards British history, omitting, amongst other things, accounts of Arthur and Merlin, the mission sent by Pope Eleutherius to convert the Britons, and the career of Anselm (*Popes and Emperors*, 12). Such omissions suggest that the primary source of interest in the *Chronicon* was its record of the two major institutions of the medieval West – papacy and empire – and their interaction.

Several different motivations for translation during this period can be discerned. Occasionally the translator draws attention to the status of English as a 'mother tongue', as opposed to the language of the original text. In a colophon to his translation of an account of the murder of James I of Scotland, John Shirley specifically notes that 'this moste pietevous cronicle of th'orribill dethe of the kyng of Scottes [was] translated oute of Latyne into owre moders Englisshe tong bi youre symple subget John Shirley in his laste age after his symple vnderstondyng' (Shirley, 56). In somewhat similar terms the anonymous early sixteenth-century translator of Titus Livius' *Vita Henrici Quinti* notes the pains he has taken 'to reduce [Titus' history] into our naturall English tongue'; he goes on to state that he has 'translated and reduced into rude and holme [sic] English, from whome all pratique and famous inditinge is farr exiled' not only Titus 'out of facound Latine', but also French accounts of the war with France (Translator of Livius, 3; cf. Gransden, 217–19). This pose of the reduction of high and ornate language to a rude, uncultivated tongue is familiar to students of much fifteenth-century English literature. It should be noted though that such a pose may only superficially be one of self-disparagement: the 'rude and homle English' is also 'naturall', and its exile from 'famous inditinge' may make it better suited for the purposes of instruction, correction, and political engagement that both Shirley and the translator of Livius had in mind.

Translation of historical works from Latin into the vernacular in a sense brings full circle the process that Geoffrey of Monmouth claimed, in his prologue to the *Historia regum britannie*, to be following. Geoffrey asserted that he was translating into Latin a 'very ancient book written in the British language', which had been given to him by Walter, archdeacon of Oxford (*Historia*, 1); Geoffrey also emphasised the simple style of his translation. The ostensible purpose of this act was to communicate the history of British kings to a wider audience, and the obvious language in which to do so was Latin. By the fifteenth century, though, an increasingly large audience seems to have wanted to read such matter of Britain in a vernacular language – not the British speech referred to by Geoffrey (i.e. Welsh), but what by the fifteenth century had become the 'mother' or 'natural' tongue, English.

Indeed the first part of Geoffrey's *Historia* (up to the wrestling match between Corineus and Gogmagog) was itself translated into Middle English, probably around the middle of the fourteenth century (London, College of Arms MS Arundel 22). In the translation Geoffrey's witty and provocative introduction to the text is rewritten. Instead, a sermon-like opening emphasises the nationalistic significance of the history, and at the same time reconfigures it, claiming British kings as English:

> God þat nath no bygynnyng no never schal haue endyng he spede vs now in
> our worchyng and euer help vs at our nede ffor of þe story of þe kynges of
> brytayne þat now y clepyd englond y wol yow telle. (fol. 8r)

The history is located by the translator in the time of Henry I, but the material is, it is implied, much older, consisting of 'olde storyes of englond translaty[d] out of speche of Brytonys'. In fact the Middle English version manages to erase any mention of Geoffrey himself, instead suggesting that his putative source, Walter of Oxford, made the translation (see further Caldwell, 646). The Middle English translator makes the point that he is translating the sense of the Latin and not word for word, but there is no apology for the act of translation and indeed the implication is that the old stories of England have been properly restored to the vernacular.

Other translations seem to have been motivated more by an interest in specific aspects of England's dealings with its neighbours. Part of book four of Froissart's *Chronicles*, rich in detail of the English court, and Anglo-French relations between 1393 and 1400, was translated into English in the late fifteenth or early sixteenth century, prior to the translation made by John Berners (1523–25) (Kennedy, 2673–74). An interest in the history of English military intervention and colonisation in Ireland seems to have prompted a (very loose) translation of Gerald of Wales' *Expugnatio hibernica* (Conquest of Ireland). Gerald's *Expugnatio* was initially composed prior to 1189, but was then revised during the reign of King John; the precise date of the translation is difficult to discern, but it seems to have been made at some stage in the fifteenth century. The dialect of the surviving copies suggests that it circulated among, and was quite possibly expressly translated for, an Anglo-Irish audience (*English Conquest*, vii–xiii; Kennedy, 2670–71). Both Froissart and Gerald's *Expugnatio* had clear resonance for a contemporary audience, but biblical history and prophetic material, such as the *Revelations* attributed to the early fourth-century bishop, Methodius, were also deemed worthy of translation (Kennedy 1989, 2664–65). Pseudo-Methodius provided a condensed narrative of biblical history, but also offered a scheme for ordering history, and for envisioning future time. That interest in apocalyptic literature could also extend to a desire to know the details of secular history: BL, Additional MS 37049, a richly illustrated Carthusian miscellany from Yorkshire, includes the *Liber Methodius*, but also precedes it with historical notes on the cities of Babylon, and an account of the rise of Rome from its primitive origins up to Tiberius, all translated from Polonus' *Chronicon* (Embree, 193–200).

Religious debate seems to have produced relatively little by way of Middle English historiography, however. The so-called 'Lollard Chronicle' is remarkably lacking in doctrinal polemic, a fact that has led its most recent editor to posit its circulation among an audience of Lollard preachers, already familiar with Wycliffite theology, but keen to be supplied with the historical details to back it up (*Lollard Chronicle*, 16). An equally plausible explanation is that the text was not intended to be restricted to a Lollard audience (the title was given to it by its first editor, Talbot, in 1942 with no manuscript authority). It may instead have been aimed at a more general audience, interested in important questions of ecclesiastical history.

Innovation

For all its derivative qualities, Middle English historical writing is in fact characterised by a high level of formal and stylistic innovation and experimentation. In the first place, one or two works evince an interest in the use of short, exemplary historical narratives as a form of moral instruction for rulers. John Lydgate's *Serpent of Diuisioun*, written in 1422 apparently at the behest of Humphrey, Duke of Gloucester, is an account of the civil war between Julius Caesar and Pompey, drawn from a range of sources, including Eusebius, Vincent of Beauvais two thirteenth-century French prose texts, Trevisa's translation of the *Polychronicon*, and Chaucer's *Monk's Tale* (Nolan, 102–10). If seen as a fairly lonely example of a fleeting English humanist interest in the classical past fostered by Humphrey, the text is no doubt disappointing. On the other hand, when seen in terms of an emerging discourse of civic responsibility and pacifism (but not republicanism), it becomes more interesting. It is not quite, as its editor described it in 1911, 'one of the very earliest political pamphlets in English history' (Lydgate, 2); but in it Lydgate does attempt to make a political point about the dangers of a culture of military expansionism. Instead of a successful military leader and emperor Caesar is presented in the terms of a fall-of-princes narrative, as a leader doomed to fail both himself and the Roman people by his reliance on violence and by his overweening ambition. In his exordium to the work, Lydgate explicitly locates the text within the mirror-for-princes tradition, exhorting 'wise gouernours of euery londe and region make a merowre in here mynde of þis manly man Iulius', to consider the harms of division, the destruction caused by pride, envy, and greed, and finally 'what hit is to begynne a werre' (65–66). Such words, written at a time of extensive English military expansion into France, seem to amount to something more than conventional pieties about the need for rulers to be humble, and to preserve the peace and the well-being of the realm: they seem to enunciate the view that the cost of political violence and expansionary wars is the very integrity of the polity.

Lydgate's text actually has strong similarities in purpose, if not in content, with Shirley's *Dethe of the Kynge of Scotis*. Perhaps the most gripping of all historical narratives rendered in Middle English prose, Shirley recounts the events that led up to the murder of James I in 1437, as well as the grisly end of the king, assassinated in his bed-chamber at Perth (while hiding at the bottom of a privy, according to the account), and the execution of his murderers. Shirley's *Dethe* is much more than a titillating narrative of an 'orrible' murder: it is in fact a treatise on monarchical tyranny and the legitimacy of regicide (Brown, 24–44). For while the king's principal enemy, leader of the assassins, and the man who deals James his death blow, Sir Robert Graham, is described as an 'odious and fals traitour', he is also cast as an opponent of the tyrannical behaviour of the king. The climax of the narrative is not, actually, the king's death, but rather the speech made by Graham at his subsequent trial, addressed to 'alle ye wrecched & mercilez Scottische folke', in which he justifies his murder of James on the ground that he was 'so crewell a tirrant, þe grettest enemye þat Scottez or Scotland myght haue' (Shirley, 51). During his pre-execution torture (described with almost gleeful precision), Graham denounces the 'immesurable tyrannye' of his tormentors (Shirley, 53). While not explicitly endorsing Graham's criticisms, Shirley echoes them in noting that 'vnsaciable coveytice was þe ground of the kingez deþe', and issues a final warning to princes, in the form of some lines from the *Roman de la Rose* (Shirley, 55–56). In short, then, the *Dethe of the Kynge of Scotis* raises issues of political theory by means of a narrative of an important contemporary event, and it does so, it may be inferred, not in order to resolve them, but to stimulate further debate.

Shirley's account of the death of James I bears affinities to a genre of historical writing that seems to have gained increasing popularity in the fifteenth century: the newsletter. These texts provided their audience (usually a select group, although they could be circulated widely) with a brief narrative of recent national or international events. A good example of this type of historical writing is the 'newsletter of John Stodeley', dated 19 January 1454, at London, which for the benefit of a provincial audience gives a digest of recent political machinations and controversies, court gossip, and parliamentary business, culled from a number of different informants (Gairdner 1904, ii. 295–99). Somewhat similarly, certain reports of overseas 'news' seem to have circulated and been translated into English, such as Guillaume Caoursin's account of the Siege of Rhodes in 1480, translated by John Kaye, possibly for Edward IV, or the account of the capitulation of Granada to the Spanish in 1492 (Gairdner 1880, 86–87). In a slightly different category are the fairly numerous accounts of particular events, such as battles or sieges, tournaments, and ceremonies – particularly royal entries into towns or cities and coronations, but also other epochal events such as the deposition of Richard II. Such narratives were made partly to inform a contemporary audience, but also presumably to provide a detailed record for posterity of important events in the social and political life of a town, city or nation. They could be incorporated (usually in abridged form) in larger historical narratives, such as the chronicles of London, as well as circulating independently. They could also be reworked as shorter narratives of particularly crucial events, such as the crisis of 1470, when Edward IV returned from exile in Burgundy to reclaim the crown from Henry VI. Two texts, the *Chronicle of the Rebellion in Lincolnshire*, and the *History of the Arrivall in England of Edward IV* provide a detailed account, primarily from the Yorkist perspective, of Edward's recapture of the throne. As Gransden notes, 'both . . . have much reportage which relates them in genre to contemporary newsletters'

(261–65); indeed the text of the *Arrivall* is an expanded version of one or more newsletters (Thomson, 84–93; Visser-Fuchs, 167–227).

Stylistically, the *Arrivall* stands very much in the *Brut* tradition. Apart from the occasional flourish, it uses parataxis to move a linear narrative along fairly swiftly. Beginning with the departure of Edward from Zeeland, it proceeds with a series of conjunctions: 'and after', 'and then', 'and when', 'and soon after all this doon', 'whereuppon' (*Arrivall*, ed. Green). Unlike the *Brut*, however, it ends the narrative with an air of pious finality:

> Wherethrough ys trusted that, with the helpe of Hym that hath not faylled the
> kinge sethe his begynninge hederto, he shall in shorte whyle so pacyfy the
> subgectes throughoute his sayde [realm] that pease and prosperyte shall dayly
> growe in the same to the honnor and laude of Almighty God . . . with confu-
> sion to all his ennemys and evell-wyllers (*Arrivall*, ed. Green, 331–32)

As an autonomous historical account, the *Arrivall* is interested in narrative closure, consistent with the theme of dynastic restoration, rather than the *Brut*'s open-ended structure.

Innovation did not take place simply in the content of historical writing, or in the means of its circulation, but also in its physical form. A large number of genealogies (dynastic and noble) survive in the form of parchment rolls. These rolls show the descent of a royal or noble house by means of a line or lines connecting the names (sometimes illustrated by drawings) of the house. The genealogy is often accompanied by a short text, which elaborates on the deeds and contexts of these illustrious ancestors. The outstanding example of this form of text is the Rous roll, written prior to 1485, which traces the lineage of the earls of Warwick from their mythical origins to the reign of Richard III. There are, however, numerous genealogical rolls that show the lineage of English royalty (divided into four types – the Long Latin and Long English pedigrees, and the Short Latin and Short English pedigrees), most of which seem to have been produced during the reign of Edward IV (Allan, 172–74). They therefore reflect the Yorkist interest in, and sensitivity to, genealogical matters, and more generally the Yorkist encouragement of historical writing as a means of substantiating Edward's claim to the throne. Indeed the identical nature of many of these genealogical chronicles suggests their origin in a single workshop (Matheson 1984, 217). The use of the roll rather than book form enables the idea of a line, and of a linear progression, to be grasped by the viewer. Unlike the leaves of a book, the roll can theoretically be viewed in its entirety at one time, so that genealogical connections between generations are not obscured: the line is not, in other words, disrupted by the demands of the book form. The roll is also a form of text that, by virtue of its form and its asso-ciations with official legal records and scientific works, may have imparted a degree of historical authority to the genealogies presented within it. Undoubt-edly too the complexity of much genealogy could be made more intelligible by the roll form; parallel lines could be depicted alongside one another, as on BL, Additional MS 29502, a roll that extends from the Anglo-Saxon heptarchy to John of Gaunt, on which the lines of the dukes of Normandy, and later the house of Lancaster, appear alongside the English royal line.

If the roll is conducive to a linear form, it is also geared to a highly visual style of historiography. The rolls frequently feature drawings of key ancestors, or historical personages. The English translation of Peter of Poitiers' *Compendium Historiae in Genealogia Christi* contained in BL, MS Add. 20010, for example, is a roll chronicle that runs from Adam to Christ; its illustrations include drawings of Adam and Eve, Noah's ark, David, and Christ. Rous' roll too, of course, is notable for its line-drawn portraits of the Earls of Warwick, as well as coats of arms. And the 'Beauchamp pageant', a roll that was created in the 1490s to celebrate the life of Richard, Earl of Warwick (1382–1439), is essentially a series of illustrations with explanatory glosses. So detailed and so many are the illustrations (there are 53, plus two genealogies) that the effect is to create a comic-book style immediacy. This effect is enhanced by the presentation of Earl Richard as an all-action military hero. Young Richard leads the charge at the battle of Shrewsbury, before (now a Knight of the Garter) emerging victorious from a seemingly interminable succession of jousts. International celebrity soon follows, as Richard hobnobs with popes and emperors, is received by the Doge in Venice, and sups with the Sultan's lieutenant in Jerusalem while on pilgrimage. When he returns to England, he gives sage counsel to Henry V on how to stamp out a conspiracy of heretics. Richard's only supine moments are at baptism (godfathers Richard II and Richard Scrope), and on his deathbed. Ultimately, the purpose of this roll is, also, genealogical: its final images show Richard in a family tree with his two wives and their descendents, including Anne, wife of Richard Nevile ('Warwick the Kingmaker'), as well as Isabel, wife of George, Duke of Clarence, and Anne, wife of Richard III. These two Warwick rolls are outstanding, but still representative of a more general move towards illustrations and visual display in historical writing of this period. Rickart's Bristol chronicle, it is worth noting, was designed to be illustrated with portraits of seven kings up to and including Edward IV, as well as its plan of Bristol. At times, it seems, it was important for history to be seen as well as read, and for historical personages to be drawn as well as described.

The differences between these forms of historical writing – chronicle, short narrative, newsletter, roll – can be explained by the different function that each had to play, and by the different means of structuring historical time that each adopted. The chronicle was the vehicle of major histories of lines of kings, of popes and emperors, of cities. The genealogical roll in fact is the epitome of the chronicle's concern with chronology, with descent and progression. That linear structure was well suited to substantiating ideological claims – claims to the throne, to territory, to civic franchises, to immunities and independence. Such was the value of the chronicle that even though it was by the fifteenth century unconvincing evidence in a court of law, it seems to have become an important way of establishing a regime's legitimacy. Certainly the literature of the fourteenth and fifteenth centuries that emerged from the long-running Anglo-Scottish conflicts is testimony to the self-generating nature of much historical writing. The Scottish chronicle tradition that developed in the fourteenth century can be seen to have arisen in direct opposition to English chronicles in the *Brut* tradition, which insisted that the king of England was, by ancient law and custom, overlord of Scotland. Although most of the Scottish counter-history is written in Latin or in English verse, some works, such as the *Scottis Originale*, a short chronicle possibly translated from a Latin original around the mid fifteenth century, or the *Auchinleck Chronicle*, are in English prose. These pro-Scottish works construct a history in which Scotland emerges as historically and legally an independent nation. They set out, moreover, to recast as villains such stock figures of British history as Brutus and Arthur. Indeed, the central premise is of the duplicitous nature of whatever peoples dwell south of Scotland – Britons, Romans, Angles, Saxons, Danes, Normans – a duplicity with it roots in their Trojan ancestry, in contrast to the noble Greek and Egyptian lineage claimed by the Scots. As the 'Part of the Ynglis cronicle', a Scottish rebuttal of the tenor of *Brut*ish histories, confidently asserts: 'in the first we understand how ye ar cummyn of brutus that is the mast faltyf pepill of all the warld that was the tresonable tratouris of troye . . . and we ar cummyn and discendit of the mast noble peple that evire was in all the warld baith of our manhed and treuth That Is of the noble grekis' ('Part', 197).

On the other hand, as the examples of Lydgate and Shirley show, other purposes and historical models result in quite different narrative forms. The mirror-for-princes genre conceives of history moving in a circular rather than linear direction, with the rise and fall of powerful men occurring throughout history. This is the historical sensibility that informs Lydgate's and Shirley's short, exemplary, narratives. But it is also the case that the chronicle form itself was various, flexible, and open to innovation. Martinus Polonus' *Chronicon*, for example, was meant to be copied with entries for popes and emperors on facing pages, and with 50 lines allocated per person. Hence the biographies of trivial popes and emperors were filled with a range of inconsequential material, while those of the most important had to be drastically curtailed. Capgrave's *Abbreuiation* was similarly intended to follow a strict format: the chronicle was arranged by year (Anno Mundi, and then Anno Domini after the birth of Christ); each year was listed in a column, and if Capgrave found any remark to make about the year, he would write it alongside the date in a parallel column (Capgrave, 7). Readers were invited to write in entries where Capgrave had left a blank.

Such structures are predicated on the availability of a relatively small amount of historical information. The consequence of the surge of historical writing in English in the fourteenth and fifteenth centuries was that any chronicler attempting to give a concise account of British history found, instead of a single helpful source, a mass of often contradictory material. Such a mass posed a challenge to linear narrative, since it became more difficult to discern clean lines of inheritance, or to know which of a number of accounts of the same issue or event to accept. Robert Fabyan's *New Chronicles* is therefore much more of a departure from tradition than has previously been acknowledged. The *New Chronicles* were first printed by Pynson in 1516, and attributed to Fabyan in its 1533 reprinting with continuation by Rastell, though this attribution has recently been questioned, and its identity within the (anonymous) London chronicle tradition asserted (McLaren 2002, 264–65). The chronicler divided his work into seven books to commemorate the seven joys of Mary; although many sources are acknowledged, until 1189 it draws heavily on the traditional *Brut* narrative, but thereafter becomes essentially a London chronicle, written in annalistic form, up to the reign of Henry VII (Kennedy, 2654–55; Gransden, 245–48; McLaren 2002, 264). The work was later updated to include the reign of Henry VIII. Where the *New Chronicles* differs from previous compilations is in its inclusion of a history of the kings of France, derived mostly from Robert Gaguin's *Compendium super Francorum gestis* (1457), alongside its account of the English polity. The two – French and English – narratives do not intersect but alternate. The effect of alternation is to disrupt the linear progression of the chronicle by drawing the reader back in time: history read from the perspective of one kingdom is then immediately re-read from the perspective of the other. What the *New Chronicles* indicate, I would suggest, is that by the beginning of the sixteenth century the notion of a universal history – of the kind produced by Higden and Capgrave in the fourteenth and fifteenth centuries – was showing signs of fragmenting into a number of different, less grandiose histories. The bigger the record, the more to record, the more history accumulated, the harder it is to represent the universal. At the same time, the 'new' chronicler's aim is explicitly a 'concordance' of histories, and that dream of reconciling discordant historical accounts within a single work was to continue to exert a powerful influence on historians to the end of the sixteenth-century and beyond.

Historical writing, in conclusion, is in a state of constant mutation from the middle of the fourteenth to the sixteenth century. It changes form; it translates; it preserves – and adds as it preserves. That degree of mutation may reflect in large part changes in the audience and authorship of histories: no longer concentrated in monasteries or courts, vernacular historical writing both fosters and responds to an expanded lay readership. Hence it is the vehicle of kings and princes, but also the means by which they might be reformed; it is the *sine qua non* of a noble family, but also a prosperous city; crucially, it tends towards a model of communal compilation by encouraging its readers to continue its narratives. The foundations laid in this period for the development of a national history in English were substantial, through the translation of monumental texts as well as detailed, small-scale narratives. Above all, English prose took historical writing away from the genres of epic and romance, towards the speed and ease of composition of the newsletter, and towards the authority of official written record.

WORKS CITED

Editions

Arrivall. The Historie of the Arrivall of King Edward IV, ed. John Bruce, Camden Society os 1 (London, 1838); short version in Richard F. Green, 'The Short Version of *The Arrival of Edward IV*', *Speculum* 56 (1981), 324–26
The Brut or The Chronicles of England, ed. Friedrich W.D. Brie, EETS os 131, 136 (London, 1906, 1908)
Capgrave, John. *John Capgrave's Abbreuiacion of Cronicles,* ed. Peter J. Lucas, EETS os 285 (Oxford, 1983)

Chronicle of the Rebellion in Lincolnshire, ed. John G. Nichols, Camden Society os 39 (London, 1847)

The English Conquest of Ireland, ed. Frederick J. Furnivall, EETS os 107 (London, 1896)

Fabyan, Robert. *The New Chronicles of England and of France*, ed. Henry Ellis (London, 1811)

Gairdner 1880. *Three Fifteenth-Century Chronicles*, ed. James Gairdner, Camden Society ns 28 (London, 1880)

Gairdner 1904. *The Paston Letters A. D. 1422–1509*, vol. 2 (London, 1904), pp. 295–99

Geoffrey of Monmouth. *The Historia Regum Britannie of Geoffrey of Monmouth*, ed. Neil Wright, vol. 1 (Cambridge, 1985)

The Great Chronicle of London, ed. A.H. Thomas and I.D. Thornley (London, 1938)

Kay, John. *Caoursin's Account of The Siege of Rhodes in 1480. Translated into English by John Kay, the Poet-Laureate to King Edward IV*, ed. H.W. Fincham, Order of St John of Jerusalem Historical Pamphlets 2 (1926), 1–35

Lollard Chronicle. The Chronicles of Rome: An Edition of the Middle English Chronicle of Popes and Emperors *and* The Lollard Chronicle, ed. Dan Embree (Woodbridge, 1999)

Lollard Chronicle. 'A Lollard Chronicle of the Papacy', ed. E.W. Talbert, *Journal of English and Germanic Philology* 41 (1942), 163–93

Lydgate, John. *The Serpent of Division*, ed. Henry Noble MacCracken (London, 1911)

Pageant of the Birth, Life, and Death of Richard Beauchamp Earl of Warwick K.G. 1389–1439, ed. Viscount Dillon and W.H. St John Hope (London, 1914)

'Part of the Ynglis cronicle'. *The Asloan Manuscript: A Miscellany in Prose and Verse*, ed. W.A. Craigie (Edinburgh, 1923), pp. 197–214

Popes and Emperors. The Chronicles of Rome: An Edition of the Middle English Chronicle of Popes and Emperors *and* The Lollard Chronicle, ed. Dan Embree (Woodbridge, 1999)

Ricart, Robert. *The Maire of Bristowe is Kalendar*, ed. Lucy Toulmin Smith, Camden Society ns 5 (London, 1872)

Rous, John. *The Rous Roll*, transcribed by L. Larking (London, 1859; repr. 1980); text printed in *Historia vitae et regni Ricardi II*, ed. Thomas Hearne (Oxford, 1729), pp. 217–39

Shirley, John. *Death and Dissent: Two Fifteenth-Century Chronicles:* The Dethe of the Kynge of Scotis, *translated by John Shirley, and* "Warkworth's" Chronicle: the Chronicle attributed to John Warkworth, Master of Peterhouse, Cambridge, ed. Lister M. Matheson (Woodbridge, 1999)

Translator of Livius. *The First English Life of King Henry the Fifth*, ed. Charles Lethbridge Kingsford (Oxford, 1911)

'Warkworth's Chronicle'. *Death and Dissent: Two Fifteenth-Century Chronicles:* The Dethe of the Kynge of Scotis, *translated by John Shirley, and* "Warkworth's" Chronicle: the Chronicle attributed to John Warkworth, Master of Peterhouse, Cambridge, ed. Lister M. Matheson (Woodbridge, 1999)

Secondary Literature

Allan, Alison, 'Yorkist Propaganda: Pedigree, Prophecy and the "British History"', in *Patronage, Pedigree and Power in Later Medieval England*, ed. Charles Ross (Gloucester, 1979), pp. 171–92

Bean, J.M.W., 'The Role of Robert Fabyan in Tudor Historiography of the "Wars of the

Roses" ', in *Florilegium Columbianum: Essays in honor of Paul Oskar Kristeller*, ed. Karl-Ludwig Selig and Robert Somerville (New York, 1987), pp. 167–85

Brown, M.H., ' "I have thus slain a tyrant": The *Dethe of the Kynge of Scotis* and the Right to Resist in Early Fifteenth-Century Scotland', *The Innes Review* 47 (1996), 24–44

Caldwell, R.A., 'The "History of the Kings of Britain" in College of Arms MS Arundel XXII', *PMLA* 69 (1954), 643–54

Carley, James P., and Julia Crick, 'Constructing Albion's Past: An Annotated Edition of *De Origine Gigantum*', *Arthurian Literature* 13 (1995), 41–114

Delano Smith, Catherine, and Roger J.P. Kain, *English Maps: A History* (London, 1999)

Drukker, Tamar, 'Readings in the Middle English Prose *Brut* Chronicle' (unpublished doctoral dissertation, University of Cambridge, 2002)

Edwards, A.S.G., 'Geography and Illustration in Higden's *Polychronicon*', in *Art Into Life: Collected Papers from the Kresge Art Museum Medieval Symposia*, ed. Carol Garrett Fisher and Kathleen L. Scott (East Lansing, 1995), pp. 95–113

Embree, Dan, 'The Fragmentary Chronicle in British Library, Additional MS 37049', *Manuscripta* 37 (1993), 193–200

Gransden, Antonia, *Historical Writing in England II: c. 1307 to the Early Sixteenth Century* (Ithaca, 1982)

Kelly, Stephen and Jason O'Rourke, 'Culturally Mapping the English *Brut*: A Preliminary Report from the "Imagining History" Project', *Journal of the Early Book Society* 6 (2003), 41–60

Kennedy, E.D., 'Chronicles and Other Historical Writing', *A Manual of the Writings in Middle English 1050–1500*, ed. Albert E. Hartung, vol. 8 (New Haven, 1989)

Kingsford, Charles L., *English Historical Literature in the Fifteenth Century* (Oxford, 1913)

McLaren 1992. Mary-Rose McLaren, 'The Textual Transmission of the London Chronicles', *English Manuscript Studies* 3 (1992), 38–72

McLaren 1994. Mary-Rose McLaren, 'The Aims and Interests of the London Chroniclers of the Fifteenth Century', in *Trade, Devotion and Governance: Papers in Later Medieval History*, ed. Dorothy J. Clayton, Richard G. Davies, and Peter McNiven (Stroud, 1994), pp. 158–76

McLaren 2002. Mary-Rose McLaren, *The London Chronicles of the Fifteenth Century: A Revolution in English Writing* (Cambridge, 2002)

Matheson 1984. Lister M. Matheson, 'Historical Prose', in *Middle English Prose: A Critical Guide to Major Authors and Genres*, ed. A.S.G. Edwards (New Brunswick, 1984), pp. 209–48

Matheson 1998. Lister M. Matheson, *The Prose* Brut: *The Development of a Middle English Chronicle* (Tempe, 1998)

Matthews, William, 'Martinus Polonus and Some Later Chroniclers', in *Medieval Literature and Civilization: Studies in Memory of G.N. Garmonsway*, ed. D.A. Pearsall and R.A. Waldron (London, 1969), pp. 275–88

Nolan, Maura B., 'The Art of History Writing: Lydgate's *Serpent of Division*', *Speculum* 78 (2003), 99–127

Ralph, Elizabeth, 'Bristol *circa* 1480', in *Local Maps and Plans from Medieval England*, ed. R.A. Skelton and P.D.A. Harvey (Oxford, 1986), pp. 309–16

Spiegel, Gabrielle M., *The Past as Text: The Theory and Practice of Medieval Historiography* (Baltimore, 1997)

Taylor, John, *English Historical Literature in the Fourteenth Century* (Oxford, 1987)

Thomson, J.A.F., ' "The Arrival of Edward IV" – The Development of the Text', *Speculum* 46 (1971), 84–93

Visser-Fuchs, Livia, 'Edward IV's "memoir on paper" to Charles, Duke of Burgundy: The So-called "Short Version of the Arrivall" ', *Nottingham Mediaeval Studies* 36 (1992), 167–227

12

Wycliffite Prose

FIONA SOMERSET

Anne Hudson's introduction to Wycliffite Prose in Edwards's *Middle English Prose* guide published in 1984 clearly registers a sense of how far this field of study had progressed in the previous forty years.[1] All English works with Wycliffite sympathies had usually been attributed to Wyclif up until the early twentieth century – yet with some uncertainty, and sometimes with the sense that being in English made them less worthy of notice. By the 1980s, English Wycliffite writings were recognized as an extensive body of writings produced by a well defined and remarkably persistent group of heretics – now referred to interchangeably as Lollards or Wycliffites, since there seemed to be no valid distinction between the terms. And these writings were now seen as a valuable resource for investigating the activities and beliefs of Wycliffites, more reliably and in closer detail than had previously been possible when relying solely on documentary sources such as chronicle accounts and episcopal records of heresy trials. The close links between Lollard tenets of belief and Wyclif's own heretical views, between the English writings and materials in Latin, and between supposedly far-flung groups of village Lollards and the views of heretics with close links to Oxford, were already becoming apparent.

It would be no exaggeration to state that since the 1980s this field has been revolutionized all over again – nor that Hudson's own extensive publications have been crucial to this change. New critical editions of several of the most important Wycliffite writings have appeared, and more are under way. A large body of analytical work based in these writings, and in closer dialogue between the insights they can provide and the evidence provided by documentary sources, has been (and continues to be) produced. Newer possibilities for in-depth study provided by computer technology are being explored (see Peikola, Pitard). And perhaps most importantly for Middle English scholarship in general, our perspective on the potential contribution that these writings can make to our understanding of medieval English writing more broadly has been altered forever. No longer are Wycliffite writings a marshy borderland, unrelated to mainstream manuscript production, readerships, writers, genres, and concepts except in cases where a more familiar writer or one of his characters should (or emphatically should not) be subsumed to Wycliffism. Instead, the

---

[1]   For help in preparing this chapter – or in preparing to prepare it – I would like to thank Anne Hudson, Margaret Aston, Christina von Nolcken, Andrew Cole, Derrick Pitard, Jill Havens, and David Watt.

greater accessibility and wider study of Wycliffite writings has shown, and continues to multiply, their close interconnections with other, more familiar aspects of medieval English culture.

Concern to identify the authors of specific Wycliffite texts has receded even further, in nearly all quarters, than it had in 1984.[2] Shifting interests within the study of Middle English, as well as in the study of literature more generally, have made the anonymity and indeterminate dating of nearly all Wycliffite works easier for critics to stomach. But this does not mean that critics have become content to view Wycliffite prose as an undifferentiated mass. Granted, Wycliffite writings have a 'certain sameness' that goes some way toward explaining earlier impulses to attribute groups of works to one or another specific author (von Nolcken 1995) Yet that sameness gives way upon closer scrutiny to considerable variety, of a kind that permits new kinds of comparisons both within and outside the Wycliffite oeuvre. New attention is now being devoted to aspects of particular works such as their literary qualities or generic affiliations, and to closer-grained similarities between certain groups of writings which suggest that they were produced and/or read together – they are found together within several manuscripts, for example, or they claim common author-ship, or cite unusual sources in common, or comment on a specific event; simi-larly, manuscripts considered as a whole may share contents or common characteristics that suggest production in the same place or by the same people.[3]

Difficulties of precisely defining the boundaries of the Wycliffite oeuvre remain. Indeed, they may even have been compounded by increased attention to manuscripts of works written (or were they?) prior to the advent of Wycliffism in the 1380s and then apparently provided with 'Lollard interpolations'; to manuscripts containing Wycliffite material (sometimes expurgated) that we know were owned by non Wycliffites; and to apparently Wycliffite-owned manuscripts containing a mixture of Wycliffite and nonWycliffite (or are they?) materials. To be sure, both Wyclif and the Wycliffites drew on previous satire and complaint, and certainly, they do not always state all the same heretical views in the same way, though whether such apparent inconsistencies may be attributed to circumspection or to variations or developments of opinion is a matter for debate. Yet while some scholars may derive new insights by attempting to establish a non-Wycliffite or Wycliffite origin for a specific text regardless of its Wycliffite use (see e.g. Clopper 2003), many others are now

---

2   Rare exceptions to this general rule may be found among scholars interested in the Wycliffite bible translation. See, for example, Fristedt, Lindberg, Yonekura.

3   For attention to literary qualities and genre see, for example, Bose, Lindberg 1995, and forthcoming work by Elizabeth Schirmer on the narrative style of the *Testimony of William Thorpe*, by Bruce Holsinger on *Piers the Plowman's Crede*'s use of ekphrasis, by Katherine Little showing how Hoccleve aims to counter what he sees as Lollard stylistic choices, and by Nicholas Watson on the prose style of the *Lanterne of Liȝt*. The first three were presented as papers at the International Medi-eval Congress at Kalamazoo in May 2002, the third at the same conference in 2000; a full session on the literary qualities of Lollard writings took place in 2003. One investigation of closer-grained simi-larities between a small group of Lollard writings may be found below, pp. 204–6. Probably the most important investigation to date of a group of Wycliffite manuscripts' common characteristics has been Hudson and Gradon's study of the manuscripts of the *English Wycliffite Sermons*: see below, pp. 200–1, for references and a brief summary of their conclusions.

content with the necessarily fuzzy boundaries of the Wycliffite oeuvre – which facilitate, if anything, the study of Wycliffism's relations with other Middle English writings.

To begin from somewhere near the centre rather than at those fuzzy boundaries, the writings most famously or notoriously Wycliffite (with a bias toward those available in print) include the Bible translations (together with translated or newly composed prefaces and prologues, works of biblical commentary, and tracts defending biblical translation); the long sermon cycle (and texts associated with it in manuscripts, as well as occasional sermons and smaller sermon collections); the Middle English *Rosarium Theologie*; declarative polemical lists of conclusions and/or answers to hostile questions (including the *Twelve Conclusions*, *Sixteen Points*, *Twenty-Five Articles*, *Lollard Disendowment Bill*, *Thirty-Seven Conclusions*, and *Apology for Lollard Doctrines*); confessional writings produced by defendants or sympathizers, usually in association with examinations for heresy (Wyclif's confessions on the Eucharist, the testimonies of William Swinderby and Walter Brut, the *Testimony of William Thorpe*, the letter of Richard Wyche); important catechetical or instructional writings (*The Lanterne of Liȝt*, *Omnis Plantacio*, *Tractatus de oblacione iugis sacrificii*, 'Of Dominion,' 'De Blasphemia'); and works that have been associated with the Chaucer or Langland traditions (the *Upland Series*, *Pierce the Plowman's Crede*, *Mum and the Sothsegger*, the *Plowman's Tale*; the Lollardy of these last two is less universally accepted). This is a representative, but far from an exhaustive list: the corpus of miscellaneous tracts of more or less uncertain Wycliffism is vast, and many of these works remain unprinted.[4]

I will focus here on the members of this canon that are in English prose, though the writings excluded by this overview should be noted, as well as the difficulties of hard and fast exclusion. Along with English prose writings, Wycliffites produced both writings in Latin and works in verse. Some works are extant only in Latin, such as the commentary on the Apocalypse known as the *Opus Arduum* or the Latin sermon cycle (see Hudson 1978b, von Nolcken 1986; for other Latin works see Aers 2003, Hudson 1978b, 1985c, 1991, 1994, Scase, Somerset 1998). Several works appear in both English and Latin versions, though the relationship between the two is not always simple: the *Dialogue between Reson and Gabbynge* is a translation and adaptation of Wyclif's *Dialogus*, for example, and the Middle English *Rosarium Theologie* is a translation of the Latin *Rosarium* (an abbreviation, in turn, of the Latin *Floretum*) in all versions an alphabetical distinction collection of the sort typically used as a reference work by preachers and others needing quick access to a range of authorities on a given topic (Hudson 1971b, von Nolcken 1979, 1981). Yet there are Latin versions of both *The Testimony of William Thorpe* and *The Sermon of*

---

4   In addition to writings by scholars such as Anne Hudson and Ralph Hanna III, the best source of up-to-date information about unprinted Wycliffite materials is the growing *IMEP* handlist series. Catalogues of individual manuscript collections are also valuable, especially if published relatively recently. Represented in the bibliography, but not discussed here, are the tracts *A Tretise of Miraclis Pleyinge* and *Of Wedded Men and Wifis* (see Clopper 1990, Davidson, Davis, Keleman, Nissé 1997, Salisbury). Whether these works are Wycliffite is undecided, but what is certain is that their topics are not particularly representative of Wycliffite concerns across the corpus as a whole.

William Taylor, each apparently a translation into Latin from English intended for continental audiences; while in the case of the *Twelve Conclusions*, or of the *Thirty-Seven Conclusions*, it is not clear whether Latin or English was the language of composition (Hudson 1993, 1995a, Hudson 1978a, Compston). As well, many works classifiable as English prose contain extensive quotations from Latin, usually translated in full, and sometimes accompanied by instruction in the meanings and even the grammar of specific words. Verse and prose are similarly difficult to disentangle: the *Upland Series*, for example, includes material in both prose and verse, and several prose works contain alliterative, metrical, or lyrical passages.[5]

As for newer and older editions of Wycliffite works, since the large selection of miscellaneous shorter works that they include do not appear in print anywhere else, Thomas Arnold's *Select English Works of Wyclif* volume 3 and F.D. Matthew's *English Works of Wyclif Hitherto Unprinted* are still frequently read and cited, even though these editions have obvious deficiencies (very little provided by way of annotation or index, rarely do they consult or even list more than one version or manuscript, introductory material is based on premise of Wyclif's authorship, etc.). Some other relatively new editions, though their critical apparatus may be more substantial, should nonetheless be used with caution since their commentary and their editorial choices in establishing the text predate the systematic study of this field (e.g., Genet, Heyworth). New, well annotated critical editions of Wycliffite writings are still sorely needed, even though much has been accomplished in this direction in recent years. Inexpensive editions of excerpts and/or short texts intended for students are of course valuable by way of introduction, and some are exceptionally well annotated (see especially Hudson 1978a), but they can do little to fill this need, especially if they do not fully re-evaluate manuscript evidence and previous commentary (e.g., Dean 1991 and 1996).

Despite the historical importance of the Wycliffite biblical translation, it continues to receive less attention than one might expect – perhaps because the translation in and of itself is not polemical; perhaps because of the daunting size of the editorial and descriptive tasks at hand. There are around 250 partial or full copies of the bible translation, and although work on cataloguing their contents and collating the evidence they can provide has proceeded piecemeal, much remains to be done. Efforts to replace Forshall and Madden's complete parallel-text edition of what they identified as an Early Version (EV) and Late Version (LV) together with prologues and prefaces appearing in varying numbers of the manuscripts have so far proceeded solely from Conrad Lindberg, who has produced an eight volume edition of EV as found in Bodley 959 and Christ Church 145 (1959–95); three volumes of parallel-text EV, LV and Latin Vulgate for Jerome's prefatory epistles, Baruch, and Judges (1978, 1985, 1989); as well as the first two volumes of a projected four volume edition of LV as

---

5   For texts making extensive use of Latin and texts whose literary qualities deserve attention, see below on *Omnis plantacio*, *De oblacione*, and *The Lanterne of Liȝt*. On the *Upland Series* see Somerset 1998, 135–78, 216–20.

found in Bodley 277 (1999, 2001). Lindberg's provisional catalogue of the Bible manuscripts (1970), has not yet been replaced, though an updated list of additions to it (and thorough new descriptions of the Middle English prose in some of its members) may be traced through the volumes of the *IMEP*. This is a significant gap, since several avenues of promising research are more difficult to pursue without a full descriptive catalogue. There has been interest, for example, in identifying more stages in the translation than Forshall and Madden's EV and LV – the first slavishly literal in its rendition of the Latin but unidiomatic in English to the point of being difficult to understand without reference to the Latin, the second freer and more idiomatic. Regardless of the conclusions that may be reached in this regard, study of the stages in the development and revision of the translation will illuminate other contemporary efforts at Latin-to-English translation. Research on the ownership and use of this Bible and on the production of its manuscripts will be an important contribution to the history of vernacular book production and reception in England more generally (see Hanna 2003). Much work remains to be done on the General Prologue as well as other prefaces, prologues, glosses, summaries, tables of readings, and other apparatus found in varying numbers of manuscripts: many of these are more polemical than the translation, and all promise new insight into methods of Wycliffite scholarship and study (see Hargreaves 1961 and 1969, Hunt).

Other valuable resources as-yet unpublished that would help us to understand Wycliffite biblical study are the Lollard revisions of Richard Rolle's Psalter translation and commentary and the Lollard commentary on the gospels known as the *Glossed Gospels*. Hudson's summaries of the published and unpublished work on the Lollard Rolle manuscripts (1988a, 259–64, 1992) suggest that while previous scholars may be correct that three versions can be distinguished (two of the full text, one much longer, extant in only one copy divided between two manuscripts, and covering only psalms 84:6 to 118), it may finally be impossible to reach any certain conclusions about whether each version was produced independently, whether the first two descend from a common original, or whether there is some even more complicated explanation for the shifting relations between the versions. The content of the added commentary in each case, even though some of it may have been drawn from previous unattributed sources, is plainly Wycliffite, but the tone of the first two is castigatory and polemical, while the third seems focused on offering comfort to those suffering persecution: Hudson suggests it 'comes closest of any Wycliffite text to a devotional work, dedicated to a spiritual purpose' (1988a, 263–64; see also Kuzcynski. Hudson is now at work on an edition of the two full-text versions). The *Glossed Gospels*, more simply, are three related versions of a commentary on Matthew, one of a commentary on Mark, two related versions on Luke, and one on John. These texts consist of exhaustive commentary from patristic sources on specific words and phrases drawn from each short section of biblical text (quoted from EV) in turn. All sources are attributed, and other than perhaps in the selection of topics and authors, there is no overt evidence of Wycliffism: direct comment by the Lollard writers themselves is reserved to the prologues. Short extracts from both versions of the Luke commentary and from the John commentary were published in Hudson 1978a (see in addition Hargreaves 1979, Hunt, Nevanlinna).

As for writings defending or describing biblical translation, the part of the 'General Prologue' to the LV that discusses the issue has been recognized as one of the most important of these, and has received much attention (see e.g., excerpts in Hudson 1978a, Dean 1996). Additions to the corpus of edited tracts and prefaces defending biblical translation include an important thesis by Simon Hunt, which presents the series of twelve tracts defending biblical translation from Cambridge University Library MS Ii 6 26 together with related texts from other manuscripts. This manuscript presents by far the most extended attention to the topic of translation, though there are several tracts in which the subject is important in passing, e.g. the 'Tractatus de regibus' (Genet, 5), an exposition on the Pater Noster (Arnold III, 98–100), a prologue to John (Forshall and Madden, IV, 685b), and the tract 'De Officio Pastorali' (Matthew, 429–30).[6] There is, as well, a widely circulated tract devoted to the subject, extant in seven manuscripts and printed repeatedly during the Reformation (Hudson 1975; ed. Deanesly, Bühler). Previously ascribed to John Purvey, this tract consisting of a series of arguments in favour of translation has been shown to be a partial translation and adaptation of the nonWycliffite Richard Ullerston's Latin determination on biblical translation (Hudson 1975). Ullerston's lengthy determination is commonly cited, but rarely read in full or compared closely with its partial English translation. This may have something to do with the fact that the one extant copy in Vienna, Österreichische Nationalbibliothek, Codex Vindobonensis Palatinus 4133, fols 195–297v is in an especially difficult, highly abbreviated script: an edition is badly needed.

The comprehensively annotated critical edition in five volumes of the long Wycliffite sermon cycle by Anne Hudson and Pamela Gradon has now been completed, bringing these sermons into the mainstream for critical studies (see Ghosh, Little). There are 294 sermons in the cycle, and these comprise five sets covering different kinds of occasions during the liturgical year, following the Sarum missal, for which a sermon might be required. Set one includes 54 sermons on the Sunday gospel readings, set two has 31 sermons on saints of general types (apostle, martyr, virgin, etc.), covering the lections provided for these in Sarum, set three has 37 sermons for specific saints again covering lections from Sarum, set four has 120 sermons covering all the holy days and special occasions for which the Sarum rite provides specific readings, set five has 55 sermons on the Sunday epistle readings. Although there are some minor differences in the handling of the biblical translation and in tone and approach between the five sets, on the whole the editors find an overwhelming consistency across the whole of this vast cycle. Probably produced in the late 1380s to 1390s, the sermons are distinctively and strongly Wycliffite. Their author(s) display(s) extensive familiarity with Wyclif's works, and in addition to the

---

6   Thanks to Andrew Cole for some of these references, drawn from his reconsideration of what Chaucer's attitude to translation in the *Treatise on the Astrolabe* has to do with Wycliffite attitudes: see Cole 2002.

suspicion of nonbiblical saints evident in the brevity of sets two and three, the sermons eschew any use of entertaining narratives and exempla of the sort Wycliffites deplored in the sermons of the friars. The editors hypothesize that if not composed as a single unit, the cycle was certainly composed in five sets that were then bonded into a single whole; and they suggest that if multiple authors were involved, then they probably each played a specific role in the composition of each sermon, rather than each working alone on a certain number of sermons (Hudson and Gradon IV, 8–40). In addition to the 31 manuscripts containing either the whole of the cycle or some liturgically coherent selection from within it, four cases have been discovered in which materials from the cycle were expurgated or adapted by nonWycliffites for less controversial uses. (Hudson 1971c, Hudson and Gradon I, 98–123, Evans) A volume of *Lollard Sermons* has also appeared (Cigman); however, although these sermons' use of the Wycliffite distinction collection known as the *Rosarium* has been demonstrated (von Nolcken 1981), other evidence of their Lollard affiliations still awaits investigation. Also recently edited are occasional sermons by Nicholas Hereford and William Taylor, a fragment of 'þe sermoun of þe Horsedoun,' and a lengthy sermon titled *Omnis Plantacio* which might equally be viewed as an instructional tract, but which contains a passage which appears to refer to the visits of an itinerant preacher (Forde, Hudson 1993, Hudson 1993, Hudson 2001; for the passage on preaching see also Hudson 1978a, 96; Copeland 2001, 128–29).

Declarative lists and confessional writings have been the subject of much interest in recent critical writings on Lollards, and have been both edited and anthologized, some repeatedly. Although declarative writings are typically refreshingly forthright, and confessional writings seemingly comprehensive, neither should be regarded as a straightforward summary of Lollard beliefs. One moment's defiance, or even one occasion for establishing defiant answers, can scarcely sum up all Lollard thought on a given issue or issues. And even our sense that a confessional text presents one defendant's convictions at a given point in time should be shadowed by the awareness that their presentation may be distorted by the agenda of his or her questioners and by the circumstances. Bearing this in mind, the *Twelve Conclusions* (Hudson 1978a) and the *Testimony of William Thorpe* (Hudson 1993) are useful for introductory study, and have recently been edited with commentary that is attentive to their commonalities with other Lollard writings. Posted (according to hostile observers) on the doors of Westminster and St Paul's in 1395, the *Twelve Conclusions* appeal to Parliament to return current ecclesiastical institutions and practices to the state of the primitive church. Included in their complaint are abuses associated with the priesthood, the sacraments as well as other rites and rituals, vows of continence, crusades, and the multitude of unnecessary crafts. Thorpe's *Testimony* refers to one particular occasion on which the writer claims to have been examined for heresy by Archbishop Arundel and his three clerks/henchmen; yet upon this circumstance is built an exemplary response to hostile questions that would have been accessible and enjoyable reading for a wide range of sympathetic readers. The coverage of topics is plainly intended to be comprehensive: Thorpe defends Lollard views on the nature of the church, freedom of preaching, the eucharist,

images, pilgrimages, tithing, oaths, oral confession, and the sources of authority
a Christian should accept.

Thorpe's *Testimony* is a good example of a Wycliffite work which has helped
to intensify critics' awareness of variations in style, genre, and intended audience among Lollard writings, of these writings' literary qualities, and of their
sometimes close affiliations with contemporary writings produced outside the
Wycliffite movement. Granted, many Wycliffite writings are grimly in earnest,
and it is common for their authors to address an audience already 'in the know'
rather than attempting to prosthelytize: some writings (such as the *Upland
Series*) treat their topics of debate so allusively that outsiders can understand
what is going on only with great difficulty. Yet the wider our reading in
Wycliffite writings, the more variety we find. Attention to catechetical and
informational writings and to those writings associated with the Langland and
Chaucer traditions has been facilitated by new critical editions of some of these
works, and has similarly improved our understanding of the breadth of
Wycliffite prose. Most writings traditionally associated with the *Piers Plowman*
and/or Chaucer traditions lie outside the purview of this chapter (though the
well annotated recent edition of some of them (Barr 1993) should be noted in
passing), since among the medieval members only two are in prose: *Jack
Upland*, a set of antifraternal questions which begins the *Upland Series*, and *The
Praier and Complaynte of the Plowman vnto Christ*, an apparently medieval
tract (though extant in no manuscript) consisting of a lengthy prayer/complaint
covering a selection of social concerns also evident in *Piers* (Heyworth, Dean
1991, Parker 1997). But catechetical and informational writings will require
extended attention.

At first glance, the quantity and content of catechetical Wycliffite works
available might not seem to justify this statement. Aside from the 'Exegetical
and Didactic Treatises' printed in Arnold (III, 3–182) and consisting of a set of
commentaries on the Cantica Sacra, the Pater Noster, the Ave Maria, the
Apostles Creed, the Ten Commandments, the Seven Deadly Sins, the Five Inner
and Outer Wits, the Seven Works of Spiritual and Bodily Mercy, as well as other
less catechetical topics, and the tracts on the Pater Noster, Ave Maria, and the
Works of Mercy and Five Senses (the last two entitled 'How Satan and His
Children . . .') in Matthew (197–218) the only candidates would seem to be the
The Lanterne of Liȝt and the Wycliffite version of the *Lay Folks' Catechism* –
whose eligibility, however, has been cast into doubt by Anne Hudson (1985b,
1988b). From the point of view of individual manuscript descriptions, however,
this category looks far more promising. Pastoral instruction seems to have been
an especially productive interface between Wycliffite thought and more mainstream religious culture (see Hanna 1997, xix–xxiii).

The Lanterne of Liȝt may be Wycliffism's only example of a coherent,
unified, polished catechetical product, in which coverage of topics such as the
Creed, the Seven Deadly Sins, and the Ten Commandments is smoothly integrated with a distinctively Wycliffite explanation of the membership of the true
church. Unusually, we even have a fairly precise probable date of composition
(1409–1414) and some evidence about an early reader, John Claydon, who was
illiterate but in his heresy trial of 1415 was said to have had the book read to

him often.[7] Yet Wycliffism-tinged pastoralia such as Arnold's commentaries (and others which remain unprinted) appear in varying manuscript contexts that suggest broad interest among Wycliffites in this sort of reading – and even suggest that others, too, read Wycliffite versions, whether by design or by accident. Contexts for Wycliffite pastoralia include manuscripts containing portions of the Wycliffite bible translation, manuscripts that also include hard-edged polemical tracts, idiosyncratic pastoral collections such as those found in Manchester, John Rylands English 85 or Westminster School 3, and pastoral collections that are standardized enough to be assigned a title (though the precise content in individual manuscripts varies) such as the *Pore Caitif* and the *Lay Folks' Catechism*. Some of these manuscripts seem orthodox apart from their Wycliffite components, whose affiliation may not have been recognized by their compilers; others are strongly Wycliffite: in others, the ideological cast is uncertain, or even confused – here, along with Lambeth Palace Library 408 version of the *Lay Folks' Catechism* discussed by Hudson (1985b), the Lollard (or is it?) version of the *Ancren Riwle* in Magdalene College Cambridge Pepys 2498 should be mentioned.[8] Yet the full range of these examples deserves attention, and to omit even fully orthodox (yet clearly related) versions from consideration would be to skew the picture.[9]

Incorporating polemical sideswipes, heretical content, and/or new kinds of information into a kind of pastoral instruction that was already widely available was one Wycliffite tactic, visible in the catechetical writings just surveyed; another tactic was to instruct unschooled lay readers about the methods and content of intellectual argumentation underlying controversial topics in the course of polemical writing on those topics, thus providing them with better tools to engage in debate. While some Wycliffite writings do not make efforts at this sort of inclusiveness, many do: far too many to be surveyed here; and they deserve to be compared with other adventurous attempts to make learning available to vernacular readers, found in writings as diverse as those of Richard Fitzralph as translated by John Trevisa, Richard Rolle, and Julian of Norwich (see Somerset 1998, 93–100, Watson 1997). Although available only in editions which do not provide commentary that makes evident their relations with university learning, the tracts 'De Blasphemia' and 'Of Dominion' are clearly good examples (Arnold III, 402–29, Matthew, 282–93). Beginning from a clear general definition of blasphemy as 'sclaundring of God' (402/8), 'De Blasphemia' proceeds to explain three ways in which the friars are blasphemers: in their theories on the Eucharist, mendicancy, and letters of fraternity (403/2–7). Especially in the section on the Eucharist (403–10), the tract instructs its readers in philosophy, encouraging them to rely on the clear evidence provided by their senses in rejecting the friars' explanation, as here: 'feythe of þo gospel techis us to trowe

---

7   See Hudson 1988a, 211–13, for the most recent assessment of the evidence about the *Lanterne*.
8   This version was edited by A. Zettersten; see also Colledge, Hudson 1988a, 27–8, and von Nolcken (forthcoming).
9   Thus, Simpson may be correct in *IMEP Handlist VII* when he notes that Bibliothèque Sainte Geneviève 3390 does not have any overt Wycliffite content (24–25). But this should not exclude it from comparison with its more Wycliffite relations.

þat þis is verey bred after þo sacringe, for Crist hymself seis, þis bred is my body; bot what foole con not se þat ne þen hit is bred?' (404/27–30). Similarly, 'Of Dominion' appeals to, and builds upon, lay powers of discretion. Its chapter on judgment (289–91) gives instruction in the various kinds of false judgment in a way that places considerable reliance on lay persons' inner and outer wits:

> [S]um good iugement is of mennes out-wittis, as þei iugen whiche mete is good & whiche mete is yuel, & sum men iugement is of mennes wit wi þinne, as men iugen how þei schal do, by lawe of conscience; as cristen men schal iuge to whom þei done here almes, and þat þei feden nouȝt fendis children among here owne heed. (291/1–7)

Anyone who can tell good food from spoiled, it is implied, will have an similarly easy time deciding which are the 'fendis children' whom they should not feed.

Two newly edited tracts, *Omnis plantacio* and *De oblacione* (in *The Works of a Lollard Preacher*, Hudson 2001), use the same tactic of beginning from skills their lay readers would already possess, but go to extraordinary lengths to instruct their readers.[10] The tracts claim to have been written by the same author, and internal references allow them to be very probably dated between 1409 and 1414. In addition to their date, the tracts share other characteristics with *The Lanterne of Liȝt* that may at the very least suggest closely related audiences and writers. All three draw extensively on biblical commentators and patristic authorities in first-hand translations that are plainly their own; all three complain about practices in the ecclesiastical and civil courts, and/or about canon and civil law, in a kind of detail that can only be born from considerable familiarity.[11] All three eschew non-biblical narrative used merely for entertainment (thus conforming with Wycliffite complaints about preachers who use irrelevant stories in their sermons) but nonetheless have literary qualities that might surprise critics who think Wycliffite writings are strident and boring. They revel in the earthier possibilities provided by the vernacular: consider, for example, *De Oblacione*'s description of Antichrist's negative effect on the cleansing fires of contrition: 'antecrist haþ nouȝ pissid out þe fire bi his yuyl ensample and stopping of Goddis lawe, and wiþ cold muddi water of his owne tradicions' (194/1446–50). They make colourful use of adventurously interpreted biblical narratives: see for example the *Lanterne*'s eighth chapter's extended allegorical exposition of Matt.13:47 (43–47) on how the kingdom of heaven is like a net cast into a fish-filled sea, where the perils presented both by the sea and by 'greet fisches' are feelingly detailed on the way to the hopeful promise of those 'fisches [that] ben riȝt quiuer & quik in plente of þe watir & dreden not þe hidouse wawis whethir þei risen hiȝe or fallen lowe' (47/1–3). And as this example also shows, these texts are not infrequently lyrical, achieving heightened emotional effects through such devices as alliteration, rhyme, and rhythmical prose.

---

[10] I am summarizing a longer discussion of the shared characteristics of these works, and a more detailed exposition of their various instructional impulses, from Somerset 2003b.

[11] For more details see Somerset 2003b, nn. 4–5.

Returning, though, to these texts' mode of instructing their readers, the second two tracts expand the *Lanterne*'s more catechetical impulse in order to provide some of the most extensive instruction in Latinate university learning to be found anywhere, whether in English or Latin. Among the three (and indeed perhaps amidst the whole of the Wycliffite oeuvre), *De Oblacione* is the most intent on imparting academic information. This is scarcely surprising, considering that the text's focus on teaching its readers and listeners to reject certain arguments about the eucharist and accept others. In addition to many passages which teach readers argumentational techniques using scholastic terminology – notably, an explanation of contraries and contradictories (199/1663–200/1700) – it also quotes, translates, and teaches specific Latin words, aiming to impart understanding of Latin to lay users, and even to introduce them to controversies over how to translate specific words and phrases. The work's exposition and evaluation of various theories about the proper translation and interpretation of Christ's statement 'hoc est corpus meum,' for example (see 207/1989–208/2024), is the fullest treatment I have found anywhere, in English or in Latin, of a topic treated allusively in a wide range of contemporary writings (see Somerset 2003a). *De Oblacione* cannot give its readers a systematic knowledge of grammar or adaptable fluency in the reading of a wide variety of learned writings. Yet it does induct its readers and listeners into a number of specialized language practices previously confined to university-educated clerics, and allows them to understand the translation possibilities of certain specific Latin words. And as in 'Of Dominion' or 'De Blasphemia,' this teaching attempts to build upon the powers of discretion that readers already possess:

> Sum seien þat þis word of Crist in Laten *hoc est corpus meum* betokeneþ þus þat þis accident wiþout soiect or substaunce signifiiþ sacramentalli Cristis bodi, so þat þei wol not graunt þat her sacrament is Cristis bodi in forme of brede, but an accident wiþout soiect or substaunce þat betokeneþ Cristis bodi. Naþeles, antecrist and his special lemys ben in a grete perplexite what accident in kinde is þis sacrament, wheþur it be a quantite as is lengþe, brede and þiknes of þis oost, or ellis a qualite; and, if it be a qualite, in what special kinde þis sacrament schuld be – þei ben not ȝit fulli determened, þat is to seie, wheþur it be whitenesse, roundenesse, heuynes or liȝtnesse, sauour or odourre, or any seche þat ben to mannys witt wiþout numbre. But up hap þes lemys wiþ þe heed schal drawe hemself togedur and determene þis douȝte whan þei seen her tyme, and multepliȝe inconuenientis [i.e., absurdities] mony and newe!

This excerpt from the conclusion of the 'hoc est corpus meum' discussion is a *reductio ad absurdum* argument; but in leading readers or listeners to delight with the writer in rejecting the absurdities multiplied by the limbs of antichrist it draws on a sense of what it means to say something plainly, in whatever language, that does not require – and might even by impeded by – university learning. Along with their new learning in scholastic techniques of argument, lay readers and listeners are encouraged to rely on their nose for the ridiculous – in rather the same way that in *Omnis Plantacio* their ears are trained to perceive the fallacy in a 'to short' argument (88/1856–90/1881). This is truly a vernacularization of knowledge: a mode of teaching which builds on the capabilities of the untrained with the goal of enabling them to engage in debate. It demonstrates an impulse toward vernacular instruction in late medieval English prose which although not unique to Wycliffites, certainly achieves in their prose its fullest realization.

BIBLIOGRAPHY

This bibliography aims to cover all important editions of Wycliffite prose and its closest relations, but only a small selection of more recent and important secondary sources. Collections of articles cited more than once are cited in full under the editor's name, and in short form under the contributors' names. For a wider-ranging, regularly updated bibliography of printed materials for the study of Wycliffism, to which I am indebted, see Derrick Pitard's online bibliography, <http: //lollard.home.att.net/biblopri.html#bibs> (for a shorter version see Pitard in Somerset, Havens and Pitard). Hudson's 'Contributions' article (1973) explains the inadequacies of the most recent previous attempt at a bibliography of Wycliffite writings (Talbert and Thomson), and lists corrections. A comprehensive bibliography of theses relevant to the study of Wycliffism has been compiled by Jill Havens and is available through the Lollard Society. A new bibliography focused on manuscript sources for the study of Wycliffism is being prepared by David Watt and Fiona Somerset.

Wycliffite Prose and Other Important Primary Sources

[Ancrene Riwle] A. Zettersten, ed., *The English Text of the Ancrene Riwle, Edited from Magdalene College, Cambridge MS Pepys 2498*, EETS os 274 (London, 1976)
[Apology] James Henthorn Todd, ed., *An Apology for Lollard Doctines Attributed to Wicliffe*, Camden Society os 20 (London,1842)
Arnold, T., ed., *Select English Works of John Wyclif*, 3 vols (Oxford, 1868–71), III
Barr, Helen, ed., *The Piers Plowman Tradition* (London, 1993)
[Bible] Josiah Forshall, and Frederick Madden, eds, *The Holy Bible . . . Made from the Latin Vulgate by John Wycliffe and his Followers* (Oxford, 1850; repr. New York, 1982)
[Bible] Conrad Lindberg, ed., *MS Bodley 959 Genesis-Baruch 3.20 in the Earlier Version of the Wycliffite Bible*, Stockholm Studies in English 6, 8, 10, 13, 20 (Stockholm, 1959–69)
[Bible] ——, *The Earlier Version of the Wycliffite Bible . . . Edited from MS Christ Church 145*, Stockholm Studies in English 29, 81, 87 (Stockholm, 1973–95)
[Bible] ——, *The Middle English Bible: Prefatory Epistles of St Jerome* (Oslo, Bergen, and Tromso, 1978)
[Bible] ——, *The Middle English Bible: The Book of Baruch* (Oslo, Bergen, and Tromso, 1985)
[Bible] ——, *The Middle English Bible: The Book of Judges* (Oslo, Bergen, and Tromso, 1989)

[Bible] ———, *King Henry's Bible: MS Bodley 277, The Revised Version of the Wyclif Bible*, Vol 1: Genesis-Ruth. Stockholm Studies in English 89. Stockholm, 1999

[Bible.] ———. *King Henry's Bible: MS Bodley 277, The Revised Version of the Wyclif Bible*. Vol 2: *Kings–Psalms*, Stockholm Studies in English 94 (Stockholm, 2001)

Blamires, Alcuin and C.W. Marx, 'Women Not to Preach: A Disputation in British Library MS Harley 31', *Journal of Medieval Latin* 3 (1993), 34–63

Bowers, John, ed., *The Canterbury Tales: Fifteenth-Century Continuations and Additions*, TEAMS Middle English Texts Series (Kalamazoo, 1992)

Brut, Walter: see Swinderby

Bühler, Curt F., 'A Lollard Tract: on Translating the Bible into English', *Medium Aevum* 7 (1938), 167–83

Cigman, Gloria, ed., *Lollard Sermons*, EETS os 294 (Oxford, 1989)

Clanvowe, John, 'The Two Ways', in Scattergood, V.J., ed., *The Works of Sir John Clanvowe* (Cambridge, 1975), pp. 57–80

Dean, James M., ed., *Six Ecclesiastical Satires*, TEAMS Middle English Texts Series (Kalamazoo, 1991)

———, ed., *Medieval English Political Writings*, TEAMS Middle English Texts Series (Kalamazoo, 1996)

Deanesly, Margaret, *The Lollard Bible and Other Medieval Biblical Versions* (Cambridge, 1920), Appendix 2.3, pp. 437–45 [Tract on translation also edited by Bühler]

Dymmok, Roger, *Liber Contra Duodecim Errores et Hereses Lollardorum*, ed. H.S. Cronin (London, 1922)

Embree, Dan, ed., *Chronicles of Popes and Emperors and the Lollard Chronicle* (Woodbridge, Suffolk, 1999)

Evans, Ruth, ed., 'An Edition of a Fifteenth-Century Middle English *Temporale* Sermon Cycle in MSS Lambeth Palace 392 and Cambridge University Library Additional 5338', 2 vols (unpublished Ph.D. thesis, University of Leeds, 1986)

[*Fasciculi Zizaniorum*] W.W. Shirley, ed., *Fasciculi Zizaniorum Magistri Johannis Wyclif cum Tritico*, Rolls Series 5 (London, 1858)

Forshall, J., ed., *Remonstrance Against Romish Corruptions*: see *Thirty-Seven Conclusions*

Genet, J.P., ed., *Four English Political Tracts of the Later Middle Ages*, Camden Society 4th ser. 18 (London, 1977)

[Hereford, Nicholas] Simon Forde. 'Nicholas Hereford's Ascension Day Sermon, 1382', *Mediaeval Studies* 51 (1989), 205–41

Hudson, Anne, ed., *Selections from English Wycliffite Writings* (Cambridge, 1978a)

———, *Two Wycliffite Texts*, EETS os 301 (Oxford, 1993)

———, *The Works of a Lollard Preacher*, EETS os 317 (Oxford, 2001)

Hudson, Anne, and Pamela Gradon, eds, *English Wycliffite Sermons*, 5 vols (Oxford, 1983–96)

Hunt, Simon, 'An Edition of Tracts in Favour of Scriptural Translation and of Some Texts Connected with Lollard Biblical Scholarship' (unpublished D.Phil. thesis, University of Oxford, 1994)

[*Lanterne of Li3t*] L.M. Swinburn, ed., *The Lanterne of Li3t*, EETS os 151 (London, 1917)

[*Lay Folks' Catechism*] Simmons, T.F., and H.E. Nolloth, eds *The Lay Folks' Catechism*, EETS os 118 (London, 1901)

Lindberg, Conrad, ed., *English Wyclif Tracts 1–3*, Studia Anglistica Norvegica 5 (Oslo, 1991)

———, *English Wyclif Tracts 4–6*, Studia Anglistica Norvegica 11 (Oslo, 2000)

Matthew, F.D., ed., *The English Works of Wyclif Hitherto Unprinted*, 2nd ed., EETS os 74 (London, 1902)

Parker, Douglas H., ed., *The Praier and Complaynte of the Ploweman vnto Christe* (Toronto, 1997)

———, *A Proper Dyalogue betwene a Gentillman and a Husbandman* (Toronto, 1996)

Salisbury, Eve, ed., *The Trials and Joys of Marriage*, TEAMS Middle English Texts Series (Kalamazoo, MI, 2002)

[Swinderby, William, and Walter Brut] *Registrum Johannis Trefnant Episcopi Herefordensis*, ed. W.W. Capes, Canterbury and York Society 20 (London, 1916)

[*Thirty-Seven Conclusions*] J. Forshall, ed., *Remonstrance Against Romish Corruptions in the Church Addressed to the People and Parliament of England in 1395* (London, 1851)

[*Thirty-Seven Conclusions*] H.F.B. Compston, 'The Thirty-Seven Conclusions of the Lollards', *English Historical Review* 22 (1907), 292–304

[*Tretise of Miraclis Pleyinge*] Clifford Davidson, ed., *A Tretise of Miraclis Pleyinge*, Early Drama, Art, and Music Monograph Series 19 (Kalamazoo, MI, 1993)

[*Twelve Conclusions*] H.S. Cronin, ed., 'The Twelve Conclusions of the Lollards', *English Historical Review* 22 (1907), 292–304

[*Upland Series*] P.L. Heyworth, ed., *Jack Upland, Friar Daw's Reply, and Upland's Rejoiner* (London, 1968)

von Nolcken, Christina, ed., *The Middle English Translation of the Rosarium Theologie* (Heidelberg, 1979)

Winn, Herbert E., ed., *Select English Writings*, with a preface by H.B. Workman (London, 1929)

[Woodford, William] Eric Doyle, 'William Woodford O.F.M. (c.1330–c.1400): His Life and Works, together with a Study and Edition of his *Responsiones contra Wyclevum et Lollardos*', *Franciscan Studies* 43 (1983), 17–187

[Wyche, Richard] F.D. Matthew, 'The Trial of Richard Wyche', *English Historical Review* 5 (1890), 530–44

Wycklyffe's Wycket (Nuremburg, 1546), repr., ed. T.P. Pantin (Oxford, 1828)

Writings on Wycliffite Prose and its Place in the Study of Wycliffism

Aers, David, and Lynn Staley, *The Powers of the Holy: Religion, Politics, and Gender in Late Medieval English Culture* (University Park, PA, 1996)

———, *Faith, Ethics and Church: Writing in England, 1360–1409* (Woodbridge, Suffolk, 2000)

———, 'Walter Brut's Theology of the Sacrament of the Altar', in Somerset, Havens, and Pitard 2003, pp. 115–26

Aston, Margaret, 'Works of Religious Instruction', in Edwards 1984, pp. 413–32

———, *Lollards and Reformers: Images and Literacy in Late Medieval Religion* (London, 1984)

———, *Faith and Fire: Popular and Unpopular Religion, 1350–1600* (London, 1993)

———, 'Lollards and the Cross', in Somerset, Havens, and Pitard 2003, pp. 99–113

Aston, Margaret, and Colin Richmond, eds, *Lollardy and the Gentry in the Later Middle Ages* (Stroud, Glos., and New York, 1997)

Barr, Helen, *Socioliterary Practice in Medieval England* (Oxford, 2001)

———, 'Wycliffite Representations of the Third Estate', in Somerset, Havens, and Pitard 2003, pp. 197–216

Benskin, M., and M.L. Samuels, eds, *So Meny People, Longages, and Tonges: Philolog-*

ical Essays in Scots and Mediaeval English Presented to Angus McIntosh (Edinburgh, 1981)

Boffey, J., and John J. Thompson, 'Anthologies and Miscellanies: Production and Choice of Texts', in Griffiths and Pearsall, pp. 279–315

Bose, Mishtooni, 'Reginald Pecock's Vernacular Voice', in Somerset, Havens, and Pitard, pp. 217–36

Bowers, John M., 'Piers Plowman and the Police: Notes toward a History of the Wycliffite Langland', *Yearbook of Langland Studies* 6 (1992), 1–50

Brady, Sr M. Theresa, 'Lollard Sources of the Pore Caitif', *Traditio* 44 (1988), 389–418

——, 'Lollard Interpolations and Omissions in Manuscripts of the Pore Caitif', in Michael G. Sargent, ed., *De Cella in Saeculum: Religious and Secular Life and Devotion in Late Medieval England* (Woodbridge, Suffolk, 1989), pp. 183–203

Catto, J.I., 'Religion and the English Nobility in the Later Fourteenth Century', in H. Lloyd-Jones, V. Pearl and B. Worden, eds, *History and Imagination: Essays in Honour of H.R. Trevor-Roper* (London, 1981), pp. 43–55

——, 'John Wyclif and the Cult of the Eucharist', in Walsh and Wood 1985, pp. 269–86

——, 'A Radical Preacher's Handbook', *English Historical Review* 115 (2000), 893–905

Clopper, Lawrence, 'Miracula and *The Tretise of Miraclis Pleyinge*', *Speculum* 65 (1990), 878–905

——, 'Franciscans, Lollards, and Reform', in Somerset, Havens, and Pitard 2003, pp. 177–96

Cole, Andrew, 'Chaucer's English Lesson', *Speculum* 77 (2002), 1128–67

——, 'William Langland and the Invention of Lollardy', in Somerset, Havens, and Pitard 2003, pp. 37–58

Colledge, E., '*The Recluse*: A Lollard Interpolated Version of the Ancren Riwle', *Review of English Studies* 15 (1939), 1–15, 129–45

Copeland, Rita, ed., *Criticism and Dissent in the Middle Ages* (Cambridge, 1996)

——, *Pedagogy, Intellectuals, and Dissent in the Later Middle Ages: Lollardy and Ideas of Learning* (Cambridge, 2001)

Davis, Nicholas, 'Another View of *The Tretise of Miraclis Pleyinge*', *Medieval English Theatre* 4 (1982), 48–55

——, '*The Tretise of Miraclis Pleyinge*: On Milieu and Authorship', *Medieval English Theatre* 12 (1990), 124–51

Dinshaw, Carolyn, *Getting Medieval: Sexualities and their Communities, Pre- and Post-Modern* (Durham, NC, 1999)

Doyle, A.I., 'University College, Oxford, MS 97 and its Relationship to the Simeon Manuscript (British Library Add. 22283)', in Benskin and Samuels, pp. 265–82

Edwards, A.S.G., ed., *Middle English Prose: A Critical Guide to Major Authors and Genres* (New Brunswick, NJ, 1984)

Fletcher, Alan J., 'John Mirk and the Lollards', *Medium Aevum* 56 (1987), 217–24

——, *Preaching and Politics in Late Medieval England* (Dublin, 1998)

Fristedt, Sven L., *The Wycliffe Bible*, 3 vols, Part I: *The Principal Problems Connected with Forshall and Madden's Edition*, Part II: *The Origin of the First Revision as presented in 'De Salutaribus Documentis'*, Part III: *Relationships of Trevisa and the Spanish Medieval Bibles*, Stockholm Studies in English 4, 21, 28 (Stockholm, 1953–73)

Galloway, Andrew, 'Chaucer's Former Age and the Fourteenth-Century Anthropology of Craft: The Social Logic of a Premodernist Lyric', *English Literary History* 63 (1996), 535–53

Ghosh, Kantik, *The Wycliffite Heresy: Authority and the Interpretation of Texts* (Cambridge, 2002)

Gillespie, Vincent, 'Vernacular Books of Religion', in Griffiths and Pearsall, pp. 317–44

Gradon, Pamela, 'Langland and the Ideology of Dissent', *Proceedings of the British Academy* 66 (1980), 179–205

Griffiths, Jeremy, and Derek Pearsall, eds, *Book Production and Publishing in Britain 1375–1475* (Cambridge, 1989)

Hanna III, Ralph, 'The Difficulty of Ricardian Prose Translation: The Case of the Lollards', *Modern Language Quarterly* 51 (1990), 319–40

———, *Pursuing History: Middle English Manuscripts and their Texts* (Stanford, 1996)

———, ' "Vae Octuplex", Lollard Socio-textual Ideology, and Ricardian-Lancastrian Prose Translation', in Copeland 1996, pp. 244–63

———, *IMEP Handlist XII: Smaller Bodleian Collections* (Woodbridge, Suffolk, 1997)

———, 'English Biblical Texts before Lollardy and their Fate', in Somerset, Havens, and Pitard 2003, pp. 141–53

Hargreaves, Henry, 'The Marginal Glosses to the Wycliffite New Testament', *Studia Neophilologica* 33 (1961), 285–300

———, 'The Wycliffite Versions', in G.W.H. Lampe, ed., *The Cambridge History of the Bible* (Cambridge, 1969), pp. 387–415

———, 'Popularising Biblical Scholarship: The Role of the Wycliffite Glossed Gospels', in W. Lourdaux and D. Verhelst, eds, *The Bible and Medieval Culture* (Leuven, 1979), pp. 171–89

Holsinger, Bruce, 'The Vision of Music in a Lollard Florilegium: *Cantus* in the Middle English *Rosarium Theologie* (Cambridge, Gonville and Caius College MS 354/581)', *Plainsong and Medieval Music* 8.2 (1999), 95–106

Hudson, Anne, 'A Lollard Sermon-Cycle and its Implications', *Medium Aevum* 40 (1971a), 142–56

———, 'A Lollard Quaternion', *Review of English Studies* ns 22 (1971b), 451–65; repr. in Hudson 1985a, pp. 193–200

———, 'The Expurgation of a Lollard Sermon-Cycle', *Journal of Theological Studies* ns 23 (1971c), 407–19; repr. in Hudson 1985a, pp. 201–15

———, 'Contributions to a Bibliography of Wycliffite Writings', *Notes and Queries* ns 20 (1973), 443–53; repr. as 'Contributions to a History of Wycliffite Writings' and 'Appendix: Additions and Modifications to a Bibliography of English Wycliffite Writings' in Hudson 1985a, pp. 1–12 and 249–52

———, 'The Debate on Bible Translation, Oxford 1401', *English Historical Review* 90 (1975), 1–18; repr. in Hudson 1985a, pp. 67–84

———, 'A Neglected Wycliffite Text', *Journal of Ecclesiastical History* 29 (1978b), 257–79; repr. in Hudson 1985a, pp. 43–65

———, 'Wycliffite Prose', in Edwards 1984, pp. 249–70

———, *Lollards and their Books* (London, 1985a)

———, 'A New Look at the Lay Folk's Catechism', *Viator* 16 (1985b), 243–58

———, 'A Wycliffite Scholar of the Early Fifteenth Century', in Walsh and Wood 1985c, pp. 301–315

———, *The Premature Reformation: Wycliffite Texts and Lollard History* (Oxford, 1988a)

———, 'The Lay Folk's Catechism: A Postscript', *Viator* 18 (1988b), 307–309

———, 'The Legacy of *Piers Plowman*', in John Alford, ed., *A Companion to 'Piers Plowman'* (Berkeley, 1988c), pp. 251–66

———, 'Lollard Book Production', in Griffiths and Pearsall 1989, pp. 125–42

———, 'The Mouse in the Pyx: Popular Heresy and the Eucharist', *Trivium* 26 (1991), 40–53

———, 'The King and Erring Clergy: A Wycliffite Contribution', in Diana Wood, ed., *The Church and Sovereignty c.590–1918: Essays in Honour of Michael Wilks*, Studies in Church History, Subsidia 9 (Oxford, 1991), pp. 269–78

———, 'The Variable Text', in A.J. Minnis and Charlotte Brewer, eds, *Crux and Controversy in Middle English Textual Criticism* (Woodbridge, Suffolk, 1992), pp. 49–60

———, 'Laicus Litteratus: The Paradox of Lollardy', in Peter Biller and Anne Hudson, eds, *Heresy and Literacy, 1000–1530* (Cambridge, 1994), pp. 222–36

———, 'Piers Plowman and the Peasant's Revolt: A Problem Revisited', *Yearbook of Langland Studies* 8 (1995b), 85–106

Hudson, Anne, and Helen L. Spencer, 'Old Author, New Work: The Sermons of MS Longleat 4', *Medium Aevum* 53 (1984), 220–38

Hudson, Anne, and M.J. Wilks, eds, *From Ockham to Wyclif*, Studies in Church History, Subsidia 5 (Oxford, 1987)

Jones, W.R., 'Lollards and Images: The Defense of Religious Art in Later Medieval England', *Journal of the History of Ideas* 34 (1973), 27–50

Jurkowski, Maureen, 'New Light on John Purvey', *English Historical Review* 110 (1995), 1180–91

———, 'The Arrest of William Thorpe in Shrewsbury and the Anti-Lollard Statute of 1406', *Historical Research* 75 (2002), 273–95

Justice, Steven, *Writing and Rebellion: England in 1381* (Berkeley, CA, 1994)

———, 'Lollardy', in Wallace 1999, pp. 662–89

Keleman, Erick, 'Drama in Sermons: Quotation, Performativity, and Conversion in a Middle English Sermon and the *Tretise of Miraclis Pleyinge*', *English Literary History* 69 (2002), 1–19

Kellogg, A.L., and Ernest W. Talbert, 'The Wycliffite Pater Noster and Ten Commandments, with Special Reference to English Mss. 85 and 90 in the John Rylands Library', *Bulletin of the John Rylands Library* 42 (1960), 345–77

Kendall, Ritchie D., *The Drama of Dissent: The Radical Poetics of Nonconformity, 1380–1590* (Chapel Hill, 1986)

Kenny, Anthony, *Wyclif*, Past Masters Series (Oxford, 1985)

———, *Wyclif in his Times* (Oxford, 1986)

Kerby-Fulton, Kathryn, 'Prophecy and Suspicion: Closet Radicalism, Reformist Politics, and the Vogue for Hildegardiana in Ricardian England', *Speculum* 75 (2000), 318–41

Kuzcynski, Michael, 'Rolle among the Reformers: Orthodoxy and Heterodoxy in Wycliffite Copies of Richard Rolle's Psalter', in W.F. Pollard and R. Boenig, eds, *Mysticism and Spirituality in Medieval England* (Woodbridge, Suffolk, 1997), pp. 177–202

Lawton, David, 'Lollardy and the Piers Plowman Tradition', *Modern Language Review* 76 (1981), 780–93

———, 'Englishing the Bible, 1066–1549', in Wallace 1999, pp. 454–82

Lindberg, Conrad, 'The Manuscript and Versions of the Wyclif Bible', *Studia Neophilologica* 42 (1970), 333–47

———, 'The Break at Baruch 3:20 in the Middle English Bible', *English Studies* 60 (1979), 106–10

———, 'Reconstructing the Lollard Versions of the Bible', *Neuphilologische Mitteilungen* 90 (1989), 117–23

———, 'Towards an English Wyclif Canon', in L.E. Breivik et al., eds, *Essays on English Language in Honour of Bertil Sundby* (Oslo, 1989), pp. 179–84

——, 'From Jerome to Wyclif. An Experiment in Translation: The First Prologue', *Studia Neophilologica* 63:2 (1991), 143–45

——, 'Literary Aspects of the Wyclif Bible', *Bulletin of the John Rylands Library* 77.3 (1995), 79–85

Little, Katherine C., 'Catechesis and Castigation: Sin in the Wycliffite Sermon Cycle', *Traditio* 54 (1999), 213–44

McFarlane, K.B., *John Wycliffe and the Beginnings of English Nonconformity* (London, 1953)

——, *Lancastrian Kings and Lollard Knights* (Oxford, 1972)

McHardy, A.K., 'The Dissemination of Wyclif's Ideas', in Hudson and Wilks 1987, pp. 361–68

McNiven, Peter, *Heresy and Politics in the Reign of Henry IV: The Burning of John Badby* (Woodbridge, Suffolk, 1987)

McSheffrey, Shannon, *Gender and Heresy: Women and Men in Lollard Communities 1420–1530* (Philadelphia, 1995)

Martin, Anthony. 'The Middle English Versions of the Ten Commandments, with Special Reference to Rylands English MS 85', *Bulletin of the John Rylands University Library* 64.1 (1981), 191–217

Martin, C.A., 'Middle English Manuals of Religious Instruction', in Benskin and Samuels, 283–98

Minnis, A.J., ed., *Late Medieval Religious Texts and their Transmission: Essays in Honour of A.I. Doyle* (Woodbridge, Suffolk, 1994)

Nevanlinna, Saara, 'Distribution of Glosses in MSS of the Wycliffite Gospel of John: The Class of Paraphrase', *Neuphilologische Mitteilungen* 102.2 (2001), 173–83

Nichols, Ann E., 'Books for Laymen. The Demise of a Commonplace: Lollard Texts and the Justification of Images as a Continuity of Belief and Polemic', *Church History* 56 (1987), 457–73

Nissé, Ruth, 'Reversing Discipline: *The Tretise of Miraclis Pleyinge*, Lollard Exegesis, and the Failure of Representation', *Yearbook of Langland Studies* 11 (1997), 163–94

——, 'Staged Interpretations: Civic Rhetoric and Lollard Politics in the York Plays', *Journal of Medieval and Early Modern Studies* 28 (1998) 427–73

——, 'Prophetic Nations', in Wendy Scase, Rita Copeland, and David Lawton, eds, *New Medieval Literatures* 4 (Oxford, 2001), pp. 95–115

Patterson, Lee, 'Chaucer's Pardoner on the Couch: Psyche and Clio in Medieval Literary Studies', *Speculum* 79 (2001), 638–80

Peikola, Matti, ' "And after all, my Aue-Maria almost to the ende": *Pierce the Ploughman's Crede* and Lollard Expositions of the Ave Maria', *English Studies* 81 (2000), 273–92

——, *Congregation of the Elect: Patterns of Self-Fashioning in English Lollard Writings*, Anglicana Turkuensia 21 (Turku, Finland, 2000)

Pitard, Derrick, 'A Selected Bibliography for Lollard Studies', in Somerset, Havens, and Pitard, pp. 251–319

Powell, Sue, 'The Transmission and Circulation of the Lay Folk's Catechism', in Minnis, pp. 67–84

Scase, Wendy, ' "Strange and Wonderful Bills": Bill-Casting and Political Discourse in Late Medieval England', in Rita Copeland, David Lawton, and Wendy Scase, eds, *New Medieval Literatures* 2 (Oxford, 1998), pp. 225–48

——, ' "Heu, quanta desolatio Angliae praestatur": A Wycliffite Libel and the Naming of Heretics, Oxford 1382', in Somerset, Havens, and Pitard 2003, pp. 19–36

Scase, Wendy, Rita Copeland, and David Lawton, eds, *New Medieval Literatures* 1 (Oxford, 1997)

Simpson, James, *IMEP Handlist VII: Parisian Libraries* (Woodbridge, Suffolk, 1989)

Somerset, Fiona, *Clerical Discourse and Lay Audience in Late Medieval England* (Cambridge, 1998)

———, ' "As just as is a squyre": The Politics of "Lewed Translacion" in Chaucer's *Summoner's Tale*', *Studies in the Age of Chaucer* 21 (1999), 187–207

———, ' "Mark him wel for he is on of tho": Training the "Lewed" Gaze to Discern Hypocrisy', *English Literary History* 68 (2001), 315–34

———, 'Here, There, and Everywhere? Wycliffite Conceptions of the Eucharist and Chaucer's "Other" Lollard Joke', in Somerset, Havens, and Pitard (2003a), pp. 127–38

———, 'Expanding the Langlandian Canon: Radical Latin and the Stylistics of Reform', *Yearbook of Langland Studies* 17 (2003b), 73–92

Somerset, Fiona, Jill C. Havens, and Derrick G. Pitard, *Lollards and their Influence in Late Medieval England* (Woodbridge, Suffolk, 2003)

Spencer, Helen Leith, 'The Fortunes of a Lollard Sermon Cycle in the Later Fifteenth Century', *Mediaeval Studies* 48 (1986), 352–96

———, *English Preaching in the Late Middle Ages* (Oxford, 1993)

Steiner, Emily, 'Inventing Legality: Documentary Culture and Lollard Preaching', in Emily Steiner and Candace Barrington, eds, *The Letter of the Law: Legal Practice and Literary Production in Medieval England* (Ithaca, NY, 2002), pp. 185–201

———, 'Lollardy and the Legal Document', in Somerset, Havens, and Pitard 2003, pp. 155–74

Strohm, Paul, 'Chaucer's Lollard Joke: History and the Textual Unconscious', *Studies in the Age of Chaucer* 17 (1995), 23–42

———, 'Counterfeiters, Lollards, and Lancastrian Unease', in Scase, Copeland, and Lawton 1997, pp. 31–58

———, *England's Empty Throne: Usurpation and the Language of Legitimation, 1399–1422* (New Haven, 1998)

Summerson, Henry, 'An English Bible and Other Books Belonging to Henry IV', *Bulletin of the John Rylands Library* 79.1 (1997), 109–15

Swanson, R.N., 'A Small Library for Pastoral Care and Spiritual Instruction in Late Medieval England', *Journal of the Early Book Society* 5 (2002), 99–120

Talbert, E.W., and S.H. Thomson, 'Wyclif and his Followers', in J. Burke Severs, ed., *A Manual of the Writings in Middle English 1050–1500* ii (Hamden, CT, 1970), pp. 354–80, 521–35

Thomson, J.A.F., *The Later Lollards, 1414–1520* (Oxford, 1965)

von Nolcken, Christina, 'Some Alphabetical Compendia and how Preachers used them in Fourteenth-Century England', *Viator* 12 (1981), 271–88

———, 'An Unremarked Group of Wycliffite Sermons in Latin', *Modern Philology* 83 (1986), 233–49

———, 'Another Kind of Saint: A Lollard Perception of John Wyclif', in Hudson and Wilks 1987, pp. 429–43

———, 'Piers Plowman, the Wycliffites, and Pierce the Plowman's Creed', *Yearbook of Langland Studies* 2 (1988), 71–102

———, 'A "Certain Sameness" and our Response to it in English Wycliffite Texts', in R. Newhauser and John Alford, eds, *Literature and Religion in the Later Middle Ages: Philological Studies in Honor of Siegfried Wenzel* (Binghamton, 1995), pp. 191–208

———, 'Richard Wyche, A Certain Knight, and the Beginning of the End', in Aston and Richmond 1997, pp. 127–54

———, 'Lay Literacy, the Democratization of God's Law, and the Lollards', in K. Van

Kampen and John L. Sharpe III, eds, *The Bible as Book: The Manuscript Tradition* (London, 1998), pp. 177–95

———, '*The Recluse* and its Readers: Some Observations on a Lollard Interpolated Version of *Ancrene Wisse*', in Yoko Wada, ed. A Companion to *Ancrene Wisse* (Woodbridge, 2003), pp. 175–96

Wallace, David, ed., *The Cambridge History of Medieval English Literature* (Cambridge, 1999)

Walsh, Katherine, and Diana Wood, eds, *The Bible in the Medieval World: Essays in Memory of Beryl Smalley*, Studies in Church History, Subsidia 4 (Oxford, 1985)

Watson, Nicholas, 'Censorship and Cultural Change in Late-Medieval England: Vernacular Theology, the Oxford Translation Debate, and Arundel's Constitutions of 1409', *Speculum* 70 (1995), 822–64

———, 'Conceptions of the Word: The Mother Tongue and the Incarnation of God', in Scase, Copeland, and Lawton 1997, pp. 85–124

Wawn, Andrew N., 'Chaucer, *The Plowman's Tale*, and Reformation Propaganda: The Testimonies of Thomas Godfray and *I Playne Piers*', *Bulletin of the John Rylands Library* 56 (1973–74), 174–92

Wenzel, Siegfried, 'Robert Lychlade's Oxford Sermon of 1395 (Lollard Sympathies and Heretical Teachings in England)', *Traditio* 53 (1998), 203–30

Wilks, M.J., 'Misleading Manuscripts: Wyclif and the Non-Wycliffite Bible', *Studies in Church History* 11 (1975), 147–61

Yonekura, H., *The Language of the Wycliffite Bible: The Syntactic Differences between the Two Versions* (Tokyo, 1985)

———, 'John Purvey's Version of the Wycliffite Bible: A Reconsideration of his Translation Method', *Studies in Medieval English Language and Literature* 1 (1986), 67–91

13

Prose Romances

HELEN COOPER

The romance was the last genre to enter the field of Middle English prose. Secular fiction is now so automatically assumed to be prose that it is hard to imagine a time when the association did not exist, yet up until the fifteenth century its medium in English was just as automatically assumed to be verse, usually metrical, occasionally alliterative. Epic still carries such an association with verse, and romance, which largely took over the generic space of epic in the late Middle Ages and Renaissance, was similarly thought of as a poetic mode. Epic in literate Europe was however a form dominated by Classical authority, Homer and Virgil, and it is their practice that has kept the perception of verse as its natural generic medium; romance, by contrast, is a much more amorphous form, with no dominating generic model or authority, and with correspondingly greater freedom to respond to social movements and altering tastes. The change in medium did not happen all at once, and English romance made a late entry into prose compared with France. From uncertain beginnings in the second quarter of the fifteenth century, prose gradually encroached on romance in England, though it was to be many centuries before its takeover was to be complete. Yet by 1400 in France and by 1500 in Spain and England, prose had become the dominant new fashion for secular fiction, and proved an explosive driving force through the sixteenth century and beyond. Far from being regarded as a backward-looking form, the medieval prose romances were held to offer a release into new worlds, even a model for the conquest of the New World (R. Cooper 1990; Goodman 1998; Leonard 1949). The age of humanism was also the age that read them with the greatest avidity, with scant regard for our own habits of drawing boundaries between the literary and intellectual traditions represented by the medieval and the new learning. The shift to prose, and the accompanying shifts in both subject-matter and readership that that brought in its wake, in turn made possible the later move from romance into novel: a change that some fifteenth-century romances are already beginning to adumbrate.

Despite the contemporary popularity of the form and its importance for the later development of fiction, the English prose romances of the fifteenth and early sixteenth centuries have remained largely unread and unstudied (Hume 1974; Keiser 1984; Pearsall 1976; Scanlon 1977). Only Malory's *Morte Darthur* retains any widespread recognition now, and that is often treated as if it were an isolated phenomenon. It is sometimes described as being a nostalgic or reactionary work written after the vogue for things Arthurian had passed; yet not only was Malory in the forefront of the shift from verse to prose fiction in English, but Caxton's publication of his work was the first of numerous prints of Arthurian prose romances across Europe – not least in France, where the *Lancelot-Grail* texts and the prose *Tristan* were given unparalleled dissemination through the new vogue for printed chivalric romance. That prose romance entered English writing so late meant that its arrival only narrowly preceded the new medium of print. It was indeed Caxton himself who turned it from struggling emergence to a new fashion, and led that fashion with a spate of romance translations of his own. The printers who followed him, especially Wynkyn de Worde, took up the new form with some enthusiasm (Meale 1992). English prose romance was the first genre to be disseminated *primarily* by means of print, with the consequence that the works were read almost from their inception by an enlarging audience of townspeople and merchants as well as by the aristocratic and gentry audiences more traditionally associated with romance. Tradition is not altogether accurate in such matters, of course, and English-language romance had appealed across a considerable social range since its first appearance (that wide appeal was indeed part of the point of writing in English rather than Anglo-Norman); but by the end of the fifteenth century, the target audience of prose romance was being recognized as middle-class even while the implied audience was still formulated as 'gentle'. The high status of the works is none the less indicated by the high proportion of early editions printed in folio format. Cheaper quartos became the norm only in the sixteenth century.

The shift of romance into prose reflects the same increase in literacy that was recognized and encouraged by the printing press. In pre-literate societies, verse is the memorable form. Germanic and, almost certainly, Frankish epics were in verse, just as Homeric epic was, and for similar reasons: verse can be passed down through an oral culture, and there is no reason to change medium once those works or their later equivalents can be recorded or composed in written form.[1] The metrical romances were composed as written works and were disseminated largely in the same way, but oral transmission still seems likely to have played a part in the circulation of at least some of them in a way that could not happen with the prose (Putter 2000). The sheer length of many of the prose romances compared with verse texts underlines the point: it may be possible to memorize five hundred lines with some accuracy, but not five hundred pages. The audiences of both forms may have been more likely to have heard them read rather than to have read them privately on the page, but the authors of the prose romances took written circulation and an increasingly literate readership for granted.

The move to prose in secular fiction emphasized its overlap with history – with secular non-fictional narrative – and with historical legend accepted as fact. Prose had long been the dominant medium for historiography, and the composition of narrative in prose immediately suggested the historical. Verse was more likely to be the medium of what was recognized as legend, or at least

[1] The early preference for verse was not universal: Welsh and Irish both preferred prose as the medium for narrative, but their influence on English literature was trivial compared with French and Anglo-Norman, or even Old English.

of history reshaped with more attention to imaginative development than to fact. The writing of factual history, whether chronicles of the past or annals of the present, furthermore took place within literate communities, which after the fall of Rome primarily meant monastic communities. Its sources, whether written records or spoken report, were themselves prose, and its medium of memorability was parchment. Prose narrative kept that association with fact, with history or pseudo-history; and the concern of romance for the past, for reasons to do with its interest in origins as much as with the exoticism of the distant, perpetually drew it towards chronicle, just as chronicles had greater freedom for invention as they delved further back in time, beyond what could be certainly known. The formal demarcation between romance and history is accordingly much more attenuated than any attempts at definition or classification can control. The development of Arthurian narrative demonstrates the fluidity of the boundary. Arthur's origins, for the purposes of both chronicle and romance, lie in Geoffrey of Monmouth's *Historia Regum Britanniae* (c. 1138) – not exactly a work of hard fact, but widely believed to be so, and that belief was aided by the fact that its choice of language was Latin and its medium was prose. The work was none the less transformed into French verse by Wace around 1155, and, by way of Wace, into English alliterative verse by Layamon. Wace also inspired some three generations of inventive verse romance in French before the composition in the early thirteenth century of the vast Vulgate Cycle, the *Lancelot-Grail*, which despite its use of prose frequently enhances the fantasy element beyond the bounds of credibility. When stories from those prose redactions were translated into English, they were put into verse as a matter of course for over two centuries. The first prose translation from the *Lancelot-Grail*, the anonymous *Merlin*, was made around the middle of the fifteenth century. For Malory, who finished what was to prove itself the definitive English version of Arthurian romance, his prose *Morte Darthur*, in 1471, verse must have presented itself as a serious option, and it is only familiarity and hindsight that makes his choice for prose seem inevitable. How far that is from being true is illustrated on the romance side by Spenser's choice for verse for his Arthurian romantic epic in the sixteenth century, and by Tennyson's similar choice for his elegiac treatment of Arthur three centuries after that. Prose was not the only possible medium even for history: Malory's contemporary John Hardyng retold Geoffrey's quasi-historical account, along with some further episodes deriving directly from the *Lancelot-Grail* (notably the Grail itself), in a *Chronicle* in rhyme royal. 'Thystoryagraphes', Caxton comments in his preface to *Godeffroy of Boloyne*, 'haue wreton many a noble hystorye, as wel in metre as in prose.' This easy overlap of both medium and subject-matter makes it unsurprising that many of the fifteenth-century prose romances have a strong historical element in them, or what was taken for historical; it is also unsurprising that medieval historiography concerned with the distant past is regarded by modern historians with the same scepticism as they would bring to romance.

Not only did a high proportion of the early English prose romances concern themselves with historical material; their authors had no interest in drawing the kind of boundary between the genres that modern distinctions between them take for granted. Most of the prose romances that date to the first half of the

fifteenth century are of this kind. What may be the earliest such texts, *The Siege
of Thebes* and *The Siege of Troy*, composed some time after 1422 and copied in
sequence in the same manuscript (Bodleian MS Rawlinson D 82), are brief
retellings of Lydgate's substantial poems on the same subjects, his *Siege of
Thebes* and *Troy Book*. There is little space for originality here, since such material was taken to be essentially historical; our own inclusion of the stories of
Thebes and Troy under the broad heading of romance partly stems from our
re-classification of them as legend. There are still, however, different ways of
presenting such topics, and these epitomes, like Lydgate and his own earlier
medieval sources, all treat it with the imaginative freedom of fiction rather than
with the emphasis on factual record such as characterizes chronicle. The two
Siege texts furthermore promote the secular values of chivalry and love (Jason
and Medea, Paris and Helen, and Achilles and Polyxena all receive concentrated
attention); and their aristocratic characters, their settings distant in space and
time, and their readiness to incorporate magic (as shown by the detailed account
of the five charms given by Medea to enable Jason to overcome the beasts that
bar his way to the Golden Fleece) are all typical generic markers for romance.
The Classical subject-matter of these texts associates them with Latin even
though their direct source was English, but two others of these early texts work
directly from Latin legendary histories. The *Life of Alexander* preserved in the
Lincoln Thornton manuscript gives the romanticized biography of a historical
character whose career was itself an acting out of fantasies, and those fantasies
lost nothing in later retellings. Also taken from Latin is the English *Pseudo-
Turpin Chronicle* recently brought to light by Stephen Shepherd (1996, and
forthcoming EETS edition), an account of the legend of Roland, which was
translated in the mid-fifteenth century for a Lancastrian gentry family of
Gloucestershire. The same Latin text had served as the source of the very first
of the French prose romances, around 1202 (Spiegel 1993). History is much
more likely than romance to end in disaster, and both the defeat at Roncesvalles
and the story of Thebes operate at the limits of romance; but although prose
romances show a much greater readiness than metrical ones to end unhappily
(H. Cooper 1997a), there are still some historical legends that fall outside those
limits altogether. The late fifteenth-century prose *Siege of Jerusalem*, which has
as its central events not just the destruction of the city but the cannibalism to
which its starving inhabitants resorted, has none of the idealizing markers of
courtesy or love or adventure that set audience expectations for the genre.

The ease with which romanticized fiction could be built on historical foundations is evident in the case of the Nine Worthies, supposedly the nine greatest
warriors or conquerors of all time. Three were pagans (Alexander himself,
Hector and Julius Caesar), three Biblical (David, Joshua and Judas Maccabeus),
and three Christian (Arthur, Charlemagne, and Godfrey of Bouillon, leader of
the First Crusade). The Biblical Worthies were largely treated within the broad
field of religious writings rather than with the secular emphasis of romance; but
the other six were all given romance treatments, and the modern distinction that
separates off the historical Caesar and Godfrey from the legendary Hector and
Arthur did not exist. It is thus possible for Julius Caesar to get a mention in the
far from historical *Huon of Bordeaux* (technically a Charlemagne romance,

though the king does not have much to do with it once the story has been set in motion), his part in the story being that he fathered the fairy king Oberon on the fairy 'lady of the pryuey Isle'. Even more sober treatments generously mix historical and fictional material. Caxton's choice of subjects suggests that he may have had in mind a project to print prose accounts of the non-Biblical Worthies (in most cases indeed to translate them himself), and the generic mixture of the resulting texts again demonstrates the easy transition between fictional and non-fictional narrative. Thus Hector figures large in his *Recuyell of the Histories of Troye* (1473–74), a title that claims the work for history; but Caxton's immediate source was the Burgundian Raoul le Fèvre, who was himself working from a Latin text by Guido delle Colonne that was derived (though Guido never admits it) from one of the foundational French romances, Benoit de St-Maur's *Roman de Troie*. The *Recuyell* was the very first book in English to be printed, being produced from Caxton's press before he moved to England. It was also one of his most successful: it was reprinted every few years until it reached its optimistically-numbered eighteenth edition in 1738.

The Christian Worthies were more recent, but not therefore more easily categorizable in generic terms. Despite his appearance in Geoffrey's *History*, Arthur presented Caxton with a considerable problem of belief, as his famous preface to Malory's *Morte Darthur* testifies. He none the less argues there the case for Arthur's historicity, and, perhaps more importantly, asserts his belief in the value of the story regardless of its factual truth – so long as his readers 'do after the good, and leave the evil', then its historical authenticity is a secondary issue. It is hard to be sure how much Caxton sets out these principles as a state-ment of his personal conviction, how far as a marketing ploy (a highly successful one, given the later history of Malory's work), but there need not have been any large difference between the two. Carolingian material, like Arthurian, had already undergone several centuries of romance treatment, and even works that presented themselves as chronicles had a good deal of the romance about them. Caxton's own history of Charlemagne, *Charles the Grete* (1485), is partly drawn from chronicle sources, but its middle section comes from Jean Bagnyon's 1478 French prose redaction of the romance of *Fierebras*, itself derived from some form of the French *Pseudo-Turpin*. His other Carolingian work, *The Four Sons of Aymon*, takes as its subject the long resis-tance to Charlemagne's injustice by Raynaud de Montauban and his brothers, and retains all the grimness of tone of the *chanson de geste* that underlay its French prose redaction as well as incorporating magical and miraculous elements. His *Godeffroy of Boloyne* (1481) derives from respectable chronicle sources and is much more factual, but he still gives it a preface urging its readers ('alle Cristen princes, Lordes, Barons, Knyghtes, Gentilmen, Marchauntes, and all the comyn people of this noble Royamme'), and most especially Edward IV and his young sons, to follow the models of chivalry portrayed in it, and, in particular, to mount a new crusade to drive the Turks back from their advance across the Christian Mediterranean and to recover Jerusalem. 'Late this sayd yere', as he notes, the great Christian stronghold of Rhodes had endured the first of its two grim sieges; it was not to survive much longer. Yet Godfrey's historical importance did not prevent his greatest popular fame deriving from the fact that his grandfather's six brothers and sisters had been metamorphosed into swans when they were infants, according to a story that first emerged not long after Godfrey's conquest of Jerusalem. Five had been transformed back into humans after only a few years, but one remained in his swan form for much longer; his story too appears as one of the early prose romances, being printed by Wynkyn de Worde some three decades after Caxton's *Godeffroy* as *The Knight of the Swan*. The descendants of the family, including in England the Beauchamps, the Bohuns, and, after Henry Bolingbroke married Mary de Bohun, the Lancastrian kings, accordingly bore the swan as one of their badges. De Worde accordingly dedicates the work to one such descendant, the Duke of Buckingham.

The dedication is an indicator of how even romances set in the distant past were believed to have a relevance to the present, and indeed acquired much of their force from that relevance. A number of the prose romances are genealogical in focus, romances of origins: works set in the past to justify and authorize the present. *Melusine*, composed in French by Jean d'Arras in 1393 and translated into English a century later, is one of the most forceful instances. It not only retells the legend of the founding of the line and castle of Lusignan through the agency of a half-fairy woman who is under a curse to turn every Saturday into a serpent from the waist down; it also recounts the origins of a further curse inflicted on her lineage, and so explains in terms of fate rather than guilt the woes that were besetting her descendants. Malory offers a still bleaker connection between the Arthurian world and his own age of the Wars of the Roses, though not a genealogical one:

> Lo ye all Englysshemen, se ye nat what a myschyff here was? For he that was the moste kynge and nobelyst knyght of the worlde, and moste loved the felyshyp of noble knyghtes, and by hym they all were upholdyn, and yet myght nat thes Englyshemen holde them contente with hym. Lo thus was the olde custom and usayges of thys londe, and men say that we of thys londe have nat yet loste that custom. (ed. Vinaver, 3.1229; Caxton, XXI.2)

The reflection of the past here is not of great heroic origins for a latter-day dynasty, but of political disaster that keeps replaying itself across time. The absence of any compensating genealogical link with the contemporary Yorkist monarchy is in some ways surprising, since Edward IV was insistent on including Cadwallader, the last of the British line of kings, in his ancestry, through the marriage of one of his Mortimer forebears to a Welsh princess; but Malory's emphasis falls instead on Arthur's dying with no direct heir, as father and illegitimate son kill each other as the culminating act of the civil war. Henry Tudor famously made a greater propaganda use of his link with Arthur, but more through the Welsh belief in a 'son of prophecy' than by way of the romance Arthur. A link with the romances had to wait for his son's painting of the Round Table at Winchester with the names of its fellowship. An alternative model of romance, that of the marriage of a lost heir to an heiress and his accession to the crown, offered a more promising pattern, and it may have been with this in mind that Henry VII's mother, Lady Margaret Beaufort, commissioned a translation from Caxton of just such a romance, *Blanchardyn and Eglantine*, a story with an altogether sunnier ending than Arthur's (H. Cooper 1997b). No such intention can be identified with relation to Henry Watson's translation of *Oliver of Castille*, but its subject-matter, of a wicked duke of Gloucester who unlawfully seizes the throne, can hardly fail to have been read in the light of the events of Richard III's reign. If a justification for the present were needed that could be provided neither by lineage or analogy, old stories could always be adapted for the purpose. Caxton's *History of Jason* (before 1477), part of the prehistory of Troy, translates the redaction of the legend written by Raoul le Fèvre in connection with the founding of the Burgundian chivalric Order of the Golden Fleece, which took Jason as its Classical patron. It therefore treats him, and even Medea, rather more kindly than many other versions of the story.

This perception that the prose romances serve in part to connect the past with the present, and to justify the present in terms of the past, has as its corollary that they need to be derivative: originality of subject-matter would break those links, just as it would cut off romance from history. The material of history is not original to the historiographer or the romancer; he may introduce some originality of treatment, but the events that underlie the narrative are a given. The same principle often held true in the prose romances even when the material was more overtly fictional, but both the French and English romances vary greatly as to how much originality of treatment they introduce. A considerable proportion of the prose romances written in French were adaptations of pre-existing metrical texts, and if these were acknowledged fictions their prose redactors sometimes took advantage of the fact. *Horn et Rimenild* is almost unrecognizable in its new guise as *Ponthus et la belle Sidone*, and was probably intended by its author to look like a new work; *Valentin et Orson* declares its origins in its title, but its prose adaptor added a further huge swathe of adventures for the heroes after the initial plot of the false accusation of their mother and the restoration of the family has been completed. Such rewritings served none the less to keep in circulation much older narratives. English versions of these new prose romances, however, tended to be strictly faithful to their originals, largely restricting their alterations to some judicious abbreviation. The anonymous translators of *King Ponthus and the Fair Sidone* (perhaps two translators, depending on the as yet un-disentangled relationship of the mid-fifteenth century manuscript version and the printed text) and of *Pierre de Provence and the Fair Maguelonne*, which survives only as a manuscript fragment; Caxton, in both his more historical romances and the overtly fictional ones such as *Blanchardyn and Eglantine* and *Paris and Vienne*; Henry Watson, translator of *Valentine and Orson* and *Oliver of Castille*; John Bourchier, Lord Berners, best known for his translation of Froissart's *Chronicles*, but whose interest in all things chivalric generously extended to romances too, most particularly *Huon of Bordeaux* and *Arthur of Little Britain* – all made only minor alterations to their originals. Caxton indeed took such faithfulness as his central principle of translation: 'accordyng to the coppy . . . I have folowed as nigh as I can', as he puts it in the preface to his *Four Sons of Aymon*. He carries this accuracy through to the point of adopting syntax patterns and vocabulary such as were deeply alien to earlier English prose traditions (on which more below). His faithfulness sometimes betrayed him: he claimed his *Eneydos* to be a translation of Virgil, and may have believed his French original to have been just that; but as Gavin

Douglas pointed out with some asperity in the prologue to his own (verse) *Eneados*, Caxton's version is a long way from Virgil – 'It hass na thing ado tharwith, God wait', and is a shameless perversion of its claimed source, as shown in its expansion of the space occupied by Dido from a twelfth to a half of the whole work. The French prose version of the story from which Caxton worked was in fact already heavily influenced by medieval romance retellings, and so was far removed not only from Virgil but from whatever historical core the narrative might have been thought to have.

English sources for prose romance were treated with a much greater degree of freedom, comparable to the treatment of earlier French material by the French prose redactors, though it was well into the sixteenth century before English prose romances began to appear that were not direct adaptations of pre-existing works. Lydgate may provide the subject-matter for the *Siege* texts, but their author is very selective indeed about taking over his words. The same happens in the prose *William and Melior*, which survives only as a printed fragment. This can be shown to be based directly on the English alliterative mid-fourteenth-century *William of Palerne* (ed. Bunt 1985), rather than on the French metrical original of that or its prose redaction, but it both abbreviates the poem and removes most traces of the alliterative vocabulary. The story of young lovers who elope in the guise of white bears and are assisted by a helpful werewolf, this is one romance that moves very decisively away from history. The same is true of *Ipomedon*, the prose version of which derives from the twelfth-century Anglo-Norman original rather than from either of the two metrical English translations: the source is thus English in the national rather than the linguistic sense, if its author, Hue de Rotelande (Rhuddlan, in the Welsh Marches), can be allowed such a categorization. Like *William and Melior*, the romance concerns itself as much with the heroine as the hero – another indicator of its distance from the male-dominated events of history, and, in correlation with that, a powerful predictor of a happy ending. It tells the story of how a disdainful heiress who has sworn she will marry only the knight of most prowess in the world falls in love with the apparently useless Ipomedon, and of his final winning of her through the secret exercise of chivalry. The prose version is again considerably compressed from its original. It was probably composed around 1460: in time, at least, for Richard duke of Gloucester, the future Richard III, to own a copy (Longleat House MS 257; Sutton and Visser-Fuchs 1997). The story was none the less disseminated in print in metrical, not prose, form – the only verse romance to be so when a rival English prose version existed, though it is likely that Wynkyn de Worde did not know of the existence of the prose when he published the couplet version.[2]

In all these matters – of history *versus* fiction, translation *versus* rewriting, the treatment of French *versus* English sources – Malory is a hybrid. In contrast to Caxton, his direct translations from French are as often sense for sense as word for word; but his adaptation of the Roman War episode from the allitera-

---

[2]   The three English texts are differentiated by spelling: *Ipomadon* for the tail-rhyme; *Ipomydon* or the *Lyfe of Ipomydon* for the couplet version (in both manuscript and print); *Ipomedon*, as for the Anglo-Norman, for the prose.

tive *Morte Arthure*, at least in the manuscript version, derives so closely from its original that some lines apparently missing from the one manuscript of the poem appear perfectly preserved in Malory's prose. His principal method, with both French and English sources, is however to abbreviate, epitomize and select. His *Book of Sir Tristram* is only one-sixth the length of the French; his Death of Arthur not only reduces the French *Mort Artu* but intercuts it with the spare, ballad-like English adaptation made of that around 1400, the stanzaic *Morte Arthur*. He is exceptional among these early prose romancers for the freedom with which he combines, adapts, edits and re-orders his various sources. He is still more unusual in his readiness to compose original material of his own, of every size from narratorial interjections (the repeated similes of knights fighting like boars or other beasts, or the condemnation of the political fickleness of his contemporaries) to individual speeches (including Elaine of Astolat's dying defence of earthly love, and Lancelot's mighty defence of himself and Guinevere before Arthur) and even entire stories (such as the 'Tale of Sir Gareth', which has no identified single source).

Even where he is working solely with a French source, Malory will exercise a steady process of adaptation to bring it away from fantasy and closer to his own conception of Arthur as being at root historical, so that his work lies on the border of legendary history and the greater imaginative liberty of romance. The preface that Caxton provided for his print of the *Morte Darthur* emphasizes both the wide dissemination of Arthurian material, and its possible historicity. Every other language, he notes, has its version of the Arthurian story, but this new prose version of the French romances will restore Arthur to his British homeland. Malory's text backs up such an interpretation through the strong appeal it makes to the traces of the Arthurian past in the English present. The French *Lancelot-Grail* and *Tristan* that provide the bulk of his sources are works of fantasy; Malory turns his own work into something much more like chronicle, in the directness of its style, its identification of place names (Camelot is Winchester, Joyous Gard is Bamburgh, Ascolat is Guildford), and its insistence on the recording of events (Field 1971). Supernatural elements are abbreviated, rationalized or omitted; the more implausible flights of courtly fantasy, not least in relation to Lancelot and Guinevere, are cut. Malory's use of English sources alongside French contributes to this change of balance. The alliterative *Morte Arthure* is derived from Geoffrey of Monmouth's version of Arthurian history rather than the French romance tradition, so supplying a strong historical counterbalance to the chivalric and amorous developments of the *Lancelot-Grail*. The chronicle emphasis of the story also fits with the directness of his style, very different in both syntax and lexis from his French originals. His use of English sources provides further evidence that this adaptation of style was deliberate: when he is using the stanzaic *Morte Arthur* side by side with the French *Mort Artu*, he adopts the spareness of the English rather than the fulsomeness of the prose. 'And thus they fought all the longe day, and never stynted tylle the noble knyghtes were layde to the colde erthe' (ed. Vinaver, 3.1236; Caxton, XXI.4), paraphrases four lines of the English poem, and some ten pages of the French prose. Many of the most gripping passages in these last sections of his work – the battle, the throwing of Excalibur into the water, the final parting of

Lancelot and Guinevere – are taken from this English source rather than the French, and have the same power of suggestion, of a hinterland behind and beyond the bare statement such as grips the imagination in a way that fullness of detail never could.

Although Caxton printed Malory as a text that promoted the British member of the series of Nine Worthies, and compares it with his own recent *Godeffroy*, the prose style of the *Morte* appears as an anomaly in Caxton's published output. Caxton himself, with no single authoritative prose model in English on which to base his style, and perhaps also slightly ill at ease with English after his many years spent abroad, wrote English as if it were French; only there could he consistently find the eloquence and ornateness that he admired, in the form of abundant syntactic subordination, a polysyllabic vocabulary, and rhetorical elaboration (Blake 1968). He is particularly fond of synonymy, the coupling of words of the same meaning, sometimes taken from different etymological (French and English) roots: 'digne and worthy', 'hookes and crochettes', 'fulfylle and accomplisshe his desire and comaundement'. It is a habit that pervades both his translations and the original prose he writes in his prefaces. Malory writes in a style that owes far more to English traditions. It is paratactic in syntax and Anglo-Saxon in vocabulary, except for a clearly defined set of Anglo-French terms: legal expressions such as *assurance* and *appealed*; words associated with a wealthy lifestyle, such as *samite* and *pavilion*; martial and chivalric expressions, such as *joust*, *truncheon* and *recreant*; words that carry extra weight within the Arthurian context, such as *siege* (in the sense of 'chair'). There are, however, far fewer such words than one might expect. He prefers the Anglo-Saxon *worship* to the French *honour*, *unhap* to *misfortune*. The contrast shows even when they are describing exactly the same action, even so brutal an act as the slicing open of a man's head. Here is Caxton, from *Blanchardyn and Eglantine*, where the protagonist

> gaffe to the knyght suche an horryble and dysmesurable a strok, in whiche he had employed alle his strengthe and vertue, that he detrenched and cut his helmet and the coyffe of stele in suche manere awyse, that the goode swerde entred in to the brayne porfended. (ed. Kellner, p. 28)

And here is Malory, as Mordred fells King Arthur:

> And ryght so he smote hys fadir, kynge Arthure, with hys swerde holdynge in both hys hondes, uppon the syde of the hede, that the swerde perced the helmet and the tay of the brayne. (ed. Vinaver, 3.1237; Caxton, XXI.4)

Malory's minimalist style presents the technical facts as they would appear to a professional fighter. Caxton's emotive amplifications paradoxically reduce the imaginative impact.

At first glance, therefore, Malory and Caxton can seem to stand at the head of the opposing traditions of prose that extend forward through all later literature in English, however differently they were formulated over time: the Biblical in contrast to the Classical, Senecan against Ciceronian, Hemingway against Henry James. Yet the contrast is not so absolute as it might seem, on either side.

Caxton can produce passages of Malorian directness, not least when his subject moves from courtliness or military prowess towards the simplicity of folktale, or the traces (as in Malory) of what is *still there*. The passage in the *Four Sons of Aymon* in which Charlemagne attempts to dispose of the marvellous horse Bayard is Malorian to the point where one wonders if the *Morte*, which he had printed four years previously, were not a direct influence on the style. As part of the peace settlement with the brothers, Charles demands that Bayard be handed over to him, and then attempts to have him drowned in the Meuse with a 'horrible hevy' millstone fastened round his neck. Bayard, however, down at the bottom of the river, has other ideas:

> And whan Bayarde saw he myght none other wyse scape, he smote soo longe and soo harde wyth his fete vpon the myll stone that he braste it, and came agen above the water, and began to swimme, soo that he passed it all over at the othir side. And whan he was come to londe, he shaked hymselfe for to make falle the water from hym . . . and after, began to renne so swyftely as the tempeste had borne hym awaye, and entred in to the grete foreste of Ardeyne . . . And wyte it for very certein that the folke of that countrey sayen, that he is yet alive wythin the wood of Ardeyne. But wyte it, whan he seeth man or woman, he renneth anone awaye. (ed. Richardson, pp. 496–97)

Equally, and especially in original passages of authorial comment, Malory can produce passages that in their elaboration of syntax and abundance of synonyms bear a strong resemblance to Caxton:

> In May, when every harte floryshyth and burgenyth (for, as the season ys lusty to beholde and comfortable, so man and woman rejoysyth and gladith of somer commynge with his freyshe floures, for wynter wyth his rowghe wyndis and blastis causyth lusty men and women to cowre and to syt by fyres), so thys season hit befelle in the moneth of May a grete angur and unhapp that stynted nat tylle the floure of chyvalry of alle the worlde was destroyed and slayne. (ed. Vinaver, 3.1161; Caxton, XX.1)

The purpose of such a passage, however, is not to impress with the elegance of its synonyms, but to trick the reader into a sense of false security, in which the point is not the contrast of the delights of flowering May after the harshness of winter, but the devastation in this ironically loveliest of months of the 'floure of chivalry'. The pairings are there not for amplitude or fecundity of style, with the associated risk of redundancy, but to create a world in the imagination that is then cut down with an equal and opposite linguistic force. The beautiful world is predominantly French in lexis, though it keeps its feet on Anglo-Saxon ground; the destruction is predominantly Anglo-Saxon, with its blunter and shorter words.

This opposition between English and continental European is represented more largely in the romances of Malory and Caxton. Malory's concern is both with the Britain of the past and the England of the present, and his method is to naturalize French romance, to make it appear native. His success in doing so can be measured in the cultural centrality achieved by his version of the Arthurian legends over the next half millennium. English romance had maintained a fluid

boundary with French ever since the Angevin Empire, but the gradual demise of
Anglo-Norman as a vernacular over the course of the Middle Ages had
narrowed those channels of communication. The new fashion for prose romance
was being set in the fifteenth century at the court of Burgundy, where Philip the
Good presided over a major resurgence of chivalry and its literature. Caxton,
through his long habitation in Bruges and his connections with the Burgundian
court, was well placed to import the new fashion into England. The prosification
of metrical romances has been described as almost a Burgundian genre, not
because all such texts were written there (though a good number were), but
because its dukes, and especially Philip, actively encouraged such works, both
reworkings and original, and acquired a large number of them for the ducal
library. Some made their way into England independently of Caxton, notably the
Burgundian-composed *The Three Kings' Sons*, the English version of which
survives in a single luxury manuscript (of c. 1500) of a kind that suggests that it
was not made with any wide reading public in mind; but Caxton found such
material ideal for his new press. He has been described as 'the most influential
interpreter of the Burgundian chivalric tradition to the English reading public'
(Bornstein 1976), and romances constituted a good part of that tradition. He
translated both texts that originated in Burgundy (notably Raoul le Fèvre's originals of his *Recuyell of the Histories of Troye* and *History of Jason*), and others
of French origin such as were given a high profile as part of that chivalric renaissance. His *Blanchardyn and Eglantine* and *Four Sons of Aymon* belong to this
group, as does *Paris and Vienne*, which had been translated into French from a
Provençal original in 1432 (ed. Leach 1957). This is a delightful story of two
young lovers who remain faithful to each other through numerous vicissitudes,
though much more plausible ones than most romances offered. Its French translator, indeed, in a prologue omitted in the version from which Caxton was
working, claimed that it was the story's credibility that attracted him to the
narrative in the first place. When the aristocratic Vienne demands of her
lower-born lover that he should 'assaye one thynge, which shal be moche
dyffycile to doo and ryght peryllous' before she will marry him, it turns out to
be not the killing of a dragon, but rather,

> I wyl that incontinent ye say to your fader, that he goo to my lord my fader,
> and requyre hym that he gyue me in maryage to you. (ed. Leach p. 31)

Paris is appalled at the thought (much more, one feels, than he would be by a
demand for dragon-killing), and his father is equally horrified when Paris plucks
up the courage to present him with the demand. The ploy is indeed singularly
unsuccessful; it takes the capture of Vienne's father in the Holy Land and his
release through the agency of Paris in the guise of a Moor before he allows the
couple to marry.

Paris and Vienne is one of the first of the prose romances to give extended
space to naturalism of feeling. Its subject-matter is still chivalric, but in a work
of this kind the origins of the novel are beginning to become apparent. The
possibility for readers to make a more personal connection with the material of
such stories, as against the broad political analogies offered by the legendary
romances, is enhanced by such treatment. A number of the prose romances have

this potential to be read as a kind of sentimental education, and some may indeed have been composed as courtesy literature. The French original of *King Ponthus and the fair Sidone*, for instance, has been attributed to Geoffroi de la Tour Landry, who also wrote a collection of exemplary stories designed to fashion his daughters as good women, *The Book of the Knight of the Tower*. These works have the potential to be models of both virtuous secular life and good behaviour, of manners in the social as well as the ethical sense. The one surviving complete manuscript of the English *Ponthus* (Oxford, Bodleian Library, MS Digby 185), in which it figures alongside a prose *Brut* and good advice texts, was copied for a Yorkshire gentry family, the Hoptons, perhaps for the Sir William Hopton who became Treasurer to Edward IV (Meale 2000). *Ponthus* itself had to wait for de Worde before it was printed, but Caxton, with his sharp eye for an upwardly mobile market, was fully alert to the potential of the new prose texts in the courtly education of both men and women, whether romances or works such as *The Book of the Knight of the Tower*. Reading a work such as *Blanchardyn*, he says, is an 'honeste and joyefull' pastime, and it will in addition encourage young men to be valiant and 'gentyl yonge ladyes and damoysellys' to be faithful, to the point where its reading will be just as morally edifying as it would be to 'studye ouer moche in bokes of contemplacion'. Moralists of the succeeding generations were disinclined to agree. When around 1529 Richard Hyrd translated Vives' *Instruction of a Christian Woman* for Catherine of Aragon, with its attack on romance as too distracting from pious reading, he added to Vives' listing of continental favourites (including *Paris and Vienne*) some further English ones, which included not only traditional metrical favourites but the *Morte Darthur* and *William and Melior*.

As many of the works discussed in this chapter indicate, 1500 does not mark any kind of watershed in the production of prose romance. It was indeed at its height, encouraged by the new audiences opened up by print. Romances of all kinds found publishers and eager audiences in the early decades of the sixteenth century: works of pre-medieval origin (*King Apollyn*, the story of Apollonius of Tyre); Grail material with a strongly historical or hagiographical cast (*Joseph of Arimathy*, which has John Capgrave as intermediary with the French); abundant translations of fifteenth-century French prose romances, from the penitential (*Robert the Devil*, in which the repentant ex-diabolical protagonist finally wins the hand of the emperor's daughter) to the increasingly fantastic (such as Lord Berners' *Huon of Bordeaux* and his non-Arthurian *Arthur of Little Britain*, both of which contain a substantial fairy element). A number of the prose romances, both fifteenth- and sixteenth-century, were reprinted for decades, or, in the case of the *Recuyell*, *Valentine and Orson* and the *Morte Darthur*, for centuries. The fashion for them was overtaken only in the 1580s and 90s, by the import of Italian *novelle* and Spanish romances of the *Amadis de Gaule* variety (itself the Spanish equivalent of the earlier English prose romances), and by an increasing quantity of original prose fiction. Most of that, however, still preferred to deal with the far away or long ago, with the exotic rather than the everyday. The taste for reading about the kind of life that one lived, such as was to become the staple of the novel, was not to develop until the early eighteenth century. Prose romance made the novel possible, and the exploration of feeling and the models of conversation found in some of them provided a model for later writers to build on; but at heart it had a different agenda. Its appeal lay in its admiration for chivalric prowess, its readiness to incorporate the fantastic and the marvellous, and its creation of a world that was different from and nobler than the readers' own. It was, none the less, a world that was fully aware of its pressure towards mortality, and the weight of history.

BIBLIOGRAPHY

Primary

Alexander: The Prose Life of Alexander, ed. J.S. Westlake, EETS os 143 (1913)
Berners: John Bourchier, Lord Berners, *Arthur of Little Britain*, [ed. E.V. Utterson] (London, 1814)
————, *The Boke of Duke Huon of Bordeux*, ed. S.L. Lee, EETS es 40, 41, 43, 50 (1882–87; 2-volume repr. 1973, 1998)
Caxton, William, *Caxton's Blanchardyn and Eglantine, c. 1489*, ed. Leon Kellner, EETS es 58 (1890)
————, *Eneydos*, ed. W.T. Culley and F.J. Furnivall, EETS es 57 (1890)
————, *Godeffroy of Boloyne, or The Siege and Conqueste of Jerusalem*, ed. Mary Noyes Colvin, EETS es 64 (1893)
————, *The History of Jason translated from the French of Raoul Lefevre*, ed. John Munro, EETS es 111 (1913)
————, *The Lyf of Charles the Grete*, ed. S.J. Herrtage, EETS es 36–37 (1880–81)
————, *Paris and Vienne translated from the French and printed by William Caxton*, ed. M. Leach, EETS os 234 (1957)
————, *The Recuyell of the Historyes of Troy translated from the French of Raoul le Fevre*, ed. H. Oskar Sommer (London, 1894)
————, *The Right Pleasaunt and Goodly Historie of the Four Sonnes of Aymon*, ed. Octavia Richardson, EETS es 44, 45 (1884–85)
Ipomedon in drei englischen Bearbeitungen, ed. Eugen Kölbing (Breslau, 1889)
Joseph of Arimathie, ed. W.W. Skeat, EETS os 44 (1871)
King Apollyn: The Romance of Kynge Apollyn of Thyre, facsimile (of de Worde's ?1510 edition) intro. Edmund William Ashbee (London, 1870)
'*King Ponthus and the Faire Sidone*', ed. F.J. Mather, jr, *Publications of the Modern Language Association* 12 (1897), i–150
The Knight of the Swanne, in Thoms, ed., *Early English Prose Romances*, pp. 691–784
Malory, Sir Thomas, *The Works of Sir Thomas Malory*, ed. Eugène Vinaver, 3 vols (3rd ed. revised by P.J.C. Field, Oxford, 1990)
Melusine, ed. A.K. Donald, EETS es 68 (1895)
Merlin, ed. Henry B. Wheatley, EETS os 10, 21, 36, 112 (1865–99)
Oliver of Castille: The Hystorye of Olyuer of Castylle, ed. Gail Orgelfinger (New York and London, 1988)
'*Pierre of Provence and the Fair Maguelonne*', ed. Arne Zettersten, *English Studies* 46 (1965), 187–201
Robert the Devil, in Thoms, ed., *Early English Prose Romances*, pp. 167–206

The Siege of Jerusalem in Prose, ed. Auvo Kurvinen, Mémoires de la Société néophilologique de Helsinki 34 (Helsinki, 1969)

The Siege of Thebes, The Siege of Troy: 'Zwei mittelenglische Prosaromane: *The Sege of Thebes* and *The Sege of Troy*', ed. Friedrich Brie, *Anglia* 130 (1913), 40–52, 269–85

Thoms, William J., ed., *Early English Prose Romances*, new edition revised by Henry Morley (London, nd)

The Three Kings' Sons, ed. F.J. Furnivall, EETS es 67 (1895)

Valentine and Orson, ed. Arthur Dickson, EETS os 204 (1937)

William of Palerne: an Alliterative Romance, ed. G.H.V. Bunt (Groningen, 1985)

Secondary

Blake, Norman, 'Caxton and Courtly Style', *Essays and Studies* 21 (1968), 29–45

Bornstein, Diane, 'William Caxton's Chivalric Romances and the Burgundian Renaissance in England', *English Studies* 57 (1976), 1–10

Cooper, Helen, 1997a, 'Counter-romance: Civil Strife and Father-killing in the Prose Romances', in *The Long Fifteenth Century: Essays for Douglas Gray*, ed. Helen Cooper and Sally Mapstone (Oxford, 1997), pp. 141–62

——, 1997b, 'Romance after Bosworth', in *The Court and Cultural Diversity: Selected Papers from the eighth triennial congress of the International Courtly Literature Society 1995*, ed. Evelyn Mullally and John Thompson (Cambridge, 1997), pp. 149–57

Cooper, Richard, ' "Nostre Histoire renouvelée": The Reception of Romances of Chivalry in the Renaissance', in *Chivalry in the Renaissance*, ed. Sydney Anglo (Woodbridge, 1990), pp. 175–238

Field, P.J.C., *From Romance to Chronicle: A Study of Malory's Prose Style* (London, 1971)

Goodman, Jennifer R., *Chivalry and Exploration 1298–1630* (Woodbridge, 1998)

Hume, Kathryn, 'The Formal Nature of Middle English Romance', *Philological Quarterly* 53 (1974), 158–80

Keiser, George R., 'The Romances', in *Middle English Prose: A Critical Guide to Major Authors and Genres*, ed. A.S.G. Edwards (New Brunswick, 1984), pp. 271–86

Leonard, Irving A., *Books of the Brave* (1949; repr. Berkeley and Los Angeles, 1992)

Meale, Carol M., 1992, 'Caxton, de Worde, and the Publication of Romance in Late Medieval England', *The Library*, 6th ser. 14 (1992), 283–98

——, 2000, 'The Politics of Book Ownership: The Hopton Family and Bodleian Library Digby MS 185', in *Prestige, Authority and Power in Late Medieval Manuscripts and Texts*, ed. Felicity Riddy (Woodbridge, 2000), pp. 103–32

Pearsall, Derek, 'The English Romance in the Fifteenth Century', *Essays and Studies* ns 29 (1976), 53–83

Putter, Ad, 'A Historical Introduction', in *The Spirit of Medieval English Popular Romance*, ed. Ad Putter and Jane Gilbert (Harlow, 2000), pp. 1–15

Scanlon, Paul A., 'Pre-Elizabethan Prose Romances in English', *Cahiers elisabéthains* 12 (1977), 1–20

Shepherd, Stephen, 'The Middle English *Pseudo-Turpin Chronicle*', *Medium Ævum* 65 (1996), 19–34

Spiegel, Gabrielle M., *Romancing the Past: The Rise of Vernacular Prose Historiography in Thirteenth-century France* (Berkeley, 1993)

Sutton, Anne, and Livia Visser-Fuchs, *Richard III's Books: Ideals and Reality in the Life and Library of a Medieval Prince* (Stroud, 1997)

14

Scientific, Medical, and Utilitarian Prose

GEORGE KEISER

Twenty years ago scientific, medical, and utilitarian prose was, to a great extent, uncharted territory. It is good to report that, thanks to the continuing appearance of important bibliographical tools, we now have a fairly clear picture of the extensive corpus of writings in this area, as well as a wealth of information that permits the study and editing of texts, many of which had not been known previously. The opportunities for major advances in this area are abundant, if a sufficient number of scholars can discover the satisfaction of working on these texts.

Handlists for the Index of Middle English Prose continue to bring us fuller information about texts, as well as more accurate information about the nature and identity of these texts. In particular, the handlists for collections with manuscripts containing large numbers of texts in the area – for example, the Ashmole collection at the Bodleian Library and the collections at Trinity College and Gonville and Caius College Libraries, Cambridge – are particularly valuable for identifying little known texts or discovering new manuscripts of known texts. Perhaps there will soon be available an electronic index to facilitate the search through the mounting number of handlists.

In addition, we now have two other major bibliographical tools, both begun some twenty years ago and published recently, which use different approaches to writings in this area and which are complementary in providing information about them. Volume 10 of *A Manual of the Writings in Middle English, 1050– 1500* (Keiser 1998b) covers a very wide range of texts that have been edited or discussed in past scholarship, as well as some previously unstudied texts, offering both a commentary and a bibliography for each text, including a list of manuscripts containing it. Finally, we now have the long anticipated electronic catalog of incipits – *Scientific and Medical Writings in Old and Middle English: An Electronic Reference* (Voigts and Kurtz 2000) – which surveys the holdings of all known manuscripts in public institutions in England, continental Europe, and North America, as well as several private collections. This index, the rationale and structure of which are explained in an anticipatory study (Voigts 1995), brings to light many texts that had not been previously known and additional manuscript locations for texts that have been studied in past.

Occupying this vast terrain are multifarious works meant to address the needs of an ever-growing number of late medieval readers, professional and non-professional, for practical and useful information concerning alchemy, cosmology, astronomy, astrology, mathematics and music, medicine in many different forms and with many different specialities, hunting and hawking, the virtues of stones, cookery and household management, farming and veterinary medicine, technology and crafts, heraldry, and education. Writings in this area, even those covering similar subjects, can vary greatly in length and form and structure. Of two very popular and substantial herbals the *Agnus Castus Herbal* [234], so called for its first entry and probably derived from a fourteenth-century Latin original, covers about 250 herbs, arranged in alphabetical order, while the herbal attributed to Macer Floridus [235] has entries for about 80 herbs, ordered as they were in the Latin source, now thought to be the work of a Frenchman who lived near Meung, c. 1070–1112.[1] Scribes copying writings in this area often subjected them to revision, either by abbreviation or by amplification, and these two herbals are fine examples of such revision. The original version of the *Agnus Castus Herbal* does not continue beyond 'S', but a number of manuscripts contain entries for later letters, sometimes taken from the *Macer Herbal*. Several copies contain far fewer entries, no doubt a result of abbreviation. In some manuscripts we find descriptions of individual herbs or groups of herbs that are clearly excised from the *Macer* or the *Agnus Castus Herbals*. In one manuscript, discussed below, we find a conflation of entries from both of these herbals, though the *Macer* entries are an independent translation.

With a few notable exceptions, most writings in this area are of moderate or even very short length and use structures appropriate to the subject, which provide easy access to their contents. Two mathematical treatises, *The Crafte of Nombrynge* [214] and *The Art of Nombryng* [215], respectively cover 30 and 19 pages in modern editions and are structured according to the arithmetical functions described in each. Prognosticatory treatises, which describe the influence of the moon on human activities, usually run from 2 to 15 pages in modern editions, arranged according to the days of the moon in the 28.5-day lunar month or the zodiac as the moon passes through each sign. Books on grammar and syntax range from 3 to 34 pages in modern editions, arranged according to parts of speech or degrees of comparison or constructions of verbs. Treatises on colors and dyes and glue and ink are usually collections of recipes that fill only a few pages in modern editions, though *The Crafte of Lymnynge of Bokys* [412] is a 20-page work containing a set of recipes for colored waters for painting, as well as a few others for working with metals and dying cloth and leather.

Even in the case of longer works with more complex and sophisticated forms and structures, it is clear that their compilers and the scribes who copied them meant for them to serve utilitarian purposes. The head-to-foot structure commonly found in medical treatises is an excellent example of an organization that would permit easy accessibility to a reader. The *Liber de diversis medicinis* [272] is a very long remedybook or recipe collection (82 pages in the modern edition) which uses this structure for a large part of the work, allowing the practitioner to find therapies for particular maladies with relative ease. The Middle English adaptation of the mid-thirteenth-century *Compendium medicinae* of Gilbertus Anglicus [254] extracts from it practical information concerning

---

[1]   Numbers within square brackets are item numbers in *Manual* 10 (Keiser 1998b), where fuller information concerning the works discussed here and accompanying bibliographies are available.

diseases – their symptoms, humoral causes, and therapies – and arranges them in a head-to-rectum organization. When the head-to-foot organization does not determine the whole structure of a work, as in the case of several very lengthy surgical treatises, it is often found within one or more portions of it. In Guy de Chauliac's *Cirurgia Magna* [251] this structure appears in parts of the work devoted to anatomy, abscesses, wounds, ulcers, broken bones, and miscellaneous disorders. This very useful structure also appears within parts of *The Science of Surgery*, a translation of Lanfranc's *Cirurgia Magna* [249], the *Wellcome 564 Surgery Treatises*, a compilation drawn from the surgical treatises of Lanfranc and Henry of Mondeville [256], and *The Surgery Attributed to Thomas Morstede* [257].

The practical didactic nature of treatises in this area is evident in the use of the conventional literary form of the dialogue between master and disciple in several of them. The most extensive use of the form is in *The Boke of Marchalsi* [443], a long treatise which explains, in separate parts, the care and training of horses and the diseases of horses. This is also the form employed in a medical work identified as an adaptation of the Surgery of Roger of Parma (Saliceto), which is a dialogue between 'Brothers' – presumably friars, probably Dominicans. The best known example of a dialogue is a work of verse, not prose, *Dame Julyans Barnes Boke of Huntyng* [460], a conflation of two works, one spoken by a dame to a child, the other a dialogue between a man and his master. Alchemical works sometimes use the dialogue as a form, as in two verse works, *The Argument of Morien and Merlin* [180] and *Dialogue Between Rhazes and his Son Merlin* [187] and in at least two prose *Dialogues* [207] between master and pupil or father and son. Closely related to the dialogue is the catechetical structure of grammar books, which took over the form from the fourth-century *Ars minor* of Donatus, the basis for all grammar teaching until the sixteenth century. Still another variation on the form can be found in the amusing dialogues within treatises that intend to teach French to travellers, particularly merchants: *Une Manière de Parler* [509], *A Lytell Treatyse for to Lerne Englysshe and Frensshe* [510], and William Caxton's *Dialogues in French and English* (*Vocabulary in French and English*) (Wilson 1972, Hüllen 1999).

Similar to the dialogue in some respects, but not offering a full development of the form are works that begin with a request from a pupil to a master for information; the work itself is then a fully articulated response to that request. The *Secretum Secretorum* [6, 10–20] is certainly the best known example. Having conquered Persia, Aristotle writes to his teacher Aristotle, asking for instructions for governing the people of that land. Aristotle responds, first, with a letter, then with an encyclopedic treatise covering a vast body of information deemed necessary for a king to govern successfully. A work that pairs a ruler and a master and sustains the dialogue form is *Sidrak and Bokkus* [23], which is best known in lengthy verse translations. However, fragments of an unedited prose version do exist, including a lapidary that was not included in the verse version. Another, fuller prose version of this lapidary was printed in 1528, *A Lytell Boke of XXIIII Stone Pryncipalles* [386], but it does not retain the dialogue form. John Russell's *Boke of Nurture* [405], a verse treatise on the duties and responsibilities of household officers, particularly the preparation and serving of meals, begins in dialogue form between an old household officer of Humfrey, Duke of Gloucester, and a desperate young man. The dialogue form continues through the opening portion of the book, after which the treatise becomes a monologue by the old officer. As in the case of the *Sidrak* lapidary, when this work was transformed into prose and printed in 1508 as *The Boke of Kervyng* [406], the dialogue form was abandoned completely.

A modern reader approaches reference works, now including computer databases, with the almost inevitable expectation of finding their contents arranged alphabetically or at least with an alphabetical index. That form of arrangment, still relatively new in late medieval England, is found only rarely in Middle English works of scientific, medical, and utilitarian prose – primarily, we may suppose, because it was rarely found in the Latin and French sources of these writings. When Bartholomaeus Anglicus compiled his encyclopedic and influential *De proprietatibus rerum* [1] in the thirteenth century, he used alphabetical arrangement within several of the individual books, including those describing birds (Book 12), mountains (Book 14), geographical regions (Book 15), stones and metals (Book 16), herbs and plants (Book 17), and animals (Book 18). When John Trevisa made his English translation in the late fourteenth century, *On the Properties of Things* [2], he retained these arrangements. Bartholomaeus's use of alphabetic arrangment was anticipated by as much as a century in the *Circa Instans* of Platearius, who used it in this comprehensive and important herbal. This arrangement was retained when it was translated, at least twice, into Middle English prose.

Two other important prose herbals, like the Agnus Castus herbal described above, used alphabetical arrangement. *The Herbal* of Henry Daniel [239], compiled c. 1380, uses it for organizing an enormous body of information, including large portions translated intact from the *Macer Herbal* and *Circa Instans* and Bartholomaeus's herbal. Though two redactions of Daniel's herbal exist and we cannot be entirely sure which is the original, both are arranged alphabetically. Obvious in that herbal is a desire for comprehensiveness, characteristic of later Middle English texts, which we also find in an alphabetical herbal preserved in BL, MS Sloane 5. This herbal, with 214 entries, is attributed to John Lelamour, schoolmaster at Hereford in 1373, and described as a translation of the *Macer Herbal* [234]. In fact, it contains large portions of the *Agnus Castus* and of an independent translation of *Macer*, as well the Anonymous Prose *Treatise on Rosemary* which enjoyed a wide, independent circulation [242]. Lelamour's own work is probably better represented in another manuscript, London, Wellcome Library, MS 5650, which contains 43 entries, not arranged in alphabetical order, and quite clearly written in a Herefordshire dialect. MS Sloane 5 has several ownership inscriptions of a London surgeon, Richard Dod, but a defaced inscription suggests that he was not the original owner. Nevertheless, like that first owner, Dod was surely pleased to have a comprehensive herbal that brought together large portions of the *Macer* and *Agnus Castus* herbals and an arrangement that expedited access to information for his practice.

The influence of Bartholomaeus's alphabetical arrangement is clear in a lapidary which covers 145 stones and is preserved in Peterborough Cathedral

Library MS 33 [384]. The compiler of this text conflated large portions of Trevisa's translation of Bartholomaeus with material from a vernacular translation of the Anglo-Norman Prose Lapidary and substantial portions of *The Southern Boke of Stones* (*The London Lapidary of King Philip*) [378], one of two Middle English translations of the French Lapidary of King Philip (*Li livre des pierres*). Neither of these latter sources used an alphabetical arrangement. Indeed *The Southern Boke of Stones* contained an introduction, not taken over into the *Peterborough Lapidary*, explaining that it treats those jewels found in the breastpiece of Aaron (Exodus 28:17–21) and the foundation of the Heavenly City (Revelation 21:19–21). It too was augmented with material from the Anglo-Norman Prose Lapidary, arranged in no particular order at the end. As with the Sloane 5 Lelamour herbal and the herbal of Henry Daniel, the *Peterborough Lapidary* attests to the late medieval desire for comprehensiveness and for easy access to information.

Like alphabetical arrangement, the finding devices we now take for granted in books – chapter divisions and headings, tables containing chapter headings, running headlines, and indexes – were relatively new developments at the time that the works under discussion here took shape. Thus, we find inconsistent but growing use of them, as authors and later scribes began to experiment with this apparatus to serve the needs of readers. The *Liber de diversis medicinis*, mentioned above, is extant in almost twenty manuscripts, copied over a period of two centuries, and in these we find no consistent use of apparatus. In several we find none at all, beyond divisions of the material marked by headings and large initials. In others we find headings, large initials, and a table at the beginning, with numbered entries corresponding to numbered headings in the text. One of these is Lincoln Cathedral MS 91, copied by the famous Yorkshire scribe, Robert Thornton, which preserves unique copies of the Alliterative *Morte Arthure*, *Perceval of Galles* and other literary works. Though an amateur, Thornton was interested in experimenting with apparatus, using running headlines to indicate the maladies for which remedies appear, though only on the opening pages of the text, and, with more consistency, marginal glosses to direct the reader to recipes for the specific maladies.

A recipe book known as *Medicines for Horses* [441] exists in numerous manuscripts and printed versions, almost all of which contain tables allowing the reader immediate access to information not only about the ailments of horses, but also about the significance of the color of horses and the training and purchase of horses. Probably the text was fitted out with a table at a very early point in its history, and as the treatise itself was modified, so too was the table, indicating its usefulness was regarded as important. Collections of cookery recipes [389–400] frequently have tables at the beginning, but most of these appear to have been added by later scribes. Several manuscripts of the renowned hunting treatise, Edward, Duke of York's *Master of Game* [462] have tables to guide the reader wishing to consult this encyclopedic collection of information about the nature of animals of prey, breeds of dogs used in hunting the prey, and the practice of hunting individual prey. However, these tables often do not agree with the contents. Perhaps, as has been suggested, this translation and adaptation of *Li livre de chasse* by Gaston III, Count of Foix and Béarn (Gaston

Phoebus), is really a library piece, rather than a practical working manual. The treatise does have a distinctively literary quality, including an unusually discursive prologue, with an allusion to Chaucer, arguing the idea that hunters are virtuous men. An ironic response to that prologue appears in *Treatyse of Fysshynge wyth an Angle* [485] which, though clearly a practical treatise, has little apparatus in either its manuscript or printed forms.

Agricultural treatises would seem obviously intended for practical purposes, and the frequent presence of tables in manuscripts of *Godfridus super Palladium* [433] attests to that. The reader in search of information about the growth and grafting of trees, cultivation of fruits and vegetables, and viniculture would have an easy time finding the desired material within this fairly short treatise, even without the aid of the table. Walter of Henley [432], a treatise on farming adapted from a thirteenth-century treatise on demesne farming and estate management, is almost always presented with a table in its manuscript and printed versions. Though not a work of prose, the verse translation of *De Re Rustica* of Palladius [437] deserves notice here for its particularly eloquent testimony to the concern for the practical value of such treatises. The translator, in the presentation copy intended for Humfrey, Duke of Gloucester, provided an alphabetized table at the beginning of the work; this contained arabic folio numbers and stanza letters corresponding to those found in the text. Given the ease with which scribes might follow an examplar of a verse work, it seems likely that the translator intended the table to serve for all future copies.

Surprisingly and interestingly, copies of alchemical writings consistently lack apparatus that would help a reader discover their contents easily. BL, MS Harley 2407 is one of the few fifteenth-century miscellanies containing a significant body of vernacular alchemical prose, much of it concerned with the mysterious *Gemma salutaris* [208]. It does contain numerous illustrations, but even these are of little value in locating specific treatises. None of the manuscripts of the three translations of *The Book of Quintessence* [340] of John of Rupescissa contains a table, though there are chapter headings throughout the work. Most manuscripts that preserve Middle English alchemical prose were compiled in the sixteenth and seventeenth centuries, and even these, copied at a time when the design of books had been more fully developed, contain little helpful apparatus. Alchemists may have wished to preserve their esoteric information for the exclusive use of truly devoted practitioners of the art.

To make explicit a point that has come up several times so far: Middle English scientific, medical, and utilitarian writings are almost all translations of Latin or French works. Knowledge of their sources can often be very useful for understanding the purpose these writings were meant to fulfill. For example, the Middle English adaptation of the *Compendium medicinae* of Gilbertus Anglicus [254], mentioned above, omits lengthy parts of the original, which treated fevers, gynecology, and theoretical concerns. Obviously, one can see that the purposes of the adaptor/translator was to provide a work of great practical value, focusing exclusively on maladies and remedies for treating them. Moreover, the work was probably directed to a male audience, for though it omits the gynecological matter found in the source, it does deal with male urology. In several of the manuscripts this Middle English adaptation is found in conjunction with a gynecological treatise, *The Sekenesse of Wymmen* [323, 324], which also has an independent circulation. Thanks to the researches of Monica Green, we now know that this treatise, which exists in two forms, is a Middle English adaptation of the chapters on women's diseases found in *Compendium medicinae*. Ironically, editions of both versions had been produced by editors who were unaware of its immediate source.

In view of what the study of their sources can tell us about Middle English prose treatises in this area, we are fortunate to have recent editions of several important sources and analogues. Editions of the translations of Guy de Chauliac can now be studied in conjunction with an edition of the Latin text of Guy's *Inventarium sive Chirurgia Magna*, which is accompanied by an extensive commentary on the text (McVaugh 1997; McVaugh and Ogden 1998). Of value for the Middle English gynecological treatises, those which have been edited and others still unedited, is the work of Monica Green on the history of the Trotula materials (Green 2000) and her edition and translation of the Trotula ensemble of treatises (Green 2001, Green 2002). In view of the inadequate translations of Latin alchemical writings published in past, the appearance of a critical edition and translation of the pseudo-Geber *Summa Perfectionis* (Newman 1991) is very welcome for the study of Middle English alchemical treatises, especially claiming to be derived from 'Geber'. Richard Hoffman's edition and translation of continental fishing treatises, which gives some attention to the *Treatyse of Fysshynge wyth an Angle* [485], may prove to be of value for further analysis of that treatise or any of the several shorter English vernacular prose treatises on fishing [481–84, 486–87] (Hoffman 1997).

Finding the Latin or French source of a Middle English work is not always easy; an invaluable resource, *A Catalogue of Incipits of Mediaeval Scientific Writings in Latin* (Thorndike and Kibre 1963) is often difficult to use and incomplete, especially in its lists of manuscripts. When an on-line or CD-ROM version of this catalogue, now in progress, is finally completed, we can hope that it will contain manuscript information not available in the printed version, thus enhancing its usefulness. Now available and of much value is Ruth Dean's guide to Anglo-Norman texts and manuscripts, which gives detailed accounts of more than 100 works in this area (Dean 1999). Even when a source is known and an edition available, it may be necessary to look into the manuscript history of the source, for medieval texts are often the work of idiosyncratic scribes. As Tony Hunt has recently observed, 'It is one thing to declare a text to be a translation, another to determine exactly what it is a translation of' (Hunt 1999). Of great value for students in search of manuscripts of sources are on-line cataloguing projects, such as those underway at the British Library </molcat.bl.uk/>. Another, especially useful for work in alchemy, is the catalogue at the University of Glasgow </special.lib.gla.ac.uk/manuscripts/search/>, which makes available very detailed information about the rich collection of Ferguson alchemical manuscripts.

Peter Jones has produced two excellent examples of what can be learned from the study of sources, both concerning the transmission of the writings of John of Arderne. In one Jones examines a manuscript containing a translator's holograph of a vernacular version of John of Arderne's *Practica* in relation to the likely source manuscript from which the translator worked. Jones shows how the translator modified his source for the clear purpose of making a thoroughly practical book (P. Jones 1990). In a more recent study he shows how the tradition of illustration, often of very great importance to the text, is continued through the manuscript transmission of Arderne's writings in Latin and English (P. Jones 2002). In an earlier study, where he works on a much larger scale, Jones has fitted the illustrations of a number of vernacular prose texts on gynecology, surgery, and alchemy into the tradition of medical illustration running from the ancient to the early modern world (P. Jones 1998).

As for the texts of Middle English works, the continuing expansion of resources for locating them has facilitated production of much needed editions. Space limitations prevent a full account of the many editions published in the past two decades, which have been noticed in *Manual* 10, but several which have appeared since the publication of that volume deserve notice here. Tony Hunt has produced editions of two previously unnoticed medical recipe collections that were copied c. 1330, far earlier than any previously edited collections (Hunt and Benskin 2001). One of these is the earliest version of the well known *Liber de diversis medicinis*, which establishes a remarkably long manuscript history, from 1330 to 1530, for this text. The recent edition of the *Kalendarium* of John Somers and the Middle English canons associated with it [62] provides valuable testimony for the study of astronomy in the period (Mooney 1998b). Of great interest because it introduces a text of theoretical and therefore somewhat different character from most writings in this area is Päivi Pahta's edition of a pseudo-Galen treatise on embryology, *De Spermate*, and an accompanying astrological treatise, *De XII portis* (*De XII signis*) (Pahta, 1998). Originating in late classical times and circulating widely in its original Latin form, this treatise balances philosophy and physiology to explore the development of the soul and the body in the embryo. Pahta does an exemplary job of placing the unique copy of the treatise in the context of Cambridge, Trinity College, R.14.52, a medical miscellany dated 1458 and apparently produced by family of London stationers known to have produced numerous other manuscripts. Finally, on a smaller scale, but still significant for calling attention to oft-ignored material is Paul Acker's edition of recipes and glosses copied into the margins and flyleaves of Morgan Library, MS Bühler 17 (Acker 2002).

Despite the numerous editions of Middle English prose works completed in the past two decades, study in this area still continues to be hampered by the lack of editions of many important and influential works. There are two complete English translations of John of Rupicessa's *The Book of Quintessence* [140], neither of which has been edited. While several vernacular herbals have been edited, the multiple translations of the influential and important Mattheus Platearius herbal, *Circa Instans*, has been almost totally ignored. Though treatises on urine are abundant in manuscripts, few have been edited; in particular, we need a complete edition of Henry Daniel's *Dome of Uryns* [300]. Several learned treatises on medicine – Bernard of Gordon's *Lilye of Medicynes* (*Lilium medicinae*), the *Antidotary* of Nicolas, the *Isagoge* of Johannitius, and the adaptation of the *Surgery* of Roger of Parma (Saliceto) – await editors. Veterinary, especially equine medicine must have played a significant role in medieval life, to judge by the treatises that exist in various languages throughout Europe. Yet the most comprehensive Middle English treatise, *The Boke of Marchalsi* [443], has never been fully edited. Many hawking and hunting treatises have been edited, but we still await a modern edition of the *Master of Game* [462]. With a few exceptions, vernacular treatises on heraldry [495–506] have received little attention, even in a recent work on heraldry in later medieval England (Coss and Keen 2002). Two long and major texts – the English version of *Tractatus de Armis* of John de Bado Aureo [495] and the *De Studio Militari* translated by John Blount [504] – remain unedited. Those who would undertake the necessary job of editing these and other texts in this area might consider advice found in four essays on the editing of scientific and practical writings (Keiser 1998a), astrological and prognosticatory writings (Mooney 1998a), culinary writings (Hieatt 1998), and glosses and dictionaries (McCarren 1998).

For editors and students of Middle English prose writings in this area, language and style are of central importance. The existence of many works in multiple translations – the *Macer Herbal* [235], *Circa Instans*, *Secretum Secretorum* [6], *The Book of Quintessence* [140], Guy de Chauliac's *Chirurgia Magna* [251], John of Arderne's *Fistula in Ano* [252], the *John of Burgundy Plague Treatise* [305], *The Wonderful Art of the Eye* [255], the King Philip Lapidary [378, 379] – offers ample opportunities for potentially important studies of lexis, syntax, and style. Fortunately, several recent studies have begun to establish the foundations needed for more detailed study of scientific and technical language. In texts translated from Latin, as many of these writings are, the vernacular lacked equivalents for technical terms, and the translators had to improvise, usually by anglicizing Latin forms. Pahta's recent edition of *De spermate* has an exemplary exposition of how one English translator faced such problems. On a larger scale, a study of sixteenth-century medical terminology by R.W. McConchie provides an interesting methodology for use in studying Middle English prose (McConchie 1997). In medical writings, the names of plants, maladies, and parts of the human body often vary widely, at least in part because of the region in which the text has been written or copied. Significant contributions addressing these problems are lexical studies by Tony Hunt (Hunt 1989) on plant names and by Juhanni Norri on names of sicknesses (Norri 1992) and body parts (Norri 1998). Hunt's work on plant names shows particular cognizance of the fact that Middle English texts often exist in a bilingual or trilingual environment, a matter taken up by Voigts in two studies of code-switching in these texts (Voigts 1989b, 1996). Hunt has provided editions of numerous popular medical texts which illustrate the mixture of Latin, French, and English (Hunt 1990, Hunt 2001), as well as a study of code-switching in these texts (Hunt 2000). Of much importance for studying this problem of mixed languages are glosses and dictionaries, as we can see in the editions of numerous glosses by Hunt (Hunt 1991) and in a study of *Medulla grammatice*, which edits a fragment of this well known dictionary (McCarren 2000). Working with lexis in another area, D. S. McNab has produced a sporting lexicon based on Dame Julyan Barnes *Boke of Hunting* [460] (McNab 2003). While stylistic study of scientific and practical prose is still a largely unexplored area, there have been several interesting short studies which have attempted to explore the conventions of medical, alchemical, and cookery recipes (Norri 1989, C. Jones 1998, Carroll 1999, Taavitsainen 2001, Grund forthcoming). Finally, Constance Hieatt has discussed the language, style and content of both Middle English and Anglo-Norman cookery recipes (Hieatt 2002).

Study of the circulation and transmission of these Middle English texts can lead us to ask and answer questions about their reception among contemporary and later readers. For this purpose an awareness of manuscript contexts is most fruitful. Three medical manuscripts that were owned by identifiable practitioners have received detailed attention: BL, MS Harley 1735, a compilation of medical and other practical writings owned by John Crophill (1450–80) of Essex [282]; Cambridge, Gonville and Caius MS 176/97, a compilation of more theoretical texts owned by Thomas Plawdon (1400–25) of London (Voigts and McVaugh 1984); BL, MS Harley 2258, a mainly Latin compilation copied by Thomas Fayreford (1400–25) of Devon and Somerset (Jones 1995). Deserving of such attention are the books of the London surgeon Richard Dod, mentioned above in connection with the Lelamour Herbal: BL, MS Sloane 5, which contains, along with the herbal, the adaptation of Gilbertus's *Compendium medicinae* and the gynecological treatise drawn from the same source, and San Marino, Huntington Library, MS HM 505, which contains a text of Henry Daniel's treatise on urines. The astounding vernacular collection of astronomical and astrological learning in Cambridge, Trinity College O.5.26 has been mined for editions of *The Little Ship of Venice* [31], *The New Theorik of Planetis* [32], and Richard of Wallingford's *Exafrenon* [34], but the manuscript has never been subjected to the comprehensive and detailed analysis that might tell us about its origins and significance. So too BL, MS Add. 34111 has been the source of editions of several apparently unique texts – a recipe collection [268], *Virtutes Aquile* [269], and *Experimentes of Cophon, The Leche of Salerne* [270] – but the collection as a whole, which apparently was compiled for a Master William Somer, has had little attention.

There is reason for optimistism that we might hope to see such studies of similar compilations in two studies, one published and one forthcoming. The latter is a compilation of studies of Cambridge, Trinity College, MS R.14.52, mentioned above in connection with the recent edition of *De Spermatate* (Tavormina forthcoming). David Parker has offered a general and comparative study of four early Tudor commonplace books which preserve a number of shorter works of scientific, medical, and utilitarian nature among their contents (Parker 1998). Perhaps the richest of these is Oxford, Balliol College, MS 354, a commonplace book compiled by the London merchant Richard Hill, between 1503 and 1536, and containing numerous utilitarian treatises, including *A Good Informacion of Augrym*, *Godfridus super Palladium*, and a portion of the *Boke of Marschalsi*.

Opportunities for study of such compilations are increasing because of the digitization of important miscellanies that contain Middle English scientific, medical, and practical writings. For several decades, because of its deteriorating condition, Balliol College, MS 354 has been unavailable to students. However, it can now be easily studied because of a digitized version on a Bodleian Library website </irusan.las.ox.ac.uk/>. On its website </library.wellcome.ac.uk/> the

Wellcome Library has mounted a digitized version of WMS 8004, which had been in private hands until 2002. This very rich and interesting physician's handbook contains numerous prose texts on astrological medicine that have not been edited or studied, as well as 'A calculacion to know by of tuo men feghtynge togidere, wheþer sale be ouercomen' [8] and a Thunder Prognostication [122b].

Encouraging the study of the production of manuscripts and the history of the texts they contain – and their continuation in printed forms – are developments in the related methodologies of codicology and book-history. The third volume of *The Cambridge History of the Book in Britain* contains three chapters that examine the transmission of texts in this area during the period 1400–1558: Peter Murray Jones on medical and scientific writings (P. Jones 1999), Nicholas Orme on school-books (Orme 1999), and George Keiser on practical writings (Keiser 1999). In an earlier piece, devoted entirely to manuscripts, Linda Voigts offered a magisterial survey of vernacular scientific and medical books (Voigts 1989a). In still another piece Voigts discusses at length the 'Sloane Group' of metropolitan manuscripts, all copied in the 1450s and early 1460s, with common texts, papers, and hands (Voigts 1990), and she suggests the existence of a London 'publisher' who specialized in the production of scientific and medical books: 'an individual or a group [who] co-ordinated and exercised control over the subject matter and presentation of these books'. Two instances, a little later in the century, in which a scribe made duplicate copies of the same text – *The Book of Quintessence* in BL, MS Sloane 353, and Glasgow University Library, Ferguson 205, and *The Boke of Kervyng* in London, Society of Antiquaries MS 287, and Aberystwyth, National Library of Wales, MS Peniarth 394 (*olim* Hengwrt 92) – suggest centers or shops where those seeking such texts might turn. In addition to the study of concurrent transmission of technical writings, it is sometimes possible to study the transmission of a text over a long period of time, as in the case of a treatise on equine medicine, which had a life in manuscript and printed form from the mid-fifteenth through the seventeenth century (Keiser 1999; Keiser 2003a). Similarly, three recent articles have demonstrated the afterlives of an ophthalmological treatise, *The Wonderful Art of the Eye* [255], an alchemical treatise, *Mayster I pray yow of pacience* [207a] and two plague treatises, *The Treatise of Master Thomas M[o]ulton, Order of Preachers* [311], and *A Litil Boke for the Pestilence by Joannes Jacobi* [312], in early modern England (Eldredge 1999, Grund 2002, Keiser 2003b).

In closing this chapter, it is appropriate to notice new directions in studies that are influencing the study of Middle English prose texts as well. Three ground-breaking monographs that explore continental academic medical literature of the thirteenth and fourteenth centuries have applied complementary approaches – analyses of the language and imagery (metaphors, similes, tropes) – to explore the interrelatedness of medical thought and other aspects of culture. Two of these, one concentrating on changes in the understanding of sex and sexuality (Jacquart and Thomasset 1988) and another concentrating on the surgical writings of Henry of Mondeville (Pouchelle 1990), are representative of the explosion of studies of body, gender, and sexuality in the past twenty years. The third, concentrating on the writings of Arnau de Vilanova and his contemporaries (Ziegler 1998), explores the convergence of medicine and religion. That these approaches can be applied to the study of Middle English medical literature is demonstrated in two interesting studies by Jeremy Citrome, one on the chivalric imagery in the writings of John of Arderne and one on medical imagery in *Cleanness* (Citrome 2001a, 2001b).

Three historical monographs completed within the past decade also establish new directions for the study of Middle English scientific and medical writings. Carol Rawcliffe's social history of late medieval English medicine weaves medical treatises, letters and documents, and literary texts into a fascinating tapestry. The other two studies attempt to put scientific and medical writings into the context of the Lancastrian-York political conflicts. Making significant use of the medical miscellany mentioned above, Cambridge, Trinity College, MS R.14.52, Anthony Gross documents the encouragement of medical and alchemical experimentation in the hope of restoring the economic, physical, and mental health of Henry VI (Gross 1996). In an account of the reign of Edward IV that is destined to produce controversy, Jonathan Hughes reads Edward as 'the first English king to harness the combined influences of alchemical medicine, myths and prophecies to weld together a nation' and to establish 'a dynastic system that has continued to this day' (Hughes 2002). Indeed, in looking back at the reigns of Henry V and Henry VI, Hughes establishes a political context within which to read not only medicine and alchemy, but also a significant number of the other writings covered in this chapter.

The developments of the past two decades in the study of English vernacular scientific, medical, and utilitarian writings bode well for the future. Writings that had once seemed marginal and deserving of concern only for their philological value are now being shown to be central to an understanding of literary, social, intellectual, political, and cultural history. If scholars continue to produce editions of these writings, making them available for closer study, and to explore the transmission and circulation of these writings in manuscript and printed form, we can surely expect that two decades hence the landscape of this area will have changed as dramatically as it has in the past two decades and that the centrality of these writings will be a well established fact among students of the literature, history, and culture of late medieval and early modern England.

BIBLIOGRAPHY

Primary Sources

The following list of scientific, medical, and utilitarian writings supplements the coverage of these works in *A Manual of the Writings in Middle English, 1050–1500, Vol. 10: Science and Information* (Keiser 1998b). Works covered in that volume are followed by the entry number in square brackets. For works not covered in *Manual* 10, I have provided information about manuscripts and, where available, editions.

ENCYCLOPEDIAS

Sidrak and Bokkus
Manuscript: Bodleian Library, Digby 194, fols 153r–155v.

SCIENCE

COSMOLOGY, ASTRONOMY, ASTROLOGY
The Kalendarium of John Somer: Middle English Canons [62]
Manuscripts: Bodleian Library, Ashmole 191, Pt 4; Bodleian Library, Ashmole 391, Pt 2; BL, Cotton Vitellius A.1; BL, Harley 937; Edinburgh, Advocates 23.7.11; Aberdeen, University Library 123.
Edition: Mooney 1998.

ALCHEMY
The Book of Quintessence [140]
NOTE: *Manual* 10 (Keiser 1998b) mistakenly reports that the version found in BL, MS Sloane 73 is an abbreviated form of the translation found in MSS Sloane 353 and Glasgow University Library, Ferguson 205. The Sloane 73 text represents an independent translation.

MEDICINE

HERBALS
Circa Instans
Manuscripts: Bodleian Library, Ashmole 1477, pp. 114–95; Bodleian Library, Ashmole 1481, fols 44r–49r, 64r–83v; Bodleian Library, Bodley 178, fols 152r–155v; Cambridge University Library, Ee.1.13, fols 1r–91v; Cambridge University Library, Kk.6.33, III, fols 12r–v; Cambridge, Gonville and Caius College, 609/340, fols 204r–45v; Cambridge, Jesus College, Q.D.1, fols 75v–122r; Cambridge, Trinity College, R.14.32, fols 128r–129r; BL, Sloane 105, fols 666r–100v; BL, Sloane 297, fols 14r–23v; BL, Sloane 635, fols 35r–69v; BL, Sloane 707, fols 21r–89v; BL, Sloane 1764, fols 49r–112v; BL, Additional 29301, fols 55r–89r; BL, Egerton 2433, fols 49r–54v; Wellcome Library, London Medical Society 131, fols 3r–56v; Wellcome Library, WMS 397, fols 71r–86r; Glasgow University Library, Hunter 95 (T.4.12), fols 158r–163r; Glasgow University Library, Hunter 307 (U.7.1), fols 167r–172v; New York Academy of Medicine 13, fols 189v–94v.

TREATISES BY DOCTORS, SURGEONS, AND PRACTITIONERS
Bernard of Gordon's Lilye of Medicynes (Lilium medicinae)
Manuscript: Bodleian Library, Ashmole 1505, fols 4r–244v

Adaptation of Roger of Parma's Surgery
Manuscripts: BL, Sloane 3489, fols 39r–42r; Bodleian Library, Ashmole 1481, fols 4v–12r; Longleat 176, fols 25r–38r.

The Antidotary of Nicholas
Manuscripts: BL, Harley 2374, fols 31r–64v; Bodleian Library, Ashmole 1413, pp. 21–22; Cambridge, Corpus Christi College, 424, IV, fols 35r–41v; Cambridge,

Magdalene College, Pepys 1307, fols 1r–51r; Cambridge, St John's College, B.15, I, fols 29r–31r; Glasgow University Library, Ferguson 147, fols 1r–55v.

The Isagoge of Johannitius
Manuscripts: BL, Sloane 6, fols 1r–9r, 18r–21v; Gonville and Caius College, 176/97, fols 16r–21r (excerpts).

REMEDYBOOKS AND LEECHBOOKS
First Corpus Compendium
Manuscript: Cambridge, Corpus Christi College, MS 388, fols 1r–35v.
Edition: Hunt 2001.

Second Corpus Compendium
Manuscript: Cambridge, Corpus Christi College, MS 388, fols 36r–48v.
Edition: Hunt 2001.

GYNECOLOGY AND OBSTETRICS
De Spermate
Manuscript: Cambridge, Trinity College, R.14.42, fols 28r–36v.
Edition: Pahta 1998.

De XII portis (De XII signis)
Manuscript: Cambridge, Trinity College, R.14.42, fols 36v–40v.
Edition: Pahta 1998.

HERALDRY

De Studio Militari Translated by John Blount [504]
Manuscript: Bodleian Library, Eng. misc d.227, fols viiv–281r.

Secondary Sources

Acker 2002. Paul Acker, 'Texts from the Margin: Lydgate, Recipes, and Glosses in Bühler MS 17', *The Chaucer Review* 27, 59–85
Carroll 1999. Ruth Carroll, 'The Middle English Recipe as a Text-type', *Neuphilologische Mitteilungen* 100, 27–42
Citrome 2001a. Jeremy J. Citrome, 'Bodies That Splatter: Surgery, Chivalry, and the Body in the *Practica* of John Arderne', *Exemplaria* 31, 137–72
——— 2001b. 'Medicine as Metaphor in the Middle English *Cleanness*', *The Chaucer Review* 35, 260–80
Coss and Keen 2002. Peter Coss and Maurice Keen, eds, *Heraldry, Pageantry and Social Display in Medieval England* (Cambridge)
Dean 1999. Ruth Dean, with Maureen Bolton, *Anglo-Norman Literature: A Guide to Texts and Manuscripts* (London)
Eldredge 1999. Laurence M. Eldredge, 'The English Vernacular Afterlife of Benvenutus Grassus, Ophthalmologist', *Early Science and Medicine* 2, 149–63
Green 2000. Monica H. Green, *Women's Healthcare in the Medieval West: Texts and Contexts* (Aldershot)

────── 2001. *The Trotula: A Medieval Compendium of Women's Medicine* (Philadelphia)

────── 2002. *The Trotula: An English Translation of the Medieval Compendium of Women's Medicine* (Philadelphia)

Gross 1996. Anthony Gross, *The Dissolution of the Lancastrian Kingship: Sir John Fortescue and the Crisis of Monarchy in Fifteenth-Century England* (Stamford)

Grund 2002. Peter Grund, 'In Search of Gold: Towards a Text Edition of An Alchemical Treatise', in *Middle English from Tongue to Text*, ed. Peter J. Lucas and Angela M. Lucas (Frankfurt), pp. 265–79

────── forthcoming. 'The Golden Formulas: Genre Conventions of Alchemical Recipes in the Middle English Period', *Neuphilologische Mitteilungen* (forthcoming)

Hieatt 1998. Constance B. Hieatt, 'Editing Middle English Culinary Manuscripts', in *A Guide to Editing Middle English*, ed. Vincent P. McCarren and Douglas Moffat (Ann Arbor), pp. 133–40

────── 2002. 'Medieval Britain', in *Regional Cuisines of Medieval Europe*, ed. Mellita Weiss Adamson (London), pp. 19–45

Hoffman 1997. Richard C. Hoffman, *Fishers' Craft & Lettered Art: Tracts on Fishing from the End of the Middle Ages* (Toronto)

Hughes 2002. Jonathan Hughes, *Arthurian Myths and Alchemy: The Kingship of Edward IV* (Stroud)

Hüllen 1999. Werner Hullen, *English Dictionaries 800–1700: The Topical Tradition* (Oxford)

Hunt 1989. Tony Hunt, *Plant Names of Medieval England* (Cambridge)

────── 1990. *Popular Medicine in Thirteenth-Century England* (Cambridge)

────── 1991. *Teaching and Learning Latin in Thirteenth-Century England*, 3 vols (Cambridge)

────── 1998. 'Old French Translations of Medical Texts', *Forum for Modern Language Studies* 4, 350–57

────── 2000. 'Code-switching in Medical Texts', in *Multilingualism in Later Medieval Britain*, ed. D.A. Trotter (Cambridge), pp. 131–47

Hunt and Benskin 2001. Tony Hunt with Michael Benskin, *Three Receptaria from Medieval England: The Languages of Medicine in the Fourteenth Century*, Medium Aevum Monographs ns 21 (Oxford)

Jacquart and Thomasset 1988. Danielle Jacquart and Claude Thomasset, *Sexuality and Medicine in the Middle Ages*, trans. Matthew Adamson (Princeton)

C. Jones 1998. Claire Jones, 'Formula and Formulation: "Efficacy Phrases" in Medieval English Medical Manuscripts', *Nuephilologische Mitteilungen* 99, 199–209

P. Jones 1990. Peter Murray Jones, 'British Library MS Sloane 76: A Translator's Holograph', in *Medieval Book Production: Assessing the Evidence*, ed. L.L. Brownrigg (Los Altos Hills), pp. 21–40

────── 1995. 'Harley MS 2558: A Fifteenth-Century Medical Commonplace Book', in *Manuscript Sources of Medieval Medicine: A Book of Essays*, ed. Margaret R. Schleissner (New York), pp. 35–54

────── 1998. *Medieval Medicine in Illuminated Manuscripts* (1984; rev. repr. London)

────── 1999. 'Medicine and Science', in *The Cambridge History of the Book in Britain, Volume III, 1400–1557*, ed. Lotte Hellinga and J.B. Trapp (Cambridge), pp. 433–48

────── 2002. 'Staying with the Programme: Illustrated Manuscripts of John of Arderne c.1380–c.1550', in *English Manuscript Studies* 10, ed. A.S.G. Edwards (London), pp. 204–227

Keiser 1998a. George R. Keiser, 'Editing Scientific and Practical Writings', in *A Guide to Editing Middle English*, ed. Vincent P. McCarren and Douglas Moffat (Ann Arbor), pp. 109–22

—— 1998b. 'Scientific and Practical Writings', in *A Manual of the Writings in Middle English, 1050–1500, Vol. 10: Science and Information*, gen. ed. A.E. Hartung (New Haven)

—— 1999. 'Practical Books for the Gentleman', in *The Cambridge History of the Book in Britain, Volume III, 1400–1557*, ed. Lotte Hellinga and J.B. Trapp (Cambridge), pp. 470–94

—— 2003a forthcoming. 'Medicines for Horses: The Continuity from Script to Print', *Veterinary History*; rev. repr., with addendum, of 'Medicines for Horses: The Continuity from Script to Print', *Yale University Library Gazette* 69, 111–28

—— 2003b. 'Two Medieval Plague Treatises and their Afterlife in Early Modern England', *Journal of the History of Medicine and Allied Sciences* 58, 292–324

McCarren 1998. Vincent P. McCarren, 'Editing Glossographical Texts: To Marrow and to Marrow and to Marrow', in *A Guide to Editing Middle English*, ed. Vincent P. McCarren and Douglas Moffat (Ann Arbor), pp. 141–55

—— 2000. 'The Gloucester Manuscript of the *Medulla grammatice*: An Edition', *Journal of Medieval Latin* 10, 338–401

McConchie 1997. R.W. McConchie, *Lexicography and Physicke: The Record of Sixteenth-Century English Medical Terminology* (Oxford)

McNab 2003. David Scott McNab, *A Sporting Lexicon of the Fifteenth Century: The J.B. Treatise* (Oxford)

McVaugh 1997. Michael R. McVaugh, ed., *Guigonis de Caulhiaco: Inventarium sive chirurgia magna, Text*, Studies in Ancient Medicine 14.1 (Leiden)

McVaugh and Ogden 1998. Michael R. McVaugh and Margaret Ogden, eds, *Guigonis de Caulhiaco: Inventarium sive chirurgia magna, Commentary*, Studies in Ancient Medicine 14.2 (Leiden)

Mooney 1998a. Linne Mooney, 'Editing Astrological and Prognostic Texts', in *A Guide to Editing Middle English*, ed. Vincent P. McCarren and Douglas Moffat (Ann Arbor), pp. 123–32

—— 1998b. *The Kalendarium of John Somer*, The Chaucer Library (Athens GA)

Newman 1991. William R. Newman, ed. and trans., *The Summa Perfectionis of Pseudo-Geber: A Critical Edition, Translation, and Study* (Leiden)

Norri 1992. Juhani Norri, *Names of Sicknesses in English, 1400–1550*, Annales Academiae Scientarum Fennica (Helsinki)

—— 1989. Norri, 'Premodification and Postmodification as a Means of Term-Formation in Middle English Medical Prose', *Neuphilologische Mitteilungen* 90, 147–61

—— 1998. *Names of Body-Parts in English, 1400–1550*, Annales Academiae Scientarum Fennica (Helsinki)

Orme 1999. Nicholas Orme, 'Schools and School-books', in *The Cambridge History of the Book in Britain, Volume III, 1400–1557*, ed. Lotte Hellinga and J.B. Trapp (Cambridge), 449–69

Pahta 1998. Päivi Pahta, ed., *Medieval Embryology in the Vernacular: The Case of De spermate* (Helsinki)

Parker 1998. David R. Parker, *The Commonplace Book in Tudor London* (Lanham MD)

Pouchelle 1990. Marie Christine Pouchelle, *The Body and Surgery in the Middle Ages*, trans. Rosemary Morris (New Brunswick)

Rawcliffe 1995. Carole Rawcliffe, *Medicine and Society in Later Medieval England* (Stroud)

Taavitsainen 2001. Irma Taavitsainen, 'Middle English Recipes: Genre Characteristics,

Text Type Features and Underlying Traditions of Writing', *Journal of Historical Pragmatics* 2, 85–113

Tavormina forthcoming. M.T. Tavormina, *Sex, Aging, and Death in a Medieval Medical Compendium. Trinity College, Cambridge, R.14.52: Its Language, Scribe, and Texts* (Medieval and Renaissance Text Society)

Thorndike and Kibre 1963. Lynn Thorndike and Pearle Kibre, eds, *A Catalogue of Incipits of Mediaeval Scientific Writings in Latin*, revised and augumented edition (Cambridge MA)

Voigts 1989a. Linda Ehrsam Voigts, 'Scientific and Medical Books', in *Book Production and Publishing in Britain, 1375–1475*, ed. Jeremy Griffiths and Derek Pearsall (Cambridge), 345–402

——— 1989b. 'The Character of the *Carecter*: Ambiguous Sigils in Scientific and Medical Texts', in *Latin and Vernacular: Studies in Late-Medieval Texts and Manuscripts*, ed. A.J. Minnis (Cambridge)

——— 1990. 'The "Sloane Group": Related Scientific and Medical Manuscripts from the Fifteenth Century in the Sloane Collection', *The British Library Journal* 16, 26–57

——— 1995. 'Multitudes of Middle English Medical Manuscripts, or the Englishing of Science and Medicine', in *Manuscript Sources of Medieval Medicine: A Book of Essays*, ed. Margaret R. Schleissner (New York), pp.183–95

——— 1996. 'What's the Word? Bilingualism in Late-Medieval England', *Speculum* 71, 813–26

Voigts and Kurtz 2000. L.E. Voigts and P.D. Kurtz, *Scientific and Medical Writings in Old and Middle English: An Electronic Reference* (Ann Arbor)

Voigts and McVaugh 1984. Linda E. Voigts and Michael R. McVaugh, *A Latin Technical Phlebotomy and its Middle English Translation*, Transactions of the American Philosophical Society 74.2 (Philadelphia)

Wilson 1972. Robert H. Wilson, 'Malory and Caxton', in *Manual of the Writings in Middle English, 1050–1500*, gen. ed. Albert E. Hartung, vol. 3 (Hamden CT), pp. 757–807, 909–51

Ziegler 1998. Joseph Ziegler, *Medicine and Religion, c. 1300: The Case of Arnau de Vilanova* (Oxford)

15

Saints' Lives

OLIVER PICKERING

Introduction

Prose hagiography flowers twice in the Middle English period. It is there at the start, in the shape of the Katherine Group of c. 1200; it re-emerges in the early fifteenth century, after which it continued to flourish until the beginning of the sixteenth.[1] The early Middle English *Katherine*, *Margaret* and *Juliana* are associated with a continuation of Old English and post-Conquest writing traditions. When Middle English began to develop its own forms and genres, in the later thirteenth century, the medium for saints' lives was invariably verse. The outstanding achievement of this poetic tradition is the *South English Legendary* (*SEL*) collection of c. 1275–85, which in different manifestations appears to have met the need for hagiographical literature in English for at least a hundred years. There are no prose saints' lives in the *omnium gatherum* that is the late fourteenth-century Vernon manuscript, whose compiler gives a prominent place to the *SEL* and who includes also, presumably for the sake of completeness, a unique corpus of seven additional verse legends, in a different metre (Görlach 1998, 58–59). Indeed the *SEL* continued to be copied and revised well into the fifteenth century, by which time it must often have fulfilled functions other than its presumed original role as a compendium of instruction and entertainment for oral delivery to the less literate (Pickering 1996, 13–14).

The new function required of hagiography in the fifteenth century was to meet personal devotional needs. Middle English prose saints' lives of this period are the product of the late medieval shift towards private reading by enclosed religious and by devout, particularly female, lay people, in the wake of the spread of literacy and the growth of individual spiritual practice. A large number of prose saints' lives were written to meet these needs, and the quality of the writing is generally of good standard. It is therefore surprising that the genre has not attracted more attention from literary scholars in recent years, given the extent of the opportunities for stylistic and translational analysis.

The developments just described were manifested first in the upper levels of society, and it is likely (as will be seen) that the authors and consumers of prose saints' lives datable to the earlier fifteenth century were associated with religious houses actively supported by the aristocracy. The lives to be discussed include single texts as well as cycles, and original compositions as well as trans-

---

[1] The major surveys are Gerould 1916a, Wolpers 1964, and Görlach 1998.

lations, and they can be said, in all cases, to be consciously hagiographic, i.e. their overriding concern is to demonstrate, through narrative, the spiritual significance of the lives of their subjects.[2] Unlike with the *SEL*, which some scholars have taken to have a homiletic purpose, or with the saints' legends in John Mirk's collection of prose sermon materials, the *Festial* (dated to the later 1380s), there is no question about the essentially narrative/devotional nature of the genre in which the authors of the prose saints' lives are operating. Collections of *sanctorale* sermons are consequently excluded from the present study,[3] as is a body of material that is better classified as scriptural narrative, of which examples are the late fourteenth-century versions of the *Evangelium Nicodemi* and the life of Adam and Eve contained in the Vernon manuscript.[4] Works of this kind, more instructional than devotional, can be said to prepare the way for Middle English saints' lives in prose.

The transition, in terms of both chronology and subject matter, is exemplified by the *Three Kings of Cologne* [1], of which the main English prose version is dated c. 1400, and a second prose version, c. 1425. Combining biblically-based narrative with travelogue in the 'marvels of the East' tradition, the main version was exceptionally popular, surviving in a total of twenty-one manuscripts that preserve four separate recensions. The work is hardly a saint's life, yet the Kings were venerated, and there is an important point of contact in the shape of Lambeth Palace Library, MS 72, one of the manuscripts of the *Gilte Legende* collection, to be discussed below. The latter, in many ways the most important fifteenth-century collection of saints' lives in English prose, shows the extent to which a distinction between scriptural/apocryphal and hagiographic material was not always recognised by manuscript compilers. *Gilte Legende* manuscripts habitually conclude their cycle of saints' lives with the Conception of the Virgin, the life of Adam and Eve,[5] and 'the Five Wiles of Pharaoh', and Lambeth 72 goes further in appending a text of the *Three Kings*. Thus although prose saints' lives can be discussed without difficulty as a distinct Middle English compositional genre, it must be borne in mind that they were not always copied (or read) separately from other religious writings.

---

2   The same, of course, applies to contemporary saints' lives in verse by John Lydgate, Osbern Bokenham, and John Capgrave; see the summary in Görlach 1998, 62–66. For Capgrave's prose saints' lives, see below.
3   The *Festial* is, however, noticed in the three surveys listed in n. 1, particularly in Görlach 1998, 67–70, where it is discussed alongside two other sermon collections in which the *sanctorale* is given prominence, namely the *Speculum Sacerdotale* and the sermons in Bodleian Library, MS Hatton 96. See also the very useful 'Conspectus of legends contained in major ME collections in calendar order' (Görlach 1998, 12–13), in which the contents of these three sermon collections are included.
4   Gerould, again taking a comprehensive view, discusses the various translations of the *Evangelium Nicodemi* in so far as they contain accounts of the life of Joseph of Arimathea, and he notices and praises the Vernon manuscript's Adam and Eve (1916a, 280–82). However, neither of these works comes within Görlach's overview of saints' lives.
5   *IPMEP* 25B, different from the text in the Vernon manuscript (*IPMEP* 53).

The Early Fifteenth Century, and Syon Abbey

The earliest prose saint's life to be considered is probably that of St Antony the Hermit [2], preserved in the early fifteenth-century manuscript, BL, Royal 17.C.xvii, where it sits alongside instructional and doctrinal material in Middle English verse and prose, including two lives from the *SEL* and Mirk's *Instructions for Parish Priests*. It is a work of some length, divided into narratives of the life, invention, and translation of St Antony, but its unsophisticated style clearly betrays its author's over-literal fidelity to his Latin originals, as in:

> To þe heryng of scripetures so wele he gaf hys tent þat nothyng suld out of hys mynd; bot alle þe comamentes of god kepyng, hys mynd was to hym as a boke. & so was he lufed of all hys brethere. (Horstmann 1881, 117)

In this way, as well as in its strongly North-Midland dialect and its manuscript context, it is quite different from a number of lives, some probably datable to the 1420s, which can be broadly associated with Syon Abbey, the Bridgettine house founded by Henry V in 1415 and situated (from 1431) on the Thames upstream from London, on the opposite bank from the Carthusian monastery of Sheen.[6] This Syon-related material, apparently involving a number of authors and revisers, and of which the chronology is hard to establish, is indicative of the degree of compositional activity in the field of prose saints' lives in the years leading up to the securely dated achievement of the *Gilte Legende* in 1438.

The group of lives in question is best approached by way of a manuscript devoted solely to hagiography, written in a single hand (datable to the second quarter of the century) and now divided into four: Cambridge, St John's College N.16, which contains a double life of SS John the Baptist and John the Evangelist [3]; St John's College N.17, which contains a life of St Jerome [4]; Harvard, Houghton Library, Richardson 44, which contains a life of St Katherine of Alexandria [5]; and San Marino, Huntington Library HM 115, which contains John Lydgate's verse *Life of Our Lady*.[7] The key text for the present purpose is Jerome, which is said to be 'drawe into Englyssh to the hyghe princesse Margaret, Duchesse of Clarence' (Waters 1999, 232).[8] The same statement prefaces the copy of Jerome in the late fifteenth-century manuscript, Yale University, Beinecke 317, with the addition of the information that the author was a 'brothir and prest of þe monastery of Syon' (fol. 5), and this statement has been glossed in turn, by another hand, with the name 'Symon Wynter'; the Yale manuscript may therefore have been written at Syon, where the author's identity is most likely to have been known (Keiser 1985, 43). Margaret, Duchess of

---

6   Recent works on the intellectual activity at Syon Abbey in the fifteenth century include de Hamel 1991 and Powell 2000.

7   For discussions of the complete manuscript see Keiser 1985, 41–42, Voigts 1985, 64–66, and the introduction to Waters, forthcoming. The identification of the four dispersed manuscripts as originally one was made by Dr A.I. Doyle.

8   An edition by Claire Waters of the three prose lives in question here is forthcoming in the Middle English Texts series (Heidelberg). I quote here from Waters 1999, which contains her edition of selections from the life of Jerome, based on Cambridge, St John's College, N.17 (pp. 232–49) and a translation of the complete life (pp. 141–63).

Clarence (d. 1439), widow of Henry V's brother Thomas, was a prominent patron and lay associate of Syon Abbey in the 1420s, and Wynter (d. 1448), who may have left Syon for the Benedictine abbey of St Albans c. 1429 because of ill-health, is recorded elsewhere as having been her spiritual adviser (Keiser 1985, 36–38; de Hamel 1991, 59–60).

The prose style of Simon Wynter's life of St Jerome is markedly more fluent than that of the anonymous St Anthony, as in, for example:

> And on a tyme, as he wryteth hymself to the hooly mayde Eustache, when he studyed bysyly nyght and day [yn] bokes of poetys and of philosophres bycause they sauouryd hym bettir then bokes of holy scripture, hit happed that about myd-Lent he was smyte wyth a sodeyn and a feruent fevir, insomoche that all his body was deed and coold vnto the hert. (Waters 1999, 234)

The work begins with a lengthy prologue addressed to the duchess, in which Wynter reveals that he has composed the work 'that not oonly ye shulde knowe hit the more cleerly to youre goostly profyte, but also hit shulde mowe abyde and turne to edificacion of other that wolde rede hit or here hit' (Waters 1999, 232–33); it goes on to encourage the duchess to allow copies to be made for the benefit of others. There then follows a table of contents of the work's nineteen chapters. The same characteristics of prologue and tabulated contents distinguish both the life of St Katherine and the double life of the two SS John, with the prologue to the former having more in common with that to Jerome (first-person references to the act of translation and to the division into chapters, though without mention of a dedicatee).[9] But the lives of St Jerome and the two Johns both draw on the *Revelaciones* of St Bridget of Sweden, among other Latin sources, making it probable that both were Bridgettine productions, and it is thus possible that all three prose lives in the now divided manuscript were composed by members of Syon Abbey in the period 1415–30. The manuscript itself, however, may have been written across the river at Sheen (also founded by Henry V), given that the hand of its scribe has been identified in a manuscript undoubtedly produced in that house (Doyle 1997, 110).

The association of these prose saints' lives with the Lancastrian court and particularly with Henry V is strengthened by a rubric in another manuscript of the same version of St Katherine, namely Cambridge, Gonville and Caius College, 390/610, asserting that the work was 'sent bi a discrete maistre vnto the kyng henry the v^{te}' (fol. 56v). If true, Katherine's date of composition is pushed back to at least 1422, which is additionally significant as the Katherine in question has been classified as version (d) in a succession of recensions of this popular saint's life (Nevanlinna and Taavitsainen 1993, xix–xxii). Versions (a) and (b), which precede it in sequence, must therefore be earlier still, despite the relative lateness of their numerous manuscripts and the claims to authorship made by the writer of the prologue to the (d) version.[10] It is quite possible,

---

9   A very similar style of prologue, though without a table of contents, prefaces the religious treatise, the *Orchard of Syon*, another translation from Latin made probably in the 1420s for the first generation of nuns at Syon. See Waters, forthcoming, and Hodgson and Liegey 1966.

10   'After I had drawe þe martirdom of the holy virgyn and martir Seynt Kateryne from Latyn into

however, that versions (a) (b), and (d) were all written within a short space of time. It has been suggested that Henry V's marriage to Catherine of France in 1422 may have acted as inspiration (Nevanlinna and Taavitsainen 1993, 29), and all three versions could plausibly have been produced at Syon.[11]

Wynter's life of St Jerome occurs also (though without the dedication) in Lambeth Palace Library 432, a manuscript from the mid-fifteenth century written by a scribe named Richard Fuller and containing devotional and instructional texts, including material translated from Bridget of Sweden's *Revelaciones*; it was therefore possibly also compiled at Syon (Keiser 1985, 43). One of its other texts is a life of St Dorothy [6], in a version said to date from the beginning of the fifteenth century (Görlach 1998, 93). The same life is found in Manchester, Chetham's Library 8009, which also contains Katherine version (a), and in Cambridge University Library Ll.5.18, with which Lambeth 432 shares copies of the spiritual treatises known as the *Abbey of the Holy Ghost* and the *Charter of the Abbey of the Holy Ghost*.

Leaving aside the St Antony, there is therefore a group of prose saints' lives, preserved in textually overlapping manuscripts, that appear to date from the first thirty years of the fifteenth century and which in some cases are probably to be associated with Syon Abbey: Simon Wynter's Jerome, several recensions of Katherine, the double life of SS John the Baptist and John the Evangelist, and a version of Dorothy. To these may be added a long and elaborate life of St Barbara [7], based on a late fourteenth-century Latin *vita* by Jan van Wackerzele, which resembles Jerome in having (in Durham University Library, Cosin V.iv.4) a preface that refers both to Bridget of Sweden and to the division of the work into chapters (though it has no table of contents) and may therefore well have been written at Syon at much the same time (Görlach 1998, 80 n. 119); and just possibly a life of St Bridget herself [8], now known only in a print issued by Richard Pynson in 1516 but perhaps (it has been suggested) written by the author of the Jerome (Gerould 1916a, 288), although in its extant form it lacks a preface and dedication, and has no chapter divisions.

The Gilte Legende

An important additional factor in dating the above legends is their relationship to the *Gilte Legende* of 1438 [9], the name and date of which derive from a colophon in Bodleian Library, Douce 372:

> And also here endith the lives of Seintis that is callid in latyne Legenda Aurea,
> And in Englissh the gilte legende, the which is drawen out of Frensshe into

---

[11] For a discussion of a number of later fifteenth-century and early sixteenth-century manuscripts of versions (a) (b) and (c) of Katherine, in which the life occurs within lay 'household books', see Lewis 2000, 177–86. For a discussion of version (c), see Jacqueline Jenkins, 'Popular Devotion and the Legend of St Katherine of Alexandria in Late Medieval England' (unpublished doctoral dissertation, University of Western Ontario, 1996), pp. 60–85.

Englisshe The yere of oure lorde, a Ml CCCC and xxxviij bi a synfulle
wrecche. (fol. 163)

G.H. Gerould, in praising this collection as representing 'the best tradition of
prose translation in the fifteenth century', asserted that it stands 'in somewhat
the same relation to saints' lives as *Le Morte Darthur* stands to romances'
(1916a, 196), and it is unfortunate, given his achievement, that the 'synfulle
wrecche' was so self-effacing. According to the prologue preserved in BL, MS
Harley 4755, his purpose was 'to excite and stere symple lettrid men and
women to encrese in vertue bi the offten redinge and hiringe of this boke'
(fol. 1), and his appropriately plain style of writing (plainer than Simon
Wynter's) has been praised for its clarity (Hamer 1978, 23; Görlach 1998, 72).
The beginning of the life of St Nicholas may serve as an example:

> Seint Nicholas was borne in the citee of Patras and was come of noble and
> riche kinrede. His fader was named Epiphanus and his moder Iohanna. He was
> begoten in the furst floure of thaire age, and sithe after thei liued in chastite &
> [l]adden an [heuen]ly liff. (BL, Egerton 876, fol. 4, ed. Hamer 1978, 51)

The *Gilte Legende* is a huge and compendious work, containing 178 different
lives (or other items) in its original form, and it would seem to have been a
major undertaking by a proven writer, who was possibly a monk at St Albans.[12]
The source of the collection is predominantly the *Légende dorée* of Jean de
Vignay, a mid-fourteenth-century translation into French of Jacobus de
Voragine's thirteenth-century *Legenda aurea*. In these sources the arrangement
of material is liturgical, beginning with St Andrew, but the English collection's
separateness from the liturgy is shown by the positioning of the item on Advent
at the end, after the 'Dedication of a Church' (the final item in the French and
Latin versions) and preceding the apocryphal Conception of the Virgin, life of
Adam and Eve, and Five Wiles of Pharaoh referred to earlier (which do not
occur in the French and Latin). The *Gilte Legende* was in turn used by Caxton as
a major source of his *Golden Legend* (see below).

Eight *Gilte Legende* manuscripts survive, in varying states of completeness
(three include significant additions, to be discussed below), together with three
manuscripts that contain selections ranging in number from three to seventeen
lives. A small number of lives were also copied separately (see the Bibliography). The physical size and decorative style of the major manuscripts reflect
the extent and importance of the complete work, the most magnificent being
BL, Harley 4775, written probably in the third quarter of the fifteenth century
by a scribe named Ricardus Franciscus (Hamer 1983), and later owned by
members of the aristocratic Morley/St John families (Boffey and Edwards 2000,
72). MS Douce 372, quoted above (and from which MS Harley 4775 was
directly copied), has an additional colophon recording the bequest of the volume

---

[12] See Hamer 1978, 17–18 for evidence from the *Gilte Legende*'s life of Alban that the author could
have been from this abbey, and Tracey 2000 for evidence that the *Gilte Legende* manuscript, BL,
Harley 630, was written there.

by the London merchant John Burton (d. 1460) first to his daughter and subsequently to the nuns of Haliwell (or Holywell) Priory, London.

The *Gilte Legende*, in different ways, gathers up many of the separate prose lives discussed earlier, all in fact except the life of SS John the Baptist and John the Evangelist, which appears nowhere else. Its standard life of St Katherine, for which it exceptionally ignores the account in the *Légende dorée* and the *Legenda aurea*, is version (b) of the various recensions of this life referred to above. The thirteen manuscripts of version (b) comprise ten of the *Gilte Legende* (including all those with selections) and three others, and there is no doubt that in this case the 'synfulle wrecche' used a pre-existing prose life.[13] The pre-existing lives of SS Jerome, Barbara, and Dorothy, however, were all added to the *Gilte Legende* at a later stage, the Jerome (in Lambeth Palace 72 alone) being a substitution for the collection's standard French-derived text of Jerome, and Barbara (also in Lambeth Palace 72 alone) and Dorothy representing new material. Dorothy is in fact one of an important group of twenty-one additional legends that deserve consideration in their own right.

These additional legends (normally referred to as *ALL*) **[10]**, none of them represented in the *Légende dorée* or the *Legenda aurea*, comprise Dorothy and twenty lives of mostly English saints. Dorothy is a later recension of the earlier life of St Dorothy referred to above as occurring in Lambeth Palace 432 and other manuscripts,[14] but the other *ALL* lives are based not on pre-existing prose texts but predominantly on lives in the *SEL*, from where, remarkably, they have been deversified.[15] The *ALL* as a whole, though with some variations, occur in Lambeth Palace 72 and two other major manuscripts of the *Gilte Legende*, BL, Add. 11565 and Add. 35298. Six of them additionally occur in an appendix to the *Festial* manuscript, Southwell Cathedral 7, and thirteen of them were later taken into Caxton's *Golden Legend* via what was evidently an expanded *Gilte Legende* manuscript (see further below). It remains uncertain as to whether the *ALL* were composed especially to supplement the *Gilte Legende*; it is likely that they were, possibly in the 1440s,[16] but there are anomalies such as the presence of lives of SS Michael and Thomas of Canterbury,[17] already represented in the collection, while the Southwell manuscript testifies to the *ALL*'s having an independent textual existence.[18]

The separate inclusion in Lambeth Palace 72 of Barbara, of Wynter's Jerome, of, in fact, a version of the life of St Augustine different from the *SEL*-derived life in the BL, Add. 35298 text of the *ALL*, and of the *Three Kings of Cologne*,

---

[13] For the close links between the abbeys of Syon and St Albans, which could be significant for the transmission of texts (and which involve also Simon Wynter), see Keiser 1985, 38 and Doyle 1997, 98–100.

[14] For a third version of Dorothy, which occurs in one of the manuscripts containing selections from the *Gilte Legende*, see Bibliography [6], below.

[15] The pioneering study of this phenomenon is Görlach 1972, now incorporated into Görlach 1998, 71–145.

[16] These are Görlach's conclusions; see 1998, 127 and 132.

[17] As well as Hamer and Russell 2000, xv–xvi, see the discussions in Görlach 1998, 117–23.

[18] A preceding appendix in Southwell Cathedral 7 contains a non-*Gilte Legende* prose life of St Ursula, for which see below, and a composite version of Katherine, found nowhere else, which combines elements of versions (a) and (b) with new material; it is ed. Nevanlinna and Taavitsainen 1993.

as mentioned earlier, testifies to the habitual fluidity of the contents of legendaries, in whatever language or medium, and to the habitual urge to add new material, when of special interest to the compiler, his institution, or his patron. The late fifteenth-century Add. MS 35298 in its turn includes, in sequence, the lives of three other British saints, Edward the Confessor, Winifred, and Erkenwald, found nowhere else in these versions, but (unlike with Lambeth 72's Jerome, Barbara, and *Three Kings*) there is no evidence that these lives existed earlier, as has been suggested (Görlach 1998, 82), and nothing is known of the manuscript's provenance.[19] Lambeth 72, in contrast, has been linked with Syon Abbey, on the grounds of its inclusion of Simon Wynter's Jerome and of Barbara. However, the links between these two lives and Syon or St Bridget are (as noted above) made in other manuscripts, not this one, where the texts in question are stripped of any prefatory matter, an unlikely occurrence if the manuscript had indeed been produced at Syon. All that can be said is that the compiler of Lambeth 72 had access to lives that were most probably composed there.

Other Fifteenth-Century Lives in Manuscript

The *Gilte Legende* is the unifying factor in fifteenth-century English prose saints' lives, linking back to at least the 1420s through its re-use of pre-existing material and forwards to Caxton's 1483 *Golden Legend* (discussed below), which draws substantially from it. Surviving manuscripts show that other prose lives were written, independent of its influence and embrace, but scarcely one is preserved in more than a single copy and the majority have no literary (or other) context to rescue them from their isolation.

The main exception to this generalisation is the Augustinian friar and prolific author John Capgrave (1393–1464), who wrote two saints' lives in prose (Augustine of Hippo [11], and Gilbert of Sempringham [12]) as well as two in verse (Norbert, and, once again, Katherine of Alexandria).[20] Both of the prose lives were composed while Capgrave was a member of the Augustinian friary of Lynn in Norfolk. The life of St Augustine was written first, c. 1450, at the request (in the author's words) of 'a noble creatur, a gentill woman', who 'desired of me with ful grete instauns to write on-to hir, þat is to sey, to translate hir treuly oute of Latyn, þe lif of Seynt Augustyn, grete doctour of þe cherch',[21] thinking that Capgrave, as an Augustinian, would be more willing than others to do the job, and because she was born on his feast day. What Capgrave produced was a free translation of the *Vita Sancti Augustini* of Jordan of Saxony. It must have enjoyed some circulation, for the preface to his life of St Gilbert reveals that the Augustine came to the notice of Nicholas Reysby, the Master of the order of St Gilbert of Sempringham (forty miles west of Lynn), who, as a result,

---

[19] Görlach 1998, 132 notes, however, the 'strong Westminster flavour' of Add. 35298, because of the inclusion of its unique texts of Edward the Confessor and Erkenwald.

[20] For an up-to-date account of Capgrave's life and works, see Lucas 1997, 7–18.

[21] Quotations from Capgrave are from Munro 1910, here p. 1.

'desired gretly þe lyf of Seynt Gilbert schuld be translat in þe same forme' – not
for himself, as it turns out, but 'for the solitarye women of ȝour [i.e. Reysby's]
religion whech vnneth can vndyrstande Latyn, þat þei may at vacaunt tymes
red in þis book þe grete vertues of her maystyr' (Munro 1910, 61). For this
purpose Capgrave translated the *Vita Sancti Gilberti Confessoris* of Roger of
Sempringham 'in-to our moder tonge', dating his work, at the end, 1451 (Munro
1910, 142). He was, therefore, writing for a distinct local audience of devout
women, associated more or less formally with religious houses, and he presumably achieved some readership, even though only a single manuscript of the two
works now survives, namely BL, Add. MS 36704, which is in his own hand.[22]

With Capgrave we encounter once more the practice of writing prose saints'
lives explicitly for a female readership, the same purpose for which they were
evidently written at Syon Abbey in the 1420s and for which another East
Anglian, Osbern Bokenham, was writing his verse *Legendys of Hooly Wummen*
in the 1440s (see Serjeantson 1938 and Edwards 1993). Rather less can be
deduced about the highly unusual collection of four female saints' lives
preserved in the mid-fifteenth-century Bodleian Library, MS Douce 114. The
oddity of this collection lies in the distinctly non-standard choice of saints, of
whom three – treated at length – lived in the Belgian diocese of Liège during the
thirteenth century: St Elizabeth of Spalbeck **[13]**, St Christine the Marvellous
[14], and St Mary of Oignies **[15]**. The fourth saint is the fourteenth-century St
Katherine of Siena **[16]**.

Latin lives of the the same saints, however, by different authors,[23] occurred
together in a manuscript formerly belonging to the Augustinian priory of
Thurgarton in Nottinghamshire, as is evident from a fifteenth-century booklist
surviving from that house (Webber and Watson 1998, 421); and a similar manuscript – though lacking the Katherine of Siena – is preserved as St John's
College, Oxford, MS 182, given by John Blacman to Witham Charterhouse in
Somerset. Clearly these Latin materials circulated together, and the author of the
Middle English versions no doubt worked from a ready-made source of this
kind. On the final page of MS Douce 114 is an ownership inscription naming
the Carthusian monastery of Beauvale, north-west of Nottingham (and only a
dozen miles from Thurgarton), and the English author's apology for mixing
southern and northern linguistic forms ('vmwhile soþeren, oþerewhile norþen',
fol. 89v) suggests that the work of translation was indeed carried out in a
Midlands location.[24]

The translator contributes a preface and epilogue of his own, in which he
explains something of his motives and his methods. In his introductory 'Þe
Apologe of the compilour' he reveals in fairly standard fashion that he has made
the translations 'to the worschep of god & edificacyone of deuoute soulles þat

---

[22] For the evidence, and reproductions of manuscript pages, see Lucas 1997, 19–36 ('Capgrave as
Scribe') and 69–89 ('Capgrave as Copyist of his Own Work').

[23] Respectively Philip of Clairvaux, Thomas of Cantimpré, Jacques of Vitry, and Stephen of Siena; see
Horstmann 1885, 102–05, and Webber and Watson 1998, 421.

[24] The language of MS Douce 114 is analysed as Linguistic Profile 99 in McIntosh, Samuels and
Benskin 1986, where it is localised to the county of Rutland.

are not leeryd in latyn tunge' (fol. 1). At the end, in 'A shorte Apologetick of þis englisshe compyloure', he says he would not have presumed to undertake the work 'but if his souereyn hadde bidden hym, whome he myghte not ageyne-seye', adding a Latin tag which he then translates to make the situation perfectly clear: 'a priours preyynge til obeyand monke is a bidynge' (fol. 89v). Each of the four lives exhibits the extremes of female religious ecstasy and/or mira-cle-working, and it may be assumed that the prior and his monk had in mind, once again, a readership of local pious women with such interests.[25] The trans-lator apologises for his lack of skill in the conventional way, describing himself as 'symple-letterd' (fol. 1), but his achievement in conveying 'þe substaunce of þe story' if not always (as he says) the exact words of his original is consider-able, as in the following account of one of St Elizabeth's ecstacies:[26]

> And anoon after sche strechys oute her riȝhte arme and makiþ a fiste of her hand, and lokiþ grymly, braunysshynge hir fiste, and makes feerful tokens and bekenynges with eyen & handys, as a body þat were wrooþ and angry. And after þat anoon sche smitith her-selfe vpon the cheke, so strongly, þat alle hir body bowith to þat party ageyns þe ground for heuynesse of the stroke; þan sche smytes hir-selfe in þe nodel of the hede byhynde, now bitwix þe schuldirs, now in the necke; and þanne sche noseles downe forwarde and wonderly crokes her body and dasches her heed to the erthe.
>
> (Horstmann 1885, 108–09)

A more substantial and apparently unstudied collection of nineteen female and three male saints' lives occurs in Cambridge University Library, Add. MS 2604, dated to the second half of the fifteenth century **[17]**. There is no authorial statement of intent other than the heading 'The lyves and dethes of the martyres', and the principles of selection and arrangement are obscure. Compar-atively few of the twenty-two saints included are martyrs; the three male saints are John the Baptist, John the Evangelist, and Leonard; and eleven of the female saints are British, anticipating the early sixteenth-century *Kalendre of the Newe Legende of Englande* (item **[29]** below). All appear to depend on Latin sources, among them the *Nova Legenda Anglie*, the source of the *Kalendre*. Given the small dimensions of the book, and the shortness of some of the lives, it may be that the manuscript was written for female readership.[27]

Six fifteenth-century prose lives in manuscript remain to be noted. There is a life of St Edward the Confessor **[18]** in Trinity College, Oxford, MS 11, deversified from the account found in some manuscripts of the *SEL*.[28] A life of St Ursula and the 11,000 Virgins **[19]** survives in two manuscripts of the later

---

[25] It may be noted that reading the life of St Mary of Oignies – but evidently in Latin – was one of the factors that caused Margery Kempe's priest-collaborator to take her extremes of piety seriously; see Meech and Allen 1940, 152–53 and 322–23.

[26] For a positive assessment of the translator's style and overall achievement, see Gerould 1916b. For all four lives, see also Gerould 1916a, 289–90.

[27] I am very grateful to Dr Veronica O'Mara, who is working on the manuscript, for drawing Add. 2604 to my attention, and to Miss Jayne Ringrose, Cambridge University Library, for assistance with the description.

[28] This is different from the life of Edward the Confessor that is inserted (with lives of Winifred and Erkenwald) into the Add. 35298 manuscript of the *Gilte Legende*, for which see above.

fifteenth century, one of which is Southwell Cathedral MS 7, where it sits along-side a composite life of Katherine of Alexandria and a selection of additional lives from the *Gilte Legende* (see above and n. 18). A brief life of St Zita **[20]**, defective at the beginning, occurs in a late fifteenth-century Nottingham University Library manuscript, and a life of St Audry (Ethelreda) **[21]** in Corpus Christi College, Oxford, MS 120. Finally, two separate versions of the life of St Margaret **[22]** survive alongside saints' lives already encountered. One is in BL, Harley 4012, a religious anthology seemingly made in the 1460s for the Norfolk gentry woman Anne Harling,[29] and which also contains Katherine version (c). The other life of Margaret – a lengthy fragment – is in Bodleian Library, MS Eng. th. e.18, which was formerly part of the same manuscript (Eng. th. e.17) as contains a variant life of Dorothy.[30]

Printed Saints' Lives

Given the popularity of saints' lives as reading matter, and the plentiful manu-script materials available, in both prose and verse, it was only natural that the genre should become a staple of the output of the early English printers. Certain of the prose texts that found their way into print in the late fifteenth and early sixteenth centuries are versions of manuscript lives already encountered, namely the *Three Kings of Cologne* (Wynkyn de Worde, four editions from [1496] to 1526), Simon Wynter's Jerome (de Worde [1499?]), the (b) version of Katherine of Alexandria ([Richard Pynson, 1510?]), and the Edward the Confessor added to Add. MS 35298 of the *Gilte Legende* (de Worde, 1523). The life of St Bridget, printed by Pynson in 1516, but possibly dating from much earlier, has also already been mentioned. Early sixteenth-century printed prose lives that may or may not have had fifteenth-century manuscript antecedents include those of Joseph of Arimathea **[23]** (de Worde [1511?]), Francis of Assisi **[24]** (Pynson [1515?]), and Nicholas of Tollentino **[25]** (de Worde [1525?]).

By far the most important propagator of printed saints' lives in English was William Caxton, whose achievements as a printer were possibly rivalled (in his own eyes) by his prodigious activity as a translator. His life of St Winifred **[26]**, translated from the Latin of Robert of Shrewsbury and printed probably in 1484, has attracted most stylistic praise; according to G.H. Gerould, 'its unaffected simplicity, no less than the richness of the narrative, makes it one of the best examples of fifteenth century prose' (1916a, 291). The following passage illus-trates something of the style, including Caxton's characteristic use of doublets:

---

29 See Wilson 1977, 301–02; Dutton 2000; and Lewis 2000, 180–81.
30 The following may also be noted. Cambridge, Trinity College, MS R.14.39, part 2, fol. 1 (*IMEP* XI, 39), has a fragment of the end of an unidentified life of St Augustine of Canterbury, which concludes 'explicit vita sanctorum', suggesting a larger collection. A brief account of John the Baptist, probably an extract from a sermon rather than a saint's life proper, occurs in John Rylands University Library of Manchester MS 412, fol. 42r–v (ed. Lester 1985, 159–60). Short accounts of a number of saints are also included in the fifteenth-century translation of Etienne de Besançon's *Alphabetum Narrationum* in BL, Add. MS 25719, known as the *Alphabet of Tales* (ed. Banks 1904–05). The life of St Katherine of Sweden, listed as in Bodleian Library, MS Digby 172, in *Manual*, 2, 602, is in fact in Latin.

Whanne this hooly vyrgyne vnderstode the departynge of her mayster and
doctour, she was moche sorowful and heuy and wepte sorowfully for his
departynge and absence. Thenne the holy man Beunowe ladde her by the ryght
honde to the welle whiche sprange at the place where her hede fylle whanne
hit was smyten of, wherof we haue tofore remembryd, and made her to stande
vpon a stone which lyeth there on the brynk of the sayd welle vnto this daye.

(Horstmann 1880, 299)

Caxton does not provide a prologue explaining the motivation for his undertaking, but it has been suggested that he may have been trying to produce a work
that appealed to the Welsh interests of the new Lancastrian regime.[31] Gerould
contrasts it with the only other single prose saint's life associated with Caxton, a
version of the life of St Katherine of Siena [16] different from that found in
Bodleian Library, MS Douce 114, which he calls 'a rather thin and confused
translation, scarcely worthy of perpetuation' (1916a, 291). This legend, which
was translated from the Latin of Raymond of Capua for a nun and 'al other of thi
gostely susteren', on whose account 'poyntes of diuynyte whiche passeth your
vnderstondyng' were omitted,[32] was issued from Caxton's shop by Wynkyn de
Worde c. 1493, i.e. after Caxton's death. The translation was apparently made
earlier in the fifteenth century; there is no suggestion that Caxton was responsible.

Caxton's greatest hagiographic achievement, by far, was his version of the
Golden Legend [27], issued at the end of 1483, which he based on a
fifteenth-century revision of the *Légende dorée* from which the *Gilte Legende*
had been translated, supplementing it with legends or passages taken from the
original Latin *Legenda aurea* and from the *Gilte Legende* itself, as well as from
other sources.[33] The result is a collection of almost 250 separate legends, beginning with a separate *temporale* section (including biblical narratives not in the
source legendaries), which is easily the largest Middle English manifestation of
the *Legenda aurea* tradition. But although Caxton aimed to be compendious, he
was also concerned to rationalise his sources, frequently excising or condensing
passages in the interests of narrative and to the exclusion of speculation and
'authorities' (Blake 1969, 120).[34] From a stylistic point of view, however,
Richard Hamer contrasts Caxton's 'attempts at copiousness and aureation and
. . . more formal and elaborate sentences' unfavourably with the plainer and
more fluent prose of the *Gilte Legende* (1978, 23).

Caxton writes in his prologue that he began the work 'bycause me semeth to
be a soverayn wele to incyte and exhorte men and wymmen to kepe them from
slouthe and ydlenesse and to lete to be understonden to suche peple as been not
letterd the natyvytees, the lyves, the passyons, the myracles, and the dethe of the
holy sayntes' (Blake 1973a, 89). But he was, he says, of a mind to set it aside

---

[31] Powell 1998, 213–14, drawing on Lowry 1983, 116.

[32] The quotations are from Horstmann 1886b, 34.

[33] For an overview and a summary of scholarship, see Görlach 1998, 72–76, 93–123, 137–45. See also
Kurvinen 1959, which includes (pp. 358–63) a useful conspectus of the order of legends in Caxton as
compared to those in the original *Gilte Legende* and in BL, Add. MS 35298.

[34] See Kurvinen 1959, 372–74; Hamer 1978, 25–26; and Görlach 1998, 93–123, 137–45 for examples
of and commentaries on Caxton's translational technique.

unfinished because of the enormity of the task of translating and printing, until he was urged to proceed (with the promise of a reward) by the Earl of Arundel. From a textual point of view it is striking that the manuscript of the *Gilte Legende* used by Caxton must have contained many of the additional legends (*ALL*) discussed above, for thirteen of these were adapted for the *Golden Legend*, as Görlach has demonstrated in detail (1998, 93–123, 142–45).[35] Caxton's source manuscript has not survived, but it was evidently close to BL, Add. MS 35298, as the *Golden Legend* also contains versions of the lives of SS Edward the Confessor, Winifred, and Erkenwald, found only in that manuscript, whose suggested Westminster provenance fits with the location of Caxton's shop.[36] It cannot, however, have been Add. MS 35298 itself, for the *Golden Legend* contains a revision of the longer version of the *ALL* Augustine of Canterbury found in MS Lambeth 72 of the *Gilte Legende*, not the shorter version found in Add. MS 35298; and it includes also the *ALL* text of Thomas of Canterbury, which is not present in that manuscript.[37] For these and other reasons it is clear that the *Gilte Legende* manuscript used by Caxton contained a different selection of *ALL* from that found in any of the surviving manuscripts.

Caxton's interest in *sanctorale* material is demonstrated also by his editions of John Mirk's sermon collection, the *Festial* (1483, 1491), and of John Lydgate's verse *Life of Our Lady* (1484). His final effort in the genre was the collection of 132 lives of the desert fathers known as the *Vitas Patrum* [28], which he finished translating, according to the colophon, 'at the laste daye of hys lyff'; the book was eventually issued by Wynkyn de Worde four years later, in 1495. Like the *Golden Legend*, it is a huge work, based in this case on just one source, a version in French printed at Lyons in 1486–87. Only the first of its five parts in fact consists of legends, the other four containing exempla, precepts, moral treatises, and 'the rule and conversation of other holy fathers' (see the valuable summary in Görlach 1998, 146–48). Seventeen of the desert saints also figure in the *Golden Legend*, but, as Görlach points out, there is no sign that Caxton consulted his earlier work when preparing the *Vitas Patrum*.

The final large-scale collection of English prose saints' lives to be printed before the Reformation was the *Kalendre of the Newe Legende of Englande* [29], which was issued by Richard Pynson in 1516 and to which his life of St Bridget forms an appendix. The *Kalendre* comprises 168 epitomes drawn from the Latin *Nova Legenda Anglie* (formerly ascribed to John Capgrave), printed by de Worde in the same year. As Görlach makes clear (1998, 149), the individual texts are frequently so abbreviated as to have the nature of encyclopedia entries, and the purpose is explicitly to whet the reader's appetite for the full versions of the stories: the collection was made, says the preface, 'for theym that

---

35 The legends in question are of Dorothy, Edmund of Abingdon, Edmund king and martyr, Edward king and martyr, Alphege, Augustine of Canterbury, Dunstan, Aldhelm, Swithun, Kenelm, Cuthbert, Brendan, and Thomas of Canterbury.

36 See n. 19 above. For the characteristics of the *Gilte Legende* manuscript likely to have been used by Caxton, and for reasons why Caxton cannot have used Add. MS 35298 itself, see Hamer 1978, 20; Görlach 1998, 142; and Hamer and Russell 2000, xvii–xviii. The Winifred taken into the *Golden Legend* is a different text from that translated and printed by Caxton probably in 1484.

37 For Caxton's treatment of these two legends, see Görlach 1998, 102–05 and 120–23.

vnderstande not the Laten tonge, that they atte theyr pleasure may be occupyed therwith and be therby þe more apte to lerne the resydue when they shall here the hole legende' (Görlach 1994, 43). Strikingly, the intended readership is envisaged, later in the preface, as the whole 'people of this realme',[38] and it is significant, too, that the *Kalendre* is a deliberate collection of national saints, as the preface explains at length.

In these ways the kind of highly organised enterprise it represents – involving in effect, the two leading English printers of the day – seems wholly different from the narrower and more scattered manuscript labours of the preceding century, and yet there is continuity, too. Görlach (1994, 12) points out that the woodcut of St Bridget preceding the life of the saint has the initials of the current abbess of Syon Abbey cut into the frame, suggesting that it was printed for the abbey;[39] and as the life of Bridget was printed with a continuation of the quire system used for the *Kalendre*, implying that it was an integral part of the project, it may even be that Pynson printed the whole book for Syon. He and de Worde were certainly both engaged with producing books for the abbey and its royal patrons, and this activity often involved the printing of much earlier texts, such as the life of Bridget may have been.[40] Some of the individual saints' lives mentioned above may also have been printed for the abbey (or for people associated with it), recalling the situation a century earlier when the monk Simon Wynter was writing texts for the Duchesss of Clarence. One of the great patrons of religious book production in the early period of printing was the Duchess's granddaughter, Lady Margaret Beaufort (1443–1509), who in her own turn was closely associated with Syon (see Powell 1998, esp. pp. 211–20). If Wynkyn de Worde, in 1499?, printed the life of St Jerome that had originally been composed for her grandmother as a compliment to her, as has been suggested (Keiser 1985, 43–44), the activity of late medieval English prose hagiography completes a satisfying circle. Yet even while the printing of Jerome 'may have brought the life to a much wider audience than had previously known it' (Keiser 1985, 44), the Reformation was not far off. The *Kalendre* did not in fact represent a new beginning to the writing of saints' lives, and the circle was indeed closed.

---

[38] In context, '. . . þat [the collection] maye be as a preparatyfe or a begynnynge to reduce the people of this realme þe rather to haue the sayde blessyd seyntes in loue & honoure' (Görlach 1994, 46).

[39] Görlach quotes here from S.H. Johnston, 'A Study of the Career and the Literary Publications of Richard Pynson' (unpublished doctoral dissertation, University of Western Ontario, 1977).

[40] One example is the early fifteenth-century *Orcherd of Syon* (n. 9 above), printed for Syon Abbey by de Worde in 1519 (*STC* 4815). For a summary of de Worde's involvement with Syon Abbey, see Edwards and Meale 1993, 115–16; for his gift, in 1516, of a copy of his *Nova Legenda Anglie* to Syon, see de Hamel 1991, 102.

BIBLIOGRAPHY

Modern Editions, Secondary Literature, and Works of Reference

Axon, W.E., 'A Fifteenth-Century Life of Dorothea', *The Antiquary* 37 (1901), 53–55

Banks, Mary Macleod, ed., *An Alphabet of Tales*, EETS os 126–27 (London, 1904–05)

Blake, N.F., *Caxton and his World* (London, 1969)

——, ed., *Middle English Religious Prose* (London, 1972)

——, ed., *Caxton's Own Prose* (London, 1973) [1973a]

——, ed., *Selections from William Caxton* (London, 1973) [1973b]

Blunt, J.H., ed., *The Myroure of Oure Ladye*, EETS es 19 (London, 1873)

Boffey, Julia, and A.S.G. Edwards, 'Books Connected with Henry Parker, Lord Morley, and his Family', in *'Triumphs of English': Henry Parker, Lord Morley, Translator to the Tudor Court: New Essays in Interpretation*, ed. Marie Axton and James P. Carley (London, 2000), pp. 69–75

de Hamel, Christopher, *Syon Abbey: The Library of the Bridgettine Nuns and their Peregrinations after the Reformation* (privately printed for the Roxburghe Club, 1991)

Doyle, A.I., 'Stephen Dodesham of Witham and Sheen', in *Of the Making of Books: Medieval Manuscripts, their Scribes and Readers. Essays Presented to M.B. Parkes*, ed. P.R. Robinson and Rivkah Zim (Aldershot, 1997), pp. 94–115

Dutton, Anne M., 'Piety, Politics and Persona: MS Harley 4012 and Anne Harling', in *Prestige, Authority and Power in Late Medieval Manuscripts and Texts*, ed. Felicity Riddy (Woodbridge, 2000), pp. 133–46

Edwards, A.S.G., 'The Transmission and Audience of Osbern Bokenham's *Legendys of Hooly Wummen*', in *Late-Medieval Texts and their Transmission: Essays in Honour of A.I. Doyle*, ed. A.J. Minnis (Cambridge, 1993), pp. 157–67

Edwards, A.S.G., and Carol Meale, 'The Marketing of Printed Books in Late Medieval England', *The Library* 6th ser. 15 (1993), 95–124

Ellis, F.S., ed., *The Golden Legend of Master William Caxton Done Anew* (London, 1892)

Ellis, Roger, ed., *The Liber Celestis of St Bridget of Sweden: The Middle English Version in British Library MS Claudius B i, together with a life of the saint from the same manuscript*, vol. 1, EETS os 291 (Oxford, 1987)

Garmonsway, G.N., and R.R. Raymo, 'A Middle-English Prose Life of St Ursula', *Review of English Studies* ns 9 (1958), 353–61

Gerould, Gordon Hall, *Saints' Legends* (Boston and New York, 1916) [1916a]

——, 'The Source of the Middle English Prose St Elizabeth of Spalbeck', *Anglia* 39 (1916), 356–58 [1916b]

Gibbs, H.H., ed., *The Life and Martyrdom of Saint Katherine of Alexandria, Virgin and Martyr* (London, for the Roxburghe Club, 1884)

Görlach, Manfred, *The 'South English Legendary', 'Gilte Legende' and 'Golden Legend'*, Braunschweiger Anglistische Arbeiten 3 (Braunschweig, 1972)

——, 'A Second Version of the Huntington Prose Legend of St Ursula', *Review of English Studies* ns 24 (1973), 450–51

——, *The Textual Tradition of the South English Legendary*, Leeds Texts and Monographs ns 6 (Leeds, 1974)

——, ed., *The Kalendre of the Newe Legende of Englande, ed. from Pynson's Printed Edition, 1516*, Middle English Texts 27 (Heidelberg, 1994)

——, *Studies in Middle English Saints' Legends* (Heidelberg, 1998)

Gray, Douglas, ed., *The Oxford Book of Late Medieval Verse and Prose* (Oxford, 1985)

Hamer, Richard, ed., *Three Lives from the Gilte Legende, ed. from MS B.L. Egerton 876*, Middle English Texts 9 (Heidelberg, 1978)

———, 'Spellings of the Fifteenth-Century Scribe Ricardus Franciscus', in *Five Hundred Years of Words and Sounds: A Festschrift for E.J. Dobson*, ed. E.G. Stanley and Douglas Gray (Cambridge, 1983), pp. 63–73

Hamer, Richard, and Vida Russell, eds, *Supplementary Lives in Some Manuscripts of the Gilte Legende*, EETS os 315 (Oxford, 2000)

Hodgson, Phyllis, and Gabriel M. Liegey, eds, *The Orcherd of Syon*, vol. I, EETS os 258 (London, 1966)

Horstmann, C., ed., *Barlaam und Josaphat, eine Prosaversion aus MS Egerton 876 fol. 301* (Sagan, 1877)

———, 'Prosalegenden', *Anglia* 3 (1880), 293–360

———, 'Prosalegenden', *Anglia* 4 (1881), 109–38

———, 'Prosalegenden', *Anglia* 8 (1885), 102–96

———, ed., *The Three Kings of Cologne: An Early English Translation of the 'Historia Trium Regum' by John of Hildesheim*, EETS os 85 (London, 1886) [1886a]

———, 'The lyf of saint Katherin of Senis', *Archiv für das Studium der neueren Sprachen und Litteraturen* 76 (1886), 33–112, 265–314, 353–91 [1886b]

Ikegami, Keiko, ed., *Barlaam and Josaphat: A Transcription of MS Egerton 876*, AMS Studies in the Middle Ages 21 (New York, 1999)

Keiser, George R., 'Patronage and Piety in Fifteenth-Century England: Margaret, Duchess of Clarence, Symon Wynter and Beinecke MS 317', *Yale University Library Gazette* 60 (1985), 32–46

Kurvinen, Auvo, 'Caxton's *Golden Legend* and the Manuscripts of the *Gilte Legende*', *Neuphilologische Mitteilungen* 60 (1959), 353–75

———, 'The Life of St Catharine of Alexandria in Middle English Prose' (unpublished doctoral dissertation, University of Oxford, 1960)

Lester, G.A., 'Unedited Middle English Prose in Rylands Manuscripts', *Bulletin of the John Rylands Library* 68 (1985), 135–60

Lewis, Katherine J., *The Cult of St Katherine of Alexandria in Late Medieval England* (Woodbridge, 2000)

Lowry, M.J.C., 'Caxton, St Winifred and the Lady Margaret Beaufort', *The Library* 6th ser. 5 (1983), 101–17

Lucas, Peter J., *From Author to Audience: John Capgrave and Medieval Publication* (Dublin, 1997)

McIntosh, Angus, M.L. Samuels and Michael Benskin, *A Linguistic Atlas of Late Mediaeval English*, 4 vols (Aberdeen, 1986)

Meech, Sanford Brown, and Hope Emily Allen, eds, *The Book of Margery Kempe*, EETS os 212 (London, 1940)

Moore, Grace Edna, ed., *The Middle English Verse Life of Edward the Confessor* (Philadelphia, 1942)

Munro, J.J., ed., *John Capgrave's Lives of St Augustine and St Gilbert of Sempringham, and a Sermon*, EETS os 140 (London, 1910)

Nevanlinna, Saara, and Irma Taavitsainen, eds, *St Katherine of Alexandria: The Late Middle English Prose Legend in Southwell Minster MS 7* (Cambridge and Helsinki, 1993)

Pahta, Päivi, 'The Middle English Prose Legend of St Faith', *Neuphilologische Mitteilungen* 94 (1993), 149–65

Pickering, O.S., 'The *South English Legendary*: Teaching or Preaching?', *Poetica* 45 (Spring 1996), 1–14

Powell, Susan, 'Lady Margaret Beaufort and her Books', *The Library*, 6th series, 20 (1998), 197–240

———, 'Preaching at Syon Abbey', *Leeds Studies in English* ns 31 (2000), 229–67

Pronger, Winifred A., 'Thomas Gascoigne', *English Historical Review* 53 (1938), 606–26

Schaer, Frank, ed., *The Three Kings of Cologne, edited from London, Lambeth Palace MS 491*, Middle English Texts 31 (Heidelberg, 2000)

Serjeantson, Mary S., ed., *Legendys of Hooly Wummen by Osbern Bokenham*, EETS os 206 (London, 1938)

Skeat, Walter W., ed., *Joseph of Arimathie*, EETS os 44 (London, 1871)

Tracy, Larissa, 'British Library MS Harley 630: Saint Alban's and Lydgate', *Journal of the Early Book Society* 3 (2000), 36–58

Turville-Petre, Thorlac, 'A Middle English Life of St Zita', *Nottingham Medieval Studies* 35 (1991), 102–05

Voigts, Linda Ehrsam, *A Handlist of Middle English in Harvard Manuscripts*, special issue of *Harvard Library Bulletin* 33: 1 (Winter, 1985)

Waters, Claire, 'Symon Wynter, *The Life of St. Jerome*', in *Cultures of Piety: Medieval English Devotional Literature in Translation*, ed. Anne Clark Bartlett and Thomas H. Bestul (Ithaca and London, 1999), pp. 141–63 and 232–49

———, ed., *The Lives of St Katherine of Alexandria, St Jerome, St John the Baptist and St John the Evangelist*, Middle English Texts, forthcoming

Webber, T., and A.G. Watson, eds, *The Libraries of the Augustinian Canons*, Corpus of British Medieval Library Catalogues 6 (London, 1998)

Wilson, Edward, 'A Middle English Manuscript at Coughton Court, Warwickshire, and British Library MS Harley 4012', *Notes and Queries* 222 (1977), 295–303

Wolpers, Theodor, *Die englische Heiligenlegende des Mittelalters* (Tübingen, 1964)

Workman, Samuel K., *Fifteenth Century Translation as an Influence on English Prose* (Princeton, 1940)

Zupitza, Julius, 'Das Leben der heiligen Maria Magdalena in me. Prosa aus einer Handschrift der Kathedral-Bibliothek zu Durham' [*recte* Durham University Library], *Archiv für das Studium der neueren Sprachen und Litteraturen* 91 (1893), 207–24

Individual Texts or Collections

1. The Three Kings of Cologne
Main version: 21 MSS, comprising one unabridged text (Durham Cathedral Library, Hunter 15, part 2, unedited) and three separate recensions of an abridgement, ed. from CUL, Ee.4.32, fols 1–23v, and BL Royal 18.A.x, fols 87–119, in Horstmann 1886a. *Manual* 2, 631. *IPMEP* 290, with additions and corrections in *IMEP* XII, 10. Printed by Wynkyn de Worde in [1496], [c. 1499], 1511, and 1526 (*STC* 5572–75). Minor version: Lambeth Palace 491, fols 228–274v (ed. Schaer 2000), and San Marino, Huntington Library HM 114, fols 190v–192v (an excerpt). See also Gerould 1916a, 282–83, Wolpers 1964, 402–03, and, for the translational style, Workman 1940, 151–52.

2. Anthony the Hermit
2 MSS: BL Royal 17.C.xvii, fols 124v–133 (ed. Horstmann 1881), and Cambridge, Trinity College R.3.21, fols 257–273. *Manual* 2, 567–68. *IPMEP* 68. See also Gerould 1916a, 283, and Wolpers 1964, 403–04, where a passage illustrating the style is quoted.

3. John the Baptist and John the Evangelist (double life)
1 MS: Cambridge, St John's College N.16, fols 1–44 (ed. Waters, forthcoming). *Manual* 2, 594–95.

4. Jerome (by Simon Wynter)
4 MSS: Cambridge, St John's College N.17, fols 1–35v (ed. Waters, forthcoming; selections ed. Waters 1999, 232–49); Lambeth Palace 72, fols 188v–202 (ed. Hamer and Russell 2000, 321–65), where it is inserted into the *Gilte Legende* (see below); Lambeth Palace 432, fols 1–37 (ed. Horstmann 1880, 328–60); and Yale UL, Beinecke Library 317, fols 5–20. *Manual* 2, 593–94. *IPMEP* 567. Printed by Wynkyn de Worde in 1499?, without the prologue (*STC* 14508). See also Keiser 1985, 38–41, Görlach 1998, 80–81, and, for the translational style, Workman 1940, 154–56.

5. Katherine of Alexandria
Five versions, classified, with details of MSS, in Nevanlinna and Taavitsainen 1993, xi–xii, building on the pioneering work of Kurvinen 1960. Version (a), 6 MSS, ed. from Oxford, Corpus Christi College 237, fols 1–12, in Kurvinen 1960, 221–343, odd numbers. Version (b), 13 MSS (including 10 *Gilte Legende* MSS, for which see below), ed. from Stonyhurst Archives, XLIII, fols 1–20v, in Kurvinen 1960, 220–342, even numbers. Version (c), 1 MS, BL Harley 4012, fols 115–123v, unedited. Version (d), 3 MSS: BL Add. 35510, fols 1–68v; Cambridge, Gonville and Caius College 390/610, fols 56v–82v; and Harvard UL, Richardson 44, fols 2–125 (ed. Gibbs 1884 and Waters, forthcoming). Composite version, 1 MS, Southwell Cathedral 7, fols 175–89 (ed. Nevanlinna and Taavitsainen 1993). *Manual* 2, 601–02. *IPMEP* 28, and cf. *IPMEP* 727, which records a fragment of a printed text (Pynson? 1510? not in *STC*), based on version (b). See also Lewis 2000, *passim*.

6. Dorothy
Three versions, distinguished in Hamer and Russell 2000, xvi. (1) Early fifteenth-century version, 4 MSS, BL Royal 2.A.xviii, fols 236v–240v (ed. Hamer and Russell 2000, 233–40); CUL, Ll.v.18, fols 25–28v; Lambeth Palace 432, fols 90–93v (ed. Horstmann 1880, 325–28); and Manchester, Chetham's Library 8009, fols 1–2v (ed. Axon 1901). (2) Revised version of (1) added to three MSS of the *Gilte Legende*: see below. (3) Variant version: 2 MSS, Bodleian Library, Eng. th. e.17, fols 1–6v (defective at beginning), and Dublin, Trinity College 319, fols 2v–4v, 15–16v (ed. Hamer and Russell 2000, 241–49). *Manual* 2, 579–80. *IPMEP* 696. See also Görlach 1998, 93–97.

7. Barbara
2 MSS: Durham UL, Cosin V.iv.4, fols 1–78, and Lambeth Palace 72, fols 251–285v (ed. Hamer and Russell 2000, 381–470), where it is inserted into the *Gilte Legende* (see below). *Manual* 2, 569. See also Görlach 1998, 80.

8. Bridget
Principal version printed in 1516 by Richard Pynson as an appendix to *The Kalendre of the Newe Legende of Englande*, for which see below; ed. Blunt 1873, xlvii–lix. *STC* 4602, part 2. Formerly attributed to Thomas Gascoigne (1403–58), benefactor of Syon Abbey and Chancellor of Oxford University in 1444–45, who is known to have written a vernacular life of Bridget for the community at Syon, but the 1516 text does not correspond to information about its contents supplied by Gascoigne (Pronger 1938, 625). Gerould, in praising Pynson's text as 'one of the best pieces of prose translation from its time', remarks on the similarity of style and language with the Jerome now attributed to

Simon Wynter (Gerould 1916a, 288). A shorter life of Bridget, translated from Archbishop Gregersson's *Officium Sanctae Birgittae*, is in BL Cotton Claudius B.i, fols 1–3v
(ed. Ellis 1987, 1–5), and a brief account is in BL Cotton Julius F.ii, fol. 254. *Manual 2*,
573–74. *IPMEP* 576.

9. The Gilte Legende
In its original form, a collection comprising 178 lives, or other items, subsequently
supplemented with additional lives. Unedited as a whole. For a conspectus of the occurrence of individual legends in the different MSS, see Kurvinen 1960, 128–37, Hamer
1978, 8–11, and (selectively) Görlach 1998, 12–13. *Manual 2*, 432–36, 559–60, and, for
references to individual lives, 561–635. See also Gerould 1916a, 195–97; Wolpers 1964,
373–83; and Görlach 1998, 71–145.

Original version: 8 principal MSS, in various states of completeness (those also
containing additional lives, for which see item 10 below, are here marked *): BL Add.
11565*, fols 34–214v; BL Add. 35298* (indexed in detail in Kurvinen 1959, 358–63);
BL Egerton 876; BL Harley 630; BL Harley 4775; Bodleian Library, Douce 372; Gloucester Cathedral 12 (contains only the first half of the collection); and Lambeth Palace
72* (indexed in detail in *IMEP* XIII, 3–13). 3 MSS contain selections: Cambridge,
Corpus Christi College 142, fols 93–107v; Cambridge, Trinity College O.9.1, fols
1v–48v (indexed in detail in *IMEP* XI, 136–37); and Dublin, Trinity College, 319. For
evidence of another MS, also containing additional lives, of which only part of the table
of contents now survives (in Paris, BN, nouv. acq. lat. 3175), see Görlach 1998, 83–84
and Hamer and Russell 2000, xvii–xviii.

Individual lives from the original version, circulating separately, survive in Durham
UL, Cosin V.ii.14, fols 106–111v (Mary Magdalene), and Lambeth Palace 306, fols
127–131v (Eustace). Two fragments of Silvester survive separately, in Indiana University, Lilly Library, Poole 84, and Tokyo, Takamiya 45.17. The *Gilte Legende*'s text of
Katherine – extant in 10 MSS, all except Gloucester Cathedral 12 – is version (b) of item
5 above, which survives also in 3 non-*Gilte Legende* MSS.

For editions of lives from the original version, see Horstmann 1877 and Ikegami 1999
(Barlaam and Josaphat, from Egerton 876, fols 296–301v); Zupitza 1893 (Mary Magda-
lene, from Durham UL, Cosin V.ii.14, as above); Blake 1972, 151–63 (the Finding of the
Cross, from BL Add. 35298, fols 40–41); and Hamer 1978 (Nicholas, George, and
Bartholomew, from Egerton 876, fols 4–6v (supplemented from Harley 630, fols 3v–4),
87v–89v, and 198v–201, respectively). A partial edition of Christopher from Lambeth
Palace 72, fol. 184, appears in Gray 1985, 105–07.

10. The Gilte Legende: Additional lives
A group of 21 additional lives, mostly of English saints, is inserted in varying arrangements and degrees of completeness into three of the main *Gilte Legende* MSS, namely
BL Add. 11565, BL Add. 35298, and Lambeth Palace 72. Six of the group occur as part
of an appendix to a fourth, non-*Gilte Legende* MS, Southwell Cathedral 7. For full
details, and an edition of all 21 lives, see Hamer and Russell 2000. The lives of Edmund
of Abingdon, Bride, Edmund king and martyr, Frideswide, Edward king and martyr,
Alphege, Augustine of Canterbury, and Oswald are ed. there from Add. 35298; those of
Dunstan, Aldhelm, Theophilus, Swithun, Kenelm, Chad, Cuthbert, Faith, Dorothy,
Leger, and Brendan from Add. 11565; and those of Michael and Thomas of Canterbury
from Lambeth Palace 72. All the lives except that of Dorothy, for which see item 6
above, are derived to a greater or lesser extent from the corresponding *SEL* lives, from
which they have been deversified. Twelve of the additional lives were also taken into
Caxton's *Golden Legend* (see below).

For editions of additional lives, see Blake 1972, 163–73 (Edmund of Abingdon, from BL Add. 35298, fols 73–74v), and Pahta 1993 (Faith, from Southwell Cathedral 7, fols 201–02). A partial edition of Brendan from Lambeth Palace 72, fol. 203, appears in Gray 1985, 102–05.

Besides this shared group of additional lives Lambeth Palace 72 alone inserts Simon Wynter's Jerome (item 4 above) in place of the normal *Gilte Legende* Jerome, a life of Barbara (item 7 above), and the *Three Kings of Cologne* (item 1 above). It also has its own, longer version of Augustine of Canterbury (fols 208–12v), different from the *SEL*-derived additional life found in BL Add. 35298; this longer version, which is taken into Caxton's *Golden Legend*, is ed. Hamer and Russell 2000, 367–80 (see Görlach 1998, 105 for speculation about its possible independent existence). Along with certain other treatises BL Add. 35298 alone inserts Edward the Confessor (fols 48–53), Winifred (fol. 53), and Erkenwald (fols 53–57), which are ed. Hamer and Russell 2000, 1–38, 39–43, and 45–72. Its Edward the Confessor, which is *IPMEP* 357, is also ed. Moore 1942, 75–106. It was printed by Wynkyn de Worde in 1523 (*STC* 7500).

11. Augustine of Hippo (by John Capgrave)
1 MS: BL Add. MS 36704, fols 5–45 (ed. Munro 1910, 1–60). *Manual* 2, 569 (where the reference to Cotton Vitellius D.xiv should be omittted). *IPMEP* 7. For a literary assessment see Wolpers 1964, 404–08.

12. Gilbert of Sempringham (by John Capgrave)
1 principal MS: BL Add. MS 36704, fols 46–116 (ed. Munro 1910, 61–142). Small fragments also survive as fols 29–35 of what remains of BL Cotton Vitellius D.xv. *Manual* 2, 590. *IPMEP* 771.

13. Elizabeth of Spalbeck
1 MS: Bodleian Library, Douce 114, fols 1–12 (ed. Horstmann 1885, 107–18). *Manual* 2, 582. *IPMEP* 78. *IMEP* IV, 39–40. See also Gerould 1916b, and, for the translational style, Workman 1940, 76–78 and 91–92.

14. Christina the Marvellous
1 MS: Bodleian Library, Douce 114, fols 12–26v (ed. Horstmann 1885, 119–34). *Manual* 2, 576. *IPMEP* 808. *IMEP* IV, 40–41.

15. Mary of Oignies
1 MS: Bodleian Library, Douce 114, fols 26v–76 (ed. Horstmann 1885, 134–84). *Manual* 2, 611–12. *IPMEP* 853. *IMEP* IV, 41. For the translational style, see Workman 1940, 104, 133–34, and 156–57.

16. Katherine of Siena
2 independent versions, translated from different sources. (1) 1 MS: Bodleian Library, Douce 114, fols 76–89v (ed. Horstmann 1885, 184–95), from a Latin letter by Stephen of Siena. *Manual* 2, 602. *IPMEP* 121. *IMEP* IV, 41–42. For the translational style, see Workman 1940, 114–16. (2) Printed by Wynkyn de Worde (but with Caxton's device), c. 1493 (ed. Horstmann 1886b), from the Latin life by Raymond of Capua. *Manual* 2, 602, *IPMEP* 96, *STC* 24766, part 1. Reissued by de Worde, c. 1500, with certain pages reset (*STC* 24766.3). For the translational style, see Workman 1940, 24–28, 102–03, 110–13, 135, 138–42, and 159–60.

17. The lyves and dethes of the martyres
1 MS: CUL, Add. 2604, fols 1–132. Certain leaves are missing, rendering some of the lives (here marked *) imperfect. The saints included, in order, are: John the Baptist, John the Evangelist, Columba of Sens, Agatha*, Cecilia*, Barbara, Etheldreda, Sexburga, Ermenilda, Werburga, Erkengood (and Ethelburga), Withburga, Edith of Wilton, Edburga, Enswida*, Hilda*, Martha, Domitilla, Justina*, Benedicta*, Modwenna, and Leonard. For a brief account of the manuscript, see *British Literary Manuscripts from Cambridge University Library. Series One: The Medieval Age, c. 1150–1500. An Inventory to Parts One, Two and Three of the Harvester Microform Collection* (Brighton, 1984), p. 26.

18. Edward the Confessor
1 MS: Trinity College, Oxford, 11, fols 1–51v (ed. Moore 1942, 108–30). *Manual* 2, 581. *IPMEP* 577. *IMEP* VIII, 95. For a refutation of Moore's argument (1942, lxiii–lxxi) that this version was the source of the *SEL* life of Edward, see Görlach 1974, 135 and n. 22, and Görlach 1998, 128. An unrelated prose 'narracio' from St Edward's life occurs in CUL, Ii.4.9, fols 94–95 (ed. Moore 1942, 132–33; *IPMEP* 803). See also the separate text of Edward the Confessor noticed under item 10 above.

19. Ursula
2 MSS: San Marino, Huntington Library, HM 140, fols 154–155v (ed. Garmonsway and Raymo 1958), and Southwell Cathedral 7, fols 172–174v. *Manual* 2, 632. *IPMEP* 719. *IMEP* 1, 15 and *IMEP* XV, 54–55. See also Görlach 1973 and Görlach 1998, 86. This life is different from the standard *Gilte Legende* life of Ursula.

20. Zita
1 MS fragment: Nottingham University Library, Middleton Mi LM 37, fol. 1 (ed. Turville-Petre 1991). *IMEP* XV, 48–49.

21. Audry
1 MS: Corpus Christi College, Oxford, 120, fols 1–14. *IMEP* VIII, 19. Not in *Manual*, Unedited.

22. Margaret
Two versions, one in BL Harley 4012, fols 124–30, the other (fragmentary) in Bodleian Library, Eng. th. e.18, fols 1–19 (*IMEP* XII, 12). Neither is listed in *Manual*, and they remain unedited; both differ from the standard *Gilte Legende* life of Margaret. According to *IMEP*, Eng. th. e.18 and Eng. th. e.17, which contains a variant version of Dorothy (see item 6 above), once formed part of the same manuscript.

23. Joseph of Arimathea
Printed by Wynkyn de Worde, [1511?] (ed. Skeat 1871, 27–32). *Manual* 2, 596, *IPMEP* 228, *STC* 14806.

24. Francis of Assisi
Printed by Richard Pynson, [1515?]. *Manual* 2, 588, *IPMEP* 523, *STC* 3270.

25. Nicholas of Tollentino
Printed by Wynkyn de Worde, [1525?]. *Manual* 2, 615, *IPMEP* 737, *STC* 18528 (and 18528.5).

26. Winifred (by William Caxton)
Printed by Caxton, [1484] (ed. Horstmann 1880, 295–313). *Manual* 2, 634, *IPMEP* 382, *STC* 25853. See also Gerould 1916a, 291. Horstmann bases his edition on the copy of Caxton's edition bound into Lambeth Palace Library MS 306 as fols 188–201. For a separate life of Winifred, see item 10 above.

27. The Golden Legend (by William Caxton)
Printed by Caxton in 1483 (ed. Ellis 1892), with subsequent editions by Caxton (1487), Wynkyn de Worde (1493–1527), and Julian Notary (1503). *Manual* 2, 436–39, 560–61, and, for references to individual lives, 561–635. *IPMEP* 682, *STC* 24873–80. See also Wolpers 1964, 383–402 (especially for appreciations of prose style), Blake 1969, 117–23 and *passim*, Hamer 1978, 24–26, and Görlach 1998 (which includes a summary history of scholarship, pp. 72–74). The lives of Barbara and Brendan were reprinted separately, by Julian Notary in 1518 (*STC* 1375) and Wynkyn de Worde, c. 1520 (*STC* 3600). Short excerpts, including Caxton's prologue and epilogue, are printed in Blake 1973a, 88–96. The legend of Ursula and the 11,000 Virgins is ed. in Blake 1973b, 105–10.

28. Vitas Patrum (by William Caxton)
Printed (and with an epilogue) by Wynkyn de Worde, 1495. *Manual* 2, 426–29, 559, *IPMEP* 222, 759, *STC* 14507. See also Görlach 1998, 146–48.

29. The Kalendre of the Newe Legende of Englande
Printed by Richard Pynson, 1516 (ed. Görlach 1994). *IPMEP* 570, *STC* 4602, part 1. Görlach's introduction includes a full discussion of the collection's antecedents and printing history. See also Görlach 1998, 148–53.

16

Reginald Pecock and John Fortescue

JAMES SIMPSON

Bishop Reginald Pecock (?1395–?1460) and Sir John Fortescue (?1395–?1477), almost exact contemporaries, wrote in the almost entirely different fields of theology and political theory respectively. Despite this large difference, they are remarkably similar in this respect: both transmitted scholastic Latin learning of high technical refinement, in English vernacular prose, to mid-fifteenth-century readers. Pecock's enterprise was more personally dangerous, and his achievement was largely, though not, as we shall see, entirely lost from view until the systematic recovery of late medieval texts, from the last half of the nineteenth century. Fortescue's Lancastrian affiliations were not without their own dangers, but he survived the transition to Yorkist rule, and his works have never been ignored by English political theorists. Whereas earlier prose writers in English had transmitted large bodies of information from the late fourteenth century in particular, Pecock and Fortescue both transmitted rational argument, in whose logic vernacular readers were actively encouraged to participate. Fortescue made such participation possible through the lucidity of his prose style; Pecock's theoretical aim of lay instruction was, by contrast, defeated in part by the complex severity of his style.

Reginald Pecock

Born in the diocese of St David's, Wales, and educated in Oxford, Pecock was elected Fellow of Oriel College Oxford in 1414.[1] He was ordained priest in 1421, and in 1431 was appointed to the Mastership of Whittington College in the Vintry, London. In 1444 he became Bishop of Asaph, Wales; in the following year he received the degree of Doctor of Theology. In 1450 he became Bishop of Chichester. Pecock seems not to have been a resident bishop, and to have remained in London, where he formed part of powerful clerical and commercial networks, including strong contacts with John Carpenter, Common Clerk of London 1417–38 (Scase 1992). In 1447 he first came to notice as a controversialist, when he preached a sermon vigorously defending both his absenteeism and his failure to preach in his own diocese. Pecock's views

I thank Mishtooni Bose, Tony Edwards and Sarah James for help of various kinds with this chapter.
[1] All biographical reference here is dependent on Scase 1996.

became a real *cause celebre*, however, only in 1456–57. In 1456 he was reported to the king by the Mayor of London for suspect theological views, and Viscount Beaumont urged action against Pecock in a letter of June 1457. Pecock was arraigned for heresy towards the end of an especially unstable decade: London and its surrounds had been subject to popular rebellion in 1450; England lost its last French possessions in 1453; and the first battle of the civil wars known as the Wars of the Roses took place at St Albans in 1455. Pecock seems almost certainly to have been the victim of Lancastrian, not Yorkist influence, and primarily of temporal, not ecclesiastical pressure. By way of encouraging Henry VI to take action against Pecock, Beaumont's letter made specific reference to the one celebrated Lancastrian king, Henry V, as having begun his reign with 'mighti punischyng and suppressyng of enemies of the feith and Chirche, and after all his dayes had victoryes of his enemies and did gret thynges' (Scase 1996, 121, and Catto 1995).

The motive of bolstering Lancastrian rule by the selection of a victim seems to be behind the concerted campaign against Pecock.[2] He was convoked before Council in late 1457 for heresy, which he recanted. Despite being reinstated to his bishopric, pressure from Henry VI ensured that Pecock was unable to resume his episcopal functions. He was sent to Thorney Abbey, Cambridgeshire, where he was confined to one room and deprived of writing materials until death. Whereas Henry V had persecuted the Lollards as the evident and self-declared opponents of orthodoxy, his son persecuted Pecock as the self-declared champion of orthodoxy against the Lollards.

Six works survive; all are in English: *The Reule of Crysten Religioun* (c. 1443); *The Donet* (c. 1443–49); *The Repressor of Overmuch Blaming of the Clergy* (c. 1449); *The Poor Mennis Myrrour; The Folewer to the Donet* (c. 1453–54); *The Book of Faith* (1456). None seems to have been published before 1454 (Ball, 231). This is certainly a very small proportion of Pecock's whole production: in Pecock's obsessively self-referential writing he frequently refers to very many other works he has written, or is in the process of writing, either in Latin or English.[3] The public burning of his writings ordered by the council of bishops in December 1457 surely destroyed some works, and more would have been destroyed in the nationwide search for Pecock's writings ordered by the Archbishop of Canterbury in March 1458.

The fact that the surviving works exist in single, sometimes incomplete manuscripts attests to the effectiveness of the campaign against his writings. Pecock's own comments would suggest that he wanted many copies of his works to have been in circulation. He clearly wanted massive dissemination of his books: he says that books are a much more effective transmitter of knowledge than sermons, since readers can go back over them in the search for truth (*Reule,*

---

[2] For the more conservative theological motives for the persecution of Pecock, see Ball.

[3] Pecock refers his readers to the following, for example: *The Encherideoun; The Book of the Divine Office; The Book of the Eucharist; The Book of Penance* (in Latin); *The Book of Priesthood; The Book of the Sacraments* (in Latin); *The Just Apprising of Holy Scripture; The Just Apprising of the Doctors* (in Latin); *The Spreading of the Four Tables; The Book of Signs; The Book of Counsels; The Book of Lessons; The Forecrier; The Provoker; The Book of the Church; The Book of Lay Men's Books* (in Latin); *The Book of Faith* (in Latin); *The Improving of Men's Insufficient Forms.*

99); and that prelates should make it their business to have books copied at their own cost, and given, sent or lent among the lay folk (*Faith*, 117). He also made cheaper, 'lasse compendiouse' versions of his own works, such as the *Poore Mennis Myrrour*, since his main works might be 'ouer costiose to pore men' (*Donet*, 177).

In 1688 Henry Wharton published the second part of Pecock's *Book of Faith*, under the title *A Treatise Proving Scripture to be the Rule of Faith*.[4] This was the one of the two works of Pecock published between his death in (?)1460 and the first modern edition of his works in 1860.[5] Wharton's purpose was to use Pecock as grist for a Protestant mill of proving that most pre-Reformation Catholic thinkers conceived of Scripture as existing prior to the Church. In his preface Wharton says the following: that we must believe that Pecock's views on the priority of Scripture were the general view of the Catholic Church, since he was a pre-Reformation bishop; that if we did not believe that this was the general view, then we would be obliged to posit, absurdly, that Pecock was a Lollard; and that there was clearly no opposition to Pecock's views on Scripture, since those who did attack Pecock did not mention those particular views.

Wharton was correct in thinking that Pecock was not a Lollard, but wrong in these respects: that Pecock had nothing in common with the Lollards; that Pecock's views on Scripture were representative; and that Pecock's views on Scripture as expressed in the *Book of Faith* were consistent with the rest of Pecock's writings on the matter. He was, furthermore, probably wrong in thinking that, just because Pecock was not arraigned for his views on Scripture, his views on that matter were unexceptionable. I point out Wharton's errors not to deride his serious scholarship within the resources available to him in 1688, but rather to underline just how easy it is to go astray in using Pecock as exemplary of any larger theological stance. It is also easy to go wrong in assuming that a given position articulated by Pecock is consistent with his *oeuvre* as a whole. Pecock himself warns against holding him to utter consistency: 'Also I proteste þat y take and schal take ech argument or mocioun maad . . . bi me in eny of my writynges . . . as for argument or mocioun oonli, and not for a proof vttirli' (*Folewer*, 6). Pecock is not ordinary or representative; he is extraordinary for his profound, unflinching, and occasionally exasperating commitment to the exercise of human reason, and all that follows from such a commitment.

Scholarship on Pecock has, for the most part, focussed primarily on his trial, and secondarily on what seems to stand behind the trial: Pecock's having adopted 'heretical' practices and positions in his fight against Lollards. This kind of attention is understandable, but it distorts Pecock's much larger enterprise in two ways. In the first place, the heretical charges against Pecock were drawn wholly from what appears to be Pecock's final work, the *Book of Faith* (Patrouch, 30–35), which is unrepresentative of his *oeuvre*. Secondly, Pecock's enterprise as a whole is much more ambitious than his attempt to win Lollards back to the orthodox fold. Certainly his positions in the *Book of Faith* are

---

4   For Wharton's edition, see Douglas, chapter 7, at pp. 142–43.
5   The other example being Foxe 1554.

striking (particularly his rejection of the authority of the article in the Apostles' Creed concerning Christ's descent into Hell); and certainly he did devote enormous energy to persuading Lollards that their positions were wrong. These features of Pecock's work are, however, only a small part of a larger enterprise.

The existence of Lollardy might have triggered Pecock's vernacular theology, but it did not at all constrain it. On the contrary, he quickly developed much greater ambitions. We can see the scope of that ambition in the *Reule*, the work of Pecock from which all the other surviving works flow, except the *Repressor* and *The Book of Faith*. He begins the *Reule* by saying that he wrote it and the other books pertaining to it in English in order to convert two kinds of reader (presumably a distinction between two kinds of Lollard): those lay readers who rely solely on the New Testament at the cost of interest in any other books; and those readers who do admit other works beyond the New Testament, but unspecified works that teach 'vnseemely, vnformaly, rudely, boistoseli, vnsufficiently, suspectly' (*Reule*, 18). By the end of this huge work the scope of the desired audience has undergone massive enlargement: Pecock says that the work will of necessity convert not only any Christian who reads it, but also any Jew or 'heþen' (*Reule*, 428). *En route* he has provided both a *summa theologiae* and a practical rule of sorts for the entirety of English society, lay and ecclesiastical.

The work was conceived as seven treatises; four and an unfinished fifth survive. They treat the following matters: the existence of God as proved by reason, and the existence of the Trinity as proved by revelation; God's rewards and punishments, including a proof of the immortality of the soul; ethical governance, divided into four tables, which determine appropriate mutual interaction for each category of inferior and superior, both lay and ecclesiastical; the importance of the moral virtues; the active and contemplative lives.

It may be that the material of this work is silently determined by Pecock's address to Lollards. He usually describes Lollards with respect, using the terms 'Lollard' and 'heretic' with the greatest reluctance, preferring the phrase 'the lay party' instead. He also restricts himself to topics that were not sources of contention between the orthodox and Lollards: belief in the Trinity; in the immortality of the soul; soteriology (doctrine pertinent to salvation); and ethics.[6] The fact of writing sometimes severely scholastic theology in English is itself a sign of serious engagement with Lollards. So too are the moments of clear agreement between Pecock and well-attested Lollard views. He agrees, for example, with Lollard condemnation of excessive ornamentation of churches at the expense of the poor (*Reule* 245–46); and of the impenetrability of Latin liturgy (*Reule*, 404–6). By the same token, Pecock's almost total avoidance of discussion of the sacraments suggests that he was trying to affirm agreement in central and profound matters, and to avoid ineluctable difference. Reflection on the Trinity, he says, is more fruitful than lay reflection on the Eucharist (*Reule* 95); the sacraments will be treated elsewhere, in Latin (*Reule*, 248); and besides, priests do nothing miraculous in the Eucharist, only God does (*Reule*, 312–13).

All that implies the silent, shaping presence of implicit dialogue between

---

6   For the engagement with Lollardy, see Bose.

Pecock and the 'lay party', which is what we might expect thirty or so years after the height of official persecution of Lollards. That point should not disguise the fact that Pecock's range of concern is very much wider. He instructs princes, for example, not to tax without the consent of subjects (*Reule*, 337); husbands and wives on how to relate sexually to each other (*Reule*, 341–61); children, apprentices, parishioners, and the religious as to how they should relate to their superiors. In the *Folewer* he advocates a new morality in the treatment of animals (*Folewer*, 181). Such views became increasingly unorthodox: he claims effectively to be a Moses to the contemporary Christian, replacing the Decalogue with his own ethical system (*Reule*, 365–66).

The historical tradition that most powerfully explains Pecock's enterprise is not the fight against Lollardy; it is, rather, the long attempt to instruct the laity in the basics of the faith, through the vernacular, that is usually dated to the Fourth Lateran Council of 1215. Pecock's vernacular works marked a new and extraordinary step in that programme, by offering often undiluted academic theology to a vernacular audience. The most remarkable aspect of this programme is Pecock's increasingly explicit defence of reason. By following reason, he says, he is not writing 'of myn owen heed', without any pre-existing authority. He writes instead from 'þe largist book of autorite þat euer god made, which is þe doom of reason, and also bi þe grettist doctour þat is a þis side god him silf, which is reason'. The books of 'vttrist ground' and deepest authority are the Bible and what Pecock metaphorically terms the 'book of reasons doom' (*Folewer*, 9–10).[7]

Pecock's confidence in the authority of the book of reason both promoted and did away with the very idea of the book. It promoted the idea of the book by preserving the metaphor for reason as a 'book'; it did away with much written authority by appealing to fresh consultation of the book of reason. Pecock promised, indeed, to replace an entire programme of lay instruction in the vernacular with his own, freshly conceived and systematically ordered works: apart from Scripture, he says, the reader seeking spiritual edification needs only Pecock's own books. The reader shall have 'riȝt sufficient and riȝt cleere knowing of god and of vs silf' from these books. Such doctrines 'can not so esili be leerned in oþer bokes . . . as þei schal be found in þis book (*Reule*, 9). If some Lollards, by Pecock's account, wished to ignore all books but the New Testament (*Reule*, 17), Pecock wanted his own books to replace everything except Scripture. He elsewhere promised to show how all other moral treatises are inadequate, by writing a book called *The Improving of Men's Insufficient Forms* (*Donet*, 81).

All Pecock's surviving works except the *Repressor* and *the Book of Faith* were conceived as a single programme. He says himself that his apparently completed books could not be regarded as finished until the whole sequence was completed: 'I maad my cours fro book to book þat ech of hem myȝte helpe þe oþer to be maad' (*Reule*, 22). Writing across the fraught clerical/lay boundary, Pecock was acutely sensitive both to the need for a graded sequence of works, and for different versions of the same work for differently equipped audiences.

---

7 For Pecock's conception of reason, see Landman.

Overall, he conceived of the works for the laity as a connected sequence deriving from the *Reule*, rather in the manner of an extended house, 'as chaumbris, parlouris and manye housis of officis answeren and cleeven to þe cheef halle for to make of alle hem . . . oon formal, oon semely, beuteful, esiful and confortable habitacioun' (*Reule*, 22). Within that structure, readers will progress from easier to more demanding material. Accordingly Pecock, changing the metaphor, describes his own task of teaching readers in graded steps in the manner of a painter applying preliminary layers of paint in order to bring out the maximum beauty of subsequent layers (*Reule*, 367). It may be, however, that some readers have absolute limits. The *Folewer*, for example, properly describes itself as a more advanced version of the *Donet*; that earlier book will suffice entirely, however, for 'symple men and wymmen of witt þat þei neuer schulen mowe leerne þis present book, and to children' (*Folewer*, 2).

By following through the consequences of his confidence in reason, Pecock offered vernacular readers material to which that category of reader had never had access. He offered, that is, university ontological, soteriological, psychological and ethical learning of much greater refinement and consistency than had previously been available in the vernacular. Neither did he simply present them in encyclopaedic form. On the contrary, in the manner of a *summa*, the rational or textual grounds for each position are clarified. Pecock thereby offered the formal methods for thinking systematically about the subject he treated. In many works he outlines the irrefutable logic of the syllogism and its kinds; were syllogistic thinking 'leerned of al the comon peple in her modiris langage . . . thei shulden therbi be putt fro myche rydnes and boistosnes which thei han now in resonyng' (*Repressor*, 9). And neither are these forms of learning added extras: understanding of moral philosophy, wholly derived from reason without any necessary reference to revealed sources, is, Pecock goes almost so far as to say, indispensable for salvation (*Repressor*, 43–44).

The formal quality of Pecock's prose, wholly argumentative as it is, flows coherently from his persuasion that the laity should be taught syllogistic argument.[8] He certainly had no time for 'the fablis of poetis' (*Reule*, 32); those of his works that are presented in dialogue form (i.e. *The Donet* and *The Folewer to the Donet*) have no pretentions to fiction. Pecock wants not to explore but to persuade, or rather utterly to convince. The opening of the *Repressor* outlines the almost military quality of the campaign, in prose of unrelenting severity and precision:

> Thre trowingis or opiniouns ben causis and groundis of manie and of weel ny3 alle the errouris whiche manie of the lay partie holden, and bi which holding thei vniustly and ouermyche wijten and blamen the clergie and alle her othere nei3bouris of the lay side, which not holden tho same errouris accordingly with hem, and therefore it is miche nede forto first 3eue bisynes to vnroote and ouerturne tho three trowingis, holdingis, or opiniouns, bifore the improuyng of othere, sithen if tho thre be sufficiently improued, that is to seie, if it be sufficientli proued that tho thre ben nou3t and vntrewe and badde, alle

---

8   For discussions of Pecock's prose style, see both Gordon, pp. 67–68, and Mueller, pp. 138–47.

the othere vntrewe opiniouns and holdingis bildid vpon hem or upon eny of hem muste needis therbi take her fal, and lacke it wherbi thei miȝten in eny colour or semyng be meyntened, holde, and supportid. (*Repressor*, 5)

The metaphors at the base of this sentence are architectural, or at least structural ('groundis', 'ouerturne', 'bilded', 'fal', 'holde', 'supportid'). The sentence is itself clearly structured. It makes three steps, beginning with the declaration that three principal errors confound the lay party ('thre trowingis . . .'); it is therefore necessary to destroy the foundations of those errors ('and therefore . . .'); if that happens, all other errors founded on these three must also collapse ('sithen . . .'). While not strictly a syllogism, Pecock's favourite mode of syllogistic argument informs the tripartite structure. The aim of such a mode of demonstration is to disallow argumentative escape. The passage just cited itself takes care to block the passage of escape by predicting and explicating possible distinctions. This gives the sentence a legalistic, contractual quality, by the use of couplets or triplets ('causis and groundis'; 'meyntened, holde, and supportid'); by the use of precise distinctions ('bildid vpon hem or upon eny of hem'); and by the use of explanatory clauses ('that is to seie'). Pecock's vocabulary throughout his *oeuvre* is fundamentally Latinate; he does translate many Latin terms into English, but in such a way as to insist on their technical force, as in his adverbs, for example: 'chesingly', 'answeringli', 'needisli', 'servingli'. So sure is Pecock of the force and persuasive power of his logic that in one passage he offers to have his arm cut off if the reader, 'wole he nyle he, amagrey his heed' [in spite of all he might think], does not concede the ineluctable truth of his arguments (*Repressor*, 52).

It may already be clear why Pecock was vulnerable: his praise and practice of reason throughout his works of lay instruction sat uneasily with the official, repressive response of the fifteenth-century English Church to vernacular theology (Watson 1995). If those works exposed him to danger, the polemical works did so more obviously. Both the *Repressor* and the *Book of Faith* were explicitly addressed to 'the lay party', and designed to treat officially heretical positions with the respect of both restatement and argumentative refutation. His principal concern in the *Repressor* was with Biblical fundamentalism. The moral law is not, by Pecock's account, grounded in Scripture; on the contrary, natural reason and Scripture are adjacent discursive fields that should not interfere with each other: Scripture should 'abide withinne his owne termys and boundis, and not enter into the boundis and the riȝt of lawe of kinde; that is to say, that he not vsurpe eny grounding which longith to the faculte of lawe of kinde or of moral philosophi' (*Repressor*, 70). Once this fundamental discursive distinction has been made, Pecock goes on to point to the inadequacy of Scripture in all matters of regulating life except the tenets of faith. Scripture did not, for example, command that it be translated into Latin or English (*Repressor*, 119). In the second part he subtly defends, on the grounds of reason, the use of images and pilgrimages; in the remaining parts he defends clerical possession, degrees of rank in the Church, and religious orders. His defence of possession includes a demolition of the Donation of Constantine (*Repressor*, 350–66).

Pecock's defence of the primacy of Scripture in *The Book of Faith* was, then, at odds with his general treatment of that contentious subject across the whole of his oeuvre. Whereas the *Book of Faith* stressed the supremacy of Scripture at the expense of the Church, the *oeuvre* as a whole, and especially the *Repressor*, emphasized not only the importance of the interpretative community, but, more daringly, the irrelevance of Scripture to many aspects of ecclesiastical and lay conduct. That stress is grounded, as we have seen, on Pecock's confidence in the coherence and priority of reason. It may be that Pecock's enemies dared not to attack him for this confidence, concentrating instead on very marginal and in any case unrepresentative positions from the *Book of Faith*. Pecock's abjuration of December 1457 does, perhaps significantly, highlight the question of reason: he confesses that he has taught 'presumeng of myn owne natural witte and preferring the natural iugement of raison' above Scripture and the Church (Scase 1996, 133). But the charges themselves are silent on this, fearing perhaps that the orthodox would be made themselves to appear like fundamentalist Lollards in attacking Pecock. Whatever the motives for the precise charges, and whatever the motives for the charges in the first place, Pecock's confidence and courage made him a rather visible target for a thoroughly exhausted and fragile régime.

John Fortescue

The specific historical pressures of mid-fifteenth-century England produced in Pecock a vernacular theologian of real distinction, who drew on a tradition of scholastic writing dating especially from the mid-thirteenth century. Exactly the same can be said for Sir John Fortescue. While writing in different discursive realms, of politics and jurisprudence, Fortescue also drew on Aristotelian scholasticism to confront the radical political deficiencies of the England in which he lived, and from which he was exiled between 1461 and 1471.[9]

The first modern edition of the work now known as *On the Governance of England* was published in 1714. Its title is as follows: *The Difference between an Absolute and Limited Monarchy, as it most particularly Regards the English Constitution*. The terms of this title both specify the topic to which Fortescue is supposed to have contributed (the 'Constitution'), and imply his own desired, limited form of constitutional monarchy. Relations between a monarch and his people (as distinct from 'The Constitution') do indeed form the principal subject of Fortescue's writings, and the delicate question of Fortescue's own political disposition has dominated scholarly debate in the reception of his works.[10] The scope of his writings is, however, rather broader than this would suggest. For a start, his politics are inseparable from his comparative jurisprudence (comparing the legal systems of England and France), and his jurisprudence is itself inseparable from an account of the different material conditions and social structures

---

[9] For Fortescue's precise debts to Aquinas, see especially Gilbert.

[10] The interests of the editor of the 1714 edition are not only in political theory. His interest in the history of law leads him to Anglo-Saxon texts, and his introduction is a passionate promotion of Anglo-Saxon studies. His notes to the text are primarily philological, tracing the connections between Middle and Old English words.

of England and France. And beyond, or sometimes overlapping with his theoretical writings, Fortescue was from 1461 engaged in a very specific polemical defence of the Lancastrian dynasty against rival Yorkist claims.

The nature and sequence of the works is best understood in the light of a brief biography, which clarifies Fortescue's interests and affiliations. Born at Norris in Devon Fortescue was the son of Sir John Fortescue, who had been appointed as governor of Meaux by Henry V. He was admitted to Lincoln's Inn before 1420, becoming Governor in 1428–29, and a Serjeant-at-Law in 1430. He was twice married, in c. 1423 and c. 1436. His appointment as Chief Justice of the King's Bench came in 1442, and he was knighted in the following year. In March 1461, after the Battle of Towton and the defeat of Henry VI's forces, he fled to Scotland to join Henry VI, Margaret and Prince Edward in Edinburgh; later that year he was named in an act of attainder passed against those who had resisted Edward IV. He remained in Scotland until 1463, writing tracts in defence of the Lancastrian legitimacy. In 1463 he accompanied Margaret and Edward to France, where he wrote the *De laudibus legum Anglie* between 1468 and 1471.

While in France, Fortescue may have translated some prose works of Alain Chartier (c. 1385–1433). A fragment of a translation of a work by Chartier, *Le Traité de l'Esperance*, was attributed to Fortescue by the librarian of the Cotton library; the person who made that translation was also responsible for translations of Chartier's *Le Quadrilogue Invectif*, and *Dialogus familiaris amici et sodalis*. Certainly Chartier's laments about the state of France riven by civil war in the early fifteenth century would have been fit (and available) matter for Fortescue in France in the later fifteenth century, in flight from English civil war. The attribution is, however, far from certain.[11]

After the Battle of Tewkesbury (1471), in which Edward was killed and after which Henry VI was murdered, Fortescue submitted to Edward IV's rule. He retracted his Lancastrian allegiance, was pardoned, and presented Prince Edward with a copy of his *On the Governance of England* (c. 1471). The attainder against him was reversed. He died c. 1477, and is buried in Ebrington church, Gloucestershire.

Fortescue's works were written in both Latin and English, sometimes, apparently, both.[12] Latin may have provided a cover for dangerous sentiments in some cases,[13] but it would be arbitrary to focus on Fortescue's English works and ignore his works written in Latin, since shared interests, both political and polemical, inform works in both languages.

As with other fifteenth-century authors in England (such as Charles

---

[11] See Blayney for a very balanced account of the arguments regarding the attribution to Fortescue. For the texts of these works, see *Fifteenth-Century English Translations of Alain Chartier's* Le Traité de l'Esperance *and* Le Quadrilogue Invectif, ed. Blayney, and *A Familiar Dialogue of the Friend and the Fellow*, ed. Blayney.

[12] Thus, for example, *De titulo Edwardi Comitis Marchiae* (ed. Clermont), the original of which was, Fortescue says, written in English (p. 77).

[13] In his 'Declaration . . . upon Certayn Wrytinges', in which he changes allegiance, for example, he lays considerable stress on the fact that the *De Natura Legis Naturae* was written in Latin.

d'Orléans, Thomas Malory, and George Ashby), Fortescue wrote in enforced leisure. His first works were intensely polemical. Written from Scotland between July 1461 and July 1463, they are: *De titulo Edwardi Comitis Marchiae*; 'Of the Title of the House of York'; and *Defensio iuris domus Lancastriae*. These are short, polemically driven works designed to bolster shaky Lancastrian claims to the throne, and destroy equally fragile Yorkist claims (Gill 1971). The most significant work of this period is the Latin *De natura legis Naturae*, in which the same polemical target is no less evident and urgent, but whose means to hit that target are entirely different and very much more literary. Part II of this work is an imagined judicial deliberation, in which a judge sifts the competing claims of contestants in an imagined dynastic struggle: a king of the Assyrians has died; his brother, daughter and son each lay claim to the throne. The debate is conducted in wholly argumentative terms, with arguments proposed and carefully rebutted by each claimant, before the question is resolved, in favour of the brother, by the judge. This may seem distant from the succession question pursued so pointedly in Fortescue's other works; in fact it is directly relevant. The key question is whether or not a woman can rule, and whether the right to succeed to the throne can pass through a woman. This question is at the heart of the Yorkist position, since Edward IV based his claim on descent from Lionel, Duke of Clarence and third son of Edward III, through Lionel's daughter, Phillipa, Edward IV's great great grand-mother. Fortescue, like his contemporary John Capgrave, debates the issue of rule by a woman with great force, though finally coming down very firmly against it.[14]

The last of Fortescue's treatises on the succession question, the 'Declaration . . . upon Certayn Wrytinges', is a total recantation. Once Edward IV was the indisputable victor in 1471, Fortescue withdrew entirely from his earlier positions. As is reported by a certain 'Man of Law' at the beginning of this work, many earlier works by Fortescue 'remaynen in the handes of full euyll dysposed people that pryvely rowne and reden theym to the kynges dyshonour'.[15] 'Fortescue' (the work is set as a private dialogue) extricates himself from his earlier works by a series of deft manoeuvres. In particular, the actual copies of the works in question are said to be unavailable, since the 'Man of Law' has not brought them with him. Working conveniently from memory, Fortescue repudiates most of the charges against him as inaccurate accounts of what he actually said. The only serious point he acknowledges is his earlier denial of the possibility of inheriting a title to rule through a woman. Fortescue says that he does not want now to repudiate this argument, since denial would 'sown so lyke dowbleness'. Not at all, the lawyer rejoins, merely the normal scholastic practice of arguing *pro* and *contra*.[16] At this point Fortescue exercises an evident casuistry to contradict his earlier position.

Part I of the *De natura legis Naturae* takes a very much broader view of the

---

[14] For Capgrave's equally forceful debate, see his *Life of St Katharine of Alexandria* (c. 1445), book 2.
[15] 'Declaration . . . upon Certayn Wrytinges', ed. Clermont, p. 523.
[16] 'Declaration . . . upon Certayn Wrytinges', ed. Clermont, p. 532.

succession question, by situating it within the terms of the law of Nature itself, which Fortescue defines as 'nothing else than the participation of eternal law in a rational creature'.[17] In this discussion Fortescue first develops his distinction of polities: the regal, the political and a third category, the *'dominium regale et politicum'*.[18] This political theory stands at the centre of the two works for which Fortescue is best known: the *De laudibus legum Anglie*, written in Latin, and the vernacular *On the Governance of England* (also known as the *Monarchia*), which was possibly written for Edward IV.[19] The Latin text is written as a dialogue between Fortescue as Henry VI's Chancellor in exile, and Henry VI's son Prince Edward; the *Governance* is pure exposition, with no pretention to fictional structure.

The central doctrine for which these works have become celebrated is stated at the beginning of *On the Governance of England*:

> Ther bith ii kyndes of kyngdomes, of the wich that on is a lordship callid in laten *dominium regale*, and that other is callid *dominium politicum et regale*. And thai diuersen in that the first kynge mey rule his peple bi suche lawes as he makyth hym self. And therfore he mey sett vppon thaim tayles [taxes] and other imposicions, such as he wol hym self, withowt thair assent. The secounde kynge may not rule his peple bi other lawes than such as thai assenten unto.[20]

The same ideas are found in the *De laudibus legum Anglie*.[21] On the face of it, this statement looks strikingly like a theory of constitutionally limited monarchy. Certainly Fortescue was welcomed and deployed by defenders of Parliament in the struggles of the seventeenth century, who had access to the *De laudibus*, first printed as it was in 1543, and available in translation in editions of 1567, 1573, 1599, 1616, and 1660.[22] A Whig tradition, culminating in the triumphalist constitutionalism of the late nineteenth century, saw Fortescue as a critical forerunner of the divided powers of constitutional monarchy. For Plummer, Fortescue's editor in the 1880s, the *Governance of England* is 'the earliest constitutional treatise written in the English language'.[23]

Twentieth-century historians of England have been in flight from that late nineteenth-century retrospective constitutionalist colouring of English history (Carpenter 1995). The first voice raised against Fortescue as constitutionalist was that of Fortescue's next editor, S.B. Chrimes, who described Fortescue as a 'ready prey for constitutional controversialists and liberal sentimentalists'. So far from being the precursor of Locke, Fortescue rather foreshadowed Hobbes (Chrimes 1936, 319). By this estimation, Fortescue gave no theoretical account

---

17 *De natura legis Naturae*, ed. Clermont, I.5, p. 194.

18 See in particular, *De natura legis Naturae*, I.16. For a larger account of the relation of this treatise to the succession question, see Litzen, pp. 29–39.

19 For the argument that Edward IV was the intended recipient, see Plummer, p. 94.

20 *On the Governance of England*, ed. Plummer, p. 109.

21 *De laudibus legum Anglie*, ed. Chrimes, chapter 9, pp. 25–27. See also the translation in *On the Laws and Governance of England*, ed. Lockwood, pp. 17–18.

22 For the editions, see *STC*, 11193–11197. For Fortescue's influence, see Skeel.

23 *On the Governance of England*, ed. Plummer, p. 86.

of actually divided legislative powers; the king remained the source of law itself. The king might be limited ethically and politically, but not constitutionally (see also Gillespie 1979).

Certainly Fortescue did aim to strengthen the monarchy financially, whereby the king could 'live off his own', richer than, and therefore invulnerable to any subject, and not dependent on raising personal income through taxation. The *Governance*, indeed, is in large measure a policy document, outlining what the king's expenses are, and how he should regain his lands so as to ensure an income sufficient to his needs (*Governance*, chapters 5–14). And certainly Fortescue does not explicitly elaborate a theory of constitutionally divided powers.

That having been said, everything Fortescue says in both tracts, both theoretically and practically, is designed to constrain the king, and to ensure that he acts consensually with representative bodies of his subjects. Theoretically England is not a *dominium regale*; the maxim 'quod principi placuit, legis habet vigorem' ['what pleased the king has the force of law'] does not apply in England. Whereas the regal dominion 'beganne of and bi the might of the prince', dominion that is both regal and political 'be ganne bi the desire and institucion of the peple of the same prince'.[24] He praises the Roman republic and its senatorial rule, and accounts for the decline of Rome by reference to its becoming an empire.[25] His deployment of organicist political metaphor stresses the primacy of the body:

> The law . . . by which a group of men is made into a people, resembles the sinews of the physical body, for, just as the body is held together by the sinews, so too this mystical body is bound together and preserved by the law . . . and the members and bones of this body . . . preserve their rights through the law, as the body natural does through the sinews. And just as the head of the physical body is unable to change its sinews . . . so a king who is head of the body politic is unable to change the laws of that body, or to deprive that same people of their own substance uninvited or against their wills.[26]

These are hardly the words of any forerunner of Hobbes.

Practically, too, Fortescue stresses the interests of subjects and the need for subjects to control the king through assemblies. The very measures designed to strengthen the king's revenues are proposed precisely by way of containing the monarch. They are designed to prevent the inevitable injustice inflicted on subjects by a penurious king's corrupt manipulation of the law (*Governance*, chapter 5). And the sufficient endowment of the monarch itself demands the establishment of a powerful Council (not made up of magnates) who will control the king's expenditure (*Governance*, chapters 14–20).[27]

---

[24] *On the Governance of England*, ed. Plummer, pp. 112–13.
[25] *On the Governance of England*, ed. Plummer, chapter 16; see also appendix A of the same edition, a brief tract by Fortescue that is a version of chapter 16, making direct parallels between the Roman and English civil wars.
[26] *De laudibus legum Anglie*, trans. Lockwood, chapter 13; for the Latin text, see *De laudibus legum Anglie*, ed. Chrimes, pp. 30–32.

Fortescue in political theory, then, as Pecock in ecclesiastical theory, was influenced by Conciliarism, the early fourteenth-century movement that stressed the authority of representative church councils above that of a monarchical papacy.[28] This accent of Fortescue's politics has immediate bearing on his jurisprudence, which is inseparable from his politics. The *De laudibus* in particular is a form of comparative jurisprudence, in which the practice of English common law is contrasted with, and praised above, the exercise of civil law that Fortescue had witnessed in France. Just as the statutes of England are not made wholly by the king, but with the assent of the parliament (*De laudibus*, chapter 18), so too the judge's decision in the common law depends on the assent of a jury. Chapters 19–27 of the *De laudibus* contrast the strength of the jury system with the corruption of evidence in the practice of civil law, focussing especially on the use of torture and the easily corruptible witness system. Chapter 29 accounts for why the common law of England is not practised elsewhere. Fortescue develops what amounts to a sociology of law, by arguing that the fertility of England and its political freedoms ensure that courts are certain to be able to find twelve men sufficiently wealthy as not to be vulnerable to corruption, in all parts of England. The countryside of France, where the king's subjects are so impoverished by the exercise of regal dominion alone, and in particular by the king's ability to impose taxes at will, could not service a jury system (*De laudibus*, chapter 35).

Unlike Pecock's, Fortescue's formal choices, both structural and stylistic, are adroit. His structural choice of dialogue for each of *De natura legis Naturae, De laudibus legum Anglie*, and the 'Declaration . . . upon Certayn Wrytinges' is in each case astute. In the first treatise it allows him a personal, geographical and philosophical distance to debate the issues. In the second the use of the prince as the interlocutor allows Fortescue to address a potentially resistant yet crucial audience (i.e royalty) in the guise of an educational encounter. In the third instance (the 'Declaration') dialogue is indispensable to Fortescue's delicate manoeuvres. He exploits the dialogic situation, for example, to situate textual reference in the memory. The learned man with whom the exiled Fortescue speaks has not brought the relevant writings by Fortescue with him, and so relies on memory to recount their contents, thus allowing (the author) Fortescue the chance to present those writings in a less incriminating way. As with Hoccleve's *Regement of Princes* (1412), Fortescue imagines a private conversation in order to deal with issues of very public relevance.

The style, too, of Fortescue's prose is well suited to its presumed aim of gaining a vernacular readership for scholastic thought. His sentences are simply yet subtly structured, his vocabulary without technical difficulty:

The Romaynes, while thair counsell callid þe senate was gret, gate, through þe wisdome off that counsell, the lordshippe off gret partye of the world. And

---

[27] See also Fortescue's short policy paper to precisely this effect, in *On the Governance of England*, ed. Plummer, appendix B, written in (?) early 1471.

[28] See Doe for an argument that Pecock anticipates Fortescue's handling of the concept of *dominium regale et politicum*.

aftirward Julyus, thair ffirst emperowre, counselled by þe same senate, gate
the monarchie nerhande of all þe world. Wherthrough Octavian, þer secounde
emperour, commounded all þe world to be discribed as subget unto hym.

(Governance, 149)

This tripartite sequence, describing the extension of Roman power, makes
allowances for an unlearned reader. Each sentence preserves a straightforward
structure of subject, verb and object. Each nevertheless takes care to insert yet
not overload that basic structure with explanatory clauses or phrases ('thair
counsell callid þe senate'; 'thair ffirst emperowre'). The aim of persuading his
readers that good council produces an extension of power is subtly underlined
by the deployment of forms of the word 'counsell', firstly by repeating the word
as a noun, with the second instance receiving maximum emphasis, and then by
using the word as a past participle. The ends of each sentence subliminally
suggest that good council produces more power. The first two sentences end by
emphasising the extension of power ('gret partye of the world', 'nerhande of all
þe world'), while the third underlines the way in which the entire world can be
brought within the power of the well-counselled king (all þe world . . . as subget
unto hym'). All the technical vocabulary here is Latinate, but none of it draws
attention to itself, while Fortescue subtly elides different forms of Roman
government (republican and imperial) with an English monarchical model.

WORKS CITED

Primary

MANUSCRIPTS

Manuscripts of works by Pecock

The Book of Faith
Cambridge, Trinity College Cambridge B. 14. 45 (incomplete), fol. 127

The Donet
Oxford, Bodleian Library, Bodley 916 (incomplete), fol. 109

The Folewer to the Donet
London, BL, Royal 17. D. ix, fol. 102

The Poore Mennis Myrrour
London, BL, Additional MS 37788, fols 3–63

The Repressor of Overmuch Blaming of the Clergy
Cambridge, CUL, Kk. iv. 26, fol. 190

The Reule of Crysten Religioun
New York, Pierpont Morgan Library 519 (incomplete), fol. 192

MANUSCRIPTS OF WORKS BY FORTESCUE

The Governance of England

Cambridge, CUL, Ll. 3. 11, fols 215–241
London, BL, Cotton Claudius A. viii, fols 175–198
London, BL, Harley 542, fols 125–140
London, BL, Harley 1757, fols 196–203
London, Lambeth Palace, Lambeth 262, fols 106–128
Oxford, Bodleian Library, Digby 145, fols 133–159
Oxford, Bodleian Library, Digby 198, fols 48–75
Oxford, Bodleian Library, Laud 593, fols 1–15
Oxford, Bodleian Library, Rawlinson B. 384, fols 48–63
Oxford, Bodleian Library, Rawlinson D. 69, fols 1–20
San Marino, Huntington EL 34 C 18, fols 2–26
Yelverton 35, now London, BL, Additional MS 48031, fols 148–164

De laudibus legum Anglie
Cambridge, CUL, Ff. 5. 22, fol. 30
London, BL, Additional MS 48598, fols 25–46
London, BL, Harley 1757, fols 208–226
Oxford, Bodleian Library, Digby 198, fols 1–47

For the manuscripts of Fortescue's minor English works, see IPMEP, items 10, 15, 105, 183, 186, 498.

PRINTED EDITIONS

A Familiar Dialogue of the Friend and the Fellow, ed. Margaret S. Blayney, EETS 295 (London, 1989)

Fifteenth-Century English Translations of Alain Chartier's Le Traité de l'Esperance *and* Le Quadrilogue Invectif, ed. Margaret S. Blayney, EETS 270 and 281 (London, 1974 and 1981)

Fortescue, John, *The Difference between an Absolute and Limited Monarchy, as it most particularly Regards the English Constitution*, ed. John Fortescue-Aland (London, 1714)

———, *The Works of Sir John Fortescue*, ed. Lord Clermont (London, 1869), which contains:
De titulo Edwardi Comitis Marchiae, pp. 63*–74* (translated, pp. 77*–90*)
'Of the Title of the House of York', pp. 497–502
Defensio juris domus Lancastriae, pp. 505–10 (translated, pp. 511–16)
Opusculum de natura legis Naturae, pp. 63–184 (translated, pp. 187–333)
'Declaration . . . upon Certayn Wrytinges Sent out of Scotland against the Kinge's Title to his Roialme of England', pp. 523–41

———, *The Governance of England otherwise called 'The Difference Between an Absolute and a Limited Monarchy'*, revised edition, ed. Charles Plummer (Oxford, 1885)

———, *De laudibus legum Anglie*, ed. S.B. Chrimes (Cambridge, 1942)

———, *On the Laws and Governance of England*, ed. Shelley Lockwood, Cambridge Texts in the History of Political Thought (Cambridge, 1997)

Foxe, John, ed., 'Collectanea Quaedam ex Reginaldi Pecoki Episcopi Cicestrensis opusculis exustis conseruata', *Commentarii Rerum in Ecclesia Gestarum* (Argentorati, 1554), fols 199v–203v

Pecock, Reginald, *A Treatise Proving Scripture to be the Rule of Faith*, ed. Henry Wharton (London, 1688)

———, *The Folewer to the Donet*, ed. Elsie Vaughan Hitchcock, EETS 164 (London, 1924)

————, *The Repressor of Overmuch Blaming of the Clergy*, ed. Churchill Babington, 2 vols, Rolls Series (London, 1860; repr. 1966)

————, *Reginald Pecock's The Book of Faith*, ed. J.L. Morison (Glasgow, 1909)

————, *The Donet . . . collated with The Poore Mennis Myrrour*, ed. Elsie Vaughan Hitchcock, EETS 156 (London, 1921)

————, *The Reule of Crysten Religioun*, ed. William Cabell Greet, EETS 171 (London, 171)

Secondary

Ball, R.M., 'The Opponents of Bishop Pecock', *Journal of Ecclesiastical History* 48 (1997), 230–62

Blayney, Margaret Slater, 'Sir John Fortescue and Alain Chartier's *Traité de l'Esperance*', *MLR* 48 (1953), 385–90

Bose, Mishtooni, 'Reginald Pecock's Vernacular Voice', in *Heresy and Reform: New Directions in Wycliffite Studies*, ed. Fiona Somerset, Derrick Pitard, and Jill Havens (Boydell and Brewer, forthcoming)

Carpenter, Christine, 'Political and Constitutional History Before and After McFarlane', in *The McFarlane Legacy: Studies in Late Medieval Politics and Society*, ed. R.H. Britnell and A.J. Pollard (Stroud, Gloucs., 1995), pp. 175–206

Catto, Jeremy, 'The King's Government and the Fall of Pecock, 1457–58', in *Rulers and Ruled in Late Medieval England: Essays Presented to Gerald Harris*, ed. Rowena E. Archer and Simon Walker (London, 1995), pp. 201–22

Chrimes, S.B., *English Constitutional Ideas in the Fifteenth Century* (Cambridge, 1936)

Doe, N., 'Fifteenth-Century Concepts of Law: Fortescue and Pecock', *History of Political Thought* 10 (1989), 257–80

Douglas, David C., *English Scholars, 1660–1730*, 2nd ed. (London, 1951)

Gilbert, Felix, 'Sir John Fortescue's *dominium regale et politicum*', *Medievalia et Humanistica* 2 (1944), 88–97

Gill, P.E., 'Politics and Propaganda in Fifteenth Century England: The Polemical Writings of Sir John Fortescue', *Speculum* 46 (1971), 333–47

Gillespie, J.L., 'Sir John Fortescue's Concept of the Royal Will', *Nottingham Medieval Studies* 23 (1979), 47–65

Gordon, Ian A., *The Movement of English Prose*, English Language Series 2 (London, 1966)

Green, V.H.H., *Bishop Reginald Pecock: A Study in Ecclesiastical History and Thought* (Cambridge, 1945)

Landman, James H., ' "The Doom of Resoun": Accommodating Lay Interpretation in Late Medieval England', in *Medieval Crime and Social Control*, ed. Barbara A. Hanawalt and David Wallace, Medieval Cultures 16 (Minneapolis, 1999), pp. 90–123

Litzen, Veikko, *A War of Roses and Lilies: The Theme of Succession in Sir John Fortescue's Works*, Annales Academiae Scientiarum Fennicae 173 (Helsinki, 1971)

Mueller, Janel M., *The Native Tongue and the Word: Developments in English Prose Style, 1380–1580* (Chicago, 1984)

Patrouch, Joseph F., Jr, *Reginald Pecock*, Twayne English Authors Series 106 (New York, 1970)

Scase, Wendy, 'Reginald Pecock, John Carpenter and John Colop's "Common-Profit" Books: Aspects of Book Ownership and Circulation in Fifteenth-Century London', *Medium Aevum* 61 (1992), 261–74

————, *Reginald Pecock*, Authors of the Middle Ages 8 (Aldershot, Hants, 1996)

Skeel, C.A., 'The Influence of the Writings of Sir John Fortescue', *Transactions of the Royal Historical Society* 3rd ser. 10 (1916), 77–114

Watson, Nicholas, 'Censorship and Cultural Change in Late-Medieval England: Vernacular Theology, the Oxford Translation Debate, and Arundel's Constitutions of 1409', *Speculum* 70 (1995), 822–64

17

Private Letters

RICHARD BEADLE

In 1787 a little-known Norfolk antiquary named John Fenn caused a literary sensation when he began to issue a series of volumes entitled, in the manner of the time, *Original Letters, Written during the Reigns of Henry VI., Edward IV. and Richard III. by Various Persons of Rank or Consequence*, and ever since then the numerous surviving private letters of the fifteenth century have been one of the most widely read and cited varieties of Middle English prose.[1] Fenn's *Original Letters* soon became popularly and then generally known as *The Paston Letters*, after the Norfolk family amongst whom most of them originated, and it was under this title that they were reissued in successively augmented editions by James Gairdner between 1872–75 and 1904. Through the nineteenth and into the twentieth century the Paston collection was gradually joined on the shelf by editions of other bodies of private correspondence of the time, likewise known by the names of the gentry or mercantile families from whose archives they came, notably the *Plumpton Correspondence* (1839), *The Cely Papers* (1900) and *The Stonor Letters and Papers* (1919). Smaller collections such as some letters of John Shillingford, a mayor of Exeter, were also printed (in 1871), and similar correspondence still comes to light, notably *The Armburgh Papers*, first published as recently as 1998. In earlier periods numerous individually surviving medieval English letters of varying degrees of privacy and formality were brought forth in semi-antiquarian collections such as the *Excerpta Historica* (1831) and Sir Henry Ellis's eleven volumes of *Original Letters Illustrative of English History* (1824–46), or noticed and extracted in official historical repertories such as the Reports of the Royal Commission on Historical Manuscripts. Separate pieces and selections of medieval English correspondence have commonly been included in anthologies, or issued in modernised reprints for the general reader.[2] The Paston Letters, as well as acting as an important detailed source for fifteenth-century political, social, economic and linguistic history, have been used as material for valuable general accounts

---

Letters are cited from the current standard editions specified in the bibliography. Complete letters are referred to by their serial numbers, and extracts from letters are quoted by their serial numbers and either line or page numbers, according to the format of the edition. In some of the extended quotations the punctuation differs from that given in the editions.

[1] D. Stoker, ' "Innumerable Letters of Good Consequence in History": The Discovery and First Publication of the Paston Letters', *The Library* 6th ser. 17 (1995), 107–55.

[2] See for example L. Lyell, *A Mediæval Post-Bag* (London, 1934), and N. Davis, ed., *The Paston Letters: A Selection in Modern Spelling* (Oxford, 1983).

of their time, and they provided R.L. Stevenson with the basis for a historical romance; a recent definitive edition has paved the way for exceptionally searching investigations of the family's fortunes and *mentalité*.[3] Though the Paston Letters and their congeners have no single focus of interest or appeal, the personalities and circumstances of their writers are often powerfully but unself-consciously conveyed in their letters. No other genre can claim to bring the reader face-to-face with the people of the time in quite this way. It is fair to say that, taken as a body, the insight private letters offer into the late-medieval English past has no exact parallel, and that their potential for enquiries of various kinds is virtually limitless.

Private letters in Middle English survive in large numbers, and the texts they contain are with a few minor exceptions unique. Because of the widespread use of dictaminal formulae, their opening words are often stereotyped, and they resist classification by incipit, the normal way in which other Middle English writings have been indexed. For these reasons they have generally been regarded as 'documentary' material for bibliographical purposes, and they are not individually traceable in reference works devoted to Middle English prose.[4] The conditions in which letters were composed and transmitted, and the circumstances of their survival, also serve to mark them off from other varieties of prose, almost all of which has come down to us in codex form, copied by professional scribes, or in early printed books. No extended analysis of the palaeographical and diplomatic aspects of vernacular letters at present exists, though Norman Davis gave an important summary of the physical characteristics of those in the Paston collection, to which others are broadly similar, and published reproductions of a number of examples.[5] Many surviving letters are their authors' autographs, including drafts of various kinds retained for record as well as missives, and their composition is straightforwardly attributable. Much of the correspondence carried on in the period however is not in the hand of the nominal author, but is rather the work of a clerk or other amanuensis, who would also supply the sender's name in the subscription if he or she did not do so. In these circumstances it can be less clear as to who precisely is the author of a letter. There appears to be no external evidence, and very few signs in the texts of the letters themselves, to support the widespread assumption that dictation

[3] For Norman Davis's standard edition of the Paston Letters see the section on editions in the bibliography below. H.S. Bennett, *The Pastons and their England* (Cambridge, 1922; 2nd ed. 1932, repr. with corr. 1968), and R. Virgoe, *Private Life in the Fifteenth Century: Illustrated Letters of the Paston Family* (London, 1989) are valuable general accounts of the letters and their background. For the Paston Letters as a source for historical romance see R.M. Faurot, 'From Records to Romance: Stevenson's *The Black Arrow* and the Paston Letters', *Studies in English Literature 1500–1900* 5 (1965), 677–90. For the most searching account of the Paston Letters so far undertaken (including references to a number of letters and other documents unknown to Fenn, Gairdner and Davis) see C. Richmond, *The Paston Family in the Fifteenth Century: The First Phase* (Cambridge, 1990), *Fastolf's Will* (Cambridge, 1996) and *Endings* (Manchester, 2000).

[4] See for example *IPMEP*, p. xxviii.

[5] Davis, *Paston Letters and Papers*, Part I, pp. xxxiii–xxxix, with plates at the ends of both Parts I and II. An aspect of the material form of the letters to which Davis did not give attention is the watermarks in the paper. Fenn, however, often remarked on them, and reproduced a number of examples; see for example *Original Letters*, ii, plates VIII–XIII, iii, XXI–XXII. Plates showing the appearance of several of the Stonor and Cely letters are included the editions by Kingsford and Hanham.

was commonly practised in the composition of vernacular letters. Perhaps it
was, but it is equally likely that the drafting of much correspondence was undertaken by scribes who had been given only general directions or notes as to the
intended content. This would seem to be the case with a number of letters
penned for the war veteran turned landowner Sir John Fastolf by his secretary
William Worcester, where Fastolf's signature sometimes appears midway down
the sheet, obviously inserted long before Worcester had completed the writing
of the letter. One such concludes bizarrely with Worcester ventriloquising for
the absent Fastolf: 'And be cause I myght [not] abyde till the wrytygnges of the
materes that I commaunded Worcestre to wryte, I signed the lettre so neere the
begynnyng'. In such cases no more than the gist of the letter may be
atttributable to its nominal author, whereas the phrasing may be the work of the
person who wrote it out.[6] The widespread use of amanuenses such as household
or estate servants, clerics, or other family members makes it somewhat less
certain exactly whose linguistic usage a given letter represents, if it is not an
autograph. Because of the wide scope of linguistic variation in Middle English,
such features as a clerk's orthography and inflectional usage (to say nothing of
his lexical and grammatical choices) are unlikely to have coincided precisely
with those of the author.

It appears that most men who possessed some degree of formal education
were capable of writing letters in their own hand. Whether they did so or not
could depend on a variety of circumstances, including status, occupation, the
availability of an amanuensis, and personal inclination. Almost all of the
numerous letters of John Paston II and John Paston III to one another, and to
their mother Margaret, are autograph. Letters in the hand of their father John I
(whose handwriting was poor) are noticeably rarer, and even his letters to his
wife were usually written by a servant. Thomas Howes, a cleric, who was head
of Sir John Fastolf's household at Caister Castle near Yarmouth, was widely
engaged in correspondence, but only one letter in his own rather crude hand
(complaining in personal terms about his employer) survives. The higher a
man's social rank, the more likely he was to employ an amanuensis: 'Scribbled
in hast with mine owne hand in default of other helpe', as one of Sir William
Plumpton's correspondents put it in a letter of c. 1465, and this probably reflects
a common attitude amongst the better off. Writing was an activity which
belonged in the category of work, and it was therefore an occupation for
servants and for those who had been professionally trained to do it.[7] In the
Paston collection, the unpractised appearance of the handwriting in the autograph letters of even minor noblemen indicates that they were much less accus-

6   The Fastolf letter quoted is BL, Add. MS 34898, fol. 10, an abstract of which is given in J. Gairdner,
    ed., *The Paston Letters A.D. 1422–1509* (London, 1904), vol. II, no. 158. For an illustration of one of
    Fastolf's letters signed halfway down the page see J. Preston and L. Yeandle, *English Handwriting
    1400 – 1650* (Binghamton NY, 1992), no. 7. The evidence for dictation is discussed by Davis, *Paston
    Letters and Papers*, Part I, p. xxxviii: 'It is seldom possible to know whether a letter written by a clerk
    was taken down verbatim at dictation or composed more or less freely on the basis of instructions
    given by the author.' In the latter circumstances clerks would have been likely to use wax tablets to
    take down the notes from which a letter was to be written up.
7   Kirby, *Plumpton Letters and Papers*, no. 12, p. 36.

tomed to using a pen than the members of the mere gentry to whom they might be writing.[8] None of the 70 or so extant letters of Sir John Fastolf is in his own hand, though he signed most of them personally prior to a serious illness in mid-1451.[9] Though women were no less likely to engage in correspondence than men, their level of formal education was more limited, and they seldom added more than their name to their letters, which were normally written out by members of their household. Margaret Paston, the most prolifically represented female correspondent of the period, is nominally responsible for just over 100 missives from between about 1441 and 1478, amongst which 24 different hands are to be distinguished. Those which are identifiable belonged either to household or estate servants, to clerics within the Paston circle, or to her sons. By contrast, BL, MS Add. 43490, fol. 42, a brief note from Elizabeth, Duchess of Suffolk to John Paston III, written sometime between c. 1479 and 1483, is exceptional, being in an unskilled hand which appears to be her autograph.[10]

Many surviving Middle English letters were missives, and this usually means that the text occupies one side of the sheet only, which was then folded to form a small packet with only parts of the blank dorse visible from the outside. Tape or thread was passed through small slits in the paper, and the ends were embedded in sealing wax, which sometimes survives to show the impression of the sender's signet. The intended recipient's name and often some form of address were normally written on the other side of the packet from the seal, and the letter was then entrusted to a messenger or carrier (who was sometimes the amanuensis) for delivery.[11] Prudence and security dictated that correspondents did not necessarily write down all that they wished to convey, and letters commonly request the recipient to give credence to the carrier, 'who will tell you more by mouth', as it was often phrased. Some letters end with a request that they be destroyed or burnt as soon as the content has been taken in. From this perspective it is evident that letters were seen as exisiting in a closer relationship to the oral than other forms of prose composition. There was no necessary expectation that letters would be read privately, since recipients, depending on their level of literacy or their inclination, are known to have had their correspondence read aloud to

---

[8] Lord Moleyns' writing in BL, Add. MS 43491, fol. 5 (Davis, *Paston Letters and Papers*, Part II, no. 873, 'Wrytyn wyth my noune Chaunsery hond') is markedly inferior to the great majority of gentry, mercantile and estate servants' letters of the time. The hands of William, Lord Hastings, in BL, Add. MS 43490, fol. 44, and John, Duke of Suffolk, in BL, Add. MS 43490, fol. 49 (Davis, II, no. 795 and Gairdner, *Paston Letters*, no. 997 respectively) are no better. The latter picked up the pen merely to add a scrawled postscript demand to a tenant for rent: 'Fayle not on peyn [of] losyng off your ferme.'

[9] On the disappearance of Fastolf's signature from his letters after mid-1451 see N. Davis, 'Language in Letters from Sir John Fastolf's Household', in P.L. Heyworth, ed., *Medieval Studies for J.A.W. Bennett* (Oxford, 1981), pp. 329–46, at pp. 330–1.

[10] Women's competence at writing is inconclusively and not exhaustively surveyed by V.M. O'Mara, 'Female Scribal Ability and Scribal Activity in Late Medieval England: the Evidence?' *Leeds Studies in English* ns 27 (1996), 87–130 (see pp. 91–96 for letters; for other women's letters ignored by O'Mara see for example Lyell, *Mediæval Post-Bag*, pp. 267, 277). A table showing the incidence of hands in Margaret Paston's letters is given by Davis, *Paston Letters and Papers*, Part I, p. lxxix; the letter from Elizabeth, Duchess of Suffolk, is printed as Davis, Part II, no. 798.

[11] P.C. Pearson, 'The Paston Letters: Carriage of Mail in the Fifteenth Century', *The London Philatelist* 99 (1990), 178–83, 189–95, 232–37, 276–79, gives a valuable illustrated account of the physical aspects of letters and of the practicalities of their conveyance.

them, and some letters were addressed jointly to several persons. Carriers were often difficult to find or could not wait, and to judge by the surprisingly large number of letters signed off as 'written in haste' (though this was sometimes probably an epistolary cliché), letter writing was evidently an activity often constrained by pressure of time. Unlike most types of Middle English prose, letters are sometimes precisely dated, or prove to be more or less closely datable from the information that they contain, and this gives them special value in charting the diachronic development of the language.

The body of missives that has survived can only represent a very small fraction of those that were actually sent,[12] and letters were plainly regarded for the most part as ephemeral, notwithstanding that injunctions to destroy them were sometimes ignored. In addition to missives, large numbers of letters were deliberately preserved, often in draft form, as file copies. On occasion missives were copied by their recipients for purposes of record, or to be forwarded to others (known in Sir John Fastolf's circle as 'doubles'), and they might also be enrolled, to provide evidence in litigation. Though these everyday vernacular letters have become matter for general reading and research in posterity, no notion of such activities would have formed a motive for their preservation. In this as in many other things they differ from the sophisticated Latin epistolatory traditions of earlier periods, aimed at enshrining fine writing for the admiration of succeeding generations, which as we shall see below impinged only to a limited and variable extent on vernacular modes of composition.[13] Margaret Paston's well-known injunction to her engaging but somewhat feckless son John Paston II is as good a statement as any of the purely pragmatic reasons for the survival of Middle English prose in this particular medium:

And in alwyse I avyse you for to be ware that ye kepe wysly youre wrytyngys that ben of charge, that it com not in here handys that may hurt you heraftere. Youre fadere, wham God assole, in hys trobyll seson set more by hys wrytyngys and evydens than he dede by any of his moveabell godys. Remembere that yf tho were had from you ye kowd neuer gyte no moo such as tho be for youre parte.[14]

Once established, the habit of keeping vernacular correspondence with a view to its evidentiary value in relation to property, marriage and litigation (alongside more conventional documents of record such as deeds and court rolls), was inevitably subject to a natural human inattention and inertia that would seem to ensure the hoarding of a wide spectrum of letters, from those containing information crucial to the family's fortune, down to the trivial and ephemeral: as Richard Cely put it to his brother George in a letter of 1478, 'Syr, I wryte to you of aull thyngys, as well of japys as sad mattars, lyke as I

12 Pearson, 'Carrriage of Mail', pp. 193–94, gives a table showing that some 32 letters passed amongst the Pastons from May to October 1465, which allude to at least 22 others that have not survived.
13 Earlier medieval epistolary writings are surveyed in G. Constable, *Letters and Letter Collections*, Typologie des Sources du Moyen Âge Occidental, Fasc. 17 (Turnhout, 1976).
14 Davis, *Paston Letters and Papers*, Part I, no. 198, lines 3–8.

promysyd you at owr departyng'.[15] Several bodies of correspondence have
survived in a form almost entirely restricted to matters of business (for example
those of the Plumpton family, Sir John Fastolf's, and the great majority of the
Armburgh letters), but many letters between family members in the Paston,
Stonor and Cely collections have something of the mixed complexion suggested
by Richard Cely's remark. Nonetheless, paper was a limited resource, and the
primary motive for writing a letter was to convey essential information, usually
of a private but sometimes of a public nature. Letters written from London, for
example, or by those in the vicinity of the king, court or government often
included a section devoted to 'tidings' or 'novelties'. Only in rare cases can one
point to a letter which might have been preserved with posterity in mind. The
Duke of Suffolk's famous parting letter to his son, framed in a distinctly literary
manner and purportedly written shortly before his assassination en route into
exile in early May 1450, is an otherwise somewhat unaccountable presence
amongst the papers of the Pastons (who had scant reason to mourn his passing),
being as it is neatly penned, and carrying an appreciative early endorsement that
reads 'The Copie of a notable Lettre, written by the Duke of Suffolk to his
Sonne, giving hym therein very good Counseil'.[16]

The private archives of gentry and mercantile families, which towards the
close of the fourteenth century were beginning to include letters in English
alongside documents in Latin and French, were doubtless informal imitations of
those found in the larger, professionally staffed baronial and noble households.[17]
Whilst Sir John Fastolf's estate papers and correspondence were held in a muniment room at Caister Castle, overseen by William Worcester and others, the
Pastons kept their 'wrytyngys that ben of charge' in various chests, boxes and
bags at several manor houses in Norfolk.[18] Annotations and endorsements added
to some of the letters by John Paston I and his two sons of that name suggest that
they had developed a basic filing system. The family's retention of large quanti-
ties of their personal correspondence long into the post-medieval period was
unusual, and the scope, variety and interest of the Paston papers is consequently

[15] Hanham, *Cely Letters*, no. 19, lines 31–33.
[16] BL, Add. MS 43488, fol. 12, reprinted by Gairdner, *The Paston Letters A.D. 1422–1509*, no. 117, from Fenn, *Original Letters*, I, p. 32. The document is obviously the work of a professional scribe whose hand is not otherwise recognisable amongst the Paston papers; it may one of a number of copies put into circulation after the duke's death. The rhyming subscription, including a line in elegant iambic pentameter, is also unusual: 'Wreten of myn hand,/ The day of my departyng fro this land.'
[17] The earliest surviving private letters in English are generally thought to be two sent from Florence to London in 1393 by the *condottiere* Sir John Hawkwood, which were produced before the mayor and aldermen in 1411, and copied into the civic records (A.H. Thomas, 'Notes on the History of the Leadenhall, A.D. 1195–1488', *London Topographical Record* 13 (1923), 1–22, at pp. 10–13). It is of note that other especially early examples of English letters are from women, e.g. Joan Pelham to Sir John Pelham, 25 July 1399 (Lyell, *Mediæval Post-Bag*, pp. 267–8), and the group found in the small archive of Elizabeth Despenser, dating from 1398 to 1403, now in the Public Record Office (P. Payne and C. Barron, 'The Letters and Life of Elizabeth Despenser, Lady Zouche (d. 1408)', *Nottingham Medieval Studies* 41 (1997), 126–56).
[18] When Bishop Wainfleet obtained the administration of the residue of Fastolf's massive estate and diverted it to his Oxford foundation at Magdalen, William Worcester took care that the Fastolf Papers in his possession found their way to the carefully designed muniment tower at the college, where they still remain in their medieval boxes; see Richmond, *Fastolf's Will*, pp. 270–1.

greater than that of the smaller collections of the Stonors, Celys and Armburghs, where the letters owe their survival to specific episodes in politics and litigation, and of the Plumpton letters, which now exist only in selected transcripts made in the early seventeenth century. The retention of the Stonor letters and papers amongst the public records may be because they were seized in connection with the attainder of Sir William Stonor (d. 1494) for his implication in Buckingham's rebellion in 1483, whilst the presence of the Cely letters in the Public Record Office is attributable to their having been taken (as part of a larger body of family papers) into Chancery in 1489, as evidence in a dispute over trading debts. The Armburgh papers were effectively archived in their own time: letters and other documents of the first half of the fifteenth century were assembled from the family's file copies in the late 1440s or early 1450s, and written out on a roll as a digest of information about a complicated and protracted dispute over landholdings in Hertfordshire, Essex and Warwickshire. The letters of the mid-fifteenth-century mayor of Exeter John Shillingford are concerned with the conduct of a somewhat Trollopian dispute between the corporation of the city and its bishop between 1447 and 1450, and they survive mostly in the form of drafts held in the civic archives.[19]

Even a cursory sketch of the circumstances in which private letters were composed, transmitted and received, and of their various adventitious modes of survival, makes it clear that in some major respects they need to be read and analysed in different ways from other varieties of Middle English prose. Such letters manifest themselves to us as fragments from or momentary glimpses into continuing narratives of the lives of the people whom they concern, narratives which may often be partly reconstructed from other documentary sources of the time, especially where the letters survive in the company of other kinds of material from the family's archive. Interpretation of the tone and intent of a particular letter also needs to be developed in the light of information about the social and economic milieux of the correspondents concerned, or in some cases of the broader political and cultural complexion of the world in which they moved. K. B. McFarlane's prescient and exemplary demonstrations of the kind of historical 'thick description' required to contextualise individual letters of Henry Beaufort and Thomas Chaucer, or of William Worcester, established the most effective mode of enquiry into this aspect of these writings.[20] Supplementary information from the drier realms of formal documentation is usually called for in order to understand a letter's content and intent, but it may also prove to be a significant factor in judging the subtle variations which can occur amongst the apparently stereotyped epistolary formulae and clichés which form a significant element in this type of writing. It is thus important to consider what kind of generic expectations we can adopt in approaching prose belonging to an avow-

---

[19] Kingsford, *Stonor Letters and Papers*, I, pp. xxxiii, xxxvi; Hanham, *Cely Letters*, pp. viii–ix; Carpenter, *Armburgh Papers*, pp. 3, 56–7.

[20] K.B. McFarlane, 'Henry V, Bishop Beaufort and the Red Hat, 1417–1421' and 'William Worcester and a Present of Lampreys' in his *England in the Fifteenth Century: Collected Essays* (London, 1981), pp. 79–113, 225–30. The essays were first published in 1945 and 1961 respectively.

edly ephemeral medium, written with no thought of a posterity or a reading public in mind.

The traditional and popular notion that medieval private letters are characterised by an artless directness, that their writers merely set down what was going through their minds in an easy and unforced manner, more or less as they spoke, is too simplified a view to sustain, and has no doubt been fostered by the repeated anthologising of a few celebrated items.[21] Margery Brews's first 'Valentine' to her fiancé John Paston III in 1477, and Thomas Betson's letter of 1476 to his twelve-year-old betrothed Katherine Ryche, a small masterpiece of tactfully expressed affection, have rightly given modern readers hardly less pleasure than they must have given their original recipients.[22] Both letters however play artfully upon exisiting epistolary conventions. John Paston would be expected to note that Margery's 'And yf it please ȝow to here of my welefare, I am not in good heele of body ner of herte' is an inversion of a common dictaminal formula whereby writers would routinely wish their correspondents good health, assure them of their own; and her 'I beseche ȝowe þat this bill be not seyn of non erthely creature safe only ȝour-selfe' would have gained a wry piquancy from his recognition that the hand of the letter was not hers, but that of Thomas Kela, a priest, probably chaplain in her father's household. Likewise Thomas Betson signs off in a playful embroidery upon the conventional terse business subscriptions of the Calais wool merchants, e.g. 'Written at Calles the xix day of October, per yowr seruaunt, William Cely':[23]

> At greate Cales on this syde on the see, the fyrst day off June, whanne every man was gone to his dener, and the cloke smote noynne, and all oure howsold cryed after me and badde me, 'Come down, come down to dener at ones!' And what answer I gaveffe hem ye know it off old.
>
>   Be your feiȝtheffull cossen and loffer,
>   Thomas Betson.
> I sent you this rynge for a token.[24]

Very personal letters such as these recognise certain conventions, even if they do not always exactly conform with them, but they are inevitably few and far between in the exisiting bodies of correspondence. Similarly the graphic spontaneity that we associate with proximity to everyday speech is generally present only under certain conditions, for example where extended actions are described, or where direct speech is quoted. In 1448 Margaret Paston wrote to her husband John I describing a *Romeo and Juliet*-type street brawl in Norwich, involving the family chaplain James Gloys, and John Wyndham, at that time a local adversary aligned with the Duke of Suffolk's affinity, bent on insulting the Pastons with a reminder of their humble origins:

---

[21] '. . . they wrote almost exactly as they spoke, with a remarkable freshness and spontaneity which is lacking in their more elaborate predecessor and successors' (Lyell, *Mediæval Post-Bag*, p. 13) is representative. Cf. the extracts from Virginia Woolf and H.S. Bennett in N. Davis, *Paston Letters* (Oxford, 1958), pp. xxvii–xxviii.

[22] Davis, *Paston Letters and Papers*, Part I, no. 415; Kingsford, *Stonor Letters*, no. 166.

[23] Hanham, *Cely Letters*, no. 198, lines 21–24.

[24] Kingsford, *Stonor Letters*, no. 166, ii, p. 8.

And Jamys Gloys come with his hatte on his hede betwen bothe his men, as he
was wont of custome to do. And whanne Gloys was a-yenst Wymondham he
seid þus, 'Couere thy heed!'. And Gloys seid ageyn, 'So I shall for the'. And
whanne Gloys was forther passed by þe space of iij or iiij strede, Wymondham
drew owt his dagger and seid, 'Shalt þow so, knave?' And þerwith Gloys
turned hym and drewe owt his dagger and defendet hym, fleyng in-to my
moderis place; and Wymondham and his man Hawys kest stonys and dreve
Gloys into my moderis place. And Hawys folwyd into my moderis place and
kest a ston as meche as a forthyng lof into þe halle after Gloys; and þan ran
owt of þe place ageyn. And Gloys folwyd owt and stod with-owt þe gate, and
þanne Wymondham called Gloys thef and seid he shuld dye, and Gloys seid he
lyed and called hym charl, and bad hym come hym-self or ell þe best man he
hadde, and Gloys wold answere hym on for on. And þanne Haweys ran into
Wymondhams place and feched a spere and a swerd, and toke his maister his
swerd. And with þe noise of þis a-saut and affray my modir and I come owt of
þe chirche from þe sakeryng; and I bad Gloys go in to my moderis place
ageyn, and so he dede. And thanne Wymondham called my moder and me
strong hores, and seid þe Pastons and alle her kyn were <charles of
Ge>myngham <and w>e seid he lyed, knave and charl as he was. And he had
meche large langage, as ye shall knowe her-after by mowthe.[25]

Most letters, however, consist of more than breathless paratactic reportage,
and exhibit an impulse to assume a more 'literary' or through-written
demeanour that strives uneasily with colloquialism to produce a mixed style. A
few of the more personally couched of the Armburgh letters, for example,
embed spontaneous and direct expression within a heavily subordinated syntax
which is combined with other features unrelated to normal speech. Several of
them consist of demands for money, sometimes including fairly blunt threats,
whilst others involve downright invective and abuse of a kind not generally
found in other collections.[26] In about 1429–30 Joan Armburgh wrote as follows
to John Horrell of Essex, who is said to have played something of a
Heathcliffe-like role in the Armburghs' affairs, having been brought up in her
own family before helping to cheat them (as they believed) out of part of their
inheritance:

Bare frende, in suche maner wise as thu hast deseruyd I grete the, for as
moche as yt is not vnknowen to the, and oopynly knowen in all the cuntré, that
thi chef makyng hath be thorough the maner of Radewynter, first be my lady
my modres day, and sithern in my tyme. And notwithstondyng that thu, as a
kukkowsbird devouryng the heysogge [hedgesparrow] whan she hath bred
hym vp, and as an vnkynd bird that foulyth his owne nest, hast labouryd fro
that tyme in to this with myn aduersarie John Sumpter and with hem that haue
weddyd his tweyne bastard doughtres, noisyng hem al aboute the cuntré for

25 Davis, *Paston Letters and Papers*, Part I, no. 129, lines 7–27, with modifications in the light of Part II,
    p. xxv. For the circumstances surrounding the events narrated in the letter see C. Richmond, 'What a
    Difference a Manuscript Makes: John Wyndham of Felbrigg (d. 1475)', in F. Riddy, ed., *Regionalism
    in Late Medieval Manuscripts and Texts* (Cambridge, 1991), pp. 129–41.
26 A letter of *c.* 1430–32 from Robert Armburgh to Thomas Mylde and Thomas Bernard is so grossly
    insulting that it has to be read to be believed: Carpenter, *Armburgh Papers*, pp. 130–1.

mulirers [*legitimate*] and right heires, there-as thu knowest wele the contrarie
is soth; so fer forth that thu, as the develes child, fadre of falshode, whos
kynde is alwey to do evil a-yenst good, hast forsworn the diuerse tymes before
chetours and justices to yeue the cuntrés fals enformacion that shuld passe
betwene vs in disherityng of me and of myn heires of the moyté of the modres
enheritance in al that euer in the is, the which with the grace of God shal neuer
ly in thi power nor in no javelys [*knaves*] that han weddid thoo fals bastardes.
. . . In so moche that, whan thu sittiste in tauernys among thy felowys, thu hast
a comyn byword in maner as a fals prophete, saying that thu hopist to se the
day to do an hare stirtyn vpon the herthstone of Radewynter Halle. But I trust
to God, or that maner that hath ben an habitacion and a dwellyng place for
many a worthi man of myn antisesters from the Conquest in to this tyme, and a
long tyme beforn, be so desolate as thu desirest, that thu shalt se, be leue of
myn husbond, a peire galweys set vp with-yn the same fraunchise for thi
nekke . . .[27]

Despite the attempt at modern punctuation above, perhaps only liberal use of
parentheses and dashes in Sterne's manner might do something to meet the
writer's desire to combine subordination with indignation. 'Thou' and 'thee',
'tweyne bastard doughters', 'javelys', 'fals bastardes' and 'Bare frend' (an intu-
itive assonantal variant on the Armburghs' usual, but otherwise unusual greeting
line, 'Dere . . . frend'[28]) and so on, alternate with the use of more calculated
allusions and devices. The similes comparing Horrell with the cuckoo and the
devil's child; the folkloric allusion to the hare on the hearthstone (an emblem of
destruction); the 'fals prophete' allusion; the reference at the end of the passage
quoted (by this time effectively 'historical') to the ancient feudal right of
infangenthief; the ornamental doublet 'an habitacion and a dwellyng place'; all
of these features hang together to disclose a mind familiar with modes of
discourse on levels other than the colloquial.[29]

As has been said, the primary purpose of private correspondence was to
convey necessary information, and the great majority of letters, including those
between family members, possess some degree of formality. Many are quite
impersonal, and are often scarcely distinguishable from the voluminous official
correspondence of the time, much of which was issued in the names of individuals such as kings and queens, magnates, bishops and mayors, and penned by
professional clerks. From about the 1420s-30s, business letters generated by the
Crown and its offices, by aristocratic and baronial households, by the various
branches of regional administration, by the Church, and by the educational and
legal systems, were increasingly written in English, as well as in Latin or
French.[30] The writers of official correspondence, and many of those whose

---

[27] Carpenter, *Armburgh Papers*, pp. 120–21.

[28] Both the *OED* and the *MED* agree that the modern-sounding 'Dear' as an preliminary greeting in
letters is very rare in this period, but the Armburghs prove to use it regularly. Thomas Howes wrote to
Sir John Fastolf on 9 May 1451 describing an unreliable lawyer as 'your bare frend' (BL, Add. MS
34888, fol. 68).

[29] Compare Norman Davis's comments on the marked echoes of some types of contemporary religious
and moral discourse in the letters of the Paston women in 'Style and Stereotype in Early English
Letters', *Leeds Studies in English* ns 1 (1967), 7–17, at pp. 10–12.

[30] C.L. Kingsford, *English Historical Literature in the Fifteenth Century* (Oxford, 1913), pp. 193–227,

private letters survive, were trained to adopt a conventional framework of expression, or if they were not so trained, were able to imitate some basic elements of received epistolary style from letters they had seen or heard read. As we shall see below, such sets of stylistic conventions were taught as part of a formal education, especially in the 'business schools' associated with the universities and cathedral schools, and the standard features of the opening and conclusion of a letter were easily memorised and reproduced.[31] Within this sometimes elaborate envelope of dictaminally prescribed greeting and leavetaking some latitude of style was possible in composing the body of a private letter, about which it is difficult to generalise. Many correspondents saw no need for, or were not given to grammatically sophisticated forms of expression, and letters relying heavily on clichés of strained *politesse*, on haphazardly applied dictaminal formulae and (an especial vice of business letters) on pseudo-legal turns of phrase, are the norm for much epistolary prose, which need not be illustrated here.[32] On the other hand, it has long been recognised that there any many letters or passages in letters in a direct, unelaborated style, characterised by readily identifiable grammatical and lexical restrictions, which, far from being a weakness, produce similar patterns of expression to those that give (for example) Malory's literary prose its peculiar strength.[33] Beyond this, it was quite possible for an individual like Richard Calle, the Pastons' able and articulate chief estate servant to whom the 'business' style was familiar, to write at a level of resonance quite out of the ordinary when the occasion arose. Nothing in the writings of any of his employers compares with the moral weight and conviction that shapes the style of his admirable letter to a daughter of the family, with whom he had contracted a forbidden but binding betrothal, a letter which was alas quite possibly intercepted and witheld by her mother and brothers as 'evidence' before she was able to see it:

> Myne owne lady and mastres, and be-for God very trewe wyff, I wyth herte full sorwefull recomaunde me vnto you as he that can not be mery, nor nought schalbe tyll it be otherwice wyth vs thenne it is yet; for thys lyff þat we lede nough is nowther plesur to Godde nor to the worlde, concederyng the gret bonde of matrymonye þat is made be-twix vs, and also the greete loue þat hath be, and as I truste yet is, beywix vs, and as on my parte neuer gretter. Wherfor I beseche Almyghty Godde comfort vs as sone as it plesyth hym, for we þat ought of very ryght to be moost to-gether ar moost asondre; me semyth it is a m^l yere agoo son þat I speke wyth you. I had leuer thenne all the goode in the worlde I myght be wyth you. Alas, alas, good lady, full litell remembre they what they do þat kepe vs thus a-sonder; iiij tymes in the yere ar they a-cursid

as well as describing the then known collections of private letters, also gives references to various sources for the official correspondence of the time. Numerous examples of royal Signet and Privy Seal letters of the earlier part of the fifteenth century are given in J.H. Fisher et al., *An Anthology of Chancery English* (Knoxville, 1984).

31 H.G. Richardson, 'Business Training in Medieval Oxford', *American Historical Review* 46 (1941), 259–80.

32 Davis, 'Style and Stereotype in Early English Letters', pp. 7–10, identifies some of the most fequently used conventional expressions.

33 See the examples collected in P.J.C. Field, *Romance and Chronicle: A Study of Malory's Prose Style* (London, 1971), pp. 38–39, 58–59.

that lette matrymonye. It causith many men to deme in hem they haue large
consyence in other maters aswele as herin. But what, lady, suffre as ye haue do
and make you as mery as ye can, for j-wys, lady, at the longe wey Godde woll
of hys ryghtwysnes helpe hys seruauntys that meane truly and wolde leue
accordyng to hes lawys.[34]

A notable feature of Richard Calle's heartfelt letter to Margery Paston is its
freedom from the traditional dictaminal formulae, which are frequently but
(contrary to some claims) far from invariably present in early private letters. In
an important article published in 1963, Norman Davis observed that the letter
that Chaucer's Troilus sends to Criseyede (in Book V, lines 1317–1421 of
Troilus and Criseyde) is not a direct translation of its source in Boccaccio's
Filostrato. It is instead an adaptation that systematically incorporates a set of
conventions that derive ultimately from the Latin *ars dictaminis* widely practised in European letter writing from the eleventh century onwards. The
vernacularised versions of these formulae that Chaucer attributes to Troilus as
this very early stage (*c.* 1385) in the development of letter writing in English are
often to be observed in many of the more formal private letters of the ensuing
century, as well as in the official correspondence of the time.[35] The question of
precisely how far private letters were composed in accordance with strict
patterns derived from the professionally cultivated dictaminal traditions of
earlier periods still calls for detailed investigation.[36] Davis was in large measure
correct to suggest that such conventions found their way into English during the
fourteenth century either directly from Latin or via French, but evidence (admittedly of a later date) has since come to light that dictamen was also taught
through the medium of English itself. A dictaminal formulary of the latter half
of the fifteenth century in Harvard, Law School Library, MS 43 preserves two
model letters in English that closely resemble the numerous Latin and French
examples that have long been known through the extensive illustrations and
discussions of C.H. Haskins and others.[37] One of the model letters, which drolly
demonstrates the correct way that a student should write to his parents
requesting the unlikely sum of £20 as a 'yerys yeft' (Christmas present) for his
tutor, is worth quoting at length, since the dictaminal components of the letter

---

[34] Richard Calle to Margery Paston, 1469; Davis, *Paston Letters and Papers*, Part II, no. 861, lines 1–17.
[35] N. Davis, 'The *Litera Troili* and English Letters', *The Review of English Studies* ns 16 (1965), 233–44. The *Gawain*-poet also shows familiarity with a particular English epistolary formula in an appropriate context in *Pearl* (see the reference in n. 40 below to the study by Davis). M. Camargo, *Ars Dictaminis, Ars Dictandi*, Typologie des Sources du Moyen Âge Occidental, Fasc. 60 (Turnhout, 1991) offers an up-to-date survey of the very numerous treatises.
[36] M. Richardson, 'The *Dictamen* and its Influence on Fifteenth Century English Prose', *Rhetorica* 2 (1984), 207–26, proposes a 'unity of fifteenth century epistolary style' (p. 215) which is surely wide of the mark, and there are no real grounds for such statements as 'Even the casual reader of late medi-eval English correspondence can see that the letters are almost exclusively formulaic' (p. 214). Though dictaminal procedures shaped much official correspondence, they were very far from deter-mining the form of all private letters, as the examples quoted above are sufficient to show.
[37] L.E. Voigts, 'A Letter from a Middle English Dictaminal Formulary in Harvard Law Library MS 43', *Speculum* 56 (1981), 575–81. C.H. Haskins, 'The Life of Mediæval Students as Illustrated by their Letters', in *Studies in Medieval Culture* (Oxford, 1927), pp. 1–35; H.G. Richardson, 'Letters of the Oxford *Dictatores*', in H.E. Salter, W.A. Pantin and H.G. Richardson, *Formularies which bear on the History of Oxford c. 1204–1420*, Oxford Historical Society ns 5 (1942), pp. 329–450.

are entered as they appear (in a different script in the original, emboldened here), and alternative formulations are offered after *vel*:

Ad patrem et matrem

Worchipfull and reverenceful fadere and modere, with lowly subieccion and seruise mekely I comende me to youre worthy reu[er]ence, **Ecce salutacio** desyryng hertyly to knowe of þe good hele and prosperité of youre sowl and body *vel* of yow or yores *vel* of yow and alle yowres, welwillyng the which I prey Jesu ful of myght kepe with encrese of honour and vertu *vel* of worchip and vertu *vel* of vertuous lyf long duryng, and yf yowre gracious excellence desire to knowe of my symple estat *vel* of my symple gouernance, I am in good hele of body at Caunterburé, I thanke þe Fader in hevene; **Ecce status affectus** thankyng yow aftyr my symple power hertily for the gret cost and kyndnes þat ye dede to me, and euere I yow beseche of contynuaunce. **Ecce clausula regratioria** Furthermore, dere fader and moder, as witnessit holy wryt, the fader and moder blessyng is the lyf and þe prosperité of the chyld. **Ecce exordium** Therfore every chyld by þe maundement of Almyghty God shulde and owte do reuerence and worschype to his fader and moder. **Ecce narracio** Wherfore my knen I sett on þe growne, I beseche every day hertili yowre blessyng. **Peticio** Also, I prey yow sende me xx li. in hast for my master yerys yeft. **Ecce conclusio** No more at þis tyme, but God þat made al of nothyng brynge yow to þe blesse þat is evere lastyng. Amen. **Ecce subsalutacio**[38]

Many official letters conform with dictaminal prescriptions of this type, but their appearance in private correspondence is much more sporadic, and strict adherence to fixed formulae is the exception rather than the rule. Recent research has shown that, as one would expect, the opening forms of address lent themselves to significant variation according to social and relational factors, and that they changed as time went by.[39] The *salutatio* (or *captatio benevolentiae*) was not necessarily fixed as the second component of a letter, and the inclusion of remarks about the writer's and recipient's state of health were as likely to be determined by the nature of specific relationships as by standard formulae. Margaret Paston almost invariably remembered to include the parental blessing mentioned in the formulary letter above when writing to John Paston II and John III, but Richard Cely the elder never used it when writing to his sons, which again suggests that received frameworks of expression could be varied according to such factors as personality, family tradition, gender and class.[40]

---

[38] See the plate in L.E. Voigts, 'A Handlist of Middle English in Harvard Manuscripts', *Harvard Library Bulletin* 33 (1985), 78.

[39] H. Raumolin-Brunberg, 'Forms of Address in Early English Correspondence', in T. Nevanlainen and H. Raumolin-Brunberg, eds, *Sociolinguistics and Language History: Studies based on the Corpus of Early English Correspondence* (Amsterdam and Atlanta GA, 1996), pp. 167–81, esp. pp. 168–69; also the same authors' 'Constraints on Politeness: the Pragmatics of Address Formulae in Early English Correspondence', in A.H. Jucker, ed., *Historical Pragmatics* (Amsterdam, 1995), pp. 541–601.

[40] T. Sánchez Roura, 'What's Left of the *Captatio Benevolentiae* in 15th Century English Letters?' *Neuphilologische Mitteilungen* 102 (2001), 317–37, at pp. 324–25 and 328 n. 9. The Pastons evidently attached some importance to the parental blessing, which in letters took the form of a time-honoured and widespread formula. Between 1463 and 1465 there was a major crisis in their rela-

Most private letters exist at the intersection of personal, social and sometimes political dimensions of their writers' lives, of which we have at best only a fractional knowledge. Whether one is reading them for historical, linguistic or literary reasons it is unwise to adopt anything less than a multidimensional approach to any one of them. To take a concluding example: in 1447 John Shillingford in his capacity as mayor of Exeter was representing the corporation before the Lord Chancellor in London in their dispute with the bishop, and found himself being personally libelled by his opponents. The part of his letter to the corporation about this, where he turns to the matter of his expenses in rebutting the charges brought against him, is quietly eloquent of the real human complexity of having to ask for £20 under difficult circumstances in the mid-fifteenth century:

> The morun Tuysday Al Halwyn yeven, y receyved the answeris to oure articulis at Westminster, of the whiche y sende yow a true copy; yn the which articulis, as hit appereth, they have spatte out the uttmyst and worst venym that they cowde seye or thynke by me. Y-blessed be God, hit is nother felony, ne treson, ne grete trespas, and thogh hit hadde be, so they wolde have don, and werce yf they cowde. But as for trawthe of the mater that tocheth me, meny worthy men stondeth on the same cas, and have do moche werce than ever y didde, thogh that be to me none excuse. As touchyng the grete venym that they menyth of my lyvyng, y may and purpose be at my purge, as y may right well apon my sawle of alle wymmen alyve excepte oone, and of hire a righte grete while. Therfor y take right noght by, and sey sadly *si recte vivas* &c., and am right mery, and fare right well, ever thankyng God and myn awne purse. And y, liying on my bedde atte writyng of this right yerly [*diligently*], myryly syngyng a myry song, and that ys this: 'Come no more at oure hous, come, come, come'. Y woll not dye nor for sorowe ne for anger, but be myry and fare right well, while y have mony; but that ys and like to be scarce with me, considerynge the bisynesse and coste that y have hadde, and like to have. And yet y hadde with me xx li. and more by my trauthe, wherof, of trauthe, not right moche y spende, but like &c. Constre what ye will . . . Wherfor y sende home to yow attis tyme William Hampton, berer of this writyng, for this cause most specially: that ye, how that ever ye do, sende me xx li. in hast, as ye wolle the spede of youre mater and the welfare of the cité – y nat shamed, but pleased attis tyme – and that ye faill yn no wyse. Mervaillyng moche, for as moche as y departed fro yow withoute eny mony of youris, that ye ne hadde sende to me sithenesse some mony by Germyn, Kyrton, or some other man &c.[41]

---

tionships, when John I withheld his blessing from his elder son and banished him from home (Davis, *Paston Letters and Papers*, Part I, nos 72, 175, 178, 234). For the 'God's blessing and mine' expression in letters from parents to children, see N. Davis, 'A Note on *Pearl*', in J. Conley, ed., *The Middle English* Pearl: *Critical Essays* (Notre Dame, 1970), pp. 325–34.

41   Moore, *Letters and Papers of John Shillingford*, no. IV, pp. 16–17.

BIBLIOGRAPHY

Surveys, Bibliographies and General Studies

Camargo, M., *Ars Dictaminis, Ars Dictandi*, Typologie des Sources du Moyen Âge Occidental, Fasc. 60 (Turnhout, 1991)

Cherewatuk, K. and U. Wietaus, eds, *Dear Sister: Medieval Women and the Epistolary Genre* (Philadelphia, 1993)

Constable, G., *Letters and Letter Collections*, Typologie des Sources du Moyen Âge Occidental, Fasc. 17 (Turnhout, 1976)

Davis, N., 'The *Litera Troili* and English Letters', *The Review of English Studies* ns 16 (1965), 233–44

——, 'Style and Stereotype in Early English Letters', *Leeds Studies in English* ns 1 (1967), 7–17

——, 'A Note on *Pearl*', in J. Conley, ed., *The Middle English* Pearl: *Critical Essays* (Notre Dame, 1970), pp. 325–34

Daybell, J., ed., *Early Modern Women's Letter Writing, 1450–1700* (Houndmills, 2001)

Kingsford, C.L., *English Historical Literature in the Fifteenth Century* (Oxford, 1913), 'Correspondence: Private and Official', pp. 193–227

——, 'English Letters and the Intellectual Ferment', in *Prejudice and Promise in XVth Century England* (Oxford, 1925), pp. 22–47

Laering, J. and R.J. Utz, 'Letter Writing in the Late Middle Ages (c. 1250–1600): An Introductory Bibliography of Critical Studies', *Disputatio* 1 (1996), 191–219

Lyell, L., *A Mediæval Post-Bag* (London, 1934)

Nevanlainen, T., 'Constraints on Politeness: The Pragmatics of Address Formulae in Early English Correspondence', in A.H. Jucker, ed., *Historical Pragmatics* (Amsterdam, 1995), pp. 541–601

Nevanlainen, T., and H. Raumolin-Brunberg, eds, *Sociolinguistics and Language History: Studies based on the Corpus of Early English Correspondence* (Amsterdam and Atlanta GA, 1996)

Richardson, M., 'The *Dictamen* and its Influence on Fifteenth Century English Prose', *Rhetorica* 2 (1984), 207–26

Sánchez Roura, T., 'What's Left of the *Captatio Benevolentiae* in 15th Century English Letters?' *Neuphilologische Mitteilungen* 102 (2001), 317–37

Taylor, J., 'Letters and Letter Collections in England, 1300–1420', *Nottingham Medieval Studies* 24 (1980), 57–70

The Paston Letters

Standard edition: N. Davis, ed., *Paston Letters and Papers of the Fifteenth Century*, Part I (Oxford, 1971), Part II (Oxford, 1976); Part III (ed. R. Beadle and C. Richmond) will be published by the EETS (with re-issues of Davis) in 2006.

J. Gairdner's 'new and complete library edition', *The Paston Letters A.D. 1422–1509* (London and Exeter, 1904) is still sometimes cited, though a significant number of the documents have since been re-dated or re-attributed, and the texts for the first time accurately transcribed, by Davis. Gairdner printed many more letters than the first editor of the Paston correspondence, John Fenn, in *Original Letters, Written during the Reigns of Henry VI. Edward IV. and Richard III.*, vols I and II 1787, vols III and IV 1798, vol. V 1823. However, because certain manuscript collections from which Fenn had worked were not available to him, Gairdner was obliged to reprint extensively from the earlier edition, in which some of the texts are abridged, often without notice.

Barron, C.M., 'Who were the Pastons?' *Journal of the Society of Archivists* 4 (1972), 530–35

Beadle, R., and L. Hellinga, 'William Paston II and Pyson's *Statutes of War* (1492)', *The Library* 7th ser. 2 (2001), 107–19

Bennett, H.S., *The Pastons and their England* (Cambridge, 1922; 2nd ed. 1932, repr. with corrections 1968)

Britnell, R.H., 'The Pastons and their Norfolk', *Agricultural History Review* 36 (1988), 132–44

Davis, N., 'The Language of the Pastons', *Proceedings of the British Academy* 40 (1955), pp. 119–44, reprinted with minor revisions and corrections in J.A. Burrow, ed., *Middle English Literature: British Academy Gollancz Lectures* (Oxford 1989), pp. 45–70

——, 'Scribal Variation in Late Fifteenth-Century English', in *Mélanges . . . Fernand Mossé in Memoriam* (Paris, 1959), pp. 95–103

——, 'The Epistolary Usages of William Worcester', in D.A. Pearsall and R.A. Waldron, eds, *Medieval Literature and Civilization: Studies in Memory of G.N. Garmonsway* (London, 1969), pp. 249–74

——, 'Margaret Paston's Uses of DO', *Neuphilologische Mitteilungen* 73 (1972), 55–62

——, 'On Editing the Paston Letters', *English Studies Today* (1973), 135–48

——, 'Language in Letters from Sir John Fastolf's Household', in P.L. Heyworth, ed., *Medieval Studies for J.A.W. Bennett* (Oxford, 1981), pp. 329–46

——, 'The Language of Two Brothers in the Fifteenth Century', in E.G. Stanley and D. Gray, eds, *Five Hundred Years of Words and Sounds: a Festschrift for Eric Dobson* (Cambridge, 1983), pp. 23–28

Faurot, R.M., 'From Records to Romance: Stevenson's *The Black Arrow* and the Paston Letters', *Studies in English Literature 1500–1900* 5 (1965), 677–90

Haskell, A.S., 'The Paston Women on Marriage in Fifteenth Century England', *Viator* 4 (1973), 459–71

Lester, G.A., 'The Books of a Fifteenth-Century English Gentleman, Sir John Paston', *Neuphilologische Mitteilungen* 88 (1987), 200–17

Maddern, P., 'Honour among the Pastons: Gender and Integrity in Fifteenth Century Society', *Journal of Medieval History* 14 (1988), 357–71

Pearson, P.C., 'The Paston Letters: Carriage of Mail in the Fifteenth Century', *The London Philatelist* 99 (1990), 178–83, 189–95, 232–37, 276–79

Stoker, D., ' "Innumerable Letters of Good Consequence in History": The Discovery and First Publication of the Paston Letters', *The Library* 6th ser. 17 (1995), 107–55

Richmond, C., *The Paston Family in the Fifteenth Century: The First Phase* (Cambridge, 1990); *The Paston Family in the Fifteenth Century: Fastolf's Will* (Cambridge, 1996); *The Paston Family in the Fifteenth Century: Endings* (Manchester, 2000)

——, 'Landlord and Tenant: The Paston Evidence', in J. Kermode, ed., *Enterprise and Individuals in Fifteenth-Century England* (Stroud, 1991), pp. 25–42

——, 'What a Difference a Manuscript Makes: John Wyndham of Felbrigg (d. 1475)', in F. Riddy, ed., *Regionalism in Late Medieval Manuscripts and Texts* (Cambridge, 1991), pp. 129–41

——, 'Elizabeth Clere: Friend of the Pastons', in J. Wogan-Browne et al., eds, *Medieval Women: Texts and Contexts in Late Medieval Britain* (Turnhout, 2000), pp. 251–73

————, 'The Pastons and London', in S. Rees Jones et al., eds, *Courts and Regions in Medieval Europe* (York, 2000), pp. 211–26

Rosenthal, J.T., 'Looking for Grandmother: The Pastons and their Counterparts in Late Medieval England', in J.C. Parsons and B. Wheeler, eds, *Medieval Mothering* (New York, 1996), pp. 259–77

Virgoe, R., *Private Life in the Fifteenth Century: Illustrated Letters of the Paston Family* (London, 1989)

Whitaker, E.A., 'Reading the Paston Letters Medically', *English Language Notes* 31 (1993), 19–27

The Stonor Letters

Standard edition: C.L. Kingsford, ed., *The Stonor Letters and Papers 1290–1483*, Camden Society 3rd ser. 29–30 (1919) and *Camden Miscellany*, Camden Society, 3rd. ser., 34 (1924); reprinted, with an introduction by C. Carpenter, as *Kingsford's Stonor Letters and Papers 1290–1483* (Cambridge, 1996). See also A. Truelove, 'The Fifteenth-Century English Stonor Letters: A revised text with notes, a glossary, and a collation of those letters edited by C. L. Kingsford in 1919 and 1924' (Ph.D. dissertation, University of London, 2001).

Carpenter, C., 'The Stonor Circle in the Fifteenth Century', in R.E. Archer and S. Walker, eds, *Rulers and Ruled in Late Medieval England: Essays Presented to Gerald Harriss* (London and Rio Grande, 1995), pp. 175–200

Truelove, A., 'Commanding Communications: The Fifteenth Century Letters of the Stonor Women', in J. Daybell, ed., *Early Modern Women's Letter Writing, 1450–1700* (Houndmills, 2001), pp. 42–58

The Cely Letters

Standard edition: A. Hanham, ed., *The Cely Letters 1472–1488*, EETS 273 (1975). The letters were originally published by H.E. Malden, ed., *The Cely Papers*, Camden Society 3rd. ser. 1 (1900).

Hanham, A., *The Celys and their World* (Cambridge, 1985)

The Plumpton Letters

Standard edition: J. Kirby, ed., *The Plumpton Letters and Papers*, Camden 5th ser. 8 (Cambridge, 1996). The letters were originally published by T. Stapleton, *Plumpton Correspondence*, Camden Society (1839).

Taylor, J., 'The Plumpton Letters, 1416–1552', *Northern History* 10 (1975), 72–87

The Shillingford Letters

Standard edition: S.A. Moore, ed., *Letters and Papers of John Shillingford, Mayor of Exeter 1447–1450*, Camden Society 2nd ser. 11 (1871).

The Armburgh Papers

Standard edition: C. Carpenter, ed., *The Armburgh Papers* (Woodbridge, 1998).

Other Letter Collections

Fisher, J.H., et al., *An Anthology of Chancery English* (Knoxville, 1984)

Lyell, L., *A Mediæval Post-Bag* (London, 1934), includes letters of Joan Pelham, Jane Roos and William Marshall

Monro, C., ed., *Letters of Margaret of Anjou, Bishop Bekynton and others* Camden Society 86 (1863)

Payne, P., and C. Barron, 'The Letters and Life of Elizabeth Despenser, Lady Zouche (d. 1408)', *Nottingham Medieval Studies* 41 (1997), 126–56

Voigts, L.E., 'A Letter from a Middle English Dictaminal Formulary in Harvard Law Library MS 43', *Speculum* 56 (1981), 575–81

18

Caxton and After*

ALEXANDRA GILLESPIE

Introduction

William Caxton was a mercer of London who became governor of the English
nation at Bruges in 1464 after some years working on the continent. He is
famous for having returned to England in 1476 to set up shop near Westminster
Abbey with a small printing press, and so for effecting a permanent change in
way that books were made in England. He is also famous because he left a
remarkable number of written traces for posterity. In the early 1470s, Caxton
travelled from Bruges to Cologne, apparently with the intention of learning the
new art of printing and applying it to his recent translation of the *Recuyell of
Troy* – a text with which, according to his prologue, he hoped to leave his
literary mark on the Burgundian court (Blake 1969; Painter 1977). He sought to
advertise as well as to distribute his own literary works in printed books; the
promotional prologues and epilogues he added to his editions have been separately treated as examples of late Middle English prose writing by both editors
and critics (Crotch 1928; Blake 1973; Blake 1991, 89–106, 119–47). In this
sense Caxton is an important figure in a history of medieval vernacular prose
writing. His compositions constitute a significant contribution to English literature and he can be assigned primary responsibility for the first editions of prose
works within many of the major generic categories of the period: devotional,
didactic, and liturgical religious pieces; philosophical and moral works; statutes;
geographies, histories, and encyclopaedias; scientific and medical writing;
Chaucerian prose; and romances and chivalric literature.

However, the importance of Caxton should not be overstated. Crucial developments in the commercial use of the press for the mass production of books
were left to Caxton's contemporaries and successors, especially Richard Pynson
and Wynkyn de Worde. Their output and its impact on the tradition of prose
writing in England has rarely been considered, and yet it was they, not Caxton,
who issued the first editions of mystical texts, including extracts from the *Book
of Margery Kempe*, works by followers of Richard Rolle, and Walter Hilton's
Scala Perfectionis; the first version of the *Ancrene Wisse*; the first travel writing
in English, including the *Book of John Mandeville*; the first Lollard texts; the
first school and law books; and much of the popular vernacular religious and

* I wish to thank Barbara Walshe and Jean Rumble for assistance with the bibliography for this chapter
and Professor A.S.G. Edwards for advice and guidance.

utilitarian material that filled the manuscripts produced in increasing numbers in England in the fifteenth century. Moreover, it was Caxton's successors, both writers and printers, who were active up to the 'end' of the Middle English period – however scholars arrive at that rather arbitrarily designated moment.[1] Caxton's choice of texts and his presentation of them suggest a certain bibliographical and literary nostalgia as well as interest in the commercial benefits of technological innovation (Kuskin 1999b). Printing provided a new context for the production of the materials of literary culture in the late medieval period, but it did not change that culture fundamentally. Humanist change to intellectual fashions and, perhaps more importantly, successive reformations of religion would have a more radical and more lasting effect on prose writing in England (Shrank 2004). It was those who succeeded Caxton who witnessed and participated in the process – however incomplete or partial – by which the literary products of the England's Middle Ages were rendered obsolete.

The scope of this chapter is, accordingly, not just texts written or printed by Caxton but prose produced by the writers who followed him, and issued from local and continental presses up to (and sometimes beyond) the English Reformation. Gaps and omissions are inevitable in such a broad and broadly new discussion. Firstly, in discussing prose works written or translated after 1500, the limit set in the standard bibliographies, and in my account of textual, critical, and historical approaches to the books and works described here, I have sought to be representative rather than comprehensive. Secondly, I have not extended my survey of printed prose much beyond the useful work of Blake, Edwards, and Lewis in the *Index of Printed Middle English Prose*. An updated version of IPMEP that takes account of the revision of STC and recent editorial work is needed; so is more detailed discussion of the fifteenth- and early sixteenth-century editions of English prose. As space is limited here, I supply IPMEP and STC numbers for each text and/or early printed book, and identify only the most recent scholarly editions. And I hope that this chapter will serve as a guide to future research rather as a summary of what is already known. The after-life of Middle English prose writing is potentially a vital field. It promises to yield important insights into English literary culture at an epochal moment in its history.

Caxton's Prose – Translations, Additions, Editions

It is possible to characterise recent critical discussions of Caxton as interested in his contradictory or at least competing concerns as a printer and a writer. Scholars link the style of his prose compositions to his consistent choice 'either of translations or of work based on foreign models' for his press (Blake 1991, 128). The 'aureate' features of his own prose, his use of doublets, Latinate diction, and French and Flemish loan-words, are evidence of the influence of

---

[1]   1500 is the date chosen by IPMEP; in this chapter, 1534 and the break with Rome is the critical moment (see Simpson 2002).

continental archetypes on his writing and of recent developments in English stylistics: especially the rhetorical embellishment and lexical enrichment of the language by famous writers such as Chaucer and Lydgate (Bornstein 1977; Blake 1966; Blake 1991, 231–58). Echoes of fifteenth-century writers' tributes to Chaucer the rhetorician; expressions of concern about the adequacy of Caxton's own, 'rude', Kentish English; his attempt to embellish his language, sometimes by the addition of 'over-subtle' terms; and, conversely, his dislike of prolixity have all been described as features of Caxton's prologues and epilogues, and as a kind of index to his approach to prose translation (Blake 1991, 119–85; Keiser 1987, 17–18).

Caxton's prose style is also often described as 'courtly' – a gesture to the influence of Burgundian and English aristocratic culture on his literary tastes. The first book that he selected for translation and printing at Bruges, the *Recuyell of Troy*, was written in 1464 by Raoul Le Fèvre, a chaplain to the Burgundian prince and bibliophile Phillip the Good. His second Bruges edition of Middle English prose was a translation the *Game and Play of Chess*: seven manuscript copies of the French original can be traced to Philip's court (Painter 1977, 52, 64–67). The vernacular romances, histories, and works of moral and religious instruction that were the staple output of Caxton's Westminster press were likewise to be found on the shelves of the libraries of Edward IV, Richard III, Henry VII, and their courtiers (Meale 1989, 202–4; Sutton and Visser-Fuchs 1997). Of even more importance was the impetus that courtly patrons – prospective or real – gave to Caxton's endeavours. In his prologue to the *Recuyell*, Caxton famously seeks the approval and promotes the name of Margaret of Burgundy, wife of Charles the Bold (Philip's successor) and sister of England's Edward IV. He encountered Margaret and a great many other Burgundian and English noblemen and women while serving as a diplomat and as the head of the English nation; he perhaps hoped for her protection during the turbulent political events of 1471, around which time he ceased to be governor (Painter 1977, 43–71). But equally, Caxton may simply have responded, in his dedication of this and other books, to a traditional literary economy in which gifts were a writer's principal pecuniary reward, and in which noble patrons were to be sought or gestured to as a matter of course (Lucas 1982). The press, it seems, did not initially dislodge the *idea* of a courtly standard for literary achievement – or the complex late feudal affinities of vernacular writers. His prologues and epilogues show that Caxton was insistently interested, and to a varying extent involved, in courtly contexts for book production – in noble authors and translators and in a succession of unnamed knights and ladies who, along with Edward IV, the young Edward V, Richard III, Elizabeth of York, Margaret Beaufort, and Henry VII formed an ideal readership for the books Caxton printed (Blake 1973, 28–31). Among Caxton's translations are those – his *Ovid*, for instance – that were never printed but instead copied into lavish, decorated manuscripts. Caxton sold or gave several such books to his patrons, and the likes of Anthony Wydeville, Earl Rivers, had manuscript versions of texts that Caxton had printed at his behest scribally copied for presentation at court (Kekewich 1971, 486; Scott 1976; Blake 1969, 98). The work of England's first printer-translator seems to look back – towards a courtly economy for bespoke literary and book production, and away from the transitional world of print.

However, Caxton's career had a dynamic aspect, as well as a nostalgic one. In his work as a maker of books and as a writer he was among those who forged new cultural links between the Yorkist and Burgundian courts in the third quarter of the fifteenth century (Bornstein 1976; Kipling 1977). He also made use of the sort of paratextual promotional material that was ultimately standardised by printing. He responded to the exigencies of mass production by developing an 'enunciation' of the book – finding new ways to advertise a book's content and producer (Hanna 1996, 37). Caxton's paratextual additions thus bear witness to his commercial as well as his literary work. Especially after his arrival in Westminster in 1476 he worked in a mercantile as well as a courtly *milieu*. He imported printed books from continental producers, and he competed with those producers for a share of the English market when he issued books (Kerling 1955; Armstrong 1977; Sutton 1994; Needham 1999). An English library filled with Caxton editions might have resembled that of a Burgundian ducal palace, but Caxton's *shop* must have resembled that of his Bruges business partner, the former scribe Colard Mansion, or that of fellow merchants in London (Saenger 1975). A well-known English prose text is a useful illustration of these points. Chaucer's *Boece* was a translation of a Latin work that had been circulating for some time in finely printed, continental editions. It had been printed in French by Mansion just a few months earlier, like many of the prose texts produced by Caxton (Blades 1861–63, 1: 45–61). In his prologue, Caxton identifies an unnamed 'gossib' probably a fellow merchant-class Londoner, who encouraged him to print the text. Caxton also appended a humanist epitaph for Chaucer, the famous English translator of the text (Lerer 1993, 147–75). The epitaph had been composed by an Italian laureate then in England, Stefano Surigone, and was presumably designed to match the learned, humanist commentary increasingly found in continental Boethius editions and the life of Boethius in Mansion's edition. It also served as a reminder of Caxton's English, metropolitan locale. The epitaph was to be found at Westminster Abbey, near Caxton's shop, hanging from a pillar like one of Caxton's posted advertisements for the *Sarum Ordinale* (*STC* 4890).

A changing and expanding London-based commercial trade in books; the use of promotional devices alongside and within prose texts; and the influence of the continental book trade and of humanism were all features of fifteenth-century literary culture before the arrival of the press (Christianson 1989; Mooney 2000; Rundle 2002). But Caxton's approach to marketing suggests that printing impacted upon the pace and the extent of change. It was conventional for medieval authors to refer to a readership beyond the immediate, known audience for their texts. It was imperative, however, that Caxton actually reach a wide market for printed books, which were produced in tens, even hundreds of copies. A patron might reward a printer for an edition, or take some copies for private distribution, but the rest would have to be sold.[2] This transi-

---

2   See, for instance, Doyle 1989 on monastic writers's direction of texts to a wide readership and

tion, as well as literary tradition, informs Caxton's paratext – his allusions to members of the court and famous *auctores* are endorsements, as are his generalised accounts of 'diverse gentlemen', 'persons of noble estate and degree', 'princes, lords, barons', but also 'merchants' to whom his books are recommended (Blake 1973, 30–31; Edwards and Meale 1993). Caxton produced a new kind of book – but his promotion of that book relied on old ways of thinking about literary culture (Kuskin 1999b).

We know a limited amount about the way the way that Caxton's customers responded to these tactics. Yu-Chiao Wang's important work on the provenance of Caxton's romances demonstrates that the printer reached each of the groups of book buyers and readers that he identifies in paratext. Clerics owned some copies; noble patrons left marks on others. Most inscriptions, however, were left in Caxton's books by the sort of folk – 'diverse' in their allegiances and their methods of self-definition – with whom Caxton himself can be associated: urban gentry, merchant travelers, men and women in the service of the aristocracy, and minor provincial landholders (Wang 2004; cf. Ford 1999). Takako Kato's development of Lotte Hellinga's study of the compositors of Caxton's edition of Malory's *Morte D'Arthur* (STC 801) serves to remind us of the work of those who inhabited the shop floor rather than the merchant hall or gentle household (Hellinga 1982; Kato 2002). By looking beyond Caxton, new scholars have found vital evidence about the history of his books and the complex, layered 'human presence in every recorded text' (McKenzie 1999, 29).

Caxton's Trace – Printers and Translators, Paratext and Text

In 1512, the printer-translator Robert Copland described himself 'gladly folowynge the trace of my mayster Caxton' (IPMEP 361, STC 708.5, A2r). Copland's remark is significant for several reasons. Firstly, it moves Caxton away from centre-stage. Copland and other printers did take up, and transform, Caxton's 'trace' in their editions of English prose writing. During Caxton's lifetime, the St Albans Printer, William de Machlinia in London, Thomas Rood in Oxford, and Gerard Leeu in Antwerp printed some English prose texts (Duff 1906 and 1912b; Blake 1991, 57–73). But it was Caxton's associate, Wynkyn de Worde, Richard Pynson (printer to the king after about 1506), and their associates and competitors in the book trade, Robert Copland, Julian Notary, Robert Redman, and Henry Pepwell among them, who accomplished what Caxton had merely begun, realising the potential of the press to invigorate the tradition of prose writing at the end of the Middle Ages. They printed a greater range of Middle English prose works, and their books were more often illustrated and more often in a quarto format that made them increasingly accessible as book prices fell (Bennett 1969, 231–33). Biographies and bibliographies for printers

Bennett 1969, 40–64 on patrons. On commercialization of book production and the marketing of printed books, see Blayney 2003 and McKitterick 2003.

of English works of the late fifteenth and early sixteenth centuries are available in Duff (1912a), STC, and the new *Oxford Dictionary of National Biography*. Moran's book on de Worde and his contemporaries has been reprinted (1976 repr. 2002). Hellinga has updated the chronology of de Worde's early editions (2002). But the two major studies of Pynson's career are unpublished and Blayney's definitive work on the early Stationers' Company is still anticipated (Johnston 1978; Neville-Sington 1990; Blayney 2003). In general, scholarship on the English printers who followed Caxton lags behind recognition of their importance.

Caxton's successors also followed him in consistently preferring translation, especially from French, to original composition (Bennett 1969, 152–77; Boffey 2000). Copland's 1512 *Appolyn of Tyre* was adapted from the French, as was his *Knyght of the Swanne* (STC 7571) and *Knyghtes and Syege of Rhodes* (STC 15050). He translated advice for the courtier or prince in the 1528 *Secret of Secrets* from an abbreviated French version (STC 770) and the utilitarian *Rutter of the Sea* from a French *Routier de la Mer* (STC 11550.6–11550.8) (Erler 1993, 36–37). Henry Watson produced versions of the French romances *Oliver of Castile*, *Ponthus*, and *Valentyne and Orson* (IPMEP 107, STC 18808; IPMEP 609, STC 20107.5–20108; IPMEP 52, STC 24571.3–25473) but he also translated the cautionary and didactic *Chirche of the Evyll Men and Women* (IPMEP 464; STC 1966–67). Brian Anslay, a yeoman of Henry VIII's cellar, chose a text by Christine de Pisan for translation, as Caxton and Earl Rivers had before him. His *Book of the City of Ladies* was printed by Henry Pepwell in 1518 (STC 7271; Summit 2000, 93–107). John Bourchier, second Lord Berners was another prolific translator of romances and historical material; perhaps because private, coterie circulation was preferred within a noble *milieu*, many of his works remained in manuscript during his lifetime (Blake 1971; Boro 2004). Margaret Beaufort, the king's mother, was named as a patron of many de Worde editions, including those of her own translations of the *Mirroure of Golde* and an *Imitatio Christi* (co-translated with William Atkinson) (IPMEP 704, STC 6894.5–6897.5; IPMEP 838, STC 23954.7–23960; Powell 1998). Another translator, Andrew Chertsey, was responsible for five religious translations for Copland's occasional collaborator, de Worde, each of them 'from french in prose / of goostly exemplayre' as Copland put it in a verse prologue to Chertsey's 1521 *Passyon of Our Lord* (STC 14558, A1v). In contrast to these ascribed texts are dozens of anonymous translations supplied to meet an ever-increasing demand among the laity for vernacular books of religion (Duffy 1992, 77–87).

Thirdly, paratextual traces left by book-producers who followed Caxton, like his prologues and epilogues, were innovative in form but conservative in their rhetoric. Copland often complains in verse and prose that the average reader prefers 'tryfles and toyes' to 'olde morall bokes' (Erler 1993, *Assemble of Foules*, 16a). They must be promoted differently, but with an eye to the 'olde': to medieval literary and manuscript traditions. The monumental 1532 edition of Chaucer's *Works* edited by William Thynne, clerk of the royal kitchen, is one outcome of these concerns. Its preface and Thynne's dedication to Henry VIII establish a Chaucerian history of English cultural sovereignty in traditional terms: the gentleman editor works within a noble household, making a new books out of old manuscripts because he believes this is his 'dewtie' to king and country (STC 5080, A3r). Several important prose works in Middle English were ascribed to Chaucer in the 1532 *Works* and as such made available for a new Tudor history of English letters (Edwards 1995). In the antiquary John Leland's *Scriptores*, a list of English writers compiled in the 1530s, Usk's *Testament of Love* (see Middleton 1998), *Boece*, the *Astrolabe*, and the *Canterbury Tales*, which includes two prose texts, as Leland carefully notes, could appear alongside the great Latin writings of the English Middle Ages (Simpson 2002, 7–33).

Finally, Caxton's own 'traces' – the prose texts he issued from his press – form a basis for a discussion of the production of Middle English prose (printed or otherwise) in the years immediately prior to English Reformation. The remainder of this chapter deals briefly with the content and audience for such works, the persistent influence of manuscript traditions on certain genres of writing, and the impact of the press in the decades during which printing became a major industry in England, before turning to the events that followed the break with Rome in 1534.

Vernacular Books of Religion

The Middle English texts that were printed most often in the fifteenth and early sixteenth centuries have received the least editorial or critical attention. In the early decades of its operation, the English press was engaged in the dissemination of thousands of religious books. Caxton printed some of these: while they seem to make up only a small proportion of his total output, they are representative in their content. Like Gutenberg, Caxton printed indulgences containing English prose for the remission of buyers' sins as soon as he set up his press. They were by nature ephemeral and survive only as binding fragments. New editions and new indulgences issued by de Worde and others probably represent only a fraction of this lucrative business (STC 148; e.g. IPMEP 104; Needham 1986). Rapid fifteenth-century growth in the production of manuscript service books and primers or *Horae* carried over into print (Duffy 1992, 209–32; Erler 1999, 495–509). Caxton's contributions to the market were in Latin and were apparently anticipated by his continental peers: a Sarum breviary was produced for the English market in the Netherlands in about 1475 (*STC* 15794). It was Caxton's English and continental successors who first printed English prose within manuals of the Sarum Use (Erler 1984). Among the vernacular texts incorporated into service books were reprints of Caxton's *Fifteen Oes* (prayers ascribed to St Bridget) and the *Gret Sentence* on excommunication that Caxton had printed alongside John Mirk's *Quattuor Sermones* in 1482–83 (IPMEP 489, e.g. in STC 15875; IPMEP 122, e.g. in STC 16145).

As the inclusion of such material in service books suggests, at the end of the Middle Ages the laity sought to participate in the liturgy, sacramental celebrations, and the calendar of observances. Caxton's edition of the *Ars Moriendi* contains a 'syngular prayer to be sayde in the fest of the dedycacyon of ony chirche' but also to be said 'at ony other tyme' (IPMEP 818, STC 786, A7r). But it was Caxton's assistant de Worde who produced the most works over his long career concerned with the proper ordering of the 'tyme' and the affective devotional experience of the Christian lay reader. He developed the market identified by Caxton for treatises for the *Dyenge Creature* (IPMEP 44, STC 6033.5–6033.5a) or those anticipating doom and the *Byrthe and Comynge of the Antechryst* (IPMEP 93, STC 670). He printed the *Ordynarye of Crysten Men* (IPMEP 165, STC 5198–99); texts such as the *Shedynge of the vii. Blood of Crist* that advanced the popular cult of Christ's wounds (STC 14546); and a wide selection of saints lives, meditations, contemplations, and prayers on the sacraments, sin, tribulation, and salvation in English prose. Such books were mostly quartos and were often illustrated by woodcut images, some of which de Worde printed separately as images of pity (Driver 1989, 1996; STC 14077 for images of pity). The devotional material they contained could also be found in almanacs like the *Kalendar of Shepherds*, jostling for space with prognostications, recipes, treatises on bloodletting, astrological diagrams, and poems about snails (STC 22408–23; Driver 2003). A flood of printed religious material promoted fashionable, if not sanctioned, religious practices – 'how euery man & woman ought to faste and absteyne from flesshe on ye Wednesday', for instance (STC 24224, A2r) – until reformers explicitly outlawed them (Duffy 1992, 37–52).

Pastoral guides, works of catechetical instruction, and sermon collections are another important category of Middle English prose writing. The freedom with which didactic texts moved between clerical communities and a lay readership determined their successful marketing in print. Designed, as Caxton puts it in his prologue to the *Doctrinal of Sapience*, for 'prestes to lerne and teche to theyr parysshens and . . . for simple prestes that understonde not the scriptures' (IPMEP 748, STC 21431; Blake 1973, *Doctrinal*, 148–49), they provided models for preaching and for maintenance of the educational programme laid out by Archbishop Pecham for the English people in 1281. But manuscript and printed copies of popular works such as John Mirk's sermon collection, the *Liber Festialis* (IPMEP 734, STC 17957–75), and Nicholas Love's *Speculum Vitae Christi* (IPMEP 553, STC 3259–68) had identifiable lay readers as well as owners among the regular and secular clergy (Doyle 1989). De Worde, Pynson, and their contemporaries capitalised on and expanded this wide market for didactic material, printing a range of texts from sermons by John Alcock (e.g. IPMEP 418, STC 284–285.5) to translations of Latin pastoral manuals like the *Exornatorium Curatorum* (IPMEP 399, STC 10627.5–10634.3). Caxton's successors issued texts for the regular clergy written within religious foundations, most famously a series of works from Syon Abbey (printed by Pynson, de Worde, and Richard Fawkes): among these the *Orcherd of Syon*, retrieved from an old manuscript at the abbey and sent to printers at the cost of its steward, Richard Sutton, in 1519 (IPMEP 561, STC 4815); an *Image of Love*, translated for the Syon nuns by John Gough, an associate of de Worde's (STC 21471.5); Thomas Gascoigne's *Myroure of Oure Lady* (IPMEP 798, STC 17542); and the 'wretch of Syon' Richard Whitford's *Lyfe of Perfection* and *Rule of Saynt Augustyn* (IPMEP 267, STC 25421; IPMEP 268, STC 922.3–922.4). Whitford's very popular *Werke for Housholders* went through seven editions between 1530 and 1537 (STC 25421.8-25.5). The possibility of financial support from religious institutions such as Syon, and the lay audience that the Brigittines anticipated and found for their texts, apparently encouraged printers to invest in these editions (Rhodes 1993; Edwards and Meale 1993; Erler 1999).

Nuns were among the readers of all of the Syon books just described, and gender was an important factor in the production of religious prose in print, as it was a vital aspect of earlier manuscript cultures (Erler 2002). However, Nicholas Watson's statement that printed editions of texts by Middle English mystics were 'aimed primarily at women religious' needs revision (1999, 561). Certain contemplative texts – a *Tretyse of Loue* derived from the *Ancrene Wisse* (IPMEP 751, STC 24234) and the *Chastysing of Goddes Chyldern* (IPMEP 343, STC 5065), for example – addressed a cloistered, female readership directly. But just as the Syon monk Thomas Betson wrote his *Treatyse* 'compendiously drawen out of many & dyuers wrytynges of holy men/ to dispose men to be virtuously occupied in theyr myndes & prayers . . . religious people [and] laye people' (IPMEP 664, STC 1978, A2r), so did early printers identify and develop multiple markets for contemplative and visionary texts, as they did for catechetical and didactic books. Caxton did not print any mystical prose. De Machlinia printed a translation of Eynsham's Latin account of his *visio* as a *Revelacion* in 1483 (IPMEP 695, STC 20917; Easting 2002) but it was the second generation of printers who printed the works of the best-known mystics (Keiser 1987). De Worde printed parts of the *Book of Margery Kempe* as a *Shorte Treatyse of Contemplacyon* in about 1501 (IPMEP 592, STC 14924): the extracts transform the book a conversation between Christ and a pious 'doughter' (A1r) (Holbrook 1987). The only extant copy if this book was formerly part of the sort of *Sammelband* (tract volume) in which late medieval readers often gathered printed pamphlets. The *Sammelband* once contained a range of devotional prose items – Margaret Beaufort's translation of part of an *Imitatio Christi*; the contemplations of an anchorite; Andrew Chertsey's account of the Passion; and a text ascribed to Richard Rolle (A. Gillespie 2004b). Similar anthologies and miscellanies were characteristic of late fifteenth-century manuscript culture and the readership for the works that they contained extended beyond communities of pious or cloistered women (V. Gillespie 1989). Printers sometimes gave such compilations mass-produced form. De Worde printed the first edition of Walter Hilton's *Scala Perfectionis* separately, at the request, he says, of Margaret Beaufort but perhaps also with a view to the sort of gentle and merchant-class lay readers, male and female, that the text had found in manuscript (IPMEP 255, STC 14042; Sargent 1985). After that, the *Scala* was always printed with Hilton's *Medled Lyf*, and no patron was named (IPMEP 147, STC 140141–45). The latter work was also printed in 1516 alongside the *Kalendre of the Newe Legende of Englande*, and a *Lyfe of Seynt Birgetta* (IPMEP 147, 570, 576, STC 4062). In 1518, Pepwell printed an even larger contemplative compilation, containing a reprint of de Worde's edition of Kempe's book, ascribed to an 'ancresse'; a translation of Richard of St Victor's *De Preparatione Animi ad Contemplationem* by a follower of Rolle; Hilton's *Anehede of Godd*; and several other pieces (IPMEP 4, 146, 429, 252, 240, 592, 255; STC 20972). There is evidence, then, of the promotion of old and new devotional material together; of the production of new kinds of devotional miscellanies in print; and of a flexible approach to the marketing of mystical texts.

Books of Chivalry and Romance

It was Caxton rather than de Worde who first sought, or at least alluded to, Margaret Beaufort's support for an edition of a religious text: he writes that his *Fifteen Oes* was produced following 'commaundementes' by the king's mother and his queen Elizabeth (IPMEP 489, STC 20195; Blake 1973, *Fifteen Oes*, 1–2; Powell 1998). However, in his prologue to *Blanchardyn and Eglantine*, also said to have been produced at Margaret's behest, Caxton describes or at least feigns a preference for secular reading matter: it is better for 'gentyl yonge ladyes and damoysellys for to lerne to be stedfaste and constaunt in their parte to theym that they ones have promysed and agreed to'; than reading 'overmoche in bokes of contemplaycion' (IPMEP 795, STC 3124; Blake 1973, *Blanchardyn*, 20–25). Many of Caxton's books deal with the edification of 'courtly' subjects: his romances; the *Order of Chivalry* (IPMEP 794, STC 3326); the *Knight of the Tower*, a courtesy manual directed to the daughters of noblemen (IPMEP 385, STC 15296); and the *Curial*, a translation of a 'lettre whyche Maistre Alain Charetier wrote to his brother whyche desired to come dwelle in court' (IPMEP 300, STC 5057; Blake 1973, *Curial*, 1–3), among others.

Caxton does make reference to the readership that such books found outside of the court (Wang 2004). His translation of Christine de Pisan's *Fayts of Arms* is directed to soldiers needing schooling in chivalry, for instance (IPMEP 106, STC 7269). The *Book of Good Manners* is said to have been printed 'that it myght be had and used emonge the people for th'amendement of their maners and to the'encrease of vertuous lyvyng' (IPMEP 820, STC 15394; Blake 1973, *Book of Good Manners*, 16–18). But the active promotion of books about courtesy and chivalry for both a noble or courtly market and an even broader readership is more evident in the work of later printers. The *Book of St Albans* is a useful example. Printed in an elaborate multi-colour folio by the St Albans printer in 1486, it contains the *Liber Armorum*, a treatise on equine medicine, and texts on the courtly pursuits of hunting, hawking, and serving (STC 3308, IPMEP 3, 390–91). It was reprinted in folio by de Worde in 1496, augmented by a *Treatyse of Fysshynge wyth an Angle*, 'for by cause that this treatyse sholde not come to the hondys of eche ydle persone whyche wolde desire it yf it were enprynted allone' (STC 3309, 14v, with IPMEP 611 added; Keiser 1999). The printer's subsequent actions belie his rhetoric. Material taken directly from de Worde's 'greter volume [for] gentyll & noble men' and similar practical books for gentle and noblemen were also separately issued 'allone' as cheap pamphlets: the *Noble Book of Cookry* printed by de Worde and Pynson (IPMEP 630, STC 3297–3297.5) and de Worde's separate prints of the *Proprytees and Medycynes for Hors* (IPMEP 3, 718, STC 20439.3–20439.7), for instance. The latter text was reprinted throughout the sixteenth century and edited anew from manuscripts and printed sources thereafter (Keiser 1995). Caxton's successors also expanded the market for English prose by providing new editions – of romances such as *Melusyne* (IPMEP 363, STC 14648) and *William of Palernoe*, adapted from an alliterative version of that text (IPMEP 534, STC 25707.5) (Meale 1992); of new advisory texts, such as a translations of Christine de Pisan's *Body of Polycye* (IPMEP 332, STC 7270); and of siege narratives that perhaps appealed to metropolitan readers for whom the War of the Roses was a recent memory. John Kay's c. 1482 translation of an eyewitness account of the *Siege of Rhodes* was soon printed, probably by Lettou and de Machlinia (IPMEP 776, STC 4594), as was the *Dystruccyon of Iherusalem by Vaspazian and Tytus* (IPMEP 241, STC 14517–19). It is of note that several romances printed in the Marian and early Elizabethan period by William Copland were reprints of earlier editions that have been lost or survive as fragments (Edwards 2003). Humanist reformers' rejection of medieval romance and other medieval models for the education of the courtier may have produced such gaps in the bibliographical record, and the gaps may account for scholarly neglect of such texts (Adams 1959). There has been little written on Tudor prose romances, or on the many other early printed prose narratives designed for the improvement of the realm – or its amusement – from Caxton's *Aesop* (IPMEP 179, STC 175) to Berthelet's jest book *Tales, and quicke answers* (STC 23665).[3]

Books of Information

Caxton claims that he is concerned about the edification of courtly readers, and those who might emulate court culture. His didacticism did not, however, extend to an interest in books for the school market. He may have imported grammars from the continent. He did print a Latin version of Donatus (STC 7013) and a *Doctrine to Learn French and English* (IPMEP 514, STC 24865).[4] But Rood and de Machlinia were much more closely engaged in the business of learning. They printed several grammatical works in Latin and a *Vulgaria* containing Latin and English sentences derived from the plays of Terence, probably by the English schoolmaster John Ankwyll. Ankwyll's work was reprinted by Leeu in Antwerp and revised for de Worde in 1529 (STC 23904–08; Brodie 1974). It anticipated Erasmian humanist reform of Latin teaching, and that reform, while it emphasised the substitution of classical for medieval texts, nevertheless generated a significant market for the Middle English writings of another early Middle English writer, the fifteenth-century schoolmaster John Leland. If the number of editions is to be the measure, adaptations by John Stanbridge of Leland's *Accidence*, *Comparacio*, *Formula*, and *Sum es fui* and Stanbridge's own *Vulgaria* were the most popular books containing Middle English prose in the

3 For a survey of popular fiction of the period see Sullivan and Woodbridge 2000.
4 Texts of this sort appear in merchant-class household books of the period such as the commonplace book of Richard Hill, Oxford, Balliol College MS 354 (Collier 1997).

decades before the Reformation, surviving in well over one hundred editions (Orme 1999; Weiss 1941, 169–72).[5]

Middle English prose was deemed a suitable medium for the dissemination of scientific information as well as grammatical instruction (Voigts 1989).[6] Caxton's *Governal of Health* was the first of many medical texts that had circulated widely in manuscript to appear from the English presses (IPMEP 407, STC 12138). Plague treatises, such as de Machlinia's *Passing Gode Lityll Boke Necessarye and Behouefull Agenst the Pestilence* (IPMEP 91, STC 4589–4593.5); 'mirrors' of health by translators such as Thomas Moulton and Andrew Borde (on the latter, see Shrank 2000); and dozens of editions of anatomies, urinaries, dietaries, astrometeorological prognostications, and herbals, printed until the middle of the sixteenth century, were often taken or adapted from Middle English prose sources (Murray Jones 1999; Mooney 1997).

Geographies, encyclopaedias, and histories of the world and nation were also popular in the early decades of printing. Information for various purposes was supplied by Caxton's edition of Trevisa's translation of Ralph Higden's *Polychronicon* (IPMEP 605, STC 13438), from which he derived his *Description of Britain* (IPMEP 605, STC 13438), and by his version of the prose *Brut*, the *Chronicles of England* (IPMEP 374, STC 9991–92). Perhaps the most important of these purposes was the self-consciousness of the English reader, who was able to locate or identify his or herself by means of such texts within the boundaries of a nation state and within a history of the Christian and non- or pre-Christian world. Caxton's texts were sufficiently popular to attract notice, and new editions, from later printers. De Worde reprinted the *Polychronicon* in 1495 at the behest of the mercer Roger Thorney (STC 13439). De Worde describes Thorney as his sponsor in the 1495 edition of Trevisa's version of *De Proprietatibus Rerum* as well (IPMEP 785, STC 1536). Trevisa's translation of Bartholomeus Anglicus's great encyclopaedia was reprinted by Thomas Berthelet in 1535 and then edited against Latin sources by the Elizabethan scholar-antiquary Stephen Batman for the printer Thomas East in 1582 (STC 1537–38).

Caxton's English *Chronicles* and his *Description of Britain* were also reprinted in adapted, combined, and separate forms, first by Caxton's competitors in St Albans and London, and then well into the sixteenth century (STC 13440b, 9993–10002). The medieval chronicle was perhaps the most vital of Middle English prose traditions in the Tudor period. Lord Berners translated Froissart's French *Chronicles* in the 1520s; it was reprinted until 1611 and also circulated in manuscript (STC 11396–400; Blake 1971; Boro 2004). The boundaries between manuscript and printed production of historical texts seem to have been especially permeable. A fifteenth-century London chronicle was abbreviated c. 1500 by a citizen, Richard Arnold, as company for the recipes and poems in his manuscript commonplace book. The manuscript does not survive, but the

---

5   Stanbridge's *Vulgaria* is IPMEP 270, STC 23195.5–23198.7; for some of Leland's work, see IPMEP 308, 349; STC 23163.6–23175.5.

6   Cf. the argument that the vernacular was regarded as suitable for technical writing only after humanist reform and the advent of printing (Jones 1953).

book was printed in its entirety by Van Berghen in Antwerp in about 1503 (IPMEP 365, STC 782). The printed version was then available to another citizen, Richard Hill, who adapted the chronicle for his household book, Oxford, Balliol College, MS 354 (Collier 1997). Manuscripts of London chronicles and other medieval histories also formed the basis for the great Elizabethan historiographical projects of John Stow and Raphael Holinshed and his collaborators (Gransden 1982, 220–48; A. Gillespie 2004a).

Another medieval source of information about worldly matters, the *Book of John Mandeville*, was first printed in 1496 by Pynson and subsequently had a continuous history of publication until the early eighteenth century (IPMEP 233, STC 17246–54; Seymour 1964; Kohanski 2001). Its enduring popularity is best explained by the shift in cultural horizons that accompanied European global expansionism from the time of Columbus's voyage, and by the catalogue of 'wonders of the East' that appeared alongside Mandeville's guide for pilgrims to Jerusalem (Greenblatt 1991). Pamphlets such as *Informacion for Pylgrymes unto the Holy Londe* (IPMEP 85, STC 14081–83) had a shorter shelf life. They were more explicitly practical in their concerns: 'At Calays ye shal haue as many plackys for half a noble englysshe or for a dukate xxiij plackes. That is beste money in Brugis' (STC 14081, A2r). There was little reason to print them after the Henrician injunctions against pilgrimage were issued in 1538.[7]

The Impact of Reform

The discussion so far has considered the importance of Middle English prose traditions to the writers, book producers, and readers involved in the transition from manuscript to print – and from the period scholars describe as medieval to that designated early modern. The discussion has not reached much further than 1534, however. Henry VIII's break with Rome marked an end for the printing of much Middle English religious prose, excepting occasional Marian and recusant editions, until the scholarly editions of the nineteenth century. If it was inevitable that the production of orthodox catholic works end with the Reformation, it is perhaps surprising find so many other genres of Middle English prose out of print after 1534 – from prose romances to plague treatises. The reasons for this change are manifold: the religious content and periphrasis of Middle English writing (Dalrymple 1995); the impact of humanism and reformist polemic on the choice of texts for the press; printers' uncertainty about religious policy and the impact of censorship; and the radical ideology of reform, which required that a breach be represented between post-Reformation England and its own past (Simpson 2002).

But if the Reformation was, in this sense, a 'cultural revolution', it was one characterised by a degree of inconsistency and uncertainty. Not all texts from the Middle Ages proved irrelevant to the reformist cause. Mary C. Erler

---

[7] Their influence may be traced, however, in the fraught accounts of pilgrimage to be found in Andrew Borde's *Introduction of Knowledge*, published in about 1547 and about 1562 (STC 3382–85; Shrank 2000).

describes the utility of Robert Copland's 1529 prose text, the *Maner to Lyue Well*, for French printers who produced *Horae* and service books for English readers, and sought both to avert censorship, and to compete with the earliest all-English primers (Erler 1984). Fourteenth- and fifteenth-century Lollard works and writings incorporating medieval anti-clerical and proto-protestant positions also found a new audience from the 1530s. They were first printed in Antwerp and distributed secretly by followers of Luther. After 1534 they were issued by English presses in the context of more moderate English reformist policy (Hudson 1985, 227–48). Printers and reformers represented such texts as evidence of the antiquity and purity of the English Church or as brilliant exceptions to England's dark, papist past, but in doing so they complicated representations of the medieval period. Chaucer was corralled into support of the reformist movement. The first of several Lollard texts to be spuriously ascribed to him was the prose dialogue *Jack Upland*, printed in 1536 (IPMEP 782, STC 5098). But these were conservative as well as reformist gestures, a way of sanctioning radical texts. As the printer of the Lollard text the *Prologe for Alle the Bokis of the Bible* tells the reader, they should not 'blame' him: 'I haue folowed myne orygynall and olde copy . . . I wrote it not blamyng no person nowe lyvyng' (IPMEP 205, STC 25587.5, A7r). In the context of unstable religious policy it was useful for printers to ascribe 'blame' to authors, and the best author was a famous, safely dead one. The approach of post-Reformation printers to Chaucer's genuine prose works was equally cautious. Grafton, nervous about the content of his 1542 edition of Chaucer's Parson's Tale, especially its exhortation to pilgrimage, added a note in the margin of the prose tract: 'This is a Caunterbury tale' (STC 5071, C1r). A 'Caunterbury tale' was, by the mid-sixteenth-century, a term for fictional nonsense (OED, s.v., Canterbury). The reformers' Chaucer was, it seems, at once a radical proto-Protestant, a famous writer of the English past whose *Works* were a safe haven for all manner of texts, and a maker of pilgrims' tales in verse and prose, no longer to be taken seriously.

Other important texts appeared in post-Reformation contexts. William Copland's editions of prose romances in the 1550s and 1560s and late editions of works by Mandeville, Trevisa, and Stanbridge have already been mentioned. Political writings can be added to the list. The decade of the 1530s was a crucial time for the development of the English press, and English prose, as political and administrative tools (Neville-Sington 1999). Caxton and his competitors and successors had already identified the market for political material. Caxton printed the *Statutes* of Henry VII in English in about 1489 (IPMEP 686, STC 9348); Machlinia issued the *Promise of Matrimony* in 1483, declaring the union of the York and Lancaster to a wide audience (IPMEP 443, STC 9176); and Pynson printed *Ordenaunces of Warre* and other works against the French in 1513, the year of Henry VIII's invasion (IPMEP 225, STC 9332). The *Ordenaunces* were reprinted often up to 1544. Likewise, Lydgate, 'monk of Bury', most of whose poems had been out of print since 1534, lasted longer as an author of a prose political tract (A. Gillespie 2000). His *Serpent of Division*, a treatise on the fall of Caesar, was printed by Redman in about 1535 (IPMEP 835, STC 17027.5) – apparently apposite to the events of that year, just as Lydgate's verses on the entry of Henry VI were suitable for incorporation into the entry of Edward VI in 1547, and just as his *Fall of Princes* was deemed an appropriate model for the Edwardian and Elizabethan authors of the *Mirror for Magistrates* (Thompson 2001). The *Serpent* was issued again by Owen Rogers in 1559, edited by John Stow, and then modernised and printed with a humanist preface alongside the *Tragedy of Gorboduc* in 1590 (STC 17028–29; Ringler 1961). The Elizabethan editions of the Serpent bring this discussion to its conclusion. On the one hand, Lydgate's work was matched with that of Thomas Sackville and Thomas Norton, whose play *Gorboduc*, an analogue for Shakespeare's tragedies, was performed before Elizabeth in 1562 and intended as a statement upon the matter of the royal marriage. In the 1590 edition, the meanings of the Roman and medieval past and the enduring legacy of Middle English prose writing are opened to revival and reconsideration. On the other hand, Stow's carefully attributed edition of the *Serpent* – that of a Tudor antiquary and a collector of medieval books – suggests that by 1559, the process by which Middle English prose would be written out of a vital literary, religious, and political culture, and into scholarly histories like this one, was well underway.

BIBLIOGRAPHY

Primary Works

Full bibliographical details for all books named can be found in STC: images are available on Early English Books Online, although bibliographical details in this database are not always to be trusted.
The best list of Caxton's books is that found in Needham 1986, Appendix D. Modern editions of his prose are identified in Blake 1969, pp. 224–39. Some more recent editions are listed below.
Modern editions of prose writing issued from presses other than Caxton's are given in IPMEP; some more recent editions are listed below.

Secondary Works

Adams, Robert P. 1959. 'Bold Bawdry and Open Manslaughter: The English New Humanist Attack on Medieval Romance', *Huntington Library Quarterly* 23, 33–48

Armstrong, Elizabeth. 1979. 'English Purchases of Printed Books from the Continent, 1465–1526', *English Historical Review* 94, 268–90

Bennett, H.S. 1969. *English Books & Readers 1475 to 1557*, 2nd ed. (Cambridge)

Blades, William. 1861–63. *The Life and Typography of William Caxton, England's First Printer, with Evidence of his Typographical Connection with Colard Mansion*, 2 vols (London)

Blake, N.F. 1966. 'Caxton's Language', *Neuphilologische Mitteilungen* 67, 122–32
——. 1969. *Caxton and his World* (London)
——. 1971. 'Lord Berners: A Survey', *Mediaevalia & Humanistica* ns 2, 119–32
——, ed. 1973. *Caxton's Own Prose* (London)
——. 1991. *William Caxton and English Literary Culture* (London)

Blayney, Peter W.M. 2003. *The Stationers' Company before the Charter, 1403–1557* (London)

Boffey, Julia. 2000. 'English Printing of Texts Translated from French', in *Vernacular Literature and Current Affairs in the Early Sixteenth Century: France, England and Scotland*, ed. Jennifer Britnell and Richard Britnell (Aldershot), pp. 171–83

Bornstein, D. 1976. 'William Caxton's Chivalric Romances and the Burgundian Renaissance in England', *English Studies* 57, 1–10

———. 1977. 'French Influence on Fifteenth-Century English Prose', *Mediaeval Studies* 39, 369–86

Boro, Joyce. 2004. 'Lord Berners' Books: A New Survey', *Huntington Library Quarterly* 66 (forthcoming)

Brodie, A.R. 1974. 'Ankwyll's Vulgaria', *Neuphilologische Mitteilungen* 75, 416–27

Christianson, C. Paul. 'The Rise of London's Book-Trade' in *The Cambridge History of the Book in Britain*: Volume III (see Hellinga and Trapp), pp. 128–47

Collier, Heather. 1997. 'Richard Hill – A London Compiler', in *The Court and Cultural Diversity: Selected Papers from the Eighth Triennial Congress of the Courtly Literature Society*, ed. Evelyn Mullally and John Thompson (Cambridge), pp. 319–29

Crotch, W.J.B. 1928. *The Prologues and Epilogues of William Caxton*, EETS os 176 (London)

Dalrymple, Roger. 1995. 'The Literary Use of Religious Formulae in Certain Middle English Romances', *Medium Aevum* 64, 250-63

Doyle, A. I. 1989. 'Publication by Members of the Religious Orders', in *Book Production and Publishing in England 1375–1475* (see Griffiths and Pearsall), pp. 109–23

Driver, Martha W. 1989. 'Pictures in Print: Late Fifteenth- and Early Sixteenth-Century English Religious Books for Lay Readers', in *De Cella in Seculum: Religious and Secular Life and Devotion in Late Medieval England*, ed. Michael G. Sargent (Cambridge), pp. 229–44

———. 1996. 'The Illustrated De Worde: An Overview', *Studies in Iconography, Medieval Institute Publications* 17, 349–403

———. 2003. 'When is a Miscellany not Miscellaneous? Making Sense of the Kalendar of Shepherds', *Yearbook of English Studies* 33, 199–214

Duff, E.G. 1906. *The Printers, Stationers and Bookbinders of Westminster and London from 1476 to 1535* (Cambridge)

———. 1912a. *A Century of the English Book Trade* (London)

———. 1912b. *The English Provincial Printers, Stationers and Bookbinders to 1557* (Cambridge)

Duffy, Eamon. 1992. *The Stripping of the Altars: Traditional Religion in England c.1400–c.1580* (New Haven and London)

Easting R., ed. 2002. *The Revelation of the Monk of Eynsham* (Oxford)

Edwards, A.S.G. 1995. 'Chaucer from Manuscript to Print: The Social Text and the Critical Text', *Mosaic: A Journal for the Interdisciplinary Study of Literature* 28, 1–12

———. 2003. 'William Copland and the Identity of Printed Middle English Romance', in *The Matter of Identity in Medieval Romance*, ed. Phillipa Hardman (Woodbridge and Rochester, NY), pp. 130–47

Edwards, A.S.G., and Carol M. Meale. 1993. 'The Marketing of Printed Books in Late Medieval England', *The Library* 6th ser. 15, 95–124

Erler, Mary C. 1984. '*The Maner to Lyue Well* and the Coming of English to Francois Regnault's Primers of the 1520s and 1530s', *The Library* 6th ser. 6, 229–43

———, ed. 1993. *Robert Copland: Poems* (Toronto)

———. 1999. 'Devotional Literature', in *The Cambridge History of the Book in Britain: Volume III* (see Hellinga and Trapp), pp. 495–525

———. 2002. *Women, Reading, and Piety in Late Medieval England* (Cambridge)

Ford, Margaret Lane. 1999. 'Private Ownership of Printed Books', in *The Cambridge History of the Book in Britain: Volume III* (see Hellinga and Trapp), pp. 205–28

Genette, Gerard. 1997. *Paratexts: Thresholds of Interpretation*, trans. Jane E. Lewin (Cambridge)

Gillespie, Alexandra. 2000. 'The Lydgate Canon in Print, 1476 to 1534', *Journal of the Early Book Society* 3, 59–93

———. 2004a. 'John Stow's 'Owlde' Manuscripts of London Chronicles', in *John Stow (1525–1605) and the Making of the English Past*, ed. Ian Gadd and Alexandra Gillespie (London), pp. 57–67

———. 2004b. 'Poets, Printers and Early English *Sammelbände*', *Huntington Library Quarterly* 66 (forthcoming)

Gillespie, Vincent. 1989. 'Vernacular Books of Religion', in *Book Production and Publishing in Britain 1375–1475* (see Griffiths and Pearsall), pp. 317–44

Glasscoe, Marion, ed. 1987. *The Medieval Mystical Tradition in England: Exeter Symposium IV* (Cambridge)

Gransden, Antonia. 1982. *Historical Writing in England II: c. 1307 to the Early Sixteenth Century* (London)

Greenblatt, Stephen. 1991. *Marvellous Possessions: The Wonder of the New World* (Chicago)

Griffiths, Jeremy, and Derek Pearsall, eds. 1989. *Book Production and Publishing in Britain 1375–1475* (Cambridge)

Hanna, Ralph. 1996. 'Miscellaneity and Vernacularity: Conditions of Literary Production in Late Medieval England' in *The Whole Book: Cultural Perspectives on the Medieval Miscellany*, ed. Stephen Nichols and Seigfried Wenzel (Ann Arbor, MI), pp. 37–51

Hellinga, Lotte. 1982. *Caxton in Focus* (London)

———. 2002. 'Tradition and Renewal: Establishing the Chronology of Wynkyn de Worde's Early Work', in *Incunabula and their Readers: Printing, Selling and Using Books in the Fifteenth Century*, ed. Kristian Jensen (London), pp. 13–30

Hellinga, Lotte, and J.B. Trapp, eds. 1999. *The Cambridge History of the Book in Britain, Volume III: 1400–1557* (Cambridge)

Holbrook, Sue Ellen. 1987. 'Margery Kempe and Wynkyn de Worde', in *The Medieval Mystical Tradition in England* (see Glasscoe), pp. 27–46

Hudson, Anne. 1985. *Lollards and their Books* (London and Ronceverte)

Johnston, S.H. 1978. 'A Study in the Career and Literary Publications of Richard Pynson' (unpublished Ph.D. thesis, Western Ontario University)

Jones, R.F. 1953. *The Triumph of the English Language* (Stanford)

Kato, Takako. 2002. *Caxton's Morte Darthur: The Printing Process and the Authenticity of the Text*, Medium Aevum Monographs n.s. 22 (Oxford)

Keiser, George R. 1987. 'The Mystics and the Early English Printers: The Economics of Devotionalism', in *The Medieval Mystical Tradition in England* (see Glasscoe), pp. 9–26

———. 1995. 'Medicines for Horses: The Continuity from Script to Print', *Yale University Library Gazette* 70, 111–25

———. 1999. 'Practical Books for the Gentleman', in *The Cambridge History of the Book in Britain*: Volume III (see Hellinga and Trapp), pp. 470–94

Kekewich, M. 1971. 'Edward IV, William Caxton and Literary Patronage in Yorkist England', *Modern Language Review* 66, 481–87

Kerling, Nellie J. M. 1955. 'Caxton and the Trade in Printed Books', *The Book Collector* 4, 190–99

Kipling, G. 1977. *The Triumph of Honour: The Burgundian Origins of the Elizabethan Renaissance* (Leiden)

Kohanski, Tamarah. 2001. *The Book of John Mandeville: An Edition of the Pynson Text* (Tempe, AZ)

Kuskin, William. 1999a. 'Caxton's Worthies Series: The Production of Literary Culture', *English Literary History* 66, 511–51

———. 1999b. 'Reading Caxton: Transformations in Capital, Authority, Print, and Persona in the Late Fifteenth Century', in *New Medieval Literatures 3*, ed. Rita Copeland, David Lawton, and Wendy Scase (Oxford), pp. 149–83

Lerer, Seth. 1993. *Chaucer and his Readers: Imagining the Author in Late-Medieval England* (Princeton)

———. 1999. 'William Caxton', in *The Cambridge History of Medieval English Literature* (see Wallace), pp. 720–38

Lucas, Peter J. 1982. 'The Growth and Development of English Literary Patronage in the Later Middle Ages and Early Renaissance', *The Library* 6th ser. 4, 219–48

McKenzie, D.F. 1999. *Bibliography and the Sociology of Texts* (Cambridge)

McKitterick, David. 2003. *Print, Manuscript and the Search for Order, 1450–1830* (Cambridge)

Meale, Carol M. 1989. 'Patrons, Buyers and Owners: Book Production and Social Status', in *Book Production and Publishing in Britain 1375–1475* (see Griffiths and Pearsall), pp. 201–38

———. 1992. 'Caxton, de Worde and the Publication of Romance in Late Medieval England', *The Library: Transactions of the Bibliographical Society* 14, 283–98

Middleton, Anne. 1998. 'Thomas Usk's "Perdurable Letters": The Testament of Love from Script to Print', *Studies in Bibliography* 51, 63–116

Mooney, Linne R. 1997. 'English Almanacks from Script to Print', in *Texts and their Contexts: Papers from the Early Book Society*, ed. John Scattergood and Julia Boffey (Dublin), pp. 11–25.

———. 2000. 'Professional Scribes? Identifying English Scribes Who Had a Hand in More Than One Manuscript', in *New Directions in Medieval Manuscript Studies*, ed. D. Pearsall (Cambridge)

Moran, James. 1976 repr. 2002. *Wynkyn de Worde: Father of Fleet Street*, 2nd ed. (London)

Murray Jones, Peter. 1999. 'Medicine and Science', in *The Cambridge History of the Book in Britain*: Volume III (see Hellinga and Trapp), pp. 470–94

Needham, Paul. 1986. *The Printer & the Pardoner* (Washington DC)

———. 1999. 'The Customs Rolls and the Printed-Book Trade', in *The Cambridge History of the Book in Britain: Volume III* (see Hellinga and Trapp), pp. 148–63

Neville-Sington, Pamela. 1990. 'Richard Pynson, King's Printer (1506–1529): Printing and Propaganda in Early Tudor England' (unpublished Ph.D. thesis, University of London, Warburg Institute)

———. 1999. 'Press, Politics and Religion', in *The Cambridge History of the Book in Britain: Volume III* (see Hellinga and Trapp), pp. 576–607

Orme, Nicholas. 1999. 'Schools and School Books', in *The Cambridge History of the Book in Britain*: Volume III (see Hellinga and Trapp), pp. 449–69

Painter, George D. 1977. *William Caxton: A Biography* (New York)

Plomer, H. 1925. *Wynkyn de Worde & his Contemporaries from the Death of Caxton to 1535: A Chapter in English Printing* (London)

Powell, Susan. 1998. 'Lady Margaret Beaufort and her Books', *The Library* 6th ser. 20, 227–33

Rhodes, J.T. 1993. 'Syon Abbey and its Religious Publications in the Sixteenth Century', *Journal of Ecclesiastical History* 44, 11–25

Ringler, William. 1961. 'Lydgate's *Serpent of Division*, 1559, Edited by John Stow', *Studies in Bibliography* 14, 201–203

Rundle, David. 2002. 'Humanism before the Tudors: On the Nobility and Reception of the *studia humanitatis* in Fifteenth-Century England', in *Reassessing Tudor Humanism*, ed. Jonathan Woolfson (London)

Rutter, Russell. 1987. 'William Caxton and Literary Patronage', *Studies in Philology* 84, 440–70

Saenger, P. 1975. 'Colard Mansion and the Evolution of the Printed Book', *The Library Quarterly* 45, 405–18

Sargent, Michael G. 1983. 'Walter Hilton's *Scale of Perfection*: The London Manuscript Group Reconsidered', *Medium Aevum* 52, 189–216

Scott, Kathleen L. 1976. *The Caxton Master and his Patrons* (Cambridge)

Seymour, M. C. 1964. 'The Early English Editions of *Mandeville's Travels*', *The Library* 5th ser. 19, 202–7

Shrank, Cathy. 2000. 'Andrew Borde and the Politics of Identity in Reformation England', *Reformation* 5, 1–26

———. 2004. *Writing the Nation in Reformation England, 1530–1580* (Oxford)

Simpson, James. 2002. *The Oxford English Literary History, Volume II: 1350–1547, Reform and Cultural Revolution* (Oxford)

Sullivan, Garrett, and Linda Woodbridge. 2000. 'Popular Culture in Print', in *The Cambridge Companion to English Literature, 1500–1600*, ed. Arthur E. Kinney (Cambridge), pp. 265–86

Summit, Jennifer. 2000. *Lost Property: The Woman Writer in English Literary History, 1380–1589* (Chicago and London)

Sutton, Anne F. 1994. 'Caxton was a Mercer: His Social Milieu and Friends', in *England in the Fifteenth Century: Proceedings of the 1992 Harlaxton Symposium*, Harlaxton Medieval Studies, IV, ed. Nicholas Rogers (Stamford), pp. 118–48

Sutton, Anne F. and Livia Visser-Fuchs. 1997. *Richard III's Books* (Stroud)

Thompson, John J. 2001. 'Reading Lydgate in Post-Reformation England', in *Middle English Poetry: Texts and Traditions: Essays in Honour of Derek Pearsall*, ed. A. J. Minnis (Woodbridge and Rochester, NY), pp. 181–209

Thrupp, Sylvia L. 1948. *The Merchant Class of Medieval London* (Ann Arbor)

Voigts, Linda E. 1989. 'Scientific and Medical Books', in *Book Production and Publishing in Britain 1375–1475* (see Griffiths and Pearsall), pp. 345–402

Wang, Yu-Chiao. 2004. 'Caxton's Romances and their Early Tudor Readers', *Huntington Library Quarterly*, 66 (forthcoming)

Watson, N. 1999. 'The Middle English Mystics', in *The Cambridge History of Middle English Literature*, ed. David Wallace (Cambridge), pp. 539–65

Weiss, R. 1941. *Humanism in England during the Fifteenth Century* (Oxford)

Index

'AB' language 6–8
Abbey of the Holy Ghost 137, 141, 253
Adam and Eve 254
Adys, Miles 182
Aegidius Romanus, *De Regimine Principum* 117, 119, 124
Aelfric 4, 11
Agnus Castus 232
Alan of Lille, *Summa de Arte Praedicatoria* 9
Alcock, John 314
Alkerton, Richard 156, 161
Allen, Hope Emily 83
Alliterative *Morte Arthure* 223
Amadis de Gaule 227
Ancren Riwle see Ancrene Wisse
Ancrene Wisse group 1–13 *passim*, 132, 137, 162, 203, 315
Andrew, St 254
Ankwyll, John 317
Anslay, Brian 312
Antony, St 251
Apology for Lollard Doctrines 197
Appolyn of Tyre 312
Aquinas, *Thomas, Summa Theologica* 41
Argument of Morien and Merlin 233
Armburgh papers 289, 295, 297–98
Arnold, Richard 318
Art of Nombryng 232
Arthur of Little Britain 227
Arundel, Thomas 54, 57, 135, 143, 156, 157, 158
Ashby, George 280
Atkinson, William 312
Auchinleck Chronicle 190
Audry, St 259
Augustin, St 2, 6–7, 134, 256

Bagnyon, Jean 219
Bale, Robert 18, 233
Barbara, St 253, 255, 256
Barnes, Dame Julian 2, 233, 239
Bartholomaeus Anglicus, *De Proprietatibus Rerum* 117, 118, 121, 123–4, 234–35, 318
Batman, Stephen 125, 318
'Beauchamp pageant' 189
Beauchamp, Richard 119, 189
Beauchamp, Richard, bishop of Salisbury 125
Beaufort, Lady Margaret 220, 262, 309, 312, 315
Beaufort, Thomas 295
Beauvale, Notts 257
Benjamini see Treatise of the Study of Wisdom called Benjamin 43–44

Berkeley, Gloucs 118
Bernard of Clairvaux 2, 43, 135, 163
Bernard of Gordon, *Lilye of medicynes* 238
Berners *see* Barnes, Bourchier
Berthelet, William 317, 318
Betson, Thomas 296
Bible, Wycliffe *see* Wycliffe Bible
Byrthe and Comynge of the Antichryst 314
Blacman, John 257
Black, Merja 7, 8
Blanchardyn and Eglantine 220, 221, 226, 227, 316
Blount, John, *De Studio Militari* 239
Bohun, Mary de 220
Bokenham, Osbern, *Legendys of Hooly Wummen* 257
Bolingbroke, Henry 220
Bonaventura, St 53, 62, 89, 135
Book for a Simple and Devout Woman 130–31
Boke of Good Manners 316
Boke of Kervyng 233, 241
Boke of Marchalsi 233, 239, 240
Book of Privy Counselling 43
Book of Quintessence 236, 239, 241
Book of St Albans 316
Book of the City of Ladies 312
Book of the Knight of the Tower 227
Book of Vices and Virtues 129
Book to a Mother 142–43
Borde, Andrew 318
Bourchier, John, lord Berners 221, 227, 312, 318
Brews, Margery 296
Bristowe Chronicle 183
Bridget, of Sweden, St 69, 89, 252, 253, 259, 262, 313, 315
Brinton, Thomas, bishop of Rochester 155
Bruen, John 164
Brunham *see* Burnham
Brut chronicle 56, 176–181, 227, 318
Brut, Walter 197
Buckingham, Duke of 220
Burham, John 84
Burton, John 254
Butler-Bowdon, William 83

Cade, Jack 182
Calle, Richard 298–99
Canonsleigh, Devon 3
Cantor, Peter 9
Capgrave, John 256, 280
    Abbreuiacion of Chronicles 176, 183–84, 190, 191, 227

Carpenter, John 271
Cathay 100
Catherine of Siena 127
Caxton, William 63, 119, 125, 130, 153, 154,
    178, 216, 217, 219, 220, 221, 222–23, 224–25,
    259–60, 307–313, 314, 316, 320
    Aesop 317
    Ars Moriendi 313
    Chronicles of England 318
    Doctrinal of Sapience 314
    Golden Legend 254, 255, 256, 260–61
    Governal of Health 318
    Mirror of the World 317
    Ovid 309
    Doctrine to French and English 233, 317
Cecilia, St 70
Cely letters 289, 293–94, 295, 300
Chambers, R. W. 8
Charles d'Orléans 280
Charles the Grete 219
Charter of the Abbey of the Holy Ghost 253
Chartier, Alain 279, 316
    Dialogus familiaris amici et sodalis 279
    Le Quadrilogue Invectif 279
    Le Traité de l'Esperance 279
Chastising of God's Children 35, 132, 133,
    138–9, 315
Chaucer, Geoffrey 39, 88, 99, 101, 151, 166,
    312, 320
    Boece 310
    Treatise on the Astrolabe 110
    Troilus and Criseyde 300
Chaucer, Thomas 295
Chaworth, Sir Thomas 125
Chertsey, Andrew 312
Chirche of the Euyll Men and Women 312
Christine, St 257
Chronicle of the Rebellion in Lincolnshire 187
Claydon, John 202–03
Cloud of Unknowing 33, 35, 43–49
Cole, King of England 109
Cobham, Eleanor 182
Conisford, Norfolk 67
Contemplations of the Dread and Love of God
    28, 138, 141
Copland, Robert 311, 312
Copland, William 317, 320
Crafte of Lymnynge of Books 232
Crafte of Nombrynge 232
Cressy, Serenus 69
Crophill, John 240
Curial 316

Daniel, Henry
    Dome of Uryns 238
    Herbal 234
De oblacione 204, 205
De XII portis 238
Deguileville, Guillaume de, Pilgrimage of the
    Human Soul 140
Deonise Hid Diuinitie 42, 43, 47
Derrida, Jacques 92

Dialogue between Reson and Gabbynge 197
Dialogue between Rhazes and his Son Merlin
    233
Disce Mori 132
Disticha Catonis 140
Dobson, E. J. 6
Dod, Richard 234, 240
Dominic, St 10
Dorothy, St 253, 255, 259
Donatus, Ars Minor 233
Douai 64
Douglas, Gavin 222
Dyeng Creature 314

East, Thomas 106, 107, 125
Edmund of Abingdon, St, Speculum Ecclesie
    130
Edward IV, King of England 178, 187, 188, 219,
    220, 309
Edward V, King of England 309
Edward, duke of York, Master of Game 235–36,
    239
Edward, the Confessor, St 256, 258, 259, 261
Egbert of Liège 167
The Eight Ghostly Dwelling Places 141–42
Eleanor, Duchess of Gliucestershire 3
Eliot, T. S. 77
Elizabeth, Duchess of Suffolk 292
Elizabeth of Spalbeck, St 257–58
Elizabeth,, of York 309
Ellis, Sir Henry 289
Eneydos 221–22
Epistel of Meidenhad 4, 9
Epistle of Prayer 43
Epistle of Discretion of Stirrings 43
Erkenwald, St 256, 261
Etheldreda see Audry
Exeter College, Oxford 117
Experimentes of Cophon, Leche of Salerne 240
Eynsham, Monk of 140, 315

Fabyan, Robert 182, 190–91
Fastolf, Sir John 291, 292, 294
Fawkes, Richard 314
Fayreford, Thomas 240
Felton, Sibilla de 56
Fervor Amoris see Contemplations of the Dread
    and Love of God
Fèvre, Raoul le 219, 221, 226, 309
Fierebras 219
Fifteen Ooes 316
Fishlake, Thomas 34
Five Wiles of the Pharaoh 254
Flete, William, Remedies Against
    Temptations 28, 35, 57, 131, 132, 133
Floretum 197
Foliot, Hugh 10
Font, Lluis de 34
Forster, Stephen 182
Fortescue, John 271, 278–84
    De laudibus legum Anglie 281, 283
    De natura legis Naturae 280, 281, 283

De titulo Edwardi Comitis Marchiae 280
'Declaration . . . upon Certayn Wrytinges'
  280, 283
Defensio iuris domus Lancastriae 280
*The Difference between an Absolute and
  Limited Monarchy see The Governance of
  England*
On the Governance of England 278, 279,
  281, 282–83, 283–4
'Of the Title of the House of York' 280
Fourth Lateran Council 6–7, 9–10, 11, 12,
  129–30
Four Sons of Aymon 219, 221, 225, 226
Francis of Assissi, St 259
Frobisher, Martin 106–7
Froissart, Jean 185, 221
Fructus temporum 184
Fuller, Richard 253

Gaguin, Robert, *Compendium super Francorum
  gestis* 191
Gallus, Thomas 43
Game and Play of Chess 309
Gast of Gy 140
Gaston, de Foix, *Livre de chasse* 235–36
Gemma salutaris 236
Genealogical rolls 188–89
Geoffrey of Monmouth, *Historia regum
  britanniae* 177, 184–85, 216, 219
Geoffroi de la Tour Landry 227
Gerald of Wales, *Expugnatio hibernica* 185
Gibbs, Marion 9
Gilbert of Sempringham, St 256–57
Gilbertus Anglicus, *Compendium
  medicinae* 232, 236, 237, 240
Gilte Legende 153, 154, 250, 251, 253–56, 259
Godfridus super Palladium 236, 240
Godeffroy of Boloyne 217, 219–20, 223
Golden Legend 153, 154, 261
Gospel of Nichodemus 121, 122
Gough, John 314
Grafton, Richard 320
Great Chronicle of London 181–83
Gregory I, the Great 2, 167
Gregory, William 182
Greenhalgh, James 33
Grosseteste, Robert 21
Guido delle Colonne 219
Guigo II, *Scala Claustralium* 38–9, 40
Guy de Chauliac, *Cirurgia Magna* 233, 237,
  239

Hall, John, *Chronicle* 178
Halliwell, James O 103
Hampole *see* Rolle
Handling Sin 129
Hardyng, John 217
Helen, St 109
Henry VI, King of England 187
Henry of Mondeville 233, 241
Hereford Cathedral 7
Hereford, Nicholas 119, 201

Higden, Ranulf, *Polychronicon* 117, 118, 119,
  120, 121, 122, 183, 184, 191, 318
Hildegard of Bingen 153
Hill, Richard 240, 319
Hilton, Walter 33–49 *passim*, 131, 132, 141
  Bomun Est 35, 69
  De imagine peccati 34
  Eight Chapters on Perfection 34, 35
  Epistle of the Mixed Life 34, 42, 315
  *Epistola ad Quondam Seculo Renunciare
    Volentem* 34
  Epistola de Utilitate et Prerogativis Religionis
    34
  Of Angel's Song 35
  A Pystille Made to a Christene Frende 34
  Qui Habitat 35, 69
  Scale of Perfection (Scala Perfeccionis) 33,
    35–42, 56, 57, 69, 89, 307
History of Jason 221
History of the Arrivall in England of Edward IV
  187–88
Hobbes, Thomas 281–82
Hoccleve, Thomas 160, 283
Holand, Thomas, Duke of Surrey 54
Holcot, Robert, *Moralitates* 166
Holinshed, Raphael 319
The Holy Book Gracia Dei 28, 137
Horn et Rimenild 221
Hue de Rotelande 222
Hugh of Lincoln, St 59
Humfrey, duke of Gloucester 234, 236
Huon of Bordeaux 218–19, 227
Huxley, Aldous 77
Hyrd, Richard 227

Imitatio Christi 312
India 100
Informacion for Pilgrymes unto the Holy Lande
  319
Informacion of Augrym 240
Ipomedon 222

Jack Upland 320; *see also Upland Series*
Jacob's Well 155
Jacobus de Voragine, *Legenda Aurea* 153, 254
Jacques de Vitry 88, 90
James of Milan 35, 132
James of Vitry 12
Jean de Bourgogne 100
Jean de Long 100
Jean de Vignay, *Légende dorée* 254
Jerome, St 251, 255, 256, 259, 262
Joan, countess of Kent 56
John, of Arderne, *Practica* 237–38, 242
John, of Bado Aureo, *Tractatus de Armis* 239
John of Burgundy, plague treatise 239
John, of Rupescissa, *The Book of Quintessence*
  238
John, the Baptist, St 251, 253, 255, 258
John, the Evangelist, St 251, 253, 255, 258
Jordan of Saxony *Vita Sancti Augustini* 256

Joseph of Arimathy 227
Joseph of Arimathea 259
Julian of Norwich 67–79 *passim*, 83, 132, 203
Juliana, St *see Seinte Iuliene*

Kalendar of Shepherds 314
Kalendre of the New Legende of Englande 258, 261, 262, 315
Katherine Group 3–13 *passim*
Katherine, St 251, 252, 253, 255, *see also Seinte Katerine*
Katherine of Alexandria, St 256, 259
Katherine of Siena, St 257, 259
Kaye, John, *Siege of Rhodes* 187, 317
Kela, Thomas 296
Kempe, John 84, 87
Kempe, Margery 68, 71, 77, 78, 79, 83–94 *passim*, 166, 307, 315
King Apollyn of Tyre 227
King Ponthus and the Fair Sidone 221
Kirkby, Margaret 20, 21, 23
Knyght of the Swanne 312
Knight of the Tower 316
Knyghtes and Syege of Rhodes 312

A Ladder with Four Rungs 137
Laing, Margaret 7
Lancaster, Roger 178
Lancelot-Grail 217
Lanfrance, *Cirurgia Magna* 233
Langton, Stephen 10
Lanterne of Li3t 197, 202, 204–05
Lay Folk's Catechism 202–03
Layamon 177, 217
Leonard, St 258
Lelamour, John 234, 235, 240
Leland, John 317
Lettou, John 317
Leversedge, Edmund 140
Liber de diversis medicinis 232, 235, 238
Life of Alexander 218
A Litil Boke for the Pestilence 241
A Lytell Boke of XXIII Stone Pryncipalles 233
A Lytell Treatyse for to Lerne Englysshe and Frensshe 233
The Little Ship of Venice 240
Lofsonge of ure Louerde 5
Locke, John 281
'Lollard chronicle' 183, 186
Lollard Disendowment Bill 197
Lollards 53–55, 56–60, 71, 85–86, 94, 128, 168, 273, 274, 275, 278, 307, 320
Lombard, Peter 20
London chronicles 180–83
London Lapidary of King Philip 235
Love, Nicholas 53–64 *passim*, 85, 314
Lydgate, John 222
    Fall of Princes 320
    Life of Our Lady 251, 261
    Serpent of Division 186, 320, 321
    Siege of Thebes 218
    Troy Book 218

Macer 232, 234, 239
Machlinia, William de 311, 315, 317, 318, 320
Malory, Thomas, *Morte Darthur* 91, 215–16, 217, 219, 220, 222, 224–26, 227, 254, 280, 311
Mandeville 99–111 *passim*, 319, 320
Mansion, Colard 310
Marbod of Rennes 5
Margaret, St 259, *see also Seinte Margarete*
Margaret, duchess of Clarence 251–52, 262
Margaret, of Burgundy 309
Martin of Troppau *see Martinus Polonus*
Martinus Polonus, *Chronicon Pontificum et Imperatorum* 183–84, 185, 190
Mary, of Oignies, St 88, 257
Medicines for Horses 235
Melton, William 161
Melusine 220
Merlin 217
Michael, St 255
Mirk, John, *Festial* 56, 153, 157–8, 250, 251, 261, 314
    Quattuor sermones 313
Mirroure of Golde 312
Mirror of Our Lady 128
Mirror of St Edmund 136, 137
Morstede, Thomas 233
Moulton, Thomas 241, 318
Mount Grace Charterhouse, Yorks 54, 83
Mum and the Sothsegger 197
Murdoch, Iris 77

Neville, Thomas 19
Nicholas of Tollentino 259
Nicolas, *Antidotary* 238
Nine Worthies 218
Norbert St 256
Norton, Thomas 320
Nova Legenda Angliae 258, 261
N-Town plays 63

O'Brien, Sarah 11
Odo of Cheriton, 12, 167
Odoric of Pordenone, *Relatio* 100
Oldcastle, Sir John 85, 160
Oliver of Castile 221, 312
Omnis Plantacio 197, 201, 204, 205–06
Opus Arduum 197
Orcherd of Syon 127, 314
Order of Chivalry 316
Ordynarye of Crysten Men 314
Oresiun of Seinte Marie 5
Owl and the Nightingale 94

Palladius, *de Re Rustica* 236
Paris and Vienne 226–27
Pasfield, Robert 164–65
Passing Gode Lityll Boke Necessarye and Behouefull Agenst the Pestilence 318
Paston letters 289–90, 291, 292, 293, 294–95, 296–97, 300
St Patrick's Purgatory 140

Pecham, archbishop John 314
Pecock, Reginald 271–78, 283
  The Book of Faith 272, 273, 274, 277, 278
  The Donet 272, 276
  The Folewer to the Donet 272, 276
  The Poor Mennis Myrrour 272
  The Repressor of Overmuch Blaming of the
    Clergy 272, 276, 277
  The Reule of Crysten Religion 272, 274,
    275, 276
Pepwell, Henry 311, 312, 315
Peter of Poitier, Compendium Historiae in
  Genealogia Christi 189
Pepwell, Henry 84
Peterborough Lapidary 234–35
Philip, King, Lapidary 235, 239
Philip, Nicholas 161
Phillip, the Good 309
Pierce the Plowman's Crede 197
Pierre de France and the Fair Maguelonne 221
Piers Plowman 202
Pisan, Christine de 312, 317
Platearius, Circa Instans 234, 238, 239
Plawdon, Thomas 240
Plowman's Tale 197
Plumpton letters 289, 291, 294
Ponthus et la belle Sidone 221, 227, 312
Pore Catif 132, 136, 137, 143, 162, 203
Porete, Margery, Mirror of Simple Souls 69
Prester John's Land 100, 111
Prick of Conscience 28, 129
The Prickynge of Love 35, 132
Proprytees and Medycynes for Hors 316
pseudo-Anselm, De custodia interioris hominis
  4
pseudo-Bonaventure, Meditaciones 55
pseudo-Dionysius, De mystica theologia 43, 47
pseudo-Geber, Summa Perfectionis 237
pseudo-Methodius 185
pseudo-Turpin Chronicle 218
Pynson, Richard 106, 253, 259, 261, 307, 311,
  314, 319, 320

Queen's College, Oxford 117, 119

Raby, Durham 19
Ralph of Maidtsone 10
Ransom, John Crowe 36
Raymond of Capua 260
Raynaud de Montauban 219
Recoyell of the Histories of Troye 219, 226, 227,
  309
Redman, Robert 311, 320
Remedies Against Temptations see Flete, William
Revelation of Purgatory 140
Reysby, Nicholas 256–57
Ricardus Franciscus 254
Richard I, King of England 109
Richard II, King of England 187
Richard III, King of England 309
Richard Fitzralph, Defensio curatorum 117, 118
Richard of St Victor 24

Benjamin Minor 44
De Preparatione Animi ad Contemplationem
  315
Richard of Wallingford, Exafrenon 240
Robert of Shrewsbury 259
Robert the Devil 227, 315
Roger of Parma 233, 238
Roger of Sempringham, Vita Sancti Gilberti
  Confessoris 257
Rogers, Owen 321
Rolle, Richard 19–28 passim, 39, 57, 69, 134,
  135, 141, 203, 307, 315
  'The Commandment' 21, 24, 25, 27
  Ego Dormio 21, 22, 24, 25, 27
  Emendatio vite 20
  Form of Living 20, 21, 22, 27, 28
  Incendium Amoris 20, 89
  'Meditation of the Passion' 27
  Melos Amoris 20
  'Oleum Effusum' 25
  Psalter, Prose Commentary on 20, 21, 26,
    199–200
Roman de la Rose 187
Romances 215–228 passim
Rood, Theodoric 311, 317
Rosarium theologie 197, 201
Rosemary, Treatise on 234
Rous roll 188
Russell, John, Boke of Nurture 233
Rutter of the Sea 312
Ruysbroek, Jan, Treatise of Perfection 69, 132

Sackville, Thomas 320
St Omer 64
Saints' lives 249–62 passim
Samuels, M. L. 11
Sawles Warde 3, 4, 5
Scottis Originale 190
Scrope, Stephen, Liber de moralibus
  philosophorum 140
Secreta Secretorum 233, 239
Seinte Iuliene 3, 4, 5, 249
Seinte Katerine 3, 4, 5, 249
Seinte Margarete 3, 4, 5, 249
The Sekenesse of Wymmen 237
Sermons 151–70 passim
Seven Points of True Wisdom see Suso, Heinrich
Shedynge of the vii. Blood of Christ 314
Shillingford, John 289, 295, 302
Shirley, John, Dethe of the Kynge of Scotis 184,
  186–7
Sidrak and Bokkus 233, 234
Siege of Jerusalem, prose 218
Siege of Thebes, prose 110, 218
Sinclair, May 77
Sisam, Celia 11
Sixteen Points 197
Sixtus, St 7
Somer, William 240
Sorg, Anton 106
South English Legendary 153, 249, 250, 251
Southern Boke of Stones 235

Speculum sacerdotale   153, 154, 169
Speculum Vite   28
Spenser, Edmund   217
Spiritus Guidonis see Gast of Gy
Spryngolde, Robert   92, 94
Stanbridge, John   317, 320
Stanzaic *Morte Arthur*   223
Stavensby, Alexander   10
Stevenson, R. L.   290
Stimulus Amoris   132
Stodeley, John   187
Stonor letters   289, 295
Stow, John   319, 321
Stranton, William   140
Suso, Heinrich, *Horologium Sapientiae*   69, 132, 143–44
Sutton, Richard   314
Swinderby, William   197
Syon, abbey of   128–9, 131, 153, 251, 256, 257, 262, 314

Talkyng of the Loue of God   5
Taylor, William   60, 156, 160–61, 197–98, 201
Tennyson, Alfred Lord   217
Thirty-Seven Conclusions   197, 198
Thomas, of Canterbury, St   109, 255
Thomas of Cantimpré, *Liber de naturis rerum*   167
Thomas, Lord Berkeley   118–119, 125
Thorney, Roger   318
Thornton Dale   19
Thornton, Robert   28, 235
Thorpe, William   197, 201–02
Three Kings of Cologne   250, 259
Three Kings' Sons   226
Thurgarton, Notts   34, 257
Thynne, William   312
Tiptoft, John   309
Titus and Vespasian   316
Tolkien, J. R. R.   6, 8
Tractatus de oblacione iugis sacrificii   197
Treatise of Fysshynge wyth an Angle   236, 237, 316
Treatise of Ghostly Battle   140
Treatise of Love   315
Treatise of the Discretion of Spirits   43
Treatise of the Study of Wisdom called Benjamin   43
Treatise of the Three Arrows   136
Trevisa, John   117–125 *passim*, 203, 234, 318, 320
Tristan   216
Twelve Conclusions   197, 198, 201

Twenty-Five Articles   197

Underhill, Evelyn   36
Upland Series   197, 198, 202
Ureisun of God Almihti   5, 11
Ursula, St   257–58

Valentin et Orson   221, 227, 312
Velser, Michael   106
Vernon Manuscript *see* Bodleian Library MS Eng. poet. a. 1
Virgil   109, 222
Virtutes Aquile   240
Vitas Patrum   261

Wace, *Roman de brut*   177, 217
Walter of Henley   236
Watson, Henry   221, 312
Warkworth, John   178
Waterton, Robert   156
Wharton, Henry   273
Whitford, Richard   314
Wigmore Abbey, North Herefordshire   3, 6
Wimbledon, Thomas   153
William and Melior   222, 227
William of Blois   10
William of Boldensele, *Liber de quibusdam ultramarinis partibus*   100
William of Ockham, *Dialogus inter militem et clericum*   117, 118
William of Palerne   222, 317
Williams, Charles   77
Winifred, St   256, 259, 261
Witham Charterhouse   257
Wohunge of ure Lauerd   5, 9
Wonderful Art of the Eye   239, 241
Wooing Group   3
Worcester, William   291, 294, 295
Worcester Cathedral   10
Worde, Wynkyn de   63, 83, 106, 125, 216, 220, 222, 259, 261, 262, 307, 311, 313–14, 315, 316, 318, 320
Wulfstan   4, 12
Wyclif, John   53, 119, 120
Wycliffe Bible   54, 56, 119, 197, 198–99, 200
Wycliffite prose   195–206 *passim*
Wycliffite sermons   154–55, 157, 158, 200–01
Wynter, Simon   251–53, 255, 259

Yeats, W. B.   77
Yedingham, Yorks   21

Zita, St   259

Index of Manuscripts

Aberystwyth, National Library of Wales MS
  Peniarth 394 241
Cambridge
  Corpus Christi College MS 402 2, 3, 6
  Gonville & Caius College MS 176/97 240
  Gonville & Caius College MS 234/120 3
  Magdalene College Pepys MS 2498 3, 203
  St John's College MS N. 17 251
  Trinity College MS O. 5.26 240
  Trinity College MS R. 14.52 238, 242
  University Library (CUL)
    Add. 2604 258
    Dd.5. 64 21, 27
    Ii.6.26 200
    Ll. 5.18 253
Cambridge, Mass., Harvard University, Houghton
  Library, Richardson 44 251
Cambridge, Mass., Harvard Law School MS 43
  300–01
Durham, University Library MS Cosin V.i. 4
  253
Edinburgh, National Library of Scotland MS
  18.1.17 56
Foyle MS 56
Glasgow University Library, Ferguson 205 241
Lincoln Cathedral 91 28, 235
London
  British Library (BL)
    Add. 3971 34
    Add. 11565 255
    Add. 16165 119, 121
    Add. 20010 189
    Add. 24194 119
    Add. 29502 188
    Add. 34111 240
    Add. 34193 140
    Add. 35298 255, 256, 259, 261
    Add. 36704 257
    Add. 37049 185
    Add. 37790(A) 69
    Add. 43490 292
    Add. 61823 83
    Arundel 286 135
    Cotton Cleopatra C. vi 2, 3
    Cotton Nero A. xiv, 2, 5, 10
    Cotton Titus C. xvi 102, 103, 107, 111
    Cotton Titus D. xviii 3, 4, 5
    Cotton Vitellius F. vii 3
    Egerton 650 178
    Egerton 1982 108
    Harley 1706 131, 140
    Harley 1735 240
    Harley 2261 183

    Harley 2407 236
    Harley 2258 240
    Harley 4012 259
    Harley 4755 254
    Royal 8. C. i 3
    Royal 17 A. xxvii 4, 5
    Royal 17 C, xvii 251
    Sloane 5 234, 240
    Sloane 353 241
    Sloane 1464 103
    Sloane 2499 69
    Sloane 3705 69
London, College of Arms, MS Arundel 22 185
London, Lambeth Palace MS 72 250, 255, 256
London, Lambeth Palace MS 408 203
London, Lambeth Palace MS 432 252, 255
London, Lambeth Palace MS 487 5, 11, 12
London, Society of Antiquaries MS 287 241
London, Wellcome Library, MS 5650 234
London, Westminster School MS 3 203
Longleat House, Marquess of Bath MS 29 21
Longleat House, Marquess of Bath MS 257 222
Manchester, Chetham's Library 8009 253
Manchester University, John Ryland Library, MS
  85 203
New Haven, Beinecke Library MS 317 251
New York, Columbia University MS 263 125
New York, Pierpont Morgan Library MS
  M875 125
New York, Pierpont Morgan Library MS Bühler
  17 238
Oxford
  Bodleian Library (Bodl.)
    Bodley 34 3, 4, 6, 7
    Bodley 806 155
    Digby 185 227
    Digby 233 118
    Douce 114 141, 257, 260
    Douce 262 33
    Douce 322 131
    Douce 372 253–54
    e Musaeo 116 110
    Eng. poet. a. 1 3, 128, 130
    Eng. th. e. 18 259
    Holkham Misc. 41 131
    Laud misc. 286 20
    Rawlinson A. 389 21
    Rawlinson D. 82 218
    Rawlinson D. 99 110
  Balliol College MS 354 240, 318
  Corpus Christi College MS 120 259
  Queen's College MS 383 107
  St John's College MS 182 257

Trinity College MS 11   258
Paris, Bibliothèque Nationale, MS fond
   anglais   40
Paris, Bibliothèque Nationale, nouv. acqu. Fr.
   4515   99
Peterborough Cathedral Library MS 33   234–35
San Marino, California MS HM 115   251
San Marino, California MS HM 149   56

San Marino, California MS HM 505   240
Southwell Cathedral MS 7   255, 259
Tokyo, Takamiya MS 8   56
Tokyo, Waseda Library MS NE 3691   56
Vienna, Österreichische Nationalbibliothek,
   Codex Vindobensis Palatinus 4133   200
Winchester Cathedral 4   69